SHELTER, SETTLEMENT, AND DEVELOPMENT

Titles of related interest

SHELTER, SETTLEMENT, AND DEVELOPMENT

EDITED BY

Lloyd Rodwin

Department of Urban Studies and Planning,
Massachusetts Institute of Technology

Boston
ALLEN & UNWIN
London   Sydney   Wellington

Allen & Unwin, Inc.,
8 Winchester Place, Winchester, Mass. 01890, USA
the U.S. company of
Unwin Hyman Ltd
PO Box 18, Park Lane, Hemel Hempstead, Herts HP2 4TE, UK
40 Museum Street, London WC1A 1 LU, UK
37/39 Queen Elizabeth Street, London SE1 2QB, UK

Allen & Unwin (Australia) Ltd,
8 Napier Street, North Sydney, NSW 2060, Australia

Allen & Unwin (New Zealand) Ltd in association with the Port Nicholson Press Ltd,
Private Bag, Wellington, New Zealand

First published in 1987

Library of Congress Cataloging-in-Publication Data

Shelter, settlement, and development

A study sponsored and financed by the United Nations/
  International Year of Shelter for the Homeless – T. P. Verso
Bibliography: P.
Includes index.
1. Housing — Developing countries.
2. Housing policy — Developing countries.
I. Rodwin, Lloyd.
II. United Nations/International Year of Shelter for the Homeless.
HD7391.S54   1987   363.5′09172′4   87–1038
ISBN 0–04–711023–6 (alk. paper).

British Library Cataloguing in Publication Data

Shelter, settlement, and development.
  1. Housing — Developing countries
  I. Rodwin, Lloyd
  363.5′09172′4   HD7391
ISBN 0–04–711023–6

Typeset in Zapf by Oxford Print Associates, Oxford and printed in Great Britain by Mackays of Chatham

Foreword

IN SPITE OF the national and international efforts during the past decade, there has not been any material improvement in the settlements conditions of the poor and the disadvantaged. This continuing deterioration of the living conditions of the majority of people in both urban and rural settlements in the developing countries is a matter of great concern. The General Assembly declared 1987 as the International Year of Shelter for the Homeless with the aim of securing renewed political commitment to the improvement of the shelter and neighbourhoods of the poor and disadvantaged. The year provides an opportunity to assess the results of the efforts of the past decade, and to decide on new directions and approaches for national policies and strategies that will bring closer the objective of shelter for all by the year 2000.

Towards this end, the United Nations Centre for Human Settlements commissioned a group of eminent academicians and practitioners to put together an analysis of the past efforts and identify the critical areas requiring urgent action. This publication reviews key shelter and settlement experiences and policies, and suggests hard decisions that have to be made to come to grips with the massive problems that loom ahead in the next decade. The analyses are provocative, critical, challenging – and hopeful! The authors believe there are ways not only of confronting far more effectively the explosive population pressures and shelter crises almost everywhere in evidence in Third World cities but, in the process, of spurring constructive advances in economic and social development.

The lessons spelled out are grounded in the actual experience of nations seeking solutions to their shelter problems, subject to political and institutional constraints. The authors take cognizance of the grim economic situation faced by many nations. What makes these findings especially persuasive is that they are realistic. This is not to say that there will not be sharp disagreement with some – perhaps even many – of the views expressed.

I wish to express my sense of indebtedness to Professor Rodwin and the group for producing analyses and findings which so clearly serve the main purposes for which they were intended, i.e., to challenge much of our conventional wisdom, to broaden perspectives and clarify issues, to sum up policy choices that lie ahead and thus to help all of us in decision influencing and decision-making rôles to do our job better in the future.

Dr. Arcot Ramachandran

Preface

WHEN THE United Nations General Assembly designated 1987 as the International Year of Shelter for the Homeless (IYSH), there were several aims. One was to highlight the plight of millions of people with no home: the pavement dwellers; those who must sleep in streets and doorways, in the recesses of public buildings, or in other nondescript areas; and those rendered homeless by natural and man-made disasters. Another was to identify measures and to demonstrate activities in various countries which can alleviate the plight of hundreds of millions who lack a real home – one which provides protection from the elements, has access to safe water and sanitation, provides for secure tenure and personal safety, is within easy reach of centers for employment, education and health care, and is available at a cost which people and society can afford.

A small staff was appointed by the United Nations Center for Human Settlements (UNCHS) – Habitat – to promote these aims. The program was divided into two phases:

Up until the end of 1987, the leadership of IYSH will promote several efforts: to increase the awareness of the pivotal rôles of shelter and human settlements in reinforcing economic and social development; to spur nations to make or to review their assessments of the needs, prospects and priorities of the poor in terms of shelter and neighbourhoods; and to devise realistic national shelter strategies.

In the subsequent period, from 1988 to the year 2000, the objective is to challenge nations to carry out on a reasonable scale the national shelter and settlement strategies which they have devised. The United Nations is also urging governments and nongovernmental organizations (NGOs) to identify IYSH activities – legislation, policies, programs and projects – that demonstrate ways and means of augmenting the efforts of the poor to upgrade their shelter and neighborhoods. Success hinges on the ability to spur as many nations as possible throughout the world to respond with vigor and imagination to these possible forms of action.

To date, 110 nations have identified a national housing agency, or some equivalent organization, to spearhead their IYSH national action plans and national and local action committees. Some 130 IYSH projects have been designated in nearly 70 countries. In addition, a number of international and national NGO groups are devoting much time, energy, and resources to IYSH activities. No doubt, some of these efforts will come to naught. Still others will prompt a verbal repackaging of existing ideas. In most countries, however, the time is ripe for rethinking the main ideas and programs of the last two decades.

Partly to serve these ends, UNCHS has sponsored this reassessment of critical shelter and human settlement problems. The mission is to point up what has been learned from the past efforts, what must be learned now to enhance the effectiveness of current efforts, and the kinds of feedback needed to ensure that shelter and settlement planning and activities play a more constructive central rôle rather than a peripheral one in the development process from now until the year 2000.

This reassessment was planned as a joint effort of scholars, professional practitioners, and policy-making officials; it was scheduled for completion within a year.[1] The study director, this writer, a Ford International Professor at MIT and Director of the Special Program for Urban and Regional Studies of Third World Countries (SPURS), was appointed on December 1, 1984. Several aspects of shelter, settlement, and development were proposed for examination by the staffs of UNCHS and the officials responsible for carrying out the aims of IYSH. These broad themes involved basic conditions and trends; the impact of shelter and settlement investments on economic and social development; and some of the crucial component elements of shelter and settlement problems, such as problems of financing and of structural and institutional change. Following further discussion of these ideas between Dr. Arcot Ramachandran, Undersecretary-General and Executive Director, UNCHS, John E. Cox, former Director, IYSH, and Professor Lloyd Rodwin, these themes were converted into the 15 chapters of this book.

From the very start it was clear that a one-volume study could not cover all the relevant aspects of shelter, settlement, and development. But a more comprehensive scope was simply not feasible at the time. Aside from limited resources, two other factors restricted the coverage. One was the likely unavailability of certain desired specialists; the field of urban management, for example, posed problems in this regard. In still other cases – for instance, the issues related to the rôle of women or problems related to the environment – the leadership of UN/IYSH concluded that the subjects should be dealt with in other ways either by UNCHS or by related organizations such as the World Commission on Environment.

The tight schedule for the completion of the study was another critical constraint. Nonetheless, we were able to attract to this enterprise many senior scholars and practitioners with exceptional experience in dealing directly or in an advisory capacity with different aspects of shelter and settlement problems in Third World countries.

In the course of the study two major changes occurred in the direction and plans. John E. Cox, the IYSH Director, completed his assignment, and his successor, Ingrid Monroe, required a brief period to become familiar with what was done and to help decide, together with Dr. Ramachandran, how this study would be used. Also, the original plan was to have an evaluation of the overview chapter and all the other contributions by a single panel of high-level Third World officials. The results were to be incorporated into the final version. Ingrid Monroe proposed instead to submit the overview chapter and policy recommendations to several high-level panels at important subregional meetings: in New Delhi in December 1985; in Dubai for Arab states in mid-January; in Bogotá, at the end of January, for Latin American states; then during February, March, and April for several African meetings. Since the initial reactions at these meetings to the overview analysis and recommendations were exceptionally positive, plans proceeded for prompt publication.

The careful reader will note some differences in emphasis and perspective among the authors. What is more noteworthy, however, is that, despite these differences, a very substantial consensus was achieved by the participants. In part, the common denominators reflect the fact that in making the reassessment the contributors were asked to take account of the five basic concerns and perspectives summarized below.

The first was the view that investments must reflect realistic and feasible development potentials. In the judgement of all concerned effective progress cannot, and does not, depend on a massive increase in foreign aid and government expenditures. The level of investments for shelter and settlements must reflect ability to pay, productivity, and family preferences (as expressed in existing or likely expenditure patterns and as constrained by political feasibility). We believe estimates of vast needs based on unrealistic standards without regard to opportunity costs are neither meaningful nor compassionate; nor are they likely, especially today, to prove persuasive to top-level decision makers and their economic and financial advisers, particularly of developing nations and of agencies providing international aid.

The second concern was that in most developing and some developed countries, regardless of the sophistication of the government structure, the effective decision-making power tends to be concentrated at the top and in a few central agencies of government (the finance ministry, a national planning commission, a bureau of the budget, etc.). The decisions of many such central agencies are constrained by the monetary and lending policies of international agencies. Within these agencies, both domestic and international, decisions are normally made without any consideration of their impact on human settlements and the poor, particularly their effects on shelter and neighborhoods. Hence, a key aim of this study is to help decision makers in these agencies become aware of and sensitive to the adverse effects of their decisions on population distribution, on settlement patterns and on shelter and neighborhood conditions.

The third guiding perspective involved the myths or illusions people have had about shelter and settlement problems in the past. We wanted to explain how and why these illusions took root and the extent to which they contributed to policies that failed. In particular, these analyses show that many of the problems have their sources in economic, social, and sectoral policies. The resolution of these problems and their future prevention should help to cope with issues of primary importance to people and governments (e.g., problems of water, food, health, employment generation, domestic capital formation, sociopolitical stability, etc.).

The fourth perspective reflects our faith. We believe that significant improvements in housing conditions are feasible for most nations. We asked the authors, therefore, to consider the critical changes – in policies and programs, in institutions and in management – which stand a good chance of being effective. We acknowledge, of course, that the necessary conditions for such changes will vary in different countries and that in some countries decisive changes will not occur without explosive social, political, and economic pressures or without profound changes in such basic institutions as land ownership, financial systems, or in the coalition of forces that manage the economic and social system.

Our final, and perhaps most important, emphasis was on learning processes. Each facet of the study sums up what we infer from past experience: what worked in the past and what did not and why; what ideas are in currency today; what changes in direction are likely in the future; and, most important of all, what efforts are needed to avoid quick fixes or one-shot solutions. These concerns are reflected in every chapter; but, for emphasis, our final chapter examines the learning processes which are likely to be necessary so that whatever action is taken is more likely to be self-correcting in the light of subsequent experience, reflection, and changing circumstances.

Lloyd Rodwin

Contents

III SETTLEMENT ISSUES

IV   RETHINKING POLICY, IMPLEMENTATION
AND MANAGEMENT

APPENDICES

I
Overview

1

Shelter, settlement, and development: An overview

LLOYD RODWIN and BISHWAPRIYA SANYAL

Synopsis

THIS STUDY DEALS with ways of addressing more effectively the problems of shelter, settlement, and development in Third World countries (TWCs). We have three aims: to explain where the TWCs are now and why, with regard to shelter, settlement, and development; to distinguish processes and policies that are working from those that are not; and to suggest measures which would encourage learning and increase the likelihood of effective responses to the problems that lie ahead.

The following summary indicates the substantial consensus which the contributors to this volume have reached on a few core ideas:

(a) We believe that most TWCs want and need to redirect their settlement and shelter policies. The time appears ripe for decisive action, in part because of the disenchantment with the experiences of the past and in part due to severe economic pressures.

(b) In confronting these issues, a critical concern is how to change deeply entrenched views concerning the low productivity and high costs of shelter and settlement. These misconceptions have been reinforced by shelter and infrastructure policies of public agencies based on inappropriate standards and ineffective methods which have inflated the costs and cut the volume of shelter produced. Actually, the contribution of shelter to GNP, savings, investment, and income – especially, shelter built incrementally with rudimentary materials – is much greater than most economists and central government planners have realized.[1,2,3] In addition, incrementally built housing provides much more effective means than the provision of public housing by the government to increase the volume and improve the quality of shelter and infrastructure and public services, at affordable costs, for all elements of the population, particularly low- and moderate-income families.[4]

(c) As for settlements, the group is skeptical about the benefits of unfettered urbanization which has resulted in the demand – impossible to satisfy – for employment, housing, transportation, and other services. We are also concerned about the growing regional inequalities exacerbated by the movement of labor and capital towards the large urban centers. However, it is important to recognize that these same centers are a critical component of the economic base of TWCs and have continued to provide individuals and business establishments opportunities to become integrated into the urban, national, and international economy. Despite the many difficulties, these cities are functional: investments are made; goods and services are produced and sold; and shelter is built and upgraded. Large urban centers have the advantages of large markets and make use of diverse technologies and varied transportation and telecommunications linkages. These activities generate jobs and income. They nourish new ties, new institutions, and possibilities for learning. They create needs which stimulate all sorts of small enterprises, thus mobilizing savings and unleashing fresh opportunities.

(d) In many ways public policies favor these huge cities, often unfairly and unnecessarily. But experience suggests that, except in very special circumstances, spatial planning strategies designed to slow down or change these trends take too much time, are costly, and are hard to implement. The benefits, too, are less conclusive than claimed. There are cheaper, more effective ways to decelerate the trends favoring big cities and to encourage development in other cities and regions.[5,6]

(e) This group proposes two alternatives for the public sector: (1) to eliminate or reduce the effects of government policies and programs which bias development in favor of big cities; and (2) do less constructing of housing and more facilitating, institution building, and land development. The former would require eliminating subsidies for infrastructure, public services, and energy that favor large cities. The latter would require more emphasis on land assemblage and preparation and infrastructure investment, the creation of a specialized national financial system for shelter, and the encouragement of small builders and suppliers of indigenous building materials serving low- and moderate-income families. These ways of promoting the building and upgrading of settlements are likely to be not only cost effective but competitive with other approaches to the promotion of jobs, income, growth, and development.

(f) We take the position that a fundamental change of perspectives is required regarding shelter built by the poor. The present shelter and settlements of the poor must no longer be perceived only as problems. They are also solutions, i.e., extraordinarily flexible adjustments to problems which neither the government nor the formal private sector have been able to solve. Instead of blocking or neglecting these settlements, there is a great need to understand them better in order to facilitate their eventual transition into healthful, productive, and efficient components of the urban community.[2]

(g) We also suggest that a necessary condition to carry out these changes will be the building of institutions. One example is the need to strengthen local government. Along with the guidance and assistance of the central government, local governments must supervise land management and infrastructure development programs. In addition, they must be responsible for setting appropriate standards for materials, building, and land use and for providing basic public services. In setting standards, local authorities must be sensitive to the different propensities among households to spend for housing. In the past unrealistic standards based on overly optimistic notions of affordability either required unsustainable subsidies to induce low-income groups to participate or led to higher-income groups benefiting from the projects.[7] Local authorities must also initiate institutional reform to improve the access of the poor to finance, land, and stable tenure. In the formulation of policies towards this end, it is necessary to distinguish and identify target groups not only on the basis of income but also on the basis of gender, since shelter needs and constraints of women in general and women-headed households in particular have often been neglected in the past.

(h) Since we still have a great deal to learn about these activities and proposed policies, much experiment and learning as well as pragmatic research will be necessary. It is best to acknowledge these gaps in our knowledge and understanding, even if we feel confident about the main directions to follow.[1,8,9,10] This candor would facilitate more deliberate program experiments and help to improve performance as the program proceeds.

We now turn more specifically to the problems – new as well as old – that have led to these views.

Some lessons of the past

Macro spatial planning and mega cities

As urban growth and development have proceeded in Third World countries, there has been growing apprehension about several trends: the increase in the population of primate cities; the high levels of real and disguised unemployment; the soaring demand for infrastructure, shelter, and services; the persistence of lagging and declining regions; the neglect of development opportunities; and politically explosive regional and social disparities.[5,11]

Over time, the positive image of the city changed, at least to the official eye. What once symbolized modernization and progress was now increasingly identified with chaotic growth, uneven distribution of benefits, and mounting social costs.

The response of the TWCs was to try to redirect urbanization through macrospatial planning. The spatial strategies implemented on the basis of these plans varied in name, scope, emphasis, and practicality. Typical examples are growth poles, satellite cities, new towns, development corridors, intermediate cities, optimum size cities, and so on. All of these variations relied on the same logic, i.e., because socioeconomic forces affect spatial forms, so, too, by spatial strategies the state might reshape the socioeconomic forces.

Such strategies proved difficult to implement. When applied with a limited objective as, for example, the promotion of a region with an exceptional resource endowment, or with the intention of strengthening a few regional centers competing with the primate city, or as a complementary effort to reinforce agricultural development through the promotion of local service centers, these approaches had some prospect of success. But, when applied without some appropriate principle of stress and sacrifice, these spatial strategies proved ineffective and expensive and sometimes lead to misallocation of investment. In any case, they failed to counter the central and sectoral policy decisions shaping public and private investments and could not offset the powerful market trends favoring spatial concentration of social and economic activities.[5,6] Worse still, when misapplied, these forms of planning scattered scarce government resources to small dispersed centers without producing significant effects.

Meanwhile, big cities continued to grow. To the surprise of many who feared the worst (outbreaks of disease, fires, and social turmoil), they have continued to provide significant economic and social infrastructure and other opportunities for their population. Although the cities do continue to function and yield net social benefits, their costs are in many ways objectionable and probably much higher than necessary. A large number of people live in extremely overcrowded conditions; most squatter compounds lack bare minimum services; a large percentage of the urban labor force survives on very small unpredictable incomes; and health and education facilities remain outside the reach of a large number of people. Moreover, the primate and other large cities usually absorb a significant amount of subsidies (both concealed and blatant) at the expense of other cities and regions; and they may perpetuate an urban bias in development policy that distorts resource allocation and encourages further migration to the cities.

Shelter, public housing, standards, and shantytowns: changing images

We have also learned much from some of the mistakes that have occurred in previous thinking and programs relating to shelter. Earlier notions, once held with much confidence, now appear to be gross oversimplifications, if not outright misconceptions. Consider four of these notions: that housing is consumption, not a productive investment; that public housing is the best way to rectify market failures; that high standards will improve the quality of shelter; and until recently, that shanty settlements are evidence of blight and failure which must be eradicated.

Housing and productivity In the competition for capital, shelter for low-income families has generally been at the end of the queue. The formal private sector ignored this segment of the market because the yield was too low. However, industry and other "economic" investments, endorsed by economists due to their higher returns, received the necessary capital and other forms of encouragement.

Today, even economists are reevaluating their position. A new point of view is that such investments in self-help housing make particular sense in TWCs "because they demand less of such scarce factors as highly skilled labor, capital, and foreign exchange, using instead relatively abundant factors of production".[3] Further, if employment is a key goal, small-scale incremental self-help shelter programs hold out the most promise for spurring direct and indirect employment creation in the poor countries.[3]

Several of the chapters in this volume also emphasize the notion that shelter is an essential part of the infrastructure of a productive society. Its contributions in terms of generating savings, investment, and income are rather significant, even when constructed incrementally with rudimentary materials. Some recent studies have also shown that with more realistic and accurate treatment of costs and benefits, shelter for low- and moderate-income families yields returns which compare favorably with productive economic activities. The evidence calls attention to the inadequate accounting concepts, the faulty treatment of benefits, the neglected backward and forward linkages, the multiplier effects of investments in complementary infrastructure and household equipment, and the need to take into account the small enterprises often carried on in, or adjacent to, the shelter and settlements of the poor.[1,2,3]

Public housing   Government responded to housing shortages, particularly for middle-income families, by building public housing. However, the actual number of units provided has been constrained by the relatively high standards (and accordingly high costs) of the shelter actually provided.[4,7] Since most of the intended residents could not afford these units, the rents have been subsidized. More often than not, even with subsidies only middle-income families could afford them. The fact that the authorities often lacked the management capabilities and/or political will to collect rents from tenants reinforced the image of public housing as a diversion of productive capital for "welfare".

However well intended, public housing has been picayune in volume, exorbitant in cost, and inefficient in administration.[1,4,7] Even in the face of this evidence, many countries still regard this alternative as their chief means for housing the poor. Inadequate financing and the very low repayments from the inhabitants made it impossible for local authorities either to augment or to maintain their housing stock. The present trend towards privatization of this housing and de-emphasis of further governmental construction is becoming acceptable, even to supporters of public housing.

High standards   The housing movement throughout the world has been based on the idea of improving the quality of shelter and settlements by condemning or eliminating units or areas that fall below "minimum" standards. The goal makes sense if shelter and infrastructure and settlements meeting these standards can either be afforded by occupants or provided by others. The goal is neither feasible nor desirable when these conditions cannot be satisfied. This happens to be the problem in most TWCs.[2,4,7]

In some instances, prevailing standards have not been a conscious choice; they simply mirrored the inherited colonial standards and ways of thinking. In other cases, high standards were demanded as evidence of modernization and economic progress, particularly if shortage of foreign exchange was not an immediate problem. Still others argued that the high capital costs required to meet high standards were preferable to high maintenance costs. The implications of high standards for low-income families somehow did not enter into these calculations; neither did the notion of cost recovery which was later to become an issue for public administrators.[4,7,12]

Much has changed in our perception of high standards. Although they now are increasingly regarded as one of the major barriers blocking the provision of shelter for low-income families, the formulation of more appropriate standards remains a difficult task. Perhaps one of the most important reasons is because it is no longer a technical but an institutional problem.[12] Official standards are supported by important groups – engineers, administrators, and other professionals, many of whom benefit in some form by retaining them. Politicians, for example, consider them a visible symbol of their efforts to provide benefits for their constituencies. Engineers often adopt high standards to avoid risks of construction failures for which they might be held responsible. Professionals who work on a percentage-of-cost-fee basis benefit accordingly from high standards; so do administrators whose budgets are increased.[12] It is often overlooked or ignored that these standards inflate costs and cut the quantity of shelter and infrastructure produced. Thus, without intending to do so, professional elites act to perpetuate ultimately inefficient standards.

Extralegal settlements Whatever the limitations of the shanty settlements may be, they have added significantly to the supply of shelter for the poor.[1,2,3,4,8] To be sure, much of this housing, constructed with scrap or rudimentary materials, is located on invaded land, or the hills, tidelands, refuse areas, and the outer edges of the city.[11] Occupied by large numbers of low-status, low-income people, they detracted from the image of modernization and aroused forebodings about crime, neighborhood change, property value decline, and loss of control by the authorities who no longer could count on traditional measures, including static blueprints of the land-use maps, to guide urban development.

Many of the chapters in this volume review some of what we now know about these incrementally built dwellings and their inhabitants. In contrast to the "myths of marginality" that had guided much of government policy during the last two decades, owners and renters of these dwellings are a cross-section of the citizenry, minus only the upper-income elite who inhabit modern residential districts.[2] The inhabitants of this housing are workers in large firms and self-employed persons, recent migrants and those who have lived in the city many years, relatively well-to-do families, and the poor. The inability of cities to prevent squatting has made it possible for even some of the latter to own homes of a sort – dwellings put together by family efforts out of cheap and scavenged materials. Meanwhile, those who can afford permanent building in better-grade materials generally employ paid carpenters and masons, generating a lively and diverse construction industry of petty contractors and craftsmen and of building materials and components.[8]

The dwellings provide shelter for the owners and contribute significantly to the rental stock.[1,2,3] They often provide working space for home-based production of goods and services which generate significant levels of income. Much of this income is used for savings and capital formation, the benefits of which remain localized. In contrast to much state-initiated development from above, these incremental settlements have helped the cities to cope with rapid urbanization, and have created investment opportunities through efficient use of local resources.

The primary source of strength of incremental building rests on the initiative and driving energy of individuals and small groups. Their autonomy, expressed in their own decisions and actions, is the key to their innovative responses in the face of repeated rejection by the authorities in the past. Over the years, this has produced a structure of organizations composed of individuals and groups connected together not by written directives of centrally administered systems but by mutual interaction and collective actions.

Administrative overcentralization and weak local government

When the first UN decade of development was launched in 1955, it was taken for granted that low-income countries with weak private sectors, stunted local and provincial governments, and internal conflict and instability needed, above all, capable leadership and strong central governments. National planning was the chosen instrument for central resource allocation; and it was generally believed that the process of development was a well defined task which could be planned and managed with central directives. But the effectiveness of such planning faltered in the face of overwhelming responsibilities.

All over the world, nations have begun to rue administrative over-centralization. This is true for socialist as well as mixed economies. The grounds for dissatisfaction vary. The most widespread criticism is that overcentralization creates apoplexy at the center and anemia at the edges. Another problem is that it usually produces cumbersome bureaucracies: in their slowness to react and their drive to maintain power, they often defer rather than accelerate progress. Third, pragmatic experience has shown central agencies to be distant from the problems to be solved, inflexible, and lacking in knowledge. Such limitations are especially crippling for locally grounded investments. These require expert knowledge of local conditions as they affect the building of shelter, the investment of infrastructure, the management of local urban centers, and the provision of public services.

In response to these well known hazards of overcentralization, a growing concern in the developing world has been how to encourage more local effort and initiatives. The "popular energy," so far trapped at the local level, must be released to provide new momentum in the development process. This will require increased responsibility and local autonomy with all of the inherent risks and errors – as well as promise. Some observers advocate a reorientation of development planning from its current preoccupation with top-down centralized planning to a bottom-up approach tied to local action and sustained through mobilization of local resources.

Unfortunately, the task is not that clear-cut: in developing countries where markets for capital, labor, and commodities are not yet well developed, development neither trickles down from the top nor effervesces from the bottom. Development comes from a combination of locally rooted innovative actions coupled with strategic central guidance directed towards efficient, equitable, and, as far as possible, agreed upon use of scarce resources.

An effective approach to shelter and settlement policies must respond to the limitations and possibilities of top-down directives and bottom-up impulses. Solutions cannot come through centralizing mechanisms into ever larger pyramidal structures. Nor can they come through local planning, which often reflects the preferences of the locally powerful and cannot guarantee efficient and equitable use of scarce resources. Central authorities can improve the functioning of the settlement and shelter system through local assistance and through the initiation of structural changes and redistribution policies. However, they must also encourage *more* local autonomy and initiatives, without which no durable response to the many problems of shelter and settlement is likely.

The problem is essentially how rôles might be redefined to strengthen both central and local government. That involves identifying the activities which the central government cannot do well and should either abandon or turn over to local or provincial governments and strengthening activities which the central government can and should pursue. It is equally important to increase the scope and effectiveness of the local government. These problems will not be solved immediately. In some cases, all that may be feasible might be greater decentralization of central government functions and headquarters. In other cases, local responsibilities for public services, revenue raising, and land-use regulations and management may be enhanced. In still other instances, the central or local government may need to relinquish control of activities that can be better performed by individuals or communities acting on their own. Ironically enough, in most environments this can occur – in the short term at least – only with the active help of the central governments.

The current crunch: crisis and opportunity

The years immediately ahead for TWCs are apt to be particularly difficult. Nevertheless, we are cautiously optimistic. The fact is most TWCs have coped with many, often fearful problems in the past. We believe that they will cope at least as well in the future. But effective reshaping of settlement and shelter policies under these conditions will not be easy.

Why should this be so? One reason is that today's development goals have become more diversified and complex. Growth and industrialization, the two main aspirations of the 1950s, remain major concerns of developing nations. In subsequent years, the issues of international economic integration, rural development, redistribution, social stability, appropriate technology, and institutional change have attained equal importance. Keeping these concerns in some reasonable balance is often baffling.

At the international level, integration with the global economy is more necessary now than ever before; yet, the need to reduce national vulnerability to international fluctuations has never been felt more strongly. At the national level, economic growth (via industrialization) remains a major objective, particularly in view of the sluggish growth experienced during the last few years. Simultaneously, the need for broad-based, rural development has emerged as a crucial component of the development process. Increased efficiency in the allocation of limited resources is likewise vital, yet redistribution and equity demand spreading of resources across sectors and regions, regardless of relative returns. Technology, too, has to be upgraded to compete on the international market, yet its choice must be mindful of the acute need for employment generation. In addition, political stability is essential to encouraging investment; yet development may require potentially disruptive institutional change. Finally, the relative confidence and decisiveness characteristic of the early years is generally missing.

Another complication is the growth of population and particularly of large cities.[10] In 1950, there were 76 agglomerations of over 1 million people. About 50 percent were in Europe and North America. In the year 2000, the number of such megacities is expected to increase to 440. About 98 (22 percent) will be in South Asia, 83 (19 percent) in East Asia, 63 (14 percent) in Africa and 46 (10 percent) in Latin America. Overall, in the developing world, 36 percent of the total population of 4.5 billion or so will be living in cities of over 100,000 people. These cities will need shelter and infrastructure at a scale unprecedented in human history. The requirements will be staggering even though megacities are expected to contribute between 30 to 70 percent of the national income of their countries.

In responding to this situation, Third World governments are currently constrained by several trends – adverse and converging. Terms of trade have run against the non-oil exporting countries of the developing world. Protectionism on the part of the industrialized countries is on the rise. Debt financing is absorbing larger percentages of export earnings, leaving less and less for investment. And although the levels of foreign aid and grants have remained approximately the same, they have been reduced as a percentage of national income.[4]

Low-income countries also face severe balance of payment problems. In a few, foreign debt has even increased to the level of GNP. Interest payments on foreign debt have steadily grown during the last decade, and some countries are clearly in difficult straits. Debt service payments, as a percentage of exports of goods and services, have increased to as much as 50 percent for many of the developing nations, particularly the primary exporters. In some cases their average reserves have dwindled to only a few weeks of imports.

The situation was in many ways different in the past. For example, between 1950 and 1975 many developing countries had experienced even more favorable growth rates than the more developed countries during their periods of industrialization. There was also evidence of clear increases in per capita income, rapid growth of education systems, increasing literacy, improvements in nutrition and health conditions, modernization of agriculture, and creation of new, important institutions (for example, extension agencies, vocational training programs, and development banks). However, even during that period, the gap between rich and poor countries tripled.

Today, it is not certain that even the limited progress of the past will be sustained in the future. Undoubtedly there will be some exceptions to the current general trends. A handful of developing nations – almost all from Asia – have managed to fare better, despite the slowing down of the international economy. These are either large countries, such as India, where exports constitute not more than 10 percent of national income, or countries with diverse export items.

But, for most developing countries, the immediate future appears gloomy. The projections are particularly disturbing for sub-Saharan African countries, where the World Bank foresees no real growth in per capita income for the first half of the coming decade; for the remaining part, a real growth of only 1.1 percent per annum per person is foreseen even under the most optimistic assumptions. Under pessimistic projections, growth per person is expected to be negative at first and negligible after that, resulting in a lower per capita income in 1990 than in 1980.

The impact of such sluggish growth on urban employment must be of major concern to settlement and shelter planners. In most developing countries, the rate of increase in urban formal sector employment is expected to be very low at best, whereas the increase in the urban labor force is projected to continue at the current rate. Three factors will sustain the growth in the labor force: rural–urban migration will continue; natural increase will constitute as much as 50 percent of the increase in urban population in some countries; and more women will join the labor force.

Those persons employed in the informal or nonwage employment sectors will be subjected to severe pressure from new entrants. This might lead to market saturation of suppliers and consequently lower the already slim profit margin for most producers.

What are the implications of these trends for the shelter and settlement problems of the Third World cities? The largest part of the additional pressure for shelter will be from low- and moderate-income households with very limited ability to pay for shelter and related services. In some countries, especially in Latin America and parts of Africa, nearly 50 percent of these households are expected to be women-headed households in which the main partner is absent, either temporarily due to migration or permanently due to separation or death. Hence, the need for shelter will be all the more important as many will use their homes for small-scale production of goods and services to supplement their income.[2] In the past, these households found accommodations either in the deteriorating city centers or in peripheral squatter communities. Now in most developing countries there is not much empty land left in the city centers.[5,13]

Even access to the peripheral land is increasingly restricted. This is only in part due to the shortage of public land. In most countries peripheral land has become a prime vehicle for the storage of capital by all social groups. This is because there are few alternative investment opportunities and/or secure and inflation-proof investment institutions. This land hoarding drastically limits the availability of land for actual use for shelter or for commerce, industry, and other activities.[13]

How may Third World cities absorb the growing number of low- and moderate-income residents? Many "austerity measures" are currently being implemented in developing countries – sharp fiscal retrenchment, restrictions on money supply, reduction of imports, devaluation of the local currency, and other related policies. Central assistance to local authorities will also be reduced. These measures, all deemed necessary to counteract the fluctuations in the balance of payments caused by the current trends in the global economy, are sure to reduce significantly the resources previously directed towards urban settlements and the shelter sector.

Despite the forbidding prospects, some of the effects could be constructive.[9] The austerity measures will put tremendous pressure on governments to improve the efficiency of their operations through more selective use of their resources. With severe resource squeezes and increasing demands, governments at both central and local levels must search for alternative revenue sources when cutting expenditures. For the central governments, this could lead to a fresh look at various subsidies which may be regressive and drain government resources. Capital-intensive projects for spatial planning will be discouraged.[6,9] The cuts will curtail expensive large-scale public housing projects and, probably, curb initiation of new projects.[4]

Austerity measures imposed by local government will include more efficient collection of charges and taxes, development of independent revenue bases, and withdrawal of subsidies. Localities will put a premium on shelter policies that would facilitate access of the maximum number of households to jobs, services, and facilities. This will encourage a redirection of emphasis from housing provided through public subsidy to shelter built with private resources. To some extent, import restrictions and devaluation of national currencies may impel building materials industries to decrease their reliance on imported materials in favor of appropriate local substitutes.[8]

The redirection of shelter, settlement, and development policies

In this period of searching reappraisal, thinking may change in other ways. For example, our group believes we should recognize human settlements as a part of the physical infrastructure essential for development – a kind of societal machinery which it is the task of governments to maintain and improve. The job of urban planners requires a deeper understanding of how cities work and how governments can help them work better, both for the people who live in them and for the local and regional functions they perform.[2,5]

Shelter, as well, will be viewed differently. Families require shelter just as machinery requires industrial buildings. Shelter is an indispensable part of the infrastructure of a productive society. The shelter systems of cities encompass public regulation, the interaction of private and public building, and the provision of infrastructure and services by the state. The way shelter is produced, managed, and regulated determines much of the framework for city life. The way in which people get access to shelter has, therefore, important social and political implications. A creative shelter policy must serve these multiple and interrelated functions.

Given these changing perspectives on the rôle of shelter and settlements, what policy guidelines might TWCs explore?

Settlement policy

Let us first consider settlement policy. The fact is we do not really know when a city is too big or too congested, rather than poorly organized or managed. Furthermore, we have as yet learned little more than the rudiments of how to convert a settlement into a growth center and how to radiate so-called growth impulses from such centers to surrounding hinterlands. To be sure, decision makers often have to manipulate forces they do not fully understand, but given what we know, spatial planning strategies should be applied with caution. The evidence suggests that *eventually* "urban dynamics will lead to deconcentration from the central core to the outer ring within the mega urban region; and *eventually* – they will lead to a slowing down of the region's growth at the expense of second order cities. But there is nothing mechanical or inevitable about the timing of this process: it may occur sooner or later".[5]

Government intervention in this process of transformation must be extremely sensitive to powerful market trends. This group believes that aiding deconcentration of the primate city or of large metropolitan areas makes sense only when the advantages of concentration are clearly diminishing.[2] In the meantime, governmental efforts can be directed towards reducing congestion, taking account of the accessibility requirements of intra-urban activities, and generating a broad tax base for the maintenance of infrastructure in all areas. The management mechanisms employed should be particularly responsive to the needs of low-income households, whose spatial access to income-earning opportunities must be improved significantly.

There are circumstances in which the containment of primate cities is desirable and justified. Experience indicates, however, that in these cases the most effective measures often may be indirect. Above all, government should not create programs that might unjustifiably increase the attractiveness of these cities. For example, subsidized urban infrastructure (especially transportation and services) and price controls on energy are policies and activities which are expensive, of dubious value, and extremely difficult to terminate once begun. In addition, the criteria for allocating the pool of national urban infrastructure investments merits the most critical scrutiny, and, no doubt, sturdy resistance to primate city pressures. Over the long term, still other measures such as adoption of family-planning programs may well be warranted. Of course, none of these measures is feasible if the appropriate political climate does not exist for pursuing such a policy.

The promotion of secondary cities is another issue. As a tool for countering primacy, it has had virtually no impact. The efforts have been too dispersed, controls on the big cities have proved ineffective, and generally inappropriate methods have been used (e.g., expensive industrial estates in cities with little industrial potential). However, the promotion of secondary cities might be a viable strategy if the aims and scope were more limited and the methods more realistic.[6] This might be the case if the policy were harnessed to rural development. The government might contribute to this specific focus by improving servicing centers for agricultural needs and by promoting processing centers for procurement and marketing of agricultural products. There could also be less expensive and more specific targets. For example, the programs could be made more dependent on the contribution of local resources and might offer credit assistance and management training for small enterprises and other indigenous activities.

Governments today are also disposed to favor broad-based rural development which could facilitate the flow of goods and services from the core to the periphery and vice versa. Well conceived, labor intensive programs aimed at increasing rural income, such as farm-to-market roads or economically sound irrigation projects, could yield substantial savings in shelter and service costs by retaining population in the periphery, where the cost of provision of shelter is usually lower. They would also expand agricultural output and provide significant long-term rural employment. The contributors to this volume share the view that well conceived rural and urban development strategies are not conflicting but fundamentally complementary priorities, each contributing to the productive base of both rural and urban areas.

The suggestions summarized above should be spelled out more explicitly and in more detail as a national settlement policy.[3] Having a settlement policy would not be novel: close examination reveals significant but implicit settlement policies in most countries. However, it would be valuable to make them explicit and realistic. Explication would make each nation's policy easier to confront, to examine for inconsistencies, and to coordinate internally. It would then be possible to explore the effects of tax, trade, transportation and other policies on settlement aims.

Shelter policy

Both the traditional private and public sector programs have failed to provide shelter in adequate volume at prices the poor can afford. The only way the bulk of the poor are now sheltered in TWCs is through incremental house building by the urban poor themselves. In the past, governments have insisted on demolishing the consequent shanty towns. However, sooner or later the shanty towns reappeared and, for lack of an alternative, they have been grudgingly tolerated.

Our attitudes to incremental building by the urban poor are now changing. Though deplored by officials and the public, such building is, and must be seen as, an efficient component of the shelter delivery system.[1,2,3,4,8] Given the acute resource scarcities they face, Third World governments must recognize incremental building as the functional substitute for the incremental paying that takes place in countries with mortgage systems reaching the working class.

We noted earlier the significant contributions of incremental building to generating savings, investment, income, and employment, even when constructed with the most rudimentary materials. Our group recognizes that such an acknowledgement may imply a blanket approval of the entire process of incremental building and explicit rejection of standards to ensure shelter quality. We understand the severity of the problems created for the local authorities by haphazard and illegal patterns of urban growth.

However, since it is no longer possible to deny or ignore these extralegal building processes, we believe one of the tasks of shelter policy is to prepare a process well in advance of the future growth of urban population that can utilize the tremendous energies embodied in incremental building and incorporate them more effectively and equitably into the productive structure of the urban system.

In the formulation of shelter policy it is necessary to recognize and understand the particular housing needs of women and women-headed households, who are disproportionately represented among the poorest of the poor. Ironically, at present in many countries there are specific constraints which limit women's access to shelter on the basis of their gender, although they take primary care of the home. We cite only three examples of ways in which redirection of policy is necessary. First, women should be allowed to possess titles to land and not be denied access to credit. Secondly, project site location and physical planning ought to be responsive to women's as well as men's income-earning activities. Third, is the need to eliminate the many obstacles to the participation of women-headed households in low-cost shelter projects.[2,13]

Even if the general thrust of redirected shelter policy must focus on the poor and be sensitive to the particular needs of women, it must also address the housing demand of moderate-income families. In part, this is because a viable shelter policy requires political support, and a shelter policy focused *only* on the needs of the poor cannot count on enough political support. In addition, a surplus of moderately priced housing would benefit the poor through filtration processes, whereas a shortage of such units would not only reduce the total stock of housing for low- and moderate-income families but also bid up the prices of this portion of the housing stock. We must not forget that middle-income families have been the main, if not exclusive, beneficiaries of public housing programs. If government construction of public housing is drastically curtailed, there will be pressure to provide an appropriate alternative for this segment of the market. Since most of these families want to be homeowners, the appropriate alternative might be based on these aspirations.

New home construction for this group, to the extent that it is possible under current conditions, must be undertaken by private builders, who need encouragement. One very effective way may be to reduce through public and private sector policies the risks in serving moderate-income families. One reason why developers serve mainly upper-income households in countries with little or no long-term finance is that only these households can afford to buy. Another reason may be that larger margins make up for the real risks of unsold inventory. In the present period of slow growth and scarce financing, many builders of housing may be willing to trade these margins for much smaller risks in return for emphasis on moderate-income shelter.

However, for housing finance agencies to take this initiative, they must greatly improve their ability to evaluate the financial, technical, and commercial risks of the development projects they are expected to finance. They must be able to negotiate quickly and effectively appropriate new arrangements with the developers when some of these risks begin to materialize.[9]

Land and tenure

To encourage investment in shelter by the urban poor, rules for establishing provisional as well as long-term property rights must be firmly established. In the past, clouded titles often seriously inhibited the efforts of the urban poor, who value ownership and may require it for credit eligibility. Experience has confirmed that self-builders only invest substantially in an asset they perceive as secure. Of course, the degree of property rights needed to achieve a perception of security varies with the culture and circumstances. For example, in the African countries, cadastral surveys are often limited to former colonial enclaves and traditions of tribal ownership remain deeply rooted. Therefore, tenure arrangements approximating de facto ownership may provide sufficient security for investment. In Latin America, where civil (Roman) law prevails, a status close to legal tenure may be necessary. The decision to invest may also be determined by other factors, e.g., the pattern of police attitudes towards squatters and the extent of neighborhood organizations, which varies from place to place.[1,13]

The cities of the developing world now have had one great advantage over those of the industrialized countries in respect to their shelter. This advantage is the high incidence of at least de facto home-ownership among people with relatively low incomes. This circumstance came about not through government policy but through the inability to implement policy. Avoidance of fixed shelter costs is important to people with fluctuating and undependable income; but vast cities of poor tenants are bound to be politically and socially volatile and difficult to manage. Because it was impossible to prevent squatting and to enforce building codes, rather poor families were able to acquire land and to build incrementally within their means. Right of tenure, which had no status in law, nevertheless became established in usage. As land markets and regulatory systems tighten up, this situation is likely to alter. Policy makers, therefore, must try to hold on to the existence and the advantage of ownership as much as possible.

To retain this advantage evolving land policies will have to deal with their own version of the "standards" issue. Poor people, like other people, want security of tenure; and indeed some security of tenure seems required for people to invest in their housing. Furthermore, cities need to regularize and to tax their real property. But, there is evidence that legalizing the tenure of land formerly held by irregular arrangements outside the legal system raises the price. As in eliminating substandard housing, eliminating irregular tenure may remove a low-cost option and cut some persons out of the market. In addition, it is customary in many cities for low-income occupancy to be tolerated in central locations, potentially of high value, on the understanding that such rights are only temporary and are terminable when government or the private owner wants to make another use of the property. Each group of policy makers must experiment with ways of managing these difficult conflicts and of devising a variety of tenures which can grant some security without, necessarily, involving permanent fee simple. Among these arrangements there is probably room for a number involving various kinds of collective use and responsibility.

To a significant extent, the tenure arrangements to be made depend on the way the poor households are provided access to land. One way is through government procurement of land by such means as compulsory purchase (financed in part or whole by taxation of capital gains and idle land). Another method is by opening up new land through the provision of public infrastructure, especially water, waste disposal, and transportation. A third approach is to increase the efficiency of existing use by encouraging potential owners to rent rooms.

A word of caution must be mentioned about government acquisition of land in advance, commonly referred to as land banking. It is understandable that when land prices are rising there are advantages for local communities or government agencies to buy land in advance of need for the purpose of either shaping a desired land-use pattern or to influence land prices. And if the process is coordinated with the extension of urban services to new land, the resulting price of serviced sites will be reduced.

A number of difficulties, however, make our group reluctant to recommend this policy, except when the circumstances are clearly exceptional. To be successful, land banking requires administrative capabilities which many municipal governments in the TWCs do not have at this time. Land purchases also presuppose ample funds at low interest rates. Just the opposite is now the case. There are also the uncertainties of advance planning, land management, and price setting, not to mention the increased risk of squatter invasion which can be resisted only at some political cost.

Finance

Unable to tap institutional financing services, low-income households rely on informal financing methods (e.g., selling assets and borrowing from friends, family members, money lenders, and the like). Since these services are limited and expensive, the problem is how to create better alternatives – in the main, more capital on better terms.

In the past, governments have tried, by regulation, to keep interest rates low. These efforts have turned out to be self-defeating. They dry up the source of funds because households will not make deposits in institutions; or else because of the underpricing of financial services, the institutions become dependent on subsidy which must be very limited in TWCs. To be sure, increased accessibility of the poor to adequate shelter is, and rightly should be, a critical concern for policy makers, but so are the various hazards faced by financial institutions in an inflationary environment. There are risks for institutions and savers inherent in unattractive interest rates, long-term maturities, problems of liquidity, and dangers of default. Little is gained in subsidizing a few borrowers at the expense of many depositors and the ability to attract savings.[9,14]

At present formal housing finance institutions finance only a modest amount of housing construction in TWCs. However, in the longer term such institutions must play a more important rôle which requires that they begin by mobilizing the savings of the people who will eventually receive loans. This will make the institutions more acceptable to the community, spread an understanding of financial practices, and give the institutions much needed market information about their potential borrowers. However, those housing finance institutions which do exist in developing countries currently rely predominantly on wholesale funding, and it seems that this must remain the case at least in the short run. In the long run, when the institutions have been firmly established, they can experiment with retail fund raising, though this will be a long and difficult process.[14]

There is a possibility of drawing on nonmarket sources of funds through "directed" credit programs. This involves drawing into the financing of shelter either tax-based "social housing" funds and/or retirement system funds. Still other examples are "directed credit" policies applied to commercial banks, plus forced deposit schemes. How feasible it may be to deploy these methods depends on the priority accorded to housing and the degree of development of the nation's financial system. For many countries the use of these funds for housing may be a way of mobilizing household savings that would not otherwise occur. By doing so it may even free other funds for nonresidential investment. This explains, in part, why these funds constitute the most likely source of finance for shelter beyond the resources of household income plus voluntary savings and deposits.

It is tempting to recommend channeling a portion of these funds into the building or improvement of shelter. The great fear, however, is that these schemes may simply dissipate scarce financial resources and possibly undermine their original purposes.[9] Some in our group consider this too risky a proposition, especially for inflation-prone economies. However, these directed programs are already playing a significant rôle in several countries, and they may be one of the more important ways of increasing the volume of credit for shelter.

Aside from the difference in views within our group on this subject, we do agree on three basic matters. The first is that successful housing finance policies are severely handicapped, if not impossible, without macroeconomic policies favoring relative price stability.[9,14] Second, if financial institutions wish to mobilize funds, they must keep their interest rates close to the market cost of funds.[7,9,14] On the lending side, it might be better to experiment with more flexible lending arrangements adjusted to different market segments and household needs. Possible examples are loan-to-value ratios, debt–income ratios, amortization periods and indexing rates rather than an exclusive focus on interest rates. Third, there is increasingly persuasive evidence that even very low income households shrewdly change their financial strategies to improve their shelter when they can count on affordable standards, minimal infrastructure and public services, and some reasonable security of tenure. Then many of these households alter their consumption patterns and convert their few assets, often kept in sterile but moveable form, to obtain additional resources from their friends and relatives. To generate an additional stream of income to pay for the improvements, some households may also rent out rooms. This adds to the number of low-priced accommodations and helps to speed up the pace of construction. All too often governments attempt to *freeze* the rental market with the objective of protecting tenants. The effect, however, is very often the opposite: it discourages the provision of rental accommodations and thereby drives up the price of existing accommodations.[1,9,14]

The construction industry and building materials

Most governments have tended to support large firms, both private and public, over small firms and informal enterprises in the construction and building materials industries. In the past, government policies included: transportation subsidies to large-scale producers of building materials; preferential treatment to large-scale firms in awarding contracts for construction and building materials; preferential treatment for imports of capital-intensive materials and equipment; and the overprotection of nascent domestic industries from foreign competition.[8]

The avowed reason for the preference was that large-scale firms provided economies of scale. Currently this assumption has come under close scrutiny.[8] A number of studies of large-scale firms have underscored distinct disadvantages. They create less employment because they are capital intensive. They are a drain on scarce foreign exchange because they require imports. They also consume significant amounts of energy and have large financial requirements.[1,8]

Small-scale firms, on the other hand, offer benefits that are particularly significant for developing countries currently confronted by macro-economic constraints. For example, small firms have lower overhead costs and are therefore more competitive. They also reflect relative factor prices, and they generate more jobs across the board, particularly for low-skilled labor.[1] Small firms depend less on large, concentrated markets and large deposits of raw materials, thus minimizing the need for transport of both raw materials and finished products. They also consume less energy, use fewer imported materials, and are generally more flexible in responding to localized demands. For these reasons, this group recommends a shift in emphasis away from large private firms and state-supported monopolies and toward small-scale builders and suppliers of building materials who cater to low-income households.

There are several ways Third World governments may encourage small firms and the use of indigenous building materials. Foremost is the reformulation of standards for materials, zoning, and building designs. These must be affordable by low-income households and still be consistent with their health and safety requirements. Other policies may include augmenting sources of financing for small-scale builders and producers, allocation of low-rent plots for informal enterprises in or very near low-income housing areas, and extension services for technical assistance and managerial training. Furthermore, the government's system of distributing raw materials must be sensitive to the needs of small builders. Also, the costs and benefits of regulations, which require informal enterprises to obtain licenses and obey labor regulations, should be re-examined. They often hinder firms whose competitive edge is the informality of their production system.[8]

What next? Implications for implementation

We believe the new emphases in policy proposed here – more modest in some respects and more ambitious in others – will appeal both to government officials and to officers of international assistance agencies who have become discouraged with the discrepancies between aims and achievements in existing shelter and settlement programs.

Nonetheless, the prospects for these ideas, too, depend on how they are implemented. To be sure, whatever is done will vary and, indeed, should vary in different countries. It might be helpful to spell out some of the more important specific actions that are often likely to be required on the part of central governments, local governments, community groups, nongovernmental organizations, and international agencies.

We have already explained why most central governments in TWCs have neither the financial and human resources nor the institutional capacity to build shelter on a significant scale to an adequate standard at prices that poor or even moderate-income households can afford. However, there are tasks they can or must handle which might provide even greater leverage in achieving their aims. First, national policy regarding the rôles of settlement and shelter in development must be clarified. These policies should provide guidelines for the public and private sector activities generally and promote collaborative efforts. They should also eliminate any gender bias in national policy that does not allow women's rights to land and shelter.

In addition, as already noted, one of the main jobs of central governments should be to provide the infrastructure for settlement and shelter, or to provide the funds to local authorities for land and infrastructure development. Central government can also create a more flexible and innovative system for shelter finance, encourage indigenous building material industries and small construction enterprises, and break up public sector construction projects into much smaller components that small firms could undertake.

There are other tough issues ahead. For example, central governments need to evaluate, and try to offset, the indirect effects of national policies and sectoral programs that intensify regional inequalities or development bias in favor of particular regions or cities. Governments also need to examine the priority given to servicing existing settlements over new developing areas. It may be necessary to provide for maintenance in order to reduce the much higher capital investment costs when maintenance problems are not anticipated.[4] Re-examination of pricing policies and the privatization possibilities for infrastructure provision may help eliminate subsidies for households that do not require them. There are still other innovations governments may wish to promote: for example, more realistic building codes and shelter standards which may be adopted by local authorities; also, experiments with more varied mortgage instruments involving flexible terms and interest rates. These efforts would serve the needs for shelter of moderate-income households as well as low-income ones.

Local governments

The actions of central governments are not the only condition necessary for successful implementation. Effective redirection of shelter policy must come from invigorated local governments. Only they can respond to the particularities of local problems and requirements. At present, in most developing countries local authority is stunted. To handle increased responsibilities, these authorities need more power.[11]

For example, local authorities must be able to increase the availability of serviced land through the provision of infrastructure, especially water, waste disposal, and transportation. They need to find new ways of providing such infrastructure on a skeletal basis at first, without too high a front-end cost. For transportation, for instance, this might be done through the reservation of reserved bus rights-of-way on existing streets. For water and liquid waste disposal, a significant infrastructure cost is entailed and subsidy in the early years may often be inescapable. Local authorities must also ensure that rules are set for establishing provisional and long-term priority rights to encourage investment in shelter. At some stage this will require land survey, mapping, and an orderly process for land subdivision and granting of titles.

To facilitate incremental building by the poor, local governments will have to alter local building codes and regulations and provide some guidelines or assistance to low-income communities for home building and for postoccupancy upgrading and management problems. They will have to encourage rather than penalize the creation of housing and rooms for rent. Residents of the previously built shantytowns will need to reach agreement with the larger community on balancing the costs of the desired infrastructure and services in return for value added by upgrading and/or legitimation of current occupancy.

To carry out these and other functions, local governments need a revenue base largely independent of central authorities. Adequate revenue may require more effective property tax rates, adequate fees for services, user charges, and the capacity to recover at least the maintenance and some portion of the amortization costs of infrastructure provision. If subsidy levels for site and service projects are to be reduced from their current level, which is more than 50 percent in many cases, it will take a combination of political will and effective planning.[7] In achieving the latter, priority should be placed on identifying the level of shelter and infrastructure standards that are truly affordable, and this must be based on careful surveys of effective demand conducted at the local level. When low-income families contribute such support, local authorities will be hard pressed to ensure more direct participation by the poor in the local political process and decision making.

These are tall orders. The local government will require shrewd, innovative and knowledgeable management. Most of the experience and skills needed will take time to acquire. The local authorities will need assistance and training from the central government. Bilateral and multilateral agencies should be able to provide help on these matters.

Community groups

Shelter provision often requires cooperation between low-income communities and agencies carrying out programs and projects. Success may depend on how this occurs.[1] In the traditional approach, there was virtually no cooperation between households and implementing agencies. Agencies did not invite occupant participation since it was thought to delay getting things done. Sometimes tenant involvement was added as an afterthought, if the funds allocated for community development had to be used up. We think community involvement is an indispensable tool for the government acting as a facilitator, rather than as a constructor, in the provision of shelter.

Such cooperation can conserve public resources by shifting some of the responsibilities to the people involved. For example, once local authorities provide low-income areas with basic infrastructure, the residents there share in or make the decisions about internal roads, location of water stand pipes, and other details. The residents may negotiate with the local authorities regarding the level of services to be provided and on arrangements for payment. Such cooperation in planning, design and postoccupancy management often earn participants significant rewards: participation, like ownership, increases their sense of control over the process and generates innovative responses that may be cost effective.

Such involvement will not happen spontaneously: it requires much effort by energetic and sensitive staff. In the past, this requirement was often treated as a "soft component" of projects – last on the list of project items and the first to be reduced if cost overruns needed to be checked. This practice must change if we want to encourage and sustain widespread community improvement.

Nongovernmental organizations (NGOs) and private voluntary organizations (PVOs)

NGOs and PVOs are usually small in scale and less subject to the inertia or interagency rivalries that often reduce the effectiveness of bureaucracies in implementing programs. They are more prone to experiment with innovative ideas which are often shunned by established agencies more vulnerable to criticism. NGOs and PVOs have been successful in encouraging private initiative in solving local problems. They usually rely on appropriate (locally learned) technologies more than government agencies do and have proved to be remarkably cost effective in activities ranging from agricultural production schemes and women's income generation projects to programs related to shelter. For these reasons, the rôle of NGOs and PVOs should be enhanced. To do so would require more responsiveness to their activities and needs, as well as better means of keeping informed about and learning from their efforts.

International agencies

International donors, bilateral and multilateral, have made significant contributions to the ongoing policy dialogue about shelter and settlements. They have financed experimental programs and technical assistance; they have propagated important concepts innovated in the field, such as site and service and shelter upgrading schemes; and in joint ventures with universities in the TWCs, multilateral and bilateral agencies, such as the UN, the World Bank, USAID, and many other bilateral programs, have trained personnel from the developing countries to support institutional development requirements.[4] In particular, the current focus on increasing public and private managerial skills is likely to yield long-term benefits.[1] Over time, too, the diverse international workshops and seminars for TWC professionals are contributing toward building an international consensus on shelter policy issues.

However, in terms of allocation of substantial financial resources, the international donor community has never assigned a particularly high priority to shelter compared to other sectors.[4] In the current international environment of expensive capital and scarce domestic savings, there is actually much pressure for the donor agencies to reduce their allocations for shelter.[1,9] But there will be much resistance too in some quarters to these trends. Some policy makers in the developing world have even suggested that an international housing bank should be created to provide seed capital for a revolving fund to provide shelter for the poor. The proposal is still rather vague and opinions are mixed on this score. For example, some members of this group think the problems of shelter in the developing world are due more to institutional weaknesses than to lack of resources. Others feel that even limited additional resources for the shelter sector can be extremely useful, particularly if used to reinforce the shift of policy in favor of providing serviced plots instead of finished shelter units. During this International Year of Shelter, relevant professional and policy meetings should consider this critical issue.

Monitoring and evaluation

Although there is considerable evidence to support the recommendations made, the directions for shelter and settlement policies proposed by this group are only general guidelines. If agreed upon, specific policies must still be tailored by each nation to respond to their unique needs and sociopolitical conditions. Unforseeable problems in putting these ideas into effect will surely arise. Every interested country must quickly identify these problems and make the alterations in policies necessary to improve their effectiveness. This will require monitoring and evaluation at both central and local levels.

At the central level, the question is whether the shelter and settlement programs proposed can meet the guidelines of efficiency, equity, and compatibility.[1] Analysts evaluating programs on the basis of efficiency may ask: Does the program provide maximum services per unit of cost? Is it flexible enough to withstand changes in the market forces? Does enough administrative capability exist to implement the program? Evaluating on the basis of equity, policy makers may ask: Will the programs serve low-income groups? Are production costs low enough to allow shallow subsidy? Do programs broaden the asset base by permitting ownership? To evaluate compatibility, one might ask: Are the programs congruent with the participants' cultural background in general and with their land systems in particular? Does the program complement or conflict with other programs, policies, and sectors?

Monitoring and evaluation at the local level might emphasize still another orientation. If governments are serious about acting as facilitators in a shelter and settlement system with many local and private actors, government policies must be seen as experiments to be tested in the field.[15] In this process the formation of policy cannot be neatly separated from its implementation. Quite the contrary! Wherever feasible, policy should be iterative, i.e., tentative and subject to careful review and reformulation at local as well as central levels after close observation of local reactions.[15]

To achieve flexibility and specificity at the same time, the monitoring required at both the central and the local levels may de-emphasize the collection of data on project costs or on the number of beneficiaries, even though such figures will be useful in honing emerging policies.[2] Instead, empirically grounded descriptions should be written of how shelter is created, managed, and maintained and what invisible systems govern these processes. Collection of information on the trade-offs made by households among different elements of the housing infrastructure bundle (e.g., relative preferences for size and location of plot, size and quality of structure, proximity to community facilities, quality and type of infrastructure) will also be helpful in improving project design and shelter sector strategies.[7] Such refined data can be acquired through interviews with program recipients and the staff involved in carrying out specific projects. This kind of case study approach will provide a rich base of information to use in refining policy instruments for future action.

The approach we are proposing involves improved management and programming at the municipal as well as central level, and it requires local governments to exercise more responsibility. As already noted, austerity conditions may prompt the central authority to promote more local power. Only case studies of specific circumstances can elucidate the best ways to achieve such reorganizations of central and local government activities.

Another essential area of inquiry is the nature of the interaction between conventional and incremental building, credit, and land systems. Several chapters in this volume recommend policies both to foster this interaction and to coordinate the conventional and incremental systems. At this time we do not have an adequate understanding of either system. We need to know how governments can lend their support without creating undue risks for the conventional system and without neutralizing the freedom of action, the spontaneity, and the capacity to improvise that have made the incremental systems worth promoting. Furthermore, governments committed to legality must find ways to cope with unregistered shelter activities outside the customary categories and procedures of the legal system. We need more information on how this has been handled in different circumstances.

A third area concerns the appropriate balance between the needs of low-income depositors and the needs of borrowers. To originate a mortgage, an institution must at some earlier stage collect a large number of small deposits. Many policy discussions during the past 15 years have concentrated exclusively on the financing of beneficiaries and remained indifferent to the sources of funds. In the late 1980s such policies need to be challenged.

Many other fruitful areas for investigation are suggested in the chapters that follow. We shall, therefore, conclude with one last set of questions: Who should be involved in the monitoring and evaluation system that will attempt to find answers to these kinds of problems? How should qualitative research on shelter and settlement systems be institutionalized? Most agencies do not have much experience in the kinds of fieldwork-based research that we propose. Comparative evaluation of how institutions function must not be done by people who are closely identified with a particular program of action.

One option is to utilize international agencies, such as the United Nations or the World Bank. One participant suggested that, since the kind of research required will have substantial public good attributes and since its benefits will have considerable international spillovers, international agencies should sponsor this type of research.[1] However, as with national agencies, evaluation must be performed by analysts not associated with the programs under scrutiny.

Another option is to base research in local universities, to be assisted by universities in the developed world, if such joint or collaborative arrangements can be made as part of international assistance. Unfortunately, such research tends to move according to the wrong timetable for action and to respond to the incentives for academic success, namely a theoretical rather than a practical focus.

Given the wide range of views on these subjects, perhaps this issue of research monitoring and evaluation, best illustrates one of several important questions that ought to be included in the extensive and critical agenda for discussion with top policy makers in settlement and shelter agencies in TWCs. They should be encouraged to express their views on the importance of the problems raised in this volume and on the approaches that best reflect their particular needs and experience.

II

Shelter issues

2

Economic impact and implications of shelter investments

LEO H. KLAASSEN, JAN G. D. HOOGLAND and MICHIEL J. F. VAN PELT

Introduction

ECONOMISTS HOLD different views on the question of how much funding developing countries should allocate to shelter or habitat (here defined as a dwelling, plus necessities directly linked to shelter such as water, sanitation, electricity, and local roads). This difference of opinion exists mainly because they do not agree on two other questions: the economic nature of habitat outlays and the optimal policy for economic development.

In the traditional sense, consumption means spending money now on goods and services that will not, through further productive processes, induce benefits in the future. *Present* welfare increases without consequences for the generation of future welfare. Investments, on the other hand, contribute to the capital stock and are made to increase production (by raising productivity) and therefore raise *future* welfare. Grossly, investments are financed out of savings; people (or governments or private firms) limit their present consumption in the belief that consumption from their future income will more than compensate for the sacrifice.

How does habitat fit in? Its position is somewhat ambiguous. On the

one hand, spending on habitat is an investment inasmuch as the capital
stock increases. On the other hand, at least in the traditional view, it does
not increase productivity; hence future production and welfare. Apart
from rents, only welfare increases directly: by "consuming" the services
of their house, the occupants feel better. Habitat may be defined, then, or
be looked upon as *consumptive* capital.[1] In that view, building new
houses is an investment, though not a productive one.

This traditional approach has been criticized by a number of authors,
who state that better housing does have positive impacts on productivity
and therefore spending on habitat is investing in *productive* capital. In
their view the chain of economic impacts does not end with the direct
consumption of the habitat services, the crucial argument being that by
living in a better house the occupants will perform better in their work. In
other words, their productivity will rise, and so will future output and
income. In this way, habitat belongs to a category, the existence of which
makes the relevance of the traditional consumption–investment dichot-
omy rather doubtful. Like food, medical care, and education shelter is a
necessary consumptive good with important productive aspects that
influence future welfare.

Now let us turn to the question of development policy: Should
economic development be attained by rapid economic growth, the
traditional point of view, or by a basic needs strategy, a more recent
approach that incorporates distributional aspects? These are two
extreme positions, but they illustrate our purpose. The advocates of rapid
growth feel that resources should be allocated to sectors with the
greatest future returns, especially certain types of manufacturing
industry. Or, referring to the investment–consumption distinction, they
propagate nonconsumptive capital accumulation. As for the distribution
of income, their assumption is usually that the benefits of growth will
"trickle down" to the poor in future. Advocates of the basic needs
approach concentrate on relieving poverty in a country. Unconvinced by
the trickling-down argument, they believe the poor should be helped
now by, among other things, generation of employment and provision of
social services such as education and shelter. In short, they put more
emphasis on present income and consumption and their distribution.

What about habitat? People who defend rapid economic growth
usually do not see it as a sound investment opportunity. A number of
industrial opportunities offer far greater direct returns and thus
contribute more to economic growth. Improvement of the habitat
situation is at best a goal of development to be reached by economic
growth. It is certainly not a tool of development. Defenders of the theory
that habitat investments do have productive impacts will disagree,
pointing out that these impacts contribute to growth. As a consequence

they see better and better serviced houses not only as a goal but also as a tool of development.[2]

Supporters of the basic needs approach set less store by the debate on the categorization of funds spent on habitat, concentrating instead on the other effects of habitat investments. Poor people will be supplied with a basic need – better habitat. In addition, a number of poor people will see their income raised as new employment in the construction sector and other sectors is created. In that way, habitat is certainly also a tool of development.

In reality, most developing countries will seek to combine the growth and basic needs approaches. Growth and provision of basic needs are often seen as goals that are not necessarily mutually exclusive. Therefore both the impacts of habitat investments on productivity and the wide range of impacts on present income and its interpersonal distribution are legitimate means for development.

In this chapter two questions are dealt with that are important for the problem of how much a country should spend on habitat and to which kind of project it should allocate the available habitat funds:

(1) What are the economic impacts habitat investments may have?
(2) What kinds of habitat projects are likely to produce the greatest benefits?

Let it be stressed that the analysis is not confined to purely financial benefits to the investor; in fact, emphasis is on the benefits to the nation. They are judged with a view to alternative development strategies. The available space only permits a tentative outline of the answers. In addition, we disregard related topics dealt with elsewhere in this book, such as implementation, administration and finance.

Figure 2.1 summarizes in a very simple way the direct and indirect impacts a habitat investment may have on economic variables. It shows that the ultimate macroeconomic changes are influenced by economic, social, and spatial factors. We do not intend to discuss the whole system, but will confine ourselves to some basic parts of the model.

In the following sections three important kinds of impacts of shelter investments will be highlighted:

(1) impacts of the investment itself on employment in formal and informal habitat and nonhabitat sectors;
(2) impacts of the resulting quantitatively or qualitatively improved habitat stock at the microlevel on the income of occupants and other groups;
(3) impacts that result from (1) and (2) at the macrolevel – income, income distribution, balance of payments, prices.

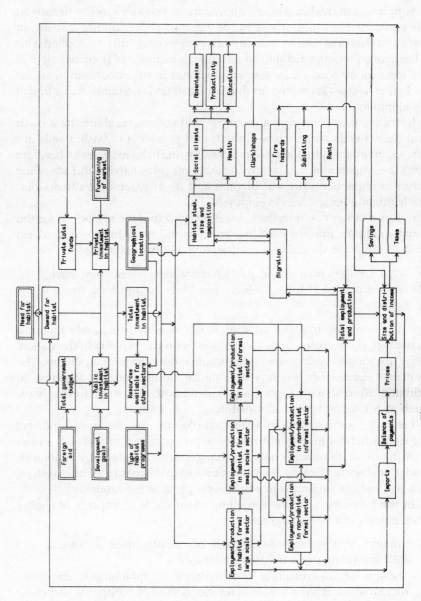

Figure 2.1 A socio-economic habitat model.

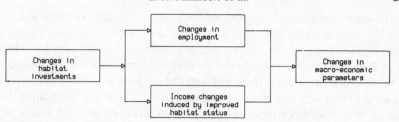

Figure 2.2   Interaction of habitat investment impacts.

Thus attention will be given to the relations shown in Figure 2.2.

We emphasize that we analyse the economic *potential* of habitat investments here. Real world circumstances may prevent the full realization of this potential. The final section, especially, refers to determining factors in this respect.

Impacts of investments on employment

Introduction

If the decision is made to invest more in habitat, how much more employment will be created? This is an important question, especially in developing countries where unemployment and, even more, under-employment prevail on a large scale. The answer will be that it depends to a great extent on the type of habitat projects on which the money is spent.

We aim here at giving a broad picture of the possible employment impacts of a habitat investment. For that purpose we start in the next subsection with a description of the most common types of habitat projects. Next, attention is given to the sectors in which directly (in the construction sector) or indirectly (in other sectors, following backward linkages) employment could be created. Then, the effects of the alternative habitat projects on these sectors are treated; first in a study of the relation between the type of project and direct employment creation is studied, and secondly in a treatment of the indirect employment impacts. The penultimate subsection deals with differences in impacts between urban and rural areas.

Types of habitat projects

Some decades ago local governments became seriously worried about the existence of districts where people lived in very bad conditions. The slums, mostly legally built in the older parts of cities, and squatter settlements, in general illegally created by immigrants or others, upset the government officials. These quarters did not fit into their image of development. Moreover, the squatters usually occupied land for which they had other uses in mind. The reaction of the authorities consisted in going against, and often demolishing, the settlements. The people were chased to districts way out of the center of town, staying there until they got driven away once more. This attitude could not prevent slums and squatter settlements growing considerably. Grimes[3] mentions that in cities in developing countries from 10 to 90 percent of the population is living in these areas. A relatively high number of cities have about half their population living in slums and squatter settlements.

Although demolition programs still exist in a great number of countries, another "positive" approach has come up. Supporters of this new approach feel that slums and squatters are phenomena that are inherent to urban development. They acknowledge the existence of the settlements and feel that the *government* should help the poor. A first action was to introduce *public housing programs*. Because the *private sector* in fact only catered for middle- and higher-income classes, the idea was for the government to build for the lower-income classes. Unfortunately, public housing, which has not been carried out on a large scale anyway, has not benefited the poor either (except in medium-income countries like Singapore and Hong Kong, where the local conditions are quite atypical). One important explanation is that governments tend to develop high-standard programs, usually favoring the construction of highrise buildings. Social services, building codes, regulations etc. are all drawn up to satisfy rigorous criteria, raising the costs of shelter so much that one in three, or sometimes two in three, of the population cannot afford to live in the "low-cost" public buildings.[4] Public programs set up to upgrade existing slums and squatter settlements have often failed for similar reasons.

That experience gave rise to a second tendency in the positive approach to shelter: if neither the private nor the public sector succeed on their own in providing cheap habitats for the poor, the *people* themselves have to get involved. At the same time more modest standards would have to be set. *Self-help* is the central notion. Self-help can be related to the upgrading of existing slums and squatter settlements and to sites-and-services schemes. With the latter schemes, the government makes available a piece of land and a package of services such as roads, water and electricity. The occupant can then build his own house, making use of the services of the construction sector, or not using them. For upgrading no new land is needed, but governments provide what individuals cannot supply themselves in the way of services and infrastructure, and the occupant contributes his labor and money.

Thus in self-help projects private as well as public funds and efforts are involved. As sites-and-services schemes usually demand greater investments from the people involved than upgrading does, it is not amazing that upgrading projects reach a greater part of the poor population.[5] There are many forms of self-help: mutual help, aided self-help, etc. We will not go into such details here. In contrast to the traditional notion of low-cost housing, self-help schemes may be called low-income projects.

In conclusion it can be said that by a trial-and-error process a kind of circle has been followed. The self-help projects can be seen as a legalized form of the fomerly spontaneous squatter settlements. After history has shown that expensive public and private approaches are not feasible, again the poor themselves are responsible for building their houses. However, this time the government has taken up the responsibility of offering the poor a legal and physical framework to operate in.

How and where can employment be created?

To get an idea of how and where employment can be created, two distinctions are useful: that between direct and indirect employment and that between employment in the formal and in the informal sector.

Too often the distinction between direct and indirect impacts on employment is not made, the focus being on direct effects. Krishnamurty[6] states that indirect effects, though sometimes substantial, are nevertheless neglected in many cases. That is surprising because government schemes often have employment generation as one of their objectives. In general, most attention is given to employment that is related to the construction work on the site itself. This involves the part of the construction sector engaged in building houses and the related infrastructure, to be referred to henceforth as the habitat sector. New investments mean more orders for and thus more employment in the habitat sector. This holds for the short run, when new houses are built or older ones upgraded, as well as for the long run, in view of the necessity of maintenance. Employment creation does not stop there, however: direct employment will be followed by indirect employment. Several other sectors will benefit from the need for inputs in the habitat sector. The building materials industries will get more orders as will, for instance, the transport sector. These firms in their turn will demand more inputs. In other sectors, chains of similar effects on production and employment can be observed. A substantial investment in the habitat sector induces an increase in the demand for labor in related sectors. If these were already working near to capacity, they will recruit more laborers.

The other distinction refers to the formal and the informal sector. Since its first appearance in the literature in the early 1970s, much has been written on the dualistic nature of the economy in developing countries, particularly in cities.[7] Many definitions have been proposed. Sethuraman[8] states that the difference between formal and informal sectors can be explained by their orientation. The former is motivated by profit maximization, the latter by employment (income) generation. Because the informal sector is hampered by serious constraints on physical and human capital, it differs from the formal sector in mode of production (use of simple technology, labor-intensive, mainly unskilled or semiskilled workers), scale of production (usually small-scale), and in other respects. Although this picture of a dual structure does of course not fully represent reality, it is useful in that it throws light on the principal characteristics of economies in developing countries. One aspect that should not be neglected, however, is that there are significant linkages between the two sectors.[9]

Let us now combine the two notions described above. A habitat investment first creates employment in the formal or the informal habitat sector. Following Hardoy & Satterthwaite,[10] we divide the formal sector into large-scale and small-scale units. In addition, we recall that people often, partly, build or work on their own houses. As to the sectors that benefit indirectly, only a distinction between formal and informal units is made.

Here we can reintroduce the types of habitat projects mentioned before: private (for people with medium and high incomes), public (meant for low-income people, but in effect usually out of their reach), and self-help (in which both the government and the occupant participate). Private projects usually give rise to orders for the formal large-scale construction sector and sometimes for the formal small-scale construction sector. The same holds for public housing projects. With self-help schemes, obviously the future occupants themselves will work on their dwellings. As has frequently been observed, however, they cannot do all the work themselves because they have their normal jobs to do, lack the necessary skills, or are pressed for time.[11] In that case they engage workers from the habitat sector, mostly from its informal part or formal small-scale establishments. Moreover, formal and/or informal units will be involved in the construction of such public facilities as roads and electricity networks.

In addition, sometimes a large-scale formal company contracts out some of the work to small-scale units.

As to the indirect effects, in general informal units will get more orders from formal units than the other way round.

Figure 2.3 summarizes the foregoing.

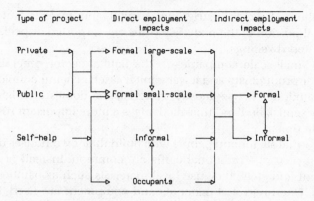

Figure 2.3   Direct and indirect employment effects of habitat projects.

Direct employment impacts

To assess the direct employment impacts of habitat investments, one has to consider the production function. In other words, how are capital, labor and materials combined? What is the building technology? In former days employment impacts were traced by looking at the capital–labor ratio. When the ratio is high, relatively little labor is involved; when it is low, relatively much labor is needed. More and more, however, a third aspect has come into focus, that of the materials used in the construction process. For labor can be replaced not only with capital, at least to a limited extent, but also with materials. Strassmann[12] draws attention to the complex process of substitution. Rising wages and standards, mechanization and better materials are all factors that can cause a switch from labor to materials. Hence it is important to know how the various groups we distinguished earlier feature in that respect. Moreover, to know what kind of materials are used is vital to the assessment of indirect employment impacts. Before we turn to the employment effects of various types of habitat projects, what can be said about differences in this respect between the habitat sector and other sectors in general? In developed countries it was found that the habitat sector is more labor intensive than most other sectors.[13] For developing countries little information is available, but it seems that this picture is valid there too. For Mexico for instance, Urquidi & Rocha[14] found that the habitat sector is one of the most important sectors from the point of view of employment.

Turning to the habitat sector itself, formal large-scale firms usually construct the more complex and the highrise buildings. To do so, they must have large capital assets and use industrialized building techniques based on sophisticated technology. They also need relatively much high-skilled labor. These industries are capital and material intensive. A substantial portion of the materials is usually imported, especially so for prefabricated dwellings.

Formal small-scale companies in the habitat sector generally have a lower labor productivity and fewer capital assets. Their technology is less sophisticated. They use mostly materials of domestic origin. Labor, especially semiskilled and unskilled, plays a more important rôle than in large-scale units.

The informal sector and people who build their own houses offer quite a different picture. Traditional crafts are common. Instead of materials like cement and steel, they use local materials such as bamboo, timber, and mud. Often recycled materials and equipment are used. Relatively much labor is needed, but only unskilled and semiskilled.[15]

In summary, from the point of view of direct employment investment in cheap dwellings is best. The cheaper shelter is, the more labor is involved in the construction process. That was confirmed, for instance, in a study of various types of habitat projects, though not self-help ones, in Mexico.[16]

The question is, however, whether investments in cheap building still score best if the aggregate employment impacts of all feasible habitat investments are considered. The answer is, of course, related to the "market" for the various types of habitat projects. Strassmann[17] has explained why building in industrialized systems has failed in most developing countries. For one thing, it is too expensive. In general, formal large-scale companies have prospects only in countries where considerable numbers of people can afford the houses they build, starting with the middle-income countries such as Hong Kong and Singapore already mentioned. Indeed, Hardoy & Satterthwaite[18] in their extensive study found no other developing countries in which favorable results have been achieved. The majority of people can afford only cheap to very cheap shelter. Here lies a challenge to the small-scale formal companies and the informal sector, both of which apply labor-intensive building techniques.

The conclusion must be, then, that self-help projects hold out the best promises for direct employment creation in poor countries. Labor-intensive firms can be involved and the projects are appropriate for many more people than the programs aiming at more expensive shelter. In higher-income developing countries, large-scale firms and consequently more luxury building will be relatively more important. Or, taking a dynamic point of view, the higher the income a country attains the more expensive projects will become appropriate.

Indirect employment impacts

In the previous section we stressed how important the choice of materials is for the creation of direct employment. The choice of materials also largely determines, through backward linkages, the creation of indirect employment. The effects are most significant in the building materials sector, but other sectors will also benefit. In general, tableized input–output relations can lead to estimates of indirect employment generation. The tables show which sectors will benefit as the habitat sector gets more orders. Increases in employment can be computed on the basis of this information. A number of studies[19] have shown that the backward linkages of the habitat sector are higher than those of most other sectors. It should be noted that most input–output studies are based on official data, which do not reflect the informal sector activities.

Less indirect employment will be generated as more materials are imported, for orders going abroad will hardly if at all profit domestic sectors.[20] We have already pointed out that formal large-scale construction companies tend to use expensive, sometimes prefabricated, materials from abroad. As Krishnamurty[21] observes, the indirect employment effects of an expansion of cement-intensive and steel-intensive houses will remain below those of an expansion achieved with the intensive use of indigenous materials, such as brick and wood. Moreover, in the latter case the benefits will accrue to the small-scale formal sector and especially to the informal sector; both sectors are in general labor-intensive. Table 2.1 gives some examples.[22]

Of course, employment generation does not stop there. The firms that deliver materials need inputs themselves. Further, in addition to shelter, amenities such as schools and health clinics may be needed, which

Table 2.1 Source and labor intensity of various materials.

Material	Source of material		Labor intensity in production and processing
	Place	Sector	
mud and wattle	local	informal	high
sundried clay blocks murrain-enforced blocks } black cotton bricks	local	informal or formal	
stones	local	informal or formal	high
timber	local	informal or formal	intensive use of skilled labor
precast concrete panels	local or imported	formal	medium
cement blocks with a chemical additive	local or imported	formal	low

implies another indirect employment impact. Employment is also indirectly created by the increased consumption of those laborers whose income has increased. Full evidence is not available, but the assumption seems reasonable that most indirect employment is created by low-income projects.

In considering direct effects in Chapter 1 of this volume, Rodwin and Sanyal state that self-help projects promise the most significant employment impacts for a given outlay as well as in the perspective of national markets. This seems to be the case for indirect effects as well. In large, middle-income countries where formal sectors import a relatively small portion of their materials, however, the indirect employment created by more expensive habitat projects may be considerable.[23]

Employment impacts in rural areas

The discussions above relate in principle to urban areas in developing countries and are only partly relevant to rural areas. The habitat situation in rural areas differs quantitatively and qualitatively from that in urban areas.[24] Among the differences are the following:

(a) The absolute need for shelter grows faster in urban than in rural areas; indeed, in many rural areas quantitative needs do not grow at all.
(b) In rural areas people are more accustomed to building their own dwellings. The houses, scattered over a large number of smaller towns and villages, are very rarely built according to government standards.

The first point indicates that in rural areas upgrading is likely to be relatively more important than new building. From the second point, formal large-scale construction industries are very unlikely to be invited to build habitats in rural parts of the country. In most cases people will build themselves, possibly helped by local small enterprise. The conclusion is that investing in shelter in rural areas at most induces employment benefits in this type of enterprise, apart from creating extra work for the owner or the builder. Other rural characteristics (lack of transportation systems, lack of high-skilled labor, seasonal unemployment, and lack of financial means) reinforce that conclusion.[25]

Conclusions

The foregoing teaches us two important things. The first is that the not unusual neglect of indirect employment effects leads to an unrealistic and too pessimistic picture of the employment that may be created by a habitat investment. The second, even more important, is that the extent to which investments lead to increased production and employment generation depends on the way the money is spent. Public or private projects applying high standards and sophisticated techniques seem to induce the least employment in most countries. Governments who, by means of habitat investments, want to increase employment, especially among the poorer sections of the population, probably do best by investing in habitat projects that are directed to the poor. Technically speaking, such a policy will generate much employment. Still, to make the most of the potential benefits, a large number of these same governments will have to change their general habitat and nonhabitat policies substantially. The last section of this chapter refers briefly to that matter.

Impacts of improved habitat at microlevel

Introduction

Section II treated the question of who would construct new houses (or upgrade older ones) and how many people would be employed through backward linkages. The outputs produced in the process result in a positive quantitative and/or qualitative change in the habitat stock. What are the benefits and to whom do they accrue? In trying to answer those questions, we will emphasize the effects on the occupants, the so-called *internal* impacts. Some of these internal impacts are of a social nature, but the fact that they ultimately also induce economic benefits is stressed here. Some benefits accrue to others as well. These *external* benefits as well as some factors that influence the intensity of the impacts are discussed below.

Internal effects: impacts on the occupants

In Section I we mentioned two basic approaches to shelter. Some people used to see and still see habitat as a consumptive good only. Others have criticized that approach, pointing at productive aspects. We think that the productive potential of habitat improvements should be stressed; this approach constitutes the basis of this chapter.

Among the first in recent times to point to the productive aspects of habitat improvements were Klaassen & Burns.[26] But, as Klaassen & Eizenga[27] mention, classical economists like Smith and Marshall had already observed that the quality of the houses people occupy influences their performance at work; in fact, a good and well serviced dwelling is an "input" for a worker enabling him to produce "outputs." Klaassen and Burns formalized that approach into two assumptions:

(a) housing is an investment good capable of generating income and influencing the productivity of the occupants at their work;
(b) housing is therefore not only a goal of development policy (as it is in the traditional view) but also a tool of this policy.

Burns,[28] setting out to explain why improved shelter increases productivity, points at some social consequences, such as more stable families, increased privacy, improved mental and physical health, improved social climate. Evidently, recognition of the relation beween living conditions and work performance, and thus economic growth, implied a plea for spending more on habitat.

Once the theoretical foundations were laid, empirical research was started. The extensive International Housing Productivity Study (IHPS), with L. S. Burns as supervisor and L. H. Klaassen, one of the authors of this chapter, as an external adviser, was especially innovative in its methods and unique in two aspects. First, it identified and covered various hitherto unnoticed benefits of housing; second, it was based on case studies carried out all over the world. Five case studies were executed in developing countries (at two sites in Mexico and at single sites in South Korea, Kenya, and Venezuela) and three in poorer regions of the United States. In all cases a group of people were moved to a better dwelling (test group), whereas others continued to live in their old houses (control group). Care was taken to ensure that the two groups were similar, except for the rehousing aspect.[29] For both groups, the variables assumedly dependent on shelter were assessed before and after the rehousing to the test group, and the change in a variable in the test group compared with that in the control group. The difference was attributed to the rehousing.

The purpose of the cast studies was to test the hypotheses that shelter improvement

(a) raises productivity at work,
(b) lowers absenteeism from work,
(c) raises the level of health,
(d) increases the productivity of education,
(e) lowers the incidence of social deviation.

Not all hypotheses were tested in every case study; for instance, the relation between habitat and social behaviour was tested only on one site. The results of the various studies did not firmly confirm all five hypotheses. Although really negative correlations were not found, the number of significant positive relationships was limited. As Burns and

Grebler put it: "...in no single case did better housing make matters worse for the rehoused populations studied. On the other hand, there are remarkably few cases where location in new housing generated unequivocably favourable results."[30]

Others have tried to assess the social benefits of housing to the occupants, but not on the scale of the IHPS. Most studies have concentrated on the relation between habitat and only one other variable especially health.[31] Few studies set out to measure more than one variable at a time, like the IHPS. Wegelin[32] made some extensive cost-benefit analyses of six housing schemes in Peninsular Malaysia. For lack of data the study had to focus on traditional low-cost housing projects only, leaving sites-and-services schemes out of consideration. Wegelin positively discerned impacts in some cases, notably improved health and improved performance at work and at school. These impacts, however, were often estimated crudely, with the help of proxies that it was hoped would represent the factor under study.

Jørgensen[33] applied a specific sort of cost-benefit analysis to a sites-and-services scheme for Dandora, just outside Nairobi. In that framework he measured some modest social benefits.

What is true of the IHPS is true of most other studies: their results neither warrant a rejection of the various hypotheses on links between habitat and various social and economic factors nor firmly confirm them. Does that mean that those linkages do not deserve our attention? In our opinion, that would not be a wise attitude. For one thing, the number of studies is too limited for such a conclusion. For another, the fact that there is no full proof of certain potential aspects does not mean they do not exist or are not important. Logically, the relations must exist, for how can people work well if their health is weak owing to bad living conditions? The problem is that the impacts, especially on productivity, are hard to quantify in practical research.[34] The change that is attributable only to the change in habitat is very difficult to separate from other influences. If a worker moves to another house in a different environment, his productivity can change owing to both factors, habitat and environment, or owing to still other factors. Moreover, the changes in productivity tend to be preceded by changes in some intermediate variables that depend directly on the shelter situation, namely mental and/or physical health; and that makes the former even harder to relate directly to the habitat improvement. In sum, for a conclusive study of the relation between shelter and certain internal benefits many conditions have to be fulfilled and many data covering a long period of time are needed. It is not surprising, therefore, that the number of suitable case studies in the field in limited and their results ambiguous.

In spite of such measurement problems, we maintain our opinion that the internal benefits of improved shelter should not be neglected, conform for instance the World Bank.[35]

Does the chain of impacts end here? The ‚answer is no. As a "translation" of the internal benefits, the occupant's income is likely to rise: first, because he is able to work more days a year (provided work is available and he is paid according to his production); second, because his employer may reward him for his improved performance by raising his wage (the chance of low-income workers preferring leisure to more money is small). The normal income multiplier effects on the economy of this income increase are to be attributed to the habitat investment.

Before we end our necessarily superficial treatment of the benefits accruing to the occupant, a few more benefits must be mentioned. In many developing countries, especially in Latin America, people are wont to create shops and workshops in or around their home; better shelter may enliven habitat-related business activity and hence lead to more income. Moreover, whether they are owners or not, occupants may add to their income by subletting part of their dwelling. Finally, because houses are built with more durable materials, the occupants will suffer less from fires around their habitat, which means a rise in disposable income.[36] The conclusion to this section can be that habitat is a necessary condition for the proper economic performance of the occupants either inside or outside the house.

External effects: impacts on those other than the occupants

Others besides the occupants may benefit from the improvement of the habitat stock in two ways. The first category of external benefits follows from the internal benefits discussed in the previous section; the second is directly related to the ownership of the houses.

The first group of people enjoying external benefits are the employers of people whose productive capacity rises or whose absenteeism decreases.[37] Some of the increased profit may, however, accrue to the workers as their wage payments are raised.

Governments of countries with some form of a social security system will also benefit. Improved shelter can be expected to diminish fire hazards, and can thus lower municipal outlays for fire brigades and payments in support of victims. As the health of the population improves, less needs to be spent on hospitals, medicine, and social security payments. The negative effects of crime and deviant behavior and the cost of combating them will also be less than before.

Among the nonoccupants who tend to receive benefits are, as it happens, the people who have invested in the improvement of the quantity or quality of the habitat stock; they will benefit by the returns on their investments. Rent used to be, and for lack of data often still is, the usual and only yardstick for the benefits of habitat investments.[38] In part, of course, increases in rents are the expression of the increases in benefits from improved habitat to the occupants. Rents are important as a direct yield to the investor, whether he is an owner-occupier or an absentee landlord.[39]

Factors influencing the magnitude of impacts

Little can be said in a general sense about the absolute magnitude of the various impacts, but some tentative judgements of the relation with the type of project can be derived from the IHPS. The findings of that study suggest that the benefits of successive shelter improvements are descending in magnitude. In other words – and not overly unexpected – marginal benefits are decreasing. The comparison of different test groups has moreover shown that the greatest benefits occur where the initial shelter conditions were worst.[40] This is a sure indication that the greatest benefits directly or indirectly related to the occupants are reaped from habitat investments for the poorest. Therefore, both Wegelin[41] and Burns *et al.*[42] suggest avoiding relatively expensive "low-cost" constructions and choosing "second-best" solutions. In that view, self-help projects are the best option. For one thing such projects improve the worst housing conditions, so that significant benefits can be expected, as explained above. For another, such second-best solutions will be within the financial reach of many more people than so-called "low-cost" solutions. The benefits of building for middle- and high-income groups will be less, as original living conditions are usually not particularly bad, improvements are more expensive, and numbers are smaller.

Other factors that both Wegelin and the IHPS refer to are local culture and institutions. Mental attitude, aspirations, habits, etc. can considerably influence the benefits.

A final factor is the location of new dwellings. Benefits will surely be less when jobs and facilities are lacking in the vicinity. Without proper physical planning, projects may show disappointing results.

No effort has been made to mention all the relevant factors, but the above certainly seem to be among the most important, apart from some general aspects to be mentioned in the conclusions at the end of the chapter.

Macroeconomic impacts

Introduction

Macroeconomic parameters will change through the impacts of habitat investments on production and employment (see p. 39) and the improved habitat situation at the microlevel (see p. 47). The problem of quantifying employment and microimpacts renders the changes in macroeconomic performance rather problematic, and there are other factors adding to the uncertainty. Nevertheless, in this chapter we will try to highlight some macroeconomic and socioeconomic changes that may occur, once more without pretention to completeness.

In the following subsection we recall the ways a habitat investment may be beneficial to an economy through its impacts on capital formation and on present income and consumption. In the next subsection the impacts on income and income distribution are analysed, starting from certain simplified working assumptions. Later some of these assumptions are relaxed, the focus being on inflation. Then impacts on the balance of payments are discussed. Finally, these findings are combined in a general picture.

Capital accumulation versus present income generation

At the beginning of this chapter we indicated the distinction between investments, or capital accumulation, leading to increased productivity and future production and consumption, and present consumption. The position of shelter was said to be somewhat ambiguous. On the one hand, national capital is accumulated as houses are built. On the other hand, the future income derived from habitat investments is modest,[43] and usually supposed to consist of rents only. The other impacts such as the rise in productivity and improved educational performance, can be added; but even if these often neglected advantages are duly considered, investments in a number of other sectors are probably more profitable. Far more significant and certainly important in comparison to the impacts of investments in other activities are the impacts on employment, leading to increased present income and consumption. The micro-impacts mentioned earlier leading to increased consumption at a much later date, will be treated in less detail.

Income multipliers

In discussing the impacts of investment on employment a distinction was made between direct and indirect impacts. Once employment has been created on the site, indirect employment ensues from the need for materials and other requirements. The resulting increase in employment in turn generates second-order employment. Thus, an investment creates various rounds of employment generation and consequent increases of income. The total income finally created is a multiple of the initial investment – the income multiplier. The usual assumption is that this multiplier depends on marginal propensities regarding savings, taxes, and imports; if most inputs are imported and taxes as well as savings are high, domestic income generation is limited. On the other hand, if inputs are locally made, and people tend to consume a large portion of their income, the income multiplier is likely to be quite high.

Starting from a number of assumptions, to which we will return in due course, income multipliers for investments in habitat and other opportunities can be assessed. In general, the multiplier for habitat investments has been shown to be quite high compared to those of other sectors. Estimates for such countries as Colombia, India, Korea, Mexico, and Pakistan all resulted in figures of about two,[44] the explanation being the usually lower import content of habitat outlays compared with those of other sectors. Moreover, the habitat sector is relatively labor intensive, and unskilled labor generally tends to save relatively little. Finally, income taxes are comparatively low for the lower income brackets concerned.

On average, habitat investments show a high income multiplier. But different types of habitat investments will produce different multipliers. Recall that habitats for poor people usually call for domestically produced materials and much unskilled and semiskilled labor. Habitats for higher income groups, on the contrary, often require imported materials and high-skilled labor. Thus, higher income multipliers can be expected from more emphasis on investments for low-income shelter. In addition, investing in shelter for the poor makes for a more equitable income distribution because directly and indirectly it involves more unskilled labor.

Wegelin[45] mentions a few limitations attached to estimating income creation by a simple multiplier formula. Its static nature makes the multiplier concept ill suited to accommodate the successive rounds of income increments over time. The problem of taking account of changes in (relative) prices should be mentioned. Finally, supply constraints in the economy are assumed to be nonexistent. The last assumption concerns the fact that new resources are being used, inducing no

negative consequences for other economic activities. If, however, resources
have to be shifted towards the habitat sector, the value of the multiplier
will decrease, probably mostly so in the case of expensive habitat
projects, which usually demand relatively scarce factors of production
(see also next section).

On top of the income multiplier described above, there is another one
relating to the impacts on income (and thus consumption) of the
improved habitat stock, as discussed on page 47. Incomes of house
owners, occupants, and their employers are raised, and their ampler
spending on goods and services will lead to successive rounds of income
generation. Although the multiplier effects will occur later in time and
presumably be smaller that those discussed before, they should not be
neglected. The micro-impacts of improved shelter are greater when they
benefit poor people, and so will be the corresponding income multiplier
effects.

In the following sections we will discuss two topics that are
disregarded in simple multiplier analysis – inflation and balance of
payments.

Inflation

Is it true, as some people maintain, that increased habitat investments
lead to inflation? There are several factors involved. Let us first consider
the impacts of increased activity in the habitat sector and then go on to
make a few remarks on the relation between the socioeconomic effects of
an improved habitat stock and inflation.

Unless domestic resources are utilized, increased investments in
housing induce an increased demand for inputs. The important
questions then are to what extent bottlenecks are encountered on the
supply side and how flexible the prices in the economy are.[46] Whether
bottlenecks arise depends on the elasticity of supply of the inputs and
the size of the additional demand in relation to the total demand for
inputs. The relative size of additional demand in real terms in its turn
depends on the magnitude of the habitat investment, the input
proportions, the extent to which resources are shifted from other sectors
to the habitat sector, and the degree to which the inputs that are released
can be efficiently used for the habitat sector.[47]

No labor bottlenecks, and consequently no rise in wage levels need
occur when underemployed or unemployed workers are engaged.[48] This
seems to be the more likely case when investments are directed towards
shelter for the poor because in that case mostly unskilled labor is
required. Both in cities and in rural areas unskilled workers often make
up the majority of the total work force. In addition, the number of

unemployed, underemployed, or misemployed people is significant in a number of countries. It seems unlikely that the involvement of this category of workers will lead to wage rises. Increased investment in expensive shelter, on the contrary, through its demand for generally scarce skilled labor, is likely to induce higher wages and thus inflation.[49] If inputs were previously underused, in general their engagement will not lead to inflation. The chances of that occurring are greater in the case of unskilled labor than of materials, for which supply constraints and hence rising prices are more likely. As more expensive habitat projects generally need relatively scarce materials, inflation in that case will certainly be higher than in the case of low-income projects.

If the inputs required for the construction of dwellings are scarce, they could be obtained by withdrawing them from use in one or more other sectors. If the factor proportion is the same in both sectors, there will be neither bottlenecks nor price rises.[50] Still, should the factor proportions differ, there are two possibilities. If prices in the economy are flexible, they will go up for the goods for which demand rises and down for goods less in demand. Inflation is not likely to be substantial, if it occurs at all. If prices are not flexible downwards,[51] the general price level will rise with any use of scarce resources. As expensive shelter demands more scarce resources than cheap shelter, in the former case inflationary tendencies will be higher. Of course, in all cases inflation will be higher when the habitat investment is larger; and the factor intensity differs more between the nonhabitat sector from which the resources are withdrawn and the habitat sector.

If, finally, habitat investments are financed from credits and aggregate demand increases, inflation is certain and will be higher than in the cases described above. Yet, poor people usually have little access to credit and finance their habitat investments out of their own savings. Various authors have indeed pointed out that many people are willing to forgo present consumption to invest in habitat;[52] in that way tendencies for inflation are lower. More expensive building programs on the other hand generally imply institutionalized credits and an increase in the supply of money. Therefore, inflation is much more probable in the latter case.

We can be brief as to the inflationary effects following from investments financed from foreign sources. If the finance is "tied" to purchases outside the country, there will for part of the investment be no claim on domestic resources; more final goods will be available, spelling deflation. For the other part of the investment the claim on domestic resources does exist and thus the chance of a rise in prices. Net inflation, if any, is probably low, especially if the tied part is great. If finance is not tied, inflation is very likely, its extent depending on the type of project. The more it demands scarce resources, the more prices will rise.

Whatever the situation, inflation is unlikely to be very high in the case of investment in cheap shelter, though an underdeveloped habitat sector or building materials industry might be a dangerous factor in this respect. Some proof has been given by Burns *et al.*,[53] who estimated what impact on prices an ambitious habitat program in Mexico and Korea would have if the investment increased aggregate demand. Inflation would be very modest: 0.2 percent for Mexico and 1.55 percent for Korea. These results should not be generalized; on the other hand, neither does economic analysis lead to the conclusion that habitat investments necessarily bring about the burden of inflation.

Finally, what can be said about inflation induced by the microeconomic impacts of improved shelter? Little or no research has been done in that field, although these impacts were included in the figures cited above on inflation in Mexico and Korea. At any rate, the inflation they could produce is not likely to be very high, as the changes in income are probably modest and occur at different times. In fact, prices may well not change at all, increases in income and consumption being counteracted by increases in productivity and production.

Balance of payments

Another anxiety often voiced in relation to habitat investments is that the balance of payments could deteriorate because imports would increase, exports being unaffected. First let us deal with exports. Habitats cannot be exported, but that does not mean that total exports do not change. First, they may rise as a result of the increased productivity of the workers in export industries. Especially labor-intensive export industries could see their receipts increase.[54] Second, exports could be negatively affected when the resources of export sectors are shifted to the habitat sector.[55]

Regarding imports, more factors can cause changes. Imports decrease when workers in import-substitution sectors become more productive as a result of improved habitat. Imports will rise when the resources of import-substitution sectors are shifted to the habitat sector. When resources are shifted from a nonhabitat sector to the habitat sector, imports will rise if the former has a relatively lower import share (and vice versa) or if the import share in sectors that are indirectly linked are lower in the former than in the latter. Imports will also rise if a credit-financed habitat investment increases effective demand. Finally, the nature of the habitat investment is important: the more expensive houses are, the more imported materials they will usually directly and indirectly need.[56]

From the above it is clear that the change in net imports depends very much on the shift of funds from other sectors to the habitat sector and therefore on the nature of these sectors and on the type of habitat project. The size of the country matters too: generally, the smaller the country the sooner it will have to resort to imports. Finally, the stage of development will also influence the need to turn to imports.

These theoretical considerations lead to the conclusion that deterioration of the balance of payments is not likely if investments are focused on cheap habitat. Burns *et al.*[57] confirmed this conclusion, and it need not be greatly altered when the microeconomic impacts of improved shelter are taken into account as well. Still, an important qualification has to be made here. The conclusions hold only if it is presumed that no bottlenecks exist on the supply side, in the habitat sector, and in the building materials sector. In reality, small and very poor countries often face difficulties in this respect.

Conclusions

A country that is totally growth oriented will not invest much in habitat (although no country can grow considerably in the long run without healthy, well housed workers). Countries with an eye for a more even distribution of welfare, and thus for basic needs, may do well to invest more in shelter than they are now doing. Income multipliers are high for investments in habitat, and the danger of inflation and deterioration of the balance of payments seems slight, provided no supply constraints exist. That argument holds more for investments in cheap shelter than for investments in dwellings for the rich. However, these potential benefits will manifest themselves only if the supply constraints and certain other bottlenecks can be removed from the economies. In the final section we will briefly go into the conditions to be fulfilled to take full advantage of the potentials of habitat investments.

Conclusions and policy implications

It is hoped that the preceding sections have contributed to the understanding of the economic potential of habitat investments. On the one hand, we have highlighted important categories of benefits, some of which are often neglected. On the other, efforts have been made to indicate which kinds of habitat projects may produce the greatest benefits. Our conclusion is that the most promising habitat policy for most developing countries seems to be to prioritize projects directed at the poor and based on self-help. Only in middle-income developing countries may other possibilities, such as public and private sector housing, be tentatively considered as equally important.

The above does not at all imply, however, that from a private, purely financial point of view investing in low-income shelter is generally the best choice. In actual life, the private sector often neglects shelter for the poor because its financial yield is too low. What we mean to say is that investing in low-income shelter could be a healthy policy from a national socioeconomic point of view. Investments in shelter for the poor are sound because they demand less of such scarce factors as high-skilled labor, capital, and foreign exchange, using instead factors of production that are essentially relatively abundant. In addition, the marginal utility of shelter improvement is highest when projects benefit the poor segments of the population.

Of course, the net benefits of habitat investments and investments in other sectors have to be weighed one against the other. Besides the question of how to measure all direct and indirect impacts (which is a problem we cannot deal with here), the fact remains that a fair balance should somehow be struck. We hope to have shown that the benefits of habitat investments are at any rate more widespread than is usually supposed. Habitat investments do fit into development strategies, especially in a basic needs approach, but to some extent they also fit into strategies with rapid economic growth as the primary goal. They certainly are relevant if a combination of growth and distribution is aimed at. The often supported idea of a contradiction between nonproductive investments in shelter and productive investments, in manufacturing industry is exaggerated.

So far we have talked about the *potential* impacts of investments. The extent to which the potential will materialize, however, depends largely on a number of broad government policies concerning habitat and other fields. It is not just a matter of increasing direct investments, as the failure of several self-help schemes clearly illustrates. This is not the place to point out the steps that should accompany the investment itself. Literature on the subject has grown considerably lately (see for instance Shah,[58] Ward,[59] Murison & Lea,[60] and Peattie,[61] and other chapters in this book). However, some points are worth recalling:

(a) Habitat policies should be directed towards the possibilities and the wishes and aspirations of the poor. Too many projects have failed because governments set standards too high, because the location was wrong, or simply because they were far too expensive.
(b) Until this moment the informal sector has often been passed over in favor of the formal sector. That policy should be reversed.
(c) Efforts should be made to promote and support the informal and small-scale formal habitat sector and building materials sector.
(d) A more fundamental necessity is the removal of basic inequalities

from the institutionalized economic system related to habitat. Access and opportunities for the poor in the field of finance, tenure, subsidies, land, etc. should be drastically improved.

(e) The location of new dwellings (in cities or within the country as a whole) should be chosen carefully, for it may considerably influence the ultimate impacts. A spatial structure which provides people with access to jobs, transport, etc. contributes largely to the efficiency of settlements.

Finally, we would like to stress that the success of habitat investments depends in general on the wider context of development policy. There is a definite need for a planning system in which shelter policies are attuned to other socioeconomic policies and spatial policies. For instance, the achievements of policies in the field of habitat rely partly on population policy: a small population growth means that families need smaller houses and have more income per capita available, whereas governmental outlays for habitat can be lowered or spent otherwise. Other examples can be found, for instance, in the field of income distribution and employment. Spending on habitat can, of course, never be *the* tool of development; it can only be *a* tool, an important one as long as policies in other fields do not block the opportunities.

3

Household preferences and expenditures

STEPHEN K. MAYO

UNTIL THE EARLY 1970s major government housing policies often followed the model of many developed nations, relying on heavily subsidized blocks of public housing flats with high standards of construction and infrastructure, zoning and building standards that discouraged production of housing with lower standards, and, in many cases, destruction of slum areas and squatter settlements in the name of either "law and order" or "urban renewal". By and large, such policies did not work.

Such public housing did not reach most of the rapidly growing urban populations where most such housing was provided. High unit subsidy levels meant that housing could not be extended to more than a fortunate few. Yet despite high subsidy levels, public housing often went unoccupied for long periods of time – a result of poor location, failure to provide for trunk infrastructure, or costs to beneficiaries which, even after accounting for subsidies, were higher than could be afforded and hence discouraged participation. At the same time, zoning and building standards were widely flouted, with squatter settlements proliferating. Indeed, informal, illegal, or unregistered housing became the predominant source of new housing in many developing country cities.[1] Such was the vitality of the informal shelter sector that in many cities the numerical output of dwellings has actually outstripped population increases in recent years.[2]

By the late 1960s and early 1970s the contrast between the largely ineffectual housing policies of the previous decades and the quantitative successes of informal housing gave rise to an innovation in shelter policy in developing countries that tried to build on the model of progressive development afforded by the informal sector. Sites and services projects and slum upgrading projects, encouraged by the World Bank and other international aid organizations, represented a sharp break with previous policies as they tried to establish project design standards on the basis of what households would be willing and able to pay for shelter and services rather than on the basis of an often arbitrary and inflated notion of "housing need". A principal goal of such projects was to reach a broader portion of low-income and moderate-income households than would be reached under conventional public housing. The route to this goal involved two important principles: "affordability" of the shelter and services by the intended beneficiaries and full cost recovery. Recovery of costs was seen as necessary to ensure that projects could be replicated on a large scale as the modest surpluses of early projects were recycled to finance later projects.

In general, sites and services projects and upgrading projects that were undertaken by developing country governments involved lowering standards (zoning and building codes) from preexisting levels in order to meet affordability criteria. At the same time, initiatives were broached regarding the use of relatively more self-help in construction of shelter and community facilities and the production and use of low-cost building materials.

In attempting to make the sites and services model work, a number of explicit or implicit assumptions were made concerning the effective demand for housing. In many cases, exigencies of project implementation or a lack of data on willingness-to-pay for housing forced project planners to use rules of thumb, often somewhat arbitrary, as the basis for setting standards of affordability and physical design. It was common, for example, in both World Bank financed projects and those financed by other aid organizations to assume that low to moderate income households could spend from 20 to 25 percent of their incomes for shelter and related services.[3] In fact, of World Bank sites and services projects financed between 1972 and 1984, nearly three-quarters of the projects were planned on the assumption that households could spend 20 to 25 percent of income for the housing provided in the projects.[3] More careful examination of the application of such rules of thumb indicates that the same approximate rule of thumb was used regardless of a country's income level and regardless of the relative income level of the target population within a country.

The major point of this chapter is that, despite the overall validity of the sites and services concept, use of such rules of thumb in planning sites and services projects is inconsistent with evidence on what households actually spend on housing around the world, and can lead to downstream consequences that frustrate some of the most fundamental goals of low-cost shelter projects. In particular, use of inappropriate affordability assumptions can lead to missing the intended beneficiary population or to necessitating subsidies of a magnitude that frustrates the goal of large-scale project replicability. If planners are to serve the shelter needs of the poor, more careful attention must be paid to establishing the level of effective demand for housing and then planning in a way that is consistent with demand. A second point is that proper reckoning of housing demand is important not only at the level of project design but also at the level of national housing planning. Specifically, relationships between housing investment and GNP, which often serve as targets in national housing plans, depend heavily on underlying housing demand relationships. As I indicate below, ratios of housing expenditure to income among households strongly influence ratios of housing investment to GNP at the aggregate level. Thus information on the former can provide an important element of realism in deciding on appropriate housing investment targets.

In what follows, I will review briefly a number of major findings concerning the demand for housing which have emerged from a major ongoing World Bank study. Following that I will point out some of the major implications for housing project design and for national housing policies.

Housing demand in developing countries

"Housing demand," as considered here, is simply housing need backed up by ability and willingness-to-pay. In contrast to a definition of demand couched in terms of normative standards, the definition used is based on the demonstrated behavior of individuals and is revealed by surveys of how households actually spend their limited resources on housing and on other goods and services. Studies of the effective demand for housing attempt to relate actual spending patterns to a number of measurable influences on spending, e.g., household characteristics such as income and family size, the relative price of housing compared to other goods and services, and the condition of the overall housing market, including, for example, the general level of economic development, inflationary expectations, and the existence of government policies such as rent control which might influence spending on housing.

Less than a decade ago, there were only a handful of published analyses of housing demand in developing countries, and fewer yet that tried to compare observed patterns of behavior across countries. As recently as 1977, for example, Burns and Grebler labeled their seminal cross-country study of housing consumption "a first effort to chart new territory".[4] Since that time the pace of research has grown, and a few additional landmarks have begun to appear on Burns and Grebler's early chart. Studies by Follain *et al.*,[5] Ingram,[6] and Jimenez & Keare[7] are particularly noteworthy for the care with which they were conducted and the conclusions they reached. Taken together with Burns and Grebler's work, these studies suggested a number of regularities in patterns of housing demand which, were they to be confirmed in broader cross-country studies, would offer the possibility of developing general explanations of housing demand and would lay the foundation for developing prescriptive policies for housing market interventions.

In particular, two major speculative conclusions seemed to be emerging from these studies, each of which has major implications for the design of housing projects and policies. First, as Jimenez and Keare noted, the sensitivity of housing expenditures to household income (the income elasticity of demand) appeared to be quite similar in a number of developing countries, indicating in particular that, within a given housing market, as income increases housing expenditures generally increase less than proportionately (e.g., the income elasticity of demand is less than one). As indicated by Burns and Grebler, however, when the general level of development increases, as measured by GNP per capita, it appears that the average fraction of income spent on housing also increases. Were such observations to be confirmed in other cross-country studies, they would suggest that (1) no single rule of thumb for the fraction of income that can be earmarked for housing is appropriate, and (2) despite this, regularities exist that can be used as the basis for more appropriate rules of thumb for use in housing project design and strategy formulation.

In an attempt to extend the limited range of empirical analysis of housing demand in developing countries, a major comparative study was initiated in 1981 at the World Bank. In that analysis high-quality data were collected for 16 cities in 8 countries (Colombia, Egypt, El Salvador, Ghana, India, Jamaica, Korea, and the Philippines) and were used to estimate housing demand relationships using relatively comparable variable definitions and a standardized analytical approach. For comparative purposes identical econometric models were estimated for two US cities. The results of this study are discussed extensively in Malpezzi *et al.*[8] however, some of the most important findings can be summarized by referring to the evidence presented in Figure 3.1.

Figure 3.1 illustrates graphically the estimated relationship between

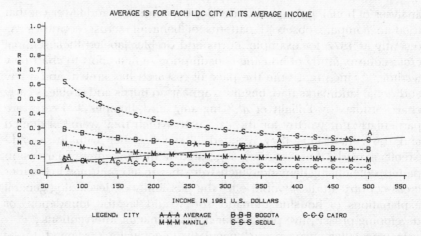

Figure 3.1   Rent-to-income ratios (by income) for renters (average is for each LDC city at its average income).

the rent-to-income ratio in each of four developing country cities (Bogota, Cairo, Manila, and Seoul) and monthly household income. In each city it is seen that as household income increases the observed ratio of rent to income declines. In economic terms this is a concomitant of estimated income elasticities of housing demand less than one. In fact most estimated income elasticities cluster within a range of 0.4 to 0.6, indicating that housing expenditures increase only 40 to 60 percent as far as income. Results for the other 12 cities included in the analysis present a similar picture, and results are similar for owners and renters.

When one compares results across cities, however, an entirely different view of housing demand emerges. Specifically, as the general level of development increases (as measured by average household income), the average fraction of income spent on housing also increases. This is indicated by the upward shift in the curves relating the rent-to-income ratio to income; as income increases among cities from Cairo to Manila to Bogota and then to Seoul, so too does the average fraction of income allocated to housing. This is shown by the upward-sloping line in Figure 3.1, which represents the relationship between the average rent-to-income ratio for each of the 16 developing country cities and average monthly household income in each city. Although there is some evidence that the upward-sloping relationship shown here eventually turns down at higher levels of development,[9] the relationship shown is a good approximation among countries that are the focus of most international assistance efforts.

The two overall tendencies shown here may be interpreted as indicative of short-run (within city) and long-run (across city) demand relationships. In the short run, housing is treated as a necessity, with low-income households willing to spend higher fractions of income for housing than are higher-income households. As economic development proceeds, however, the share of household budgets allocated to housing increases among households at all income levels.

Implications for project design and housing strategy

The major implication of these tendencies is quite clear: the fraction of income that households allocate for housing is highly variable, depending in particular on household income and on the level of economic development.[10] Thus in setting design standards in housing projects it is inappropriate to use a single universal "affordability ratio" such as 20 or 25 percent. If a single value is used, particularly if it is higher than normal spending patterns would indicate, then unsustainable subsidies might be required to induce low-income target groups to participate and higher-income groups might find their way into projects, either initially or by purchasing from initial allotees.

Some idea of the potential problems created by choosing inappropriate design standards are illustrated in Figure 3.2 and 3.3, which indicate respectively estimates of (1) the minimum subsidy (as a percentage of unit costs) necessary to induce moderate-income (35th percentile) households to participate in sites and services projects, and (2) the income percentile of households that would be most likely to participate in a project in the absence of subsidies.[11] In each figure a family of curves is shown which allows one to see how subsidies or participant income levels are related to the average income level in a city (the horizontal axis)

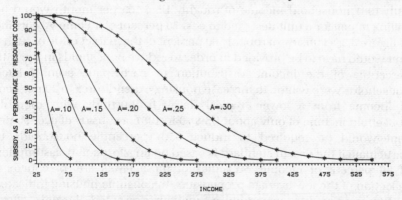

Figure 3.2 Minimum subsidies necessary to induce participation of 35th percentile households at alternative design affordability ratios (average monthly, household income in 1981 US dollars).

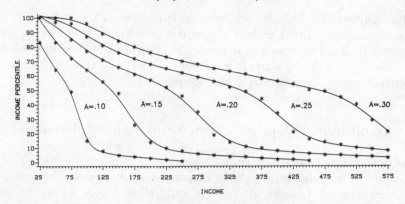

Figure 3.3 Income percentile of participating households with no subsidy at alternative design affordability ratios (average monthly household income in 1981 US dollars).

and the design affordability assumption.[12,13] The latter is represented by "A" which is the assumed proportion of income that target income group households will allocate to housing – the amount that serves as the basis for physical design standards in a project. Each of these figures is derived from the empirical evidence taken from the World Bank study cited above and hence each represents a "best guess" about actual behavior of households that might be the intended beneficiaries of sites and services projects.

Figure 3.2 indicates clearly the effect that project standards (as derived from "design affordability levels") have on target-group households' incentive to participate, and on the need to provide subsidies to induce participation when standards are set too high. For example, suppose that it were assumed that households in a typical African country, say Kenya, with 1981 household income of roughly US $ 100 per month would be willing to pay for a unit designed to cost 20 percent of income. According to Figure 3.2, a subsidy of roughly 60 percent of the market value of such a unit would have to be provided in order to induce households in the 35th percentile of the income distribution to participate, even if such households were willing to increase housing expenditures to 20 per cent of income from a lower "typical" level. In Burundi, with monthly household income of only about US $ 70 in 1981, a subsidy of over 90 per cent would be required to induce 35th percentile households to participate if the design standard is based on an affordability assumption of 20 percent of income. Subsidies of these levels are, of course, a reflection of the low average propensities to consume housing indicated by the cross-country expenditure functions presented above. In effect, households must be offered significant bribes in the form of subsidy payments to induce them to willingly allocate higher than "normal" fractions of income for housing.

In higher-income developing countries by contrast, a 20 percent affordability standard may be entirely appropriate. For example, for countries (cities) with average household monthly income above about US $ 175, subsidies of less than 20 percent would appear to be adequate to induce target groups to participate. Required subsidies are, however, extremely sensitive to the choice of design standards. Although the difference between 20 percent and 25 percent of income may not sound like much to a project planner, such a difference represents a 25 percentage point difference in monthly shelter costs and can easily mean the difference between required subsidies in the range 60 to 70 percent rather than the range of 20 to 35 percent. Depending on whether subsidies of the required magnitude are forthcoming or not, target income groups may not even participate or, if they do, they may have strong incentives to sell out to higher-income groups.

Figure 3.2 portrays the estimated subsidy levels necessary to induce low-income households to participate in projects with different design standards, but it is also useful to estimate the way in which the income levels of households that would participate in the absence of subsidies would vary in response to varying design standards. To do so we can use the information on housing demand portrayed in Figure 3.1 to infer the income level that would typically be associated with housing spending implied by a given design standard; this then is the estimated income of project participants in the absence of any subsidy.

Figure 3.3 illustrates the effect of alternative design standards of unsubsidized projects on the income of probable participants. Not only does increasing the design affordability ratio increase the income level of likely participants, but it does so with particularly dramatic effect at various thresholds. For example, for households in low-income countries (e.g., income of US $ 100 per month), setting the design standards on the basis of an assumption that households are willing to spend 20 percent of income on housing implies that households in approximately the 80th percentile of the income distribution could afford to participate without subsidies. Dropping the standard to one based on 15 percent of income has only a modest effect, inducing participation down to the 65th percentile in the absence of subsidies. Dropping the standard still further to one based on just 10 percent of income permits reaching even below the original target group, all the way down to the 15th percentile. Similar thresholds exist at each level of income, suggesting that dramatic improvements can be realized in the ability to reach the poor through sites-and-services projects by finding the "correct" design standard – the one that reflects true willingness-to-pay by low-income groups.

The empirical findings on housing demand have implications that transcend project design considerations. For example, it is straightforward to show that overall levels of housing investment relative to GNP are strongly related to the household-level demand relationships portrayed in Figure 3.1. Thus knowledge of the pervasiveness and regularity of these underlying demand relationships can add an element of realism to countries' investment planning regarding housing.

Often country investment planning for housing is cast in terms of target fractions of GNP that should be allocated to housing investment. Indeed, since Burns and Grebler's important work, it has been common for planners in many countries to set investment targets on the basis of the empirical relationship observed by Burns and Grebler relating the housing investment to GNP ratio and GNP per capita. This relationship, shown here as Figure 3.4, indicates that the share of housing investment in GNP first rises with ENP per capita but then declines as countries pass about $ 1,600 per capita in 1970 US dollars (or about $ 3,400 in 1981 US dollars, the benchmark units used in deriving Fig. 3.1.[14] To put this in perspective, upper middle-income developing countries such as Argentina, Uruguay, South Africa, and Yugoslavia were approaching this estimated turning point in 1981, and Venezuela, Greece, Israel, and Hong Kong had recently passed it.

Here it is important to note the microeconomic foundations of the Burns–Grebler relationship in order bolster its legitimacy as a planning

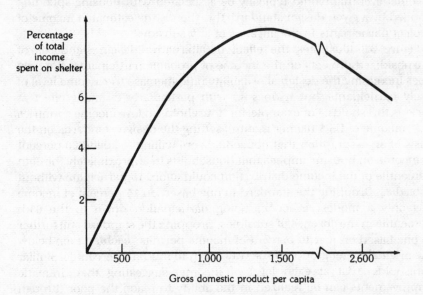

Figure 3.4 The relation between the level of development and the share of housing investment in total output.
Source: Burns, L. S. & L. Grebler 1977. *The housing of nations: analysis and policy in a comparative framework.* London: Macmillan. (As reproduced in World Bank (1980) *Shelter* September – p. 30.)

tool. The microeconomic basis for the Burns–Grebler relationship may be seen by realizing that housing investment is what is known as a derived demand – the result of a mismatch between effective demand and available supply. In the aggregate there are three sources of housing demand that give impetus to housing investment: (1) demand for housing by new households, (2) replacement demand for housing removed from the standing stock, and (3) demand for better housing by existing households. Each source of aggregate demand depends on prevailing housing standards in a country and hence, since standards (implied by housing expenditure to income ratios) have been shown to be related to the level of development in a systematic way, on a country's level of economic development.

The simplest expression of housing investment, for example, is that it is equal to the average value of a new housing unit multiplied by the number of units built. Recent research (Annez and Wheaton) has shown that the number of new units built in a country (relative to population) is largely insensitive to a country's income level but varies proportionately with the rate of population increase.[15] Housing value, on the other hand, is very sensitive to the level of development and indeed follows directly from the sorts of demand relationships portrayed in Figure 3.1. Value is simply equal to the capitalized value of rent; thus the relationship between value and income will follow from the relationship between rent and income. Thus just as the average rent-to-income ratio rises with economic development, so too will the ratio of housing investment to GNP.[15] That is, the ratio of housing investment to GNP is to a considerable degree an aggregate manifestation of the rent-to-income ratio and hence may be expected to follow a comparable path as economic development proceeds. In consequence, planners who base their housing investment targets on the sort of relationship discovered by Burns and Grebler may do so secure in the knowledge that that relationship is well rooted in strong microeconomic regularities among countries.

Another implication of the Burns–Grebler relationship for housing strategy is that it represents as much a constraint on the prospects for effective government intervention in the housing market as it does an opportunity. The powerful regularity between housing investment and GNP, rooted as it is in pervasive behavioral differences among households in different markets, cannot be easily transcended by governments that wish to employ housing investment to serve other goals, such as stimulating overall economic performance. Recent research on this is quite clear. One of the most telling recent analyses of the impact of government intervention to stimulate housing production was provided by Murray, who analyzed the impact of new publicly subsidized housing in the United States on the growth of the total housing stock. That analysis indicates that, largely because of linkages through the demand side of the housing market, new subsidized housing starts displaced a considerable number of new private unsubsidized housing starts that would otherwise have occurred. The net effect was that for each new subsidized unit provided by the government, private production decreased by an amount equivalent to 85 percent of a unit for a net gain of only 15 percent of the number of presumably "incremental" subsidized units.[17] Thus massive government investments in housing appeared to have little overall effect on the ratio of housing investment to GNP. Although Murray speculates that alternative forms of housing subsidy could have been more effective in stimulating new net investment, his findings illustrate the difficulty of trying to work against the forces of the market so strongly imbedded in the sorts of household-level and aggregate-level housing demand relationships discussed above.

Summary and conclusions

Only by providing truly affordable housing to low-income families, which is provided at little or no subsidy and with costs fully recovered, can there be any hope of replicating on a broad scale the limited but genuine successes of sites-and-services and slum-upgrading projects.

A principal goal of this chapter has been to illustrate some of the problems inherent in achieving these objectives. As shown here, empirical evidence on the effective demand for housing suggests that the definition of "affordable housing" will be highly variable from place to place and among different sorts of households. Within cities the fraction of income that households are willing to spend for housing typically declines as income increases, but as the general level of economic development increases, the average fraction of income allocated to housing increases. These observations suggest that no universal rule of thumb is appropriate in designing affordable housing. Instead, a highly differentiated policy should be followed among countries at different levels of development and, when planning within a given country, account should be taken of different propensities among households to spend for housing. Aggregate investment targets for housing should similarly be set differentially, depending on a country's level of economic development.

Unless these things are done, predictable and undesirable consequences will be forthcoming even in housing projects that meet all technical goals of implementation. In particular, planning physical standards on the basis of the typical rule of thumb that households can spend 20 to 25 percent of income on housing will run the risk of either requiring large, unsustainable subsidies in order to encourage participation of low-income target groups or will result in a continuation of one of the major undesirable outcomes of earlier policies – provision of housing intended for low-income groups to higher-income groups. Mayo & Gross[3] have explored in some detail the actual practice of the World Bank and some other organizations regarding design affordability assumptions and project outcomes regarding subsidy levels and the effectiveness of targeting low-income groups. Their conclusions, which are consistent with the analysis discussed here, are (1) that affordability assumptions and hence physical design standards have generally been set at levels higher than appropriate based on evidence on effective demand (this problem is most acute in very low income countries); (2) there has been some leakage of benefits in sites and services projects to higher-income households; and (3) subsidy levels well above 50 percent have occurred in many projects. Subsidies of this magnitude have evidently been necessary to reach intended target groups in the face of overly ambitious planning and affordability standards. In the best of circumstances, subsidies of this magnitude frustrate the ability of authorities to extend the benefits of sites and services to the vast numbers of truly needy households; in the current perilous economic conditions of many developing countries, such subsidies are pure folly.

If subsidy levels are to be reduced it will take a combination of political will and effective planning. In achieving the latter, a major priority should be placed on discovering the level of shelter and infrastructure standards that are truly affordable in each country where low-income housing is to be provided. This effort can be aided by the sort of international comparative studies discussed here, but should be based primarily on careful surveys of effective demand conducted at the local level. Methods for designing, conducting, and analyzing local housing surveys are presented in papers such as those by Malpezzi *et al.*[18] and by Malpezzi.[19] Simply getting the "affordability assumption" right can go a long way toward bringing standards and subsidies down to the appropriate level in many countries.

Reducing standards to an appropriate level is not by itself sufficient to reduce subsidies, however. Pricing policies for sites and services projects must be revised to reflect true resource costs. This means costing project elements (land, building materials, infrastructure, administration, and recurring costs) at their full resource costs and charging accordingly. Loans to beneficiaries should also be made at market rates of interest in order to allow loan-granting organizations to generate a sufficient surplus to ensure their institutional viability and growth.

If there are to be departures from resource-cost-based pricing in order to subsidize some households, these should be explicitly recognized, analyzed, and discussed by project planners. Subsidies, rather than being treated in the *ad hoc* or accidental ways that now characterize their use, should be explicitly justified and should, to the extent possible, be rationalized to serve equity, efficiency, and project impact criteria. Procedures should be established for identifying subsidy elements, for quantifying them, and for estimating their incidence and impacts on project beneficiaries and their consequences for institutions responsible for them. Evaluating incidence and impacts with precision depends on having a better notion of housing demand parameters than has heretofore been available; this is another reason for conducting careful local studies of effective demand for housing.

Another way to reduce subsidies is to provide households with a bundle of shelter and services that maximizes the perceived benefit for a given level of cost of provision. For example, if information is available on the tradeoffs made by households among different elements of the housing infrastructure bundle (e.g., relative preferences for size and location of plot, size and quality of structure, proximity to community facilities, quality and type of infrastructure, etc.), it may be possible to design a package of shelter and infrastructure characteristics for which households are willing to spend a good deal more than they normally do but costing no more to provide than shelter they already occupy. Providing infrastructure rather than shelter *per se* may be a more cost-effective form of government intervention in many countries. In some cases, dealing with capital market and land market imperfections by making available long-term finance or secure tenure may induce significant changes in household willingness-to-pay for shelter. Research on such tradeoffs in developing countries has been conducted recently by Quigley,[20] Follain & Jimenez,[21] and with particular reference to the demand for secure tenure, by Jimenez[22] and by Friedman *et al.*[23] Related work by Gross[24] looks not only at the tradeoffs made by households among shelter and infrastructure attributes, but also at the influence of providing different bundles of characteristics on groups most likely to participate in a project. More empirical research into the nature of such tradeoffs and their implications for project design could be of great benefit in improving project designs and housing sector strategies.

4

The construction industry

FRED MOAVENZADEH

THE CONSTRUCTION industry is unique in its ability to facilitate
development by providing directly for human needs or stimulating
investment, or by generating employment, which can accomplish these
objectives; but these things can be done only if the nature of the building
industry and its function in the national economy are well understood.
This chapter provides an overview of the current context of development
as it affects domestic construction; the structure of the construction
industry as the supplier of shelter and infrastructure in developing
countries; the industry's potential to contribute to development; and the
factors that determine the demand for its products.

The second part of the chapter examines the policies and market
forces that have constrained the growth of the construction industry. In
particular, an attempt has been made to answer the following questions:
Should the public sector produce the bulk of the shelter and infrastructure
in developing countries, or is the private sector better suited to this rôle?
Within the appropriate sector, should firms be large-scale or small-scale,
formal or informal? Are the norms and standards that govern the
construction and building materials industries in developing countries
realistic? What are the consequences of ignoring the maintenance and
rehabilitation of the housing that already exists in the cities of the
developing world?

The answers to these questions all point toward the desirability and
feasibility of encouraging small-scale enterprises, both formal and

informal, in the construction and building materials industries in developing nations. The chapter concludes with a discussion of policies that can loosen the constraints on such enterprises, including the adoption of more realistic standards for building materials and designs, and programs to increase the maintenance and repair of low-income housing. For each of these activities, we suggest that the appropriate rôle for the government is as facilitator rather than primary agent.

The current context of development

The rapid rise in commodity prices in the 1970s ended abruptly with the severe global recession at the turn of the decade. Though prices have recently begun to make a modest comeback, they are still lower than they were in 1960. Moreover, prolonged unemployment in many developed countries has intensified protectionist sentiments, which threaten to undermine recent attempts to liberalize world trade. The repercussions have been felt acutely by middle-income developing countries in their need to service their large foreign debts.[1]

Low commodity prices, daunting trade barriers, and heavy debt burdens have forced many middle-income and poorer countries to restrict their domestic spending, investments, and imports, and to divert capital from development programs to the service of debt. The gloomy prospects for new commercial borrowing by many developing countries will further restrict their capacity to import the inputs for industrialization.

These economic restrictions on current development, coupled with the high price of energy, indicates that nations wishing to sustain the progress of the past must turn their attention to industries that: (1) create stable markets for the products of other domestic sectors (backward linkages) and produce goods necessary for the growth of key consumer industries (forward linkages); (2) rely as much as possible on domestic inputs and production techniques consistent with national factor endowments: and (3) rely as heavily as possible on production methods that are thermally efficient and sources of energy that are locally abundant. Any industry that also provides employment and basic human needs for a significant number of people will be even more attractive as a candidate for development.

Throughout this chapter it will be contended that the construction and building materials industries satisfy these criteria. Although few countries will be able to install domestic capacity in every sector of these industries, nearly every developing country has the potential to compete in several sectors; this will have the dual benefit of increasing the supply of low-cost shelter and stimulating the national economy. We will now examine the structure of the construction industry as it relates to this first function, as the supplier of housing and related infrastructure: we will follow this by a discussion of the industry's potential to contribute to development.

The structure of the construction industry

Fragmentation

The construction industry is organized around the project, which is immobile, long lasting, and relatively expensive. Production is primarily on site rather than in a plant, making it impossible to stockpile products; this is especially problematic since demand is highly seasonal. In contrast to manufacturing, in which the designer and producer collaborate from start to finish, the engineers, architects, and contractors who carry out a construction project will usually work independently. The process is complicated by the participation of investors, subcontractors, suppliers of equipment and materials, potential users of the facility, and government agencies, which will regulate nearly every step of the process. In response to seasonal and geographic fluctuations in construction demand, contractors also rely on a floating pool of labor.

In this separation of responsibilities lies a crucial constraint on the provision of construction. Each participant in the process may be from a different organization, or even a different country. Each engages in the project only when needed and has little opportunity to establish ties with other participants that will outlast the project.

Firm size and geographic concentration

In most market-economy-developed countries, the construction market is composed mainly of small- and medium-sized companies, with 5 to 200 employees. In the planned-economy countries, large, state-run enterprises are common, with payrolls of 600 to 4,000. The construction industry in developing countries is crudely divided into a formal sector, dominated in many cases by a few firms which use advanced technologies, and an informal sector, which will be discussed in detail below. Here we will examine the composition of the formal market in developing countries to get an idea of its ability to satisfy the demand for construction.

Although information on the size of construction firms in developing countries is sparse, the data that are available allow the generalization that special trade firms have small payrolls whereas civil construction firms employ large numbers of workers.[2] Nothing, however, need preclude a large firm from building houses or a small firm from building roads and bridges: in Malaysia, large firms predominate even in residential construction.

Although the building materials industry in developed countries is characterized by intense competition in some parts and oligopolies in others, the market in developing nations, outside the informal sector, is thin and usually dominated by a state-run firm, one or two private firms, or a few foreign companies. The manufacture of steel and cement throughout Latin America, Asia, Africa, and Europe is often by state-run monopolies.

In most developing countries, the construction industry is concentrated in one or two large cities. Such patterns have left a large percentage of the population, especially in rural areas, outside the reach of the formal market.

Public versus private ownership

Ideally, the public sector can promote human welfare and investment in construction where private firms have shown themselves unable or unwilling to do so. In practice, however, public firms have not been successful or efficient in producing shelter for the poor. Developing countries must therefore weigh the advantages of directly engaging in construction against helping the private sector fulfill the nation's social and economic goals. Several options are available. Here, five of the most common possibilities are offered, though these options are not mutually exclusive. Each allows a different balance between the rôles of the public and private sectors.

First, the public sector might construct and deliver complete units and their necessary infrastructure – streets, lighting, sanitary facilities, and community centers for health and education. Since the standards for such homes are often higher than those in the informal market, costs will be far beyond the poor and the government will have to make up the difference. Many governments have committed themselves to such programs; however, most came to realize that the cost as a percentage of their national products was too high. As a result, these governments have built fewer houses than planned, each house of a higher standard and cost than was needed, leaving the poor with as little affordable housing as before.

A second option is to build the shell of an apartment building – a walk-up that might be as high as eight stories, if land is costly – and install central cooking and sanitary facilities. The family that buys each apartment is then responsible for finishing its unit; but the government must still bear the brunt of the cost of the project, which may be nearly as onerous as the cost of providing finished units. Also, the technology and designs that the formal public sector normally uses to produce an apartment building will not favor local materials and labor; again, standards, and prices, will be higher than necessary.

An alternative that has shown promise is the sites-and-services project. The first step in such a project is to level a vacant lot, provide it with streets, lighting, and communal sanitation facilities, and allow low-income families to buy small plots of this land. The agency in charge of the project might leave each family to its own devices in building its house, or give technical instruction or loans for materials. Some cities have followed a fourth option – to renovate substandard housing in slums and squatter settlements. Both sites and services and upgrading programs will be discussed in more detail below.

A fifth choice, of course, is to delegate the provision of housing entirely to the private market, which would mean that the poorest families would be able to afford housing only through the informal sector.

The informal construction sector

Definition The importance of the informal sector in producing shelter and commercial structures for the urban poor has been recognized for more than a decade and has been increasingly well documented, especially in studies by the International Labor Office (ILO); but a review of such studies[3] reveals little agreement even as to the definition of the sector. For instance, a problem appears when the informal sector is viewed in terms of location. In rural areas, the unregulated construction of shelter is centuries old. But defining this activity as the "informal" market seems meaningless, as it is often the *only* market in rural areas; the term "traditional" might be more appropriate.

The urbanization of the developing world brought many traditional industries from the countryside to the cities. Since the formal construction industry was hard pressed to provide shelter for so many new inhabitants, most migrants continued to rely on the methods of the village. Were these methods still to be called traditional or could they now be defined as informal, in contrast to the methods of the formal urban market? As the inhabitants of squatter settlements adapted traditional techniques to urban conditions, improving them with materials and methods from the formal urban sector, the lines of distinction blurred further.

If the definition of the informal construction industry is murky, the outlines of its subsector, the informal building materials industry, are even fuzzier, for it is rarely treated apart from its parent sector. Nor does the informal construction industry rely solely on building materials produced in the informal sector; builders may buy, scavenge, or steal materials produced by formal manufacturers. Similarly, formal contractors may buy materials from informal producers to save money, to obtain products for which no formal substitutes are available, or to evade taxes or labor regulations. The relationship between the formal and informal building materials industries is also somewhat arbitrary. Firms in both sectors may use the same production factors, and these inputs may come from either the formal or informal market. Both sectors may chafe under the same constraints, and both may claim similar linkages to the rest of the economy.

Neither contractors nor materials suppliers in the informal sector can be defined solely by the number of workers they employ: though the average firm in this sector employs few people, a formal, capital-intensive operation may employ even fewer. Instead, most researchers have resorted to an operational definition of informal contractors and producers of building materials in the form of a list of typical traits: small number of employees; small volume of output; low capital investment; reliance on locally available raw materials; and service to local markets whose conditions fluctuate widely. Clearly, more work is needed to identify the limits and function of the informal sector. Here, only a rough idea of its extent is given.

Extent   The informal construction sector is not an anomaly of developing countries. Although few houses in developed nations are built entirely by workers from the informal sector, and almost no building materials are manufactured by unregulated companies, informal activity is pervasive in maintenance and home improvement, which is often performed by the owner of a structure, a union worker who is moonlighting for a lower-than-union wage, or a neighbor who is working for barter.

In developing countries, where the formal sector is less regulated and less entrenched, the informal production of shelter and building materials is extremely widespread. Riedel and Schultz[4] suggest that the average number of dwellings built by the informal sector in developing countries is about four times the number counted by formal statistics. The government of Honduras has estimated that 90 percent of its dwellings were built by the informal sector, and a 1971 study of Ivory Coast revealed that the informal sector accounted for 30 percent the value added by the entire construction industry in the country, as well as 39 percent of the intermediate consumption of materials and services, and 35 percent of the total value of the output of the industry.[5]

The study by the United Nations Centre for Human Settlement (UNCHS) found that a substantial amount of the building materials in developing countries are produced by small-scale units using domestic resources. These materials "sometimes meet all the needs of small-scale private developers in rural trading centers and peri-urban areas, not only for shelter, but also for ... workshops, commercial cooking areas, market stalls, kiosks, private clinics, restaurants, day nurseries, etc."[6] In addition, small-scale suppliers of lime, aggregates, and laterite "have contributed immensely to the construction of civil engineering projects."

The rôle of construction in development

Contribution to GDP

The contribution of construction to gross domestic product (GDP) is typically 3 to 8 percent in developing countries. In the industrialized nations, the mean share of construction in GDP is substantially higher – 8 percent.[7] Time-series data show that construction activity increases faster than per capita income, with each change of 1 percent in per capita GDP accompanied by a 1.2 percent change in the per capita value added by construction.[8] The picture is different in developed nations, where the construction sector has grown more slowly than GDP since the mid-1960s. Such generalizations, of course, do not take into account the fine-scale differences between countries, which depend on the economic and political climate in each country, wars, natural disasters, national priorities, and the expectations of the people.

Contribution to GFCF

Construction also plays a dominant rôle in gross fixed capital formation (GFCF), which includes the outlays of industries, government, and private nonprofit institutions for their stock of fixed assets; this includes the infrastructure for vital social and economic activities, such as the provision of safe drinking water, adequate sanitation and power, transportation and communications, schools and hospitals, and facilities for a wide range of industrial activities.

In most developing countries, construction contributes 40 to 70 percent of GFCF. In countries with relatively high per capita GDP, the rôle of construction in GFCF is toward the lower end of this range, whereas countries that are less developed approach the upper limits.[9] As with the share of construction in GDP, such patterns are modified by the circumstances of individual nations.

Although data as to the economic effects of each dollar invested in the formation of fixed assets is virtually nonexistent for developing countries, a recent simulation based on an econometric model[10] of the United States has shown that a total investment of $ 60 billion in public facilities over the next six years could increase the potential output of the US economy by nearly $ 40 billion through its formation of fixed capital alone. This same investment could contribute an additional US $ 141 billion through increased spending in all sectors, induced by the greater income paid to construction workers, for a multiplier of US $ 2.35 for each US $ 1 invested. The total boost to the US economy from an investment of US $ 60 billion would therefore be US $ 181 billion, a result remarkably close to an independent estimate obtained with a dynamic input–output model of the economy.[10] Even if the growth in the output of the economy and the generation of income are lower in developing countries, they are no doubt substantial, for the construction industry clearly has strong linkages to the rest of the economy in nations at all ranges of per capita income.

Backward linkages

Backward linkages are measures of the demands created by one economic sector for the products of other sectors. For construction, backward linkages usually represent a value which exceeds the value added by the sector itself. The intermediate inputs to construction as a percentage of the total value of the sector's output in 11 developing countries from 1970 to 1975 averaged 55 percent of the value of the sector's output.[2]

As shown in Table 4.1, the Kenyan construction sector has strong backward linkages with the sectors that produce metals and machinery, petroleum, and nonmetallic goods. A comparable breakdown for each 1,000 pesos of gross output of construction in Mexico is given in Table 4.2. Here, the principal intermediate input is nonmetallic products, which provide about 10 percent of the value of the gross output of the sector. Total intermediate deliveries, which were 51 percent in Mexico, fall far below the 71 percent registered in Kenya. Table 4.3 provides similar data for Greece, though the Greek data include repair and maintenance as well as new construction. Mining, nonmetallic minerals, and metallic products again dominate the inputs to construction. Total intermediate deliveries were 52 percent of the gross output of the sector, comparable to the figure for Mexico.

Figure 4.1 displays less precisely but more graphically the backward linkages of the construction sectors of many other countries. The strongest demand for construction inputs in virtually all countries is in building materials, especially stone, soil or clay, iron, steel and other

Table 4.1 Construction sector purchases from other sectors per thousand Kenyan pounds of gross output: Kenya, 1976.

Sector	Increases in intermediate output
mining	42
wood furniture	26
paper and printing	7
petroleum products	92
rubber products	7
paint and detergents	14
other chemicals	17
nonmetallic products	86
metals: machinery	156
transport: bus and rail	14
electricity: supply	5
construction	119
trade	47
transport services	17
restaurants and hotels	12
financial services	30
businesses: premises	5
other intermediate	17
total intermediate	713
wages and salaries	233
other inputs	54
total primary inputs	287
gross output	1000

Source: CMT, Incorporated 1982. *Rôle and contribution of construction industry to the socio-economic growth of developing countries.* Paper prepared for the United Nations Center for Human Settlements, Cambridge, Mass., n.p. 1980, revised 1982.

Table 4.2 Construction sector purchases from other sectors per thousand Mexican pesos of gross output: Mexico, 1970.

Sector	Increases in intermediate output
quarrying	12
wood processing and other wood products	45
oil refining	18
other chemicals	17
rubber and plastic products	11
glass	4
cement	29
nonmetallic mining products	103
basic iron and steel	63
nonferrous metals	7
furniture	3
metal structures and other metal products	38
equipment	12
electricity	3

Table **4.2** – *continued*   Construction sector purchases from other sectors per thousand Mexican pesos of gross output: Mexico, 1970.

Sector	Increases in intermediate output
trade	78
transport	38
financial and other services	20
other intermediate	9
total intermediate	510
wages	304
other value added and indirect taxes	186
gross value added	490
gross output	1000

Source: as for Table 4.1.

Table **4.3**   Construction sector purchases from other sectors per thousand Greek drachmas of gross output: Greece, 1980.

Sector	Increases in intermediate output
agriculture	6
mining etc.	41
wood	44
plastic	14
chemicals	6
oil	13
cement	49
glass	12
nonmetal	84
basic metal	34
metal	86
electrical	59
transportation	21
trade	30
financial	6
other intermediate	15
total intermediate	520
wages and salaries	221
social security	32
other income	176
indirect taxes	51
total primary inputs	490
gross output	1000

Source: as for Table 4.1

metals, processed wood, and the residual category "other manufacturing," which includes glass. Also figuring prominently are mining, trade, and construction itself.

Forward linkages

Forward linkages, the patterns of consumption encouraged by the production of intermediate goods, are more difficult to establish for construction than backward linkages. The value of investment in most structures is nearly impossible to separate from the value of the activities inside. Almost every business and public service has to be housed in some structure, but no clear, measurable relationship exists between the structures themselves and the social benefits of the activities they shelter; the same is true for housing. Planners must assign new structures an arbitrary weight or their current market valuations. The accounting traps in either method are numerous.[11] The task is further complicated by national accounting practices that treat construction as a final product, and so fail to record the deliveries that the construction industry makes to other sectors. None of this means that the sector *has* no forward linkages; the logic and the empirical evidence for their existence are presented in other chapters of this volume.

Employment

On average, construction accounts for 5 percent of the employment in developing nations. In southern Europe and many of the industrialized economies, the contribution is higher – from 7 to 9 percent.[12] In the United States the industry employs 5.5 per cent of all workers;[13] if indirect employment is also counted, nearly 17 percent of all Americans can be said to owe their jobs to the construction industry.[14]

The large number of unskilled workers in the construction industry gives it a great capacity to absorb labor, especially from the agricultural sector; in the low-income African countries, construction is the most important sector in this respect.[7] The success of national plans to generate employment by investing in construction lends further credence to the capacity of the sector to absorb labor.

Investment in construction also can generate jobs in other sectors through its consumption of intermediate goods. In the housing sector in Mexico in 1970, the ratio of direct to indirect employment varied from 3:2 to 5:2.[15] A study of housing construction in Rio de Janeiro[16] found that one job would be created indirectly for every three created directly in the construction sector. In India, the National Buildings Organization has estimated that an investment of Rs. 10 million (Rs. 9.80 = US $1) in

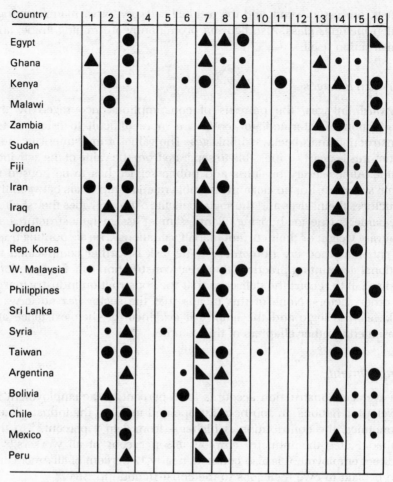

Country	1	2	3	4	5	6	7	8	9	10	11	12	13	14	15	16
Egypt			●				▲	▲	●							◣
Ghana	▲		●				▲	•	•				▲	•	•	
Kenya		●	•			•	●		▲		●			▲	•	●
Malawi		●														●
Zambia			•				▲		•				▲	●	•	▲
Sudan	◣													◣		
Fiji			▲				▲						●	●	•	▲
Iran	●	•	●				▲	●						▲	▲	
Iraq		▲	▲				◣							▲		
Jordan		▲					▲	▲						●	•	
Rep. Korea	•	•	●		•	•	▲	▲		•				●	●	
W. Malaysia	•		▲				▲	•	●			•		▲		
Philippines		•	▲				▲	●		•				▲		●
Sri Lanka		●	●				▲	▲						▲	●	
Syria		•	▲		•		▲							▲		•
Taiwan			●				◣	●		•				●	●	
Argentina			▲			•	◣	▲								●
Bolivia		▲				●								▲	•	•
Chile		●	●			•	◣	▲							•	•
Mexico			●				▲	▲	▲					▲		•
Peru			▲				◣	◣								

^aFor sector definitions and explanations of symbols, see Figure 1(b).

Source: Reidel and Schultz, Bauwirtschaft, pp. 56-57.

Figure 4.1 Construction sector's domestic purchases from other sectors: share of supply sectors. (For sector definitions and explanation of symbols, see key on facing page.).
    Source: Reidel, J. & S. Schultz 1978. *Bauwirtschaft und Baustoffindustrie in Entwicklungslandern.* Munich: Weltform – pp. 56–7.

Key to Figure 4.1: Sector definitions and explanation of symbols

No.	Sector	ISIC – 1968[a]
1	agriculture, forestry, farming	11 – 13
2	mining and quarrying	21 – 23, 29
3	wood, furniture, paper, printing	33, 34
4	rubber	355
5	chemical, plastic products	351, 352, 356
6	petrochemicals	353, 354
7	nonmetallic minerals	36
8	basic metals, metal products	37, 381
9	nonelectrical machinery	382
10	electrical machinery	383
11	transport equipment	384
12	electricity, gas and water	41, 42
13	construction	50
14	trade	61, 62
15	transport, storage, communications	71, 72
16	other services	63, 81 – 3, 91 – 4, 951 – 3, 959

[a] Classification from the Statistical Office of the United States,

ISIC Statistical Papers, Series M, No. 4, Rev. 2, Add. 1, 1968.

Symbol	Explanation
●	3 – 7 percent
●	8 – 13 percent
▲	14 – 25 percent
◣	26 – 50 percent

building construction at the 1980–1 wage rate generated 624 person-years in on-site employment (420 by unskilled laborers, 204 by skilled), and 999 person-years in indirect employment in the building materials industry and other support sectors. Studies in the United States[17] have estimated that each on-site construction job generates an equal number of off-site jobs and induces nearly three times that number of jobs through corporate expenditures and the spending and respending of wages.

Rôle of the informal sector

As we have seen, the size and output of the informal sector in most developing countries is substantial. It provides not only shelter for the poor but also commercial structures for retail outlets, the repair of vehicles and machinery, the manufacture of tools, and the operation of commercial laundries; in many cases, the same structure provides both shelter and a commercial facility. In rural areas, the informal sector supplies farmers with barns and silos and in other regions it contributes to the building of infrastructure. In Kenya in 1976, 60 percent of the capital formation in dwellings and 16 percent in all categories of construction was contributed by the traditional sector.[2]

Since the informal production of building materials uses almost no imported inputs, it conserves scarce foreign exchange and stimulates the demand for domestic resources, machinery, and labor rather than foreign inputs. The sector has strong backward linkages to both the formal and informal economies, creating a demand for providers and carriers of raw inputs (i.e., sand, lime, stone, and sawn lumber); makers of simple tools such as wheelbarrows and pickaxes; mechanics; suppliers of fuel, chemicals, and adhesives; and manufacturers of more complex tools and machinery.[18]

Such linkages have not been quantified, but the logic for their existence is strong. The production of building materials is well suited to small-scale techniques and local resources; it is therefore able to bring jobs and commodities to rural areas. Its labor-intensive nature allows it to generate jobs in cities as well. For instance, the production of 10 million bricks per year by traditional methods employs 160 workers, whereas an automated plant with the same output employs only eight. Similarly, the production of Rs. 1 million worth of in-country tiles for roofing might employ 960 workers, whereas the production of an equivalent value of galvanized iron sheets, also for roofing, would create jobs for only seven workers.[19] As a result, the informal sector provides a high share of the total employment for the construction industry: in Ivory Coast in 1970, the informal sector accounted for 60 percent of the workers in the construction industry as a whole.[20]

Jobs created in the informal sector would also heighten the demand for the goods and services of other small-scale enterprises, multiplying the effects of job creation. Moreover, workers who produce building materials, even with traditional techniques, acquire skills that can be transferred to the formal sector.

The demand for construction

Determinants of demand

No matter how great the real need for construction in a country, the effective demand for the sector's products will depend on the ability and willingness of private households, businesses, and public agencies to pay for those products. Among the most important determinants of this effective demand are population and its division between cities and the countryside, per capita income, and the distribution of income. For instance, in most developing countries the poorest 40 percent of the population will be unable to afford housing from any formal producer.[21] As Table 4.4 shows, owning a home even in a public project can be beyond the reach of the poorest quarter of the population of a city (in this case, San Salvador).

Table 4.4 Accessibility of formal and informal housing programs to the urban poor of San Salvador, 1977.[a]

Type of housing	Lowest percentile who can afford option
tenement housing, poorest quality	6
extralegal subdivisions, poorest quality	10
FSDVM,[b] basic core unit	24
tenement housing, adequate quality	24
IVU,[c] marginal housing in squatter areas	27
extralegal subdivisions, adequate standard	42
FSV,[d] normal program (1975–8)	48
IVU,[c] two-bedroom houses	52
IVU,[c] four-bedroom houses	beyond 60th percentile
IVU,[c] apartments	beyond 60th percentile
FSV,[d] normal program (1978–)	beyond 60th percentile

Source: Bamberger, M. E. Gonzalez-Polio & U. Sae-Hau 1982. *Evaluation of sites and services programs: the evidence from El Salvador.* World Bank Staff Working Paper No. 549, World Bank, Washington, D.C. – p. 29.

Notes

[a] Represents conditions before the 1979 coup in El Salvador.

[b] Fundacion Salvadorena de Desarrollo y Vivienda Minima, a private, nonprofit organization.

[c] Instituto de Vivienda Urbana, a government housing agency.

[d] Fondo Social para la Vivienda, a government housing agency, an extension of El Salvador's social security system.

A second broad determinant of the demand for construction is the national propensity to mobilize income and savings and channel them into capital formation and investment. The scarcity of capital in developing countries may force owners and contractors to secure financing abroad. Although bilateral and multilateral aid may foster development, it may also stipulate that the borrowers must purchase goods and services in the donor country.

Types of construction

The resources available for the construction of shelter will be affected by the demand for nonresidential buildings and infrastructure. Typically, 35 to 40 percent of the demand for construction in a developing country is for residential dwellings, 22 to 27 percent for nonresidential buildings such as offices, and 35 to 38 percent for civil works.[22] Regression analyses have shown[11] that infrastructure fades from about one-half of all construction in the first stages of development to 30 percent in higher-income societies, but the share of residential construction rises almost as quickly as infrastructure falls – from around 28 percent at US $ 200 to nearly 40 percent at US $ 2,000 per capita. The nonresidential share, which begins near the residential share in poor societies, climbs slowly but more steadily than the residential share, moving from around 23 percent at US $ 200 to about 28 percent at US $ 3,100. The two converge in societies with incomes around US $ 10,000.

New construction versus maintenance

Construction activity may also be categorized according to whether it produces a new facility or maintains or repairs an old one. In developing nations, repair and maintenance generally account for less than 10 percent of total construction, as opposed to 25 to 40 percent in developing nations.[7,23] In Great Britain, for instance, building maintenance accounts for about 40 percent of construction expenditure.[24] In the United States, improvements to housing alone amounted to US $ 50 billion in 1983, exclusive of the value of self-help labor, compared to the US $ 86 billion spent on new housing that year. The demand for repairs and maintenance thus provides a substantial market for contractors and suppliers of building materials, a buffer for workers in times of slack demand for new construction, and a stabilizing force in the demand for materials.[25]

The relatively modest share of maintenance in developing countries can be partly attributed to the younger age of its facilities; but if this were the principal cause, the proportion of repair and maintenance would rise as these facilities aged; and a look at 14 developing countries with a wide range of per capita incomes reveals no such pattern.[26] Visits to many developing countries confirm that facilities are simply not being maintained.

Constraints on the supply of low-income housing

Construction projects almost always need land, financing, equipment, labor of various types and levels of skill, building materials and supplies; but the mix of resources in a given project will vary with the type of the project (i.e., single-family housing, a skyscraper, a rural road), the stage of development of the host country, the policies and priorities of the government, and the relative prices of labor and machinery. Here we discuss each factor in turn, though we leave the problems that owners have in acquiring land and commercial financing to other chapters in this volume.

Financing within the construction industry

Like owners, contractors of construction projects and suppliers of building materials must also obtain financing for their operations, both through investment and working capital. The difficulties that owners have in obtaining reasonable financing exacerbate the difficulties of contractors and manufacturers of building materials. Contractors are almost universally paid in installments on the basis of work completed – a figure which is often deliberately underestimated by the client. Moreover, a portion of the payment due the contractor is almost always withheld by the owner as a guarantee against poor workmanship and hidden defects.

For small contractors in developing countries, these difficulties are compounded. Unlike developed countries, where suppliers often extend short-term credit to contractors, materials and supplies in developing countries must be paid for on delivery, or even in advance. Payment from the client may be unreasonably delayed, even when the client is the government. Equipment rentals, which would reduce the requirements for investment capital may be nonexistent; equipment purchases and repairs may be expensive, especially when spare parts must be imported.

Commercial banks have only partially filled the need for operating capital in developing countries. Many banks in developing countries are reluctant to extend credit to contractors or manufacturers of building materials, especially if such firms are small or new. The shortage of commercial credit is especially serious for firms that need to buy imported goods and services. The universal need for bonds and for liability and property insurance impose additional financial difficulties and risks on contractors in developing countries, where such bonds and policies may be available only at exorbitant premiums.

Equipment

Developed and developing countries show similar patterns of consumption of construction equipment; but developing nations must fulfill nearly 100 percent of their needs for heavy construction equipment through importation. The levels of equipment needed for domestic construction are difficult to determine. If a firm carries too little equipment, it may be forced to cancel a project or turn it over to a foreign contractor. If a firm buys enough equipment for a large project, the machines may sit idle thereafter.

An enormous investment would be needed to launch the domestic manufacture of heavy construction equipment. Since one of the best prospects for decreasing the need for imported equipment is to substitute indigenous labor for capital investment, we will now discuss the supply of construction labor in developing countries, and the possibilities for substituting capital for labor in construction.

Labor

Composition of the labor force Labor is the second most important input to construction (19 to 27 percent of the total value of output); only building materials represent a greater expenditure (37 to 55 percent).[2] Construction labor is not homogeneous. Workers may be classified according to their levels of skills by their functions (i.e., mason, plumber, electrician) or by their unions (in the United States there are more than 70 unions for construction workers).

The pool of construction workers in developing countries has a higher percentage of unskilled workers than in developed nations. Ensuring an adequate supply of skilled construction labor is extremely difficult for many developing countries for several reasons: (1) the low monetary value attached to construction labor relative to other sectors; (2) the minimum full-time staffs carried by most firms as a hedge against the uncertainty of demand; (3) a large agricultural sector which draws large numbers of laborers away from construction at critical periods; (4) the migration of construction workers to the oil-producing countries of the Middle East.

The major means of acquiring skills in developing countries is through informal training on the job or through apprenticeships. On-the-job training, however, produces at best semiskilled workers with project-specific abilities. Implementing formal training programs has been difficult. Construction firms are generally unwilling to invest in such programs, fearing that newly skilled workers, under no obligation to the firm that paid for their training, may leave for jobs elsewhere. Commonly, the public sector has been expected to provide training programs, but most of these programs have been unsuccessful.

Also important, though largely ignored, is the training of supervisory personnel. The unavailability of indigenous managers who have been trained, as opposed to managers who have risen from the ranks of workers, is not easily compensable. Capable managers play a crucial rôle in supervising unskilled workers, and so are vital to the success of labor-intensive construction techniques.

The substitution of capital for labor   Not only is the scarcity of heavy equipment, skilled craftsmen, and trained managers a fact of life in many developing countries, but the infrastructure needed for capital-intensive operations may also be inadequate. It therefore becomes imperative to ask whether a mix of capital and labor exists such that these scarcities are rendered less critical. Fortunately, the technologies of the construction and building materials industries are extremely flexible; many ways of producing the same project or material are possible, each with a different ratio of capital to labor.

Studies by the World Bank have shown that 60 developing countries would benefit from the greater use of labor-based construction. Even countries that might not appear suited to such methods on the whole may have many regions in which labor-based methods would be beneficial.[27] Similarly, estimates performed across the building materials industries of many nations and within various countries across wide time spans provide convincing evidence that labor and capital are highly interchangeable in the face of differentials in factor prices.[28]

Within this broad range of possible ratios of capital to labor, the actual ratio used in a given project (i.e., the provision of housing to 1,000 people) will be determined by the technology chosen (i.e., 1,000 single-story houses as opposed to a multistory building with 1,000 units). The choice of technology will then determine the ratios of light to heavy equipment, of skilled to unskilled workers, and of domestic to imported materials (i.e., bricks and prefabricated components for single-family houses as opposed to steel and glass for a skyscraper). Data from Rio de Janeiro in the early 1970s, for example, showed that five times as many skilled laborers and six times as many unskilled laborers were employed in medium-cost, four-story housing than in low-cost, single-family housing.[29] Table 4.5 indicates how building materials can vary according to project type.

Table 4.5 Materials inputs as a percentage of total expenditure for three types of construction projects in Kenya.

Type of input	Residential	Nonresidential	Civil works
sand	4.6	6.4	3.0
aggregate	5.6	5.2	10.0
cement	10.0	13.4	3.0
hydrated lime	–	–	2.4
concrete products	6.0	3.8	2.8
hardcore filling	1.5	0.9	–
wood products	8.9	3.0	0.4
steel products	3.0	17.9	22.9
hardware: windows	4.5	2.9	3.0[a]
paints	8.2	2.2	–
glass	1.0	1.3	–
floor tiles	5.2	1.6	–
roofing materials	4.1	2.3	–
plumbing: sanitation fixtures	7.8	5.0	–
electrical installations	5.2	2.0	–
explosives	–	–	3.0
fuels, bitumen, etc.	–	–	2.4
Total: all material	75.6	68.2	52.7

Source: as for Table 4.1.
Note
[a] Includes paints.

The most common criterion by which a firm selects a technology for a given project is by minimizing the marginal costs of capital and labor. In some developing countries, constr⁹.ction wages may be only 5 to 10 percent of the wages offered in industrialized countries, leading firms to rely as heavily as possible on labor. Many firms, however, are biased against labor-intensive production, despite its low cost, because of the difficulties they have experienced – or imagine they would experience – in mobilizing large forces of unskilled laborers.

One way to overcome this bias might be to show contractors that labor-intensive methods can be technically efficient. This could be done by comparing the productivities of various technologies, each with its own ratio of capital to labor. Unfortunately, most productivity indices measure labor productivity alone. When Kassimatis[30] devised a joint labor–capital index for construction, he found that the productivity of capital declined from 1956 to 1965 and was made up for only by the increase in the productivity of labor during that time.

A second reason for the unfounded bias toward capital-intensive methods in developing countries is that most estimates of the costs of labor-based technologies are made on the basis of project designs geared toward equipment-based methods. Moreover, in most developing countries, wages and equipment prices are distorted by monopolies, artificially high wage floors, excess capacity, rampant unemployment, tariffs, overvalued currency, and uneven rates of inflation in various sectors. As a consequence, the correct choice of technology by a firm may be incorrect with respect to the national economy. To compensate, policy makers often use "shadow prices," which more accurately reflect the relative scarcities of inputs and the development goals of the country.

Labor-intensive methods of construction often show themselves capable of satisfying these goals. Perhaps the most important advantage of labor-based production in the 1980s is its ability to save scarce foreign exchange. The true cost of importing heavy equipment may be even higher than its nominal value, if the price in hard currency requires export promotion schemes, which inevitably mean curtailing domestic consumption.

Identical arguments speak in favor of the labor-intensive production of building materials. Since the availability of building materials is the most crucial factor in providing housing to the poor, any strategy for the development of a domestic construction industry must give heavy consideration to the conditions that influence the supply of this input.

Building materials

Import substitution Although expenditures on building materials represent only 3 to 5 percent of the GDP of developing countries, they account for 5 to 8 percent of the total value of the imports of these countries. The developing world recently has made great strides in overcoming its dependence on imported materials. For virtually every material, developing countries collectively improved their share of global production during the 1970s; but the distribution of these gains has been uneven. Although imports of building materials in countries such as Mexico are as low as 5 to 10 percent, in other countries they are 60 percent. Building materials are therefore a drain on foreign exchange at a time when developing nations can least afford it.

The recent recession in world trade has led many economists to take a closer look at the effects of export instability on growth, with the result that planners in many developing countries are finding local autonomy increasingly attractive; but if new strategies of import substitution are to be successful, planners must learn from the past, for the history of import substitution is replete with unfortunate stories.

First, the protective measures that developing nations have imposed on building materials have grown much larger than those of developed nations. Although a policy of shielding domestic infant industries has theoretical validity, in practice it has created walls behind which private firms have raised their prices with impunity and maturing industries have relaxed their efforts to become more efficient. Barriers designed by developing nations to protect their infant industries from competition by developed countries have also inadvertently restricted trade with other developing nations.

History has shown that the basic principle of comparative advantage cannot be overthrown by fiat. A nation must develop those sectors favoured by its factor endowments. Although attempts by relatively small economies to achieve autonomy can be worth while, the development of complementary industrial bases within a region may be still more productive, resulting in larger markets and the increased exchange of goods between neighboring countries.

Constraints on the formal supply of building materials   Since many developing countries have been forced to limit their foreign trade so they can service their external debts, any strategy for establishing a domestic industry in which the major supplies of raw materials and energy must be imported will be impractical. The requirements for energy is especially severe for building materials, which are more energy intensive than many other products.

A second major constraint on the domestic manufacture and distribution of building materials is poor transportation. The low value–weight ratio of most building materials can make the cost of transporting certain materials higher than the cost of producing them. In the Sudan, Honduras, and Botswana, for instance, the cost of transporting cement more than 100 miles exceeds its value.[31] This means that a single, centralized producer will find it more economical to service a small but concentrated urban area than a diffuse rural area.

In many countries, the development of a building materials industry is also hampered by the inadequacy of support industries, such as skilled repairmen and suppliers of spare parts for heavy capital goods. Equipment breakdown is one of the many reasons for the underutilized capacity that has been a long-standing problem in the production of building materials in developing countries. A second important cause of underutilization is the lack of a demand sufficient to support full-capacity production, and the instability of that demand.

The shortage of skilled workers and trained managers described earlier in regard to the construction industry also affects the building materials industry. Large-scale, capital-intensive technologies seem to need more skilled workers and managers than small-scale, labor-intensive tech-nologies. Statistics indicate that "small enterprises with a lower level of investment per worker tend to achieve a higher level of productivity of capital than do large, more capital-intensive enterprises".[32] When the scarcity of financing in developing countries is taken into account, the high cost of capital-intensive technologies is exacerbated.

Constraints on the informal supply of building materials The owners of small, unregistered firms are even less likely than registered firms to receive institutional financing. Owners who cannot obtain loans from banks usually turn to relatives, personal savings, chit funds, private financiers – or to moneylenders, who may charge interest rates as high as 10 percent per week. Complaints about shortages of storage facilities, factory space, and efficient machinery indicate that owners have problems obtaining money for capital expansion as well as working capital.[33]

Informal producers are in a weak bargaining position relative to large-scale firms. They are less visible to the government and so receive few subsidies; they do not have licenses to import raw materials and spare parts and so must go without these items or buy them at high prices from large firms. Informal producers also are at a disadvantage in marketing their wares, especially to large buyers such as the government.

The market for the goods of the informal sector is sometimes limited by their uneven quality, since handmade items may lack regularity and smoothness. Regardless of the actual quality of these products, the public perception that they are inferior to the goods of the formal sector may create a bias against them. Although developing countries have conducted a great deal of research to improve the productivity of workers and the quality of goods in the informal sector, the results have rarely been disseminated with success, and the formal construction industry has remained reluctant to use innovative domestic materials. Such failures are not surprising, since the informal sector is so little understood. If its potential is to be fully realized its needs, operation, and capacity must first be determined. This and other recommendations for promoting the domestic manufacture of building materials, mostly through small-scale production, as well as recommendations to enhance the supply of low-income housing, again through small-scale production, are presented below.

Overcoming constraints on the supply of housing

We have seen that the construction policies of the past have left the poorest 40 percent of the developing world unable to afford housing through the formal sector. Any re-examination of these policies must consider the following three vital questions.

Who should produce housing for the poor?

Initially, many governments viewed urbanization as a threat to economic growth rather than as a necessary consequence of new social and economic opportunities and a condition for continued development. As it became apparent that it was futile to fight urbanization, developing countries and multinational aid groups began to consider ways to provide shelter for the new inhabitants of overcrowded cities. The undertaking seemed massive when viewed in terms of aggregate need and formal supply, and the private sector seemed poorly equipped to fill the need for housing for the poor, especially when the profit motive for doing so seemed small. The public sector seemed the only logical choice.

Unfortunately, public companies have proved to be inefficient or completely ineffectual in providing affordable housing to the poor. They are prone to monopolistic behavior, with the concomitant waste of resources, high prices, and other market distortions. Often, public construction has been a disincentive rather than a complement to private construction. Public firms that have been treated preferentially by the government have performed weakly and wastefully, raising concern that subsidizing such firms at the expense of private domestic firms has not been cost effective.

Disenchanted with the public sector, policy makers have recently turned to the private sector. The question remains as to which firms in this sector – large scale or small scale, formal or informal – are the best agents to produce shelter for the poor. The magnitude of the problem once again would seem to indicate that large-scale firms are needed to solve it; but large-scale private firms have shown themselves to be vulnerable to the same weaknesses as their counterparts in the public sector.

Although the need for housing in the cities of the developing world is tremendous, the only hope of meeting that need is through the efforts of many small-scale firms, some in the formal sector, others in the informal sector; since the two sectors share so many characteristics, it seems pointless to try to judge which is the better provider of low-cost shelter. Policy makers are beginning to recognize that even as they have debated the best way to provide shelter to the poor, the informal construction sector has quietly been fulfilling a staggering percentage of the demand for urban housing. If this housing does not often meet the standards of government agencies, the question arises as to whether these standards are too high.

What standards are appropriate for low-cost shelter?

Traditionally, government agencies have set unrealistically high standards for building materials and construction designs. Many of these regulations, i.e., that materials be of the highest grades possible and that each unit of public housing have indoor sanitation, were either imported from developed countries or formulated by people who were educated in the Western tradition, if not the West itself. Such regulations have often been inappropriate to local conditions; they have limited the number of homes that could be built, raised unit costs beyond the reach of the poor, and prevented the use of local resources and labor. Standards for building materials have sometimes made it necessary that these materials be produced by large-scale facilities, with the attendant requirements of imported machinery and skilled workers.

For each building material, a government can require either a single national standard or a range of strengths according to specified uses. Although a universal standard might seem justified on the basis of safety, this is probably unnecessary and wasteful; for example, only about 20 percent of the world's construction projects demand cement that would meet the international standard for full-strength portland cement, and most of these are not housing projects.

To permit the use of various grades of materials, building codes must be performance oriented rather than prescriptive. Instead of requiring 20 cm brickwork in a party wall, a performance standard would specify how fire resistant, load bearing and soundproof the wall must be. A builder could then use any combination of materials that fulfilled these specifications, though government guidelines could suggest wise choices. Performance standards would encourage not only the use of local materials but also the reduction of design requirements to levels appropriate to local conditions: a house in an arid climate may not need a roof that sheds water, though a building code imported from a developed nation might have mandated one.[34]

As standards become more reasonable, small-scale firms will be in a better position to satisfy them and so to compete in the housing market. The informal sector by definition would not be directly affected by a change in government regulations, but if standards were made more flexible, an informal firm might find it easier to meet these requirements and so enter the formal market. At the very least, the products of the informal sector would suffer less of a stigma in the eyes of government officials and the poor when compared to the products of the formal sector.

Consider the standards for lot size in housing projects. Since urban land is so expensive and difficult to acquire, developing countries might find it beneficial to increase the density of settlement in housing projects; this could be done without threatening the health of residents or violating their minimum requirements for acceptable shelter. In Bogotá, the World Bank found that the distribution of roads and open spaces that grew up under relatively free market conditions in illegal subdivisions was far below government standards, but was acceptable to residents, who would not have been able to afford lots at all if these had been divided according to legal standards. The World Bank decided that the system needed to be guided, but was fundamentally a good strategy for increasing the supply of affordable housing to the poor.[35]

What is the cost of neglecting maintenance and repair?

As shown earlier, the repair and maintenance of the existing stock of housing in developing nations is largely ignored. Such neglect can have serious economic and social consequences; extensive repairs will be more costly than routine upkeep, and will require higher capital expenditures and more advanced labor skills. If repairs are ignored completely, the house may be lost. In most major cities, the rate at which housing for the poor is built is slower than the rate at which it collapses or must be demolished because it is unsafe.

On the other hand, if substandard housing is upgraded and decaying homes are rehabilitated before they collapse, the net gain of acceptable shelter will be tremendous. The cost would be a fraction of that required for new facilities and there would be little dislocation of the current residents of slums and squatter settlements. A program of repair and maintenance would have the added social value of being more labor intensive than a program of new construction; it would require virtually no foreign exchange and would be more amenable to the use of the unskilled workers, local contractors, and locally produced materials.

Implications for new policies

The answers to all three questions indicate that small-scale enterprises in the private sector have the greatest potential to provide housing for the poorest inhabitants of the developing world and that the government can best assist in this process by facilitating the natural operation of such firms. Governments may be unwilling to accept this rôle, since the conventional wisdom for many years has been that small-scale firms cannot compete against large-scale firms because they cannot reap the advantages of economies of scale. Yet the lessons of the past controvert this "wisdom". Even if a large-scale plant were able to achieve economies of scale when located in a well-developed region, that same plant, transposed to an underdeveloped region, would not be able to produce its product as cheaply, given the difficulties it would encounter in trying to serve a large market – difficulties such as the high cost of transportation, the added requirements for complex machinery and skilled personnel, and the need for large sources of energy. Even in the developed world, similar factors have made large-scale plants less attractive than they once were, and their construction has declined.

The main reason for the waning enthusiasm for large-scale firms is that they are only efficient when operating near their design capacities, which has not been the case for many facilities, especially in developing countries. Forecasting demand is fraught with uncertainty, even in the most stable of industries, and the construction and building materials industries are among the most unstable. Bottlenecks in production are another major contributor to underutilization. In developing countries, where most of the equipment, raw materials, and spare parts for large-scale plants must be imported, supplies of these items can be difficult or costly to obtain. Although a large-scale firm may be better able to attract skilled repairmen and technicians than a small-scale firm, a large-scale firm may have machinery that is much more complex than the small-scale firm's, so that even the total supply of trained mechanics in a region will be inadequate to its needs.

In addition to the economies of scale that may or may not exist within a single firm, economists recognize economies of scale within an industry. For example, as an industry grows and creates a large and stable demand for a certain intermediate good, a domestic support industry may develop to meet this demand, causing the price of that intermediate good to fall. If such external economies of scale exist, they should accrue as readily to an industry composed of a large number of small-scale firms as to an industry composed of a few large-scale firms.

Some economists are calling into question the entire theory that supports the existence of economies of scale. As Bela Gold pointed out in a recent UNIDO report, the very definition of scale is ambiguous in the minds of most researchers and manufacturers; Plant B might be called "large scale" in relation to Plant A when it merely carries out the same number of activities as Plant A in greater number, or carries out a greater number of related activities. Rather, scale effects must be tied to the level of specialization in a plant as well as its output.[36]

In general, support for the existence of economies of scale is too weak to substantiate the bias of many officials towards large-scale firms; when taken together with the dismal history of large-scale construction and building materials firms in developing countries, the rationale for encouraging small-scale firms in these sectors is clear. We will now look at three programs that could increase the supply of housing in developing countries in a manner consistent with the policies suggested in this section; in each case, we discuss the strengths of the program and ways in which it might be made more effective.

Sites-and-services programs

In some cities, sites-and-services programs have been able to increase the national production of low-cost housing by 50 percent, with homes affordable by families down to (but not below) the lowest 20 percentile of income.[37] The benefits of sites-and-services programs have also extended to others besides the occupants of the houses. A sites-and-services project in El Salvador generated US $ 500 of income per unit (in 1980 prices) for a total of 3,700 person-years of employment and US $ 4.1 million in wages, whereas a project in Zambia generated 667 person-years of employment and more than US $ 1 million in wages.[38] Studies of these and other projects have shown that families are more likely to hire laborers from the informal sector than to perform the work completely by themselves.

In this and other ways, experience has shown that the private market has as great a rôle to play in sites-and-services programs as the sweat equity of residents. First, hiring a builder may be a wise choice for a family, especially since more low-income families seem to be employed outside the home than once was predicted. Similarly, participants may do as well to buy materials from a project warehouse or a local supplier as to make their own bricks and cement.

Hiring workers and purchasing materials from the informal sector may also enable families to construct safe multistory housing on their sites, which would lower the unit cost of their land. Although multistory housing should not be encouraged if it would preclude the use of domestic labor and materials, evidence from the Tondo project in Manila indicates that builders in the informal sector are capable of constructing buildings several stories high. In Cairo, the inelastic supply of land has led the informal market to build houses from two to five stories tall, at a lower cost than a one-story house on the same plot of land.[39]

Multistory homes would also create more rental units in projects, leading to a second opportunity for income transfers in sites-and-services programs. Allowing participants to rent out rooms in their new homes not only increases their incomes but also provides decent housing to migrants who otherwise would be unable to afford it; this has not opened the door to absentee landlordism, as had previously been feared.[40]

Third, more private financing may now be available for sites-and-services programs than before their effectiveness was demonstrated. The

Housing Guaranty program of the Agency for International Development (AID) has been extremely successful in attracting long-term loans from private US investors to finance sites-and-services programs, the construction of core housing, and the upgrading of urban slums. AID helps the host country design a workable shelter program, then notifies the American financial community that it is willing to guarantee 100 percent of a loan to the host country for this program. Once financing is secured, AID continues to offer technical assistance to the host country, which in turn promises to repay its loan in full, even if the agency administering the program cannot collect its entire cost from its tenants. Of AID's portfolio of US $ 1.3 billion, only 1 percent has been lost to default.[41]

A fourth rôle for the private sector is in implementing a program. The project in El Salvador showed that if a private nonprofit organization runs a program, the chances of recovering its costs may be greater than if a public agency is in charge, since the continued operation of a private organization depends on its success in this task.[42]

But even with greater participation by the private sector, sites-and-services projects may still be a second-best option for the creation of low-cost urban housing – a compromise between the natural operation of the informal sector and the highly controlled operation of the public sector. Although policy makers now realize that the informal sector can be a powerful mechanism for the provision of shelter to the poor, the limits that govern institutional investment in housing make it difficult to finance this sector. It is easier to give large amounts of money to a few well defined recipients, whose resources and operations can be readily determined, than to give small amounts of money to a great many recipients whose operations are hard to monitor, assess, or even define. Institutions are unable to finance the construction of homes on land to which the occupants do not hold title. Yet under natural conditions, the informal sector almost always builds homes first and worries about land tenure later.

Similarly, most programs require that services be in place before a family can build its house on a site, whereas the informal sector first occupies a given territory, builds its shelters, and only later tries to obtain services for the territory, either by pressuring the government, threatening violence, or becoming a hazard to the safety and health of the rest of the city. Although there is nothing sacred about the order in which the informal sector chooses to acquire the necessities of decent shelter, it is possible that the choices and natural activities of millions of people may be as wise as the decisions of a handful of bureaucrats. Failure to recognize that the sites-and-services projects are in many ways designed for the convenience of the institutions that finance and manage them rather than the people who live in them could result in a landscape dotted with well serviced sites that are empty of residents and surrounded by shantytowns and squatters' settlements bustling with families and small businesses.

Some multinational aid groups have begun to recognize this danger. The World Bank, in reviewing the first ten years of its urban program, has found that the social and economic systems of most cities are so complex, and their needs so overwhelming, that a site-by-site approach cannot satisfy a significant percentage of the demand for low-income urban housing, especially if local institutions are too weak to operate and maintain the services the Bank has provided. The Bank has decided that it is more important to leave behind effective policies and institutions than a few new housing sites.[43]

How can even the most effective institutions help the informal sector acquire the resources it needs to operate effectively if the rules that govern institutional investment are so ill suited to financing such enterprises? No simple answer is apparent. But this does not mean we can stop looking for at least a few partial answers. Policy makers tried for decades to ignore the informal sector because it was difficult to define, but they finally had to recognize its existence because it proved to be the only viable means of producing low-cost shelter for the urban poor. In the same way, policy makers will have to find methods to facilitate the activities of the informal sector, as difficult as that now seems.

Upgrading substandard housing

We have seen (Table 4.4) that even sites-and-services programs do not reach the poorest 20 percent of most city residents. Programs to upgrade urban slums, however, can and have improved their housing significantly. Given the limited resources available in most countries, conserving and upgrading the existing stock of housing is an economical, immediate remedy to the housing problems of the poor, without displacing them. Such programs may focus on upgrading tenements, squatter settlements, or extralegal subdivisions.

In El Salvador, a nonprofit developer bought a tenement, renovated the rooms, and improved the water and sanitation facilities. Tenants were then able to buy the apartments they had previously rented, though this meant a 20 percent increase in their monthly payments.[44] In Thailand, programs by the National Housing Authority annually produce 10,000 new housing units and upgrade another 6,000 units in the slums; ten years ago, the annual production of housing by the government was 500 units.[45] These are merely examples of what can be done; they are not indicators of a widespread movement toward renovation, a movement that could be accomplished efficiently and cheaply by small-scale construction firms, both formal and informal.

Increasing the supply of building materials

Even the most successful sites-and-services and upgrading programs have been plagued by shortages of low-cost building materials, for their planners failed to recognize that any program to improve the supply of housing must include measures to develop a domestic industry in building materials. Fortunately, the distribution of natural resources necessary for the production of most building materials is widespread enough to allow nearly all nations to develop domestic capacity in several important sectors. A country can develop a cement industry, as long as it does not view large-scale factories with rotary kilns as its only option but also considers mini cement plants with vertical shaft kilns. For many materials, small-scale, labor-intensive methods will have the best chance of overcoming the constraints on production outlined above; the rôle of the government is to encourage the formation and healthy operation of private firms that use such methods.

Encouraging small-scale production   Impressive statistical and empirical evidence substantiates the economic viability of the small-scale production of most building materials. This is especially true for brickmaking: the total investment and production costs for making one brick in a small (300,000-per-year capacity) plant in Gambia in 1980 was US $ 0.29, as compared to US $ 0.43 per brick in a large (10-million-per-year) plant. Even cement and steel can be produced economically in miniplants and minimills; the capital investment per ton of installed capacity for a domestic plant producing 1,200 tons of cement per day in India in 1978 was US $ 77, but only US $ 61 for a plant with a 50-ton-per-day capacity. Moreover, miniplants can be brought on line more quickly than large-scale plants, and have lower costs for upkeep.[46]

The severity of the macroeconomic constraints in developing countries increases the competitiveness of small-scale plants in at least two ways. First, a small-scale plant will be less dependent on a large, concentrated market than a large-scale plant; it will also be less dependent on large deposits of raw materials, thus minimizing the need to transport raw materials and finished products long distances and increasing the distribution of factories to rural areas. For some activities, notably limeburning, sawmilling, the production of cement, and the precasting of concrete, mobile plants have been developed which allow factory owners to move their plants when sources of raw materials have been depleted or the construction needs of a small market have been met. Second, small-scale plants, especially in the informal sector, are more labor intensive than large-scale plants; therefore they are less dependent on imported equipment and support industries to maintain this equipment.[47]

Small-scale plants also demand less energy than capital-intensive plants, and in some cases may be converted more easily to bulky, nontraditional fuels such as coconut husks and wood wastes. Although large-scale plants have made great strides in the conservation of energy, small-scale plants may be still more conservative. Steel minimills are three times as energy efficient as their integrated, large-scale counterparts,[48] and mini cement plants with vertical kilns are able to minimize heat losses more effectively than large plants with rotary kilns.

Fostering opportunities for secondary production   The evolution of the building materials industry in developed nations indicates that the opportunities for small-scale enterprises are much more numerous than is commonly thought, and that such enterprises have been an increasingly favored response to the economic pressures of recent years. This becomes apparent if the industry is divided according to the final uses of its products: structural, such as beams, outer walls, and foundations; semistructural, such as partitions, floors, roofs, and claddings; and auxiliary, such as doors, windows, insulation, and fixtures.

Though the sector producing basic structural materials (i.e., steel, cement, and wood) in developed countries has traditionally been dominated by large-scale, capital-intensive plants, this domination is being eroded by smaller, specialized factories, such as miniplants for steel and cement. Moreover, an enormous market exists for the secondary fabrication of structural materials into forms that are useful for a given project. Nearly all such fabrications can be accomplished by small-scale, labor-intensive firms. Steel, for instance, must be fabricated into frames for walls, doors, and windows, and bars for the reinforcement of concrete. The capital investment for a fabrication shop is relatively low, and the requisite skills are relatively easy to learn.

Similarly, cement must be made into concrete and concrete products before it can be used in a building. Suppliers of ready-mixed and precast concrete products consume roughly 80 percent of the cement made in the United States, yet most of these suppliers are small firms.[49] Opportunities exist all over the world for small-scale businesses that sell concrete blocks and precast products such as sewerage systems, steps, floors, roofs, curbs, etc.

The fabrication of semistructural products is also rife with opportunities for small-scale enterprises. Suitable materials for roofing may be the most expensive and scarce component of a low-cost home in a developing country; the production of ferrocement and cement–fiberboard panels for this purpose holds great promise not only for fulfilling the need for roofing materials but also for creating small-scale businesses. The fabrication of secondary lumber products (i.e., window frames and sashes, door frames and jambs, roofing panels, partitions, sheeting, upper-storey floors, and forms to hold concrete) is also suitable to small-scale production with simple mechanical or hand tools.

Although the domestic demand for auxiliary materials, such as plumbing and sanitary fixtures, electrical equipment, and elevators, may not be as high as for roofs, walls, and doors, a failure to develop domestic supplies of these items may result in a perpetual reliance on imports. Auxiliary products may take more know-how to manufacture than structural and semistructural materials, but the preponderance of small-scale suppliers of these items in developed nations may indicate that this means of production and distribution is viable in developing countries as well.

Augmenting informal production   The informal sector is even more amenable to small-scale production and the use of domestic resources than the formal sector. In Sri Lanka, the average capital–labor ratio for the traditional production of building materials is 1 to 700 rupees per worker (in 1973 prices), as opposed to 2,500 to 24,000 for medium-scale producers in the formal sector and 3,300 to 182,000 for large-scale units.[50] Informal producers use virtually no foreign exchange in their inputs.[50] Raw materials are almost always obtained locally, and products are distributed locally, so that transportation is usually by low-cost vehicles, such as animal-drawn carts.

The mix of factors in the informal sector may sometimes result in a lower productivity per worker than in the formal sector, but the ratio of output to capital may be higher.[51] Although the informal sector is subject to the constraints discussed earlier, its potential to create low-cost building materials from domestic resources would indicate that the governments of developing countries would do better to try to remove these constraints than to ignore the informal sector altogether, or to place it in competition with the public sector.

Institutional barriers

Implementing the policies and programs described in the previous section will be difficult without strong institutions. Most developing countries will need a national planning body to coordinate the myriad and fragmented subsectors of the construction industry to assess the capabilities of this industry and the demand for its products. Since the marketplace functions imperfectly in most developing countries, it may be necessary for the planning board, in concert with the private sector, to try to balance supply and demand.

Critical in the developing world has been a comparative lack of institutions to provide financing to small-scale firms. Without such institutions, the market for financing is not free but anarchic, and entrepreneurs must turn to moneylenders. If a developing country makes sure that legal financing is available, most entrepreneurs will be only too glad to shun the loansharks. It is also likely that most borrowers, when provided with a loan at a reasonable interest, will have the very human response of trying to clear themselves of debt by paying their loans back.

The scarcity of professional associations, institutes for research and development, and agencies for the dissemination of technical information have also held back the construction industry in the developing world. Relatively few agencies exist to initiate training programs for workers or managers, to formulate and enforce standards and specifications suitable to local needs and conditions, and to propagate the use of appropriate designs and domestic materials.

Where government institutions have concerned themselves with the domestic construction industry, they sometimes have created market distortions. Tariffs designed to protect infant industries have become entrenched as sources of revenue. Labor laws to raise wages have led factory owners to employ machines instead of people. Subsidies to guarantee equal prices for building materials countrywide have robbed rural industries of their primary advantage over centralized producers. The procedures by which governments have awarded construction contracts have discouraged the use of domestic resources. Finally, public institutions have not fully appreciated the ability of the private sector to contribute to the growth of the building materials industry, especially in the manufacture and fabrication of wood, steel, and concrete products.

Conclusions and recommendations

A domestic construction industry that is productive and efficient is essential for the provision of housing at the lowest cost possible. Such an industry will need to rely as heavily as possible on resources that are available locally; in most developing countries, these resources are unskilled labor and domestic materials. Similarly, a shortage of skilled managers, engineers, and other professionals in the construction and building materials sectors will make it worth while to encourage the development of small-scale enterprises, since these require fewer skilled workers and less capital than large-scale firms. The failure of the public sector to be productive and efficient has led policy makers to place their hopes in the private sector, with the government acting as facilitator for this sector's operations. In this capacity, the government will need to strengthen its institutional support of the construction industry.

To increase the supply of low-cost housing, the minimum standards for materials, zoning, and building designs should be more realistic, though standards should remain consistent with the health and safety of occupants. Sites-and-services programs have sometimes proved effective in providing homes for the poor in many countries, but could be even more successful through greater reliance on the private sector and greater attention to the supply of low-cost building materials; it must be remembered, however, that sites-and-services projects are as much a product of the needs and practices of institutions as of the poor. In many cases, developing countries will be able to further stretch their resources by maintaining, repairing, and upgrading the current stock of housing.

Such policies will require several institutional changes; chief among them will be an increase in the supply of affordable financing to worthy small-scale producers. As discussed earlier, the rules that govern most financial institutions will not make this easy, especially in the informal sector. This should lead not to despair but to a search for creative solutions.

These might entail regional finance markets, state guarantees of loans, direct financing through state banks, and modifications of the commercial banking system, such as a decentralization of banking services. Making loans available only through a few state-run institutions can encourage abuses in the allocation of the limited supply of low-interest credit. Setting too low a ceiling on interest rates could actually decrease the capital pool by making commercial banks even less willing than before to offer loans to small businesses; entrepreneurs in developing countries are probably less concerned about a few percentage points difference in commercial rates than a dearth of financing which sends them to moneylenders. More effective than ceilings might be a campaign to inform entrepreneurs how to approach a bank, a reduction in the paperwork necessary to apply for a loan, and guidelines to help bank personnel objectively evaluate the risks and capital requirements of small businesses and to devise payback schemes that are reasonable, given the volatility of the market.

Encouraging commercial banks to handle loans for working capital as well as fixed capital (the former being less risky) would allow a bank to reduce the overall risk on its investment in a given business and induce it to develop a more lasting and effective involvement in the firm's operation. Banks might also offer mortgages on machinery rather than money to buy it outright; since the capital would remain the property of the bank during the firm's start-up period, the risk to the bank would be reduced.

Extension services, which can increase the viability and profitability of small businesses, would also make banks more inclined to lend them money. Many small firms will need help not only in obtaining capital but in choosing equipment and production methods and setting up bookkeeping systems. At later stages, they may need advice about how to train employees and managers, acquire and handle subcontracts, and fulfill government regulations. An agency independent from financial institutions but working closely with them is probably the best means to provide technical assistance to small businesses. An independent agency is less likely to promote capital-intensive methods than the consultants and salesmen from industrialized nations who are now the main sources of information to businesses in developing countries; however, extension services must include advisers aware of the broad range of methods suitable to the various sectors of the construction and building material industries, specialists in important subsectors, workers who can be of practical use in the field, and people who are experienced in running small businesses.

Attempts to improve the productivity of small-scale firms should lead developing countries to establish programs of research and development in conjunction with the private and academic sectors, with the goal of designing new technologies for small-scale businesses and new, inexpensive materials for domestic production and use.

Tied to the dissemination of technical and managerial know-how is the development of programs to train workers for the construction and building materials industries, especially craftspeople, managers, engineers, and other professionals. Apprenticeship systems for small firms, and incentives for the return of expatriated workers and professionals, could be especially helpful; however, the encouragement of small-scale enterprises, with their reduced need for skilled workers and managers, remains the best bet for mitigating the shortage of technical and managerial talent in developing countries.

Since workers in the informal sector are already experienced in the manufacture and use of domestic materials and the construction of low-cost housing, any program to improve the housing conditions of the poor would profit by their inclusions. This will first entail studies to define more clearly the nature and scope of the informal sector; but even the evidence now available indicates that increasing the supply of the sector's inputs would go a long way to increasing its productivity. This might mean augmenting sources of low-interest seed capital, working capital, and loans for expansion; allocating low-rent plots for informal enterprises in sites-and-services projects; and finding more effective ways to disseminate technical assistance, managerial training, and the results of laboratory research to entrepreneurs in the informal sector. Urging informal producers to organize would give them bargaining power to obtain lower prices for their inputs; reforming governmental systems for distributing raw materials could keep these from discriminating against informal producers. Several studies have shown, however, that requiring informal enterprises to obtain licenses and obey labor regulations can hinder firms whose competitive edge is the informality of their productive systems.[52]

Finally, developing countries may want to examine their economic policies to make certain that these policies are not distorting the domestic market for construction and building materials. Among such policies might be artificially high wage floors for construction labor; transportation subsidies to large-scale producers of building materials; preferential treatment to large-scale or public firms in awarding contracts to construction contractors and producers of building materials; preferential treatment for imports of capital-intensive materials and equipment; and the overprotection of nascent domestic industries.

Policies that favor small-scale production, and institutional mechanisms that support such policies, will not only promote the social and economic welfare of the poor but also generate growth and employment in nearly all sectors of a developing nation.

5

Land policy

WILLIAM A. DOEBELE

Introduction

LAND IS, WITH capital and labor, one of the the three classic elements of production. When urban land policies are defective, economic productivity immediately suffers: adequate land is not available for industrial production and commercial activities of all sorts are impaired.[1] Failure to check urban expansion can result in a loss of agricultural production as vital areas in the peripheries of cities are converted from agricultural to urban uses. In nations with very limited agricultural areas such losses may be quite serious. For example, in Egypt, it is estimated that 10 percent of the most productive land was lost to urban expansion from 1950 to the 1970s.[2] The loss of cropland may also result in diminishing agricultural exports and lower earnings in foreign exchange.

In a broader sense, true economic development means the creation of institutions under which each person is able to develop his or her abilities to the utmost, and which offers channels by which even the very poor may, through their own efforts, move up in economic and social status. Numerous studies have shown that access to land is a critical element in providing the upward mobility. It is through the acquisition of a small parcel of land that people establish themselves in an urban economy. It is on this parcel that they engage in "brick-by-brick" capitalization, gradually accumulating the materials for a house, or, in later stages, the addition of a rental unit that not only brings them income but adds to the housing stock of the city without the use of public funds.

A secure parcel and house can be the basis for small commercial and industrial enterprises, in which the whole family may become economically productive. The same parcel and house provide a financial cushion against loss of outside employment through illness or economic downturns. They also provide security for obtaining credit, often essential to small enterprises and individual efforts to become productive members of society.

Effective action to assure access to parcels of land in cities is therefore not only necessary for social justice, it is fundamental to assure that all members of society are as economically productive as their talents and energies permit them to be.

This theme was recognized at the conference on Habitat sponsored by the United Nations in Vancouver, Canada, in 1976. However, in the years since that conference, access to urban land has in fact become more difficult. Today, not only the poor are effectively excluded, but many members of the middle classes are finding the obtaining of a parcel for house construction almost impossible. Even governments themselves are often encountering severe difficulties and delays in obtaining land for critically needed developmental projects.

How this has come about, and what might be done about it, are major themes of this chapter.

The future demand for land

Data developed by the United Nations show that world urbanization is far from being over, especially in Africa, Central America, and South Asia (see Table 5.1). Although it is difficult to project precise demand for urban land, Table 5.2 indicates that many world cities are still far from reaching the areas they may occupy by the year 2000, in terms of the base dates of the information shown. In fact for TWCs in general, overall demand for urban land is expected to be about 118 percent, or more than double present sizes, in the years 1980 to 2000.

Nor does demand slacken with economic growth, since families with higher incomes tend to increase expenditures on housing. Even in Europe, where urban populations are not growing significantly, there is demand for more housing because of reductions in household sizes.[3]

However, the most significant fact is not that future demand is so high but that it will occur in the face of very different conditions for supplying urban land than those that have generally prevailed in the past.

Table 5.1 Projected increases in urban population in major world regions, 1980–2000 (thousands).

Region	Urban Population 1980	Urban Population 2000	Absolute increase	Percentage increase
World	1,806,809	3,208,028	1,401,219	77.6
Less developed regions	972,408	2,115,558	1,143,150	117.6
More developed regions	834,401	1,092,470	258,069	30.9
Africa	132,951	345,757	212,806	160.1
Eastern Africa	21,303	70,535	49,232	231.1
Middle Africa	17,598	45,235	27,637	157.0
Northern Africa	49,557	111,914	62,357	125.8
Southern Africa	14,959	32,561	17,601	117.7
Western Africa	29,534	85,513	55,979	189.5
Latin America	240,592	466,234	225,642	93.8
Caribbean	15,653	28,760	13,107	83.7
Middle America	56,275	124,610	68,335	121.4
Temperate South America	34,157	45,741	11,584	33.1
Tropical South America	134,507	267,163	132,656	98.6
Northern America	183,281	239,199	55,918	30.5
East Asia	359,457	622,441	262,984	73.2
China	230,652	443,216	212,561	92.2
Japan	91,970	114,128	22,158	24.1
Other East Asia	36,835	65,100	28,265	76.7
South Asia	329,760	790,685	460,925	139.8
Southeast Asia	85,863	207,672	121,809	141.9
Middle South Asia	214,900	517,642	302,742	140.9
Western South Asia	28,997	65,371	36,374	125.4
Europe	369,286	476,953	107,667	29.2
Eastern Europe	65,028	85,688	20,660	31.8
Northern Europe	71,276	82,119	10,843	15.2
Southern Europe	111,141	165,002	53,861	48.5
Western Europe	121,841	144,144	22,303	18.3
Oceania	17,829	27,145	9,316	52.3
USSR	173,653	239,614	65,961	38.0

Source: World Population Trends and Policies: 1979 Monitoring Report, Vol. I. Population Studies No. 70 (ST/ESA/SER. A/70), United Nations publication (Sales No. E.80.XIII.4) – table 56, p. 125. Table taken from U.N. Center for Human Settlements (Habitat), Nairobi, Kenya, *Land for human settlements*, Hs/Op/83–15/E, p. 23.

Table 5.2 Projected increases in the built-up areas of selected cities and regions by the year 2000.

| City or region | Initial period | | | Gross density | Year 2000 | | Annual increase in built-up area (hectares) | Percentage increase over base year |
	Year	Population (thousands)	Built-up area (hectares)		Population (thousands)	Built-up area (hectares)		
Hong Kong	1973	3,691	11,749	314	5,210	16,590	180	41%
Ahmadabad, India	1980	2,451	10,073	243	5,196	21,380	565	112
Tunis, Tunisia	1975	960	4,560	211	1,994	9,450	196	107
Djakarta, Indonesia	1979	6,500	31,304	208	16,591	76,760	2,307	155
Lagos, Nigeria	1976	3,050	16,177	189	11,950	63,230	1,960	291
Moscow, USSR	1975	7,408	41,160	180	9,087	50,480	373	23
Bogotá, Colombia	1981	4,500	28,260	161	11,663	72,440	2,325	156
Colombo, Sri Lanka	1980	586	3,803	154	1,125	7,310	366	92
Mexico City, Mexico	1970	8,889	58,000	153	31,025	202,780	4,826	250
Teheran, Iran	1966	2,720	18,000	151	11,329	75,030	1,677	316
Bangkok, Thailand	1981	5,331	44,428	120	11,936	99,470	2,897	124
Valencia, Venezuela	1981	730	12,167	60	1,387	23,120	576	90
less developed regions	1980	972,408	8,103,400	120	2,115,558	17,659,650	476,310	118
more developed regions	1980	834,401	6,953,340	120	1,092,470	9,103,920	107,530	31
World total	1980	1,806,809	15,056,740	120	3,208,028	26,733,570	583,840	78

Sources: Patterns of urban and rural population growth. Population Studies No. 68 (ST/ESA/SER.A/68), United Nations publication (Sales No. E.80.XIII.9) and Corr. – Table 48, pp. 125–54; and numerous country publications. Table taken from U.N. Center for Human Settlements (Habitat), Nairobi, Kenya, *Land for human settlements*, HS/Op/83–15/E, p.24.

Note: In calculating the estimated built-up area for the year 2000, densities are assumed to remain the same during the intervening period. Densities for regions were independently estimated, based on existing densities in towns of different sizes.

The future supply of land

If one considers the percentages of urban growth that have occurred in the past three decades, the extraordinary thing is not that access to land is now difficult but rather how adaptable urban land markets have been under pressures that are historically unprecedented. Consider the fact that many major cities of the world have tripled (4 percent annual growth), quadrupled (5 percent annual growth), or even multiplied by six (6 percent annual growth) in the period from 1950 to today.[4] The amazing thing is not that they have difficulties but that they function at all.

How, then, have cities been able to absorb growth greater in percentages and much greater in absolute numbers than the urban growth of Europe during the Industrial Revolution? There have been both physical and economic reasons.

From the physical point of view, it has been possible because of what might be called the "porous" qualities of most Third World cities at the end of World War II. In their centers there were often relatively large dwellings that could easily be transformed into many smaller units. Frequently center city houses were on large lots, in which additional dwellings could be installed. Through historical accident, public and charitable organizations owned large tracts of well located land. In short, most cities in TWCs had been built in an unplanned and loosely structured way, with many vacant interstices in the fabric of development.[5]

In the peripheries, land was sometimes owned in the form of large farms, which lent themselves to easy conversion to urban uses. In cases where ownership was more numerous (small farmers), there was a competitive supply situation that often acted to keep prices relatively low. Moreover, substantial amounts of peripheral land were in the hands of public agencies.

In short, the acquisition of central and peripheral land was mainly a matter of individualized transactions between a large number of buyers and many sellers, operating in many submarkets. At times, energetic entrepreneurs were able to purchase large tracts from farmers, subdivide them, and offer building plots at fairly reasonable prices. At times, individual farmers would sell directly. Even though such illegal sub-divisions generally only had the most primitive services, they offered enough sense of security of title to encourage their owners to use them as economic resources in the fashion described above.[6] Moreover, public agencies, for political reasons, frequently chose not to vigorously defend their parcels, thus permitting the poor to acquire some claim to land through invasion and squatting. In many African cities these conditions still prevail.

Today, in most of the larger cities of TWCs all this is changing. After several decades of rapid urban growth, central city locations have enormously increased in price. Sites have become too expensive for low-income residential occupancy, and there have been great pressures to push out even those who had been well established.[7] For new migrants to the city, there is little hope of getting more than a small rental room. Central areas have been saturated: their vacant land has been used up and what is left is so high in price as to be unavailable to the poor, even at high densities.

From the institutional and economic point of view, as wealth has increased, upper- and middle-income persons with surplus funds have seen the purchase of peripheral land as the most secure of all investments.[8]

Construction companies who have prospered from urban growth buy in the periphery to assure adequate sites for future projects. Financial institutions see land as sound security for loans and thus encourage its acquisition. In short, a set of self-reinforcing processes have been established that have resulted, in many cities, in the assembly of rights in peripheral lands in the hands of relatively few owners, who view it mainly as a vehicle for investment profit and are reluctant to make it accessible to low-income families. To quote a recent United Nations Center for Human Settlements (UNCHS) publication:

> Land and housing markets are becoming integrated and monopolized. There are indications that land development, housing development and housing finance are becoming increasingly integrated in large corporations with substantial land reserves, managerial capacities and access to short-term and long-term finance. Those organizations are usually favoured by Governments, because they are able to comply with government regulations, to take advantage of government incentives and to operate on a large scale. The growth of large developers tends to reduce the number of small-scale developers, make it unattractive for them to engage in informal subdivisions and make it· difficult for them to find land for low-income settlements...
>
> Governments can no longer rely on informal processes to provide land for the growing numbers of low-income and disadvantaged groups in human settlements. All of the trends ... point to the fact that the processes for supplying land to house low-income groups are being increasingly constrained. By turning a blind eye to land-delivery processes outside the legal systems, Governments in the past have allowed the poor to house themselves through a variety of illegal and semi-legal processes. This was possible because most settlements had an absorptive cushion in the land-supply market, and entrepreneurs in

the informal sector could operate within that cushion. In most cases, this will not be feasible for very much longer: the informal arrangements which have provided the cushion for absorbing low-income and disadvantaged groups in settlements over the past three decades are under pressure, and there is a need for action to relieve that pressure.[9]

With respect to government lands, public agencies have begun to realize that their holdings, particularly the more central ones, are, in a practical sense, virtually irreplaceable. They feel that they can no longer tolerate invasion and squatting as they once did when they seemed to have more land than they could use.[10]

Urban land markets that 20 or even 10 years ago seemed relatively responsive to demand are now inelastic.[11] Private owners, who formerly were willing to enter informal agreements with the poor for cultural or ethnic reasons, now often find their land in a premium position for commercial development and can no longer afford to offer it on the basis of social obligation or religious principle. All over the world, markets are being consolidated into fewer and fewer owners, who will have correspondingly greater power over its disposition. In many cities an era has ended, and policy makers can no longer depend on the flexible structure of the city, its institutions, and its landowners to provide an accessible supply of land.[12]

All of these trends still have many exceptions, and there is great variety among cities and countries. However, the general trend seems clear, and it is that one that must be taken into account by policy makers.

One measure of this tightening has been absolute increases in land prices.[13] See the worldwide data shown on Table 5.3.

The result of these developments is a growing class of urban landless, whose access to land and shelter is becoming more difficult each passing year. We have entered what might be called "second generation urbanization." As difficult as the transition has been for past urban migrants, they have been the lucky ones, if the obstacles that future migrants will confront are considered.

New approaches must be found.

Economic and social consequences of landlessness

The budgets of many TWCs have been based on the premise that most of the shelter problems of the poor will be solved by the poor themselves. the fact that low-income families have been so ingenious in dealing with their own problems in the past has led to the assumption that this will continue to be the case.

Table 5.3   Increases in urban land prices compared to increases in consumer price indices in selected cities and countries.

City or country	Period	Increase in land price		Increase in consumer price index		Real land price increase	
		As multiple of original price	Annual percentage increase	As multiple of original index	Annual percentage increase	As multiple of original price	Annual percentage increase
all cities, Japan	1976–81	4.93	37.6	1.36	6.3	3.63	29.4
Tokyo, Japan (residential areas)	1976–81	4.35	34.2	1.36	6.3	3.20	26.2
San Salvador, El Salvador (land for social housing)	1975–77	2.75	40.0	1.43	12.7	1.92	24.2
Seoul, Republic of Korea	1963–74	26.10	34.5	3.43	11.9	7.61	20.2
New Delhi, India (middle-income residential area)	1957–77	77.28	24.3	3.43	6.4	22.53	16.9
Caracas, Venezuela	1973–77	2.50	25.7	1.38	8.4	1.81	16.0
large cities, France (residential suburbs)	1975–77	–	–	–	–	1.54	9.0
Manila, Philippines	1973–77	2.18	21.5	1.65	13.3	1.32	7.2
12 metropolitan areas, USA	1975–80	1.97	14.5	1.45	7.7	1.36	6.3
all cities, Federal Republic of Germany	1970–80	2.67	10.3	1.65	5.1	1.62	4.9
Urban areas, Norway (land for terrace housing)	1965–1981	6.96	12.9	3.22	7.6	2.16	4.9
Lagos, Nigeria (public land)	1960–70	4.20	15.4	3.20	12.3	1.31	2.8

Sources: Country publications and published studies. Where consumer price index was not given, estimates were obtained from World Bank, 1980. *World Tables*, (2nd edn). Baltimore: Johns Hopkins University Press. Table taken from U.N. Center for Human Settlements (Habitat), Nairobi, Kenya, *Land for human settlements*, HS/Op/83–15/E, p. 28.

Note: Real price index refers to the rise in land price in constant prices. It is obtained by dividing the increase of land price by the increase in the consumer price index.

In fact, however, the ability of the poor to solve their own problems has been, to a large degree, based on the possibility of their obtaining access to a plot of land. If, as suggested above, such access is becoming more and more difficult, the possibilities of self-help shelter are correspondingly reduced. Studies have shown that a sense of security of possession in a parcel of land will release surprisingly large amounts of capital.[14] If, however, the best that most migrants are able to expect is rented quarters, this capital will not be forthcoming. Those who create the rental quarters will, of course, be adding to capital stock in the process of constructing such units. However, the number of families participating in this form of wealth creation will be greatly reduced.[15]

Moreover, people who are not able to obtain land and create their own shelter are much more vulnerable to economic vicissitudes. House ownership is, for the poor, one of the best insurance policies against the hazards of intermittent employment, ill health, unexpected expenses, and the other threatening contingencies of life at the bottom of the economic scale.

Thus the economic implications of landlessness for the poor are:

(a) Lack of access to employment. With lands in the center city and immediate peripheries "locked up" in a way not known before, new migrants have a choice of the insecurity of renting, or locating their shelter far from the centers of employment and thus necessitating lengthy journeys to work that are costly in money and time. In São Paolo, for example, the highest-income zone is 4.3 km from the center, whereas the lowest-income zone is 14.5 km away. In Bogotá, the average low-income traveller spends more than two hours per day in travel.[16] (It should not be assumed that the condition of poverty means that the poor put a low value on their time. When every penny counts, the hours of seeking or doing work may be even more critical as one descends the economic scale.)

(b) Loss of ability to convert surplus labor into increased capital (the dwelling). As has been mentioned, lower-income families customarily use small savings to accumulate building materials. In spare time, these are converted into valuable capital: their own shelter, or a rental unit. No other mechanism except the feeling of security of possession in land is capable of mobilizing petty amounts of capital in this way. The erosion of this system will not only hurt those affected, but in a larger sense, deprive the whole society of an efficent system of capital mobilization for which there is no adequate substitute. It will also affect unemployment, because "self-help" building in fact normally involves not only the immediate family but an elaborate network of small contractors and material suppliers, who are themselves generally of low income.[17]

(c) Loss of access to credit. As explained in Chapters 7 and 8 of this volume, access to credit is essential if the poor are to put themselves on the road to economic security. One of the keys to such access is possession of an asset recognized by the credit-granting body as being secure collateral. A plot of land and dwelling with good title are generally recognized as being sound security, and as such can release funds which may enable a family to set itself on the road out of poverty. Tenants never have this possibility and are therefore permanently burdened in their struggle for fiscal independence. Lack of access to land leads directly to the creation of an ever larger dependent and permanently poor urban population. As the numbers of this economically insecure population grow, there are likely to be increased political pressures on governments.[18]

(d) Loss of ability to convert surplus labor into small commercial or industrial enterprises. Recent data about cities in TWCs increasingly emphasizes the importance of the so-called "informal sector" in economically supporting what is often a majority of an urban population.[19] One important aspect of this sector is the wide range of small commercial and industrial activities carried out inside structures that also serve as dwellings. When such activities are carried out in rented quarters, there will be a tendency for rent payments to be increased as the commercial or industrial enterprise flourishes, thus transferring part of its profitability to the landlord.

(e) Less on-plot food production. In some cities in TWCs, the owners of individual plots in residential neighborhoods still have enough land to do intensive gardening. Individual amounts produced may be small, but their collective contribution to the total food supply may be an important element in a nation's balance of trade and ability to become self-sufficient.

Future directions

Introduction: learning from the past

It has for many years been believed that the best way to deal with the shortage of urban land for shelter was to reduce demand by means of attractive programs outside major cities that would stem migration. We now know that although some modification of migration behavior may be possible, it is unrealistic to assume that any policy can substantially decrease net migration to major urban centers.[20] Indeed, even if new migration were to cease entirely the natural increase of persons in major cities can be one-half or more of total growth, and this factor alone would continue to create the problems already described.

Given that a continuing high demand is a fact of life for most countries, basic economics tell us that the only fundamental and lasting solution can come through policies that will lead to a substantial increase in the supply of land directly available for low- and moderate-income families. Because land markets are highly complex, increasing the supply of land for urbanization is a more difficult undertaking than relieving shortages in most other commodities. There, are, however, at least three approaches available:

(a) increase in supply through direct public actions;
(b) increase in supply through improved interactions between the public and private (including the informal) sectors; and
(c) increase in supply through the more efficient use of existing urban land resources.

Let us now discuss each of these.

Increasing supply through direct public actions

Accelerated construction of service systems and improvement of transportation   As shown in Table 5.3 above, there is evidence that urban land prices increase more rapidly than the general consumer price index. In particular, land in the growing peripheral locations (where low-income demand is often greatest) has been subjected to the greatest upward pressures on prices.[21] In one of the most thoughtful articles on the nature of the urban land market, Alan Walters argues that there are three factors that cause land values to exceed prices that would otherwise be created by a free market: (1) institutional, administrative, and financial deficiencies that prevent the installation of necessary infrastructure and services, (2) planning and land-use controls, and (3) other forms of rationing restrictions.[22]

Although planning and other types of land-use controls are often essential for carrying out necessary economic, social, and ecological objectives, the installation of services networks, and their pricing, are normally subjects over which governments have considerable discretion.

It is important to understand that the supply of land available for urbanization is usually not something that is fixed by outside forces but is a product of human decisions to connect certain areas to the urban system by extending transportation facilities, and making them habitable by providing an appropriate level of urban services (infrastructure). It is true that in some major cities, such as Caracas and Lagos, there are indeed major physical barriers. In most cases, however, there is no absolute shortage of land for urbanization, only a limit on willingness or ability to extend service systems. Additional supplies of land will be available if there is careful long-range planning and capital budgeting for this purpose by the public and semipublic agencies concerned.

The pursuit of this policy is of course constrained by financial limitations, by the need to protect valuable agricultural land, and by a host of other complex political and equity considerations that will vary greatly from city to city.[23] However, it is important not to lose sight of the fact that an integrated program of good land-use planning, sound transportation strategy, and aggressive extension of primary urban infrastructure in areas suitable for low-income occupation is the most basic and effective response to the problems of scarcity and high price.[24]

South Korea adopted this course by establishing in 1979 the Korea Land Development Corporation, a parastatal agency with broad powers, charged with the duty of almost doubling the urban land supply of that country. This is to be achieved through a vigorous program of land acquisition and installation of services on a scale seldom attempted at a national level.

Improved methods of cost recovery   The fiscal ability of authorities to extend services and to make associated transportation improvement will often depend heavily on their ability to establish systems to recover the costs of such programs from the increases in land values that they inevitably create.

The resolutions of the 1976 Vancouver Conference, subscribed to by 132 states, called for the appropriate recapture by public bodies of all the unearned increment resulting from public investment. This recommendation has not been widely followed.

The present suggestion is not for the recapture of all the increments arising from public investments and population increases, but the much more modest goal of recapturing enough of the increments to pay for the actual cost of construction (including administration, interest costs, and other charges directly associated with construction).

In general, in cities in which there is an overall shortage of serviced land at reasonable prices, the creation of new serviced land will produce increases in prices in substantial excess of the installation costs of those services. The practical consequence is that the owner still has received a greatly increased land value, even after payment of his or her share of the cost of construction to the public agency concerned. Thus, a situation is created in which both owners and public agency gain; in contrast to devices for the recovery of all unearned increment, which leave an owner with no benefit from the development of his or her land, an understandably unpopular measure, and a disincentive to initiative.

The mechanisms for this more limited type of cost recovery are varied and involve technical considerations beyond the scope of this chapter.[25]

However, their implementation can be crucial to achieving real progress in increasing the effective supply of land.[26]

Reducing the attractiveness of urban land as a vehicle for the storage of capital   In virtually all TWCs, urban land is considered to be the safest of all domestic investments, and for this reason begins to acquire values not related to its physical use. Just as the price of gold is determined by demand for it as an investment rather than its physical use (in jewelry, dentistry, etc.), so urban land values often accumulate a part of their value from the same psychological seeking for security. Particularly in countries in which there is serious inflation, and/or weak institutions for other forms of investment, land, like gold, participates simultaneously in two economic markets, and its price is set both by the demand for it as site for some actual activity and the demand for it as a storage place for surplus funds.

A few countries, such as Sweden, the Netherlands, and Singapore, have regulatory and taxation systems that make urban land unattractive as a fiscal investment. In most others, however, the rôle of land as an investment vehicle has heavily affected urban development. For example, in Greater Buenos Aires, Argentina, 72 percent of all existing plots remain vacant; in Metro Manila, the Philippines, 64 percent of land was undeveloped in 1973; in New Maadi and Nasr City (both in Greater Cairo, Egypt) 75 and 50 percent respectively remained underdeveloped in 1977; and in Brazil vacant lots represent one-third of the total areas of cities.[27]

It can be argued that land "speculation" of this type is normal and healthy, since it creates a reserve supply of a scarce commodity that will be released in the future when its owner calculates that its best use (and therefore highest price) has arrived. It thus also tends to offset the trends toward saturation discussed earlier in this chapter. There are, however, so many imperfections and distortions in urban land markets, particularly in TWCs, that ordinary market forces cannot always be relied upon to bring the supply of land into the market in an economically rational way.[28]

A fully adequate supply of urban land can never be achieved unless measures are taken to make alternative investments as attractive in security and expected rate of return as land now is. Because so many members of the middle and upper classes in almost all nonsocialist countries have invested directly or indirectly in land, the political will required to make major modifications will be difficult to obtain. The suggestion, therefore, is not to penalize investment in land as such but simply to devise and install new institutional arrangements that will make other investments competitively attractive. Strengthening alternative investment markets may indeed be one of the most important steps any government can take to make the supply of land more responsive to the needs of all income groups.[29]

There are four ways in which this can be done.

(a) *Taxation.* The imposition of taxes or development charges that reduce the profitability of land transactions to the levels typical of other investments. Such measures can take many forms, including capital gains taxation, taxation of land suitable for development but being held off the market ("vacant-land taxation"), and "site value" taxation in which all land similarly situated pays the same tax. (The latter system has been quite effective in reducing land prices in the Netherlands.)[30] Although such taxes exist nominally in a number of countries, they generally have not been high enough to be effective.[31]

(b) *Land-use controls.* If land-use controls are firmly set for relatively limited uses, and/or low densities, the margin of future profitability will be narrowed and speculative investment discouraged. Such policies must, of course, be compatible with overall physical planning objectives.

(c) *Credit controls.* The banking system in virtually all countries is under national regulation, which may specify that no loans or credits are to be given for the purpose of purchasing land without proof that it will be physically developed in the immediate future. Such legislation is somewhat difficult to enforce, since in modern economies money flows easily from one catergory into another. It also makes it possible for persons already wealthy and having ample personal funds to invest in vacant land while others are excluded. Nevertheless, the control of credit is an important and often overlooked tool for directing investment into more productive channels.

(d) *Price freezing.* Governments can impose direct control over land prices as with any other commodity. Widespread use of this mechanism, as with all price controls, will lead to market distortions in the long run. Japan has a system of flexible government interventions to stabilize land prices when they threaten to "heat up" in a specific area, but its effectiveness is yet not clear.[32] However, selective price controls have apparently had some success in South Korea, at least in preventing excessive land speculation in the surroundings of a proposed New Town.[33]

Prevention of unnecessary destruction of existing low-income settlements
All too often governments still consider low-income settlements (particularly those located in downtown areas) as a blight and somehow representing national failure. Although it is certainly true that some relocation is inevitable as cities grow and change, governments should be

aware that the international experience has been that the destruction of low-quality residence in one part of the city does not solve the problem but merely displaces people into another area, which is likely to be bad for them personally and often destructive of their potential to contribute to economic development.

A more enlightened view is to see low-quality areas as locations for upgrading projects. The success of the Kampong Improvement Programs in Indonesia (now affecting over 3.5 million people) show that improvement in place is a far more effective approach. As carried out in Indonesia, upgrading consists of the improvement of drainage, access roads, footpaths, water supply, clinics, schools, and other social services. Once these are in place, pride in the neighborhood usually leads to further private improvements. At an investment of about US $ 37 per person, it has been a very cost-effective program.[34]

Another approach is to use regularization of tenure as a means for stimulating physical improvement. Although governments are rightfully reluctant to issue legal titles to invaders and squatters, in many countries it may be desirable to have legislation to provide for gradual transfers of legality when settlements have been established for certain periods of time, with complete legality being awarded at the end of a defined period. This principle is in fact incorporated into the customary law of many cultures; its modern readoption could be based on national traditions. Turkey, Peru, and Hyderabad State (India) have already taken steps in this direction.[35]

It must be noted, however, that granting tenure may produce "upward filtration," that is, the buying out of lower-income persons by middle-income households who also have severe problems of securing land and housing. Whether or not this is socially desirable is a complex and controversial issue.[36]

Centrally located areas occupied by low-income families present special problems, but also special opportunities, if location advantages can be turned to their benefit. Projects in Bangkok have had success, where such areas were along a major road, in adjusting lot lines so as to provide valuable commercial frontage on the road, the income of which can be used to cross-subsidize the occupancy of the rest of the parcel by lower-income families.[37]

A similar method is to make the issuance of permits for downtown redevelopment projects conditional upon the initiators providing a specified percentage of such housing.[38]

Legislation can also require that any developer who displaces a local population must find or provide equivalent living accommodations for those displaced, or otherwise provide compensation that realistically covers all aspects of relocation costs.[39]

The need to modernize cadastral and land registration systems Good systems for measuring and recording land boundaries (cadastral information) and for the registration of titles seem, at first glance, to be simply technical matters, They are, however, fundamental to any strategy for improving the supply of land and assuring its most beneficial economic use.

Breakdowns in cadastral (land boundary measurement) and land registration systems are frequent in TWCs, since the methods inherited from the past were geared to a much slower pace of urban growth. Such breakdowns are quite serious. The security of registered title, with a clear delineation of boundaries, is, of course, essential to maximum private investment in commercial and industrial activities. Moreover, some form of security is basic to housing investment.

What is often not recognized is the direct and heavy fiscal costs that the lack of such systems imposes on effective *public* action for all types of economic development projects. Since constitutions typically require that government purchases (either voluntary or compulsory) give fair compensation to the owners of the property, all government activities requiring new land can be seriously delayed if it is impossible to identify quickly who the owners are, and exactly what they own. In the Philippines, for example, the need to litigate to establish titles for land for low-income housing projects will often require two years and increase total construction costs by 30–40 percent, correspondingly decreasing the number of persons that can be served.[40]

In addition to the general problem, the growing importance of rental dwellings (discussed above) is beginning to raise very interesting and important issues of tenure and registration, as it becomes important for lessees to have some security of occupancy. According to one commentator, this is already a major problem in Africa, and it has been observed in many other countries as well.[41] The usual response – rent control – is either extremely difficult to enforce or inequitable in its long-range effects, possibly favoring the middle-income groups rather than the low-income groups.[42] One of the great challenges to innovative thinking in the next decade may be to devise realistic regulations for the protection of families who rent.

In terms of economic development, a good cadastral and land registration system are as vital a part of infrastructure as a road network, yet many TWCs still have institutions that are totally inadequate.[43]

Better legislation for compulsory acquisition Although all countries have laws for compulsory acquisition "in the public interest," it is not always clear that legislation covers land acquisition for the purpose of providing land for shelter. Where this is not the case, appropriate revision should be made. (It may also be useful to follow the example of Taiwan, where the compulsory acquisition price is tied to the value declared by the owner for purposes of taxation.)

Inventories of all publicly owned land   Another step that should be taken by all governments is the preparation of an inventory of all public lands. The number of ministries, parastatals, provincial, municipal, and other governmental units holding land is generally very large, and it is difficult to determine the areas and locations of all holdings.[44] When an inventory is done, policy makers are normally surprised at the amount of land already in government hands. This does not, of course, imply that these holdings should be immediately sold for development purposes. However, an accurate picture of what exists is a first step in creating effective interministerial cooperation and establishing a reasonable policy about supply. For example, land exchanges may be possible between governmental agencies, leaving a net surplus that can be put on the market.

Increasing supply through improved interaction of public and private (including informal) sectors

Supporting informal systems   Perhaps one of the most important understandings that has emerged since the Vancouver Conference in 1976 (and in other chapters in this volume) is a much greater respect for the importance of private and informal systems of furnishing urban plots in almost all major cities (see Table 5.4). Just as specialists in employment have found that the so-called "informal sector" is one of the most important factors in understanding the economics of urban life, so those concerned with land have come to realize that nongovernmental and nonconventional factors are critical to dealing with the land question. Although, as has been discussed above, the increasing "commercialization" of urban land markets may be diminishing the rôle of informal systems, they still represent a very important proportion of the total land being supplied for shelter. Indeed, the evidence indicates that these informal systems frequently operate more speedily and efficiently than government bureaucracies charged with the duty of providing shelter.

The paradox of the current situation is that we have not learned well from the experience we already have. Almost every city in the world has its informal land delivery system, sometimes providing the basis for housing for the majority of the entire population, yet in very few cities are these systems fully understood by public officials. A primary task, therefore, in the formulation of a truly relevant policy is to work with local universities and institutes to carry out well designed research into the exact mechanisms by which families actually acquire plots through

Table 5.4 Recent estimates of the percentage of city populations residing in informal settlements.

City	Population 1980 (thousands)	Estimated population in informal settlements	
		Number (thousands)	Percentage
Addis Ababa, Ethiopia	1,668	1,418	85
Luanda, Angola	959	671	70
Dar es Salaam, United Republic of Tanzania	1,075	645	60
Bogotá, Colombia	5.493	3,241	59
Ankara, Turkey	2.164	1,104	51
Lusaka, Zambia	791	396	50
Tunis, Tunisia	1,046	471	45
Manila, Philippines	5,664	2,266	40
Mexico City, Mexico	15,032	6,013	40
Karachi, Pakistan	5,005	1,852	37
Caracas, Venezuela	3,093	1,052	34
Nairobi, Kenya	1,275	421	33
Lima, Peru	4,682	1,545	33
São Paolo, Brazil	13,541	4,333	32

Sources: Patterns of urban and rural population growth, Population Studies No. 68 (ST/ESA/SER. A/68, United Nations publications (sales No. E.80 XIII.9 and Corr.) – table 48, pp. 125–154; and numerous UN country publications and published studies. Table taken from U.N. Center for Human Settlements (Habitat), Naioribi, Kenya, *Land for human settlements*, HS/Op/83–15/E, p. 9.

such systems. Such research must be based on fieldwork, perhaps through extensive use of participant-observers rather than by the mere analysis of data in a research office.[45] Although additional studies are often resisted by impatient governments, in this case taking time to gain better insights might be wise policy. *In the face of the current urban land crisis it is imperative to understand how and why all of the systems now in place actually do work.*

Understanding such systems will permit governmental programs to be designed to facilitate and encourage them. Such interventions may be among the most economical of all possible governmental actions, since successful merging of private sector intitiatives with supportive governmental actions are often highly cost effective.

To give a simple example, most of the low-income houses in Bogotá, Colombia, are built of cement blocks with heavy reinforced cement roofs. Iron rods are left exposed to permit the easy addition of second storeys. However, lack of money frequently means that it will be some time before the second storey can be finished. A number of years ago a program was suggested for giving credit for the construction of second storeys, using the existing first storey as collateral. Although this proposal was never put into operation, it had the potential for adding more units in a shorter time to the housing stock of Bogotá (and other cities) than almost any other type of program. It illustrates how public and informal sectors might effectively work together.

Informal systems by their nature are subject to abuses. However, the objective should not be to stamp such systems out of existence but to harness their best qualities while limiting their less desirable characteristics.

Illegal subdividers, for example, often offer the most reasonable prices available for urban land but typically provide only the most primitive services. It should be possible to legitimize the basic activity of such subdividers, though imposing on them a duty of preparing street alignments and plot layouts that could be easily furnished with proper services in future years.[46] Perhaps the threat of punishment combined with a promise of delivery of municipal services would be an effective method.

Direct competition between the public and private sectors has recently been tried in the Philippines. A unit of the Ministry of Human Settlements has been given the responsibility of stimulating private landowners to form partnerships with land developers for the creation of serviced sites, 70 percent of which must be affordable by 70 percent of the population. Short-term and long-term credits are then made available for financing the project. Although the program is only just getting underway (as of early 1985), it could be a significant test of whether the private sector (which does not have the power of eminent domain and other government prerogatives) can effectively compete with similar programs of the National Housing Agency.[47]

More imaginative experiments of this type are needed.

Joint private–public development   Many governments have placed very few demands on private developers, even though the construction of public services is often critical to the development of land in new areas, or even in redeveloping portions of the central city. One effective and equitable method of increasing land for shelter for the homeless is to make it a condition of negotiation between governments and developers in major projects.[48] A special type of institutionalized public–private development is "land readjustment," which permits the recovery of costs for the installation of infrastructure through an exchange of land rather than cash. It has played an important rôle in the urban development of Japan, the Republic of Korea, and Taiwan, and may be worth examination in other countries.[49]

Making existing supply more efficient

The need to re-examine the question of appropriate standards for plot sizes, building codes and infrastructure As has been mentioned by several other contributors to this volume, a continuing issue has been the question of what level of regulations should be imposed on urban development. All governments are rightly concerned with a lowering of standards that will lead in the long run to the creation of future slums. On the other hand, if initial standards are too high, land will be beyond the financial reach of its intended low-income beneficiaries (see Chapter 6 for further discussion.) This controversy in fact involves a number of separate categories:

(a) *Lot sizes.* Nowhere has the standards controversy been more intense than in the case of appropriate sizes for lots. On one side it is argued that small lots economize on the most expensive utility systems (infrastructure). On the other side, it is said that small lots automatically lead to overcrowding, with all its attendant problems. Furthermore, it is argued that large lots will permit low-income families to supplement incomes with gardens for food, and, more importantly, with space to create rental units to supplement monetary income. To the extent that shelter for rental is capitalized by the small savings of thousands of families, it will reduce demands on the government to use its own scarce capital resources for this purpose. There is no single answer to the lot size controversy, which is highly dependent on local conditions. As, however, it becomes clear that rental shelter is becoming more important as a source of housing for new urban migrants, the question of providing lot sizes that will expedite the rapid and efficient production of rental units becomes more critical, adding a new dimension to discussion. The fundamental consideration is not only the immediate future but to set lot sizes that will in the long run be most effective in increasing the total amount of shelter on the low-income market, since greater supply is the only ultimate answer to lower prices and greater availability.[50]

(b) *Excessive building codes and standards for infrastructure and services.* In general, building codes and standards for infrastructure and services have been much too restrictive to be suited to the shelter needs of lower-income families. The pragmatic result has been the creation of vast areas of shelter that are, de facto, serving the need of large portions of the urban population but which are, technically, illegal. This illegality not only contributes to the economic insecurity of those concerned but may permanently cloud the titles of large areas, removing them from effective interaction with the general land market, impeding its responsiveness in supplying the needs of all classes.[51]

Community participation: mobilizing the energies and ideas of local organizations   Many of the land problems in growing cities involve the upgrading and densification of older settlements now absorbed in a much larger urban system. Normally corrective programs involve the introduction of new roads and services, rearrangement of densities, etc. Where community organizations are strong, they can be quite valuable in establishing priorities for action and in mediating between the government and the community and among the members of the community themselves. When they work well, the savings in time and public funds can be substantial.[52]

Their existence can also be of major importance in assuring adequate maintenance and the protection of public investments after construction is completed.[53]

Cooperative ownership   Condominium and cooperative ownerships are well known and increasingly popular in developed countries. In such ownership the land and common facilities are owned in common, but the individual units are privately held, This separation of rights in land from rights in structure has many interesting possibilities that have not yet been fully explored in TWCs. It can, for example, greatly facilitate the granting of credit, since a cooperative as a whole will normally be more creditworthy than any individual member.

In addition to making the assembly of capital easier, cooperative land ownership can directly curb land speculation and lower prices.[54] The discussion of Shann Turnbull on this subject in *Land for housing the poor* is especially interesting.[55] The Government of New South Wales, Australia, has recently been formulating special legislation to permit this to be done.[56] Although the current Australian proposal is aimed primarily at rural communities, there is no inherent reason why it could not be applied to urban settings as well.[57]

Summary and conclusions

Assuring access to urban land by all income groups is an essential aspect of economic development, since it permits all members of society to make a maximum contribution to the development process. In spite of their obvious deficiencies, most cities in developing countries have, in the decades just past, been remarkably adaptable in their capability to absorb an historically unprecedented number of in-migrants. This capability was not so much based on government actions (which at best have only dealt with a tiny fraction of the problem) as on the creation of a complex set of informal arrangements and institutions, frequently on the margin or outside the law, that responded to demand, particularly for lower-income groups.

In recent years, there has been a trend in most countries for control over the supply of land to become concentrated. The informal arrangements that once prevailed may be being superseded in favor of a formalization and commercialization severely detrimental to the poor.

The problem of obtaining access for current and future urban migrants is therefore far more difficult now than it was only a few years ago. Similarly, government attempts to intervene will be now more complex and costly than ever.

There are no panaceas for this situation. However, there are steps that all governments can immediately take to make the situation better. Among these are:

(a) A recognition that the ultimate key to the problem is to increase, as rapidly as possible, the total supply of land accessible to low-income and moderate-income families and to facilitate better use of the considerable amounts of land now underutilized.

(b) The use of imaginative public policies with respect to transportation and the coordinated expansion of infrastructure to increase substantially the amount of new land coming onto the market in locations accessible to the poor.

(c) Improved methods for recovering the costs of providing transportation and infrastructure.

(d) Better understanding of, and cooperation with, the informal systems that exist, including the immediate mounting of empirical research to determine how much systems *do*, in fact, operate.

(e) The creation of effective disincentives to reduce the attractiveness of urban land as a storage place for surplus capital.

(f) Improved interaction and cooperation between public and private (including the informal) sectors.

(g) Prevention of unnecessary destruction of existing low-income housing.

(h) The critical examination of all legal standards relating to land subdivision, services, and building codes.

(i) Improved cadastral, registration, and expropriation procedures to lubricate both private and public land transactions, but carried out only after careful field studies to assure that such procedures do not make the economically weak more vulnerable than they already are.

(j) Mobilizing the ideas and energies of local organizations.

(k) Exploration of the possibilities of cooperative patterns of land ownership.

(l) A more thoughtful and coordinated policy among government agencies as to their policies about the considerable amounts of urban land that they, collectively, own or control.

Although all these tasks are indeed difficult, there are two great forces always at work, which, if harnessed, can enormously facilitate all policies and programs. One force lies in the basic truth that the settlement process itself is constantly creating wealth and value. The mere concentration of people in one place increases demand, and hence price. Every public action to construct roads, install infrastructure, and provide social services adds to value – almost always greater value than it has cost. The key to success, therefore, lies in public policies that will recover costs and thus create the possibility of the continual renewal of programs. (Singapore has demonstrated one way in which this can be done.)[58]

A second force is the vitality of the population itself, not only the migrants who have been forced by necessity into inventive types of shelter but also the thousands of entrepreneurs in every major city who, when given the opportunity, have created systems for supplying land, materials, and shelter whose efficiency has been largely limited only by the inappropriateness of institutional systems under which they frequently must operate.

Because of the powerful vested interests that have grown up around the existing laws and practices, it would not be politically easy to carry out any of the policies recommended. However, the worsening conditions that will be created by a failure to act may well lead to the creation of political forces more intractable and dangerous than any now existing.

Without attempting to go into technical detail, this chapter has tried to outline major trends and possibilities and to indicate in the notes section some sources of further information for those interested in reading more.

Surveys of the poor in several countries have shown that access to land and land tenure is a matter of high priority (higher, in fact, than better shelter *per se*).[59] Perhaps better than governments, those directly affected understand clearly how important land is to economic survival and meaningful social participation. There is nothing to be gained (and a great deal to be lost) in delaying the effort to address land issues.

6

Infrastructure standards

RALPH GAKENHEIMER and
CARLOS HENRIQUE JORGE BRANDO

An unintentional conspiracy

STANDARDS FOR design and equipment are important aspects in encouraging "appropriate technology" for urban water and sewerage systems in developing countries. Appropriate standards have been discussed so far mostly as a technology problem. Here we argue that it is mostly an *institutional problem*.

The basic objective is to provide adequate water and sewerage service to more people in the cities of the developing world. There are two ways to do this (1) make a higher investment; (2) make better choices of equipment, better design configurations of components, and better construction procedures to provide a larger amount of satisfactory service on a limited budget. Without denying that raising the investment is very important, we focus here on the second problem.

What are standards? The term is used in many ways.[1] Here standards are constraints on the equipment specification (e.g., maximum porosity of the drainage pipes), on design specifications (e.g. maximum and minimum distance between manholes on sewerage lines), and on construction procedures. On the one hand they are to avoid unsatisfactory service or failure of service and on the other to forestall excessively expensive equipment, design, or procedures imposed by misdirected efforts to produce higher-quality service.

Excessively high standards is the classicial problem of the developing countries. They sometimes double the cost of service.

Why does this occur? The conventional perspective is that consultants and contractors from the developed countries encourage the use of expensive equipment and practices to replicate the unnecessarily high quality of service and cautious practices of the developed countries and to induce costly purchases abroad. But the analysis is not so easy.

Our research on infrastructure in Egypt and our experiences in several other countries have given rise to an alternative model. There are several strong forces in the developing countries themselves that tend to escalate infrastructure standards. The much maligned international engineering community is and has been, in at least a few cases, the only source of advocacy for appropriate standards.

What are the escalated standards we speak of? They include standards requiring the use of excessively large pipes for sewage collection. The requirement of unnecessarily high-quality material in pipe manufacture, spacing manholes closer together than necessary, using heavier covers for them than necessary. Sometimes the use of such standards together creates a special irony. In Egypt designers fear there will be no maintenance and therefore use large sewer pipes intended to avoid clogging. On the other hand, they are likely to place manholes (whose sole purpose is to facilitate maintenance, i.e., unclogging) only 30 m apart, whereas they could be used to rod out (clean) the intervening sections of sewer equally easily if they were twice or three times as far apart. And the manhole is topped by a cover weighing 285 kg rather than a weight of the order of 80–175 kg used in other countries. The matter is important because manholes are a significant part of the total cost of sewerage. Possible savings are suggested by case study computations in our Appendix.

Water supply is susceptible to the same kinds of problems. Engineers may be so concerned about water quality that they are willing drastically to reduce the number of people served on a fixed budget, perhaps by ruling out standpipes in the interests of hygiene. They may insist on looping the network (so that each location is part of a closed circuit, connected at both ends to the rest of the network, to ensure retention of service in the case of a break in the pipe), even though it reduces the number of locations that might have been served by a tree-shaped network. They may uncritically assume high levels of consumption that are the average in prior locations where half the water is lost because of inferior or aging construction.

Are more appropriate standards always lower standards? The answer, of course, is "no." In the environment of uncertainty of developing countries higher standards may be appropriate in many uses. For example, rapid intractable urban growth induces high demand forecasts, unneeded in the developed world. We are dealing here, however, with the large part of applications in which more appropriate standards are lower standards.

Note also that we are dealing here with urban areas, not rural environments. In urban areas there is a need to use higher technologies and there are fewer alternatives than in localities where low population densities still permit tapping natural water sources, and some use of the holding capacity of the earth for disposal may be possible.

What is the unintentional conspiracy leading to these problems? It is simply a set of mutually reinforcing behaviors in which engineers seek substantial, modern solutions, in which responsible government agencies seek the safety of strong, failure-proof, maintenance-free construction, and in which policy actions required to change standards are not taken because of a tendency for elected officials to leave them to technicians and to avoid a sense of "demodernizing" the service. We will look at the actors more closely.

Actors in the standards stalemate

The problem of standards must be understood through the positions of a number of interacting participants.

Project designers and contractors

These are for the most part domestic engineering and construction firms, led by civil engineers. They are at the center of the process creating national infrastructure standards. These people have the relevant education, the applicable experience, and membership in the national collegium that controls professional practice. As private sector designers and builders of infrastructure they have stakes in the process.

In a developing country they are a national technical elite that is custodian of a belief in modernity and substantial technology. They reject the pursuit of minimum adequacy as an objective. They would rather conceive engineered construction as grounds for a take-off toward a generically different level of development. They are likely to be disciplined people, accustomed to forms of analysis that do not adjust easily to uncertainties. (In many developing countries they are some of the few people who keep appointments on time!) They are likely to have the sense of being surrounded by large – perhaps exaggerated – uncertainties, and therefore to hedge heavily against them. In any case their reputation as a profession is damaged by infrastructure breakdowns, but not by the limited portions of populations that are served by high-standard facilities. They have little motivation to stretch fixed budgets.

The textbooks from which they learned the field were likely to have been foreign, conservative, and old – not updated by more recent critical thinking about technologies.

Of course, there are important positive aspects to this professionalism. In a world where public projects are exposed to outright quests of vested interests and political advantage, rational evidence often becomes so distorted that there is no basis for evaluation by summary overview. In such an environment there is an important rôle for professionals schooled to professional ethics, professional pride and matter-of-factness.[2] They can be a healthy source of stability in the elusive visibility of objective concerns in the developing world. The unfortunate side of this professional socialization is that it can lead to a pride in complexity of practice. How often have engineering students been told by impatient instructors: "You wouldn't want this to be easy, would you? Then anyone could do it." That complexity is taken to distinguish the engineer from a simple construction technician, whose skills are gained in service or in a more modest institution. Here is another source of high infrastructure standards.

The professionals' point of view leads to a number of at least partly justifiable tendencies that further complicate the problem of appropriate standards. Engineers are likely to resist progressive standards with an insistence that the job should be done "right," and now, though the high opportunity cost of capital may argue, at least theoretically, for postponing some phases until later years.[3] They are likely to overlook important secondary objectives of projects, such as employment creation or ease of maintenance, in favor of the solution that is the most robust in its initial technical form.

Several of these points can be summarized as perspectives on uncertainty. Uncertainty is postponing anything that might be finalized under the current contract – thus the resistance to progressive standards. Who knows what resources may be available at the more appropriate future date? Uncertainty is consigning anything to unfamiliar technologies, however "appropriate" – such as the traditional, labor-intensive construction. Uncertainty is releasing anything of the control of centralized surveillance system. Labor-intensive methods involving local hires may fail because of unpredictable learning capabilities on the part of the volunteers, exposure to the interests of local elites, the financial fragility of subcontractors with insufficient working capital, exposure to unaccustomed claims on bribery, etc. This is the flip side of the prevalent view that high technology is uncertain because of the need for high skills and special parts. What is "uncertain" depends on one's point of vantage.[4] And it is not surprising that this is the one that usually prevails.

It is not surprising, then, that analysts of project experience have concluded that use and dissemination of appropriate standards might best be undertaken by second-rank engineers, those who attended trade-oriented schools, who do not speak the dominant developed country language, who do not live in the capital city, and who do not have the connections that enable them to aspire to high professional status.[5] They may be in the best position to see the right compromise between available technologies and economic reality.

Several factors combine in developing countries to make engineering design and construction firms remarkably large scale, independent, and powerful, as compared, for example, with the United States, where the industry is generally characterized by small, specialized firms. Since access to contracts is likely to be aided by personal influence, public construction attracts elite groups in the society. The construction itself is the main source of profit, but construction firms find it practical to create affiliated engineering design firms to help get contracts and to prepare projects cooperatively with the construction phase. In some cases regulations even require that design and construction be let in a single contract (e.g., until recently, for transportation structures in Egypt).

Large scale is induced by conditions of credit for working capital. Foreign aid donors and lenders generally will not finance it.[6] For one thing, it is mostly in the local currency part of the project, and they prefer to fund only the foreign currency part.[7] As pointed out by Moavenzadeh in Chapter 4 of this volume, unlike in developed countries, suppliers will not provide credit and in fact may require payment in advance of meeting an order, based on a strategy of minimizing inventory and risk. Their strategy is often facilitated by the fact that they are state-run monopolies or are a few firms dominating a whole construction supply market, therefore lacking the motivation to be competitive. Equipment cannot be rented in many countries, so it has to be bought – more need for capital. Payments on contract may be based on portions of the project completed, estimated very conservatively and with a portion of the amount held back for hidden defects. Payments are often delayed because of unexpected public budget reductions, or because practice caused by reductions in the past encourages bureaucrats to play loosely with their financial obligations.

All this adds up, like so many circumstances in the developing world, to strongly favor large-scale, well capitalized interests. In Egypt, over half the public infrastructure construction is reportedly in the hands of a single firm. Because of their scale, the coherence of their engineering leadership, and their elite connections, these firms have a great deal of influence in the sector. It is not unknown for them to prepare unsolicited facility project designs (at their preferred standards, of course) and then persuade public agencies to undertake them.

More concretely speaking, the fees for design and also the profit from construction are likely to be computed as a percentage of the total project cost. Thus there is little motivation to minimize the project cost. Where the design fee is not computed that way, it may in any case be paid directly to the designer by the construction company. This effect is especially noticeable in the turnkey projects, of course, which are very common in the least developed countries. Further, these are not the people who will be eventually responsible for operation and maintenance. Operators may be working for a lower level of government and are likely to be people of considerably less preparation and skill, on seriously limited and unpredictable budgets. Designers may then, for good reason, have very cautious expectations of the effectiveness of these people. This encourages striving for a facility that is as maintenance free as possible and as easy to operate as possible – which means high standards.

Of course, all this tends to be exacerbated by any success of the current fashion to increase the rôle of the private sector.

The responsible government agencies

Since we are dealing here with substantial quantities of new construction, the principal agencies involved are important visible ones, often national, sometimes regional or municipal. These agencies are led by members of the same professional corps discussed in the last section, responsive to bureaucratic authority, but probably also practicing in the private sector part time or during other periods of their career development. Agency leadership in some countries is subject to so much pressure by competing political interests, both national and local, that they may resemble elected officials in their behavior. In general, agency leadership is likely to be fragile and weak when compared with genuine political leadership and strong private sector interests. Design and construction are likely to be isolated from operating and maintenance responsibilities, even when they are the responsibilities of the same agency.

More so than the other participant groups, agency leadership is likely to be very risk averse. They are sure to bear the responsibility of any major system failure, no matter whose fault it really is, because they are the most accessible to politicians in need of a scapegoat and to the users they serve. In particular, they must be concerned with adjusting plans to allow for the possible absence of reasonable maintenance since they do not have the budget or organizational strength to insist on improved maintenance policies.

This is not to ignore cases of heroic professionals, known to many of us, who have made efforts to improve the situation from the inside, but the number of them whose efforts are eventually appreciated is surely very small when compared to the vast majority who eventually become martyrs of the bureaucratic process.

As a means of hedging against outside intervention into their duties, given their weak position, agencies are likely to favor strong standard operating procedures and to be very hesitant to consider changes in them.

Agencies often resist different standards for special localities because of a general disapproval of "project orientation".[8] This is a term widely used to ridicule special local solutions that ignore the wisdoms of system-wide vision and are easily maneuverable by political interests.

Perspective on the budget is another key issue. The outside observer may reason that, on a fixed budget, lower standards means that more people can be served. But from the vantage of agency leadership the budget is not fixed, it varies widely from year to year depending on the attractiveness of particular projects in terms of their political importance, the need for them as compared with other parallel projects, and so forth. Some projects lever foreign donor contributions whereas others do not, and so forth. In brief, the strategy of agency leadership is to maximize the attractiveness to political leadership of the budget package, not to stretch a fixed annual budget. This will be a very important strategic issue in pursuing appropriate standards.

Finally, agency views are necessarily conditioned by the membership of principal personnel in the same professional collegium discussed in the last section. Political responsibilities notwithstanding, other members of their profession are the people they are closest to intellectually. They share the image of modernization and the quest for levering development.

In some countries agency actions are brought into alignment with contractor interests through bribes. This will not be examined here, but is always a great temptation in developing countries, especially since civil servants earn such low salaries in comparison with the value of the contracts they handle. In Egypt (as of 1982) a junior-level sanitary engineer working for the government has a monthly wage about equivalent to the value of two and a half meters of laid seven-inch sewerage line!

The elected officials

We deal here with the behavior of members of the national parliament, or in any case of officers at high levels who are exposed to interparty political conflict, external pressures on government, and public response to government. Definitive standards ultimately must be legislated by these officials.

The first problem is that they are likely to consider infrastructure standards to be a largely technical, nonvisible matter best left to engineers. Standards are never likely to be an important political issue except when suddenly and visibly lowered, especially if only in a limited area.

Secondly, political leadership may itself be drawn from an elite that shares the modernist preference for high technologies, favoring its image as an indication of progressive development. The widespread interest of leadership in the developing world for urban subways surely is one expression of this attachment to "demonstration effect." There are unambiguous cases of changes of technological standards with changes in elected leadership.[9]

A third point on the behavior of political leadership is more in the form of a hypothesis than a confident observation. Political leaders may consider themselves to be holders of a "social contract" with the citizenry, an agreement including the promise of high infrastructure service levels as conspicuous government largesse. They may be very hesitant to contravene this "social contract." In the case of lowering standards, the dissatisfaction of people poorly served would not be outweighed by the additional ones served by the stretched budget. Dissatisfied users are much more vocal than those who get new service.

Finally, support of the engineering design and construction interests may be politically important to elected officials, since they are often linked to the wealthiest and most influential national groups. Furthermore, the design and construction community favors high standards.

The suppliers

The suppliers of materials have the most obvious self-interest in highest standards. For foreign suppliers, the developing world presents an environment with high marketing costs (because of the distances and disorganized purchasing practices), but potentially high payoffs. A product accepted by a national agency may be bought in very large quantities and become a standard not jeoparized by comparative analysis for many years. Where suppliers are local the situation is variable. If they are monopolies or state owned, they may make no effort to raise standards. (In that case economies may be lost by failure to take advantage of new efficient technologies.)

We know a case in a Latin American country, however, where a large firm bought foreign technology for the production of low-absorption pipes; this was immediately followed by a public action that raised permeability standards accordingly. At a later time the relaxation of these standards occurred roughly at the time the firm went bankrupt.

In general, then, suppliers are a clear case of vested interest in higher infrastructure standards.

The users

Last and, most unfortunately, perhaps least, in their contribution to the national dynamic bearing on standards of infrastructure design are the users (and would-be users). We refer simply to people in households or business establishments who have need of infrastructure service. If served, their concerns are the cost of connections, the price rates of service, and the level and reliability of service. If not served, their concern is for the eventual availability of service, the cost of connection, and whether connection will be obligatory, possibly replacing a satisfactory individual substitute for public service (such as a water well and septic tank).

It is possible for infrastructure to become an issue of community participation – and it has been in certain upgrading projects. Significant participation is rare, however, for at least two reasons: (1) the active government agencies and private firms are likely to be conservatively oriented and to find management of meaningful participation difficult; (2) given the infrastructure configuration surrounding the site of intended extension, there are likely to be few meaningful choices in the hands of the community. The big question, under typical circumstances of high deficit, is who to serve and who to leave unserved. This is difficult to manage as a participatory question.

Anyway, decision makers themselves are users. They are likely to order the best facilities for neighborhoods of their own income level and to find it awkward to recommend different standards for other parts of the city. The service shortfall is a more tolerated form of favoritism.

There is the possibility of participation in a mode that involves community payment for the system extension. It is especially attractive here, since the local visibility of economies might stimulate attention to standards. This confronts certain problems in most countries. First, it breaks the "social contract." Services are supposed to be supplied, if at all, as heavily subsidized evidence of the government's largesse. Further, residents know that those already served did not pay the capital costs. They assume, reasonably, that the service charges have been computed to include the capital investment.[10] The positive prospect is that squatter settlers may see infrastructure as an important step toward the claim to tenure of their property and therefore welcome the chance to have it, even on the basis of a special charge. For the same reason, however, politicians may be reluctant to extend service to squatter settlements. It appears to condone de facto tenure. Locally paid system extension is likely to work only in special cases.

The bottom line is that there is little user dynamic involved in system extension. The most important rôle of users in the process is to complain when the service is unsatisfactory or when the rates rise. Thus they reinforce the general tendency toward conservative decision making directed toward minimizing the risk of system failure i.e., higher standards.

The international agencies

The international agencies have a potentially very important part in this game. They are active in it, of course, through the funding of infrastructure projects or more comprehensive projects in which infrastructure is a component.

There is a possibility that they may have a less distracted concern for more appropriate infrastructure standards. In the host country they are represented by members of the international engineering and planning community, who are not (usually) related to industrial interests and among whom appropriate standards is sometimes a special commitment.

In addition, the perspective of the international agencies on the effect of expenditures has a chance to approach more closely that of "getting maximum effect for a fixed budget" than that of national actors. Whether this is true in fact remains to be checked; their performance was not surveyed for this chapter.

This attracts attention to the international agencies as useful intervenors.

Breaking the stalemate

There you have it – the unintentional conspiracy. A series of mutually independent domestic actors, each pursuing an independent agenda, but ending up sustaining the same unfortunate tendency: increasingly high and unrealistic standards for urban infrastructure that make poor use of very limited national resources.

What is to be done? First, it is clear that we need a broad strategy that strikes at the institutional structure of the problem at various points. No single insight or innovation is likely to be very effective in the solution of a problem caused by various actors with various motivations.

Secondly, it is clear that a strong normative concern for sensible economy has to intervene in the matter. Private advantage and public caution have to be forced into their places.

In addition, institutional relationships will have to be restructured to overcome some problems caused by the present ones.

Again, this is all built on the case of improved infrastructure service for cities, rather than rural areas. In cities the problem is the more efficient use of conventional technologies rather than the invention of new ones.

We are dealing with extensions that need to be incorporated into existing networks, and where there are relatively few technological options.

We propose five steps toward the solution.

(1) Reorganize the planning, design, construction and operations activities

The problems have been laid out in the discussion above. The solutions are in some cases very hard to come by, but the objectives are clear.

(a) Link the responsibilities for design and operations so that agencies can consider the trade-offs between them. This is inherently difficult because it deals with two very different classes of activity, performed by professionals of different kind and status. The task seems best done where the utility has the stature of a strong local "authority" (that is, a quasi-governmental organization with substantial financial independence). At the very least it is well to strengthen the involvement of public authority in the project development, and to avoid the use of turnkey arrangements, which are surely the worst in this respect. The current cry, of course, is to privatize services. Clearly, since such a concessionaire would be in a monopoly position requiring considerable public control, the arrangement might well come out looking like the authority recommended above.

(b) Separate the design and construction components so designers are not tempted to favor configurations that put the construction contractor to financial advantage. This is hard to accomplish because of the associations naturally created between these two interrelated activities. A beginning, in the case of countries where contracts are required to include the two together, is to contract them separately. There may be possibilities in creating bodies of design consultants attached to the national banks or other bodies who normally lend the domestic part of the capital for infrastructure projects. The use of these designers could then be required, or become desired because of the belief that their participation would favor consideration of the project loan. The consequences of such an arrangement would have to be considered in each country and sector. Naturally, it would be steadfastly resisted by the industry in most countries. It resembles the consulting industry in France.

(c) Pay for design and construction by some measure of effort, rather than as a percentage of the value of the final construction. This is perhaps the most achievable of the recommendations. It would entail greater administrative effort in costing services, of course, but it is not difficult in principle.

(d) Increase the feasibility of labor-intensive construction methods. There is a substantial techno-institutional literature on this matter and some recent efforts to summarize it.[11] It is not a simple matter of urging good intentions. It involves complicated questions of manageability, uncertainty, economy, and quality of product. The need for numerous small punctual payments to local workers may introduce difficult cash flow and money management problems. Several projects of this sort are believed to have failed on this account, such as the Colombian Pico y Pala Program.[12] The small contractors working in this technology are likely to be more fragile than larger ones. Hence, for example, discontinuities caused by the in-stream budget modifications typical of developing countries are more likely to be damaging, the more so still because failure to pay marginal local employees can cause collapses of confidence difficult to restore. There is a dilemma: the preference is to use small firms in the interest of better administrative control. But small firms are the most susceptible to the disadvantages and uncertainties of this technology. It may be best to sacrifice this preference in the interest of creating local employment and local engagement. Larger, more stable, firms might be attracted. At present, administrative preference notwithstanding, they often refuse even to bid on labor-intensive projects. Their reluctance might be reduced by (1) including labor expenditures in foreign loans, even though they are within the local currency component of the project: (2) creating special organizations responsible for the financial management of this component, thus freeing the construction contractor from the problems related to it; and (3) raising the overhead on labor that is paid to contractors. The problem at present is that contractors much prefer materials-oriented project components, where they buy from suppliers and "retail" to clients at an easier profit. Of course, each issue mentioned here bears separate examination in each local environment. The general dilemma should be emphasized: the international community shows preference in many sectors for small, yeoman-like firms that seem to personify economic opportunity, spread the rewards of labor, attain greater economic efficiencies, and promise more responsiveness to administrative direction. But the other perspective is that they are often punishingly confining work units, with little learning capability, lacking skills to survive unexpected demands, and vulnerable to uncertainties in general because of limited backup resources and no access to supporting institutions (e.g., banks or wider labor pools). As a result, the real welfare consequences of engendering networks of small firms should be held in serious question; so should their potential effectiveness for infrastructure construction.

(e) Prepare and build projects in a series of small contracts (not necessarily by smaller contractors) rather than a few large contracts. This may be an important means of facilitating administrative control, including control over the standards in use.[13] This is no doubt an effective and desirable practice. It should be attempted even though it would surely be opposed by administrations and contractors alike. From the administration's point of view, especially in a rapidly inflating economy, it makes sense to contract the full span of a project as soon as possible in order to both assure and minimize its final cost. From the point of view of the contractor, the process of seeking, bidding, negotiating, and contracting a job is often long and uncertain. Further, it occupies the highest paid senior staff. For this reason, contractors typically make very strong efforts to incorporate as much as they can in as few contracts as possible. Dividing a project into several independent contracts would substantially raise their costs per unit of earnings. In fact, it might work against including smaller firms. Though they might be more appropriate to the scale of the contract, they may not be able to afford the marketing costs.

All these actions contribute to an important general goal linked to better standards: that of increasing the strength of public agency control over the process. This objective is a delicate and perhaps controversial one. On the one hand, strong, autocratic agencies are often a source of insistence on high standards and inefficient procedures. On the other hand, this may in large measure simply reflect the convergence of many of the pressures outlined in our analysis of these agencies. How can we start the improvement of the situation without a strong, self-confident central agency to assert itself in the interest of better infrastructure design?

(2)   Reorganize the budgeting process

As suggested in our descriptions of actors' positions, there is little motivation in the budgeting process to stretch a fixed budget. Individual projects are likely to get funded on the basis of their individual significance or the need for them. Very high service deficits weaken the resolve of agencies to make significant gains on the problem. With perhaps 50 percent of recent construction unserved by sewerage, as in Egypt, the bureaucrat may ask "What is the use?"

Significant contributions have been made in cases where projects on a fixed budget found their budget reduced but had to meet the originally planned requirements anyway. Judith Tendler reports such a case in Brazil, where an authority with a grant to increase the electrical service for a specific project area got an unexpected reduction in budget, and then discovered that the structures to carry the cable were planned to be placed much closer together than necessary.[14]

The strategy is to put agencies in "fixed budget" situations by delineating service subareas and assigning reliable appropriations to those subareas. Thus agencies are encouraged to strive for the level of total effect gained from specified area budgets, rather than emphasizing the attractiveness of their budget package in the hope of getting a higher budget. In a realistic political environment, the former is likely to lead to appropriate standards, the latter to secularly rising standards.

There are a couple of special elements in this simple but elusive strategy. One is the need for international lenders and donors to include local currency components in their project arrangements. It is very difficult to deal with a local sectoral budget as a whole to be economized upon when efforts are diverted by the need to maneuver the local currency part to maximize the "free" foreign currency part. This problem has been discussed in detail by Tendler.[15] A second is the need to budget for maintenance together with project capital requirements – the financial aspect of the problem mentioned above as an organizational one.

The principal obstacle is the chaotic nature of the budgeting process. Validity of the "fixed budget exercise" depends on a good level of confidence in the budget that was initially established. But budgeting in the developing world is full of politics, unknowns, and opportunism.[16] The initially approved annual budget may change greatly as the ministry of finance reduces individual appropriations requested along the way – and their approvals are based on the competitive importance of each expenditure, not on the agency's right to an initially approved amount. Efforts to isolate individual budget terrain for protection from this effect by earmarking are likely to be resisted by budget specialists. Their hallowed principle is that budgets should be unified for maximum flexibility, never divided into single-purpose parts to which management access is denied. (This is one principle widely followed because it conforms also to the vested interests of political leadership.) Formal economic evaluations are likely to miss the point because of emphasizing efficiency to the whole economy, which is not the best context for these decisions. International lenders also distort the effort by engendering strategies intended to maximize windfalls rather than to garner known resources. Still, for specific subterrains of infrastructure budgeting, it may be possible to initiate the fixed budget that encourages minimum standards.

(3) Revise the "social contract" of infrastructure service toward a concern for welfare and development

We mentioned the social contract as a tacit agreement by which people expect high-quality service, however few may receive it. We believe this is a reasonable portrayal of public expectation from government in many developing countries. Infrastructure is seen by those who receive it as a personal accommodation, more than as an urban service. We need to turn this toward an appreciation of the positive externalities of infrastructure – the reduction of communicable disease, the attainment of a more effective work force through better health, contribution to the improvement of property. If the budgeting problem is seen as an instrument of community development and welfare, there is a better chance to pose it as: how to get the most service for a fixed investment.[17]

(4) Show the savings and improvements resulting from more appropriate standards

Focusing on the institutional problem should not make us cynical about the need for convincing research. However, independent the vested interests are, proven benefits are essentially efforts to change practice. It must be shown that you can save some 30 percent of sewerage projects costs by using fewer manholes, economical materials, and judicious pipe sizes. The result of analysis must indicate significant savings on water-supply system capital investments with more appropriate technologies for water intake and pumping, simplified design of water treatment plants, elimination of elevated storage (by pressurizing stations at surface level), etc.

The discussion has suggested many topics in need of analysis toward more informed standards. In many cases it has to be performed in individual localities of intended application – the answers can be very different for slightly different environments.

Usually we know very well the directions that should be taken by revision of standards. The problem is focusing a consensus on some single choice among several options known to be better. There are many cases in which everyone knows there are several options superior to the one in use, but in the absence of agreement it is least disruptive to simply use the existing one. Another tendency under these circumstances is to a kind of satisfying choosing of any apparently better standard than the one specified, with the assumption that any visible gain over it is a satisfactory design since the gain is a bonus anyway.[18] Adequate standards are not likely to appear without research.

Research must deal especially with uncertainty. The issue is delicate.

Should poor countries permit higher risks of failure than rich ones? The answer may be "yes," because the rich ones have used abundant resources to reduce risks to extremely low levels. Why not? In those countries, water bills for most consumers are trivial. In developing countries this may not be so. Anyway, the rich country is fully served, so there is no trade-off. *In poor countries risk is lowered in one locality at the cost of fully exposing another.* Thus the terms of the problem of uncertainty are entirely different. Finally, the most important contribution of research on uncertainty is to simply induce the understanding that uncertainties are in some ways contemplatable, rather than being detached phenomena that may be dealt with only by maximizing the hedge against them.

Another rôle of research is to reveal the value of those savings from the use of appropriate infrastructure standards. The quantity of additional service available from such savings might be surprising to a designer who always assumed they would be lost in a sea of unserved additional demand.

The job is not easy, but identifying the tactical issues that will untangle the unintentional conspiracy is the first step.

Appendix

Tables 6.1 and 6.2 indicate results from case studies in Egypt performed by Carlos Brando and Professor Ibrahim El Hattab of Cairo University. Beni Suef, where one locality for study was chosen, is a medium-sized city about 50 miles south of Cairo. Kafr El Shokr is a small city in the Nile Delta. The study was sponsored by the MIT Technology Adaptation Program.

The alternatives estimated include:

A   The base design done for the National Organization for Potable Water and Sanitary Drainage (NOPWSD) of Egypt, in conformance with the usual national standards.

B   A design declining allowance for storm drainage. There is very little rainfall in Egypt, and it occurs in a cool season when sewage from household water consumption does not make maximum demands on the system.

C, D, and E   These were hypotheses concerning minimum pipe size and maximum porosity allowances. They were abandoned when it became clear that adjustments of pipe size standards would not be considered on any account by the authorities.

F   Household connections made to the nearest point of the sewer line, accomplished by cutting the pipe and providing special fittings. This reduces the length of connection in comparison with the traditional practice of connections only at the nearest manhole.

G   Longer spacing between manholes, which does not reduce their effectiveness for cleaning the pipes.

H   The combination of F and G.

J   Lighter standard manhole covers than the 285 kg ones currently required (e.g., compared with the 175 and 80 kg ones used in São Paulo).

Table 6.1 Costs of individual design variations (figures are percentages of the total cost of alternative A for each column).

Alternative	Beni Suef		Kafr el Shokr	
	No connections[a]	With connections[b]	No connections[a]	With connections[b]
A recommended by the NOPWSD	L.E.[d] 127,379.28 100.00%	L.E. 150,702.70 100.00%	L.E. 235,880.10 100.00%	L.E. 287,585.85 100.00%
B no storm water	99.25%	99.37%	100.00%	100.00%
F household connections made directly to sewer lines (instead of at manholes only)	100.00%	92.41%	99.56%	90.27%
G manhole spacing 50% larger than that recommended by the NOPWSD	95.38%	97.75%	96.23%	98.02%
H manhole spacing 50% larger than that recommended; direct houshold connections	93.47%	86.89%	90.69%	82.99%
J lighter manhole covers and modified steps	95.37%	96.08%	95.25%	96.10%
K no manhole at upstream dry end of branch sewers ("rodding eyes")	91.66%	n.a.[c]	94.45%	n.a.[c]

Notes
[a] Costs of household connections are not included in the cost calculations.
[b] Costs of household connections are included in the cost calculations.
[c] Not available.
[d] L.E. = Egyptian pounds: about (US) $ 1.40 in 1980.

Infrastructure standards

Table 6.2 Costs of combined design variations (figures are percentages of the total cost of alternative A for each column).

Alternative	Beni Suef		Kafr el Shokr	
	No connections[a]	With connections[b]	No connections[a]	With connections[b]
A recommended by the NOPWSD	L.E.[c] 127,379.28 100.00%	L.E. 150,702.70 100.00%	L.E. 235,880.10 100.00%	L.E. 287,585.85 100.00%
B + G + J no storm water; manhole spacing 50% larger than that recommended by the NOPWSD; lighter manhole covers and modified steps.	90.79%	93.88%	92.01%	94.56%
B + H + J no storm water; manhole spacing 50% larger than that recommended; direct household connections; lighter manhole covers and modified steps	89.12%	83.21%	87.20%	80.13%
B + H + J + K no storm water; manhole spacing 50% larger than that recommended; direct household connections; lighter manhole covers and modified steps; no manhole at upstream dry end ("rodding eyes")	82.09%	77.27%	82.52%	76.29%

Notes
[a] Costs of household connections are not included in the cost calculations.
[b] Costs of household connections are included in the cost calculations.
[c] L.E. = Egyptian pounds: about (US) $ 1.40 in 1980.

Replacement of constructed steps in the manholes with steel ladder brackets.

K Exclusion of manholes at the beginnings of branch sewer runs. Substitution by angular pipes to the surface for the insertion of flexible rods to clean pipes.

These proposals were conservative in view of economical practices proven elsewhere in the world. It would be possible to space the manholes considerably further apart than proposed by item G, or even to replace them all with rodding eyes, at considerable increase in savings.

Thus the maximum combined saving suggested here for sewerage collection networks, about 25 percent, is still less than could confidently be attained by yet further reduced standards.

7

Housing finance institutions

MARK BOLEAT

Introduction

COMPARATIVELY LITTLE attention has been paid to the housing finance constraint to dealing with severe housing problems. That is, even if there are projects which can improve housing conditions, and even if affordable housing units can be built, progress still may be frustrated if financial mechanisms are inadequate to enable house purchase and improvement to be effected. Here the differences between developing and industrialized countries can be as significant as those in respect of housing itself.

In most industrialized countries there is no longer a housing finance constraint to the achievement of housing objectives. That is, where people can afford to buy houses there are financial mechanisms which will help them to do so.

However, even this does not hold true in all industrialized countries today, and only recently have housing finance obstacles been removed in others. For example, the maintenance of interest rate controls in New Zealand has made for an inefficient housing finance market which has filtered through to the housing market itself. In the United States, regulations which forced savings associations to borrow short and lend long led to massive problems in the housing finance industry in the early 1980s, which fed through into housing itself, and the recent adoption in the United States of the adjustable rate mortgage is held to have contributed to the recovery of housing starts. In France the establishment of the mortgage market in the 1970s contributed to an easing of the problems which people faced in acquiring homes, and much the same applies in respect of the establishment of mortgage insurance in the 1960s in Australia.

This brief analysis in itself suggests that developing countries can learn from industrialized countries, particularly their mistakes. However, it is clear that developing countries face far more severe problems in respect of housing finance that are specific to them. These problems basically are the lack of financial markets generally and unfamiliarity with basic concepts such as long-term loans, interest, and repayments.

This chapter begins with a brief analysis of types of housing finance institution in order to put the position of developing countries in context. It then goes on to consider the development of retail financial institutions and housing finance in developing countries, before concentrating on the need to encourage the mobilization of savings and how this can be achieved.

Types of housing finance system

A housing finance system is a mechanism by which funds can be transferred from those with savings to those who need to borrow. Four basic types of system have been identified.[1]

(a) The direct system.
(b) The contractual system.
(c) The deposit-taking system.
(d) The mortgage bank system.

Of the four systems it is the *direct system* which predominates in developing countries. Under this system the funds which house buyers require are obtained directly from those who have available funds. Often these funds will be obtained from relatives, with older people lending to younger ones to enable them to purchase homes. Even in advanced countries it is not unknown for parents to help children purchase their homes by, for example, giving assistance with the provision of the down payment.

A slightly more sophisticated version of the direct route is the provision of finance by vendors, including those responsible for developing housing units. A developer or a vendor of a secondhand house has already acquired the necessary capital to purchase or build the house, and he can effectively transfer this capital to the purchaser by operating what might be considered to be a hire-purchase arrangement, that is the purchaser occupies the house, but instead of paying the lump sum to the vendor immediately he pays it over a period of years. This form of financing is commonly used by developers in countries where the institutional framework is fairly primitive. In fact, in most developing countries where there are new housing units built by developers, the developers have to provide the house purchase finance in this way.

Even in industrialized countries, vendor finance is used when the housing finance mechanism fails to respond to the requirements of the market. For example, in the United States the difficulties encountered by housing finance institutions and high market rates of interest, which buyers perceived to be short term, led to vendor finance becoming common in the late 1970s and early 1980s. This point is developed further subsequently.

The *contractual system* is a method by which the savings of potential house buyers are used to provide the funds for house purchase. A person enters into a contract to save a certain sum of money over a period of years, generally at a below-market rate of interest. When the period of saving is completed, there is an entitlement to a loan, also at a below-market rate of interest. The system is used in just three industrialized countries, West Germany and Austria, where it is operated by the specialist Bausparkassen, and France, where the scheme can be operated by any financial institution with the approval of the government. However, the contract system is not well suited to providing a significant amount of funds in developing countries, and suffers from three more general problems:

(a) It can provide only a fraction of the finance which the purchaser requires, generally no more than a third, and therefore it has to be used in tandem with some other system.
(b) In practice, it seems to be dependent on government subsidies, and to work effectively it also requires that some people save under the scheme, but never require a loan.
(c) It is most effective only in countries where people defer house purchase to late in life.

The *deposit-taking system* is the most common. Under this system institutions which in the normal course of their business take deposits make loans to house purchasers, both operations generally being done at variable rates of interest. The institutions providing this service can be either general commercial or savings banks or specialist building societies or savings associations.

The *mortgage bank system* makes use of the wholesale markets. Institutions raise funds through bond issues and other instruments on the wholesale markets and use these bond issues to make loans to house purchasers on matching terms. This system is particularly common in West European countries.

In most developing countries there is no easily recognizable housing finance system. House purchase is financed by drawing on savings, the sale of assets and various other informal means, including a small element of direct financing and often loans within families. The deposit-taking route would seem to be the most attractive one to be adopted, but in practice the housing finance institutions which do exist use the mortgage bank principle.

Retail financial institutions and housing finance in developing countries

It is well known that the extent of financial intermediation within a country is linked with the degree of industrialization. A simple comparison of financial aggregates as a percentage of GDP with GDP per capita is adequate to show this. A country-by-country analysis tends to show a fairly uniform pattern of development for retail financial institutions as real incomes increase.

In most developing countries there are informal rotating credit societies and savings clubs. These exist under a variety of names, but basically operate in similar ways. In the case of rotating credit societies, members contribute a set amount each week or month, and each member of the society has the right to the funds under some established procedure. In Africa and the Middle East lots are frequently drawn to decide who has access to the funds, and normally no interest is charged. In Asian countries interest is generally charged, and access to funds is determined by bids rather than by drawing lots. Such institutions are very similar in nature to the early building societies in the United Kingdom and similar institutions in other countries.

In the poorest countries the one formal financial institution operating at the retail level is generally a government savings bank operated through post offices, although in some countries commercial banks are also significant. The government savings banks generally do not have a lending function.

In Thailand the commercial banks account for over two-thirds of household savings, which they collect through some 1,500 branches. The other major retail financial institution is the Government Savings Bank which has a little over 10 percent of savings and which operates through 400 branches. The Savings Bank has virtually no direct lending function, but rather 90 percent of its assets are invested in government securities.

A similar position applies in Sri Lanka. Commercial banks have 72 percent of deposits and the National Savings Bank 28 percent. The National Savings Bank operates through 450 branches and also post offices. It has over 7 million individual depositors, more than half of the adult population, but again invests almost all of its funds in government securities.

In Pakistan the National Savings Organization sells various government instruments through 7,000 bank branches, 6,000 post offices, and 3,000 national savings centers. All the funds it attracts are transferred to the government.

In Bangladesh the Post Office Savings Bank and the National Savings Bureau operate through commercial banks and 5,000 post offices, but neither has any lending function.

In the more developed Third World countries savings banks with lending as well as deposit-taking functions acquire a greater importance. However, it should be noted that even in some fairly rich countries the post office savings bank system remains extremely important. Nowhere is this more true than in Japan where the Postal Savings System, which has virtually no direct lending function, is the largest retail financial institution in the world. In the United Kingdom the National Savings Bank, which operates through post offices, is a substantial financial institution with no lending function.

Brazil is an example of a developing country with a substantial savings bank sector, and the Federal Savings Bank, which has some 60 percent of its assets in housing finance loans, is the largest institution of its type in the developing countries.

However, in most developing countries the formal institutions which provide housing finance loans tend not to be more wide ranging savings banks; rather they are small specialist institutions which raise most of their funds on the wholesale basis, a point which is developed subsequently. Examples of such institutions are the Jamaica Housing Bank and Caribbean Housing Finance Corporation in Jamaica, the Barbados Mortgage Finance Corporation, the Housing Development Finance Corporation in India, the Government Housing Bank in Thailand, the State Mortgage and Investment Bank in Sri Lanka, the House Building Finance Corporation in Bangladesh and the building societies in Malaysia.

This does raise a problem because it is the generally accepted view that financial institutions need to be able to offer a wide range of services if they are to thrive. This conflict cannot easily be resolved, except to suggest that specialist subsidiaries of general institutions may have a particularly important rôle to play and that a housing finance institution should concentrate its lending on housing, although it may need to offer wide-ranging services in respect of deposit taking.

Housing finance and economic development

The question of whether the promotion of housing and housing finance can contribute to economic development is one on which there is no unanimity between economists. What is fairly certain is that in most developing countries housing is accorded a relatively low priority, and the international aid agencies provide relatively little finance for investment in housing.

At first sight it might be self-evident that the promotion of housing is a desirable activity for developing countries. Unlike some other areas of activity it is labor intensive and can make substantial use of indigenous materials.

The argument in respect of housing finance is more complex. It is recognized that neither international nor government funds are likely to be forthcoming for housing finance on a large scale, and most of the finance which has been made available is seed capital rather than finance which can be re-lent (the activities of the United States Agency for International Development are an exception here, but even these are on a comparatively modest scale, given the size of the problem). The one Third World country which has devoted substantial resources to housing and housing finance is Singapore. However, Singapore is a relatively wealthy island and arguably it is this wealth which has made it possible to provide resources for housing.

The one source of funds for housing finance is therefore the personal sector, and if the promotion of housing itself encourages the mobilization of saving, then this must be good for the economy generally. However, even the question of whether this is the case is one that is not capable of being settled by reference to the analytical material, although research in the USA by the National Association of Realtors[2] does show that homeowners with given characteristics tend to save more than renters with the same characteristics.

Certainly, home-ownership is the highest priority in terms of asset acquisition for many people in developing countries. There is little doubt that low-income people are prepared to make sacrifices in other directions in order to purchase a home of their own. Even in the poorest countries some of the poorest people will save with the objective of home-ownership in mind. If this saving can be channeled through financial institutions, it can contribute to a strengthening of financial markets in the country as a whole. The downside risk, of course, is that any saving which is channeled through financial institutions is more capable of being preempted by the government to finance public sector investment. This follows from the natural tendency to view financial institutions as being independent organizations which have resources available at their disposal, rather than being the depository of people's savings. It is not unusual in both industrialized and developing countries for financial institutions to be forced to invest their assets in a certain way including, in some cases, housing development, but insufficient attention is given as to whether this is compatible with their duties to those who have placed their deposits with them, and whether, in the long term, such a policy discourages the mobilization of savings.

The need to encourage the mobilization of savings

Housing investment by the individual can be financed by loans, which assume some saving elsewhere in the economy, or out of income, broadly defined. In practice loans have been relatively unimportant, partly because the degree of savings mobilization is low. This will remain the case in the short term, but in the long term a higher degree of savings mobilization is essential if a dynamic housing finance market is to be created.

Personal sector savings can be the only major source of finance for housing investment, government and foreign sources being fully committed to other sectors. Potentially the personal sector has a huge capacity to save and it is a question of tapping that potential. Much savings are held in jewelry and other nonproductive assets and can be tapped to the advantage of the individual as well as the economy as a whole.

In fact, it is impossible to analyze the mobilization of savings independently of housing finance, both formal and informal, because invariably there is a direct link between saving and investment in housing rather than the two actions being brought together by an intermediary. There are examples of slum upgrading and sites-and-services projects where low-income families have mobilized financial resources from saving, borrowing from family and friends, and selling cattle or other assets. The rôle of formal and informal mechanisms to mobilize savings for house purchase is now considered in detail.

Informal housing finance systems

It is helpful to explain what is meant by formal and informal housing finance systems. Precise definitions are far from easy because the purchaser of a house will generally put in some of his own savings, will borrow from a financial institution, the loan being secured on the property, and may obtain finance from other sources. This applies in both industrialized and developing countries. For example, a typical first-time buyer in an industrialized country may provide 10 percent of the purchase price from his savings and may obtain an 80 percent loan from a bank; the remaining 10 percent might be provided by a gift from parents and a short-term bank loan. In a developing country a more typical pattern may be 50 percent savings, a 10 percent loan from a bank, 10 percent realized by the sale of assets, 10 percent borrowed from relatives, 10 percent trade credit, and 10 percent borrowed from an unregulated financial institution.

Perhaps it makes more sense to define the informal sector functionally rather than institutionally. Informal financing can be said to exist where a person cannot buy or build a house using only a loan secured on the property, at a rate of interest reflecting the security and the market, and a reasonable amount of previous savings (between 10 and 30 percent of the total cost). Loans from unregulated institutions at rates of interest above an appropriate rate as defined above, short-term bank loans at high rates, loans from relatives, the forced sale of assets (where the house buyer would rather have borrowed an equivalent amount), and trade credit are all informal. The need to accumulate on excessive down payment (in relation to the income of the borrower and his ability to repay the loan, and the value of the property) may also be regarded as informal financing. The degree of informal financing varies from 0 in most industrialized countries (although not New Zealand or Italy) to perhaps 80 percent (with most of the remaining 20 percent being reasonable savings) in most of the Third World countries. Most studies, however, would count all saving as being within the informal sector. For example, one study[3] showed that in the Philippines 86 percent of housing had been produced by informal means and that in Brazil the figure was 82 percent. Renaud[4] quotes a World Bank Study of Tunisia, which is more developed than most Third World countries, that showed that between 1975 and 1980 only 17 percent of investment in housing was institutionally financed. Generally, in developing countries under 20 percent of housing is financed by the formal sector, and in some countries the proportion is under 10 percent.

The reasons why the formal financial system has been little used in housing finance are fairly obvious. Apart from the general reasons noted in the previous section for the relative absence of formal retail financial institutions, there are the more specific problems related to housing finance. Most importantly, housing finance involves dealing with households rather than companies. This means that there are very high transaction costs, partly because many households are unaccustomed to dealing with financial institutions and do not understand simple concepts like interest. The evidence is that general financial institutions shy away from housing finance simply because it is unprofitable for them compared with their other business, and even some specialist housing finance institutions, when given the opportunity to do so, have moved away from their traditional housing rôle into more general banking. Two examples of this are the Bank of the Near East in Lebanon and the Banco Hipotecario Nacional in Bolivia.

Housing finance institutions also have to perform more difficult maturity transformation than other financial institutions. In particular, they have to borrow short and lend long, a task which has proved too much for the very sophisticated American financial system until the fairly recent past. This task has been made more difficult by high rates of inflation, particularly in the Latin American countries, which make it difficult to operate any housing finance system, let alone one where formal financial institutions are not well developed.

The strength of the informal system is such that it is not practical policy to attempt to replace it by more formal mechanisms. The following section of this chapter will consider government policy, in particular, how the informal system can be made more efficient. However, for the most part it must be a question more of understanding and facilitating informal techniques to enable house purchase and improvement to be effected, and, in the longer term, allowing the increasingly efficient formal institutions to supplant informal mechanisms.

As a starting point it is helpful to look at examples of how the informal system works. Colombia seems to have been subject to more studies than other countries. One study[5] found that only 10 percent of low-income housing in Cartagena, Colombia, had any debts against it. A detailed study of housing in Colombia[6] analyzed the pirate submarket, the illegal subdivision of plots. Purchasers generally acquired their lots, paying on an instalment basis. To the extent that capital was used, the major source was personal saving followed by cesantias. This is severance pay which, by Colombian law, every employer must pay to each employee on termination of employment and which can be used to obtain advances from the employer for specific purposes related to housing. The actual monthly instalments are generally paid out of earnings. Only 17 percent of purchasers used loans to help finance the construction. Construction work was normally undertaken by the head of the household, or at least supervised by him, and was a long-term process. One floor was built as financial resources allowed, and then others would be built which could be rented out to help pay rent. The World Bank study of Bogotá has showed a similar pattern.[7] Pirate developers offered instalment credit and accepted delayed payments. In a 1978 survey, 63 percent of households in pirate settlements bought on credit. Thirty-three percent relied on loans and severance pay for the down payment and 48 percent for the last phase of construction.

Some detailed figures, albeit based on a small sample, in respect of new

Table 7.1   Sources of finance for new houses, 1981.

Source	Surat 152 units (%)	Villupuram 47 units (%)
savings	67	53
sale of assets	6	14
loan from provident fund	1	0
loan from employer	1	0
loan from Life Insurance Company (LIC)	2	0
loan from Housing Development Finance Corporation (HDFC)	2	0
loan from banks	9	4
loan from relatives	8	5
other loans	5	24
Total	100	100

Source: Lall, V. D. 1982. *Some aspects of economics of housing in India.* Delhi: The Times Research Foundation – p. 74.

housing in two Indian towns are given in Table 7.1. The table shows the overwhelming importance of savings and the sale of assets (which can be considered as part of savings). The main source of other loans are thought to be indigenous (informal) bankers. The loans from banks are likely to be short-term rather than long-term housing loans. Housing finance loans from LIC and HDFC accounted for only 4 percent of finance in Surat and nothing in Villupuram.

Public policy to encourage the mobilization of savings

Perhaps the most important requirement for public policy is to recognize the rôle of the informal sector, from financing within families to more formal rotating credit societies and other arrangements. The fact is that informal methods of financing account for over 80 percent of housing investment in many developing countries. This is itself an indication that informal methods can be effective in generating a substantial amount of housing investment. The reasons for the success of the informal sector are obvious. Basically, it conforms to certain standards which are appropriate to those of the market. They are based on the family or the group towards which people feel some identity, rather than a somewhat anonymous financial institution. They do not require formality. For example, where loans are provided then generally no forms need to be filled in, and no collateral is required. As they are community based it may often be easier to recover loans because personal pressure can be put on a borrower by other members of the group. Most informal systems also do not use interest in the normal sense of the word because this concept is simply not understood by many people in developing countries. Above all, informal systems succeed because they are unregulated, and, as will be seen subsequently, it is government regulation that all too often prevents formal institutions from playing their proper rôle.

However, no one would suggest that informal systems of finance are satisfactory. A successful financial intermediary brings together borrowers and investors with quite differing requirements. Sums of money can be raised in various amounts and over various terms and can be lent in different amounts and over longer terms. The most successful financial intermediaries can bring down the cost of intermediation substantially. For example, in the USA the cost of intermediation has been reduced to under half a percentage point through use of the capital markets and modern technology. In other words, funds can be raised at, say, 12 percent and lent at 12.5 percent.

The rate of interest at which a viable financial institution can lend depends on four factors:

(a) The cost of savings.
(b) Management expenses.
(c) Bad debt provision.
(d) Profit, together with tax on that profit.

The final three factors together can be described as the cost of intermediation. Table 7.2 shows how these costs can vary for different types of institution in industrialized countries. The table is highly simplified, but it is sufficient to show the importance of the cost of intermediation. Danish mortgage credit institutions had the lowest management expenses and costs of intermediation. This is largely

Table 7.2 Intermediate costs for various institutions in industrialized countries.

	British building societies 1983 (%)	British finance houses 1982 (%)	New Zealand building societies 1982 (%)	Danish mortgage credit institutions 1983 (%)
cost of funds	9.1	14.0	3.8	8.7
management expenses	1.3	4.5	3.3	0.2
bad debts	–	2.8	–	0.2
profit	0.4	1.3	5.7	0.5
lending rate	10.8	22.6	12.8	9.6

Sources: Derived from Boleat, M. J. 1985. *National housing finance systems: a comparative study*. London: Croom Helm, IUBSSA; and *Credit* 23 (4, February) 1985.

because they raise their money wholesale and therefore do not have the costs of running a branch network. The figures for British building societies represent probably as efficient a situation as is possible for retail institutions.

New Zealand building societies operate in a less sophisticated market than their British counterparts, and this is reflected in high management expenses and profit and therefore a high cost of intermediation. The figures for British finance houses are included to show the effects of long-term secured lending on the costs of intermediation. British building societies lend only on the security of houses and their loans are long term. Finance houses, very sophisticated and efficient institutions, lend for shorter terms and on the security of moveable property. Compared with building societies they have high management expenses and bad debts, leading to a high lending rate. This does not make them inefficient but merely indicates that unsecured short-term lending must be more expensive, because of the higher intermediation costs, than long-term loans secured on property. This emphasizes the need for the government to provide for an efficient title system without which the advantages of secured loans cannot be obtained.

As a general proposition, it can be argued that informal systems exist where formal systems either have not developed or are prevented from working. Informal housing finance is very much a second best solution and can never be as efficient as an efficient formal system. This proposition can be illustrated by examining the experience of the USA in the late 1970s and early 1980s. In the late 1970s the specialist housing finance institutions, the savings associations, had deposit rates that were regulated with the intention that this should keep down the cost of housing loans. However, as market interest rates rose, so the savings institutions lost deposits to the informal sector, in this case unregulated money market mutual funds. Their deposits increased to US $ 55 billion by January 1980 and to US $ 142 billion by July 1981.

Savings associations were also prevented from matching variable rate liabilities by variable rate loans. The resultant earnings squeeze made them reluctant to lend and the availability of housing finance loans fell. Existing borrowers also wanted to continue to hold their below-market rate loans when they sold their houses. The result again was the partial replacement of the formal housing finance mechanism by an informal system in which vendors provided finance to borrowers. By 1981 half of all new loans on existing houses were created by vendors. Many such loans were for short periods with no amortization and badly drafted legal documents.

The effect of the regulation therefore was not, as intended, to keep interest rates down to home buyers but rather to replace partially what should have been an efficient formal mechanism by an extremely inefficient informal system. As the formal institutions were deregulated so they regained their market share at the expense of the informal system.

A major problem with the informal system in developing countries is that it is segmented. Typically no more than 100 people can be involved in any one group, and this may not allow sufficient sharing of risks, nor can sufficient capital be generated. Informal finance also tends to be short term, and this is not ideal for financing many forms of housing investment. It is for this reason that construction is often phased, according to the availability of finance. It has been pointed out that there are high default rates and intermediation costs in the informal sector. This is undoubtedly true, but the same is also true of the formal sector, and it may be the case that the greater community involvement of the informal sector can outweigh any additional costs arising from using fairly primitive accounting methods.

The aim of government should not be to prevent the informal system from working but rather to provide it with competition so as to make it more effective, and ultimately to supplant it with more successful formal financial institutions. As an economy grows one would expect the share of savings taken by the informal system to decline. Some figures are available in respect of Thailand which show that the proportion of household saving held through the informal sector fell from 57 percent in 1961–6 to 33 percent in 1979–81.[8] This could well prove to be a typical pattern. There are various ways in which the formal institutions can be encouraged. Most important is that they themselves have a community base, and that must mean lending in the community as well as raising funds from it. It has already been noted that many savings institutions in developing countries effectively hand over all funds to government, and this is likely to reduce their ability to attract funds from some parts of the community. If the institutions were given a lending function, they might well be more able to attract funds.

However, it has to be recognized that the climate facing formal financial institutions in developing countries is a far from favorable one. Among the most critical problems are economic and political stability. That many poor people in the poorest countries put their limited savings into jewelry is an indication that there is a distrust of financial institutions. Perhaps people fear that if they place their money in the savings bank, they might lose control of it. It is well known that inflation has a disincentive effect on saving, and it is wholly logical that poor people should hold their savings in jewelry rather than in bank deposits in a country where inflation is running at substantially above the rate of interest. The pursuit of economic stability is likely to be beneficial to the promotion of formal savings institutions, and, indeed, if a country is run such that there is endemic inflation, it can hardly be expected that people will entrust their savings to a savings bank unless there is some form of index-linking. Here, however, it seems that index-linking has only been used effectively in a number of countries – Israel, Colombia, and Brazil, for example – and it is probably not a suitable weapon in the poorest of the developing countries, simply because it is difficult to understand.

There is a natural inclination on the part of governments to regulate interest rates in the belief that low interest rates are desirable because they encourage borrowing and activity and that high rates are undesirable because the people with money are generally rich moneylenders. It might be noted that this attitude has prevailed not only in developing countries but also in many industrialized countries. Until recently many American states had usury ceilings, and the federal government regulated interest rates on savings deposits by means of regulation Q. In Australia, until recently, the banks were prevented from paying any rate of interest on call deposits, and in many other industrialized countries there are interest rate ceilings of one form or another. This is despite overwhelming evidence that the effect of interest rate ceilings is undesirable in terms of both the allocation of resources and the distribution of income.

These arguments apply with equal force in developing countries. If interest rates are artificially held down, naturally people will be less inclined to put their savings in those institutions with artificially low rates. As it is only the formal institutions which are regulated in this way, the informal mechanisms continue to thrive. Artificially low interest rates to borrowers inevitably encourage demand, and this leads to nonprice methods of rationing which tend to favor less risky business; alternatively, they lead to a black market. This happened even in the USA where artificially low interest rates were compensated for by points charged at the beginning of the mortgage such that the effective rate was increased to the market level.

Because financial markets in developing countries are far from perfect, some governments may feel that they simply cannot allow the market to decide rates, as this would put the moneylender in an advantageous position over the relatively unsophisticated borrower. In such circumstances, regulation of rates can be defended, but it is a dangerous path to go along because there will always be pressure to hold rates down. Where governments feel compelled to regulate rates, at the very least they should allow them to be established at positive real levels. Equally, institutions should be free to offer variable rate loans if they consider it necessary for them to do so to remain viable. Fixed-rate long-term loans, unless matched by deposits on similar terms, are financially dangerous, as the American experience showed.

It may be argued that this analysis is inconsistent with the observed fact that people in both industrialized and developing countries will save at rates of interest which are below market and substantially negative. In fact the evidence is that the total volume of savings is, to a large extent, independent of interest rates and depends more on the availability of savings instruments. This misses the point in two respects:

(a) As long as people are able to obtain a market rate by some means, then institutions forced to work below market rates will suffer a relative loss of deposits.
(b) Artificially low rates will lead to an excess demand for loans and rationing, which is likely to work against more marginal borrowers, and more generally to a misallocation of resources.

The point has been made that governments should allow savings institutions to lend funds. More generally, if they wish to encourage the mobilization of savings, they should not attempt to control credit, because this could well be counterproductive in the longer term by leading to a general distrust of financial institutions. It is accepted that there is a huge call on the financial resources of developing countries and that priority cannot be given to housing. Governments tend to use financial institutions to raise funds for their own purposes. However, financial institutions may be able to raise funds from those who will be looking to them for loans; therefore additional funds can be mobilized. If the wishes of such people are frustrated by credit controls being introduced, the whole market receives a setback, and once again the informal sector is likely to take over the functions which should properly belong to the formal sector. Governments should recognize that if people invest with a certain financial institution then it may be because they want a loan from that institution, and that new forms of savings mobilization should not automatically be used to pump additional funds into the public sector, where there is no guarantee that they will be used more efficiently than if they could be loaned back to the private sector.

A United Nations symposium came to the conclusion "that in order to be successful and to contribute to economic development savings mobilization institutions in developing countries had to operate with minimum government interference and should be free to offer all types of service demanded by the market."[9] However, it is essential that institutions should not be forced to diversify but rather should be allowed to diversify in such a way as to enhance their basic housing finance function. This balance is a very difficult one to achieve, especially given the default risk on housing loans.

This same publication also has detailed case studies of the effects of removing harmful controls on savings institutions in Malaysia, Sri Lanka, and South Korea.

One method that the government could use to encourage the mobilization of savings and to encourage financial institutions to be more involved in housing is to develop cofinancing projects with the banking sector or to lend funds through formal financial institutions. Again, some examples in industrialized countries can illustrate the benefits of this. In the United Kingdom in 1959 the government made £100 million available to building societies to lend on pre-1919 houses. The amount of money was relatively small in the context of total building society lending, but there seems little doubt that this very act encouraged building societies to take a more positive view of lending on older housing when they saw that the default rates were minimal.

In the USA, Neighborhood Housing Service projects made use of a revolving loan fund in cases where a commercial loan was thought inappropriate. The experience with these funds was such as to encourage the introduction of more liberal lending criteria.

The public sector has tremendous expertise in respect of housing projects, and where this expertise can be passed on to the private sector through cofinancing or making loans through the formal financial institutions, these institutions may be able to attract related business – for example, current accounts and also savings. This strengthens the financial system and the ability of formal institutions to mobilize savings.

Such projects can also influence the willingness of lending institutions to liberalize their lending criteria. An interesting project in Zimbabwe is relevant here. It is described in the following extract from *Habitat News*.

An innovative housing finance mechanism: Zimbabwe

The Government of Zimbabwe, UNCHS (Habitat), the United Nations Development Programme, the United States Agency for International Development (USAID) and the Beverly Building Society in Harare are implementing a unique joint venture programme to provide shelter and community facilities for low-income families in the secondary town of KweKwe and the rural growth centre of Gutu in Zimbabwe ... This article deals with an innovative housing finance mechanism which forms an important aspect of the project.

In the past the private-sector housing finance institutions in Zimbabwe served the housing needs of only the upper three per cent of the population; the public sector was left to cope with the housing needs of the remaining 97 per cent thus imposing enormous burdens on the Government's limited resources. Under this pilot programme the private sector is for the first time helping to provide housing affordable to families below the median income.

The Ministry of Construction and National Housing (MCNH) has designed the project with technical assistance from UNCHS (Habitat). The project design calls for provision of 1,000 fully serviced plots in KweKwe and 200 in Gutu to selected beneficiaries below the median income. The beneficiaries will receive fully serviced plots (with water, sewerage, roads, electricity and community facilities). In addition, each beneficiary will be entitled to a housing loan based on his or her ability to pay. Beneficiaries will also be encouraged to mobilize their own resources towards building their homes. They will be given free choice of the mode of construction: pure self-help combined with the aid of small contractors, the use of a building brigade employed by the city, or the formation of housing co-operatives. The beneficiaries will start off with a house they can initially afford, and, using the concept of progressive development, they will be encouraged to complete their housing unit within a specified time.

USAID has provided a grant for the capital financing of the programme. The USAID's grant funds are matched at a 1/1 ratio by the Beverly Building Society. These joint resources are being used to finance the KweKwe and Gutu pilot projects. The Beverly Building Society, which already has an office in KweKwe and will set up a new office in Gutu to service the loans to the beneficiaries, intends to use this opportunity to mobilize additional savings through these small accounts.

The pilot project is designed to provide learning experience to all parties. The Government of Zimbabwe, for instance, will learn how the Building Society resources can be mobilized to meet the Government's objectives of satisfying the housing needs of low-income families can best be mobilized, and will have an opportunity to look at their credit ratings and the performance of loan repayment.

If these pilot joint venture schemes prove to be successful, it is anticipated that the building societies would expand their rôle in extending access to credit to low-income families in other parts of the country with encouragement from the Government and possible future support from external donor agencies.[10]

A major question which needs consideration in respect of public policy is the use of social security funds. These are by far the most important contractual savings institutions in many developing countries, partly because other institutions are not well developed. If these are funded on a pay-as-you-go basis (as is common in industrialized countries), no surplus funds are available for investment. However, if they are fully funded (as is common in developing countries), a substantial reserve of funds will quickly be built up as the liabilities of the funds, particularly in respect of pensions, are long term. However, it should be noted that if savings are generated these are incidental to the operation of funds. Some governments effectively preempt the social security funds to finance their general activities, but in one or two countries extensive use is made of these funds and mandatory savings schemes in the housing finance system.

The Philippines provided the best example of this. In 1975 over 80 percent of all housing finance loans granted were by the Government Services Insurance System and the Social Security System, but by 1980 that proportion had fallen to 36 percent. There was no overall reduction in lending as the reduced market share of the two systems was more than made up for by the increase in commercial bank and development bank activity. It is intended that the Government Services Insurance System will withdraw entirely from the house purchase market, and the Social Security System has also been reducing its involvement. However, a mandatory savings scheme has been introduced for employees in the formal sector of the economy, although employers can ask for exemption if they can offer a better scheme themselves. The scheme became compulsory in 1981, and a contribution of 3 percent of salary has to be paid into the Home Development Mutual Fund. Interest is earned at the rate of 7.5 percent. A participant in the scheme can reclaim his contribution together with interest after 20 years. Members of the scheme are able to apply for a 25-year loan from an approved bank at a rate of interest of 9 percent. The maximum loan is 48 times the monthly salary. By the end of 1983 there were over 2 million members of the scheme.

A similar arrangement exists in Singapore through the Central Provident Fund. Employees are required to contribute no less than 25 percent of salaries, with employers contributing a further 25 percent, although there is a limit to the total monthly contribution of US $ 1,136. The fund had balances in excess of S $ 22 billion in May 1985. Until the mid-1970s the fund made direct loans for house purchase, but now funds can be drawn from the scheme to pay for housing, both the initial deposit and monthly instalments. The main owner of housing in Singapore is the Housing Development Board, which has recently been selling its units. Some 75 percent of those who purchase units from the board used their contributions from the Central Provident Fund to help meet costs.

The Brazilian system is, of course, the best known of the mandatory saving scheme systems. Employers are required to channel 8 percent of their payrolls through collection agents, largely the commercial banks, to the National Housing Bank. The funds are held in the names of individuals and receive an annual rate of interest of 3 percent with full index-linking. By June 1982 there were 41 million individual accounts. Individuals can draw on their accounts when they become unemployed, when they wish to make down payments for a house, or in order to make mortgage payments.

As housing is itself an investment, it seems not unreasonable that people should be able to draw against their social security entitlement for the cost of housing. Using the funds for investment in housing when other more profitable investments are available must be wrong because the funds have a fiduciary responsibility to their ultimate beneficiaries. There is also the question of whether forced savings through social security schemes discourage voluntary saving. The evidence is inconclusive, but there is no firm evidence that it does.[9] Generally, the use of such funds needs to be carefully planned, otherwise the objectives of the social security system itself might be frustrated. Certainly, this sort of system seems an effective way of getting housing finance off the ground, perhaps to be replaced at a later stage by more formal financial institutions when these are fully developed.

A final government policy that merits attention is mortgage insurance. There is evidence that in industrialized countries this has played a major part in the development of housing finance systems. In the USA the introduction of loan insurance by the Federal Housing Administration in 1934 is held to have played a significant part in the recovery of housing and housing finance following the Great Depression. In Australia the establishment of mortgage insurance in the 1960s contributed to a take-off in the activities of building societies.

In many developing countries it is probable that mortgage insurance would be a disaster at this stage of their development. There would be less incentive on the part of lending institutions to seek recovery of the funds, and the cost of the insurance could well be prohibitive. However, as a housing finance system becomes more developed, so the case for mortgage insurance strengthens.

Action by formal institutions

The direct action that formal institutions can take to mobilize saving is dependent on the framework within which they can operate. If they have regulated interest rates, and if government effectively controls their lending, or worse still does not allow it, then there is little scope for them to mobilize saving. If, however, they have the right framework, there are various lessons which they might be able to learn from their counterparts in other countries.

The first section of this chapter noted the existence of contractual savings schemes in France, Germany, and Austria. Arguably these schemes owe more to tax incentives than to anything else, but they do provide some elements which could be extremely successful in developing countries. Most important is that they establish a direct link between saving and borrowing. The discipline of saving is useful in helping promote the discipline of repaying a loan. For the financial institution it is helpful to be able to lend to one's investors because already the relationship has been established, and it is easier for the institution to assess creditworthiness. This point has already become established in respect of rural credit institutions.[9] Furthermore, it may well be the case that a contractual savings scheme without any interest being paid or charged could be more attractive in some developing countries than a savings scheme with a rate of interest but without the promise of a loan. This is a matter than can be decided only in each particular case. However, the importance of contractual schemes should not be over-emphasized. They can provide only a proportion of the funds which home buyers require, and they are more relevant to the development of sound financial practices than to fund raising. The experience of the Housing Development Finance Corporation in India illustrates this point. Its loan-linked deposit scheme had deposits of 8.2 million rupees at the end of June 1984 out of total liabilities of 2,164 million rupees.

A major decision that financial institutions have to take is whether to branch or not. The arguments for branching are fairly clear, and at first sight persuasive, and in the long term branching is essential if savings are to be mobilized. An institution can have a community involvement only if it is represented on the ground, and this must mean by branches. The institution which is most frequently cited as having successfully adopted a branching policy is the Housing Bank in Jordan. This was established as recently as 1973, but it already has 65 branches and is the largest financial institution in Jordan in terms of branches and the second largest in terms of deposits. It relies on retail deposits for 74 percent of its funds. However, only about 10 percent of its loans are to individuals, the remainder being credit facilities, loans to the Housing Corporation, and loans to other developers.

The problem with branching is that it may well stretch resources beyond management capability, especially if the branching policy is pursued too quickly. The branches are unlikely to attract sufficient new savings to justify their existence for many years and could well prove to be a drain on the profitability of the institution. Satellite branches, perhaps based in the home of an agent and open for only a few hours a week, may be a useful alternative to full-scale branches.

The formal institutions can use various novel ways of attracting funds. A particularly relevant one for developing countries are company savings plans. Companies can make deposits on behalf of their employees in the institution or can make a deposit to match loans made by the institution. In turn the institution can either make loans to the company to finance housing (which the company can subsidize if it wishes) or can make loans directly to the employees, guaranteed by the company. More generally, savings instruments must be specially tailored to the markets at which they are aimed and must be accessible.

The literature on financial institutions in developing countries suggests there can and should be links between formal and informal institutions. In practice, there are likely to be such links; for example, the "treasurer" of an informal institution may well place funds in the banking system. Christian[11] suggests a number of approaches by which the formal and informal systems can be linked.

(a) An outreach program. Mobile branches of formal institutions can make regular scheduled visits to squatter areas to collect savings and receive loan applications. Existing employees of the financial institutions can be offered commission for generating new accounts and servicing loans in informal sector communities during their off-duty hours. The formal sector institution can enter into agreements with a network of agents, who are not employees of the institution, to act as intermediaries between the institution and local communities.
(b) The offering of mutual accounts in the names of villages or other communities rather than individuals.
(c) Informal rotating credit societies or similar arrangements can become affiliates of a housing finance institution. This approach may make maximum use of informal arrangements, but it would require substantial modification to the method of operation of the financial institution itself.

However, despite the obvious attractive nature of these proposals, it is far from certain that they have been successfully implemented in many countries, and the evidence on this is scarce.

More generally, it is clear from close examination of housing finance institutions in developing countries that most do raise their funds predominantly from the wholesale markets, simply because there are insufficient funds that can, as yet, be mobilized from individuals. Even in a middle-income country such as Brazil, the housing finance system relies on compulsory savings for one-third of its funds. In India the Housing Development Finance Corporation obtains almost all of its resources from wholesale sources, with certificates of deposit accounting for over 60 percent of total liabilities. The Government Housing Bank in Thailand at the end of 1982 obtained some 80 percent of its funds from bank loans, borrowing, and bond issues. The Malaysia Building Society, notwithstanding its name, has only 2 percent of its liabilities in the form of deposits. The Crédit Foncier in Egypt obtains as much as 70 percent of its funds from the Central bank.

The lessons learned from this experience are fairly clear. Notwithstanding the obvious theoretical attractions of concentrating on raising deposits from people to whom loans will be made, this is not going to provide sufficient funds to enable a housing finance system to be established. Rather, it is essential that any system has access to wholesale borrowing, and this immediately raises the problem of the allocation of financial resources between the sectors of the economy. If the funds can be raised, and a lending function developed, then a deposit-taking function can be built on top of this, but this is inevitably going to be a long, slow, and far from painless task.

Raising funds is probably the easier part of the housing finance mechanism in developing countries. Making loans, and then recovering them, is far more difficult. The problems, and some potential solutions, were usefully discussed by the General Manager of HDFC:

> Coming to lending, one of the problems that HDFC has encountered is in assessing incomes of the applicants. Self-employed individuals with small incomes are not required to pay income-tax and so there is no possibility of verification of income from their tax returns. HDFC has resorted to innovative techniques for this purpose. For instance, while lending to a cooperative society of small traders in a small town in Gujarat, our credit officer had to spend hours with vegetable vendors and small grocers at their stalls by the roadside to estimate their incomes. HDFC has occasionally found that such people do not even have bank accounts; they have then to be encouraged to open a bank account and deposit a small sum every month in those accounts to enable them to service our loan conveniently.
>
> Many of these borrowers are not literate and are not even in a position to fill up an application form for a loan. The problem is further compounded because there is no uniform language for communication.
>
> HDFC has to help out individuals in deciding on the loan amount to be applied for, as well as in filling up the forms. More importantly, individuals have sometimes to be educated about the obligation to repay the loan in a timely fashion. In the past, there have been various occasions when government and government agencies have provided loans, especially in small towns and rural areas, which have then been written off resulting in individuals developing the belief that loans need not be repaid.

An interesting problem that HDFC has encountered concerns collection mechanisms in respect of borrowers whose income arises irregularly, as in certain self-employed cases, or on a daily basis, as in case of workmen. For instance, HDFC has provided loans on a pilot basis for a housing project in a tribal area of Valod. The loans range from Rs. 1,000 ($ 100) to Rs 3,000 ($ 300) per dwelling unit and the cost of the dwelling units is a maximum of Rs 5,000 ($ 500); the borrowers include agricultural laborers earning about Rs 10–12 per day during the sowing and harvesting seasons and possibly nothing for part of the year. HDFC, along with a local voluntary agency in that area, is encouraging these individuals to save on a daily basis out of their income to facilitate repayment of the loan. HDFC is also discussing with agencies the possibility of setting up a service agency in each village which would be responsible for collection of the loans for a small fee.

All these factors greatly increase the cost of servicing loans to low income individuals. Coupled with this is the fact that the loan amount is small. Therefore, the profitability of loans to low income individuals is not very attractive. In case of arrears in repayment of such loans due to illness or loss of employment, the lending agency would have little choice but to reschedule such loans. Fortunately, HDFC has not had occasion to reschedule any loan, but the possibility always exists.[12]

This extract shows the difficulty of lending and loan recovery in low-income countries and again stresses the need for specialist institutions. As they develop expertise they can help spread it to other institutions (including in other countries), thereby encouraging the housing finance system to strengthen. They can also have a desirable impact on the regulatory framework by using their practical experience to point to the need for change.

One particular problem with respect to loan terms is the percentage advance. In industrialized countries 80–90 percent loans are common, partly because of mortgage insurance. High percentage loans are particularly useful for low-income borrowers, who are simply not able to accumulate savings. However, the evidence is that specialist housing finance institutions in developing countries make only low percentage loans. The Korea Housing Bank, which has a hand in the financing of over 50 percent of all housing units, for example, loans on average only 30 percent of purchase price. In India HDFC will lend no more than 70 percent of cost, but the average loan is no higher than 41 percent, and, on average, HDFC borrowers borrow 7 percent from relatives and 6 percent from other sources. This policy means that potential borrowers without savings cannot qualify for HDFC loans. However, this very simplistic conclusion needs to be modified in two respects:

(a) There may be an income constraint which would make higher percentage loans prudentially unwise. HDFC borrowers rely less on loans from other sources than house purchasers generally. The limitation of the HDFC advance does not seem to force them to borrow from other sources, something which could threaten the ability to repay the HDFC loan.

(b) Given a shortage of savings, a higher average percentage advance would simply mean fewer loans.

It is probably the case that higher percentage advances can safely be made, but such a policy must be dependent on more savings being mobilized so that a higher average loan is not at the expense of the number of loans.

The limits of housing finance

Renaud[4] has pointed out that the housing market in developing countries can be divided into three sectors. The upper-income legal sector obtains its funding from the commercial banking system. The middle-income sector has been the main beneficiary of government subsidized funds. The informal lower-income sector has received no assistance at all. The housing problems in developing countries are so massive that they simply cannot be solved all at once, and one problem has undoubtedly been too high expectations. On the housing side this has been reflected in building to standards which people simply cannot afford. Obviously, if the housing itself is too expensive, no housing finance mechanism can overcome this. The World Bank study of Bogatá, commenting on the pirate subdivision of lots, found "the distribution of roads and open spaces resulting from relatively free market conditions are far below government standards. But they are acceptable to homeowners who could not have afforded lots divided according to legal standards."[7] Recently, there has been a more welcome concentration on slum up-grading and sites-and-services projects. However, even these may well require loans being made to individuals, for example to finance the purchase of building materials. There is some evidence to suggest that people are more willing to repay such loans if they are satisfied with the outcome, and this in turn may well involve being involved in the planning process itself. If the services that are actually provided are inefficient, it is hardly surprising if people refuse to pay for them. If the government is providing the infrastructure on which housing improvement schemes are based, the whole scheme could be threatened if the infrastructure is inadequate.

In the housing finance field there has similarly been an expectation that too much can be achieved and that all efforts should be concentrated on the poorest. In fact, the poorest must be helped by subsidized funds where these are available, and it is unrealistic to expect these funds to be provided by private sector institutions. The World Bank study referred to earlier found that even in illegal settlements home-ownership was not accessible to the lowest 30 percent of the income distribution.[7] If housing finance institutions, which already face massive problems in developing countries, are forced to lend downmarket, then this must threaten their future viability. The most that can be expected of the formal institutions is that they gradually move down the income scale, as their resources and management capability permit. They should not be forced to lend to the lowest-income people, because all that this is likely to achieve is to increase their management expenses and losses substantially, thereby threatening the ability of the institution to perform any function at all.

It may be accepted in industrialized countries that people can afford to spend 25 percent of their income on housing, but the same assumption cannot be made of all people in developing countries. If people have been paying only 10 percent for their housing, and if they are very poor, then it is unrealistic to expect them suddenly to be prepared to pay 25 percent of their income, even if they have an enhanced standard of housing. This suggests a careful evaluation of all programs to see whether they are what people want and, moreover, whether they can be afforded.

Governments and formal institutions must accept the importance of renting, both to provide reasonable housing and to help those improving or building their houses to meet the cost of the process. Again, lessons can be learned from the industrialized countries. In the United Kingdom, where people buy houses at a very early age, it is common for single people in particular to take in tenants to help pay the mortgage. The study of Bogotá may have found that the lowest 30 percent of the income distribution could not afford home-ownership, but it also commented: "Households in this category do obtain housing in illegal settlements by renting rooms. Rentals are a positive solution, not a problem."[7] It went on to say that renting of rooms provided "low cost, good quality space to renters, and that households that rent rooms tend to provide larger units".

The learning process

Housing finance remains a service provided on a national basis, and unlike other goods and services, there is very little international trade in housing finance techniques or loans, because by its very nature it is a local, or at best a countrywide, activity. Unfortunately, this also means that the learning process tends to be confined to within individual countries. The United States, the most sophisticated economy in the world, provides the best example of this. In the 1970s a number of British and other observers noted how America seemed to be building up a potential disaster by having a housing finance system relying on short-term liabilities and long-term loans. The disaster duly occurred. Over a period of years the Americans gradually developed an instrument called the adjustable rate mortgage, and this was regarded as an innovation. Such an instrument has been in operation in other countries, including the United Kingdom and Australia, for many years. The learning process has clearly been very slow in the USA. Similarly, in Europe and in other countries there has not yet been the acceptance that the processes of granting and holding loans can be separated as has been the case in the USA.

Given these circumstances, it is hardly surprising that the learning process in developing countries is somewhat tortuous. There appear to be a number of circuits involved in promoting housing finance, or at least in understanding it, and the linkage between these sectors is, at best, poor. There is the international aid circuit, comprising the United Nations, the World Bank, the International Finance Corporation, and perhaps also in this category the Agency for International Development. There are the national governments which often prefer to work independently of the international aid agencies. There are academics, often trailing years behind actual developments, not through any fault of their own but simply because they lack the available information. There are the institutions in industrialized countries which generally have little idea as to what is going on in developing countries, and finally there are the institutions in developing countries themselves.

If someone knows his way round all of these circuits, he can get various facts together. However, much of the best information is either not published (the World Bank housing sector review of Tunisia for example) or, if it is, its existence may well not be known to many. The International Union of Building Societies and Savings Associations, the Agency for International Development, the World Bank, and the United Nations Center for Human Settlements (Habitat) have published many studies, but often these are unknown to others working in the field.

Summary

(a) In developing countries, even where there are projects to provide affordable housing units, progress may be frustrated because of inadequate housing finance mechanisms.

(b) In developing countries, housing finance is largely provided by the direct system without the intermediation of financial institutions. In industrialized countries, funds for house purchase are raised by deposit-taking institutions or institutions which raise funds on the capital markets.

(c) Formal financial institutions are relatively small in developing countries. Many countries have government-owned savings banks which have no lending function. The formal institutions which provide housing loans generally work on the mortgage bank principle.

(d) There is no proof that housing and housing finance can assist economic development, although there are theoretical grounds for suggesting that this should be the case. However, there is little doubt that home-ownership is a powerful incentive to save and that people will make sacrifices to purchase their homes.

(e) Informal systems of housing finance work because they are suited to the conditions in which they operate. However, informal systems are not efficient; in particular, they cannot provide long-term loans.

(f) Governments should not try to prevent the informal system working but rather should encourage formal institutions to provide competition to it. Formal institutions are more likely to be efficient where:

   (i)   they are allowed to lend as well as raise deposits;
   (ii)   there is political and economic stability;
   (iii) there are no artificial constraints on interest rates;
   (iv)   institutions which raise retail deposits are not subject to credit controls on how they lend those funds.

(g) Social security funds and mandatory savings schemes can provide funds for house purchase or can be used as security for loans.

(h) Formal institutions can increase their housing finance activity and mobilization of savings by various measures including:

   (i)   promoting savings schemes linked to house purchase;
   (ii)   establishing branches, if management capability allows;
   (iii) establishing links with informal institutions;
   (iv)   using innovative methods of assessing income and recovering repayments.

(i)   Housing finance is best provided by specialist institutions.

(j)   In the past, expectations in respect of both housing and housing finance have been too high. Many people in the lowest income groups simply cannot afford owner-occupation, and if institutions are forced to lend to them, then their own viability is threatened.

(k)   The provision of informal rented housing is an important source of supply of affordable housing and can help finance improvements and house purchase by owner-occupiers.

(l)   The learning system in housing finance is deficient, in industrialized as well as in developing countries. In particular, there is inadequate dissemination of information.

8

Financing shelter

BERTRAND RENAUD

Introduction

URBAN DEVELOPMENT policies in developing countries are at a new threshold. In sharp contrast to the relative financial stability of the period 1965–73, the decade 1974–84 has been a period of financial instability. First, Third World countries (TWCs) experienced an expansion from 1974 to 1980 which was then followed by a period of contraction and a financial crisis beginning about 1980 and lasting into the present in many countries. Policy makers are facing a very constraining environment. Third World countries are experiencing low growth, exports are sluggish, levels of unemployment are rising, and the high levels of foreign debt are leading to stringent fiscal austerity. In spite of these economic conditions, urban areas continue to grow steadily in population and appropriate strategies to finance shelter are taking on renewed importance.

In the public discussion of shelter financing, misunderstandings abound. First, is there a difference between "housing" finance and "shelter" finance? One of the major lessons from experience in the shelter sector in TWCs is that there is a crucial economic and functional relationship between housing and its related infrastructure. It is therefore necessary in this chapter to address the problems of financing both, even if the required institutions and instruments are quite different. Second, is it possible to limit an analysis of shelter financing to a discussion of the problems of housing the poor? Again, experience shows that if housing policies are to be integrated effectively into national policy making and not confined to marginal institutions, the entire housing sector and all income groups must be considered. Third, whose problems do you analyze? There is a very wide diversity of participants in the housing market: a variety of professions involved in the production of housing, a diversity of financial institutions involved in its financing, and very different households to be served either as owners or as renters. Improving financial mechanisms in the housing delivery system of a country requires that more than the specific problems of households be analyzed with great care. In particular, with an instable financial environment the problems of developing viable and adaptable housing finance institutions have taken on a new urgency. The growth of the housing finance system cannot be separated from the rest of the financial sector.

In the demanding economic context of the present, the objective of this chapter is to review the lessons from experience and analyze directions which policy makers should consider to restructure activities in shelter finance.

Housing delivery systems in TWCs: lessons from experience

Considerable progress has been made over the last 15 years in understanding the operations of housing markets in TWCs and what might constitute appropriate policies and projects in a given country. In particular, it has become very clear that access to formal financing is not the only constraint on expanding the supply of housing. There are constraints on both sides – on the real side of the housing markets and on the side of housing finance institutions exposed to their own capital market constraints. In the formulation of policies, more progress has been made in understanding housing market constraints than financial sector constraints, so the structure of TWC housing markets is reviewed first.

Activities to be financed and the rôle of institutions

Different types of financing needed   The process of converting a parcel of raw agricultural land into a fully serviced housing unit is a lengthy and complex one. Many public sector shelter projects in developing countries take seven to eight years from planning to full occupancy. The type of financial services to be provided during the process of developing a shelter project are quite varied. Looking at an individual project, there is a need to finance the acquisition of the raw land, to finance its infrastructure (sometimes called off-site and on-site; sometimes classified as primary, secondary, and tertiary infrastructure, depending on the capacity of the networks), to finance construction, and, finally, the sale of the project.

In developed countries these financial arrangements are quite complex and involve interactions between the private project developer, local government agencies, and, often, central government agencies. The amount of lending, the degree of financial leverage, the level of equity participation among different partners, loan maturities, risks, and quality of collateral vary significantly according to the phase of the project financed and its nature.

Formal financing for private development activities is typically very difficult to find in TWC countries, even for high-income projects. Development and construction financing, which in boom periods can be quite profitable to both developers and lenders, is always risky; paradoxically, this stage of financing is rendered even more risky by the inability of most financial institutions to provide "take-out" long-term mortgage financing to households at the end of projects. In such cases, private developers typically resort to pre-sale and pre-financing by their buyers to reduce their inventory risks in addition to having equity sharing arrangements with those who contribute the land. This method, which is heavily based on the equity contribution of buyers, limits such private developments to upper-income groups during periods of prosperity when participating households can cash other assets to finance the new units. Moreover, private and public banks tend to limit their development financing to their own subsidiaries in order to maintain some control over risks. An asset-based, asset-financed demand for housing ownership is very sensitive to economic conditions and can cause sharp fluctuations in output in this segment of the housing market, depending on the impact of market conditions on the ability to sell a piece of land to finance building. It is not a very effective way to reach ownership for lower middle-income and low-income households without very significant assets but with good incomes.

The availability of long-term mortgage financing can be a very strong factor in reorienting the supply of housing toward more appropriate housing standards. Experience shows that quite a few private developers are prepared to change their product in order to reduce the large risk of unsold inventories or incomplete projects. Another great constraint is the provision of basic infrastructure services which require a large amount of financing and the intervention of the public sector. In the absence of efficient housing finance systems, households must generate resources entirely through their own saving efforts and reach ownership very late in life, if at all. In middle-income countries, there is a large incremental housing sector which is quite capable of producing buildings of good quality but not of servicing land with appropriate trunk infrastructure, road access, clean water, and sanitation.

Low levels of financial intermediation in housing   International statistics on the level of financial intermediation in TWCs are yet to be developed systematically. When intermediation is defined in terms of flows as the ratio of the annual value of new mortgage loans made to the estimated value of new housing, it is quite low and typically less than 20 percent.[1] Other measures are based on outstanding loans. For instance in Korea, which is one of the most rapidly growing and better managed TWC economies, housing mortgages represented only 6.9 percent of GNP in 1984, indicating that access to ownership is heavily dependent on the previous ownership of assets and that the housing finance system is still very little developed. In comparison, this ratio varied from 15 percent in Japan to 28 percent in France and the UK, 37 percent in Canada and Germany, 41 percent in the United States, and 64 percent in Switzerland by the end of 1982.[2]

Three-tier structure of TWC housing markets

The difficulty of obtaining financing for financial institutions, together with other major constraints regarding physical and institutional infrastructure found in TWCs, generates a typical three-tier structure of the housing markets found practically everywhere. At the top of the income scale can be found a small, well financed upper-income market entirely supplied by the private sector. In the middle can be found a fairly narrow subsidized market composed of middle-class salaried workers and civil servant households who are the main, if not exclusive, beneficiaries of public housing finance policies. Then, finally, there is a large and private incremental housing market which has had no access to formal financing services and is encompassing a wide range of incomes and of housing units. Some of it consists of good-quality buildings, other parts being destitute slums, but all of it is characterized by its nonconformity to official rules and standards. Within this incremental housing market, financial arrangements are made all the time by individuals who are trying to build their own houses. In that sense, financing is taking place and a financial market exists, but the services provided are small, expensive, very costly to provide, and unpredictable. Such a structure is shown in the case of Tunisia in Table 8.1 and Figure 8.1.

Table 8.1   Three-tier structure of a housing sector: Tunisia, 1975–80.

	Share of housing investment (millions of TD)	Number of units (1,000)	Households served	Institutional financing (including subsidies but excluding down payments)
legal private sector	urban 268 rural 4.3 total 272.3 (34.2%)	urban 58.3 rural 6.1 total 64.4 (20.5%)	100th to 80th percentile (top 20%)	TD 21 million (7.7%)
public sector controlled Con	urban 265 rural 63.2 (41.2%)	urban 38.3 rural 42.1 (25.6%)	90th to 30th percentile	TD 113 million (34.4%) including subsidies
informal sector (urban and rural)	urban 144.6 rural 50.9 total 195.5 (24.6%)	urban 96.4 rural 72.8 total 169.2 (53.9%)	50th percentile and below	zero
total	TD 796 million (100%)	314.0		TD 134 million (16.8% of column 1)

Source: Renaud, B. 1984. *Housing and financial institutions in developing countries.* Chicago, Ill.: International Union of Building Societies and Savings Associations.
Note
1 Tunisian Dinar = US $ 2.00

The Tunisian data describe the housing market over the period 1975–80 from three convergent viewpoints: (1) the relative contribution of each market tier to total housing output, (2) the position within the income distribution of those who are found in each tier, and (3) the contributions made by public and private institutions in the financing of total output. One can see that the public sector is dominant in Tunisia in terms of the value of the infrastructure and housing investment which it controls or regulates, but this is not always the case in other countries. In contrast, the public sector is involved in the production of only 25.6 percent of all units, including the incremental sector in the private sector. The reason for this contrast is that a significant proportion of public investment in housing is devoted to urban infrastructure.

The limited reach of financial institutions into the housing sector is also quite visible: institutional financing represents only 7.7 percent of the estimated value of the "legal" (fully conforming) private sector investment. Institutional financing represents only 34 percent of public

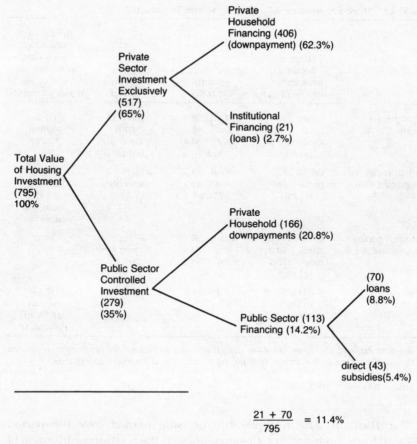

$$\frac{21 + 70}{795} = 11.4\%$$

Figure 8.1 Tunisian housing finance system, 1975–80.
Source: World Bank 1982. *Tunisia housing sector review.* Washington, DC: World Bank.

sector investment and only 16.7 percent of the entire Tunisian housing market for new housing. If one separates budget allocations from financing by institutions, the latter ratio drops to 11.4 percent. One of the implications of these figures is that in order to buy housing families have to "chase loans" from every possible source, such as social security systems, pension funds, and borrowing from their employers' social funds as well as from friends and relatives. This process is very inefficient and costly and can sometimes lead to very high debt–income ratios.[3] Paradoxically, the financial agency of the housing sector (CNEL) has been extremely successful in mobilizing housing savings and collected a large share of household savings until 1983. Clearly, during that period there was a mismatch between household demand and the financial services provided. In addition, nonfinancial constraints appeared to be quite important because households had difficulty finding affordable houses to buy once they had accumulated financial savings.

Nonfinancial constraints affecting housing supply

Whenever the rôle of financial institutions in the housing sector is limited and the value of loans made is quite small compared to the total value of the investment put in place, it is for two reasons. First, there is a crucial economic and functional relationship between housing and basic physical and institutional infrastructure. Important nonfinancial constraints on the housing sector side make it very difficult to provide financing adequately. Second, other important constraints on the provision of housing finance services arise from the state of development of financial markets and their regulatory environment. Nonfinancial constraints are examined first.

Policy makers and urban planners are often fond of saying that the problem with housing is the lack of financing, but in many countries serious weaknesses in the housing delivery systems also prevent the flow of banking funds into the sector. These nonfinancial constraints have a direct impact on the provision of financing by making it either extremely costly or simply impossible for formal institutions to provide long-term mortgages.

Poor land administration and institutions The foremost constraint on the provision of formal finance and on orderly urban development is land management and administration. Poor land administration, unclear land titles, and unclear land tenure produce unbankable, non-conforming (illegal) housing arrangements. Inappropriate land policies succeed mostly in restricting land availability and can raise the cost of housing very significantly in urban areas. It is not excessive to say that one can judge the overall urban development potential of a country (in contrast to uncontrollable growth) by the quality of its land institutions.

Mortgage lending for home-ownership can be one of the safest forms of bank lending, in spite of very long loan maturities, because of the safety of the real estate collateral. This is confirmed by the fact that, in quite a few countries, particularly in East Asia where land is scarce and values are high, commercial banking practices are often criticized for being based on the value of the real estate collateral provided rather than on the commercial evaluation of the intrinsic merits of the projects to be financed. However, the cost of registering and evaluating land can be prohibitively long and extremely expensive, even for large moderate-income projects.[4]

Uncertainty of tenure of course makes formal lending impossible. It has important additional economic and financial effects that have been observed in practically every low-income shelter project in the world. When offered security of tenure, even prior to full legalization but with clear political and technical evidence that it is being done, low-income households reduce and restructure their consumption: they convert their few assets currently kept in economically sterile but moveable form, such as jewelry and valuable durable goods; they obtain transfers from relatives; and they invest these resources into housing improvements which produce additional housing services.

Creating an appropriate institutional infrastructure and running it efficiently is the highest priority for governments. It has a direct feedback on public revenues and the financing of physical shelter infrastructure. For instance, in the case of low-income projects, the cost of slow processing of land titles can be high for governments, because in most countries the ability to recover the cost of public infrastructure and to charge user fees and taxes for its maintenance is tied to the transfer of full titles to the beneficiaries of the project. Since there is an element of subsidy in such projects and less than 100 percent of cost recovery has too often been planned, this additional resource shortfall can have a serious impact on the ability of public agencies to move on to new projects, particularly in periods of stringent fiscal austerity.

Excessively high standards and building costs Significant progress has been made over the last two decades with the growing acceptance of the necessity to do a systematic analysis of project designs and standards according to the income-carrying capacity of the target population to be served. Many countries have revised their building codes in order to eliminate some of their negative economic and social impacts. In housing it always seems to be easier to deal with visible physical issues than with equally crucial but publicly less visible institutional and managerial issues. It is not yet fully appreciated that the cost of delays in permit delivery as well as the inconsistent application of building codes can substantially raise the cost of housing.[5] The cost of delays in delivering permits is very significant in most countries because of the very high level of real interest rates prevalent in most countries. Moreover, regulators are too often indifferent to the indirect increase in administrative costs which they impose on builders for nobody's benefit. The alternative for builders is to resort to nonconforming housing construction which generally cannot be financed by formal financial institutions.

The other problems faced by financial institutions are the correct appraisal of real estate values and the respect of financial contracts implying full and timely repayments of loans as well as the possibility of foreclosure in extreme cases. These two factors combined often induce private mortgage lenders with scarce resources to offer only low loan-to-value ratios on mortgages to account for default risks. On the other hand, public lenders, particularly in Latin America, sometimes fall into the opposite situation of allowing excessively high loan-to-value ratios for low-income households.

Lack of major trunk infrastructure The provision of major trunk infrastructure is the responsibility of the public sector. It is a service that private developers do not have the legal, technical, and financial capacity to provide in most cities. A shortage of serviced land prevents private builders from producing the type of housing which could be financed by financial institutions. In the case of existing housing, whether it consists of good-quality housing on unserviced land or massive slums in depressed areas, the government is also confronted with the need to upgrade or plainly provide the infrastructure.

The sheer magnitude of these infrastructure deficiencies, combined with fiscal austerity, is leading to a fundamental reanalysis of the issue of infrastructure provision in many countries and to increased pressures for realistic approaches to the rôle of the public sector in shelter. The emerging division of labor is to reserve public sector financial resources for the provision of basic trunk infrastructure and area-wide improvements, limiting drastically the public financing of shelter units and of on-site infrastructure. On the other side, financial institutions are being encouraged to mobilize household savings for the more efficient provision of mortgage finance.

Rent-control legislation A final policy factor having a negative impact on the flow of financial resources into housing is rent-control legislation. Starting with the well-meaning social objectives of protecting low-income families and aged households, most rent control laws have had mostly negative impacts on the operation of housing markets.

Rent controls can appear to have some short-term beneficial effects, particularly for elected politicians, but in the very dynamic environment of TWC cities they have three consistent effects: (1) they reduce the rate of return on housing, thereby discouraging investment in shelter; (2) they create arbitrary windfalls and invisible asset transfers from landowners to current tenants in the short run; and (3) they induce illegal side payments in the long run. Rent-control legislation has been shown to be an inferior way to arbitrate conflicts between landlords and tenants: it represents a capricious and unpredictable way of providing subsidies to tenants without appearing to have an impact on public budgets.[6]

By discouraging the private supply of housing, rent control may progressively push the public sector into supplying more and more subsidized housing to the middle class as resources are available, causing a substitution of suppliers rather than net additions to the total housing stock. In this case funds necessary for infrastructure investment go into needless public housing construction. Moreover, there is no evidence that public builders are consistently more efficient and cheaper than private builders when taking into account their tax status, access to low-cost funds, regulatory advantages, and legal powers. The structure of the housing construction industry is also likely to become more concentrated into fewer large organizations with heavy overheads and the ability to afford the costs of dealing with various ministries and regulatory agencies.

Rôle of the public sector and shelter finance

The most radical change taking place in recent years in shelter policy is the changing view about the appropriate rôle of the public sector. Since the early 1960s many governments have taken the position that the public sector has a major responsibility in providing housing and infrastructure services. Various influences were at work including rapid growth, cheap international funds, comprehensive planning ideologies, the welfare state policies of many OECD countries, and, in many countries, colonial legacies. Experience has shown the limits of public budgets which could not accommodate large and rapidly growing urban populations and of the implementing capacity of public institutions. Developing countries have found that conventional subsidized public housing is not the answer to providing shelter for large low-income populations and that public agencies should focus their activities on the provision of infrastructure (physical and institutional), move away from the direct production of housing units, and strive to facilitate private housing construction at all income levels.

From a financial viewpoint, two issues dominate discussions of the rôle of the public sector in shelter finance: subsidies and cost recovery, which control a government's ability to maintain its programs over time.

Subsidies

There is an endless variety of ways of generating subsidies and, depending on circumstances and on the analyst, some are considered legitimate and others are not. At a time when national resources are scarce, it is imperative that the most significant subsidies be correctly measured so that governments can determine whether more could not be achieved with the same resources. This is crucial because the inefficiencies and distortive economic and financial effects of subsidies need to be controlled.

For the convenience of this review, one can re-group subsidies into two broad categories: subsidies provided through the pricing and taxation of the various phases of shelter production and subsidies provided through credit programs. Subsidies through production can include public land pricing, the provision of infrastructure below cost, subsidized construction costs through tax incentive to specially designated builders or construction services provided by untaxed public enterprises, waivers on real estate taxes, public services provided below cost, rental allowances, reduced rents, etc. Among the subsidies provided through credit programs one can find low interest rates, cash housing allowances at time of purchase, mortgage terms unadjustable for inflation and unpaid arrears.

The efficiency and equity aspects of shelter subsidies are important – after all they are their original justification. The efficiency argument arises when the public sector steps into the supply process in order to reduce market risks and encourage the supply of new shelter services or technologies not yet available locally. The difficulty is to determine at what stage and at what level of subsidies public sector activities are actually beginning to prevent the emergence of private suppliers. On the other hand, there is somewhat less difficulty in differentiating between public and private goods in the shelter sector and between infrastructure and housing.

From an equity viewpoint, it is important to return to the three-tier structure of housing markets described earlier. It can be seen that the essential beneficiaries of subsidies through housing programs are found in the second tier of the housing market where the salaried, private, or civil service middle-class households are concentrated.

If governments want to have housing programs that are sustainable over time, they should clarify their use of subsidies and contain them, particularly in periods of fiscal restraints when they are confronted with a sharp trade-off between deeper subsidies for a few or lighter ones for many. In addition, since subsidies represent a transfer of wealth between income groups, they are questionable in countries where all incomes are low. Two points seem clear. In housing programs which include an element of subsidy, this subsidy should be confined to the lowest income groups so that the impact per household can be material and the greatest number helped. In addition, such subsidy should focus most heavily on infrastructure and direct government production of housing should be avoided as far as possible. Subsidies should be transparent, i.e., easily measurable, and the sources from which the transfers will have to be made should be clearly known.

Cost recovery

Cost recovery is the mirror image of subsidies, with the qualification that there are unintended subsidies implicitly present in the failure to recover some costs. Therefore one can define the basic policy equations of cost recovery as being: (a) total project resource cost equals cost recovered plus total subsidy, and (b) total subsidy equals intended subsidies plus unintentional failure to recover costs.

The recovery of project costs can take two forms because of the mix of public and private goods present in public shelter projects as well as the mix of infrastructure and housing services provided: a direct method and an indirect one. The beneficiaries of a project can pay directly for services such as roads, water and sanitation, street lighting, and refuse collection through monthly plot charges, utility tariffs, and other user charges; construction costs and business loans can be repaid through monthly or periodical financial payments. Indirect recovery methods imply that a wider population than that benefiting immediately from a project is expected to share in covering its costs. Services whose costs are indirectly recovered are of a public good nature where users and nonusers cannot be easily segregated and user fees charged. Typically, projects with large investments in trunk infrastructure and community facilities have higher shares of planned indirect cost recovery.

The causes of failure in cost recovery are varied. In the case of low-income projects, with repeated operations and growing experience with planning as well as improved managerial ability, cost recovery tends to improve over time. The typical causes of failure to recover costs are inadequate legislation; poorly organized and supervised collection procedures; difficulties with land tenure and the transfer of titles; weak administration or unwillingness to adjust tariffs and user charges for inflation and the true cost of providing services; and sometimes plain unwillingness to pay on the part of beneficiaries. No generalization on cost recovery is entirely safe geographically or over time, but typically local governments tend to have more difficulty in enforcing cost recovery, particularly small municipalities which are used to getting most of their resources from central government grants.

The failure to recover cost has two main results: it provides a windfall to those who have already been served and threatens the viability of public programs. If governments want to be able to expand their programs of infrastructure provision, they must confront the fact that good infrastructure has to be paid for and that, without cost recovery, even the maintenance of the existing capital infrastructure is in jeopardy. During this period of scarce resources public sector savings must be raised and public sector institutions should be expected to follow sound financial practices in their internal management and to know exactly what and where their resources are.[7] Financial management in public housing authorities is greatly in need of improvement.

Financial institutions and capital market constraints

In addition to nonfinancial constraints such as poor land administration which impede the supply of housing finance, there are other constraints on the financial market side which limit the growth of housing finance institutions. If the public sector is now expected to concentrate its financial resources on infrastructure and public services, what can be expected from financial institutions? The period of financial instability which many countries are currently experiencing is bringing into sharp relief the nature of the constraints on the financing of housing.

Financial development over the last 20 years

To understand better the potential of housing finance institutions it is useful to place them within the general context of financial development. During the 1960s and early 1970s exchange rates, commodity prices, and the domestic price level were all relatively stable. Recent data compiled by the World Bank show that for a sample of 35 of the largest developing countries representing a very high percentage of the global GNP of developing countries, the average inflation rate was 7 percent per year. Only a few countries lived through periods of sustained double-digit inflation.[8] During the same period inflation in the industrial countries averaged 5 percent per year. Negative real rates of interest were a serious problem only in the high inflation countries which in fact pioneered indexation of financial assets, in particular home mortgages. It is estimated that the real rate of interest on term deposits averaged minus 1 percent. This was a period when low inflation and reasonable interest rates made the holding of financial assets possible and attractive. Most countries showed significant increases in their level of financial intermediation and the use of banking services, the ratio of M2 to GDP rose markedly, and nonbank financial intermediaries grew well. Most countries followed conservative invesment strategies and depended primarily upon their own resources to finance their investment programs. National savings provided 80 percent of investment needs.

Since 1974 and the first oil crisis, financial conditions have been quite different. Between 1974 and 1980 commodity prices rose sharply, fell abruptly, and recovered again. The oil revenues which could be seen as a heavy tax on industrial countries were redeposited at commercial banks which recycled these funds as international loans. Much of this lending was short-term and longer-term lending was increasingly done at variable rates, reflecting in part the new pattern set by fluctuating exchange rates since 1971 and the impact of US monetary policies on capital markets. High inflation spread from a few developing countries to many. The average annual rate of inflation rose from 7 to 19 percent; including the few high inflation countries of the earlier period the average was 25 percent. Inflation rose in industrial countries, but much less, to an average of 10 percent. The average real rate of interest in developing countries fell to minus 8 percent on average, thereby discouraging domestic savings mobilization through financial institutions.

During this second period most developing countries followed very expansionary policies. The average rate of investment rose from 20 to 24 percent, most of the increase reflecting additional public sector investment. Domestic savings were discouraged by negative deposit rates, but international loans were cheap and countries kept borrowing abroad to sustain their growth, finance their trade deficits, and raise investments. Domestic savings dropped to 74 percent of investment, and medium- and long-term foreign debt rose from 24 to 31 percent of GDP; in addition, countries made extensive use of short-term debt at commercial terms which amounted to an additional 6 percent of GNP in 1980. This period saw a massive internationalization of capital markets, whcih became really global in their operations.

The second oil crisis of 1979 created much more serious problems than the first one. It included a recession in industrial countries, a sharp fall in commodity prices, and deteriorating terms of trade. For the first time in 30 years the value of international trade actually declined in 1981 and international interest rates became sharply positive, increasing the debt of burden of TWCs which rose to an average of 48 percent of GNP in 1983 as a consequence of devaluations. At the same time much of voluntary international lending stopped. Because of their heavy foreign debt servicing burdens and their previous inability to increase their debt servicing capacity in step with their borrowings, governments had to tighten their fiscal policies, making domestic conditions worse. Quite frequently, the failure of the public sector to pay its bills also eroded the liquidity position of private firms and directly or indirectly that of the financial institutions. Among the most seriously affected have been the specialized, public, long-term lending institutions.

Characteristics of housing and form of financing required

Housing has characteristics which affect the form of financing it requires. There are several major reasons why a household would want to purchase a house and would take out a long-term loan: the transaction costs of frequent moves are high for families; the quality of the services provided by a house is very sensitive to the way it is used; housing is one of the most durable goods, providing a flow of services over a long period of time; and a housing unit generally costs three to four times the annual income of its occupants, making it very difficult to acquire through a pure cash (equity) rather than debt transaction.[9] From a financial institution's viewpoint, mortgage lending is costly: in addition to the long maturities required, a mortgage loan is a fairly small investment transaction compared to commercial lending, and the cost of creating such a financial asset is high. In developed countries with well developed and competitive financial systems, mortgage interest rates are marginally higher than the cost of long-term corporate funds in order to avoid shortages of funds.

The recent past has not been favorable to many housing finance institutions. As shown by recent events, because of the need for long-term financing, the biggest burden on developing viable and flexible housing finance systems is severe inflation accompanied by high and fluctuating interest rates. On the other hand, a necessary but not sufficient condition for the sustained growth of a housing finance system is an environment of sound monetary and fiscal policies.

Types of housing finance systems

There are basically four ways of channeling funds from savers to borrowers, and housing finance systems consist in combinations of these four ways.[10] The direct route (informal financing) is obviously the most widespread in developing countries; it is the only method for the large incremental shelter sector. It involves many inefficiencies and needs to be better understood. The objective of financial policies should obviously be to reduce the scope of informal financial markets, but artificially low, regulated interest rates and directed credit policies as well as taxation have helped the direct route to endure and often grow.

The contractual route, where the home buyer receives his loan from an institution collecting funds on a long-term contractual basis, is used in a variety of countries where financial markets are fragmented and not well developed; it is generally used by highly specialized financial institutions. CNEL in Tunisia is an important illustration of that approach. For a variety of financial management reasons, it is not possible to rely exclusively on this approach.

The deposit financing route where short-term savings are packaged into long-term loans by intermediaries has been popularized by the building societies, savings and loans associations, and other mutual credit institutions around the world. Their success requires low inflation rates, interest rates set freely at competitive levels, and easy access to the depositor through a network of branches. They can offer loans at moderate price but are sensitive to term-intermediation risks (borrowing short and lending long).

The mortgage bank route where the funds used to finance mortgage loans are mobilized through long-term bonds purchased by institutional investors rather than individuals is a fourth way to finance housing. The two main considerations in this approach are the cost and the volume of funds accessible from other deposit-taking institutions; funds are more expensive than from direct deposit taking, but maturity risks are small and there is no need for extensive and costly branch networks. This approach is used in Morocco and in India. It has been argued by some that the mortgage bank route followed later by deposit-taking may be one of the easier ways to create a new housing finance institution rapidly, deposit-taking being added to the institution at a later stage. In that case, dependence on long-term funds from the public sector should be carefully controlled.

Lending policies and viable housing finance systems

Lending policies are central to the viability of housing finance systems. Many discussions of housing finance are exclusively concerned with the problems of the households and with the financial techniques that can be used to make housing affordable to beneficiaries, basically in four ways: by lowering interest rates, by lengthening mortgage maturities, by using graduated payments, or by reducing the equity contribution that households must make. Although it is important to distinguish clearly between policies to improve the efficiency of housing finance systems and the desire to provide subsidies through credit programs, it must also be recognized that directed credit programs are deeply entrenched in many countries and are considered a major instrument of policy, including in housing.

By insisting on low interest policies, irrespective of current levels of financial savings, inflation, and the opportunity cost of capital, many housing ministries are greatly underpricing financial services and making housing finance institutions dependent on public subsidies for their operations. Without funds available in financial institutions, households draw none of the benefits of financial intermediation and end up paying considerably more in the informal markets. Lasting housing finance policies must address on one hand the affordability problems of the households and on the other the interest rate risk, maturity risk, liquidity risk, and default risk faced by the financial institutions; otherwise housing finance services cannot be provided in a stable and flexible way.

Expanding the volume of housing finance funds

Voluntary deposits The logic of financial institutions is such that if they are to lend at very low interest rates they are in no position to offer attractive rates to their depositors on a competitive basis. During the earlier period of large negative real interest rates imposed on many financial institutions, wealth transfers from depositors to borrowers were taking place. In the case of housing credit and agricultural credit, lending rules, particularly low loan-to-value ratios, were often such that the borrowers had considerably higher income status than the depositors. When inflation is high, loan maturities in the financial markets shorten drastically, and under the pressure to lend at low rates the only institutions remaining active in housing finance have been public institutions receiving long-term concessional loans. The importance of offering positive real rates of interest has also been demonstrated by the success of indexed deposits in the UPAC system of Colombia when the housing finance system kept expanding very successfully under inflation.[11]

Directed credit programs Given inflation and the behavior of interest rates, the problem for policy makers is to develop stable sources of long-term capital at the lowest cost possible. Money markets are short term and capital markets are undeveloped in Third World countries, offering at best only short maturities. Governments have therefore resorted to various means to generate funds that market forces alone would not provide in sufficient amount or quickly enough. The decisions to choose such techniques have depended on the degree of priority accorded to the housing sector in national policies and on the degree of development of the financial system. The need to develop some source of long-term funds explains why direct credit programs are playing such a significant rôle in many countries.

The four main nonmarket techniques used to create a supply of long-term housing finance have been tax-based social housing funds, the use of retirement systems, directed credit policies applied to commercial banks, and forced deposit schemes where people interested in purchasing housing must give proof of having opened a housing account. Depending on how they are managed, such systems can make a major contribution to housing or dissipate scarce financial resources.[12]

Current macroeconomic opportunities and constraints

The shelter sector plays a very important rôle in every TWC economy. Housing investment as a share of annual gross domestic fixed capital formation (gross investment) varies between 15 and 30 percent. Even in very depressed periods, such as in Turkey in 1981, housing investment still represented 12 percent of GDCF. Housing has other features which make it currently important. It is a major nontraded sector with limited needs for foreign exchange in most countries, except island economies. It is a labor-intensive sector able to provide employment to low-income workers. Most governments are therefore interested in stimulating investment in housing as a countercyclical tool to revive their economy and as a means of lessening the impact of the economic recession on the lower-income groups. However, there are two opposing factors which reduce considerably the scope of a housing stimulus, in spite of the pressing needs of the sector. One is the intensified competition for domestic savings and the other is the weakened effective demand for housing.

From the viewpoint of national accounts, there are four main sources of gross savings in an economy: the household sector, the business sector, the government, and the foreign sector (foreign lenders). The household sector is typically a net lender and the business sector a net borrower, whereas the net position of the government and the foreign sector can vary from period to period and country to country. With the problems of foreign debt – when so many countries have experienced net transfer of resources in favor of the foreign sector – and large government deficits, the household sector is currently the last source of savings to keep national economies growing, however slowly.

Presently, governments would prefer to see household savings go to investment activities with a more rapid capital recovery period and lower capital output ratios than housing. in addition, the need to curtail public sector deficits makes it very difficult for them to pursue vigorously through the public sector the social housing policies most beneficial to low-income groups. It must be noted in this respect that past emphasis on heavily subsidized public housing had led some economists to recommend curtailment of investment in housing as a nonproductive sector, which is not the case of infrastructure investment nor of private nonsubsidized housing.

The other major current constraint is that the demand for housing has weakened considerably with the recession. The annual supply of new housing is a small proportion of the existing stock. Relatively small shifts in real income, prices, interest rates, and expectations can lead to sharp year-to-year fluctuations in housing output. In most countries this instability is accentuated by the lack of long-term financing. At present, the problem in TWC cities is more immediately one of income generation through employment than one of housing, especially for low-income groups. Among the households which could normally aim at home-ownership, the current demand for new housing has weakened as real incomes have either stagnated or declined, inducing families to draw on their savings.

The gap between ability to pay and socially desirable housing consumption has been widening. Governments have to identify the narrow path between stimulating housing demand and avoiding using large amounts of scarce public resources as subsidies. This implies a lowering of individual household expectations and a reorientation of housing supply to more modest housing units.

Level of development and housing finance

Cross-country differences in housing investment

Microanalyses and macroanalyses concur in showing that the housing sector becomes increasingly important as the per capita income of a country rises. Housing and housing finance policies reach a peak of importance in middle-income countries that are urbanizing rapidly.

The structural characteristics of housing demand (price and income elasticities in particular) have been found to be remarkably similar across cities and countries. On the other hand, there are systematic variations in the share of housing in household expenditures as a function of the level of per capita income of countries (or cities). Similarly, all available studies show that the share of housing in GDP varies between 1 and 7 percent, these two numbers being extreme values that are not sustained over long periods of time. This share of housing investment is generally very low at the early stages of development when a country's per capita income is very low. The highest values are generally found among middle-income countries that are already significantly urbanized and with strongly growing economies, in which case both the total level of national investment and the share of housing in that investment are high. Studies also show that the systematic variation between per capita income level and housing investment is stronger than the effect of demographic variables. Among other intervening factors, indicators of financial development such as capital deepening suggest that countries with more developed financial markets invest relatively more in housing.[13]

These macroanalyses are consistent with microanalyses of households in TWCs in finding that the force that drives housing demand is a rising household income level before anything else. It is possible to interpret the levelling off of the housing share of GNP as the net result of the positive effect of rising income balanced with the negative effect of increasing housing prices with rising urbanization and population concentration.

Such findings already suggest that from a national viewpoint it is difficult to give a high level of priority to the construction of housing units in very low income countries where public resources are scarce and institutions limited. In these countries public priority should typically go to developing cost-effective, basic institutional and physical infrastructure which will organize and support private activities. The weight and complexity of housing policy both for private and public activities increases as countries move toward the middle-income level.

Regional differences in housing finance systems

As could be expected, there is a broad correlation between the level of per capita income of a country and the degree of development of housing finance systems, but as is shown by Boleat's review[10] of some 50 countries, no single approach to developing housing finance systems is clearly preferable over all the others, and the national financial history is quite important. The institutional structure originally chosen to mobilize household savings, for instance whether special systems such as postal savings or banking institutions started first, has a lasting impact on the evolution of housing finance systems. This is particularly true in small and still-fragmented financial systems.

An important element of consideration for what can be done in housing finance in the immediate future is the extent to which various national financial systems have been affected by the present period of financial instability. The overall quality of national economic management policies regarding price stability, directed credit, and interest rate policies determines the economic environment in which housing finance institutions have to operate.

Many of the sub-Saharan countries were overextended during the 1970s, and even if the aggregate volume of their foreign debt was not large on a global basis, as a percentage of GNP the debt burden is as heavy as for the Latin American group of countries that has been making headlines. The problems are severe because most countries are currently on a trend of economic decline, and per capita income is falling, implying that domestic savings rates are seriously affected. Many of the housing finance institutions in the region have been touched by the financial crisis and are dormant. Clearly, more than anywhere else, the concentration of efforts on developing the institutional and basic physical infrastructure is a priority during this period of restructuring. The problems in the shelter sector are compounded by the fact that the highest rates of city growth are anticipated in sub-Saharan Africa for the rest of the century.

The middle-income countries of North Africa and the Middle East, which had open trade and capital markets and were fairly dependent on foreign borrowing, were also seriously affected by recent international trends. But the experience of the region is heterogeneous. Some of these countries are making slow but steady progress in modernizing their shelter delivery systems in spite of the weaker economic environment. Considerably more attention is now being placed on improving housing finance institutions through better mobilization of resources and new financial services. Efforts are also being made to develop more coherent shelter support systems, starting with land management institutions.

The newly industrialized countries of Latin America have been most severely affected by the financial crisis. During the 1970s, their economies became overheated through inflation and they had become heavily dependent on foreign savings. In Chile and Brazil, the housing finance systems went through traumatic periods with nonperforming loans and unstable deposits, whose effects have not yet been fully played out. In Mexico, the fragmented housing finance system needs to be better coordinated and structured. Interest rate policies in some parts of the system are wasteful and in need of major improvement. Because of high levels of inflation, many countries in the region are heavily dependent on indexed instruments to mobilize funds, but these tools are not easy to manage and subsidies through credit programs are very large and difficult to bring under control.

The countries of East Asia and South Asia which had kept better control over their domestic economy than in other regions are not pressed by financial instability, except for the Philippines. In Asia, the issues are not issues of restructuring but of continued modernization of shelter finance. Trends toward more liberalization of the financial systems are inducing reviews of housing finance institutions, which still remain quite specialized.

In the large countries of South Asia, differences are marked. In India, the housing sector still remains a low priority, but discussions on how to modernize the housing finance system have taken place over the last few years because the housing sector is already quite important in absolute size. In Pakistan, the decision to move to a full Islamization of the financial system by 1986 is raising unusual issues: it would appear that the main approach to housing finance may be through some form of shared equity mortgages which might not be convenient, given the structure of the national housing market. In Indonesia, progress is being made in improving the shelter delivery system in a general context of improved national economic and financial management.

The experience of international agencies

International agencies have no choice but to adjust to the new economic environment of expensive international capital and scarce domestic savings by encouraging more efficient management of scarce public resources and assisting in identifying better policies. The volume of resources that they can devote to shelter finance is limited; they are therefore placing increasing emphasis on the design of viable and adaptable systems that will not be heavily dependent on foreign savings in what is essentially a nontraded sector where foreign exchange risks should be avoided.

The 1960s were marked by the take-off of efforts in favor of housing in developing countries. A lack of familiarity with the facts and processes of housing markets in low-income countries sometimes lead to unwarranted attempts to transfer policies, institutions, and procedures from high-income, slow urban growth industrial countries to Third World countries.

The 1970s were marked by the emergence of a clearer understanding of the nature and scope of urbanization in developing countries and of its implications for housing markets. The rapid growth of the world economy and the expansion of public sector institutions facilitated experiments in the housing sector and did not render the cost of mistakes too heavy.

The 1980s is a period of slow growth, high inflation, and fluctuating interest rates, with heightened competition for domestic savings. At the same time well over 50 percent of GNP originates in cities in most TWC economies, and urban institutions must therefore continue to be modernized and better managed, given their impact on the efficiency of cities which themselves have an impact on the productivity of national economies. The needs of the various regions of the world are also growing increasingly diversified, in spite of the now global nature of international financial markets.

Conclusions

The most radical departure from earlier policies regarding the financing of shelter lies in the realization that public budgets do not have the resources nor public institutions the capacity to meet all the needs of low-income households and that subsidized conventional public housing will not provide sufficient shelter for all the poor. New policies must aim at the development of viable and flexible shelter production systems based on the comparative advantage of the public sector, which lies in institutional and regulatory support as well as in infrastructure investment, and of the private sector, which lies in the production of housing and the provision of financial services.

Rôle of regulators

The rôle of governments as regulators of the shelter sector begins with the formulation of a policy framework which is not exclusively focused on what the public sector does but also on the needs of the private sector which will remain the main source of new housing. The costs of regulations caused by delays and uncertainty in the processing of permits should be reduced. Building standards should be in harmony with prevalent levels of income.

Within the context of shelter policy, the four principles which should govern both the provision of shelter and the supply of basic infrastructure are household savings mobilization, affordability, replicability, and cost recovery. Without getting into detail, we can elaborate their meaning for the present decade as follows:

(1) *Household savings mobilization.* In order to provide cheap loans, government have too often insisted on low lending rates, which cannot be sustained without also imposing low deposit rates (often negative in real terms). A few lucky borrowers are therefore subsidized by many small depositors, whereas others are driven away from formal financial institutions. The only recourse is informal financing, which is often considerably more expensive due to various inefficiencies. Artificially low lending rates are therefore harmful to the growth of housing finance.

(2) *Affordability.* The only sustainable way to increase the delivery of housing is to encourage the supply of housing of a kind compatible with the income level of the country. High standards for a few will not help.

(3) *Replicability.* Whenever governments are engaged in the production of social housing in which they want to include an element of subsidy, such subsidy should be confined to the lowest income groups, and it should focus most heavily on infrastructure elements. Subsidies should be transparent, i.e., easily measureable, and the sources from which the transfer will have to be made should be clearly known. Direct government production of housing should be avoided as much as possible in favour of infrastructure.

(4) *Cost recovery.* If governments want to be able to expand their programs of infrastructure provision, they should educate the public about the fact that good infrastructure has to be paid for and that, without effective cost recovery, even the maintenance of the existing

capital infrastructure is in jeopardy. In addition, public sector institutions should be expected to follow sound financial practices in their internal management and to know exactly what and where their resources are.

Rôle of financial institutions

The primary requirement for a successful housing finance policy consists in a set of macroeconomic policies conducive to price stability and increased domestic savings. Without price stability, housing finance policies can only be of a short, remedial, and unstable nature requiring large government interventions for rather limited and ephemeral results.

As noted earlier, the biggest burden on developing viable and flexible housing finance systems is severe inflation accompanied by high and fluctuating interest rates. In fact, as a general rule of thumb, one can say that the volume of direct government subsidies and the scope for their misallocation is in direct proportion to the level of inflation. The weakness of approaches disregarding savings mobilization has been exposed during this period of economic slowdown combined with positive real rates of interest. Heavy subsidies provided through housing finance, insolvent public sector agencies, and continuing attempts at financing public activities through inflation have been the cause of major financial instability in quite a few countries in recent years.

The strategic variable for the expansion of housing finance systems is the mortgage interest rate level. Financial institutions should keep this rate close to the market cost of funds in order to be able to pay appropriate rates on deposits and to mobilize funds. Legislative frameworks limiting the flexibility of housing finance institutions should be reviewed to permit them to experiment with more varied mortgage instruments; as a rule, all institutions should use mortgage instruments with periodically adjustable interest rates. Financial institutions should develop their project appraisal capacities with respect to the financial, technical, and commercial characteristics of the projects submitted to them for financing.

Rôle of public developers

The existence of public developers is inevitable as desired instruments of public policy. Their priority should lie in the coordination and/or production of shelter infrastructure. They should be used to determine at each level of urban development what is the appropriate balance between public and private sector activities. They should play a leading rôle in the selection of appropriate technologies and in the development of innovative production techniques. They should also play a leading rôle in the improvement of shelter regulations, particularly in the improvement of building codes. They should aim to minimize their involvement in the direct production of housing units and in any case should withdraw from loan origination and investment in long-term mortgages and leave such activities to financial institutions.

III

Settlement issues

9

Spatial strategies, the settlement pattern, and shelter and services policies

HARRY W. RICHARDSON

Introduction

SPATIAL STRATEGIES may impact on the shelter and services sector by changing (1) the investment requirements for shelter, (2) the affordability of shelter for the population, and (3) the implementability of shelter programs. Investment requirements vary with the settlement pattern because both construction costs and standards vary over space. Generally, shelter and service standards decline with movement down the urban hierarchy and out from the core region to the periphery. The spatial variation in construction costs is less clear-cut because the decline in labor costs down the urban hierarchy and out from the core region may simultaneously be reinforced by the adoption of less capital-intensive technologies but offset by higher materials costs at more remote locations (except where it is feasible to substitute cheaper local materials). Affordability may vary over space because, although household income levels vary in the same way as shelter and service standards (i.e., down the urban hierarchy and out from the core region), these variations may not be symmetric. Whether shelter and services are more affordable in big cities relative to small towns or in the core region relative to the periphery depends on the specifics of the individual country. The capacity for implementation also varies in the same way as standards and incomes, because planning and technical expertise is disproportionately clustered in the primate city and core region and because most countries remain centralist administratively so that performance in execution tends to decline with distance from the seat of national government. The urban size and core–periphery differentials in costs, standards, incomes, and technical capacity are also repeated, sometimes in even more extreme terms, in the differentials between urban and rural areas.

Spatial strategies and the settlement pattern

Over the past 20 years a great many developing countries have adopted different types of spatial policies to alter the national settlement pattern. Although the ultimate goals of such policies are the general goals of society, such as promoting efficiency, reducing interregional and interpersonal income inequities, and improving the quality of life,[1] a recurrent set of spatial policy objectives is also involved. These spatial policy goals include slowing down primacy,[2] opening up new frontier regions and improving the economic prospects of lagging regions, promoting intermediate (secondary, medium-sized) cities,[3] and reducing rural–urban migration rates via a mix of rural development strategies. In spite of the cumulative experiences drawn from all regions of the developing world, there is surprisingly little consensus about how effective these spatial policies have been. Although it is true that in *some* countries the rate of growth of the primate city has declined, rural–urban migration rates have fallen, selected secondary cities have begun to grow faster than the national urban average, and core–periphery disparities have narrowed, it is unclear that these changes have been the result of spatial policies. Moreover, the incidence of these changes in trends have been too spotty to conclude that in general policy makers have demonstrated their ability to influence the geographic distribution of population and economic activity to a major degree.

A critical problem is that population distribution outcomes are the result of three sets of forces, the individual impact of which is difficult, perhaps impossible, to unravel. These forces are market trends and the dynamics of the aggregate development process; the implicit spatial impacts of macroeconomic and sectoral economic (and social) policies;[4] and explicit spatial policies. Although there is no satisfactory methodology available to separate out these impacts, it is widely believed that explicit spatial policies are the weakest of the three sets of forces. Moreover, implicit spatial policies more often than not conflict with explicit spatial policies with the result that efforts to redistribute population and economic activity are consistently undermined by the primate city and core region biases inherent in many sectoral policies – import substitution, subsidized urban services, internal terms of trade distortions, etc. Where dispersion trends have been observed, usually in middle-income countries with a reasonably diversified economic base, these reflect much more the onset of the polarization reversal process[5] than the effects of explicit spatial policies. Thus, it would be very misleading to ascribe shifts in the settlement pattern (and the distribution of economic activity) consistent with spatial policy objectives to the impact of policy.

Although the quantitative impact of explicit spatial policies is difficult to measure, with the result that it is not possible to draw conclusions with confidence about the overall effectiveness of these policies, there is considerable qualitative knowledge about what kinds of intervention have the better prospects for success.[6] Major lessons from experience include the following:

(a) *The timing of intervention is critical.* In the earliest stages of economic development, spatial redistribution policies are likely to be ineffective because there are few alternatives to the combination of a dispersed rural population and a high degree of urban concentration in a limited number of urban centers. Policies to promote industrial decentralization or the growth of secondary cities are likely to waste scarce investment resources (empty industrial estates are a widely prevalent symptom of such policy failures). Spatial policies are much more likely to be effective at intermediate stages of development when regional markets begin to cross scale economy thresholds, pecuniary diseconomies and congestion costs may be emerging in the primate city and core region, and polarization forces show signs of weakening spontaneously.

(b) *Urban and rural development policies are complementary, not alternatives.* Much of the historical debate about an appropriate focus for spatial policies reduced to a fight between pro-rural and pro-urban schools of thought.[7] Although much of this debate has been colored by ideology, practical implications include the optimal allocation of scarce investment resources between urban and rural areas and whether or not rural–urban migration rates have been excessive. The pro–urban school argues that rural outmigration may reduce the rural labor surplus, increase agricultural output per capita, and raise rural incomes via urban–rural remittances. In the urban areas the marginal product of the migrant may be higher than in the area of origin, per capita public services costs may be lower than in rural areas, in-migration may dampen urban inflationary tendencies, and urban agglomeration economies may be reinforced. The pro-rural school, on the other hand, argues that rural outmigration is selective in age and skills, results in the export of capital, worsens the rural income distribution because remittances dispro-portionately accrue to better-off families, and may raise the cost of public services in rural areas.[8] In-migration into urban areas, especially the primate city, generates significant social costs such as higher unemploy-ment, lags in shelter and services provision, congestion costs, dampening of income levels, and risks of political instability. Both these views are extreme. The results of rural–urban migration are more likely to be mixed and may vary substantially from one country to another or in the same country over time.

The optimal allocation of investment between urban and rural areas might be defined in terms of the investment allocation which distributes population between the two sectors in a way which maximizes the discounted stream of real income and welfare levels for all the national population, regardless of where they live and their migrant status. Unfortunately, this concept has little practical significance. Alternative distributions of population may imply similar per capita income levels and income distributions, and little can be said about the welfare implications of different national settlement patterns, i.e., the distribution of population among settlements of different sizes including the rural–urban split.

The pro-urban versus pro-rural debate is arid because the only viable spatial strategies for countries still experiencing moderate to high rates of population growth and modest levels of urbanization are comprehensive strategies with both urban and rural components. In most countries rural population growth cannot all be absorbed in the rural areas, so that a strategy for urban absorption is needed if rural per capita income levels are to rise above bare subsistence level. However, rural development strategies are also crucial to increase food output and to improve rural household welfare. The implications for rural–urban migration of a comprehensive spatial strategy are unclear and may vary widely from circumstance to circumstance. The effectiveness of spatial strategies has been weakened by the failure of Third World policy makers (and international and bilateral lenders) to recognize the interdependencies between urban and rural development strategies rapidly enough. An exclusive focus on rural areas (as in Bangladesh, for example) may result in severe underinvestment in urbanization which will restrict the future growth of urban absorptive capacity. Conversely, an exclusive focus on urban development may bring about similar results though by different means – an acceleration in rural–urban migration rates and declining food production per capita indices. A comprehensive spatial strategy needs to be based on the complementarity of metropolitan (especially primate), "other urban" and rural development policies. Although this point is increasingly being appreciated by policy makers, the problem of identifying an optimal spatial mix remains simply because resources are too constrained to allocate all the investment resources needed at each spatial level at each point of time. This problem is particularly acute in the shelter and services sector, where there are many examples of limited resources being invested in the primate city or in the rural areas when the middle tier of urban centers is neglected. Whatever the benefits of this allocation, it is not a strategy for minimizing costs (see pp. 221–30).

(c) *Policies to slow primate city growth may be justifiable and effective.* Efforts to slow down primacy are such an ubiquitous element of spatial strategies that Stark suggested that population distribution policies are merely a codephrase for primacy contol policies.[9] Slowing down the growth of the primate city remained a spatial policy goal for almost all the respondent countries to the Fifth United Nations Population Inquiry in 1983. This persists in spite of the long-established association between increasing primacy and faster GNP growth and the more recently discovered positive links between the growth of large metropolitan areas and social indicators (school enrolments, literacy, declining infant mortality, nutritional intake, life expectancy, falling birth and death rates).[10] Yet developing country policy makers may still be able to make a case for efforts to slow down primacy. First, although agglomeration economies persist in many primate cities and contribute to their superior efficiency, this may be offset by higher per capita absorption costs. For example, Karachi is about 60 percent more efficient than the national urban average but is 70 percent more costly.[11] Secondly, severe congestion costs and communication diseconomies have already developed in some primate cities (e.g., Lagos, Mexico City, Cairo) and may be avoided in others, provided that growth rates are not too fast. Thirdly, and especially important in the context of this chapter, shelter and services lags may become too severe at high primate city growth rates and per capita costs may soar because of implementation problems. Finally, a societal consensus that the primate city is becoming unacceptably large relative to the national urban system as a whole may be sufficient justification for intervening.

In practice, most policies to slow down primacy have been ineffective, short of chronic underinvestment in the metropolitan capital stock (Cuba) or the forced removal of population (Kampuchea). Where primate city growth has slowed down as it has it many cases (e.g., São Paulo, Mexico City, Lima, Cairo, Djakarta), it has usually been the result of spontaneous forces or the spillover of development beyond defined metropolitan boundaries.[12] However, the measures adopted (difficult-to-enforce control strategies, weak incentives for industrial decentralization, and half-hearted attempts to divert migrants to secondary cities) have been misplaced. A multipronged strategy with much greater prospects of success might include the modification of implicit spatial policies favoring primacy (reduction in big-city subsidies and the redirection of trade policy to favor resource and agricultural products are prime candidates); controls on employment growth, though fiscal disincentives (e.g., an industrial investment levy) may be more effective than industrial licensing schemes; redistribution of the national urban infrastructure investment pool in favor of other urban areas (the primate city share is often disproportionately large, reflecting the influence of the metropolitan elites, the rôle of the primate city as a symbol of prestige, and ignorance of the extent of services deficiencies in cities in the periphery); and higher taxes on metropolitan life (wage taxes, higher or more efficiently collected property taxes, or metropolitan residential taxes as in South Korea). This particular mix of measures has not been adopted, but the obstacles are institutional and political rather than technical.

(d)　*Rural development strategies should focus on raising rural per capita incomes rather than on maximizing rural retention.* Although holding people in rural areas may generate substantial savings in urban absorption costs, including shelter and services costs (see pp. 229–30), the priorities in rural development should emphasize raising food production and increasing rural per capita incomes, factors which are unlikely to imply maximizing the rural population share. However, rural development strategies are most effective when combined with small-scale urban strategies, thereby strengthening urban–rural linkages and improving rural accessibility to public services. Any application of population targets should refer to rural regions, including their urban centers, not to the rural population alone.[13] An income-generating rural development strategy might include *effective* land reform and other institutional changes that radically redistribute rural capital assets (land, irrigation systems, etc.); the adoption of efficient labor-intensive technologies and organizational improvements (e.g., multiple cropping) which simultaneously increase agricultural output and employment; the expansion of credit and technical assistance schemes to smallholders; replication of successfully integrated rural development planning (i.e., multisectoral strategies involving agricultural development, infrastructure provision, community development, and other social activities); and an array of interventions to strengthen rural–urban linkages such as investing in farm–to–market roads, the promotion of off-farm jobs in nearby small towns, the provision of public services in small towns accessible to the rural population, improvements in agricultural marketing facilities and services, and consolidation of the rural settlement pattern.

(e) *Promotion of small towns and intermediate cities (STICs) is a dominant theme in recent spatial strategies.* The third element in a comprehensive spatial strategy, paralleling primate city deceleration and rural development programs, is the promotion of STICs (or secondary cities). STIC strategies offer some modest prospects for reducing the rate of migration to the primate city, not necessarily by attracting new migrants but by retaining past migrants who might otherwise move on up the urban hierarchy.[14] The size and functions of a STIC may vary widely from one country to another, ranging from small urban centers of less than 20,000 in a sub-Saharan African context to a major city of several hundred thousand in a country such as Brazil. A STICs strategy should not be confused with a growth-center strategy: it stresses indigenous development, such as agroprocessing, small-scale industry, and the informal sector, rather than the attraction of large-scale industry from outside; it builds on the potential interactions between the growth of the city and the agricultural character of its hinterland; and it gives relatively more attention to social infrastructure than to an almost exclusive reliance on economic and industrial infrastructure. This last point suggests that a shelter and services investment program will be a key component of a STICs strategy. Resource constraints in countries with a sizeable number of STICs rule out simultaneous interventions in all cities. The problem can be resolved by selectivity (perhaps initially focusing on a limited set of high-potential centers), replicability (finding out which measures work best – especially institutional and managerial reforms with moderate investment requirements – to permit the rapid diffusion of learning benefits to cities outside the priority set), and phasing (substitution of new cities within the priority set over time to minimize the political costs of a highly discriminatory strategy).

A successful STIC strategy might combine several of the following elements: modification of the implicit spatial policies that discriminate against secondary cities (e.g., energy subsidies which favor big cities, industrial development incentives confined to large-scale industry); the spatial restriction of industrial incentives (preferably wage subsidies) to STICs; adoption of types of economic development assistance (increasing credit, technical assistance) more appropriate to the dominant economic structure of STICs, including measures to promote domestic import substitution; a focus on relieving major bottlenecks in economic infrastructure and avoiding the risks of a supply-led investment strategy; actions to strengthen the linkages between STICs and rural areas, such as intraregional transport and communication investments and the expansion of agricultural service facilities; the decentralization of selected types of public facilities (e.g., universities, colleges, government offices) to broaden the economic base and social structure of a limited number of STICs; migration policies to induce migration to STICs, including destination-specific relocation assistance, the diffusion of information about employment and income-generating opportunities in STICs, and an emphasis on the origin community rather than the individual as the target for migration assistance and information; more attention to public services provision in STICs, not only by reallocating them a higher share of the urban infrastructure pool but even more by efforts to improve local resource generation and the implementation of workable cost-recovery schemes; and strengthening local autonomy via the decentralization of administrative functions to local governments, building up local planning and management capacity,[15] and introducing fiscal reforms to broaden the revenue resources of local governments. This list of policy requirements is a long one, and no country has adopted the full range. In some cases, institutional constraints remain difficult to overcome. In many countries STIC strategies are too new for much progress to have been made in learning what works and what does not. But the scope for successful STIC strategies is enhanced by the finding that in some developing countries (Brazil and Pakistan are two examples) selected medium-sized cities are the most productive and most efficient locations in the economy. In such cases, the trade-off between aggregate efficiency and spatial equity which has plagued most spatial interventions may be avoided.[16]

A particularly important aspect of a successful STIC strategy is action to support the rôle of the informal sector[17] in the economic structure of secondary (intermediate) cities. A reasonable hypothesis is that the share of informal sector employment in total employment declines with increasing city size, though this is a subject of some debate,[18] not least because of the difficulties in defining the informal sector and the inadequacies of its measurement. Nevertheless, regardless of whether or not this hypothesis is valid, indirect evidence on the spatial concentration of formal sector activities, including large- and medium-scale manufacturing, the finance, insurance, and real estate (FIRE) sector and government, in large cities and the scattered and incomplete statistical and field survey data on the presence of informal sector establishments in STICs make it clear that the informal sector dominates the economic base of these cities. The more dynamic components of the informal sector, such as small-scale manufacturing and construction, confer substantial economic benefits in the form of labor absorption, lower production costs, capital savings, and skill training. Also, in spite of the difficulties of formulating and implementing policies to promote informal sector activities, they offer a more viable path for secondary city economic development than attracting large-scale formal sector establishments from the primate city and other large metropolitan areas, if only because there is not enough mobile industry to go round. Of course, the well known links between the formal sector and the informal sector imply that a development strategy based on the informal sector alone is inadequate.

The policy measures needed to promote small-scale workshops, informal construction, and other informal sector activities are quite different from the standard type of industrial decentralization and location incentive policies familiar in industrial development strategies. The latter bypass the informal sector establishments because industrial incentive schemes almost always have a minimum threshold size criterion which excludes small firms. Also, an informal sector strategy primarily aims at encouraging existing enterprises to grow or to become more stable *in situ* rather than attracting new plants to one location rather than another. There are also special difficulties in designing effective informal sector policies. Almost by definition, the unregistered status of informal sector enterprises means that they have no obvious lines of access to official assistance such as state credit. Informal sector commodity and service markets tend to be very competitive, and action to limit this competition may impair their efficiency and dynamism. Some even argue the most appropriate government intervention is "benign neglect" in contrast to the harassment from which informal sector establishments in some countries still suffer.

However, there is some scope for more active policies. In many cases, the provision of financial assistance is the most critical need. The obstacles are familiar: the lack of collateral, the reluctance of commercial banks to process applications for small loans, the risks of default. But in most situations credit for working capital (or, in the construction sector, for the purchase of building materials) is the key priority; relatively small sums with rapid repayment periods are involved, the availability of credit is more important than its cost (so processing costs can be recovered), repayments may be administered by a group (e.g., a cooperative, the community) rather than by the individual, and the rôle of government may be limited to providing seed capital for a loan fund and perhaps setting up a loan guarantee scheme. The problem of collateral is less critical if the sums borrowed are small and if credit schemes are implemented locally (perhaps by commercial banks) where local knowledge can permit a more satisfactory evaluation of the credit worthiness of a potential borrower. Also, if resources allow, financial assistance may be combined with technical assistance, though the human resource requirements of an informal sector technical assistance program may be beyond the capacity of many developing countries, at least if the program is to reach a sizeable number of secondary cities.

Other components of an informal sector strategy might include management training, job skill training, the provision of worksheds, and marketing assistance. But the benefits of management training are not always appreciated by very small firms, and job training programs may be less effective than existing on-the-job training. Worksheds may be helpful in cases where production is not home based, providing the costs, and the rents, are low and they are developed in ways which exploit economies of scale (e.g., in power supply). Marketing assistance may be critical in some sectors (e.g., handicrafts) where products are potentially saleable in international or national markets. Nevertheless, availability of credit remains the key element in any program to aid the informal sector.[19]

It would be wrong to expect too much from informal sector promotion policies in secondary cities. First, the impacts on the settlement pattern may be quite modest because the major impact of such policies is to raise the incomes of existing informal sector participants rather than to expand secondary city populations. Second, the demand for informal sector goods and services will remain limited unless there is simultaneous expansion within the formal sector. In view of the restricted scope for industrial decentralization outside the relatively developed middle-income countries, the major options for formal sector growth are increases in agricultural output, the introduction of agroprocessing industries, natural resource exploitation, dispersion of government employment, domestic import substitution, tourism, and the development of small-scale export industries. Only one or two of these options may be available in a particular city. Probably, the most general policy inference is the importance of increasing agricultural incomes as a means of increasing informal sector demand. Secondary city policies are usually most effective when combined with complementary hinterland strategies, and the informal sector is a potentially critical link between urban and rural activities.

Finally, and most important, the case for a STICs strategy should be made on positive grounds, i.e., the rôle that a dynamic STIC can play in revitalizing its surrounding region, rather than on the negative ground of controlling primacy. The annual population increment for a primate city might be equal to the sum of population increments of up to 90 or more STICs, so that marginal downward adjustments to primate city growth can imply growth rates for STICs that are possibly too high to be absorbed. Hence, the impact of a STIC strategy on slowing down primacy will be modest, if not negligible.

(f) *Fertility control remains in many countries a very cost-effective urbanization policy.* The importance of family planning and population control policies to relieving urbanization problems and, in particular, to slowing down primacy should not be underestimated. Natural increase is quantitatively more important than net migration in urban growth in general, and primate city growth in particular, in many developing countries. The cost per birth averted is very small (typically between 0.5 and 3.0 percent) relative to the average urban absorption cost per capita. A few countries – China and Sri Lanka are two examples – have demonstrated that successful attempts to reduce the rate of aggregate population growth are associated with low rates of urbanization (though the absolute scale of future urbanization in China remains massive, largely because of a huge rural population surplus resulting from agricultural productivity increases).

(g) *Other possible spatial strategy components are less likely to be successful.* Occasionally, spatial strategies may include other components which are frequently either costly or risky. Examples include:

(i) *Countermagnets.* A countermagnet strategy aims to reduce concentration in the primate city by creating a second core region elsewhere in the country. A countermagnet has to be based on a large city distant from the primate city. The problem is that countermagnets can rarely be found where they are needed. Countries with candidate countermagnets (e.g., Colombia, South Korea, the Philippines) tend to have reasonably balanced national urban hierarchies, but countries with very primate city size distributions (e.g. Thailand, Peru) have no suitable cities large enough to become an effective countermagnet.

(ii) *Development corridors.* These are an extension of the growth center approach, compensating for the limited viability of individual growth centers by stressing their mutual reinforcement when two centers are located at the end points of a development axis (e.g., a major highway) with the possibility that other centers may eventually thrive at intermediate points along the axis. The idea is that transport cost reductions along a given route function in much the same way as agglomeration economies, i.e., stimulating economic activity through lower production costs. Such a strategy requires high-speed travel along the axis, a large capacity for the transportation system, and end-point cities which are not too far apart (say, less than 300 km). These preconditions are absent from many developing countries.

(iii) *Relocation of the national capital.* This is a "one-shot" strategy which cannot be replicated. The most well known examples, Brasilia and Islamabad, involved huge resource costs, though Brasilia has, in conjunction with the rapid growth of the industrial metropolis of Belo Horizonte, changed the regional population distribution of Brazil and is largely responsible for the fact that Rio de Janeiro is now the slowest-growing metropolitan area in the country. Five African countries have capital relocation projects, though some of the projects are currently stalled because of tight resources. A preferable strategy to this high-cost option is the devolution of central government functions to lower levels of government or the physical relocation to a variety of sites of routine branches of government departments.

(iv) *New towns.* These are also a high-cost strategy, but they may be unavoidable in cases where new regions are opened up for development. In these cases costs should be minimized by the adoption of modest population targets, minimum infrastructure and public services standards involving sights and services for residential development and simple, utilitarian public buildings, and the introduction of sound cost-recovery schemes. In any event, new towns programs have minimal impacts on the overall settlement pattern.

(v) *Land colonization schemes.* The most dramatic example is Indonesia's transmigration program which accounted for five-sixths of *net* outmigration from Java to the Outer Islands (especially Sumatra, which received more than three-fifths of official transmigrants) between 1971 and 1980. But the costs of the program were high (US $ 7,000 per settler family), and there have been many failures because of poor land quality, irrigation problems, and inadequate infrastructure. Land colonization schemes elsewhere have been characterized by high costs and minimal impacts (in terms of numbers moved).[20] Assistance to spontaneous colonization may be more cost effective than government-sponsored schemes.

(vi) *Border region strategies.* Many developing countries pursue border region strategies for national security reasons, to support claims to disputed territory, or to keep the support of indigenous populations who straddle national boundaries (the Kurds, the Baluchis, the New Guineans in the Irian Jaya region of Indonesia, etc.). These regions receive disproportionate shares of public investment in an attempt to increase their populations to a size larger than justified in terms of economic efficiency. However, the reasons for this priority go beyond allocational efficiency. The motivations are largely political, though it makes economic sense to charge border residents, with their more elastic demands to remain loyal, a lower tax price per unit of public investment (cf. models of spatial discrimination).

Obstacles to implementation

The analysis above suggests that it is possible to design a sound spatial strategy. Nevertheless, successful experiences have been rare. A major source of failure has been the difficulties of implementation. These difficulties include:

(a) The policy instruments used are frequently weak or ineffective. Examples include capital-intensive industrial location incentives that are nevertheless too small to overcome the attractions of the primate city; direct controls on development which are easily avoided in developing countries; allocation mechanisms for urban infrastructure investments which are biased in favor of the primate city and on an equal per capita basis elsewhere; and rural development interventions which reinforce rather than change the existing distribution of income. Location-specific instruments such as labor subsidies (financed out of core-region taxes) or migration assistance to STICs and more emphasis on the dynamic components of the small-scale industrial sector (which dominate the economic structure of STICs) might be more effective.

(b) The long-run character of spatial policies clashes with the short-run preoccupations of policy makers. The overall distribution of population changes sluggishly, suggesting a 20-year planning horizon, but policy makers may expect results within the standard 4–5 year national planning period. The consequences are overambitious expectations, insufficient political will, and policy "flip-flops." The situation is exacerbated by the long and uneven lags of impacts behind implementation and the frequency of long-run impacts being different from short-run impacts.[21]

(c) In many developing countries, there are severe conflicts of interest among regions and cities or ethnic and religious minorities which inhibit a national consensus on spatial strategies. The tight constraints of political acceptability impair implementation of spatial policies.

(d) A myopic focus on the effects of explicit spatial policies can lead to an underestimation of the geographic impacts of overall development strategy and other implicit spatial policies. Unless policy makers can get the implicit spatial impacts that conflict with spatial policy goals under control, explicit spatial policies will fail.

(e) Highly centralized administrations cannot implement spatial policies efficiently because they lack knowledge of local conditions and the flexibility to operate in many locations simultaneously. Although many developing countries have introduced administrative decentralization schemes in the last decade, these vary widely in effectiveness from paper reforms at one extreme to a major devolution of functions and personnel at the other.

(f) Public investment resource constraints are a major limitation on attempts to redistribute investment and economic activity spatially. Palliatives include reductions in infrastructure standards; cost-recovery schemes to generate new resources for public investment; spreading risks and diffusing benefits spatially by favoring many small projects over a few large ones; substituting institutional and managerial reforms for capital projects (e.g., traffic management schemes rather than new highways); the use of self-balancing tax-subsidy schemes which do not make claims on public resources; and eliciting the support of international and bilateral donors for spatial policies. However, adoption of these solutions may be constrained by political factors.

Conclusions

This review of the influence of spatial policies on national settlement patterns suggests that there have been few successful experiences. Major problems have included overexpectations of what might be achieved; a too narrow focus on specific locations or approaches and its corollary, the failure to develop a comprehensive spatial strategy; the swamping of explicit spatial policies by conflicting implicit policies; the selection of ineffective policy instruments; bureaucratic inflexibility; and poor implementation capacity.

It is not difficult to outline the general preconditions of a sound spatial strategy. It should be a long-term strategy with a high degree of consensus and should be consistently followed from one government to another. It should be introduced at a time when the forces of spatial polarization are breaking down; a dispersion strategy is likely to fail in low-income economies at an early stage of economic development. Expectations should be modest; policy impacts will be marginal, at least in the short run. An effective spatial strategy requires simultaneous action in both urban and rural areas; raising per capita incomes for all households at all locations may be an appropriate goal. If spatial policy goals aim for dispersion, the strategy should be comprehensive in scope, combining measures to slow down the growth of the primate city and the core region (without using direct controls, if possible), the promotion of development in other urban areas (particularly STICs), and equity-oriented rural development programs. Other familiar spatial strategy components such as the relocation of the national capital, growth centers, development corridors, new towns, countermagnets, land colonization schemes and border region development programs can be recommended only in very special cases. These options are too costly in terms of investment (including shelter and services costs) and have minimal impacts on the national settlement pattern.

A reasonable assumption is that a successful spatial dispersion strategy would reduce investment requirements for shelter and services because of the belief that these costs are lower in per capita terms in STICs than in the primate city and lower in rural areas than in urban areas (costs may be higher at lower rural densities, but standards are lower and the expected range of services narrower). If this is the case, economies in shelter and services costs would provide an additional rationale for the pursuit of effective spatial strategies. However, a major issue is how large these shelter and services cost savings would be. This important question is examined in the next section of the chapter.

Spatial variations in shelter and services costs

Whereas hypotheses that shelter and service costs per capita vary over national space are plausible, until recently they remained merely hypotheses because no one had ever attempted to estimate the costs of alternative settlement patterns, at least at the national level.[22] However, in 1980–2 the National Urban Policy Study (NUPS) of Egypt, financed by US/AID, estimated shelter and service costs, as well as job creation costs, for 38 urban areas over 50,000 (accounting for 85.5 percent of the urban population).[23] The approach was modified and refined in a subsequent study, the National Human Settlements Policy Study (NHSPS) of Pakistan undertaken in 1982–4, which developed shelter and services costs per capita estimates for 293 urban areas larger than 10,000 (about 93 percent of the total urban population).[24] In both studies shelter and service costs were calculated for different urban settlement patterns, ranging from a trend scenario to alternatives reflecting different spatial policy objectives.[25] Two subsequent studies, for Bangladesh and Indonesia,[26] were on a much smaller scale, though the Indonesian exercise drew upon a research study which has made available the most detailed estimates of urban shelter and services deficits for any developing country to date (see Table 9.1).[27] In addition, the Pakistan and Indonesia studies generated some information on *rural* shelter and services costs to permit a comparison of relative urban and rural absorption costs per capita.

The methodology for estimating shelter and services costs per capita was more or less the same in each study. Essentially, these costs were measured by city size class drawing upon data from Master Plans, specific projects or, in NHSPS, by developing engineering cost estimates from a representative 25-hectare site in each city size class (with varying

Table 9.1   Shelter and services deficits: Indonesia, 1984.

Subsector	Percentage deficiency	
	Urban	Rural
housing	68	80
water	81	95
sanitation	51	90
solid waste	90	–
electricity	58	94
roads and drainage	27	–
health	48	50
primary education	25	50
secondary education	70	90
Total	64	85

standards and densities). A comprehensive list of urban services was included – water, sanitation, electricity, solid waste, roads and drainage, health and education. Interurban infrastructure costs, such as power transmission, highways, and telecommunications, were calculated separately and are excluded from the analysis in this chapter. The city size class data were then adjusted for city-specific characteristics, such as topography, drainage problems, and distance from construction material sources. Estimates were made for different standards in each city size class (reflecting variations in demand levels) and for alternative aggregate standards (in Egypt and Pakistan). The infrastructure costs also include components for the rehabilitation of existing infrastructure, slum upgrading, maintenance, and (in Indonesia) eliminating all urban service deficits. In some of the analysis which follows, the focus is on shelter and service costs per unit increase of population, but it should be noted that rehabilitation, maintenance, upgrading, and deficit correction are not minor items. In Indonesia, for example, they account for 47.8 percent of total urban shelter and services investment requirements and 83.7 percent of rural requirements between 1980 and 2000. In Pakistan, the corresponding urban share is 43.3 percent (the reduced standards cost case).[28]

The argument that aggregate shelter and services costs will vary with alternative settlement patterns is not very useful in itself unless these cost variations are quantified. The key questions from the point of view of assessing the impact of spatial strategies on the shelter and services sector are: what cost savings can be generated from the settlement pattern achievable by a successful strategy compared with the trend settlement pattern (or some other policy-relevant alternative)? How large are these cost savings relative to savings from policy changes in the shelter and services sector itself (e.g., reductions in standards)? These questions are critical for most developing countries because they suffer

from capital resource constraints which may make it very difficult for
policy makers to achieve shelter and services goals in both the near
future and the long-term future. The aim of this section of the chapter is
to shed light on these questions. The implicit hypothesis to be tested is
whether or not spatial strategies can be justified in terms of shelter and
services goals from the point of view of major capital savings. Obviously, a
sample of four countries is too small to permit more than provisional
conclusions, but unfortunately these are the only data available. The lack
of a sub-Saharan African case is particularly troubling, because it is
widely held that shelter and services needs are greater in most countries
of that subcontinent and that resource constraints are even tighter than
elsewhere.[29]

Table 9.2 presents some background data for the four countries which
affect the assessment of aggregate urban shelter and services costs. The
time horizon for the estimates varies between 15 and 20 years. Although
the growth rates of urban population vary widely within the range of 3.4
percent and 5.4 percent per annum and the share of urban in future
population growth varies between 52 percent and 70 percent, the more
interesting comparison is the annual average number to be absorbed in
urban areas. From this point of view, Indonesia and Pakistan have to
absorb about 2 million per year compared with 1.25 million in

Table 9.2 Population growth and resource pool parameters.

	Bangladesh	Egypt	Indonesia	Pakistan
Demographic data				
population growth rate				
total	2.11	2.50	1.89	2.89
urban	5.40	3.40	3.98	4.89
rural	1.27	1.55	0.96	1.76
urban share in future population growth (%)	52.2	69.9	61.9	61.0
Annual average numbers to be absorbed in urban areas (thousands)	1,241	973	1,950	2,068
Primate city share (%) in				
urban population	27.5	43.3	19.7	21.5
total population	4.1	20.8	4.4	6.1
Cities of 1 million-plus share (%) in				
urban population	38.5	56.9	34.2	38.5
total population	5.8	27.4	7.7	10.9
Resource pool				
GNP growth rate (%)	4.0	7.0	5.0	6.9
gross domestic investment/GDP ratio	0.17	0.29	0.263	0.142
Time horizon	1983–2000	1985–2000	1980–2000	1983–2000

Bangladesh and less than 1 million in Egypt.[30] The absorption problem in Egypt is eased by its smaller population and its higher level of urbanization, which implies a lower urbanization rate. However, Egypt is the most primate of the four countries which might have been expected *a priori* to have resulted in higher per capita shelter and services costs (this turns out not to be the case, though the assumptions underlying the Egyptian study have to be treated with caution, if not suspicion).[31] Although primacy varies among the other three countries, the share of million-plus cities in total urban population is very similar.

The other data in Table 9.2 refer to parameters used in estimating the investment resource pool, needed because all the studies involved a comparison of the total costs of future urbanization with available resources. This is used in this chapter to estimate shelter and services costs as a proportion of the investment pool. The GNP growth rates assumed are very optimistic for Egypt and Pakistan, mildly optimistic for Bangladesh, and about right for Indonesia. The investment ratios are reasonable, though they are slightly optimistic for Egypt and slightly pessimistic for Pakistan.

Before proceeding with the analysis, a brief comment is appropriate on the shelter and services deficits illustrated in Table 9.1. Although urban deficits are less severe than rural deficits, a situation where only 36 percent of the urban population is currently served on average is hardly encouraging. Moreover, Indonesia is a relatively favorable case because she pursued a basic needs strategy throughout the 1970s, supported by high oil revenues and a sensible approach to standards based on experience with the Kampung Improvement Programme (KIP). A general inference is that it would be dangerous to base estimates of shelter and services investment needs solely on the costs of accommodating future population; the requirements of the existing population have to be attended to as well. In Indonesia urban housing deficits are a little more severe, and rural housing deficits a little less severe, than the average for other services. But housing's share in total shelter and services costs is 53 percent in urban areas and 44 percent in rural areas; the corresponding urban share in Egypt is 30 percent and varies between 29 and 64 percent in Pakistan according to city size. The point is that housing costs vary more both within and between countries than services costs because of the wide choice in standards, size, and materials used, whereas services cost variations are limited by technological constraints (at least for a given standard of service).

City size, regional and alternative scenario (Tables 9.3–6) shelter and service costs data are available for some of the four countries. The anomalous results from the Egyptian data compared to the other three countries, where the results are very consistent with each other, need to

Table 9.3 Shelter and services costs per capita by city size (primate city – 1.0).

Indonesia		Pakistan	
Size class ('000)	Cost ratio	Size class ('000)	Cost ratio
20	0.500	10–50	0.292–0.325
50	0.487		
100	0.478	50–250	0.375–0.483
250	0.604		
500	0.828	250–1000	0.511–0.628
750	0.743		
1,000	0.798	3000	0.882
2,000	0.937		
3,000	0.937	5000	1.000
6,500	1.000		

Table 9.4 Regional differentials in shelter and services costs per increment of new population.

EGYPT

Region	Existing standards	Modified standards
Cairo	1.00	1.00
Alexandria	1.45	1.61
Delta	1.21–1.67	1.81–2.59
Canal	1.69–2.14	1.41–2.75
Northern Upper Egypt	1.10–2.09	1.24–2.38
Southern Upper Egypt	1.10–1.23	1.14–1.44
Remote areas	7.24	10.81

PAKISTAN

Region	Existing standards	Modified standards
Punjab	1.00	1.00
Sind	1.10	1.09
Northwest Frontier Province	1.15	1.07
Baluchistan	1.50	1.35
Lahore	1.92	2.29
Karachi	2.45	2.38
Islamabad	2.63	3.43

INDONESIA

Region	Cost ratio
Java (excluding Djakarta), Sumatra and Sulawesi	1.00
Djakarta	1.50
Kalimantan, Maluku	1.86
Irian Jaya	2.39

Table 9.5 Pakistan: shelter and services costs by scenario.

Scenario	Costs as ratio of "least cost"
least cost	1.000
decentralization	1.026
no change	1.097
preferred strategy	1.107
efficiency I	1.192
efficiency II	1.220
centralization	1.246

Table 9.6 Egypt: shelter and services costs by scenario.

Scenario	Cost as ratio of "least cost"
least cost	1.000
preferred strategy	1.022
trend	1.095
countermagnet (efficiency)	1.199
countermagnet (equity)	1.290
multiple growth centers (efficiency)	1.177
multiple growth centers (equity)	1.323
remote areas emphasis plus multiple growth centers	1.494

be addressed. No satisfactory explanation of the lower shelter and services costs per capita in Cairo is offered in the NUPS study. However, many of the major building materials suppliers are located in the Greater Cairo area, so that construction materials costs tend to increase with distance from Cairo. The NUPS study argued that Cairo is much better provided with infrastructure and services than the other cities, which reduces the incremental per capita costs, but it is unlikely that this influence would persist over the forecasting period as a whole. Land costs are excluded from the shelter and services costs esimates (as they are for the other countries, except for Bangladesh where land reclamation costs of flood-prone land have to be included as a resource cost) on the ground that land rent is a transfer, not a resource cost. However, if the public sector provides shelter and services and has to buy land at market prices, then clearly land expenditures make claims on budgetary resources. The inclusion of land costs would shift the shelter and services costs per capita gradient against Cairo. The most important factor is that the Egyptian study does not allow for sufficient city size class variation in standards because of the adoption of relatively high standards of services in smaller cities (this conforms with practice), but the assumption of similar housing costs throughout the country is implausible. A major problem is that NUPS did not make sufficient if any allowance for income-distribution effects, by assigning higher per capita costs to the high-income population which is disproportionately concentrated in Cairo (and Alexandria). Thus, there are reasons to be suspicious of the Egyptian data, although there may also be grounds for the belief that Cairo may be less costly relative to the national urban average than the primate city in other countries.

The cross-country comparisons of shelter and services costs are summarized in Table 9.7. Although costs per capita vary widely among the four countries (by a factor of more than five) because of difference in standards, labor and materials costs and, most of all, currency exchange relationships, the differences are much narrower when shelter and services costs per capita are expressed in years of median per capita income. However, these data indicate an affordability problem, especially where it takes 8–9 years of total annual income to cover shelter and services costs.[32] An interesting question is whether a decentralized settlement pattern would ease the affordability problem. In other words, does per capita income decline with decreasing city size more slowly than shelter and services costs per capita? To the extent that the Egyptian data are valid, affordability becomes more difficult outside Cairo because costs are higher and incomes are lower. No city size income data exist for Pakistan, but it is unlikely that incomes in small cities are as low as 30 percent of the Karachi level (and this conclusion is supported by household income surveys for Sind province, which separate out Karachi from "other urban"). Thus, in Pakistan affordability becomes somewhat easier with movement down the urban hierarchy. In Bangladesh, urban income data are spotty, but incomes in small towns are probably less

Table 9.7 Shelter and services costs.

	Bangladesh	Egypt	Indonesia	Pakistan
shelter and services cost (SSC) per capita (1983 US $)	480	2598	1197	1603
SSC in years of median income per capita	5.3	8.3	3.6	8.6
SSC/job creation costs per capita ratio	1.234	0.496	0.501	1.003
SSC requirements as percentage of resource pool	23.9	24.8	17.3	54.4
small city/primate city SSC per capita ratio	0.69	1.32	0.50	0.31
cost savings of decentralization				
as percentage of trend	4.3	−37.3	5.9	6.4
as percentage of centralized scenario	9.6	−49.4	8.9	17.7

than 70 percent of those in Dhaka and Chittagong, so that affordability is more of a problem in the smaller cities. The most detailed city size data are for Indonesia, though the size class boundaries are broad.[33] They show that shelter and services costs fall from 50 percent of median household income in the 10,000 size class to 39 percent in the 100,000 size class, then fluctuate until a trough of 35 percent in the 750,000 size class is reached, after which there is a steady rise to 47.4 percent in Djakarta.[34] Despite the city size class fluctuations, this evidence suggests that there would be no significant affordability benefits from promoting a decentralized settlement pattern. Instead, the data indicate a major affordability problem at the national level regardless of the city size distribution, even though the Indonesian situation is more favorable than in any of the other countries.

Returning to Table 9.7, at the aggregate level urban shelter and services investment requirements absorb a significant proportion of the available resource pool, ranging from 17 percent in Indonesia to 24–25 percent in Bangladesh and Egypt and to 54 percent in Pakistan. Moreover, the resource claims are more severe because the shelter and services costs needed to absorb population in urban areas cannot be divorced from the job creation costs needed to absorb the workers from each household into employment. These job creation costs (converted to per capita terms) are sizeable relative to shelter and services costs. In Bangladesh and Pakistan they are approximately of the same size, but in Egypt and Indonesia job creation costs are double the level of shelter and service costs. This doubles or trebles urban absorption costs per capita.

The final two lines of Table 9.7 represent the climax of the analysis in this section of the chapter. They show the shelter and services costs savings from the most decentralized settlement pattern relative to both the trend pattern and the most centralized pattern. The "most decentralized" and the "most centralized" settlement patterns are defined not in abstract terms but as the most feasible variants of these extremes, assuming plausible growth rates. For example, it would be wholly unrealistic to derive an urban settlement pattern for a developing country based upon very fast growth rates for cities in the smallest size class combined with very slow growth rates for the largest cities. There are no costs savings from decentralization in Egypt simply because populating the Remote Areas is so expensive. There are cost savings from a decentralized settlement pattern in the other three countries, but the surprising result is that the savings are so small (4.3–6.4 percent compared with the trend). The point is that the wide differentials in city size class costs are eroded by offsetting regional cost variations and constraints on how fast small cities could grow under a decentralized strategy. Comparing decentralized and highly centralized settlement patterns, the savings are somewhat larger (9–10 percent); the 18 percent savings in Pakistan are somewhat spurious because the centralization scenario assigns too fast a growth rate to many of the larger cities, especially Karachi.

Apart from their impact on the urban settlement pattern, spatial policies may also affect the distribution of population between urban areas and rural areas, though investment strategies for the rural sector and urban-oriented sectors – which are not specifically spatial – may have a greater impact. The finding that changes in the urban settlement pattern result in little more than marginal variations in aggregate shelter and services costs is not repeated when changes in the urban–rural population split are examined. The Indonesian data show that urban shelter and services costs per capita are 2.6 times more costly than rural shelter and services costs (housing is 3.2 times more expensive and services are 2.2 times more expensive, the smaller margin of the latter being partly explained by the fact that some services, e.g., solid waste disposal, do not have to be provided in rural areas). In Pakistan, the combined total of shelter and services costs and job creation costs per capita is 6.1 times more expensive in urban areas than in rural areas at current government services standards and 3.8 times more expensive with modified standards.[35] Although these results suggest that maximizing the rural population share is an effective means of saving on shelter and services costs, there are obvious constraints on how far such a strategy can be pushed. Adverse effects on rural per capita incomes and on GNP may be anticipated if a policy of maximum rural retention is followed. On the other hand, policies to increase permanent labor absorption in rural areas, whether on-farm or off-farm, can generate significant capital savings in shelter and services provision – savings which are large enough in some cases to more than pay for the investment needed to create the new rural jobs.

The conclusions of this analysis are clear-cut. Although the majority of the evidence suggests that shelter and services costs per capita increase with city size, this tendency is partially offset by increasing costs with distance from the core region. Moreover, the need to absorb large absolute numbers means that all cities and towns have to play a rôle in absorbing urban population growth. Measures to slow down the growth of a high-cost primate city too quickly are difficult to implement, not only because controlling primacy is difficult to achieve but also because it is often impossible for alternative urban centers to grow fast enough to absorb the would-be migrants to the primate city. These feasibility constraints mean that the costs savings from a decentralization strategy are much smaller than a look at raw data on city size and cost relationships might imply. The policy inference is that spatial strategies to influence the city size distribution cannot be justified in terms of shelter goals alone. The point is that the savings from spatial decentraliz-ation, about 4–6 percent of aggregate shelter and services costs, are significantly less than the potential savings from intrasectoral policy reforms, such as standards reduction. For instance, the Pakistan data suggest that a 50 percent cut in current government shelter and services standards could be achieved, whereas the Egyptian study estimated modified standards investment requirements which were 16 percent below current standards requirements. Shelter and services costs savings may be a welcome side benefit from successful spatial policies which promote dispersion of population into smaller urban areas, but they are not a necessary or sufficient reason for the adoption of such policies.

Policies which favor rural absorption rather than urban absorption, on the other hand, can generate major shelter and services costs savings. In this case, the risks are somewhat different: potential damage to GNP growth, dampening effects on rural per capita incomes, and ignoring the economic and social benefits of urbanization. However, well conceived labor-intensive capital investment programs in rural regions which create permanent jobs, both on-farm and off-farm, may be justified in terms of the shelter and services costs savings alone. For example, estimates in Pakistan suggested that a national farm-to-market roads program could not only employ 178,000 laborers for 20 years but would also save US $ 3.7 billion in net absorption costs (after deducting the investment costs of the program). Similarly, an expanded irrigation program could employ 241,000 laborers for 20 years and save more than US $ 6 billion, not to mention the gains in on-farm rural labor absorption and the expanded output associated with the expansion in the land area under cultivation. Thus, spatial investment policies which effectively give permanent employment to rural workers may be capital saving, even where sizeable investments are involved.[36]

The settlement pattern and other shelter issues

The conclusion that the investment cost savings associated with a more dispersed settlement pattern are quite modest ones does not address the suggestions implied in several other chapters in this volume that there are other dimensions of shelter and services provision that are impacted by the settlement pattern. For example, in Chapter 10, Hall makes it very clear that the supply of urban land is a major constraint on the rate of shelter and services provision. The greatest pressures on land and the most rapid increase in land prices are experienced in the primate city and other large metropolitan areas. The land supply problem may be alleviated in situations where urban growth rates are higher in small and intermediate cities than in the primate city. Not only are land costs almost invariably lower, but the available land is more centrally located, thereby involving a much shorter commute for workers with jobs close to the city center. On the other hand, it is the availability of serviced, not raw, land which counts, and there may be implementation capacity constraints in land development which are more severe in the smaller cities because of shortages of planners, engineers, and other professional skills or because of limited financial resources. There is some evidence that management costs are higher in intermediate cities and that these offset the lower input costs and land prices.[37]

Another handicap that small and intermediate cities face in shelter and services provision in a great many developing countries is the absence of formal housing finance institutions because of the failure of the existing housing bank to adopt a branching policy for reasons pointed out by Hardoy and Satterthwaite in Chapter 13, namely the limitations of management capability and the difficulty of attracting sufficient new savings. The latter problem may be exacerbated by the siphoning off of savings generated in the peripheral regions by the financial system to the core region and the primate city. In Pakistan, for example, all cities generate larger bank deposits than advances with the sole exceptions of Karachi and Lahore, where bank advances substantially exceed deposits. Even in the relatively rare cases where branching has occurred, its impact has been limited by the relative unfamiliarity with banking practices, less education, and lower incomes of the average STIC household compared to the metropolitan household.

As argued by Peattie in Chapter 11, it will be very difficult to reduce national infrastructure and service standards because of the "unintentional conspiracy". Nevertheless, within countries there are differences in standards among city size classes (as reflected in the city size cost differentials illustrated in Table 9.3). These differences reflect variations in demand (reflecting variations in household income by city size), changes in the density of development (the infrastructure cost savings from high densities in large cities are often outweighed by the higher building costs associated with multistorey construction), and differences in the choice of construction technology and materials. Lower standards are a major explanation of the lower investment costs of more dispersed settlement patterns. However, the enforcement of *national minimum* standards provides a floor below which standards in smaller cities cannot fall, even if justified in terms of demand and costs. Moreover, the lowest standards are not always the most appropriate because of the trade-off between capital costs and maintenance costs (see Ch. 4) and the

possibly more severe problems of generating the resources for infrastructure maintenance in smaller than in larger cities. Thus, although
policies to promote a less spatially concentrated settlement pattern will
tend to reduce *average* shelter and services standards, there are limits to
the gains to be achieved from this approach.

Although there is a wide degree of heterogeneity among countries so
that generalization is difficult, it is pointed out in Chapter 4 that
construction industries, including building materials firms, are heavily
concentrated in the major cities. This limits the access of smaller cities in
peripheral regions to the formal housing market and/or, as implied by the
data in Table 9.4, tends to increase construction costs there (unless
cheap local substitutes for building materials imported from the core
region are available) because of high transport costs. This reinforces the
argument advanced above (p. 214) that the informal construction sector
is very important in peripherally located small and intermediate cities. It
is, of course, even more important in rural areas where almost all housing
is informal and service provision may be minimal (see Renaud, Ch. 8). The
urban–rural population split is consequently very critical, because a
larger rural population share will reduce aggregate shelter and services
costs and relieve demand pressures for shelter and services in urban
areas. As suggested in many other chapters (Chs. 2, 5, 8, 11, for example,
and especially Ch. 15), the informal housing sector has a very positive rôle
to play in the shelter provision task facing developing countries.

This chapter does not discuss in any detail the issue of the spatial
reorganization of metropolitan regions which is treated by Hall in
Chapter 10. There is no doubt that spatial restructuring of the metropolitan
region, especially the primate city, may be an effective means of
minimizing the impact of negative externalities associated with gigantic
city size.[38] However, it is unclear what form this spatial reorganization
should take in developing countries. The development of a few major
subcenters, based on quaternary activities, mimicking the policentric
pattern of cities in developed countries, may be inappropriate for low-
income countries. In the latter cases the promotion of a larger number of
smaller subcenters with low-cost public facilities and many small
workplaces close to informal housing settlements may be critical to
reducing the inaccessibility of the big-city poor to jobs and services.[39]
There has been very little experience with this type of spatial restructuring.
More generally, there has been very little research on the comparative
costs of alternative spatial arrangements of the primate city (or other
larger metropolitan areas), and it is not known how much variation in the
capital costs of shelter and services provision might result from different,
feasible metropolitan spatial structures. In addition, developing country
metropolitan planners have had little success in implementing plans for

spatial reorganization, partly because of the weakness of land-use controls in developing country cities.

This brief review of some of the issues analyzed in other chapters does little to modify the conclusion that dispersed settlement patterns do not make it significantly easier to implement shelter and services goals.

Shelter and services policy implications

The major conclusions of the preceding analysis are clear-cut. Although it is not difficult to identify the components of a sound spatial strategy, very few countries have adopted such a strategy. Spatial policies have been weak and limited in scope, and their effects have almost always been outweighed by implicit spatial policy impacts. One of the problems is that the ministries and agencies responsible for urban development and spatial policies tend to be on the periphery of central government decision making and have little influence on the key actors, such as the minister of finance. Where national settlement patterns have changed in a desired fashion, the explanation has more often than not been the result of spontaneous market forces and the development process itself rather than of any identifiable spatial impact.

Even if spatial policies were more successful in dispersing population and economic activity, the payoff for the shelter and services sector is probably much lower than might be expected *a priori*. Although per capita costs decline with city size because of lower shelter standards and lower labor costs, these savings tend to be offset by higher materials costs in peripheral regions. Moreover, the constraints on how fast STICs can grow and the need for the primate city to play a continued rôle in urban population absorption imply that the cost savings from a *feasible* decentralized settlement pattern are much smaller (4.3–6.4 percent) than the raw city size data might suggest.

Furthermore, there do not appear to be major gains in affordability down the urban hierarchy as in many countries incomes decline as fast as per capita shelter and services costs. A shelter and services strategy giving priority to STICs would offer prospects for reaching a higher proportion of the target poor, but not significantly unless the affordability constraints could be overcome. This reinforces the argument that nationwide reductions in shelter and services standards are a much more effective shelter solution than changing the spatial focus of shelter and services policies. Significant investment cost savings could be obtained if the rate of urbanization were slowed down because shelter and services costs – not to mention job creation costs – are much lower in rural than in urban areas, but policies for rural population retention have to be implemented with extreme caution. First, it is dubious how effective such policies can be. Second, the private and social benefits of urbanization cannot be ignored. Nevertheless, investment programs which create *permanent* rural off-farm jobs at low incremental capital-labor ratios may be justified by their shelter and services capital savings alone.

The upshot of this discussion is that shelter and services goals cannot justify the adoption of a spatial strategy aimed at dispersion but that a modest side-benefit from the successful implementation of such a strategy may be shelter and services cost savings. Moreover, successful spatial policies may have other positive impacts on shelter policy. For example, changes in the national settlement pattern alter the spatial distribution of housing demand. The pressures of shelter demand will be especially critical in rapidly growing primate cities and other large metropolitan areas because it builds up competition for scarce urban land. This encourages land speculation and regressive income gains to urban landowners with severe consequences for the welfare of the metropolitan poor. Although this problem is theoretically solvable by urban land policy reform and institutional change, the hold of the metropolitan elites may be so strong that relief of the demand pressures by slowing down primacy may be a more effective solution. Once again, however, this would be a side-benefit of, rather than a justification for, attempts to slow down primacy. The regressive income distribution impacts of competition for urban land will be less severe in rapidly growing STICs because land values increase exponentially with city size in developing countries. However, the expansion of shelter programs in STICs is not free of difficulty in the form of local resource availability, implementation capacity, appropriate standards, and cost recovery. For example, even if formal public housing programs are ruled out as unsound and ineffective in low-income countries, it may not be easy to implement sites-and-services projects in medium-sized towns because of limited planning capacity. The technical simplicity of sites-and-services projects does not make them easy to manage. Moreover, housing finance institutions which are critical for making materials loans for self-help housing rarely have a dense national network of branch offices but are concentrated in the large cities. Forging links with commercial banks may be a sensible solution, but the institutional barriers are not easy to overcome.

There may be a rôle for spatial policies in influencing shelter costs. As suggested above, the shelter cost savings from decentralization are reduced by higher construction costs in the periphery. Thus, interregional transport investments will reduce construction costs in isolated regions if they suffer from shortages of local building materials. A final question is the appropriate rôle for shelter policy instruments as a component of the spatial strategy itself. Because there is no evidence that migrants in developing countries respond to the availability of housing, this rôle is inevitably small. At best, shelter policies can play only a modest supporting rôle in improving the effectiveness of the spatial policy mix (e.g. by including a residential sites-and-services component when a new industrial area is opened up). On the other hand, the same argument can be used to support "accommodationist" policies in primate cities which provide shelter and services for low-income households without a serious risk of inducing higher in-migration rates.[40]

These conclusions on the limited impact of spatial policies on shelter strategies should not be interpreted pessimistically. On the contrary, they shift the attention of policy makers to intrasectoral shelter policy solutions. These are much more tractable than settlement policies, though the institutional and political obstacles to effective implementation remain severe. Because shelter policy requirements are examined in depth in other chapters, it is appropriate here merely to list a few of the key priorities. Because resources are scarce and shelter and services requirements absorb a sizeable proportion of the aggregate resource pool (averaging 30 percent), a viable shelter strategy must be based on the supply of serviced lots at minimum standards rather than on formal housing programs. Reducing standards to affordability levels is the key to delivering shelter and services to all the population within aggregate resource constraints. To be effective, cuts in standards may have to be combined with restrictions on the shelter and services consumption of the rich, such as lot size restrictions and limits on square meters of living space,[41] and with major reforms in urban land policy. Implementation of cost recovery schemes is critical to generate more resources, to reduce big-city subsidies, and to improve equity.[42] A sound cost-recovery scheme, backed up by institutional reforms such as shelter and services loans for low-income households, will permit cost recovery from a high proportion of households (typically down to the 20th percentile), and the need of the very poor can be accommodated via cross-subsidies. Some attention to rural shelter and services needs *in combination with* effective job creation strategies for rural areas can be justified because of savings in urban absorption costs.

With the possible exception of the last, there is nothing particularly novel about these policy requirements. Some of them have been tried in some countries, and their success has been demonstrated. Although affordability remains at least a medium-term constraint in low-income countries, the shelter problem is primarily neither economic nor technical. It is institutional and it is political. Unfortunately, these are the barriers to policy shifts which are most difficult to overcome.

10

Metropolitan settlement strategies

PETER HALL

THE MOST DISTINCTIVE feature of 20th-century urbanization is the growth of very large urban agglomerations of 1 million and more people, which by the year 2000 are predicted to contain 43.4 percent of the world's population.[1] That proportion, further, will be equalled or exceeded in several parts of the developing world: in South Asia it is predicted to be 41.2 percent, in East Asia 42.5 per cent, in Africa 46.3 percent and in Latin America, 56.4 per cent.[1]

The argument of this chapter, however, is this growth does not represent merely a challenge; it also represents an opportunity. As emphasized by Dr. Ramachandran in the Foreword of this book, investment in human settlements is a productive activity, which creates large numbers of jobs at low capital cost in the construction and service sectors.[2] This is nowhere more true than in the great urban agglomerations of the developing world, which already contribute between 30 and 80 percent of the gross national product (GNP) of their nations.[3]

Therefore, this present chapter argues, far from limiting the growth of such agglomerations we should actually be facilitating it. But we should also be guiding the growth, so as to maximize the economic gains it can bring while minimizing the negative externalities.

More particularly, the chapter will argue six propositions.

(1) There is emerging evidence that all nations – developing and developed – have tended to follow a similar path of urban evolution:

beyond a certain point in development, the degree of primacy tends to weaken, and urban areas, led by the leading urban region, begin to deconcentrate people and activities from core cities to surrounding suburban rings. This process *eventually* leads all the world's great cities to solve for themselves their most acute problems of congestion and overgrowth. But the process is not invariable or inevitable; there are many variations in the timing of the reversal.

(2) There are two main reasons for planners to intervene in this process. There is the problem of large and growing inequality between regions, and there is the problem of overgrown major cities. These two problems are different, though related. The first may be difficult to solve, except in the long run; it may be necessary to accept the fact, which means continuing growth of the central urban region. The second may best be solved, or at least mitigated, by better internal ordering of the activities within this region.

(3) In the 20th century many now-developed nations have sought to channel or to influence the growth of the giant city region, either by steering this growth to neighbouring satellite towns or new towns, or by longer-distance decentralization to planned growth centers in other regions of the country. Such attempts have met with varying degrees of success. In general, short-distance deconcentration policies appear to have been more successful than long-distance decentralization policies, probably because they went with the prevailing trend rather than against it. However, no single solution is itself likely to be succesful.

(4) Most importantly, great care is needed in trying to apply this historical experience of the developed nations to the solution of the problems of today's developing world. Today's developing cities experience problems that are differnt in kind from the great cities of the developed world a century ago. Further, when the former initiated their urban growth-management policies, these developed nations had per capita income levels close to those of middle-income countries today; this gave them sufficient resources to invest in physical and social infrastructure. These conditions obtain in some, but not all, developing countries today. The most significant difference is that today's developed nations then had a better developed administrative–legal system for their planning policies than many developing countries now possess. Therefore, only a few developing countries may find it feasible to copy the path of the developed nations.

(5) Consequently, most of today's developing nations may find it necessary or desirable to develop less dramatic solutions for accommodating urban growth, based on low-cost, low-technology

methods in the areas of the urban economy, housing, land, and transportation. Some feasible strategies along such lines, based on recent experience in developing cities, are outlined.

(6) Though these examples appear promising, they may not be universally applicable. More work is needed to research further solutions and variants of existing solutions applicable to the very different economic, social, administrative, and cultural contexts that exist in the developing world.

A general model of urban development

We first need to try to resolve a basic issue of urban development: How far do nations generally follow a similar path of urban evolution, which planning policies can affect only superficially? If this were so, it would profoundly affect our notions of what could be done and when it could be done.

Any such account of the urban development process needs simultaneously to incorporate a number of elements. Firstly, the rate of overall urban growth, which is defined as a product of the overall rate of population growth and the rate of urbanization. Secondly, the distribution of the urban population across size classes, for which the well known primacy rate (defined usually as a ratio between the first city, or the first two or three cities, and the next following cities) is a crude but useful index. Thirdly, the distribution of population within urban areas as between central city and suburban ring, measured by the rate of centralization or decentralization. It is common in developing the second and third of these analytical measures to employ a standardized urban definition such as the well known Standard Metropolitan Statistical Area of the United States Census.

Work on international urban systems[4] suggests strongly that such a general model exists. In its early stages, the predominant direction of movement is inward from regional periphery to core, upward from lower- to higher-order metropolitan areas, and inward from suburban ring (at this stage often still rural) to urban core. Then, progressively, there is a series of what Richardson[5] calls "polarization reversals." Growth first washes out from the central city into the surrounding ring, which begins to grow faster than the city; soon after, the city's population contracts. This process is initiated by the leading (primate) city. Then, at about the same time, the growth of this primate city slows down; second-order provincial cities begin to grow faster, so that the index of primacy begins to fall. Eventually, the slowing of primate-city growth is such that its whole urban system begins to lose population – a stage that has now been reached by a number of big cities in the United States and in western Europe.[6] Finally, this process spreads to urban areas generally, leading to an actual reversal of long-continued farm-to-city migration: the condition that Vining has called the Clean Break with the Past.[7]

For the advanced industrial nations, the model seems generally to hold. But for the newly industrializing nations, the evidence is less sure. Analysis by the present author suggests that though a few had reached peak primacy before 1970, most were expected to do so between 1975 and 1990.[8] From very partial and somewhat unsatisfactory data, it further appeared that several of the big metropolitan areas of the newly industrializing world had actually reached the state of decentralization as early as 1950–60, suggesting that perhaps these countries (Greece, India, Mexico, Venezuela, Brazil) had arrived at the first stage of polarization reversal by this time.[9] This indeed was an almost inevitable feature, given the very large absolute size of many of these city-regions and their continuing very rapid growth rates. Other evidence indicates that deconcentration was evident not merely in the distribution of the residential population, but also in the distribution of employment in manufacturing industry and in associated services, which tended to be concentrating in new industrial zones in the suburbs. In this regard the patterns of change in some leading Third World cities strongly resembled that of some of their First World counterparts some 50 years earlier, in the 1920s and 1930s.

Two points should be emphasized about the model. First, it is clearly not mechanical in character, but is dependent on the complex interaction of a set of forces – economic, social, cultural, technical. These forces operate in part differentially from one country to another. Thus the experience of industrialization is a common element, occurring first in one country, then in another. But in part they may operate simultaneously, or nearly so, in countries at very different stages of economic development. Thus the advent of modern mass transportation, and later of the automobile, tended to occur everywhere at about the same time, albeit affecting different numbers of people as between rich and poor countries.

Secondly, though the model may work for an individual country's development over the course of time, it may not work equally well for a point-of-time comparison between countries. Richardson has established the rather remarkable fact that there is no clear relationship between GNP per capita and the degree of urban primacy, as measured by international comparison at one point of time: the developing countries in fact display striking contrasts in primacy, all the way from Mozambique's 88 to India's 6.[10] But such variations do not contradict the general rule whereby in any country, over time, primacy first rises and then falls.

Thirdly, it is necessary to underline the fact that primacy trends on the one hand, absolute urban size on the other, are very different things: the most acute problem of managing the very large city tends to occur in countries like Venezuela and Mexico, where the balance of evidence suggests that the peak of primacy may now have passed.

The conclusion is that *eventually* the general laws of urban dynamics will lead to deconcentration from central core to suburban ring within the giant urban region; *eventually* they will lead to a slowing down of the region's growth at the expense of second-order cities. But there is nothing mechanical or inevitable about the timing of this process: it may occur sooner or later. Therefore, so long as public policy intervenes at the right stage – somewhat ahead of the trends, but not too far ahead – it can hope to influence the timing; it can also influence the character of the process.

The rationale for intervention

Against this background, we can now ask why planners have sought to intervene to check or reverse these trends. Viewed historically, the reasons fall into two main groups: one concerned with issues of national and regional disparities, the other with issues of large-scale metropolitan management.

At the national and regional scale, the main concern has been with unequal development. As Williamson first showed in 1965, during the course of development interregional income disparities tend to increase.[11] The leading city-region tends to aggrandize to itself a disproportionate part of the innovative impulses, thus attracting scarce capital and skilled labor as well as entrepreneurship. The result is the well known condition of circular and cumulative causation, identified by Myrdal and Hirschman.[12] This cannot but lead to large differences in average per capita incomes between these leading regions and the still-backward rural peripheral regions, albeit with much greater internal income disparities in the former.

These differences appear to be greater than those recorded by now-developed nations about a century ago. The resulting question is: What is the most effective way to reduce these inequalities? Is it through the conventional policy of trying to decentralize activities from the highly urbanized core region to the still-rural periphery? Or is it – a heretical view until recently, but now increasingly argued[13] – by accepting the fact of uneven development and actually facilitating migration from periphery to core?

Here the second problem becomes relevant. This, the metropolitan problem, concerns the alleged negative returns to urban scale. Very big urban areas, it is argued, generate negative externalities in the form of air and water pollution; highly segregated distributions of residential and industrial areas, resulting in long and arduous journeys to work; problems of providing adequate basic services such as water and drainage; and a vicious circle of land shortages and land speculation, which raises the costs and increases the difficulty of providing adequate shelter for low-income people. Large sums are demanded for new freeways or metro systems, water aqueducts and sewers, purification plants, and air-control schemes. The national exchequer is pressured into meeting these demands because of the penalty for urban breakdown. If the rate of growth of the first city were curtailed, it is argued, many of these costs could be avoided.

Again, some of these problems are similar to those experienced in the cities of the now-developed nations earlier this century, albeit on a much larger scale. The obvious question for policy is how far the solutions for orderly urban growth, developed by those nations then, are applicable to the cities of the developing world now.

The problem of urban externalities, then, is far from new; it has been exhaustively discussed in the literature over the last two decades, without much resolution. In the first place, it is at least possible that big cities produce higher incomes for their inhabitants, and so maximize national money income.[14] It may be that even if true this is outweighed by negative externalities, though if this is the case it is unclear why migration should continue to the primate city on the scale that is currently observed. Some observers, notably Richardson,[15] have argued that we should be very cautious in our attempts to devise a national urban development strategy.

If this is the case, the argument goes on, then it may be a more sensible policy – at least for a time – to let the leading city-region continue to grow, but to try to guide that growth so as to promote economic efficiency and to reduce negative externalities. This might involve guiding the local deconcentration process – which, as already seen, tends to be occurring spontaneously – so as to reduce the need for long and costly commuter journeys, to reduce the degree of traffic congestion, and to reduce the total volume of environmental pollution. Because such policies go with a trend that is occurring anyway – so the argument runs – they may have a better prospect of success than policies that go against the trend. That is the fundamental argument of this chapter.

I am not opposed to the argument that it may also be right to promote second-order centers as growth poles. Since, after a certain point, these cities tend to grow even faster than the leading city, it may be possible to anticipate and to encourage this process. However, the evidence –

admittedly fragmentary – suggests that only a limited number of such centers, located in the more favoured peripheral regions, will join in it. Conventional wisdom suggests that, as soon as possible, the growth of such centers should be steered outwards into the surrounding urban regions. But the empirical evidence suggests that this may occur quite late in the development process. Richardson's analysis (in Ch. 9 of this volume) has shown that shelter costs in such second-order cities are only marginally less than in the first-order city; but it does not cover negative externalities (notably traffic congestion costs) which are by definition smaller in these medium-sized cities than in the giant city. So there may be a strong argument for actually concentrating growth in them, thus increasing the degree of intraregional inequality and encouraging local farm-to-city migration. In this way, so the argument runs, migrants may generate incomes which can in part be passed back to families remaining in the nearby areas, while they are also available to supplement farm labor at critical periods such as harvest time.

All this accepted, the critical question concerns the timing of the process. The empirical evidence seems to suggest that the deconcentration of the first-order city may come somewhat earlier than the accelerated growth of the second-order cities. If that is so, even though the two processes may overlap in time, the conclusion is that the *first* effort should be to promote the orderly deconcentration of the giant metropolis, the *second* to promote the early development of selected second-order cities, and the *third* to promote spread effects into their rural and small-city hinterlands. Therefore, immediate planning efforts should be concentrated on guiding the growth of the primate metropolis in order to exploit its income-generating potential and to reduce, as far as possible, the concomitant negative externalities. Accepting that argument, in the remainder of this chapter we shall concentrate on that first priority.

The rationale applied:
strategies for deconcentration

These arguments are not merely well rehearsed in the context of the developing nations; in the developed nations they go back much further, indeed at least to the beginning of the 20th century. Long before the growth of the giant city became a major problem in the developing world, it was perceived as such in the industrialized world. Between 1890 and 1940 many of the now-developed nations were in fact going through the same phase as is today evident in the Third World; they were the newly industrializing countries of their day. As this occurred, so their great cities exploded. Greater Berlin grew from 1.6 to 4.3 million; the Ruhr coalfield from 1.5 to 4.3 million; Moscow from 0.8 to 4.1 million. In an even shorter period, 1900–40, the New York metropolitan district grew from 4.6 to 11.7 million.[16] Though the absolute sizes did not compare with present-day Third World examples, and the rates of growth were also lower, nevertheless, in terms of the perception of the problem at the time, there are clear similarities.

Faced with this perceived problem, First World planning theorists and practitioners developed a number of alternative strategies. Though the majority remained on paper, some were actually attempted and remain on the ground to be judged. We can summarize them thus:

(a) short-distance decentralization to satellite towns remaining part of the urban agglomeration;

(b) longer-distance decentralization to new towns (garden cities) outside the sphere of influence of the agglomeration;

(c) axial or corridor developments along main lines of transportation connecting the agglomeration with other cities;

(d) attempts to promote growth centers embodying industrial and urban development in peripheral regions;

(e) schemes of rural regeneration through integrated development schemes combining agriculture, industry, and power development.

(a) Satellite developments

Overwhelmingly, these were the preferred form of planned development, alike in the giant metropolis and in smaller cities. Some of the classic examples were in such smaller cities, such as Ernst May's *Trabantenstädte* (satellite cities) in Frankfurt am Main in the late 1920s or Barry Parker's Wythenshawe outside Manchester, in the 1930s. Some, however, were planned for the giant metropolis either by industrial complexes or by social housing associations, such as the great *Grossiedlungen* of Berlin of the 1920s (Siemensstadt, Bruno Taut's Onkel-Toms-Hütte, Taut and Martin Wagner's Britz), or Henri Sellier's so-called *Villes Nouvelles* around Paris in the same period. They were essentially housing schemes, but with extremely well developed community and open-space facilities, connected to the parent city by good public transport. The Stockholm suburbs, built between 1950 and 1975 under Sven Markelius's 1945 plan, and grouped like beads on a string along the lines of the new Metro (*Tunnelbana*) system, are of the same genre.

The satellites can be seen as a compromise solution that recognised the difficulty of more radical answers. But their advocates were enthusiastic about them in their own right. The *Stadtbaurat* of Berlin in the 1920s, Martin Wagner, believed that they should be physically and functionally integrated into the fabric of the city, and so they are; unlike May's Römerstadt or Parker's Wythenshawe, they are not physically separated from the main urban mass by a green belt but owe their coherence as communities to the skillful way in which their designers have grouped the buildings to focus on a central rapid-transit station or shopping center. Markelius's suburbs have exactly the same quality: they are separate units but are parts of the city.

(b) Garden city–new town solutions

The problem with this solution is to define it clearly as against the satellite alternative. Many so-called garden cities do not fulfill the formula proposed by Ebenezer Howard in his classic study of 1898:[17] they are not fully self-contained places for living and working. The two garden cities built under Howard's own influence, Letchworth (1903) and Welwyn (1920), clearly do. So do the new towns built around London by government promotion after World War II, from Stevenage (1946) onwards. All are more than 30 km (20 miles) from the center of London, that is outside the city's commuter sphere at that time (though no longer). Hampstead Garden Suburb (1907) is, however, clearly not a garden city: neither is the early German imitation, Gartenstadt Falkenberg outside Berlin, though Hellerau outside Dresden probably deserves the title.

Other cases are more difficult. Clarence Stein's famous Radburn in New Jersey, 25 km (15 miles) from Manhattan, was a satellite rather than a garden city. So essentially are Rexford Tugwell's three greenbelt towns of the early 1930s – Greenbelt (Maryland), Greendale (Wisconsin), and Greenhills (Ohio). None offered independent sources of work; all are now physically part of their parent cities. So the United States does not have true new towns, except perhaps for the miniscule Norris (Tennessee), built in the early 1930s as part of the Tennessee Valley Authority (TVA) project.[18] In fact, the remarkable fact about the garden city is how rare a species it is; few exist outside its country of origin. Even there, the London new towns account for a very small proportion of all the new housing built around London since World War II.[19]

(c) Axial or corridor developments

This again is a *rara avis*. The classic case is Arturo Soria y Mata's *Ciudad Lineal* outside Madrid (1882), which was started by a private company but was not completed as planned. The important point about the linear city was that, despite its unconventional form, it was a pure suburban commuter development; it never made any pretence to being anything other. In the 1930s Le Corbusier frequently advocated the development of linear garden cities which would have been truly self-contained, since each element would have had its own factory unit and associated housing; but, in common with most Corbusian plan-making, none was ever realized. Neither were the applications of Corbusian ideas by the Russian urbanist school of the 1920s;[20] nor the later espousal by members of the Modern Architectural Research (MARS) group in their celebrated 1939 plan for London, which remained a footnote of planning history.

Linear planning received its greatest boost after World War II in the celebrated 1948 Finger Plan for Copenhagen and its later developments.[21] Here, at last, planned urban units were slotted together along main lines of communication. Yet the original plan essentially went no further than Soria's vision of 66 years before: it was a scheme for orderly suburban development within the continuing framework of a radial–concentric city. The 1959 plan for Washington, D.C., which would have been a good deal more radical, foundered on the total lack of any means for implementation.

The high point of radial planning, however, came in the second half of the 1960s. The celebrated 1965 *Schéma Directeur* for the Paris region conceived of eight giant new cities (later reduced to five), partly but by no means entirely self-contained, strung along two parallel axes, one north and one south of the original agglomeration. They were to be joined with each other and with the center by concentric motorways and by a radial H-shaped rapid transit system (RER), following the lines of the two axes.[22] This brilliant conception, part satellite, part new town, part axial, has been very largely realized in the subsequent two decades. Whatever the qualifications about the quality of implementation, there can be no doubt that it represents a particularly ingenious solution to the problem of organizing very rapid growth for a very large metropolis.

The other case represents only a partial-success. In 1967 the British South East Regional Planning Council published a strategy for the development of the region around London, based on an appreciative analysis of the Paris, Washington, and Copenhagen plans[23] and suggesting an axial form of development along the main radial communication corridors which would link older towns, the new towns, and planned centers. In the event, the British government did not accept the proposal but instead commissioned another study which, published in 1970, took on some of the features of the earlier strategy and has provided the overall framework for planning in the region ever since.

Thus in the London region, as in the Paris region, it can be said that axial planning has exerted a profound influence. The physical expression is, however, very different: in the Paris plan, large new town units are planned close to each other and to the central agglomeration, essentially forming part of a single polycentric urban mass; in the London plan, there are large polycentric groupings along the main corridors, quite distinct from the parent agglomeration. The first represents a conscious bias in favor of the growth of the giant agglomeration; the second a continued attempt to restrict it by the development of decentralized countermagnets.

(d) Provincial growth poles

Still, although outside the daily commuting radius, such British counter-magnets – at distances up to 130 km (80 miles) from London – would form part of a wider functional metropolitan reality. They need to be carefully distinguished from another strategy: the attempt to build up growth poles as centers of quite remote peripheral regions, as an initial focus of development there. Such a strategy has a long theoretical history, going back to the classical 1940s work of François Perroux on the *pole de croissance* and its subsequent development by Walter Isard and others in the United States.[24] However, its actual applications in the advanced industrial world have been very few. The Howardian garden city concept, though it was avowedly intended to help revive the rural economy as well as to provide orderly deconcentration of the giant city, was never consciously seen as an agent of regional development. The development of territorial production complexes, in the Soviet Union in the 1930s and subsequently, came closer.

British regional development policy after 1945, despite the energy that went into it, never developed a very specific spatial focus: new towns in the development areas were each designated for rather specific local purposes – most for overspill from the provincial cities, a few as a means of restructuring colliery settlements. Perhaps the clearest application came appropriately in France with the designation in the 1960s of eight *metropoles d'equilibre*, each based on a major provincial city or group of cities, as a means of combating the excessive concentration of national life in Paris. The *metropoles* have been used as a means for channeling national investment into the regions via the regular four-year develop-ment plans, and the effects of the policy are now clear to see on the ground in such urban-industrial complexes as Lyon-St. Etienne or Marseille-Foss.

(e) Rural development programs

Here we can identify a great variety of programs in a number of advanced industrial countries, ranging from the pre-World War II TVA to the Johnsonian Appalachian Development program in the United States, and embracing also the policy for encouraging small rural development centers in the remoter rural areas of the Federal Republic of Germany.[25] All have had the general objective of trying to reduce the rate of outmigration from lagging rural regions and of simultaneously trying to raise local incomes through the injection of new forms of economic activity, located chiefly in the existing country towns. Blacksell[25] concludes that the German programs seem to be having some success, though it also needs emphasis that this may partly result from the outmovement of people from the cities into the countryside.[26]

Applying the lessons: Can planners learn from history?

To try to reach a single verdict about such varied programs is difficult, even foolhardy. But certain limited conclusions can be drawn.

The first is that there is a very basic distinction between metropolitan deconcentration policies (satellites, new towns, and axial growth) and policies for growth centers in lagging peripheral regions. The former are relatively common, the latter much less so. Even when pursued in the same country, they seldom are seen as part of a comprehensive program of regional and urban planning. Metropolitan deconcentration policies are typically conceived as primarily physical planning schemes, albeit with social and economic objectives. Development policies for lagging regions are seen largely in economic terms, generally involve a strong element of subsidy, and seldom have a very strong spatial strategy.

The second conclusion is that within the bundle of metropolitan strategies satellite and other planned suburban developments tend to dominate. Few cities in the developed world have seen the need for longer-distance deconcentration. Britain's new towns are in this regard a unique historical anomaly. It must be remembered, though, that most of the cities concerned were – and still are – much smaller than their equivalents in today's developing world – a point to which we shall return below.

To what extent, then, does the planning experience of the First World cities prove relevant or helpful to the present dilemmas of Third World ones? There are both significant similarities and important differences.

The first similarity is that planners in both contexts were dealing with urban populations that were increasing rapidly, albeit at a declining rate: the demographic transition had begun to occur. This, coupled with rural-to-urban migration, helped produce urban growth far in excess of previous experience.

The second is that in both cases planners were dealing with the problems of the poor. Per capita incomes in European cities in the 1920s were comparable with those in low-income to middle-income countries today. Housing conditions in both eras were bad, with people living at very high densities per room or per dwelling; the difference, arising in part from climate, is that in early 20th-century Europe they lived mainly at very high densities in apartment dwellings whereas now they live in low-density autonomous housing. In both cases, many of the poor worked in insecure casual employment, or in what has come to be known as the informal sector. Indeed, in both contexts it can be said that because of the lack of advanced social security the bulk of all employment was informal in today's sense.

The third is that, however low, per capita incomes were nevertheless rising. This is evident for the developed world from 1895 to 1914 and from 1924 to 1930 and for the developing world between 1960 and 1973. Growth produced buoyant tax revenues that could be applied to social programs.

But there were also differences. The first is that though rates of growth might be similar, absolute sizes were not. Greater London in 1900 had about 6 million people, Greater Paris about 4 million, and Greater Berlin between 2 and 3 million. Some cities were far smaller: Frankfurt in the 1920s had half a million, Stockholm in 1945 some three-quarters of a million. The largest metropolises of the Third World in the 1980s have 10 million and more. This is a critical order of magnitude, implying a different scale and type of spatial organization.

The second is that technologies are different. London, Paris, and Berlin were able to meet some of the challenge of growth, around 1900, through the then new technology of underground railways using electric traction. They did this when they were considerably smaller (and also in general denser) than Third World cities when they in turn adopted the same technology after 1970. These latter cities have, however, long felt the impact of mass car ownership, unknown in European cities until the 1950s. This is because of the simple availability of automobile technology, coupled with a highly unequal distribution of income which makes the car available to the top 30–40 percent of population. Problems of traffic congestion and pollution are thus more serious than in European cities around 1900, though the latter did suffer problems of horse-drawn traffic that should not be underestimated.

The third and most important difference is that administrative and, above all, planning capacities are not the same. Around 1900 the nascent city planning movement was making large gains in Europe. The garden city idea had been born in England and was rapidly spreading to France, Germany, and Russia. There were early exercises in slum removal and redevelopment. Stockholm and Amsterdam took steps to acquire land for urban development well ahead of need. Frankfurt pioneered the pooling of inner-city plots for redevelopment purposes. In contrast, the attitude in many Third World metropolises is one of benign neglect. There is neither the professional capacity, nor the political will, to control land development and associated land speculation, whether legal or illegal. Often, too, necessary resources are lacking to provide the basic infrastructural services such as pure water, sewerage, or electricity. In this regard, though standards differ, developing cities today often lag behind the capacities of European cities in 1900, let alone European cities in 1945.

To summarize: the problem that faces today's developing cities is different in kind from that which faced European cities nearly a century ago. They are far bigger and far more incohate. In particular, they sprawl over far greater areas, often with a serious lack of basic infrastructure. Travel-to-work distances and times are far greater than in the tightly bounded European city of the early 20th century. The political and professional capacity to deal with the resulting problems is, with a few conspicuous exceptions, less.

That said, it must be stressed that the developing countries are far from homogeneous either in the problems they face or in their capacity to face them. A particular difference is between the so-called middle income or newly industrializing countries and the true Third World countries. The former tend to experience the most serious problems of uneven development, inequality of incomes, and growth of very large primate cities. But in general their resources are greater and their administrative competence is more highly developed. Indeed this group includes a few countries (e.g., Singapore, Hong Kong) that offer models of how to promote orderly programs of urban development and shelter provision. These lessons may be useful for other countries in the same position, especially those that have reached the per capita income levels of Singapore or Hong Kong a quarter-century ago; they may not, however, be relevant for very poor countries, where in any case uneven development and urban growth are generally less of a problem.

A feasible strategy

What, in the circumstances, should be the strategy for the giant Third World city? It should be to adopt the lessons of the early and mid-20th-century European cities to a very different context. The nature of this adaptation is crucial.

The basis should be to recognize that, whatever can be done to divert growth to other cities and regions, the rate and, above all, the absolute size of the increment in large cities will continue to be very great. Some kind of a metropolitan strategy will therefore be necessary. This strategy will need to deal with four central problems: employment, shelter, land, and mobility.

Employment

A very high proportion of workers in the cities of the developing world – generally a large minority, sometimes an actual majority – earn their living in the so-called informal sector, without any guarantee of regular employment and income. Because of its nature, such employment tends to be concentrated in the central and inner areas of the city. One important part of it consists in hawking and peddling, which by definition clusters where market opportunities are greatest. Another consists of daily work on construction projects, which tend to be concentrated in redevelopment areas in, or just on the edge of, the central business district. Yet another consists of various casual labor jobs – in running messages, in offering instant services – within the central business district. Finally, there are a great number of low-level domestic service jobs to be found in central hotels, central offices, and in the homes of the rich – which, in typical developing cities, tend to be concentrated in one sector of the city quite close to the Central Business District (CBD).

For these various reasons, together with the density of information available in the heart of the city, the chances of informal sector work are much greater in the heart of the city. It has been suggested that this is a principal reason why new low-income migrants try to make their first homes in slums close to these job opportunities, only later – when some kind of job security has been obtained – moving out to peripheral housing areas. This may make it difficult to develop programs for orderly deconcentration. The resulting policy question is: How far is it possible to regenerate the informal economy in or around planned growth nodes, which by definition start life without it?

There is some reassurance here in the experience of two planned cities that were developed in remote locations, far from existing large urban centers: Ciudad Guayana (Venezuela) and Brasilia. In both, informal colonies very rapidly developed; indeed, the problem soon became one of controlling their growth. The copybook planned city of Brasilia is now merely the central core of a polycentric urban region in which the outer units either had completely informal beginnings or resulted from the attempts by the authorities to regulate the process.[27] If this is possible for such remote developments, then it should be possible for satellites developed within easy travelling range of the leading city.

Another cause for hope is that settled migrants tend increasingly to find formal sector jobs. Though many of these, too, are in the central business district, others have a typically peripheral distribution: in particular, modern sector factory jobs, which tend to locate on radial highways within certain sectors in the outer suburbs. Planned deconcentration schemes could be particularly successful in attracting such developments through tax incentives and infrastructure provision, coupling this with the provision of shelter schemes for the expected movement of workers. And this in turn should bring about a growth of informal sector job opportunities in the local service sector.

However, it should be recognized that – as argued below, in the discussion of transportation – such deconcentration strategies are always liable to lead to increasingly long journeys to work for at least a minority of the population. The dream of the self-contained new town, which was a key belief of the First World pioneers of the Garden City Movement, is very unlikely to be realized in the context of the great Third World city. Therefore, strategies of planned deconcentration will always bring with them a need for improved longer-distance commuter facilities.

Further, as longer-established migrants move out, new migrants are likely to take their places in the inner-city slums. Therefore planned deconcentration schemes are not a substitute for inner-city slum upgrading: both will be necessary.

Shelter

In typical developing countries many more people depend on informal housing than on the informal economy. The proportion of the total population living in informal settlements ranges upwards from 32 percent in São Paulo and 34 percent in Caracas to 59 percent in Bogotá and 60 percent in Dar es Salaam to an extraordinary 85 percent in Addis Ababa.[28] In such cities virtually all the poor, as well as many middle-income families, will live in autonomous housing, self-built on land to which the legal title is at best ambiguous.

For governments of many developing countries, this process is an embarrassing and unwelcome necessity, reluctantly accepted. The conventional view in such countries is that state intervention in housing would only encourage further rural-to-urban migration and that it would be economically unproductive, taking scarce resources from productive sectors such as agriculture. Latterly a contrary view has been heard: that migrants move for solid reasons of better economic opportunity; that housing prospects are irrelevant to their decision; and that, far from being unproductive, informal sector housing can contribute positively to the growth of Gross Domestic Product (GDP).[29]

One reason for this is that informal sector housing provision is symbiotic to other economic activities; in economic terms, its opportunity costs are low or near zero. People work on their own homes, or on those of their friends, when they have no other work – at weekends, on holidays, or when they are unemployed. This work, done for zero or low monetary reward, nevertheless contributes substantially to the total national stock of fixed capital. Further, this capital may have a direct or indirect economic value: it may be used for home work, and it is a resource for the nurture of the next generation of human capital. In terms of personal incomes, the resulting home is a capital asset which may be sold at a profit, thus producing income which may in turn be invested to improve the economic prospects of the worker and his family.

Thus, beginning with the work of Turner and his colleagues in Peru in the 1960s, a new conventional wisdom has emerged: that, far from discouraging the growth of informal settlements, official policy should actually facilitate it. This, however, demands the dismantling of many administrative barriers: rigid master plans, building regulations, infrastructure and service standards which are set at levels unattainable by the great mass of the population.[30]

This is particularly a problem for so-called planned urban developments; there, the inherited wisdom still tends to be that the state should provide public housing, as in the notable examples of the Hong Kong new towns and the Singapore satellites. But it is notable that even in Hong Kong, despite one of the largest public sector housing programs in the western world, there nevertheless remains an intractable and apparently permanent problem of some 750,000 people in squatter settlements.[31] It still remains unclear as to how a city could devise a plan for the orderly deconcentration of large numbers of people to satellites or new towns through largely informal means.

Land

Wherever such development takes place, there will remain three intractable and linked problems: land tenure, land cost, and the provision of infrastructure and services. The common element in this bundle of problems is land. As a recent Habitat report puts it: "Land is the emerging obstacle in the housing crisis facing growing settlements."[32]

The new conventional wisdom, based on the informal settlement strategy, is that "the emphasis of public policy should shift from the housing construction process to the land delivery process".[33] The resulting objective is to provide a sufficient supply of developed, well located land to meet the housing requirements of low-income groups at affordable costs.[33] In practice, this is far from easy. Increasingly, in developing cities the land market is becoming commercialized as the more affluent groups appreciate its value as an investment and as a hedge against inflation; land and housing markets are becoming increasingly concentrated in the hands of large commercial developers; and prices rise over time faster than the cost of living.[34] These developments are making it increasingly difficult for the informal settlement process to work as effectively as in the 1960s and early 1970s.[35] As a recent Habitat report concludes:

> ... the informal arrangements which have provided the cushion for absorbing low-income and disadvantaged groups in settlements over the last three decades are under pressure, and there is a need for action to relieve that pressure.[35]

The means to that end include compulsory public purchase at existing use value; trading of land, or development rights, for land in other locations; freezing of land prices; and the imposition of development gains taxes.[36] However, it needs to be recognized that none of these solutions is free of problems. The experience of countries that have instituted development land taxes, and compulsory purchase at existing use values – most notably Great Britain between 1947 and 1953 – suggests that the result may be politically very controversial, and that it may cause a freezing of the land market for a time. Further, of course, Britain had a highly developed administrative apparatus, including a reasonably uncorrupt bureaucracy, that may be lacking in some other countries. It may be easier to introduce certain measures which contain an element of self-enforcement: for instance, higher rates of taxation on land left undeveloped for speculative reasons, which have proved efficacious in Malaysia, Singapore, and the Philippines.[37]

What can be said is that in general such policies are the more likely to be successful, the smaller the difference between existing use value and forseeable speculative value. This suggests the wisdom of the original garden city concept of Ebenezer Howard: that deconcentration strategies should be based on purchase of agricultural land at low costs beyond the shadow effect of the growth of the city. This remains the ideal. Unfortunately, for reasons already examined, it may not always be practicable. This raises the question of feasible spatial planning strategies.

The physical form of deconcentrated development, in particular its location, will vary according to the size of the entire urban area. The smaller among the million-plus cities – up to, say, 5 million people – may be able to grow through satellites connected by good transit (buses, streetcars, metro) to the city centre, on the Frankfurt or Stockholm models. Larger cities should aim to decentralize modern sector employment, as well as informal sector homes, to new-town type developments on the model of London post-1945 or Paris post-1965. But, insofar as many residents will still need to seek employment in the distant central business district or the even more distant factory zones on the opposite periphery of the metropolis, the interconnected Paris model may be superior to the self-contained London one.

Transportation

Hence, the question of urban transportation becomes critical. The evidence from several developing cities strongly suggests that schemes of planned deconcentration have the effect of increasing the burden of commuting for the low-income displacees. In Dacca for instance, when refugees were moved to resettlement camps up to 24 km from the city center, many lost their jobs. In Bogotá a low-income traveller spends an average of 127 minutes per day on travel, a high-income one only 83 minutes.[38] So schemes of planned deconcentration should also include efficient means of public transportation that low-income people can afford.

As in urban housing, so in urban transport policies, there has been a fundamental shift in thinking. These, it is now argued, should be based on the need to increase accessibility to jobs and urban services for low-income people at minimum total real cost, also taking into account energy costs and environmental impacts.[39] That, the argument continues, may be best achieved through unconventional solutions including paratransit and improved personal mobility (for instance, subsidized bicycles). Though the private car provides a high degree of comfort and flexibility for those who can afford it, its use often imposes external costs – in congestion and pollution – on others. Rapid transit systems can move large numbers of people, but at very high capital costs. A fully loaded bus, operating on a segregated busway, involves costs per passenger-kilometer lower than any other mode. But the choice of the right mode will depend on local circumstances.[39] No one mode will be correct, anywhere; the aim should be to look for a rational combination of modes that are maximally efficient and are economical in use of space. The Habitat analysis of the problem concludes:

> The principles mentioned here lead to the conclusion that, for the majority of cities in developing countries and for the bulk of their population, a combination of walking, cycling, bus and paratransit constitutes a correct mix of transport modes.[40]

Additionally, for the affluent minority, the car will play a rôle; but its users should be required to pay the complete range of costs that their choice entails.

This, then, is now the conventional wisdom. The problem is that – just as with housing policies – it is far from clear how these policies would be integrated with spatial decentralization strategies, which, reflecting their First World origins, have often tended to be posited on ambitious and expensive transit or highway investments. This has obvious relevance for the Parisian model of urban development, described above, which requires a sophisticated, and expensive, mass transit system: an express metro capable of linking quite distant nodes at high speed. Such a system is likely to be completely beyond the fiscal capacity of most Third World cities in the 1980s. Additionally, the administrative capacity of the metropolitan area may preclude metro extensions beyond the boundaries of the city as strictly defined.

In such a case, the right way will be to build up an incremental system. The metropolitan area should try to set up a regional transit authority responsible for regulating, but not necessarily for operating, all kinds of transit – buses, taxis, rail. This authority should acquire rights-of-way, ahead of development and at write-down prices, on which a flexible transit strategy can be pursued. This could begin with express buses and/or jitneys and shared taxis, and could then be upgraded as necessary or feasible to guided busway, light rail, or heavy rail transit. The city of Curitiba, Brazil, offers a model: it has a combined land-use–transportation plan based on a system of "structural axes," each consisting of a "trinary" road system in which two parallel one-way streets flank a central road zoned for high-density commercial and residential development, where the central feature is a two-lane two-way reserved central busway which might eventually be upgraded to streetcar or light rail.[41]

Curitiba, with a present-day population of close on 1 million, provides a model for cities in the 1–5 million range. For larger cities, the same principles might apply, but they might require to be applied in different ways. There, the problem is to give the entire metropolitan area a polycentric structure wherein some employment is available locally, and transit makes possible a wider range of jobs in other nodes. In the very largest metropolitan areas (above approximately 10 million people), such a strategy should consciously promote the development of more distant nodes, 50 km and more from the CBD, with their own local employment. Though more self-sufficient than nearer nodes, these should possess good interconnection with the main CBD and with other nodes. Location on the main intercity rail net, if existent, would be a useful feature here. If a beltway or tangential highway is planned for the metropolitan area, such nodes should preferably be located some distance (10–20 km) outside it.

In virtually all developing countries, long-distance buses provide the basic means of interurban travel for the poor, connecting rural-to-urban migrants with their families in the countryside. In some of them (for instance Brazil, Korea), such services have been developed to a remarkable level of frequency, comfort, and efficiency. The aim should be to use them as part of a deconcentration strategy, through development of express bus services over medium range (40–150 km) connecting the central city with satellite developments. These could utilize the high-quality radial freeways that invariably exist in the near neighborhood of the capital city. Where congestion developed on these, segregated busways could be provided at relatively modest incremental cost. Provision for such busways would be built into the design of future freeways. In turn, these should be connected to express busways in the central medians of surface-level arterials, on the Curitiba model. The objective should be to build up, at fairly modest cost, a system of express bus transportation connecting the different nodes of the polycentric metropolis, in turn connecting with local bus and metro systems and paratransit services.

Such a system would provide for rapid medium-distance transit. Parts of it could be shared, as appropriate, by shorter-distance buses and paratransit vehicles. Labor-intensive policing of the exclusive busways may be necessary to prevent abuse at congested periods. For local travel, it may similarly be necessary to provide segregated bus and paratransit lanes on congested sections of city streets.

Lower-income residents, however, may not be able to afford the cost of regular use of bus or paratransit; their choice will lie between walking and cycling. For them, there is a strong case for the subsidized provision of bicycles coupled with the provision of segregated bike lanes on main streets. In many Chinese cities, where the bicycle is by far the most usual mode, it is common for bikeways to occupy half the total street space or more. On this basis, the bicycle can provide a basic low-income means of transportation, giving much of the flexibility of the private car at very low real cost for journeys of up to about 15 km – that is, for most journeys in developing cities of up to about 5 million population.

To summarize: for cities in the 1–5 million range, a combination of bicycle, local bus, and paratransit will suffice for the great majority of most people's journeys. Generous priority for such modes, by reserving street space, may be necessary to obviate the congestion effects of private car traffic. In some cases, it may be desirable to supplement this by policies designed to make the car driver pay the congestion costs: for instance, the supplementary licence system successfully used in Singapore since 1975 or the electronic road pricing system now on trial in Hong Kong. For the successful introduction of deconcentration strategies for larger cities, however, some system of low-cost express bus transportation, with reserved-track priority, will almost certainly be essential.

The organization of public transportation services in developing cities has been the subject of intensive examination and discussion by the World Bank and other interested agencies. From this has emerged yet another piece of new conventional wisdom: that in general, competing private companies can provide service at lower real cost than monopolistic public agencies.[42] The rôle of public authorities, in this view, should be limited to regulating the conditions of operation (for instance, safety standards); to providing essential infrastructure in the form of highways and reserved-access facilities; and to traffic management in order to facilitate the efficient operation of bus and paratransit operations. These arguments are not universally accepted, but they have proved difficult to refute.

The elements in concert

These elements, it can be argued, add up to a reasonably consistent and above all feasible policy for guiding the growth of the giant city. In this, the key is positive guidance that takes the strong forces operating in the private sector, works with them rather than against them, seeks to anticipate their impacts in advance, and works to channel them in ways that aid efficiency and equity rather than hindering them. The clue is to provide plenty of building land ahead of speculative pressures, at least minimally serviced, under a form of ownership that provides for a community share in any rises in value.

In many developing cities even this will not be easy. The growth of the city, and the lure of speculative gain, may cause plots to be illegally subdivided or transferred for denser forms of building, including highrise structures that lack adequate servicing. In such cases it may be necessary to adopt draconian measures, such as repossession of the land. But these should be used sparingly. It may be better, in such cases, to insist on the provision of adequate infrastructure, at the owner or developer's expense, as a condition of denser development.

This suggests a final lesson, perhaps the most important of all. In developing countries, a relative few middle-income nations excepted, the crucial feature is the lack of expertise, especially at the middle levels of the bureaucracy. A critical objective, therefore, should be to use this limited supply of talent in the most effective possible way. Self-help schemes are desirable just because they help achieve this. Ironically, it is in the developing world that we see the wisdom of the autonomous approach to development as promoted at the beginning of this century by such writers as Ebenezer Howard and Patrick Geddes. The aim, as they stressed, should be to harness the energies and talents of individuals organized in local groups, with the planner–administrator acting as facilitator and adviser.

Planners, in other words, need a due sense of their own limitations. In the developing world this is particularly important. Given the dynamism of the world's new great cities, planning should in general seek to anticipate trends and then guide them, rather than opposing them. The latter is bound to be futile: the former has just as much chance of success.

An agenda for research

Given the basic fact of scarce skills, it might appear totally inconsequential to conclude by suggesting a research agenda. But, in relation to the scale of the problem, research need not prove very costly, particularly if it is done, in collaboration with other developing countries, with the aid of funds from international agencies.

Four topics appear to be of outstanding importance. The first and most basic concerns the measurement of income differentials and of externalities. Logically, in economic analysis, people would not migrate to cities unless the resulting increase in money income more than compensated for any externalities. But they may be wrong in their expectations, or simply disappointed. We need for developing nations the kind of analysis that Hoch[14] made persuasively for the United States: What are the true income differences (not merely on average, but also for different income groups) between farm, small city, and big city? What are the externalities, and how do different groups perceive them? There is a real danger here of applying First World professional middle-class standards to the welfare of poor people in developing countries, whose priorities may be quite different. At least, if planners do assert their own standards, let them first be sure that they are shared.

Related to this is a second basic question. What sources contribute to urban incomes? In particular, how and to what extent does the urban informal economy do so? How does this economy come to be located where it is, and how mobile is it in response to changes in the location of its markets? There is increasing evidence that the so-called formal and informal economies are in fact interdependent in that the latter exists for much of the time by subcontracting for the former. Therefore, a planned shift in the modern sector might be expected to produce a shift in the informal sector also – but only on the premise that the members of the latter are both knowledgeable and able to act on their knowledge.

The third basic question concerns land and land cost. It can be argued that through autonomous housing we can go far to provide shelter quickly and economically for the urban poor, but that as we do so we automatically create a problem of mass land speculation. Useful work has been done here by agencies such as the World Bank.[28,43] But it needs updating. We need a study here that reviews the experience of different countries – developed and developing, capitalist and socialist – to see whether, and if so how, it has been possible to deal with this problem. Can it be met by policies that nationalize the land but allocate individual plots for lease? Is it, alternatively, possible to nationalize development rights while retaining individual land titles? Would it be equally feasible simply to tax capital gains on land, either at the same rate as other such gains or at a special rate? Would collective ownership of the land, in small cooperatives, have any merit? And how far would it be open to abuse? These and other solutions should be reviewed and evaluated.

There is a fourth question for research – though it is perhaps not as amenable to a definite answer as the first three. It concerns administrative competence. Clearly, some developing nations seem to have performed better in devising and implementing their urban policies than have others. Partly this reflects the greater resources available for state intervention as countries move into the middle-income range; partly, however, it reflects other, more elusive, factors. Is it possible to isolate these latter factors? Are there features in the training of professionals, for instance, that could be emulated? Does the legal tradition make a difference? Why does plan implementation appear easier in some countries, and some cultures, than in others? What helps explain why some countries have uncorrupt officials whereas others evidently do not? Is it possible to transfer traditions from one culture to another, and if so how? These might seem fanciful questions. But, it can be suggested, the chances of devising an effective urban policy turn very much on finding an answer to them.

IV

Rethinking policy, implementation, and management

11

Shelter, development, and the poor

LISA PEATTIE

WHAT DO WE know about the information and ideas involved in shelter and settlement policy? What are our areas of ignorance? How do we think about what we know? How could we improve our understanding for policy? What kinds of categories are useful for action, and what constitutes a distraction from practical knowing?

This discussion will have three parts. First will be an overview of the facts: what we know about the development of shelter for the poor in the cities of developing countries. Second will be a critical look at the economic categories which constitute the lenses through which we look at those facts. Finally, there will be some suggestions on the design of shelter programs for poor people, on the design of our schemes of program evaluation, and on research on urban shelter issues focusing on an understanding of shelter systems.

The second section, that on economic categories, will focus on the debate about trade-offs between welfare and development which underlies much of the policy debate about shelter for the poor in developing countries. This debate supposes a conflict between the alleviation of poverty now and investment in development for economic growth into the future. What part of its resources can a developing country afford to commit to the alleviation of poverty via shelter programs? And, since general economic growth must, necessarily, be a central priority, how can welfare-focused shelter programs be designed to spread the limited resources further?

It will be argued that these are the wrong questions. Further, it will be argued that such questions structure a debate on a level of abstraction which confuses rather than enlightens. An attempt will be made to review what we know about the processes which produce shelter for the poor in developing countries, to look at the way in which the debate above deforms our understanding of the issues, and to propose a framework for thinking about shelter which should be more useful in program design, as well as in evaluating and learning from the programs already in existence.

What we know

There are, of course, no plain facts, just as there is no pure ideology. What we notice and how we classify what we see is shaped by our purposes, practices, and preconceptions. However, one way to map the issues in shelter policy is to make a conceptual separation between facts, accounting categories, and economic theory. Let us begin, then, by mapping out, as closely as we can come to it, the facts upon which shelter policy must be based. What is the nature of the world with which policy has to deal?

The first category of "plain facts" has to do with the dramatic phenomena of worldwide urban migration. Shelter policy in most developing countries is dominated by what is thought of as the attempt to cope with the rapid expansion of cities. This is not the same as saying that the provision of shelter is a phenomenon necessarily centered in cities; many countries for which the preceding characterization of shelter policy is true are still predominantly rural, with most people, like most shelters for them, still in the country. However, one can easily confirm by a casual inspection of the literature that policy discussions, as in this book, almost invariably begin with an account of the increase of urban population, moving from these figures to the apparent incapacity of governments to provide services for the new urban populations and of a high proportion of the new urban populations to pay for standard housing.

These facts may be presented in two ways: via figures on incomes and on the costs of some basic standard dwelling;[1] or, more commonly, by tracing the rise and expansion of "squatter" or unregulated settlements.[2]

The problematic character of this rural-to-urban movement of population has generated a subliterature of facts bearing on the issue of whether we ought to discourage or encourage it in shelter and other policies.

One subset of this literature either models or tries to derive data on the question of whether the urban migrants are better or worse off in the city than they were back in rural areas. One form of this is a discussion of "push" versus "pull" factors in migration: Were people drawn to the city by its relative attractiveness, or were they squeezed off the land?[3] Another body of literature looks at the situation of urban dwellers and attempts to compare it to their situation in rural areas.[4] (Unfortunately for science, and no doubt also for clarity of analysis, many of the articles comparing stress, social disorganization, and other problems in the city to the situation in rural areas lack a true comparative base in that they have never looked empirically into the question as to the degree to which mental health and social harmony prevail in the country, but rather assume that they must.)[5] The Harris-Todaro family of migration models constitutes an attempt to show that migrants may well remain in the city even if worse off so long as they have some hope of achieving a more desirable position in the city with time and good luck.[6] A third approach is that of studies comparing urban incomes with rural ones. Such studies are so complicated technically that there are relatively few of them. Those I have seen all show higher incomes in the city,[7] with the consequence that an interpretation that migrants are worse off must either rest on nonmaterial values (the mental health and social harmony issue) or via a "real income" concept which takes the cost of living in the city into account. Here we encounter the very basic difficulty that those expenditures that make up the cost of urban living represent both the necessary costs of doing business in an urban location and, presumably, in some part consumer gratification. To work in the city one needs shoes and respectable clothes; but, on the other hand, the wearer is also enjoying the modern clothing. Shelter in the city typically costs a great deal more than it does in the countryside; but people may well value their urban dwelling, even a modest one, more than they would its rural earth-and-thatch counterpart. Here we encounter a point which will be stressed later: the difficulty of separating economic functions from welfare in the area of shelter.

Finally, there is a body of literature to which, again, it will be necessary to return, focused on facts bearing on the consequences for economic growth and development of the movement of people to cities. Particularly noteworthy are the reports issued over a number of years by the Economic Commission for Latin America calling attention to the occupational composition of city populations and arguing that an economy in which the ratio of the tertiary "services" sector to the secondary manufacturing sector was higher than that in Europe represented a kind of economic pathology. Urban populations were shown to be in substantial part involved in petty commerce and street vending, domestic service and unskilled and transitory work, and a rather loose category known as "disguised unemployment". These activities having been categorized, through prior reasoning, as unproductive, it followed that a substantial part of the urban population was not contributing to economic growth and development.[8] (This view is of course closely related to the Harris–Todaro family of migration models.) On the other side of the question is a literature which produces evidence to argue for many linkages and positive externalities among urban activities, such as to lead to the conclusion that urbanization is not simply a consequence but a highly positive force in economic growth.[9]

These are the major bodies of fact about urbanization within which, as noted at the outset, most of the discussion of shelter issues has its context.

Turning now to the shelter issue itself, we find two sharply contrasting bodies of fact relating to the definition of, and therefore the magnitude of, the problem. On the one hand is a body of fact, largely in statistical form, which presents data on the number of substandard dwellings, the number of new households needing housing, and the number of dwellings being produced and finds in the difference the housing needed. This figure is always substantial.[10] This approach is favored particularly by government building and planning agencies and those producing reports in support of their activities. On the other side, there is a body of evidence, largely in qualitative terms, which starts by looking at how people are currently sheltered at the time of inquiry. It sees marginal settlements not as evidence of a deficit of housing but as evidence of a process of solution. For example, in a paper on Bangkok:

> There is a system which delivers housing solutions daily to satisfy the needs of the low-income people. The low-income housing delivery system in Bangkok is made up of several subsystems. ... The workers' housing subsystem, the squatters' housing subsystem, the filtered housing subsystem, the rural commuters subsystem, and the public housing subsystem. ... The information about the magnitude of housing provision by each subsystem is still unknown. What is known is that altogether they provide housing for *all* the low-income people in the city.[11]

This category of factual evidence is put forward by those advocating government tolerance and positive support for existing shelter subsystems.

Finally there is a third body of fact which one might suppose is relevant to these discussions: the facts on homelessness in the developed countries which show that in Boston and New York (and other major cities), as in Calcutta and other cities of the less developed countries (LDC), a number of individuals sleep on the street, in stations, or in emergency shelters. Although perhaps meeting, at the margin, the definition of the housing subsystem used in the paper on Bangkok, these arrangements are socially defined as sheltering homeless persons in the settings where their users live without residing.[12] There is also in the industrialized countries a body of relevant facts being presented on the rising proportion of income being taken by housing expense. Fifty percent is now not unusual in some cities, particularly for persons at the bottom of the income scale. The argument is then made that the social issue in shelter policy is no longer "slums" or substandard housing (facts are produced to show that the proportion of housing without basic services is very much reduced) but a problem of affordability.[13]

Finally, there is an interesting fact about all these bodies of fact: the discussions of shelter policy in the LDCs and the facts relating to the LDCs tend to be carried out quite independently of discussions of housing policy in the United States and in Europe. It is not unreasonable to believe that our conceptual grasp, and thus our general understanding, would be improved by a more comparative approach. For example, the facts on homelessness in the developed world just referred to should at least help us to get beyond the simplistic view which treats the problem as that of the output failure of a "housing sector" and towards an understanding of shelter problems in the context of the functioning of a set of institutions which can be called the *shelter system*.

What do we know about how housing – in the broad sense of human shelters – gets produced? One point is clearly documented: with few exceptions (Singapore, Hong Kong, Israel) government's rôle as a direct producer is overshadowed by that of private individuals and private bodies. Indeed, the better part of housing produced in the countries of the Third World falls outside the mesh of government regulation and enumeration; a recent study found that "typically only 25% of the total growth in housing units between censuses is recorded in national construction statistics".[14]

Cuba, a socialist country with a relatively high level of development and one of the most urbanized countries in the world, has placed enormous emphasis on government-sponsored housing programs. Nevertheless, the 1970 census showed that there were some 600,000 more houses in 1970 than in 1953; only about 200,000 of these had been built by the government.[15] Alteration, upgrading, and maintenance of housing – certainly critical elements in the size of the housing stock – must be even more in private hands. On the amounts and the processes by which this investment takes place we have practically no facts at all.

It is conventional to divide housing into three categories: a government sector; a "private sector" of recognized (often called "formal sector") developments of modern standard housing; and a sector of small producers, often called "self-help" or "incremental building," more recently the "informal sector." Housing in the recognized private commercial sector is produced for that part of the economic elite not served by government; this sector is, given the distribution of incomes, rather small. The self-help component of private shelter production is generally very much larger. However, the level of our factual knowledge about these two is in inverse relationship to their contribution to shelter output. There are a limited number of studies of the construction industry[16] and surely more facts to be gathered about formal sector construction than we now possess; nevertheless, it is the actors and processes in the informal sector, or self-help component, which is, relatively speaking, the *terra incognita*.

However, facts are beginning to be collected[17] on the processes of shelter production in the marginal settlements. These facts, and their economic implications, are summarized by Klaassen *et al*. in Chapter 2 of this volume. This building is not clearly dominated by processes of self-help in the usual meaning of the term. It is in large part a sector of owner-builders, in the sense that development is mainly one unit at a time, by persons who at least at the outset intend to live in the structure being produced and who act as their own general contractors in the productive process. But although persons may frequently, even usually, put up their own provisional shacks, once it is a question of permanent materials the owner usually finds it sound policy to hire competent workmen and concentrate on the financial and managerial issues for which he has a comparative advantage. The owner and his family members may also find it sensible to do much of the painting and finishing. The building process is, therefore, found to be a commercialized one, in the sense of employing paid labor.

The facts now coming in show that building in this informal sector is commercialized in other ways also. The fact that the buildings are being produced to be used does not constitute them "production for use" in the usual sense of the term. There is a lively market for housing in the marginal settlements. People buy and sell such dwellings with great frequency; in addition, dwellings are rented in whole or in part. Investment in dwellings by owner-occupants closely reflects their actual resale value in these informal markets.[18]

At this point, the facts about real estate transactions in the informal sector seem to require integration with the growing body of facts on land tenure. The dramatic struggles between land squatters and the authorities attempting to dislodge them for some time focused attention on the building of shelter on land owned by others – usually, it turns out, by government bodies. There has been developing a body of descriptive literature on the political processes by which squatters interact with politicians to acquire legal tenure. But at the same time, studies[19] have shown that in large part persons building in the so-called self-help sector are building on land for which they have paid money to a subdivider who, though he may legally own the land, more probably than not has failed to go through the processes legally prescribed for subdividing. Thus it turns out that building goes on in a variety of land tenure situations from outright illegal occupation to legal title with a variety of more or less clouded titles in between.

We now have enough studies on the processes by which these irregular settlements come into being to know that they are not, as once thought, wholly outside the sphere of government. Instead, the occupation of land is often organized and generally involves informal negotiation with the authorities. The leaders of these settlements operate with strategies and motives in which the political and the commercial are variously combined.[20]

Meanwhile, the studies of Karst and others[21] show that legal title is not a precondition for dealing in real estate; a claim to land, however clouded, can be sold on its merits, and those who invade one day may sell their staked plot to a later comer the next.[22] These facts are, of course, far from trivial for policy. The entire range of claims to ownership by those occupying plots of land confront the claims of governments to deploy land use for their own purposes. It is a problem, but not impossible, for government to displace legal owners; it is possible, but also a problem, to displace squatters where they are numerous and visible and where government needs constituency support.

There is relatively little factual material on the firms and persons which operate commercially in this "informal" or what used to be called "self-help" building sector. Stretton says in his work on contractors in Greater Manila,

> In much of the literature the economy of Third World cities is divided into two sectors, such as the formal and the informal. However, we have seen that the buildings industry in the GMA does not fit into either of these categories. Nor can it be viewed as dualistic. The size and attitude of contractors cover a spectrum ranging from large modern firms using technology borrowed from Western countries to self-employed artisans working with a gang of laborers and using no equipment. There is considerable interdependence and/or conflict between contractors at different points of the spectrum.[23]

My own sense is that research would develop similar findings in other LDC settings, but until we have the empirical work we must recognize that we are in fact inventing in the discussions of contrasts between the formal sector of construction firms and the informal sector; these may be aspects of a single industry.

We can, of course, look at the output, the quality of housing stock in the various, however defined, subsectors of the shelter industry. The issue here is, it turns out, not simply one of relative costs. Official housing, studies show, distributes the cost in different ways from private informal building, by and large skimping on space, in comparison to "informal" building, but using more industrially produced materials than the latter.

One study of the costs issue in Egypt found that even though "savings through self-help is not a factor, since it is not common in the construction of units" costs were lowered in a number of other ways. "Contractors tend to charge lower rates largely because they substitute lower skilled labor for regular skilled workers. ... Neither architectural nor engineering services are used. ... Recycled or used materials are common, generally wood for windows and doors, and steel reinforcing bars. Expensive materials are used more sparingly. ... Less expensive fittings and finishings are used."[24] Multiunit building almost invariably turns out to be a good deal more costly per unit than the single-unit building characteristics of the informal sector.[25]

Paul Strassman has called attention to the economic implications of building in different ways: High-rise construction, in particular, by requiring steel is likely to create problems for foreign exchange; different kinds of building, by implying different capital–labor ratios and different skill mixes, also have consequences for employment.[26] A study in Pakistan developing this line of thought has looked at the economic linkages and consequences of choice of technology in building and shown that the use of high-grade standard construction not only increases costs relative to traditional building but leads to a leakage of construction expenditures out of the district or to upper-income groups rather than generating jobs through the materials industries and construction for the local poor.[27] This picture is supported by the admittedly scanty data from other settings reviewed recently by Sethuraman for the ILO.[28]

We also have relatively little good data on how building in the informal sector is financed, beyond a pretty clear understanding that the banks do not do it. Family transfers and personal savings seem major sources.[29] We do not even have factual information – and this is more consequential for policy – on how important a bottleneck financing is, compared to the availability of land and of low-cost construction materials. Our discussions produced a good deal of anecdotal evidence of *reluctance* to engage in long-term borrowing.

We do have evidence on the importance of rental units in the informal sector as a way of financing the building process itself. Families in the Nairobi sites-and-services project studied by Praful Soni[30] derived very high returns from rents – from 100 to 600 percent per year return on invested capital. This project represented a classic conflict between the interests of the families in the project and the image of the outcome held by those who had designed the project: the former tended to rent each additional room as they built it, and thus to expand as petty landlords, but the latter perceived multiple occupancy blighting what they had hoped to see as a settlement of family homes.

Such rental units are, of course, an addition to the low-income housing stock as well as a source of finance to the owner-builder, and we are coming to have enough data to see that they are an important part of the housing stock in most cities. But we are only recently seeing studies on tenancy in the LDC cities such that we can see the complexity of the issues, for neither income nor stage in the life cycle appears to clearly account for choice (Is it better thought of as choice or constraint?) between ownership and tenancy.[31]

Probably we ought to take the provision of rental stock within the informal sector far more seriously than we have. A study of landlord–tenant relations and their housing policy implications in Canada makes a point which may be quite transferable to the developing countries. The researcher contrasts a commercial real estate market "conducted by economic sophisticates seeking financial gain through bargained contracts" to the "other economy" of landladies in three-deckers and other small operators; "by using their own resources of capital and especially labor, and sometimes by exchanging labor, skills information, and advice with relatives and friends, they often provide themselves (and their tenant) with far better housing than could be purchased conventionally."[32]

Finally, the studies of tenancy lead into the studies which are moving towards an understanding of the way in which real estate submarkets are structured and interrelate in the cities of the Third World.[33] At this point it is not so much any specific bodies of fact which are the matter of interest but rather the vision that emerges of an urban *system* of shelter and investment in shelter. We see that shelter is continually changing its use and its physical form as it is maintained, altered, enlarged or, perhaps, let deteriorate and be abandoned. We do not yet have a clear analysis of the ways that public policies and regulations shape the system of shelter provision, but we can be sure from the evidence we have that public interventions are critical: roads, water lines, schools, clinics, land tenure regularization, and recognition of community organization all play into the changing values of real estate, including that in the marginal settlements, and thus affect the rate, the amount, and the manner in which investment in shelter will flow. We know, also, that to understand the shelter system for low-income families it is not enough to look at the part of the system where low-income people are living. Submarkets for real estate, like submarkets for building materials,

are substitutable at the margins. When Colombia was pushing development via a flow of funds into upper-income housing, the prices of
building materials rose not merely at the top of the scale where it was
steel, concrete, and glass; prices permutated clean down to a rise in the
cost of cardboard and used sheet metal.[34] Use of land for upper-income
developments will affect the price of occupancy in marginal settlements
in the same city. In Egypt, the allocation of cement to formal sector
construction firms means that small builders must buy on the black
market at greatly increased prices.[35]

Finally, there is coming to be a body of factual information on the use
of dwellings for income-producing activities other than the income to
owners via rental of some part of the structure. Simon Fass, looking at the
economic strategies of households in a marginal settlement of Port Au
Prince, found the use of dwellings for making, storing and/or selling of
goods for the market so universal that he decided to treat the dwelling
unit as a piece of productive infrastructure rather than as predominantly
a part of household consumption. To look at the same phenomenon in
another way: in a part of the economy characterized by self-employment
and by very small firms involving, frequently, members of a single family,
the house is often the factory, the shop, and the warehouse.[36] This is not
to argue that dwellings lack economic implications for upper-income
families. It can be argued that those whose professional careers depend
on impressing management and the maintenance of social contacts
require a suitably capacious and elegant house as part of *their* income-
producing strategies; nevertheless, any survey of the use of residential
structures in a low-income neighborhood is likely to bring out the
economic importance of what planners call "mixed use."

A study of the shoe industry in Bogotá reveals that the vast majority of
firms are very small ones, and that these are housed in rooms, garages,
and sheds throughout the deteriorated residential areas of the city. The
industry thus depends for its existence on the presence of what might be
called slums.[37] The same can be said of the extraordinarily successful
development of Hong Kong, based on a multiplicity of small firms
housed, until quite recently, very largely within apartment buildings
constructed for residential use. The Hong Kong case also brings out
another important implication for planning: it was not only the
cheapness of the space which made it possible for the firms to be
economically successful but the freedom of location, permitted by failure
to regulate, which made it possible for firms to locate in proximity to
those with which they had economic linkages.[38]

How we think about the
facts we have

The framing of shelter policy in the context of larger development strategies encounters first a very basic problem of accounting: Is housing (or shelter more generally) a productive contribution to economic growth? Or is it unproductive, perhaps a necessary accompaniment to growth strategies, but basically a welfare or consumption issue, a cost to society as a whole but a gain to individual users? The available categories – production, consumption, or the Marxist social reproduction – turn out to raise some serious issues in application.

The problem may, perhaps, best be introduced by an example taken from Ivan Szelenyi's recently translated book on urban policy in Hungary. Here the new socialist state found itself in a peculiar and internally conflicting position. On the one hand, "capitalist production and marketing of housing ceased. Housing had become a universal right, a demand sanctioned by the socialist state itself." But it was difficult for the state to satisfy the demand for the satisfaction of this right. "Housing units are so expensive, durable, comparatively indivisible, and fixed in particular neighborhoods, that consumer equality is harder to achieve in housing than in any other sphere of distribution." But even given the inherent difficulties, the state did badly on housing, and it did so by plan. Housing construction fell sharply, even below the level of the 1920s. One reason was a national economic policy which cut down on consumer goods so as to direct all available resources into extensive and rapid industrialization. The planners saw this choice as a conflict between short-term individual interests and the long-term interests of society as a whole.

In addition, Szelenyi tells us, the planner's vision was supported by a "strangely self-defeating article of faith." Since housing was seen as such a basic need, to be removed from market processes, it seemed to follow that it was not a useful economic commodity. Thus it came about that "in the competition for capital resources, ... local council officials representing housing needs were confronted by general directors of trusts in charge of huge capital movements who usually won easily." Housing was starved for capital, while the building programs of big industry had ample resources. The result was the industry-produced "mass assembly halls," "factory structures like cathedrals," and "expensive office premises," while the housing shortage got worse.[39]

Thus the system of thought which established housing as a particularly important item of consumption had the perverse effect of restricting its production. Meanwhile, "mass assembly halls," "factory structures like

cathedrals," and "expensive office premises" for bureaucratic administrators, accounted as part of the productive apparatus, could be built
with enthusiastic support from planners.

This rather amusing story should teach us a lesson about the
limitations of economic accounting categories. "Output" (whatever we
mean by it and however we measure it) is produced not by isolated
components of capital or labor or by "sectors," but rather by often very
complex institutional systems. Our accounting categories are extremely
vulnerable to the way in which the processes by which output is
produced are institutionalized. In the example given, "factory structures
like cathedrals" get counted as part of productive apparatus, whereas
housing for the workers is accounted as outside production. Similarly, a
large manufacturing firm which employs a staff to pack and distribute its
products will have these employees accounted as a part of the industry.
If the products are sold by vendors in the street, these vending activities
will be part of a different, commercial, sector in the accounts, if indeed
they enter at all. Central planning and its interministerial struggles for
budget will continue to produce sectoral planning and its debates. Let
us, however, when we design settlement and shelter programs, take
these documents with a grain of salt.

"Expensive office premises" and "factory structures like cathedrals" are
used and probably enjoyed, and are thus part of the daily consumption
package of those who work in them as well as part of the productive
apparatus. Housing may also be considered as part of the productive
apparatus, as well as of family consumption. Gary Becker[40] and Patricia
Apps[41] have both, in diverse ways, tried to develop conceptualization in
which the house is the setting where various inputs are combined into
the goods and services, like meals, which constitute final consumption.
Given the data on the use of dwellings by low-income families in
developing countries for making, storing, and selling goods for the
market, we cannot sensibly treat housing as *simply* a consumer good. It
is, rather, the task of planning to maximize the economic value of shelter.

If "housing" turns out to be a slippery item to put into an accounting
system for planning, the same is even more true for the term against
which we might think to balance it: "development." This is certainly not
the place to try to review or summarize the many and complex
discussions on this topic. Let us merely recall that this literature has
brought forward at least two very basic debates which bear centrally on
thinking about shelter policy. First, we may distinguish people-centered
approaches to development, such as those of Schumpeter and Kaldor,
from theories centered on capital. If entrepreneurship and human
capital are seen as important elements, shelter policy must be seen as
part of the strategy for developing human resources; if capital is the key,

human consumption must be minimized. Second, there is a continuing debate on the rôle of small enterprises in economic growth. "Small is beautiful" proponents, both in respect to the LDCs and in respect to the industrialized or postindustrial world confront advocates of economies of scale. The latest arena for this long-standing argument is in the discussions of the informal sector.[42] How shall we understand the microenterprises of the Third World cities? As disguised unemployment, as infant industries, or as exploited subsidiaries of enterprises of the formal sector?

Looking at the intricacy, murkiness, and imperviousness to empirical test of the current debates we should convince ourselves of one thing at least: the category "development" is cloudy enough so that we can not be sure of what we mean when we say the word, and even less confident that we would recognize it when we meet it in the street. If we are unclear as to what development is, and unclear as to how we should account investment in shelter, a discussion of the trade-offs between development and shelter investment promises to be quite unproductive. Probably more useful as a grounding for shelter policy would be a discussion at a somewhat lower level of abstraction in which the intermingling of political and economic objectives or, to put it another way, of prudential judgement and social values, is frankly taken into account.

I propose, therefore, an information and research strategy focused on developing a grounded understanding of issues in shelter policy by learning how the institutions constituting our shelter systems actually function.

Here, for example, are some issues which might serve to orient the strategies of shelter policy.

To what degree do we want to support the development of a large class of small enterprises? "Small is beautiful" is a political objective, as much or more than an economic means. Americans may recognize the political imagery as modern urban Jeffersonianism, but the idea is bound to recur as a class of small entrepreneurs confront both the big corporations and the consolidating State. To support small enterprises do we want to leave shelter provision open to small enterprise production, and do we want to leave the urban fabric open to use by little firms? Or do we believe that the State or the big corporations should dominate? What are the market niches that small firms can best exploit? What are the areas in which large firms or the State actually operate efficiently? What are the political implications of support to small firms versus support to large firms or to State monopolies?

Is government effective? If so, under what conditions? How can users and clients make their needs felt in government programs? Or will it work better to have the programs out of the control of government? Under what conditions will the State serve the poor? These are all questions which have to be asked and answered in the context of a particular national situation in a particular time and set of circumstances. They constitute the context in which policy makers must try to answer a basic question: Will social stability best be served by enlarging the mandate and responsibility of the State, and with that enlargement, an enlarging arena for conflict and dissatisfaction? Or will social stability best be served by supporting a wide range of private actors?

Some guidelines for program design

We might better deal with the trade-off between economic development and welfare by a more sensitive attention to the way in which particular programs are designed. We will recognize that shelter is always *both* welfare and an economic asset. To its owner it is a piece of potential real estate, a potential site of income-producing activities, a base of participation in the large urban economy, and a family dwelling.

Therefore let us not take advantage of people's need for shelter in its economic aspects to force them, via enforcement of standards, to pay for more welfare than they want.

Let us make it possible for people to create rental space in their dwellings; they are creating additional housing which is needed.

Let us make it possible for people to use their shelter for income-producing activities.

Let us realize that most shelter is created by private individuals and very small firms, and see that this very important "construction industry" has access to the materials and to the land it needs to function.

Let us realize that this construction industry, much of which we once misunderstood as self-help, can be in itself a major source of employment, and let us design our programs with the employment effects in mind. A program which is organized so that the poor pay professionals and highly skilled workers for their housing is inferior to one relying more heavily on unskilled and semiskilled labor from an income-generating point of view, no matter what the relative merits are of the housing produced.

Let us realize that when we try to get rid of slums and shantytowns we are doing what is clearly reducing the supply of low-income housing; we are bound to raise the price and increase crowding in the remaining stock.

Let us realistically build the convertibility of housing into cash into our program design, rather than insisting that our programs are *shelter* programs only and that people may not transfer the units to others. It is surely inequitable to permit real estate speculation only to the well-to-do. If upper-income people can sell land and houses, why frown on the attempts of the poor man to turn his asset into liquid capital? If "beneficiaries" want to sell, this suggests that government is pushing consumption of housing which is unsound economically for the beneficiaries. (Someone once complained to me: "This is not a program of loans to build houses; it is a program of houses to get (subsidized) loans." The loan, as a line of credit, would have been used otherwise – and perhaps more productively.)

Instead of debating whether participatory approaches are appropriate for shelter-building programs, we should realize that most shelter in most cities of the developing countries is being built, in a sense, with owner participation. If participation appears to be a problem in government-sponsored programs, let us look at the terms on which it is offered. Are we asking people to participate in a way which is costly to them (as when people who need to hold jobs in order to pay for land and materials are required to participate physically in building their houses) or on terms which are basically unattractive (as when participation means working in a project planned by and according to the standards of outsiders)?

Finally, let us take note of our ignorance of those uncharted reaches of the economy which we have found it convenient to call the informal sector and worry about whether in our fresh enthusiasm for its energies we are not expecting too much of it. "You cannot make bricks without straw," it is said, and even less can anyone build without land to build on. In Chapter 5 of this volume, Doebele tells us that the planners' discovery of the informal sector in the 1980s coincided with a sharp tightening up of urban land markets. Where are the political and administrative processes which will make land available to the householder and small builder?

Part of our confidence in the capacity of the informal builders is based on the experience with sites-and-services projects which – it is easy to forget this – have never reached the poorest of the poor. The people with whom we worked in these projects had jobs; they could and did hire petty contractors. What of the others excluded from these projects by the need for a steady income, who must build with their hands if they build at all, and who cannot afford standard construction materials?

It would seem that there are critical thresholds that remain unknown with regards to low-income populations and shelter needs; one threshold divides those very poor who are not concerned about housing given their immediate, daily necessities of living, the priorities of food, health and clothing being principal and full-time occupiers of time, from the next group up that begins to include housing in their range of priorities but still not as a central one. There is probably a series of further thresholds going up the income scale that we should address in designing shelter programs.[43]

A learning agenda

We should shift our attention away from those accounting categories which, as I have argued, do not tell us very much, and towards the way in which various kinds of programs work and the broader social consequences they have.

We should, for example, compare sites-and-services projects to the more common petty enterprise pattern of development with respect to a number of issues, both political and economic. What are the comparative costs to users? Who gets access to each kind of shelter? What are the consequences of location for access to the job market in the city as a whole and for the development of income-producing activities in the residential area itself? In each of these patterns of development, who benefits economically from the construction process? What are the political consequences? Does government find itself with responsibilities it cannot discharge? Or does it find its rôle a channel for productive contact with constituents and a form of leverage for useful institutional development?

We would compare the upgrading approach to the new-project approach (including sites-and-services projects) not only with respect to the cost and ease of delivery, but with respect to the social and institutional consequences. These are very different when one starts with a government initiative and a relatively clean slate from when the program starts by entering into an existing community with its existing economic and political interests. Because few cities have found it possible to carry out new projects at a rate sufficient to deal with the urbanization problem, both approaches will be necessary in most cases; still, some choice of emphasis is possible. What are the larger results of each approach?

We should take a greater interest in rental tenancy. What part should rental play in the shelter system? Should government, large enterprises, or small owners be the landlords? And what kind of urban environment is produced when one or the other dominates?

Finally, and most generally, those who think about shelter should realize that government is necessarily only one actor among many and that housing is a process by which various individuals and institutions invest or disinvest, maintain, or fail to maintain; government's rôle has especially to do with that process. Its shelter policies include the layout of roads and services, the regulations on urbanization, and the regulation of use, taxes, loans, building codes. How do policies in these areas bear on the shelter system?

This way of thinking about shelter policy suggests a different strategy of research from that usually favored by housing and planning agencies. Questions like those posed above are not readily answered by the collection of data on project costs or on numbers of beneficiaries, even though such figures will have their use in developing answers. Counting is not particularly useful when we need to get a picture of how the world works and of the linkages between phenomena. We need empirically grounded descriptions of the processes by which shelter is created, managed, and maintained and of the invisible structures which govern these processes. This means qualitative data. It means interviews, and it means a greater use of case studies from which we try to draw general lessons.

I have elsewhere[44] proposed some major research topics which seem basic to the approach outlined above. These are:

(a) *More descriptive accounts of how programs work.* By interviewing both program recipients and the staff involved in implementation, we can get a clearer sense of what the outcome really was. Who was involved and why? What were the consequences to the clients, to the agency, to the project's neighbors, and to the city as a whole? If such a program were to be done again, what would we want to do differently?

(b) *Housing markets.* As noted, a broader approach to shelter policy requires us to look at the city as a diverse, interlinked set of sub-markets of housing. To some degree, we can identify these sub-markets by visual inspection. But to plan policy, we need to dig a bit deeper. We want to know something about the people and institutions controlling these submarkets. What are their economic strategies? What incentives do they respond to? Interviews are the easiest way to get at these matters.

(c) *Subdividing and building.* Once we realize that what we thought of as a kind of personal self-help is really a construction industry of many small actors, we must realize that an industry study is in order. What are the sources of financing? What are the bottlenecks in building? How do people obtain land?

(d) *How cities work.* Studies of the informal sector have shown us at least one thing: that economists' understanding of the urban economy does not go down very far. We are just beginning to get some understanding of how the enterprises of the poor function, and how they link to other parts of the urban economy. We need more such work.

A question for discussion is: Who should do such studies? What are the consequences for placing this enterprise with the international agencies, with the local universities, or with the government agencies responsible for policy?

Sectoral programming and statistical data will continue to play the major rôle in central planning; it is the language of interministerial negotiation. But if we take seriously the recommendation that government should act as *facilitator* in a shelter system with many private actors, we need to look for ways in which learning about the system's functioning can be incorporated into central planning. Is a small strategic planning unit with a good research capacity a possible addition at this level?

Much of the approach to settlement and shelter which we are proposing involves management and programming at the municipal level. Here we guess that there is more information on how things work than academics and top-level decision makers often realize, but that it is of what an American would call the seat-of-the-pants type – not generalized and not easily passed along to others. How can we attach to the municipalities persons whose job it is to record program experience and make it available to other program planners and managers? Perhaps this is a rôle for the universities; perhaps it could be financed by international agencies like the United Nations.

Finally, we would hope that the international agencies like the World Bank would enlarge the scope of their program monitoring and evaluation to look not only at the program itself but at its context and consequences. Where are the people who are not able to get access to the program sheltered? What are the program's consequences for urban real estate markets and for municipal administration?

12

Criteria for future shelter and settlement policies in developing countries

LELAND S. BURNS and BRUCE FERGUSON

Alternative postures for shelter and settlement policy

EFFICIENCY, EQUITY, and compatibility rank as the overriding criteria for evaluating shelter and settlement policies, or for that matter, most social and economic programs and policies. They guide actions at all decision-making levels. *Efficiency* connotes steady progress in improving the quality of shelter and settlement services per unit of resource expenditure. Policies that attempt to reduce the unit costs of satisfying shelter and settlement requirements are of this type. *Equity* refers to ensuring access to shelter at prices that households can pay without excessively or continuously straining their budgets. Shelter allocation policies that satisfy the equity criterion focus especially on the lowest income groups of the population. *Compatibility* requires that shelter and settlement policy is congruent with others and that its implementation does not compromise the strategies that pursue other major goals. For example, construction methods that depend on advanced technologies may conflict with policies aimed at stimulating job formation or restricting imports. In practice, the inevitable conflicts between criteria force difficult trade-off choices. For example, equity and efficiency criteria may stand at variance when the poorest groups' default rates run high.

Policies that have been used (and abused) in the search for shelter and settlement solutions fall into four categories:

(1) Policies that *reduce need* by controlling population size and spatial distribution. Because an analysis of such policies would take us far afield, they are merely noted here as one possibility and not examined further.[1]

(2) Policies that *increase external assistance*, whether specifically targeted or for general development, have historically provided major support for Third World shelter and settlement programs. Whether grants and loans from bilateral and multilateral agencies can be counted on as major sources for increased support in the future, or possibly even for maintenance of support at current levels, seems uncertain at this writing due to the economizing pressures that characterize many of the developed nations which, in the past, have been major contributors. Again, because this form of assistance raises questions of such enormous magnitude, the option is noted without further elaboration.

(3) Policies that *shift domestic budgets* in favor of shelter and settlement projects. Policy decisions of this type include internal reallocations within overall government budgets favoring the shelter and settlement sector without changing overall budgetary allocations, or policy actions that stimulate changes in private budgets, whether of consumers or businesses. Exactions requiring private enterpreneurs to provide employee housing exemplify the latter. Policies fostering the development of financial intermediaries specialized in lending for house purchase, construction, or improvement and that stimulate capital formation through accumulating private sector savings are another example. Because policies of this type augment shelter and settlement sector allocations at the expense of other sector budgets without altering the total supply of resources available, the trade-off between gainers and losers must be confronted.

(4) Policies that *reduce or minimize unit costs* of producing shelter and settlement are of two broad types:

    (a) Policies that reduce unit costs *without sacrificing quality*. Technologies ranging from industrialized building systems ("hardware" innovations) through the so-called intermediate technologies to on-site managerial innovations ("software") are examples. Closely related are design solutions that more creatively combine and arrange spaces and materials; institutional innovations that reform landownership and legitimize property rights for those with insecure tenancy, thereby fostering spontaneous investment; cooperatives that organize communities for quantity purchases; and cooperatively owned and for-profit financial institutions that more efficiently channel financial resources into the shelter sector.

(b) Policies that reduce unit costs *with sacrifice of quality* are of two types. The more obvious requires compromising building codes, occupancy standards, zoning restrictions, environmental controls, or other regulations that aim to raise the quality of construction. The less obvious type, and one that fits somewhat awkwardly in this class, is the set of alternatives sometimes termed "second-best" solutions, or policies promoting self-help construction, upgrading of shelter and settlements, and sites-and-services schemes. Such alternatives usually require reducing quality standards, at least in comparison to "standard" housing.

The policy postures classified in this typology, and the examples, aim specifically at the provision of new shelter or the upgrading of the standing stock. They are *explicit policies* with the goal of raising quality or expanding the quantity of shelter and related services. *Implicit policies*, on the other hand, have other aims but nonetheless indirectly impact shelter and settlement. With government budgets fixed in amount, new industrialization programs or the augmentation of education budgets, for example, leave fewer resources available for shelter and settlement (or for other sectors). Job creation policies that raise wages, and in so doing increase the opportunity costs of time, discourage self-building in favor of construction by the formal sector. A general price stabilization policy could discourage investment in land or in other opportunities regarded as inflation hedges. Import controls could tilt the construction bill of goods in favor of indigenous materials. And so on. The list is almost endless for it is difficult to identify *any* public policy of consequence that fails to bear in some respect on shelter and settlement. Such policies can have significant effects, though unintended, and perhaps even greater impacts on shelter and settlement than those intended by explicit policies.

Criteria for choices at macro, meso, and micro levels

Recognizing that specific criteria differ by decision-making level, standards for evaluating decisions about investment in shelter and settlement programs may be distinguished between "macro," "meso," and "micro."

Macro decisions are those taken at the highest levels of government – ministerial, parliamentary, or executive – and involve allocating budgets between the shelter and settlement sector and all others that compete for available public and private resources. By the meso choice is meant the decisions surrounding project types. Choices between self-building by the informal sector versus dependence on the organized construction industry, between low- and high-profile development, between owning or renting, and a host of other alternatives define the components of a shelter and settlement program. Criteria used for micro choices are the standards applied in project appraisal, either for determining the feasibility of a planned project or for assessing postoccupancy outcomes.

The scheme described links shelter and settlement policy with social and economic development and exploits opportunities for learning by doing. Any fiscal year's budget is allocated in greater detail with movement down the decision tree, but information on outcomes, as governed by performance criteria, shapes the subsequent year's appropriations at higher levels of the hierarchy. Appropriations move from macro through meso to micro levels, with allocations at each level governed by the appropriate criteria (Fig. 12.1). Allocating funds according to a scheme somewhat like this would seem to be fairly standard practice in most nations. Less commonplace, however, is the practice of transforming criteria into subsequent decisions based on the counterflows of information gained from experience. Yet, if opportunities for learning by doing are to be maximized, the information feedback must play a rôle in tandem with the funding process.

The uniqueness of each shelter and settlement project is poor reason

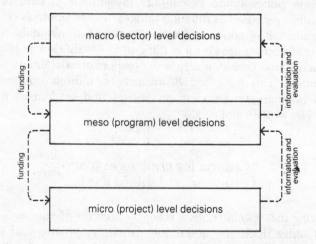

Figure 12.1 Flows of information and funds.

for failing to transmit knowledge gained from implementation in order to improve the performance of other projects. This holds no less true for pilot projects that are of an experimental nature, of demonstration projects that aim to exhibit the effectiveness of innovative new approaches in the hope of gaining more widespread acceptance, or of replicated projects that are based on successful completions. Because each project is in some respects novel, all projects are largely experimental. Each is, as Hirschman puts it, a "voyage of discovery."[2] If the discoveries are to be learned from, the knowledge must be transferred to where it is useful.

Thus, the levels are linked by information feedbacks and by reciprocal flows of financial resources. For example, appraisals of the successes and failures of built shelter and settlement projects (at micro level), based on specified criteria, influence the next round of choices between project types (at meso level); the outcomes of meso-level choices, in turn, influence subsequent macro-level decisions regarding overall allocations to shelter and settlement programs. Successive iterations generate changing outcomes.

Although the sets of criteria are meant to be consistent among levels, they are not wholly unique to a particular tier. For example, there is considerable overlap between the meso-level criteria that guide choice of project type and the micro-level criteria intended for appraising specific projects. Moreover, the criteria are not fixed. They must be modified to take into account differences in culture and custom and, because criteria reflect lessons learned from past experience, they will change with new experience.

Macro criteria

The decisions surrounding the "optimal" allocation of resources to the shelter and settlement sector can be broadly classified into the following four types:

1 *Shelter as a basic need.* Needs estimates for shelter are offered as a standard form of evidence to support claims for increasing shelter and settlement budgets. Though well intended, the estimates are less than convincing and perhaps even harmful to the cause they support. First, they fall easy prey to the economist's standard response that "needs are unlimited." Second, they fail to establish the fact that housing deficits are more pressing than unsatisfied needs for other of life's essentials including food, medical care, schooling, and jobs. Third, the method of estimating requirements – roughly, the standing stock of dwelling units less the number of substandard units and expected demolitions, plus the number of unsheltered households – assumes

that qualitatively substandard units should be replaced rather than upgraded. Fourth, they produce magnitudes that probably can never be achieved in practice; it has been calculated that meeting the developing nations' estimated shelter requirements by the end of the century would require expanding the capacity of their residential construction industries by roughly seven-fold.[3] Fifth, because the estimates are so unrealistic of attainment, they provide counter-productive information that fosters a sense of despair with making any reasonable progress in narrowing the gap between the supply of adequate dwellings and the total number of units required. Moreover, although frequently advanced as a device for underscoring the magnitude of the problem and the urgency for action, claims argued from this type of information have apparently had little effect. Research attempting to estimate the importance of determinants of housing investment for a sample of 39 nations covering the development spectrum showed that, though demographic variables that serve as the basis for needs estimates were statistically significant in explaining cross-national variance, the terms were far less powerful than level of income as a proxy for stage of economic development and a direct measure of ability to pay.[4]

(2) *Shelter as a required investment.* An adequately housed labor force is a necessary condition for economic development. According to the argument, shelter and settlement strategies must be geared to industrialization and regional development policies. "The problem is not a choice between housing and other kinds of investment," claims Millikan,[5] the position's chief exponent, "the problem is how much housing you must have in order to make some other investment actually pay off." The argument takes on special force in cases involving the development of new regions, such as Venezuela's Ciudad Guayana,[6] or new towns where shelter becomes a key component of support systems fostering industrial development. No claim is made that shelter and settlement programs have special qualities that promote economic progress, however, but only that they accommodate it.

(3) *Shelter as an economic investment.* Investment criteria that set priorities among competing sectors according to internal rates of return, capital–output ratios, cost–benefit analyses, and the like, customarily assign shelter and settlement a low priority because of the sector's presumed poor performance on those measures. Yet a number of case studies assessing the consequences of qualitative shelter improvement in developing nations indicates that, under specified conditions, their profitability is competitive with alternative uses of funds. A carefully controlled investigation of relocated Korean

coal miners, for example, demonstrates the economic feasibility of employer-sponsored housing.[7] Moreover, a compilation of rates of return on World Bank urbanization projects in 22 developing nations also shows favorable outcomes.[8] Returns, defined as increased rental or capital values of improved lots, were estimated for sites and services and upgrading projects. Although the variance in rates was sufficiently broad to discourage global generalization, within-nation comparisons showed that the projects fared well relative to industrial and commercial investments. The median rate of return was roughly 17–18 percent for sites and services and marginally higher for upgrading projects. The use of rate of return as an allocative criterion is criticized by those who counter that investment guidelines such as these disregard external or social benefits, which are presumed to be positive on balance and possibly even sizeable for social sectors such as shelter. Given the existence of net positive externalities, there will be underinvestment. This argument is obviously the mirror opposite of the first.

(4) *Shelter as a socially productive investment.* This argument asserts that improvements in shelter quality translate into real economic benefits through human resources investment.[9] Returns based solely on rents or capital gains underestimate the full complement of benefits. In addition to the direct profitability of housing investment are indirect returns consisting of (a) *unperceived internal benefits* that accrue to occupants but, because they are not perceived, fail to enter their market decisions;[10] (b) *private goods externalities* that benefit those other than residents – examples are employers who gain from possible increases in their workers' productivity when the work-force is better housed;[11] and (c) *public goods externalities* accruing as "neighborhood effects" to the broader community – examples take the form of reduced incidence of contagion or of fire hazards associated with safer and more sanitary shelter. Given positive external and internal benefits, social demand exceeds market demand and makes the case for subsidy to expand shelter allocation.[12] Although the arguments have great conceptual appeal, empirical evidence of such elusive benefits is fragmentary and inconclusive. Efforts by the International Housing Productivity Study to identify the benefits and estimate their magnitude at seven test sites in less developed areas produced these results. First, in half of the cases, positive effects on work productivity attributable to better quality shelter were observed. Second, in only two of the seven cases did better shelter contribute measurably to health improvement. Third, of the four cases where school attendance was studied, in only one could a positive result be found. Fourth, in the single case where

deviant behavior was examined, a positive outcome was observed. Although there were relatively few positive consequences of a statistically significant order, at least improvements in shelter quality turned up no negative consequences.[13] This is not to say that qualitatively improved housing fails to generate indirect benefits – it probably does – but only that the methodologies used to date have generally failed to reveal them unambiguously. The results do show, however, that "the upgrading of existing dwellings and settlements and the construction of 'second-best' new housing in low-income areas can yield social and personal benefits which the market for standard buildings does not provide."[14]

The meso criteria: program and project choice

Whether shelter and settlement programs are judged successful depends in large part on decisions that are often subjective in nature and that rely on a host of factors, differently chosen and variously weighted, under a set of widely divergent conditions. Advocates of social reform may consider their efforts worth while if their calls for action result in new policy legislation. Success in getting new programs organized and funded constitutes a higher order of achievement. Others will claim success only if there is tangible evidence of progress; in the case of shelter programs, built and occupied dwellings may signify that order of achievement. Still others will judge programs and projects successful only if the improvements have generated ongoing participation that has "empowered" residents.

Although there can be little disagreement with assigning the highest priority to ultimate output measures, such as the effect the projects have had on the quality of lives of the target groups, the interpretation of those effects is intensely subjective. An impact judged as "good" by some ranks as "bad" by others. A case in point is drawn from the results of a survey of Salvadoran residents' satisfaction with their self-built dwellings.[15] The relocated respondents indicated substantial satisfaction with the products of their labor, but new attachments to local affairs and neighborhood groups replaced their earlier concerns for political organizations and activities at higher levels. The shift in locus of concern would be welcomed by incumbent politicians but hardly by challengers seeking broadly based opportunities for social and political reform.

If there is little consensus on the nature of ultimate impacts, we are left in the awkward position of judging performance using inputs rather than outputs. This too is tricky. The world's landscape is dotted with settlements that were built but remain vacant because the potential tenants preferred to stay where they were, even if their present dwellings were qualitatively inferior to the new because the newly developed settlements were poorly located with respect to jobs, because moving required sacrificing secure tenure (whether real or only perceived), or because relocation meant forsaking an established network of supportive friends and contacts for an undefined social structure.

There are settlements too where people live unhappily. Unobtrusive indicators register the extent of their dissatisfaction. Individual units show the signs of neglect and rapid deterioration. Public areas go undermaintained and unused. Crime rates run high and neighbors organize their communities only in the event of crisis. The settlements show little evidence of upgrading, and overall there hangs a pall of apparent indifference to the quality of the environment.

Thus, whether legislation got enacted, programs funded, projects built, or dwellings occupied tells only part of the whole story. Investment made leaves unanswered the question of whether the resources were allocated to their best use. If shelter and infrastructure were built or improved at high cost, the efficiency criterion was violated, for the funds could have been better managed. If middle- and upper-income households were the chief beneficiaries, the equity criterion was compromised. If the dwellings failed to reflect indigenous cultural preferences, the project failed on compatibility grounds. In any case, the resources could have been better managed and the mere fact that substantial investments were made fails as an appropriate indicator of success. Nonetheless, in the absence of techniques for objectively assessing outcomes that are ultimately subjective, we are left in the breach with appraisals that must rely on imperfect measures or criteria – often inputs only crudely approximating ultimate outcomes.

In this section dealing with choices at the meso level – decisions intermediate between those taken at macro level where resources are allocated to the shelter and settlement sector and the micro appraisals that evaluate the successes and failures of individual projects – we suggest criteria for judging projects by type. The link between criterion and project alternative is illustrated by a matrix (Fig. 12.2). Operational criteria are itemized on lines of the matrix under the general headings of efficiency, equity, and compatibility. The list is more illustrative than definitive, for the criteria, as well as the weights attached to them, will differ among cultures. Moreover, because they reflect general lessons learned by doing, they should be subject to constant revision in the light of new experience. Programs are displayed in the columns. Although a complete list of options would include upgrading, site servicing, core construction, aided or mutual self-help, and conventional public housing, parsimony dictates limiting consideration to polar opposites, turnkey and self-help. Dots in the maxtrix indicate a continuum of other options.

Program Alternatives / Criteria	Turn-key	Self-help	Does program alternative...
I. EFFICIENCY			
1. Productivity	.....	.....	...minimize labor, land, materials, financing and transaction/administrative costs? ...increase access to serviced land, appropriate technologies and other factors of production without significant price inflation?
2. Flexibility	.....	.....	...respond to changes in urban form including private and government land use changes, and to increases in demand (including demographic trends)?
3. Administrative capability	.....	.....	...recapture program funds? ...require high level of managerial competence?
4. Standards	.....	.....	...require high standards, such as restrictive building and occupancy codes?
.....	.....	.....	
II. EQUITY			
1. Availability to low-income groups	.....	.....	...represent an affordable solution to the lowest income groups' shelter/settlement needs? ...target benefits to low-income groups? ...reduce the depth of subsidy to reach larger numbers of households?
2. Accessibility	.....	.....	...provide access to job opportunities and essential services?
3. Participation	.....	.....	...offer opportunities for broad involvement of participants/occupants in planning, design and management?
III. COMPATIBILITY			
1. With legal structure and culture	.....	.....	...respect participants' cultural traditions and preferences? ...provide security of tenure and opportunities for ownership?
2. With other programs/ policies/sectors	.....	.....	...conflict with or re-enforce other programs policies? ...make a maximum contribution to increasing employment and setting acceptable energy use patterns?
.....	.....	.....	

Note: ..... = a continuum of other options.

Figure 12.2 Matrix comparing meso criteria with program options.

EFFICIENCY

Productivity Does the program alternative provide maximum services per unit of cost? Inability to produce shelter at low cost explains why many Third World countries have made only token progress in meeting shelter targets. The occupancy of new shelter by the middle- and high-income groups, instead of by the populations they were targeted to serve, may be explained by the discrepancy between actual and anticipated costs. Cost overruns are commonplace when technologies such as industrialized building systems are used blindly, when production is frequently interrupted by bottlenecks (read: huge interrelated shortages), or when large transactions costs require channeling substantial resources into administrators' salaries rather than into bricks and mortar. The cost experience with turnkey government-built project housing may be contrasted with self-help production. Labor-intensive self-help methods usually prove to be far less expensive. Self-builders frequently acquire materials and labor services at greatly reduced prices or by barter. Because autoconstruction can progress with greater flexibility, bottlenecks are less costly.

Software technologies offer greater promise than large-scale mechanized ones, as Strassmann notes.[16] These consist of innovations in construction management both on-site and off-site; skilled assistance to aid self-builders on-site with technical tasks such as wiring and plumbing; administrative procedures and monitoring to ensure full and equal participation in communal tasks; and service aspects such as aiding the community to organize itself for postoccupancy management.

Flexibility From evaluations of a wide variety of development projects, flexibility emerges as a key ingredient of success.[17] Flexibility provides opportunities to adjust what is built and when and how it is built, and it allows for continuous redesign and even experimentation during progress and following completion. Moreover, when outcomes are difficult to predict and control, flexibility becomes a necessary condition. In particularly dynamic areas, such as the Third World's urbanizing regions, land uses often change rapidly and radically as a consequence of market forces or government interventions. Turnkey projects tend to be fixed in location and use, at least in the short run. Self-help construction, on the other hand, is more adaptable to new uses such as income production, or for expansion to accommodate renters – a common practice according to Gilbert's survey of five settlements in Bogotá[18] – and its lower cost means that less is lost if shelter is razed for other uses. Even more predictable factors, such as natural increase of the population, which may put greater pressures on space in Latin American cities than migration, can be accommodated easily if projects are adaptable. Self-help housing units lend themselves more readily to expanded household size, for example, than does the turnkey alternative.

Administrative capability   Managerial skills are often in short supply. Many shelter programs which promised much have failed due to managerial ineptitude. Program proposals requiring high levels of managerial skill should be highly suspect. Despite their great theoretical appeal, development rights and betterment taxes, for instance, will have limited use due to their formidable administrative requirements.[19] Occupancy standards to maintain health quality are often unenforceable in practice, leading to the paradox that the original objective of control is lost, although the costs of intervention remain.[20] The substantial burden on financial and human resources of maintaining public housing projects has prompted Egypt's and Singapore's housing ministries to offer tenants generous subsidies that encourage them to buy their units,[21] thus transferring costs to occupants and, in the process, probably lowering overall maintenance costs.

This is not to downplay the importance of adequate budgeting for project administration and technical assistance. Both are required in all types of projects for, all too often, on-site interruptions are excused by the absence of a technical skill at a critical point in construction. The sensitivity shown to these problems and the quality of technical services offered by El Salvador's *Fundacion Salvadorena de Desarrollo y Vivienda Minima* deserve study and emulation.[22] Relative to other shelter and settlement investment, increasing public and private managerial skills is a cost-effective strategy with potentially large and long-run benefits. Cost recapture is a case in point.

Managing cost recapture requires skill and inventiveness. Prompt and full loan repayment is required not only to recoup costs but to provide the financial resources to support new rounds of lending. The ability of private or public institutions to continue their lending programs may be determined by their records of repayments on outstanding loans. A public agency with poor collection experience will find it difficult to make its case for renewed subsidies in the subsequent rounds of appropriations. The problem is exacerbated by the legacy of colonial rule which in some areas has led to the expectation that certain public services such as water would be provided "free," thus spoiling the market in other subsidized sectors (and demonstrating that efficiency criteria have distributional consequences). If sanctions are not imposed on the delinquent, borrowers in other projects will see no reason why they too cannot be negligent.

Major problems remain in cost recovery in some countries, and in appropriately tailoring mortgage instruments in most. If credit is to reach the lowest economic strata, considerable imagination must be used in matching mortgage instruments to the special circumstances of the poor. Requiring level payments of marginal workers whose incomes are erratic and unpredictable invites default. Moreover, the poorest groups seldom have the collateral to satisfy lenders. Borrowing an idea from abroad provides a clue. In Korea, any annual renewal of the equivalent of community block grants is made on the condition that good judgement was exercised in the uses to which the funds were put in the previous year. Progressive loans might be made on the condition that the family had already used initiative in upgrading its housing, possibly through the investment of sweat equity, thus demonstrating a commitment as well as a record of success. Short of institutional arrangements that provide ready access to credit, families will have to rely on informal capital markets – families, friends, and local moneylenders – for their sources of financing.

In sum, success in recapturing costs requires a high level of managerial competence and enforcement mechanisms, as Sanyal so effectively demonstrates in his analysis of Lusaka's difficulties.[23] Still, in spite of the unresolved problems, there are successes to be reported, but rates of recapture tend to vary with project type, being generally more favorable with second best alternatives than with conventional public housing. Linn's evaluation of World Bank lending experience shows high cost recovery rates both for upgrading and for sites and services projects – rates in over half were 100 percent – but less success in recapturing the costs of public housing.[24] Major factors explaining the differences in outcomes between conventional and second-best solutions would include the lesser sense of commitment by public housing tenants through fewer opportunities for participation in project design and governance, their smaller sweat equity investments, and the generally greater proportion of their incomes required for rents.

Standards Building codes, occupancy standards, zoning restrictions, environmental controls, and other regulations that aim to raise the quality of construction in particular or the quality of life for occupants and larger communities in general also impose higher costs in the process.[25] The legislation for, and enforcement of, high standards may be well intentioned, for the object is to guarantee high-quality shelter for rich and poor alike, but enforcement frequently leads to the ironic conclusion that the poor are priced out of the market and get no housing at all. Often codes and standards are blindly extrapolated cross-nationally from the developed to the developing nations with little regard for differences in climate, culture, or ability to pay. Sometimes too they exceed industrialized nations' standards; for example, a low-income housing competition for Delhi specified separate bathrooms and WCs, "something that is not required of official housing in Great Britain,"[26] and building regulations in the Sudan specify minimum ceiling heights of 3 m.[27]

Obviously, the compromise of standards, particularly those set at unrealistic levels, can produce substantial cost economies. The case is well illustrated by settlement-serving infrastructure. Disposal of human waste, for instance, through conventional water-carried systems is estimated to cost US $ 500–600 per installation.[28] Even using intermediate technologies such as the vacuum method that depends on collection by trucks or an elaborate pipe network may be prohibitively expensive. Although its image may not be appealing to planners trained in designing more complex systems, the only cost-effective method generalizable to low-income countries, according to Dwyer,[28] is the communal facility where excreta falls into a simple concrete box that is manually emptied and carried away in animal-drawn carts.

Adherence to and enforcement of unrealistic standards produces at least two effects. First, they will maintain the relatively high costs of units produced by the organized construction sector, thus restricting consumption to middle- and high-income groups. Second, they will encourage shifts in production to the informal sector where such standards are more readily ignored. Rather than imposing standards as a condition of occupancy, a more realistic approach for public policy would be to facilitate the upgrading of occupied substandard units. Given institutional support and skilled advice, occupants can then raise their shelter standards on their own.

EQUITY

Availability to low-income groups Do programs serve low-income groups at affordable prices? Are production costs low enough to allow shallow subsidy? Do programs broaden the asset base by permitting ownership? The central issue is providing access to shelter for those least able to pay. Cases illustrating differences in program alternatives underscore the issue's importance. The Brazilian government relocated Rio de Janeiro's squatters from central sites to turnkey projects located far away. The National Housing Bank provided mortgage credit with payments pegged to inflation. Payments that escalated more rapidly than incomes led to default, foreclosure, and not infrequent takeovers by middle-income groups. In contrast, those living in the illegal private subdivisions at Rio's urban periphery can buy lots with 5–7 year mortgages, repaid under flexible conditions that take into account household crises such as illness or job loss.[29] Although clearly not a panacea, the *favela* and the lot offer a "budgetary solution."

Creative uses of windfalls and wipeouts may bring lots and shelter within reach of the poor, though to the disadvantage of the public sector. A prime example is the case of illegal private subdivisions on a Brazilian city's periphery.[30] Private developers first make available lots at extremely low prices while holding the choicest parcels in reserve. As the subdivision develops, residents pressure local politicians to provide the area's infrastructure. Once installed, the improvements radically raise the values of both the residents' properties and those reserved by the developer. In this way, the rich settling later cross-subsidize the poor.

Often, however, public action fails to distribute windfalls and wipeouts equitably. A prime example is the pervasive tendency for program benefits intended for low-income groups to be capitalized into higher values of land owned by upper-income groups. For instance, improving transportation services to low-income areas where land is owned by the middle- and upper-income groups may result in higher rents charged to the poor, thus offsetting the advantage of superior accessibility. Also, turnkey projects are often occupied by higher-income groups rather than by the poor for whom they were targeted.

Perverse consequences can result in many ways. First, cost overruns may defeat the original intentions of providing low-cost housing for low-income families. Second, middle-income people can legally or clandestinely purchase rights to units from initial program recipients. Although the sale of rights will benefit participants by providing them with resources they can use elsewhere, in the process they sacrifice an asset that is likely to produce above average returns.[31] Self-help projects, on the other hand, permit wealth and income redistribution favoring the poor. They carry less risk of loss from inability to meet mortgage payments. Ownership allows for the possibility of earning capital gains in a sale. Because self-built units do not have the exchange value of conventional project units, which are more attractive to middle-income groups, they tend to remain with targeted groups.

Accessibility The importance of accessibility to employment and services is widely – perhaps universally – recognized. Workers who are relocated to outlying sites where the land is cheap and easily assembled, but where job opportunities are limited, may sacrifice access to jobs. The losses are particularly severe for marginal workers who must be on the spot at the right moment if they are to hustle work successfully. Similarly situated formal sector workers may also be deprived of work opportunities for, according to a survey of Santiago's labor force, workers who were disadvantageously located failed to "be incorporated into work shifts outside normal working hours".[32] With inefficient transport systems, access is reduced and commuting times are lengthened – a particularly serious problem in Latin America where, maintaining the tradition of midday siestas, workers typically make four daily work trips instead of the usual two. Development of more remote locales also attracts mom-and-pop establishments that cater to consumers' routine shopping needs but at monopolistic prices. The claim is often made that scarce and expensive land requires building at high density and, because of this, low-profile autoconstruction is impractical in crowded urban centers. The work of the University of Cambridge's Centre for Land Use and Built Form Studies, showing ingenious building-land configurations, casts a long shadow of doubt on such assertions.[33] Development at the periphery may in fact offer the path of least resistance. Shoup notes that governments often locate projects in outlying areas not as the result of careful analyses of alternatives but simply because that is where the publicly owned land is situated.[19] Yet when employment opportunities are clustered in centers, workers who are relocated to cheaper outlying sites may sacrifice access to jobs. (Research could fruitfully be addressed to this issue, comparing differences in acquisition costs at alternative sites with the discounted losses in income streams; depending on relative prices, the discount rate, and the extent of job loss, the trade-off could favor paying more for better located sites.)

There are at least two solutions, though neither is costless. Formal sector jobs could be decentralized by policies that stimulate the location of new plants or the relocation of existing plants in outlying areas. Improvements in the transport system could moderate the chances of job loss. Improved urban transit and the organization of consumer cooperatives could also help to break down the monopolistic positions of mom-and-pop entrepreneurs.

Participation Shelter provision yields numerous, though frequently unexploited, opportunities for broad-scale cooperation between private and public sectors and the operating units and agencies within each. Project success may turn on the way that liaisons are worked out. Government may act more effectively as a facilitator of inputs and provider of infrastructure than as a producer of finished units. Public agencies may assist in providing land, technical assistance, infrastructure and materials financing. Self-helpers, acting as general contractors, can then hire private small-scale operators for the technically specialized construction tasks. And the self-helpers do the rest.

Aside from conserving public resources, occupants' participation yields other benefits as well. Involvement in planning, design, and postoccupancy management often earns participants significant rewards. Turner asserts that "when dwellers control the major decisions and are free to make their own contribution to the design, construction or management of their housing, both the process and the environment produced stimulate individual and social well-being."[34] The claim is supported by evidence from Turner's work in Peru. Moreover, project evaluations in El Salvador demonstrated that participants who learned by doing through active and personal involvement reported higher levels of satisfaction with outcomes than those who were denied similar opportunities.[35] Participation, like ownership, increases control. Decisions are often improved when larger proportions of populations have the chance to take part in the affairs that influence their lives. Such opportunities are more abundantly available in self-help projects than in turnkey projects. In the latter case, tenants are rarely identified before the projects get under way. Design and planning decisions have been made well in advance of the first arrivals. Their participation is limited to postoccupancy governance. Not so with self-help where participants take an active part from the very beginning and are afforded opportunities to continue their involvement in managing communities during consolidation.

COMPATIBILITY

With legal structure and culture Is the program congruent with participants' cultural background in general and with land tenure arrangements in particular?

Adaptability to high-rise living requires familiarity with urban life styles. A major element in the success of Hong Kong's highrises compared to Caracas's socially troubled superblocks has been greater cultural acceptance of that form.[28] Similarly, a study of Mexico City's *colonias populares* concludes that urban background was a significant correlate of success in consolidation.[36]

Land tenure systems rank as key elements pervading all shelter and settlement programs and accounting in major part for program perform-ance. Yet tenure arrangements vary enormously among countries. Clouded titles, a problem in many, can seriously inhibit the effectiveness of programs such as sites and services or upgrading that depend on the initiative of residents who value ownership and may require it as the basis for credit eligibility. Experience has confirmed that self-builders will only invest substantially in an asset that is perceived as secure: in fact, as Doebele[31] has pointed out, it is the perception rather than the reality of rights that governs behavior. Legalization of titles in squatter areas such as Bogotá's Las Colinas, for instance, has promoted a rapid increase in the quality of housing,[37] and the gaining of property rights was a major determinant of spontaneous investment in El Salvador's projects.[38] The degree of property rights needed to achieve a perception of security varies with culture and circumstance. In African nations, where cadastral surveys are limited to former colonial enclaves and traditions of tribal ownership remain deeply rooted, tenure arrangements approximating de facto ownership may provide sufficient security for investment. In

Latin America, where Roman law prevails, a status close to legal tenure may be necessary depending on circumstances. The decision to invest substantially may also be determined by the pattern of police attitudes toward invasion, the extent of squatter neighborhood organization, and the age of the settlement.

Hence, legalizing the property rights of those who occupy land illegally has considerable merit. First, because ownership sets the stage for spontaneous investment in upgrading, the granting of property rights offers an effective, yet relatively inexpensive, means for raising the quality of shelter and settlement. Second, because occupants of illegally occupied land usually pay no property taxes, legitimization offers the opportunity of charging for public services received. Public intervention that transfers ownership is not without its problems, for sanctioning illegal occupancy after the fact can encourage subsequent invasions. The problem can be met, however, by charging illegal settlers a fair price for the rights they gain; this, coupled with the understanding that ownership carries with it the obligation to pay property taxes, may serve to discourage continued waves of illegal occupancies.

With other programs, policies, and sectors   Does the program reinforce development of the informal sector, thus contributing to employment generation, minimal imports, lower energy consumption, and minimum financing requirements?

The informal sector reflects relative factor prices, including high capital and low labor costs. Reinforcing the informal sector, including its construction component, will aid economic integration, particularly in the key area of employment generation.

Residential construction ranks high as an employment generator. A study of 15 industry sectors in Mexico showed that construction ranked sixth in overall terms of man-years of work required per peso invested, and fifth in creating low-skilled jobs.[39] But, as Strassmann demonstrates, estimating the labor content of alternative construction methods can influence the selection of programs and techniques that maintain employment.[16] Low-cost construction gives work to relatively larger numbers than does expensive building. According to data for Mexico, the labor share declines with rising outlays per shelter unit. The labor component ranges from one-third of the total cost of a minimal dwelling to under one-fourth the cost of luxury single-family housing.[39] More importantly, labor skill distributions are substantially different between low- and high-cost units, with skill requirements dropping quite rapidly with rising cost. Because of its links with the informal sector, low-cost shelter generates more jobs across the board and particularly for low-skilled labor.

Construction also requires substantial materials inputs. Materials often account for over one-half of total building costs in Third World countries.[40] Although materials costs obviously vary by type of project, less apparent is the demand the materials bill of goods places on imports. Empirical studies of the imports required for residential construction in Mexico and Korea conclude that "while luxury housing in many LDCs has high import requirements, this does not hold for housing to accommodate those currently living at very low standards."[41] With high price elasticities of demand for imports, shifts toward lower-quality dwellings can substantially reduce payments for imports. Import substitution policies and the relative stability of domestic prices can reduce them further. Although the case for favoring indigenous materials over imports seems obvious, apparently few countries are convinced of the merits of import substitution and policies that support developing local materials industries. From their survey of shelter policies in 17 developing nations, Hardoy and Satterthwaite find "little government support for developing and promoting the use of local building materials."[42]

Energy consumption is also related to project type. High-quality shelter built with machine-fabricated components and advanced technologies generally absorb more energy per unit produced than do dwellings built to lower standards and using simpler materials.

Recourse to informal financing, and the type of channels through which it is obtained, also depends on project type. Low-cost self-help requirements are likely to be financed by informal means, if at all. A survey conducted in Lima's *barriadas* showed that housing credit ranked as least important among 26 publicly and privately provided services. Respondents were reluctant to take on the financial burden of fixed commitments, preferring instead to upgrade their dwellings piecemeal as their personal circumstances permitted.[43] (The result could be explained by the respondents' unfamiliarity with credit instruments and institutions.) Project type will generate different demands for credit, just as it does for technologies. Upgrading can be done when the family has the resources, with progress accelerated during periods of personal prosperity or postponed during bad times. The public housing project, on the other hand, straps the family into a financial straitjacket, or an "architectural mould," to use Turner's term.[44]

Micro criteria

The meso-level criteria governing choices between project types differ little from those used in evaluating individual projects, either in the planning stages where determining feasibility is paramount or in the postoccupancy phase where the assessment of actual outcomes becomes an input influencing subsequent decisions. Again, the overarching trinity of efficiency, equity, and compatibility are the major categories. To the meso criteria list in Figure 12.2 might be added more detailed components that reflect the conditions of specific projects. For completed projects, fieldwork should assess, for example, rates of consolidation and participants' satisfaction with outcomes. Given the rewards of broad-scale participation, information should be sought to determine whether the .projects resulted in the creation of ongoing neighborhood organizations, whether the participants' energies were effectively utilized, whether participation provided a sense of involvement and shared purpose. Answers to practical and detailed questions will identify bottlenecks and generate information useful to future practice. For instance, were materials, technical expertise, requisite skills, financing, and infrastructure facilities available at critical points in the production process?

Recapitulation

The macro, meso, and micro criteria are best applied as a continual process where constant evaluation of past experience feeds into the design of new shelter and settlement programs. Experience with turnkey and self-help approaches offers an example of this learning dynamic.

During recent decades, sectoral budget allocations at macro level have often been determined by needs criteria specified as numbers of new, finished units required to replace existing substandard units. Implementation at meso level meant removing squatters to turnkey projects. For reasons previously mentioned, the turnkey projects generally failed to meet the housing requirements of the poor. Failure first became apparent at micro level as projects were abandoned, became socially troubled, or, in some especially dramatic cases, were never occupied. The program response at meso level took form as a radical shift favoring second-best solutions that offered a broad spectrum of costs and methods to fit the varied circumstances of the populations they were meant to serve, providing them with a realistic budgetary solution to their shelter requirements. Program experience at meso level has in turn helped to shape housing investment decisions at the highest level. The "new" macro response reflects policies of international organizations such as the World Bank's "basic needs approach" which recognizes the potential for second best to do more with limited resources.

Self-help and the other second-best variants are by no means panaceas. Problems remain but solutions sensitive to country and culture can be found with the help of learning cycles and continual reassessment of criteria.

Progress and the challenges
for future policy

Recognition accorded the second-best solutions to meeting shelter needs ranks among the most significant events advancing progress in the struggle to improve the quality of the Third World's settlements. Sparking that recognition was the discovery that squatter settlements are the slums of hope rather than the imagined slums of despair, to borrow Stokes's terminology.[45] Neither are illegal settlements centers of political subversion and organized crime, as convention has portrayed them, nor are their residents the permanently poor entrapped by a culture of poverty. Instead the settlements are "overwhelmingly composed of poor families who work hard and aspire to get ahead legitimately."[46] The frameworks developed for dealing with illegal settlements and capitalizing on their residents' potential for upward mobility were a first step taken for translating this knowledge into action. Slums, traditionally seen as problems, were in fact the solutions. Latent resources, both human and physical, had to be tapped and institutions had to provide support for initiating an evolutionary, perhaps self-sustaining, process that would transform the settlements into self-improving neighborhoods.

The second step was convincing policy makers that indeed solution was problem and problem was solution. Shelter requirements responded to by provision of large-scale accommodations built to high standards and using advanced capital-intensive technologies were really the problem, so the argument went; the correct solution was instead to confront the "problem," as popularly but incorrectly portrayed – the slum itself. The apparently topsy-turvy conception succeeded in realization. Largely due to arguments of this type, attitudes toward squatter settlements have undergone radical revision.

Upgrading, site servicing, and self-help, the principal alternatives embraced by "second best," offered the potential for satisfying the overriding criteria for choice of shelter type. First, they were efficient for they provided shelter improvement cheaply. Using unemployed labor and indigenous materials that had few other uses meant building at virtually zero wage and materials costs. A tabulation of sites and services projects completed by the World Bank during the 1970s shows how closely the efficiency expectations were realized in practice. In the typical project, shelter cost about US $ 1,400 per plot and in some cases below US $ 300. Sites and services was a bargain, for, in cases where data permitted comparisons of alternative project types, the median shelter cost less than half that of the least expensive public housing – US $ 1,342 compared to US $ 3,300.[47]

Second, second best satisfied the equity criterion by providing even the lowest income groups of the population with the opportunities for upgrading the quality of their shelters and settlements, and the quality of their lives as well. Linn's tabulation of World Bank projects shows that public housing programs fared less well in reaching the lowest income groups than did serviced-site programs.[48] Moreover, the charges imposed on sites-and-services participants ranged from 8 percent of household income to an exceptional 50 percent but were typically only about 20 percent. Upgrading projects generally performed even better on this criterion, generally reaching larger numbers of beneficiaries.[49]

Third, second best rarely compromised other major development goals. Using indigenous materials requires no imports. *In situ* improvements can be made without dislocating families. Minimal input costs require minimal shifts in household budgets away from other necessities.

The empirical work completed by the International Housing Productivity Study has demonstrated the superiority of shallow subsidies given to many for marginal improvements compared to deep subsidies made for more costly programs that supplied finished dwellings to a few.[50] If a trend can be discerned in the support of shelter and settlement projects by international aid organizations, it is in the same direction. Grants and loans once made for the construction of high-profile developments are today increasingly made for second-best projects. Indeed, even within this group, shallower subsidies for upgrading are absorbing an increasing share of total urbanization resources committed by the World Bank, compared to allocations for the somewhat more costly sites and services and self-help programs.[51]

Despite the remarkable success record of second best in satisfying the criteria of efficiency, equity, and compatibility, formidable problems remain – and probably always will – to challenge policy making. No attempt has been made here to provide a complete inventory of issues, but problems of effectively using technology, of developing financial instruments and institutions, of devising effective cost recapture schemes, of reforming landownership and conveying rights, of better locating projects, of formulating appropriate construction standards, and of improving design rank among the most urgent.

In spite of the past two decades' progress in generally accepting second-best alternatives as appealing and workable solutions to the shelter and settlement problem, and its translation into action, the concept has yet to be recognized in other nations. "Many government officials still regard serviced-site schemes as no more than officially sponsored slum or squatter settlement construction," note Hardoy & Satterthwaite,[52] who go on to point out that, of 17 nations surveyed, in only two (the Sudan and Tanzania) has construction by the informal sector become the central part of urban housing policy. The most compelling problem is clearly convincing the majority of the wisdom of the minority.

Conclusions and recommendations

Criteria offering guidelines for the evaluation of actions spring from an empirical as well as a theoretical base. The case for shelter targets, for example, can be argued on grounds of social justice, but the arguments become operational only when framed by estimates of actual need. Although theoretically sound, the economic and productivity arguments are persuasive only when accompanied by estimates of the sector's contribution to economic progress. Advocacy of shelter as a means for redistributing wealth is convincing only in the light of evidence demonstrating that programs actually reach the poor. Claims of superiority of one type of shelter provision over another carry the ring of conviction only when supported by field evidence. Information gleaned from observation is required to give credence to the criteria proposed in this chapter and to make them operative as decision guidelines. Indeed, they have little practical meaning unless rooted in good evidence as well as good theory.

In his preface to a piece on housing need, Rodwin observes that "all problems are divided into two classes: soluble questions which are trivial and important questions which are insoluble."[53] Learning by doing provides an effective device for confronting the "insoluble" questions of shelter and settlement. Resources devoted to evaluative research that has shaped criteria and fostered new ways of looking at one of the world's oldest and most enduring problems – how to provide shelter – have probably been as well spent as resources directly allocated for the production of shelter itself.

Copyrighting or patenting most types of research – "soft technologies" in their own right – addressed to these concerns is difficult. Because beneficiaries cannot be efficiently charged, research has substantial public goods attributes. In light of international spillovers, any nation will underinvest. For the same reason that public subsidies are warranted for shelter investments that generate spillovers benefiting society at large, it falls to international organizations to sponsor research that accrues benefits at international scale. Therefore, as a contribution to the International Year of Shelter for the Homeless, it is recommended that the United Nations and related organizations accelerate their sponsorship of innovative research on the shelter and settlement sector, the monitoring of shelter and settlement programs and projects, and the broad-scale dissemination of results.

13

The legal and the illegal city

JORGE HARDOY and DAVID SATTERTHWAITE

Introduction

IF WE EXAMINE a list of the Third World's largest cities, we find that many have a colonial origin. This is especially so in Latin America where virtually all cities with more than a million inhabitants were founded by the Spaniards or the Portuguese; indeed, the ten largest metropolitan areas today had all been founded by the year 1580. It is also the case in sub-Saharan Africa, where most of the national capitals and many other cities were established by European colonial powers – Britain, France, Portugal, Germany, Belgium. To give only one example, in East Africa, virtually every urban center which had more than 20,000 inhabitants by the mid-1970s was a colonial administrative station by 1910. The British, French, and Portuguese also founded many settlements in Southeast Asia and the Pacific, and many of the region's larger cities first grew as major centers of industry, commerce, and trade under colonial rule.

But an understanding of the origin and early developments of Third World cities, and of the institutions and norms which arose to control and administer them, is not merely an interesting historical background. Such an understanding is vital in that these institutions and norms have helped shape current institutions and norms and have contributed much to what seem today to be intractable problems. In today's large

Third World cities – and indeed in many small ones too – both the theory and the practice of urban planning under the colonial powers when the cities were founded and during the decades or centuries of colonial domination are visible in the urban fabric – the central districts, the layout of streets, the location and form of the squares or public spaces, the design of avenues (often built over destroyed city walls), the architecture, and the land uses. The locations of such cities also reveal colonial priorities; the fact that so many of the larger cities are also the main seaports or on natural crossroads reflects the importance given to colonies' trade and communications with the centers of empire and the need to exercise political and administrative control. City sites were selected with such objectives in mind. To give only one among many possible examples, the five largest cities in India in the 1981 census largely owe their preeminence to developments under colonial rule.[1] Those who first founded or settled these colonial cities could not have foreseen the demographic and physical size which they would attain decades or centuries later.

Where territories controlled by the European powers were previously occupied by advanced indigenous cultures, such as in Mexico, Guatemala, and Peru, or in many Arab nations or in much of India or Yorubaland, the location of settlements (including cities) shows an often surprising continuity over time. Colonial cities so often grew within or alongside precolonial cities; after all, there were no colonial economies without serfs or slaves or at least cheap labor, and the more densely occupied areas were often selected for the construction or reconstruction of new sites of government. But these were cities where cultural and social segregation were imposed; the frequently used term in British colonial cities for the exclusively European residential areas was the "sanitary district"; it was usually only in these white enclaves that high-quality infrastructure and service standards were met. In Africa, a *cordon sanitaire* of open space where no buildings were permitted was often placed between European settlements and the "native city," in the hope that this would safeguard Europeans from the epidemics and diseases of poverty which ravaged the indigenous population. Meanwhile, the movements of the indigenous population were controlled to serve or safeguard the colonial economies and a new administrative and legal system was imposed.

Inevitably, cities still reflect these controls and policies. The symbolic values of the colonial powers are evident in the architecture which housed their institutions and their senior representatives – the palaces of Governors and archbishops, the churches and city halls, the houses of colonial administrators, wealthy merchants, mine-owners and land-owners. These are still evident in hundreds of cities.

Throughout history, the poor have always created their own habitats – their houses and neighborhoods. They have been building their settlements, whether urban or rural, for millennia. And they have been doing so outside what might be termed the "official" norms of the elite city, although these official norms clearly vary by region, culture, and time. The poor utilize when possible, techniques and settlement layouts which reveal their cultural values; these too differ from region to region and change over time. They build their settlements outside the "official city" of the elite. Tenochtitlan (now Mexico City), Delhi, or Cairo were built in defiance of official rules and practices.

As many Third World cities began to grow as centers of government or in response to growing rôles as centers for production and commerce within an increasingly interlinked world market, new neighborhoods, many largely self-built by their inhabitants, began to occupy unused land near the city center or near places such as ports where jobs were available. The poor often had little choice but to occupy sites ill suited to permanent habitation – areas subjected to periodic floods or tidal inundation such as in Guayaquil, Bombay, Lagos, Maputo, and Bangkok or on hillsides prone to landslides such as in Rio de Janeiro or La Paz or Quito or on dry lakebed as in Mexico City or even in ravines or on desert lands as in Guatemala City, Salvador, Lima, Khartoum, and Cairo. Under colonial rule and today, there were and are different degrees of poverty both inside and outside the limits of the "official city." There are also large differences in the way the poor build their own urban "popular settlements."

The city of the precolonial powers, like the city of the colonial powers and today's capitalist cities, could not function without the labor of the poor. Much of the work in which they engage may be termed "informal sector," but in reality, the goods and services this produces are essential to the functioning of the "legal city." Many of the settlements and neighborhoods of the poor may be physically segregated from the "legal city," as they were under colonial rule. But the cheap labor, cheap goods, and cheap services their inhabitants provide are central to the entire city's economy.

So the differences in the city for the rich and the city for the poor, the legal and the illegal city, are not new. They have existed in close relationship for millennia. In the past, as now, they reflect the fact that governments are seldom elected by the people over whom they rule and seldom represent their aims and interests. Perhaps it is because squatter settlements or overcrowded slums and other forms of degraded human habitats have existed for so long that many people with the power to influence their development, including many professionals, regard them as inevitable. There is also the belief that the problem will be solved, as

Third World countries develop. Such a belief is convenient in that it helps justify no action to improve conditions for the poor. But its accuracy is more in doubt as the number of people living in very poor and degraded housing conditions has grown.

Perhaps it is because the elimination of poverty, which means the elimination of hunger, endemic diseases, illiteracy, high child mortality, and a degraded human environment is seldom regarded as a collective responsibility of a nation – and much less a collective responsibility of the world. It is a truism to say that there are rich nations, rich people, rich institutions and rich urban districts who live off the efforts of poor nations, poor people, poor institutions, and poor urban districts.

Most Third World nations are becoming increasingly urban. There is often a parallel process of concentration of urban population in a few cities or city-regions. In many nations, this is happening in and around just one city. The multimillion inhabitant conurbation, which only a few decades ago was a characteristic of industrialized nations, is now worldwide. Cities of half a million or 1 million or more people even dot the landscape of regions which were sparsely settled until a few decades ago. They reveal the rapid growth experienced by many cities in regions where the breakdown of colonial empires, since World War II, has led to the formation of independent nations. They also reveal the national and international constraints faced by Third World nations in their aspirations to develop. And they reveal the difficulties faced by their governments (or their unwillingness) to implement essential reforms in rural areas. This has been and continues to be a major cause of migration flows to cities; this could have been predicted but cannot be easily reoriented or controlled.

Over 120 politically independent but economically and technologically highly dependent nations form what is now called the Third World. At least 40 of these have such a shortage of resources that one tends to think that they are not economically viable, as nation-states, unless regional integration and more equal trade agreements and technological transfers from the industrialized world and with the richer Third World nations are adopted. Many have only a few million or less inhabitants. The poorer nations' lack of a stable, viable economic base was disguised during the 1950s, 1960s and early 1970s, as most managed to survive in the wake of a rapidly expanding world economy. Under the present recession, their fundamental problems are now all too evident. Such nations are concentrated in Central America, South-central, Central and western sub-Saharan Africa and Southeast Asia and the Pacific. Most only gained independence in recent decades. Their boundaries (and thus the parameters for their nation-state) were defined by the colonial powers (although sometimes with the connivance of local elites). But this choice of boundaries was linked neither to economic viability nor to existing economic and cultural links. National boundaries defined by colonial powers frequently cut across the territories of ancient cultures and disrupted important cultural and commercial links. And when considering the problems faced by poorer Third World nations, one should not forget those whose institutional, political, and economic life is threatened by foreign powers and corporations when they try to implement basic reforms.

But there are Third World nations with better long-term prospects but which seem to have lost their course for reasons which have resisted the interpretation of national and international elites. Perhaps the explanation is that the elites discuss development with little knowledge of history and culture and thus with a poor understanding of the rôle that free people, democratic institutions, and laws guaranteeing equal rights can play in development. Even most of the more scientifically and technologically advanced Third World nations are ruled by small minorities from a handful of cities with little knowledge of the diversity of circumstances which exist within their borders. The growing gap between rich and poor nations is also present within nations between the national centers of power and peripheral regions.

The old colonial economies are still visible in current patterns of economic activities, in the large disparities between regions and between cities and rural areas in basic service provision and in connections to road and railway networks; in the location of ports and industrial centers; in the use of the best lands for cash crops with the ownership of this land so often heavily concentrated in the hands of a small elite; in the shortage of technical and administrative skills; in the destruction or suppression of ancient community organizations and systems; in the imposition of laws and institutions based on western models which deny the value of cultural traditions; even in the writing of each culture's history.

This provides the context for the questions posed by this chapter: What makes cities grow physically and demographically in ways which increasingly show the results of unequal global and national development and thus become a block to efficient democratic institutions and result in a multiplication of degraded human environments? What can Third World societies do in the context of economic crisis, when the crisis will continue to be an ingredient in their decisions, at least in the short term and for many nations in the long term too? What can they achieve in terms of addressing the most serious questions of poverty when the ending of the crisis under present development models and political blocs may depend on the recovery of the industrialized nations and drastic changes in the terms under which they can trade within the world market? Why is the Third World city so poorly understood, despite so many reports, conferences, and learned publications? And why do city problems and the problems facing the poor majority of their inhabitants receive such a low priority from governments and the elites in power? How can we build cities which help their inhabitants to earn sufficient income; which promote community participation, which is at the root of strong participatory democracy; which facilitate social exchanges and which are less expensive to build, maintain, and manage; and which make basic services accessible to all while saving energy and time?

The search for shelter

Some months ago, the United Nations circulated a poster to publicize the UN International Year of Shelter for the Homeless which is to take place in 1987. This poster showed the struggles faced by a family of recent rural migrants in finding a home in a large metropolis. Based on a well known children's game of "snakes and ladders," the poster sought to explain the political, environmental, cultural, and economic problems that had to be overcome by the family's father, Juan Ramirez, his wife Ines, and their three children. After 20 years and the loss of one of their children (who died after drinking contaminated water), the Ramirez family finally achieved their objective of their own conventional house in a legal urban development with basic services. But before this, they had had to live in one tiny room in an inner-city tenement. And when they had finally begun to establish and build their own home in a squatter settlement, they had been forcibly ejected by the police. Only after returning to live for a while in a rented room in a tenement did they manage to take part in a squatter invasion which successfully resisted eviction and eventually gained legal tenure for its inhabitants.

Tens of millions of individuals or households face comparable problems when they migrate to Third World cities. Comparatively few will be as fortunate as the Ramirez family. For many, their entire lives will be spent in an endless struggle to survive while living in a degraded environment and having little hope of finding a stable income. With no capital and often no training and little knowledge of how to move around in an unfamiliar city, their creativeness, sensibility, and will are seriously undermined. They live and move in a city setting which is strange to them because they had little alternative but to move from their own setting. Dozens of studies on migration have shown how people's movements, whether temporary or permanent, from rural areas or smaller urban centers to large urban centers (or indeed from large urban centers to rural areas) are essentially logical responses to where

economic opportunities are better or survival more certain. And it is not
the fact that they moved in from rural areas which is the problem. Long-
term city inhabitants face comparable problems in finding housing and
adequately paid jobs. Many empirical studies have shown how a high
proportion of the people in many squatter settlements are not recent
migrants at all but long-term city residents who had little alternative but
to build their own homes in such illegal settlements. For example, in San
Martín settlement and surrounding *barrios* in Greater Buenos Aires,
which were established through organized mass invasions beginning in
late 1981, most of those who took part were not homeless migrants but
long-term city residents forced out of tenements by the (then) military
government's abolition of rent control and the general deterioration in
lower-income groups' incomes.[2] Indeed, in most urban areas, natural
increase now contributes more to population growth than net in-
migration.

In order to have a roof over their heads, the urban poor frequently
build their own dwellings with the help of family or friends. But to find a
site to do so is only possible by invading public or private land or buying
a plot in an illegal subdivision; legal house plots are far too expensive. So
too is meeting the "official" standards demanded for construction. The
process by which these illegal settlements get built contributes to the
physical growth of the city. The other alternative open to the urban poor
is to rent space in which to live, for instance a room in a tenement
building or in a shack in a squatter settlement or in a common lodging
house or hostel. Or they rent a bed or a space to place some bedding.
This contributes to overcrowding rather than the physical expansion of
the city until the absorptive capacity of rental housing in the existing
housing stock (whether in legal or illegal dwellings) reaches a point
where newcomers can no longer be accommodated.[3]

Practically all forms of housing for low-income groups are illegal in
some way, i.e., outside the legislative framework of each nation. Houses in
a squatter settlement are on illegally occupied land and the layout and
the structures there probably contravene zoning laws and building codes
– quite apart from the lack of supporting infrastructure and services.
Other settlements have some aspects of legality; a house built on an
illegal subdivision is usually not illegally occupied from the point of view
of the landowner, although the land use, the layout, the structures, and
the infrastructure and service standards probably contravene official
laws and codes. Inner-city tenement buildings were often legally built
structures. Many were built as middle-class housing or apartments, but
were then subdivided when middle-income groups moved out to the
suburbs; others were custom-built slums, often constructed with
government approval or even government support. But these rarely meet

the most basic standards for lighting, ventilation, space per person, facilities for washing, cooking, and sanitation. Ironically, the dwellings which contravene all these laws and codes and which cannot be rented or bought legally are precisely the ones which the poorer individuals or households can afford.

Very few poor people obtain accommodation in public housing projects. The number of such units built annually falls far below needs in virtually all nations; in a survey of 17 Third World nations' housing policies, only in two were public housing programs (including sites-and-services schemes and core housing units) on a scale to have a significant impact on improving lower-income groups' housing conditions.[4] Ambitious targets were set but rarely met. For instance, in Kenya, the 1979–83 Development Plan admitted that "over the last plan period, only 8 percent of the low cost units planned were in fact completed and these cost on average five times the expected cost."[5] And the criteria for the allocation of the few that are built often exclude the poorer households, for they lack the proof of a regular income which is demanded by eligibility criteria or do not belong to officially recognized organizations or trade unions, whose members get first priority. Less than one third of the 202,000 public housing units planned in the Nigerian government's 1976–80 plan were built and relatively few went to lower-income groups. In Indonesia, civil servants and military personnel were receiving priority allocation for the low-cost houses or sites-and-services schemes developed by a public agency in the late 1970s. A World Bank paper published in 1979 states that half the population of Rabat (Morocco) and four-fifths of its squatters cannot afford conventional public housing. It also gives comparable examples of the exclusion of lower-income groups from public housing projects in Cairo, Manila, and Indonesia.[6]

The income of tens of millions of households living in large, intermediate, and small urban centers is so low and unstable that most if not all their daily activities have to be performed outside the law. These households constitute an increasingly large percentage of all urban households. One does not need more detailed studies to appreciate their problems; they – men, women, children – can be seen in most districts in every city selling in the streets, carrying heavy loads, performing all kinds of unskilled jobs in the houses or gardens of the rich, begging or simply standing on a street corner. If the problems are so clear and so visible, why are governments performing so poorly?

Many Third World governments still try to plan and build cities for societies which only exist in the minds of technocrats and politicians. It is one thing to build cities for those who have steady incomes and can pay for the houses and services they use. It is quite another to build cities for those with less or with unstable incomes but who nonetheless can pay modest amounts for housing and services. But it is completely different to have people who can afford to pay little or nothing for housing and services, who have little alternative but to build their own houses and neighborhoods and who subsist on such inadequate and unstable incomes that all this goes on goods, such as food, on which their survival depends. For these people, chronic illnesses and debilities often have to be untreated; the cost of paying for health services or medicines or even the time and cost involved in visiting a hospital is too great. But these are the people who are the true builders of Third World cities. For in most cities, they are responsible for the construction of most new housing units, each year. And their contribution to the housing stock is usually between a quarter and a half of the total housing stock; it is not uncommon for it to be even higher. To give just a few examples, some 40 percent of Nairobi's population live in unauthorized units.[7] In Nouakchott (Mauritania), a 1981 estimate suggested that 64 percent of the population live in largely self-built communities.[8] A 1975 study in El Salvador found that nearly two-thirds of the housing stock in the five main urban centers had been produced informally or illegally outside the formal, legal financial and institutional framework.[9] In Manila, a 1978 report suggests that there were close to 2 million people living in some 415 squatter settlements dotted around the whole urban region.[10] Some 60 percent of the population in Guayaquil live in communities built by the people themselves on stilts over tidal swamplands.[11] Comparable examples could be given for most Third World cities.

But in the process, cities and conurbations are built bit by bit. Their physical expansion is largely defined by where such people build their settlements – which in turn is much influenced by where they think they can consolidate and not be forcibly evicted. So the urbanized area grows in a haphazard and fragmented way; each *barrio*, or neighborhood, is built with no coordination with other *barrios*. As noted earlier, this chaotic and haphazard process truly represents the socioeconomic circumstances and political complexities of that nation and region throughout its recent history.

There is a growing gap between the problems created by the rapid physical and demographic growth of cities and the capacity (or willingness) of governments to provide basic solutions. For the majority of their inhabitants, cities are not developing economically and are not adequately serviced or integrated socially. Has rapid urban growth caught Third World nations by surprise and thus ill prepared to cope with such a variety of interconnected problems, especially when resources are very scarce? The answer, specially for nations which only achieved independence relatively recently, would be that they are indeed ill prepared in many ways. Many of the reasons for the poor performance of their governments relate to their colonial inheritance. Others are of their own making. But today, if governments insist on continuing with present approaches, many simply do not have the economic and human resources, the information, institutions, and technology to cope with rapid urban growth. A fresh view on how to address the problems is needed.

One major block to fresh approaches is the fact that most Third World governments are not elected and can hardly claim to have the political support of their people. A nation is defined by a number of values, life-styles, customs, and institutions; in other words, by its culture or cultures. Culture implies knowledge, i.e., experiences accumulated over a long period of time. But most governments have ignored both history and culture as essential inputs into their development plans. Governments and people do not see the problems of building and managing cities in the same way. It is the limited and often inaccurate understanding of governments – and also international agencies – which helps lead to their isolation and, as a result, to indifference, or to criticism, of their actions by the majority of people. People who are forced by circumstances beyond their control to live in overcrowded, degraded environments with no piped water, no provision for the removal of household and human wastes, no storm drainage, no roads and paved walkways, no health care and community facilities, and so on are less passive than before. They too have citizen's rights, although these are seldom acknowledged. Yet these people – so often now the majority in Third World cities – constitute the greatest and most dynamic resource to build and manage Third World cities.

However, these people have little or no idea of what governments are trying to do. Government priorities are so often entirely unrelated to their most pressing needs. City mayors may want highways, metro systems, improved parking facilities, civic buildings, pavements, and water supply systems which start from more central districts. But when those living in the poorer neighborhoods are questioned, their priorities are generally cheap and regular public transport, garbage collection, health centers and schools, protection against floods, and, of course, water supply and drains, jobs, and the possibility of obtaining small credits. Big projects have little or no appeal for them. The city in which they live and work is unrelated to the city that the mayors and technocrats want to build. The neighborhoods of the poor form a city of pragmatists. Every square metre, every scrap of material, and every unit of currency is usually put to best possible use. Community groups involved in the construction or improvement of these neighborhoods are very rational in their aims and actions. Yet the ideas, actions, and resources which might eventually improve the urban environment are in the hands of small groups of

technocrats with little power to make independent decisions and often
with little sensibility as to the programs that can benefit poorer groups.

National and provincial governments limit municipal government
actions to the provision of services. Never in the history of cities in the
Third World have there been so many projects on sanitation, conventional
housing, social services, and industrial parks. But they have contributed
very little to improving the living conditions of the poor. These projects
have favored only certain sections of the population in certain cities. For
those who can afford to pay neither for housing nor for services, these
projects have been of little or no value. Even for those who can pay
something towards acquiring or renting a dwelling but not the full
market price for a legal house or apartment, these projects have also been
of little value. Although the position varies greatly from nation to nation
(and indeed from city to city within nations), all nations face the
problems that result from rapid urban growth without the essential
investments and strategies addressed to the needs of low-income groups.
The result is that already privileged cities and the consolidated urban
districts within such cities receive a much higher share of total
expenditure and investment than do the largely self-built suburbs or
settlements around the city and the peripheral areas. One of the most
tangible pieces of evidence which demonstrates the effect is the
increasing number of health studies which show that differences in
infant mortality and life expectancy can be higher *within* a large city
when the richer and poorer neighborhoods are compared than between
the city and rural areas.[12] There is a certain confusion in the commonly
held belief that there is a strong "urban bias" in most Third World
governments' policies. But this cannot be the case when most small and
intermediate urban centers have been as starved of public investments
and as ignored by public programs as most rural areas.[13] "Large city bias"
would be more accurate for most Third World nations, yet this too is a
little simplistic for few would claim that the hundreds of millions of
inhabitants in slums and illegal housing developments in large cities
benefit from some "large city bias." The bias in public policies,
investments, and provision of services is not surprisingly in favor of the
better off and more influential inhabitants and the more powerful
commercial, industrial, and financial concerns. And since in many
nations these are concentrated in and around the largest city (or cities) it
appears as a spatial bias for large cities.

When politicians and technocrats allow free speculation with urban
land and the proliferation of illegal subdivisions, they are condoning the
establishment of chaotic and haphazard land patterns precisely where
lower-income groups will live. By segregating low-income groups in
overcrowded urban slums (often in inner-city areas) and increasingly

distant squatter settlements or illegal subdivisions, the segregation of the old colonial cities is being rebuilt. This means an acceptance of the growth of segregated urban societies ruled from above, which inevitably limits their potentials and undermines their interactions. Once established, these patterns of urban development cannot be easily changed. Integration will be more difficult; so will any official attempt to upgrade them. The haphazard development of land lots on city peripheries with many such lots remaining undeveloped or only partially developed ensures a pattern and density for which it is very expensive to provide roads, pavements, piped water, sanitation, and social services. In establishing these settlements where lower-income groups will live, we are actually deciding on the kind of culture and society we will have. We do not seem to be aware that by acting in such ways we seriously undermine people's creativeness and sensibility. By forcing lower-income groups to live, day after day, with unsatisfied material needs and with little reference to their ideas on how to use space, we also risk losing the relationship between people and their environment.

Third World cities are facing increasing difficulties in coping with the many interconnected problems caused by rapid demographic and physical growth. At the same time, most of the population live in small towns or rural areas in the majority of Third World nations, especially those in sub-Saharan Africa, South-central and Southeast Asia, Central America, and among the Arab nations. Many of those living outside cities face serious problems in getting access to essential income and services, quite apart from the fact that many face hunger. Natural population growth rates are often high and, over time, this helps put pressure on finite resource bases. This suggests a large potential for continuous and rapid urbanization in the foreseeable future. Meanwhile, in the cities, natural population growth alone creates increasing needs and puts increasing demands on limited resources. These point to a truly unprecedented challenge for national societies willing to try and cope with this problem.

The nucleus of the problem is the growing number of poor urban households. Neither rural nor urban poverty will be eliminated with foreign aid or assistance. It requires a different mentality to that persisting today, and a good beginning would be to link the elimination of poverty with disarmament and with broad political participation which includes the mass of the poor. Perhaps, in this context, strategies to cope with the challenges mentioned above will have some impact.

Poverty remains the fundamental issue in dealing with the future Third World city. Poverty is rapidly shaping the form of the city and its spatial structure. As vacant sites in central locations have been filled or their inhabitants evicted, new squatter settlements or illegal urban developments are increasingly distant from their inhabitants' source of income and from the trunk lines of transportation, water supply, and sanitary infrastructure. The result is a decline in the average plot size in new illegal settlements; often less than 50 or 40 square meters for a family. More often than not, lowlands subject to floods or steep slopes subject to landslides are occupied. This too adds to the price of providing basic services and facilities, if these are ever provided. But many cannot afford to live in illegal settlements miles from the center of the city. So many poor households try to settle in existing, more centrally located squatter settlements or slums, doubling up with family or friends or using empty spaces originally left as sites for schools and civic centers. The result is an increase in the overall density of people in many slums or squatter settlements. Some metropolises have grown to such sizes that squatters opt to invade old or unoccupied houses in central areas or to overcrowd in existing slums with controlled rents.

Rural settlements and small urban centers

Over the last eight years, the Human Settlements Programme of the International Institute for Environment and Development and its network of associated Third World institutions[14] have surveyed settlement and shelter policies in 31 Third World nations. In a first phase, 17 nations were covered, including some of the more populous nations in Africa, Asia, and Latin America. In a second phase, the concentration was on nations with relatively small populations; each of the surveyed nations had less than 6 million inhabitants in 1981. In a third phase, our program surveyed some nations which have undergone rapid social or political change. We also had direct access to similar studies undertaken by other research groups and individual researchers.[15]

A general conclusion from these studies is that governments practically never take into account housing and service requirements in rural areas and small urban centers. It is worth considering small urban centers with rural areas since, in most such centers, most employment is directly or indirectly related to rural production or to the incomes generated by such production. In the majority of nations covered by our studies – many with predominantly rural populations – governments have no interest in improving conditions in rural housing; or just a few token projects have been run. The exceptions are some socialist countries which have included the construction of rural houses and even of entire rural villages and small towns as part of their land reform and colonization programs; many have also sought to provide education and health care to a substantial proportion of the rural population.

In the capitalist Third World nations, some housing projects have been or are being carried out as part of official colonization programs, sometimes as a response to spontaneous colonization movements and occasionally as part of integrated agricultural development projects. In these official projects, many supported by multilateral or bilateral aid, investments in improving housing, services, and education form a very small share – if any share at all – of the funds invested in production, diversification of crops, the development of marketing facilities, the construction of regional infrastructure, and sometimes the training of the work force. The private sector invests very little in rural housing and rural services, other than in those related to production. When it does so, it is to house administrative or technical personnel and part of the skilled and permanently employed work force who live in hamlets near the plantations and "haciendas" dedicated to the production of food exports. Housing is thus the responsibility of rural inhabitants, who build with local materials, which vary according to region and customs (for instance, wood in Thailand, adobe and thatched roofs in different Andean regions of Latin America, coconut palm in Sri Lanka and Indonesia), and follow traditional designs and techniques. Very rarely are official loans available for rural housing. In general, no support is given to help develop indigenous building material industries.

Although every rural family has some sort of shelter, a very high percentage live without services in poor and overcrowded conditions. Accurate estimates are difficult to make; in many nations, there is little or no data since few rural censuses are taken. Even when they are taken the data are presented in such aggregated form that their value is mainly indicative of very general situations.

Poor rural housing, exemplified by overcrowding and poor ventilation, with no access to piped water and without protection from insects (or other vectors which spread diseases), is one of the principal causes of the high rural mortality rates, especially among children. If a convenient piped or protected water supply and better sanitation existed, dysentery and infant diarrhoea would decrease sharply, as would other water-borne diseases; if traditional building materials were treated and insect screens installed in houses, the incidence of malaria and other diseases spread by insect vectors could be curbed; if well designed latrines were installed, schistosomiasis and other debilitating intestinal parasites could be better controlled and the fecal–oral-related diseases might well diminish. Tuberculosis and respiratory problems could be reduced by less overcrowding, better stoves and improved ventilation in the dwellings. The incidence and the debilitating effects of most of these could be lessened with more adequate, regular and nutritious food supplies.

The physical and mental weakness such diseases cause – and most are prevalent among lower-income groups in large cities as well – also prevents millions from effectively joining the work force or drastically curtails their productive capacity. Many of these diseases are simply the diseases of poverty; they hardly ever impinge on the lives of middle- or upper-income groups.

Very few Third World countries have given serious thought to what public interventions and mix of services could improve housing conditions and reduce diseases in small urban centers and rural areas. This is despite the fact that in most Asian and African countries south of the Sahara and in some of the less developed regions of Latin America, rural population will continue to increase rapidly at least for the next generation. Without economic improvement in the rural areas and small urban centers, it is practically impossible to envisage positive changes in the living conditions of their inhabitants. Sometimes it is only a question of opening up permanent roads to break down the social isolation of many communities and to facilitate the marketing of their products. Sometimes the need is for basic technical help and very small loans. Very often it is also a question of water supply or simple forms of energy. In most cases, first it is necessary to bring to an end the exploitation of rural workers, which means guaranteeing them access to land and essential tools. But in some countries or regions within countries, such as much of India, Bangladesh, and Pakistan, perhaps there is already insufficient land to give an adequate livelihood to current rural populations, although better crop prices, better irrigation, and good agricultural extension services can give adequate livings on relatively small plots in fertile areas. In many others, among them Haiti and El Salvador, the Sahel and a number of Arab countries, and in some Andean and East African regions, the potential for the absorption of increasing numbers of rural population into agriculture or associated activities is limited and could only be brought about by prudent investments in activities which would permit an increase in the productivity of badly eroded land and well thought out programs of colonization in other areas. There is no reason to believe that the present state of affairs for the rural poor will change in the foreseeable future unless there are changes in the power relations between rich and poor social groups and between rich and poor countries.

The government of the nations covered in our surveys showed little concern about rural habitats. No major programs existed in Egypt, Jordan, the Sudan, Nigeria, Bolivia, Brazil, Paraguay, and Colombia at the time of our field trips in the late 1970s and early 1980s. There were some exceptions. In Tanzania, one of the aims of the villagization program was to concentrate rural populations into villages to allow them to be provided with basic services. The Housing Bank extended loan facilities to rural areas with the intention of funding 32,000 permanent dwellings in rural villages up to 1981. The Tunisian Development Plan (1977–81) envisaged the construction of 40,000 rural dwellings, a figure which represented half the publicly funded housing for that period. The rural housing program of Kerala State, in India, initiated in the early 1970s, was based on the mobilization of local committees, volunteers, and students giving priority to landless families. There are other initiatives which are not so well known. In Malaysia, the construction of new villages was favored; in Thailand a program to relocate inhabitants from urban tenement houses to rural areas was started; Kenya put some efforts in equipping rural villages with basic services; in India, a program has been running for years to provide landless laborers with plots to build their dwellings – resulting in 5.8 million plots by the end of 1975. There has also been a considerable effort in recent years to improve water supplies in villages. This information requires updating and expanding to cover other experiences, but how significant are these programs? What difference do a few hundred thousand rural dwellings, newly built or rehabilitated with public sector money, spread over all the countries in the Third World make when the rural population grows at an average of 30 million people per year and perhaps 60 or 70 per cent of the rural population live in inadequate shelters? We do not share the views of those who look optimistically at the situation for no better reason than that some governments are showing greater concern for rural housing in their official plans or because some projects are under way and some special agencies have been set up.

Some socialist Third World nations have taken a different view for a number of reasons. To start with, many have defined a distinct strategy for rural development and, as part of that strategy, the improvement of rural conditions has received high priority. New settlements were needed in the newly formed state or cooperative farms to house workers and to bring services to the rural population. Existing villages were modernized to serve the needs of those living in private farms in areas where land reforms had taken place. Over 1 thousand socialist villages were planned in Algeria; an extensive communal village program has been set up in Mozambique; over 300 villages were built by the Cuban government in the countryside, and many existing small settlements were provided with services, sources of employment, and links with the road system; the Sandinista government in Nicaragua has stressed housing and services in rural villages and towns; the government of Ethiopia has encouraged the formation of producers' and service cooperatives in the rural areas as well as building model villages to set an example in rural areas and to support rural settlement schemes for those in greatest need through the Relief and Rehabilitation Commission; village improvement projects in Angola were helped by traditional networks in rural areas. As noted already, in Tanzania, a villagization program brought most of the rural population into nucleated settlements. But in many of these nations, achievements have fallen below expectations and, indeed, in the case of Mozambique, Tanzania, Angola, and Ethiopia, any early achievements in terms of improving housing and service provision in rural areas has been much curtailed by serious economic crises and by wars. And how appropriate were the "solutions"? Certainly, the rural housing program in Tunisia and the socialist village program in Algeria have been criticized for the inflexible "western" concepts of housing, family organization and site lay-out these contained.[16] They, like much of Tanzania's villagization program, were not suited to the diversity of local needs, local resources and local preferences.

Rural settlements are essential components in the development of Third World countries. Through rural settlements and small urban centers, rural people are linked to wider regional and national markets. The livelihoods of a substantial proportion of the population in most nations are still related to the land and its crops, or to processing or marketing the produce. Social and economic services should be available in rural settlements and small urban centers which act as crossroads in the transport and communication networks. As Third World governments aspire to increase agricultural production for exports and to reduce food imports, a number of investments, such as in infrastructure, agro-industries, and social services, warehouses, and irrigation offices, will be required. Not all regions will benefit from such investments and actions and these will inevitably produce strong disparities. But when they take place their impact will largely be transmitted through existing or future settlement networks. In addition, the lower levels of government administration are, or will be, located in small and intermediate urban centers. If local development plans are to reflect local possibilities and needs, it is this level of government which should play a key rôle in defining needs and in influencing resource allocations at higher levels of government. Political independence requires different administrative arrangements to serve and control territories previously ignored by the colonial administration and to direct programs to a growing and more mobile population and bring them more into the political process.

It is worth recalling that three-quarters or more of the inhabitants of most Asian and African nations live in rural areas or in urban centers with less than 20,000 inhabitants. But there is often little idea in government about how to incorporate effectively their population into development initiatives and alternative strategies.

The impact of the economic crisis

The economic crisis has had and will continue to have enormous repercussions in all aspects of urban life in the Third World. Changes in the economic policies and orientations of the United States and the European Economic Community have had wider repercussions for the urban and rural poor in many countries than the foreign debt. As Third World nations found increasing problems in expanding and diversifying their exports, especially manufactures, they tended to resort to additional foreign loans, even if both sides knew or should have known the difficulties in repayment later. Then in many nations, loans were often not used for the purpose for which they were requested and contributed little to economic or social development. The way seen out of the crisis is through an increase in production. But the richest foreign markets – those of North America and Europe – are increasingly closed to Third World exports, especially manufactures. And domestically, Third World governments are faced with severe recession and very often requirements from the IMF to reduce public spending. Repayment of the debt becomes an insuperable problem because of the high rates of interest in the developed countries. And to reduce public expenditures means a decrease in the number of jobs and a reduction in the already declining purchasing power of salaries and informal incomes, leading to social and political clashes of unforeseeable dimensions. The bread revolts in Morocco and Tunis, the reported problems faced by governments in Senegal and Cameroon, and the difficult negotiations of the recently elected governments of Argentina, Brazil, Peru, and Uruguay with labor unions are some examples. But the debt of many Third World nations was contracted by the international banking system with nonelected, often highly repressive military governments. In certain instances, these only gained power with the tacit approval of some industrialized nations. How can a democratically elected government, committed to social justice, request from the population additional sacrifices to pay a debt for which they were in no way responsible? True enough it may not be just a question of shortage of resources but their misuse. Whatever the outcome of the present crisis, we are certain that those worst hit by the crisis will be the urban and rural poor and the lower-income groups among the middle classes. Cities already show in many ways the impact of the crisis.

Every economic crisis imposes growing pressures on already scant resources. It also delays the incorporation of new resources and the maintenance and extension of necessary services. In periods of crisis, all actors in urban areas rethink their individual decisions and concentrate on a policy of personal or institutional survival. This has major repercussions on the architectural and urban fabric of any city and in the quality of life of its inhabitants. To make matters worse, as sectoral or isolated decisions predominate, government policies and actions have little positive effect on the totality of the urban areas.

The economic crisis and the resulting deterioration in the urban fabric hits the poor in many ways. Many have little or no safety margin above survival. The crisis brings to the surface their unsatisfied needs. They are so concerned with surviving that they hardly have the time or inclination to think about anything else. But they are forced to organize the construction of their own shelters and create the immediate environment to their shelters, because no other housing is accessible to them. For the lower-middle classes, the economic crisis has meant a heavy blow to their expectations, and many with stable jobs have been forced to seek additional incomes, often in the informal sector. They may also be forced to compete with lower-income groups for cheap rental accommodation.

If our predictions are correct, the socioeconomic and environmental picture in most urban centers will continue deteriorating. Third World cities are being built and will continue to be built in the foreseeable future, with a great scarcity of resources. They will increasingly become centers of competition for the use of vacant areas which can be inhabited, for a place in a school or a hospital bed, for access to potable water, for parking and traffic, for a place in a bus or a train, for a corner on a sidewalk or in a square to sell merchandise, and obviously for jobs. It is difficult to predict what will happen in 10, 20, or 30 years' time. Even if the present crisis is gradually overcome, its impact will affect cities for a long time. We can expect more shanty towns, more slums, and more illegal subdivisions; we can expect the use of more dangerous sites for precarious shelters, we can expect more people forced to work in illegal or unstable jobs, poorer services, and a rise in the number of diseases related to poor and contaminated living environments.

The questions are then: Are the economic proposals discussed as ways of overcoming the recession conducive to economic and social development and can they be accepted by Third World governments from a political and social point of view? What measures should and could be adopted to lessen these problems and to establish preconditions for a more equitable and efficient urban growth in a situation of continuing economic crisis? And the implication is obvious: What must we learn to allow us to tackle some of the above-mentioned problems with a certain possibility of success?

The law is not equal for all

Not long ago, it was common to find urban planners in city agencies still representing squatter settlements as unbuilt areas or open spaces in their land-use maps, as if the heavily overcrowded but illegally held sites occupied by thousands of squatters somehow did not exist and could be represented by green shades, denoting open space. These maps illustrate the official attitude to these settlements, even though they may house a third or even a half of the city's population and work force.

Squatter settlements and other forms of illegal housing developments were considered as transitory forms of shelter which would be replaced by conventional housing, once national economies developed – as if all Third World nations are to go through linear, historical development processes comparable to those experienced by the richer Western nations; or the illegal developments could be eliminated and their inhabitants moved to less visible and more distant locations. It has taken years for governments to accept the reality that a high proportion of city populations have no alternative but illegal developments to finding accommodation. Although governments are slowly acknowledging the ways in which cities are built, many still persist in bulldozing settlements, in compulsory evictions and constant harassment to dissuade low-income groups from invading new sites and overcrowding existing ones. Some, perhaps in a desperate attempt to show they are doing something, even try to forcibly send some city inhabitants to rural areas or other regions. More troubling is the neglect with which governments regard the varied problems of illegal communities. Given present and foreseeable future economic circumstances, the problem cannot be solved by harassment, evictions, neglect, or even "trucking them to the countryside." It is a lost battle for governments that persist with such attitudes.

Over the past 30 to 40 years, urban growth in most Third World nations has been so rapid that one must think of entire new cities built in the periphery of (or over) the old ones, every 8, 10, or 15 years. In its architecture, land uses, and quality of infrastructure and services, this process reflects the privileges of the few and the poverty of many.

Governments and agencies often reduce the problem of building and managing cities to a quantitative problem; the universal solution is more money. Money to build more homes, pipes, roads, and pavements, money to buy more buses or build an underground, a hospital, or schools. Each ministry, municipal department and social group wants more money to satisfy its plans and ambitions. Each has its own idea as to the priority, for that priority serves its needs and interests. But there are few serious efforts to rethink the city in terms of a more equal distribution and efficient use of scarce resources: the use of technologies which relate to economic possibilities and satisfy general needs; norms for house construction which permit every citizen to find some legal solution but which are sufficiently flexible to encourage and support upgrading; municipal government far more based on a broader and more participatory approach. There is also a growing gap between thinking and acting across issues. The population has a right to demand that scarce resources be used more efficiently and a right to influence the planning and implementation of decisions which should help develop better human habitats. But this is not happening. The same ineffective approaches to the management of cities persist, the same criticisms are made, the same things are said in conference after conference, and the same mistakes are made in most development plans.

Official action with regard to the construction of cities is never clear. Often, the first time city inhabitants hear about a new sewer line or road is the arrival of the bulldozers to implement it in their settlement or district. Squatter settlements have preceded by many years any official policy to try and ease the social and environmental problems which their inhabitants are forced to face. Not that such policies, when they finally do come, are generous or widely put into practice. But in some nations there are new official attitudes to recognizing the rights of the inhabitants of squatter settlements to accommodation there and to basic services. Urban legislation throughout the Third World reflects the predominance of English common law, Roman law, or Islamic law. Such legislation did not anticipate the transformation in the world economy and the economic and social change in Third World nations which would lead to massive illegal settlements around most cities. For instance, under the tradition of the French Civil Code of 1804, the public or private owner of the land becomes the owner of the shelter built by the squatter and this squatter (a trespasser) can be evicted without compensation.

But the enforcement of the law, as experience has shown, brings many problems. It is worth recalling that in much of Asia and virtually all of sub-Saharan Africa, the legal system on which current urban legislation is based was imposed by colonial régimes to guarantee (and legitimize) their rights and their access to resources. The city planning tradition and the legislation which underpins it was essentially put in place to provide a tiny elite of Europeans with high housing and health standards, segregated from "natives" and to provide a legislative base for the colonial administration.

Few governments, whether national or local, have fully and systematic-ally enforced their legislation, although some have resorted to the expropriation of any private land over which illegal developments grow and full compensation to the original owner. By turning the land into public property, they resolve the conflict of interests. As an author from Venezuela commented recently:

> ...this paradox seems to reflect a broad ambiguity in state policy. On the one hand, the State recognizes that a significant proportion of the population lacks adequate housing and resorts to squatting. Plans are drawn up to resolve the problem, different measures are introduced and substantial resources are invested in low-income areas. At the same time, however, the State pays generous compensation both to the landowners and to the occupants of the ranchos (illegal settlements). One interpretation of this reaction is that rather than trying to solve the problem effectively, officialdom is concerned to disperse resources as favours to its chosen beneficiaries.[17]

But this can lead to strange distortions, as in the case where landowners actually pay people to organize the invasion of their land, since this is likely to produce a higher "price" in compensation from government than would be realized by simply selling the land.

Similar paradoxes can be witnessed on city streets. Governments acknowledge that there are not enough jobs and that most of those employed earn very low incomes. This leads to many having to earn incomes performing activities which are outside current regulations. Few of the street vendors who offer similar merchandise to that sold in legal businesses have the licences they are meant to purchase. Governments will not prohibit such illegal businesses; without them, many poor households would starve. But as a gesture towards existing regulations and established businesses, street vendors are often subjected to constant harassment by the police and are frequently taken to the police station and fined. Needless to say, some hours later, they will once again be pursuing their "illegal" activities for they have little or no other way of earning the income on which their survival depends.

In many cities, health centers, schools and piped water networks are not built within the limits of squatter settlements precisely because the settlements are illegal. The involvement of a public agency in such areas would represent, for the private landowner and for the courts, the tacit approval of illegal land occupation. Similar examples could be given for every daily activity performed by many poor households in every Third World city. Urban legislation, labor legislation, health and safety legislation, environmental legislation, commercial regulations, building regulations, etc., all aspects of the legal framework which attempt to regulate the acts of individuals within any Third World city, were originally sanctioned with some ideal situation in mind. Perhaps this was originally the correct approach. But they have become so complex, so rigid, and so unreal in relation to current circumstances and the possibilities open to the poor that they are transgressed, daily, by those in greatest need.

All too often, we assume that the law is equal for all. It was assumed, when national constitutions were sanctioned, that all citizens enjoyed equal opportunities. So legislation was based on the criterion of equity. The reality is very different, and we do not foresee much possibility of major change in the near future. Much of what we have learned – and what, essentially, low-income groups have learned – about the basic preconditions for a more egalitarian construction of cities will face enormous problems in becoming incorporated into prevailing public programs and projects. For it will cut across some of the principal precepts on which current legislation is based. Deeply rooted concepts about the ownership of land and the inheritance of privilege will have to be changed if we are to aspire to having better cities. Access to adequate housing and services and to equal employment opportunities should become a collective responsibility. And this is only feasible when each national society and the world awakens to the need for sharing. We can go on discussing how to improve the Third World city when in fact we know that current developments in such cities are producing problems of such complexity and scale that they defy any viable solution under present approaches, within existing institutions and legislative frameworks. Governments are slowly appreciating these realities, perhaps partially as a result of conferences, projects, better knowledge, and closer ties among their researchers and leaders. But a more potent pressure for governments to appreciate these realities is coming direct from the pressures of community groups that still have little or no representation in most governments.

Inevitably, most people have little faith in laws. Quite possibly, many do not even know that many laws exist. If laws are applied harshly, low-income groups simply ignore them or try to coexist with them. If the laws are too complex and threaten their survival, they try to live by their own system of values and codes. There is someting fundamentally wrong with a law if it is being transgressed so often, especially when most of the transgressors belong to low-income households, and when they can survive only by transgressing the law.

Two years ago, when visiting a squatter settlement in Delhi, we asked one of its dwellers (through a local journalist who walked with us) what had happened to the shelter which had obviously existed in what was now a small empty plot in the middle of the densely built-up settlement. His answer, as we remember, was the following:

A family lived here. During the last monsoon, the rains destroyed the shelter. As the family did not have enough money to buy the materials to build a new shelter [we estimated their cost to be some US $ 40–50], they moved out of the settlement to seek other sources of income. But they said that they plan to return. We are keeping the plot for them.

Despite the desperate shortage of land and the fact that every square meter of this settlement was crowded with huts and shacks, the community or the neighbors were assuming the responsibility to keep a place for one of their families, even if the entire community's occupation of that land was illegal.

The value of a law and its justification should relate to the benefits the population as a whole receive from its application. But laws are seldom changed to take account of new realities. So, despite fundamental transformations in most societies' economic base, a legal system implanted under totally different circumstances and often by a foreign power still remains in force, hardly changed at all. In Third World countries, there are a multiplicity of agencies at all levels of government involved in the process of setting up, administering, and reviewing urban and housing standards at the national level or within subnational areas of jurisdiction. Seldom do these agencies take into consideration the very low average income of the people, the differences in income distribution, the rural origin of many new urban inhabitants, and the diversity of cultural groups.

Furthermore, foreign colonization, foreign cultural influence, and foreign aid have resulted in a number of urban laws, especially building and zoning laws and standards, which have alienated and segregated increasingly large numbers of people. Of course, as noted earlier, for many colonial régimes, this was their purpose. But, incredibly, this same legislation, with perhaps a few changes, still remains in force. In nations which are rapidly becoming more urbanized, these issues are of great importance. Few governments have formulated adequate, realistic standards based on local possibilities and local resources. What little work has been done on this has been in large cities; few governments have given much thought to small and intermediate-size urban centers where in most nations a high proportion of the total urban population lives. If they have set standards for these, they are usually only simplified replicas of those adopted for large cities or conurbations. Urban legislation, once adopted, changes very slowly. And old colonial legislations or legislation based on imported European practices is hardly a realistic legislative basis to deal with the needs of rapidly growing and largely self-built cities.

At present, laws are simply unjust because they only threaten the most vulnerable and less privileged members of each national society. For it is their poverty which makes them unable to comply with such laws. A high proportion of urban dwellers cannot survive if they have to meet current building norms or labor or civil codes which determine working conditions and relationships, especially when the simpler acts of their lives – to build a shelter, to earn an income, the food they eat, and the water they drink – are outside established legislation. It would be wise for legislators to change such unrealistic laws and procedures and also to eliminate those that are not necessary. Urban legislation should be more generous and more flexible in adapting to the great variety of circumstances and the rate at which these can change. But it should also incorporate the particular objectives and priorities of lower-income groups as well as the experience gained by community groups in the construction and management of their neighborhoods. If building norms and codes are in principal to promote health and safety, then perhaps they would have more effect if they sought to *guide* the people who are actually managing the building of most new dwellings – as to how health and safety standards can be met at minimum cost. It is hardly appropriate for self-help builders to be told that "the level of foundation (for their new house) should be such that a minimum depth of the foundation to prevent the soil moving laterally under pressure shall be according to Rankine's theory" with Rankine's theory then set out in mathematical symbols with no diagrams, drawings, or simple explanations of what is required. Yet this is part of Madras City Corporation's building rules which apply to all buildings within the city.[18] After all, Third World governments cannot solve all problems simultaneously and more reasonable and flexible approaches are needed. To paraphrase a Masai proverb, "One government cannot hold all wisdom."

Local government

In most nations, local governments have enormous legal and institutional responsibilities in the planning, maintenance and rehabilitation of urban areas. Yet they can fulfill only a tiny portion of this responsibility. Local governments are responsible for land-use planning and also for regulating buildings, for instance height, technology, and building characteristics. They are also responsible for paving streets and sidewalks, for regulating traffic and public transport, for enforcing (and perhaps legislating on) environmental matters including sanitary measures and, at least in principle, in deciding on the location, characteristics, and sequence of public and private developments within their area of jurisdiction. In exchange for these services, local governments can exact certain taxes or revenues – typically real estate taxes and taxes or rates or licence fees on certain industrial and commercial activities. They also set rates and collect charges for many publicly provided services. Local governments are also often an important source of employment, especially for unskilled labor.

Urban plans and socioeconomic plans for cities are also the responsibility of local governments. Individually or through agreements with other local governments and provincial (or state) and national government, metropolitan or even regional plans can be initiated. So all plans, programs, and policies for an urban area should in theory be subjected to decisions by local government. In practice this is not the case. Most local governments play little or no rôle in development plans. This is even the case in Latin America where it is not uncommon to have 60 percent or more of national populations in urban areas.

Despite local government's old tradition in many regions, its rôle in the socioeconomic development of Third World nations has declined, even though it never was particularly strong or well defined. The structure of most local governments is obsolete. The professional and intermediate staff are totally inadequate for the tasks and duties assigned to them. The tax collecting systems and the ordinances which generate local revenues are usually obsolete; so too are the control systems to prevent tax evasion. A training exercise in the Philippines for local government officials included mapping many local government units, and it was found that just collecting the property tax from only a few of the largest property tax delinquents would be equal to one year's total local government revenue.[19] A comparable exercise in Ghana found that the potential returns from local revenues from a variety of fees, taxes, tolls, and licences were usually five times or more the amount collected.[19] In many instances, local governments pretend to serve cities or conurbations of several million inhabitants with structures, levels of representation, and political ideas which might have some validity for urban centers of a few thousand inhabitants; but they are totally ineffective within these larger conurbations. The capacity of local governments to negotiate with provincial or state and national governments and the private sector is also weak.

The economic and political decline of local governments reflects the growing centralization of national governments and the indifference of national governments towards subnational levels of government. Political parties and formal power groups show little interest in local government, as if a certain fear was there of its potential as a breeding ground for politicians with real popular support. In predominantly urban societies, as in most Latin American and some Asian nations, the situation is extremely serious as there is also poor coordination between different levels of government; it points to another expression of underdevelopment. It can bring with it high costs. As a recently published review of experiences with decentralization in the Third World noted:

> Central administrators cannot know the complex variety of factors that affect the success of projects in local communities throughout the country. In their attempt to cope with uncertainty, they create highly

centralized and standardized procedures; or through fear of making mistakes they do nothing about urgent decisions that are essential for implementing local projects and programmes.[20]

Parallel to the strong centralization of power in national governments is the division along functional or sectoral lines at each administrative level. Investment decisions are made sectorally in public works, health, education, housing, etc. As a result, in any urban area, there are several sectoral public budgets operating simultaneously in addition to private investments – and with no coordination between them.

Furthermore, the rigid systems of tax collection (where national government usually reserves the most lucrative and easily collected taxes for itself), the sporadic contacts between tax assessment agencies and those responsible for public services, and the low technical level of most local officials explain the low revenues which accrue to local governments, whether raised from direct or indirect sources. This is made worse in periods of high inflation and recession, but these are now common characteristics for many nations. Thus it is urgent to examine the behavior of public agencies at the local level, beginning with the tendencies observed in recent years.

Many urban planners retain a faith in planned changes as a solution to the many, interconnected problems of rapid urban growth with very scarce investments, even when most changes are taking place completely unplanned and unregulated. Most have no clear idea of how to use the traditional planning approaches learned in academic institutions. These proved ineffective even during the period in the 1950s, 1960s, and early 1970s when at least many Third World nations' economies grew relatively rapidly. They prove even less effective under the economic crisis confronting most nations and the present political circumstances. Technocrats trained in Northern nations or in Third World institutions, but with curricula firmly based on Northern models, are rarely capable of avoiding the trap of transferring to their own cultures theories and experiences based on and designed for First or Second World countries. Municipal politicians and planners have not been able to influence the land markets in their cities, especially the submarkets which could permit low-income groups to get access to cheap land sites for housing not too far from sources of employment or income. The problem for low-income people to get access to land on which they can organize the construction of their own houses is central to the housing problem in all Third World cities with mixed or market-oriented economies; historically, the market has never produced adequate urban environments for the poor. Indeed, only rarely has it catered for those social groups with a small savings capacity and some ability to pay for housing. But today the legal market does not provide even for the needs of this group.

Undoubtedly, there are political, legal, and financial difficulties involved in any state intervention – as well as managerial constraints. But there are alternative approaches, such as the release of publicly owned lands through communal or cooperative organizations, fiscal and legal measures, land readjustment programs, cadastral improvements, and changes in existing norms and standards, simplifying and speeding up the process by which private landowners can subdivide and sell building plots. Public transport can be well designed and managed to increase the amount of housing sites within cheap and easy reach of the main centers of employment. All of these could help bring benefits to lower-income groups. There are other measures too – in the long term, perhaps land banks but, in the short term, initiatives by public agencies which acquire land, install basic infrastructure and service it, and then sell the land in a rolling program. This increases the supply of serviced land sites; it has been tried with some success in Tunisia. There are other measures such as ceilings on land holdings. If, due to political and economic weakness, local politicians and technocrats cannot influence the land markets within the cities for which they are meant to be responsible, one can hardly expect them to influence decisions undertaken at higher levels of government.

Local (and national) governments tend to label squatter settlements or illegal subdivisions as "disorganized" or "unplanned." But this is only partially true. The diversity of self-built neighborhoods and the complexity of their connections to the wider city, economy and society are overlooked by traditional approaches. Each self-built neighborhood performs many functions vital to the survival of its inhabitants. Each should be understood as a particular process of social transformation, in a constant and vital period of transition. The interconnections between different neighborhoods or different settlements, sometimes weak, sometimes very strong, are much more carefully thought out and planned by their inhabitants than is often realized.

National policies

Most Third World governments have not defined explicitly what they intend to do with their human settlements. National plans have traditionally shown little concern about the spatial distribution of social and economic investments. During the 1950s and 1960s, the emphasis was on economic development, i.e., on "productive" investment, which meant mostly industry (but sometimes export crops) and the infrastructure to serve it. By the early 1970s, more national plans began to include the word "social" in their titles. An increasing interest also became apparent in slowing the growth of the large cities; one sees ambitious spatial plans to decentralize the population settled in congested areas and even to reduce Cairo's population in Egypt; the start of special programs on small and intermediate urban centers (growth centers or growth axes) in Kenya, Tanzania, Nepal, India, Thailand, Indonesia, and Panama, to name just a few. Most national governments declared themselves dissatisfied with the high (and on occasion increasing) concentration of population in large cities.

Rather than explicit policies and projects, based on careful analyses as to what was causing or contributing to current urban trends, national plans included a number of very broad objectives for the construction or management of human settlements. But rarely were they related to the economic capacity of the nation or the administrative organization which existed at provincial or state and local levels. They were also unrelated to the technical means available to implement them. There was little understanding of the direct and indirect means open to different levels of government to intervene in human settlements. There was also a great confusion between social equity and spatial equity; the claim was that pushing some industries or some developments to poorer regions would benefit the lower-income groups. Assessments of most such policies have revealed their high cost to government and their marginal benefit to lower-income groups. Given the highly centralized nature of governments, the technocratic style of national and local planning, and the political structure of most nations, popular opinion was almost inevitably excluded.

Examination as to where most new productive investment and indeed government investment in infrastructure and services was going and where most industries, services, trade, and commerce were concentrated frequently reveals that these are heavily concentrated in the very cities which governments claim they want to deconcentrate. An analysis of the impact of government policies and sectoral investments and of market forces points clearly at why such cities have grown so rapidly. If there is rapid migration to any particular city, it is because those who are moving there will probably be better off by doing so. But governments all too often try to deal with the effect rather than the cause. If governments are serious about stopping any particular migration flow from certain rural areas to certain cities, they should look to the factors causing that migration flow. In many instances, it will relate to factors such as an increasing concentration of landownership, soil erosion, drought, or low crop prices which remove rural inhabitants' livelihoods. Meanwhile, national governments' macroeconomic policies, pricing policies, sectoral plans, and tax systems are often helping to concentrate new employment opportunities in the very cities whose rapid growth they want to slow.[21]

So, although many national plans articulate worthy aims and objectives in terms of improving housing and living conditions and giving special attention to poorer regions and smaller urban centers, these human settlement objectives were not related to the real political and economic priorities of governments. Indeed, as Harris[22] observes, the invention of special programs for poor regions or small and intermediate urban centers might be judged to be no more than a way of diverting attention from the fact that a government is not addressing the fundamental causes of the poverty of the inhabitants in poor regions and the weakness in the economic base and of the local governments within small and intermediate urban centers.

Epilogue

Most Third World cities have grown so rapidly that the new districts do not seem to have the visual histories that are evident only in the consolidated and conventional urban districts. Their construction and maintenance, organized by their inhabitants, is carried out through largely uncoordinated and illegal individual efforts. Visually, Third World cities are becoming increasingly alike. Only topography introduces a visual distinction, but this disappears once squatters gain control of flat, solid lands. Not climate, building materials, cultural, nor even ecological differences are sufficient, in many instances, to allow one to distinguish one squatter settlement from another. Beset by similar problems – demographic pressures, land markets dominated by speculative interests, class structures, inadequate administrations, insufficient public invest- ments – the cities come to present an increasingly similar picture. This is so for different reasons in the residential districts of the rich, in the commercial and financial centers, in the architecture of public buildings and public housing projects; technological uniformity is everywhere. Only the historical centers and the old districts retain any of the characteristics which distinguished the Islamic city from the Hispano- American city, a Portuguese-American city from an Eastern city. The common denominator of the Third World city is the poverty of many or most of its inhabitants. Increasingly, the urban landscape is made up of recently developed neighborhoods and the districts of the lower-income workers. Meanwhile, the sameness in the architecture of the elite, whether in their homes or offices, can be seen almost as a denial of the culture and history of their city.

Two parallel histories, closely interconnected but visually very different, have emerged. One is the official history, represented by explicit concerns about the construction and management of the city and reflected in concrete measures. The second, that of low-income urban groups, has rarely been written. It is a fragmented and ill-recorded history, inevitably different from the official history. It is the daily experience of millions of anonymous protagonists who must find immediate viable solutions to ensure their survival, without any possibility of long-term perspectives.

The modern Third World cities sprawl. Their physical growth does not seem to have limits. They grow and deteriorate without receiving the attention they need from those empowered to take action to lessen the social and environmental costs of uncontrolled expansion. The historical moment through which Third World cities are living is very critical; it is part of an unprecedented transformation in the world economy which underlies an increasingly urbanized world population. But most govern-ments do not dare to adopt essential measures to cope with this transformation. They act with partial and fragmentary knowledge and information and with limited resources. But this is no excuse for the adoption of partial and fragementary solutions or no initiatives at all. Governments are showing such a lack of respect for their citizens that one has to assume that they accept their impotence or that they care little about their citizens' plight.

Governments need to inform their people about their plans and the real possibilities to allow their implementations. This might seem to many as politically dangerous, given the scarce public resources invested in cities, and the criticisms or apathy which such announcements might provoke. But more open and participatory forms of government are an essential part of being able to address the fundamental problems of Third World cities. These require a frankness and honesty which have hardly characterized the actions of most governments. To not undertake a dissemination of such information is not only dangerous but also a sure way of reinforcing governments' present isolation. As in the construction and management of cities, many positive and negative actors are involved. The concerns of the latter and the initiatives that they might undertake are predictable. But, foresight and firmness and a more efficient and honest administration, utopian as it may seem, represents the only way for governments to involve the people and their organizations. Third World cities have to be built with the resources available to each nation and its people. Multilateral and bilateral assistance can be of some help in, for instance, building up technical and administrative personnel, in the managerial and financial organization of agencies, in helping to organize data collection and to make use of the data collected, in information programs, and in funding small projects. For many of these activities, such agencies *cannot* expect full cost recovery. But agencies which insist on "big" projects, simply because it is easier and quicker, per dollar, to process the loan or grant application, to oversee progress, and to recover investment costs (where cost recovery is demanded) seem in many instances to be a misallocation of scarce resources. If such a change in direction is not viable, perhaps the only realistic alternative may be to wait until the degradation and injustice provoke explosive reactions. The "patch" approach, a project here, a project there, which prevails in official attitudes in the construction and management of cities, is not a solution.

But the economic crisis might be turned to positive use. For example, as governments (or at least a few governments) recognize their impotence to deal with the causes and effects of rapid urban growth, it opens the possibility for the permanent participation of community groups in local government and thus a change from the centralization of many decisions which impinge on people's daily activities. It could represent the end of "big" government, at least in relation to the construction and management of cities, and a respect for the rôle the people want to play (and could play), in development, if permanent, democratic organizations were permitted. It could also mean less emphasis on large urban projects – or a more significant control of them – with a higher priority for smaller kinds of projects and programs placing priority in different areas. Of course, there are large projects which are necessary and will inevitably involve large government intervention – for instance, the control of floods and other measures to improve the environmental quality of already occupied sites or the preparation of sites for new districts with site preparation and installation of infrastructure and services.

But there are many alternatives whose potential we are just beginning to appreciate. The innovative way in which public transport was improved in Curitiba (Brazil) and credits and assistance given to artisans in São Paulo in working in their homes or the hundreds of experiences from all over the world on self-construction of houses (and often even of entire neighborhoods) give some clues. Perhaps even more important are principles underlying the experience of Hyderabad Municipal Corporation's urban community development agency which works directly with community groups and nongovernment organizations in poor neighborhoods, and responds to their needs rather than imposing on them some already predetermined package. The work undertaken by informal community or neighborhood organizations in providing basic services and site improvements for themselves, when official agencies refuse to do so, is also a rich, though poorly documented, source of example. There are simple techniques, already tried and tested, to ameliorate sanitary problems for lower-income groups and to improve literacy and skills; their organization and implementation could be decentralized. Finally, there are the experiences from various governments – some positive, some negative – which have tried new approaches to city management, construction or service provision – the *kebeles* in Ethiopia, the micro-brigades in Cuba, the group dynamizers in Mozambique, the local development associations in Yemen Arab Republic.

Even combined, such actions in quantitative terms do not represent a major impact on the living conditions of the poor, still less on the employment problems faced by the inhabitants of Third World cities. If all who had benefited from these kinds of initiatives were added together, they would represent a tiny proportion of those in need – perhaps the equivalent of the population of a few middle-sized metropolitan areas. But they do point to new attitudes by government in bringing out of illegality countless cases of settlements or neighborhoods, thus changing what has hindered better relations between government and civil societies. The minimum conditions which governments must guarantee for their citizens is coherent action, a connection between what they promise and what they carry out. At the same time, community groups want more open, wide-ranging participation without hindrance from government. This would allow governments to learn from the real builders and planners of most new residential districts in most Third World cities. In this way, the discussion whether to favor big projects or community-based projects, whether it is convenient to reduce density or increase density in metropolitan areas, and many other aspects related to the construction and management of cities will also acquire a measure of reality and connection to everyday urban life.

It continually strikes us how narrowly the problems of Third World cities are presented and how little attention governments pay to city problems, as if governments in their arrogance and isolation have forgotten the reason for their existence. Researchers in the Third World have begun to reveal fresh interpretations of the city and its problems, aided by the experience of the individuals and their organizations which actually build the cities (even if their work is "illegal"). But many governments claim to be ignorant about the magnitude of the crisis in people's habitat and are reluctant to admit that there are other ways of seeking to ameliorate the social impacts. Degraded human environments will always exist if there is poverty, and poverty will not be eliminated through international aid. Industrialized nations' aid is so often oriented to the survival of friendly governments in nations for which the donor government has a strategic interest; only a small proportion helps the poor, except for funds devoted to disasters. Even a substantial increase in such aid will not address the problems of poverty because it is rooted in the ways national and international societies are organized and wealth is distributed. Like so many world problems which are the result of an uneven distribution of power and wealth, its solution should be accepted as a collective responsibility. Just as in many nations in western Europe, the provision of cheap or free health care and of a minimum income to the unemployed or disabled is accepted as a collective responsibility, so too must the world community accept a comparable collective responsibility for the world.

The improvement of human habitats requires the involvement of the "users" of those habitats. The problem is that even with the spread of community movements evident in so many squatter settlements or illegal urbanizations in Latin American cities, their organization requires time. And the rate of formation of new illegal settlements is much faster than the current capacity of existing groups to train themselves and develop their capacity to receive and work with professional assistance.

Substantial improvements could be achieved if governments acknowledged the reality of present trends in the formation and construction of settlements. As described earlier, the "illegal" sector of each city is growing and spreading more rapidly than the "legal" sector. This is growing because more and more people cannot afford the luxury of a legal plot on which to build and of being able to meet building codes. It is growing because more and more people cannot afford to go to registered doctors or hospitals. An increasing reliance on buying "street" foods is often the result of all adult members of the family having to work to ensure sufficient income for survival.

Such trends are inevitable in the foreseeable future under present political systems prevailing in the Third World and given the reluctance of First and Second World nations even to discuss some restructuring of the international economy. Much as we dislike throwing on the shoulders of the poor, the unskilled, and the poorly fed the responsibility also of building their own habitats, a total reversal of this situation will not be accomplished unless there is a sharp reversal in income distribution, both nationally and globally. The catastrophe predicted in many world models published during the 1970s may not impinge much, as yet, on the daily lives of those in western Europe and North America. But the catastrophe has been and remains the daily reality for a large part of the world's population.

In the end, we suspect that the key lies in governments no longer chaining and repressing a vast range of activities which are at present invisible to them: individuals, households, and communities building or extending their homes and creating a living for themselves through making or selling something since no other income source is available to them. This great range of activities where people are working with small amounts of capital and with both individual and collective efforts could be supported and coordinated to provide certain services, mobilize production, and improve human habitats. Of course, there have to be safeguards to protect individuals from exploitation by employers and landlords. But these and a strategy by which governments support and enable the true builders of their cities adapted to each culture and situation, requires very different attitudes towards local power and the use of power.

14

New directions for national shelter policies

ALFRED VAN HUYCK

ALL NATIONS HAVE a national shelter policy which is either explicit as a written document or implicit in the sense that it is the summation of individual laws, regulations, and budget allocations which impact the shelter sector.

There is frequently a gap between the stated national shelter policy, the policies that governments state they are following, and the real national shelter policies which are the totality of what governments are actually doing. Most often this gap occurs between an emphasis in the national shelter policy on the shelter needs of low-income groups and the reality that aggregate subsidies and budget allocations are being used to support middle-income housing.

This chapter argues that a written national shelter policy, approved by the highest levels of government, is an important part of the overall national development effort. Few countries have fully written and approved shelter policies at present. Botswana and Jamaica are two countries which have adopted national shelter policies of this sort, but few others come to mind.

The value of a national shelter policy

A written national shelter policy is of value in national development because:

(a) It achieves a national understanding of the dimensions and implications of the shelter sector issues among all of the groups concerned by providing a common data base and projections for both the public and private sector.

(b) It establishes a unity of purpose and a basis for decision-making in both the private and public sectors. In this sense, it acts as an agent for coordination.

(c) It establishes the place of shelter in the national development priorities. Shelter has often been left as a "residue" to other sectors. The formulation of a national shelter policy forces consideration of the rightful claim on resources and its relationship to other development sectors.

(d) It defines the rôles and responsibilities of the public and private sector and can contribute to the establishment of effective public–private partnerships in the shelter sector.

(e) It defines the shelter delivery system to serve the shelter needs of all income groups throughout the settlement system. It seeks to eliminate the bottlenecks and constraints within the delivery system.

The evolution of shelter policy concepts

Over the past 25 years, there has been a considerable evolution in thinking about what are relevant shelter policy objectives.

In the 1960s, most developing countries assumed that only the public sector could provide shelter for low-income groups and often stated that "safe, decent, and sanitary housing for all people" was the shelter policy objective. These objectives were interpreted to mean support for public sector shelter in walk-up flats built to high physical standards and requiring very high monthly subsidies per unit. In reality, very little such shelter was ever built when compared to the total needs of low-income groups.

During this period, the general view was that informal (or "illegal") sector shelter was below national standards and therefore should be cleared where it existed and new settlements built below national standards should be prohibited. This policy view gave rise to the tragic use of the police power to tear down "illegal" housing stock and to harass low-income people who sought to shelter themselves at standards they could afford.

Shelter policies reflecting these concepts rarely had a constructive impact on their respective shelter sectors and generally suffered from a number of serious deficiencies:

(a) they usually failed to recognize the financial resource limitations of the public sector to execute the shelter policy;
(b) they failed to consider the limitations of the administrative and management resources of government to implement the shelter policies;
(c) they usually lacked a realistic and comprehensive implementation strategy;
(d) they frequently left the private sector rôle in shelter undefined and without a specific strategy to induce the private sector to meet its responsibilities;
(e) they were negative, or ignored the potential contributions of the informal sector.

The failure of the then conventional shelter policies of the developing countries became widely recognized during the early 1970s. International donor agencies drawing on promising experiments in Puerto Rico, Peru, India, and other countries began to support new approaches for housing low-income groups. The Office of Housing and Urban Development of United States Agency for International Development (USAID), the then newly created Urban Projects Division of the World Bank, and the United Nations Center for Human Settlements took the lead in promoting new forms of shelter projects in the developing countries.

These initiatives, called sites-and-services projects, focused investment on the provision of serviced sites with a minimum structure provided, if any. Sites-and-services projects demonstrated that low-income people, when provided with secure land tenure and a serviced site, would invest in the incremental development of their own house structure. Often ten sites-and-services plots could be provided for the cost of one traditional walk-up flat built at high standards. Furthermore, these sites-and-services projects introduced concepts of affordability and cost recovery which, when implemented, would reduce significantly the subsidy element in publicly provided shelter.

The other major initiative was called settlement upgrading. This approach recognized the basic worth of informal (and often illegal) settlements regardless of its existing standard and focused investment on providing the essential minimum infrastructure which was missing. Frequently this upgrading process was accompanied with efforts to provide secure land tenure. Settlement upgrading clearly proved that, when informal neighborhoods were provided with infrastructure and security of tenure, the people themselves would invest substantially in the improvement of their own shelter.

International donor support for these kinds of projects increased dramatically throughout the 1970s. However, in many countries there was a continued resistance to adopt these techniques as national shelter policy. Often international resources were invested in these kinds of projects, whereas domestic resources continued to be invested in other higher-standard shelter projects. Nonetheless, the overall impact was a considerable reduction of standards and a growing awareness within the developing countries of the resource mobilization issues and the need for increased cost recovery.

The shelter policies of the 1960s and early 1970s were largely ineffective in dealing with the scale of real shelter problems in the developing countries. They were superimposed on extremely weak institutions. Many housing organizations were declared bankrupt or reached a point of decapitalization which permitted them to build only a trickle of housing units with annual contributions of government capital grants.

Shelter finance organizations did not exist in many developing countries with the exception of the savings and loan system which developed in Latin America through support from the Housing Guaranty Program of USAID. Almost all of the shelter finance organizations which did exist limited their lending to upper-income households for the construction of high-standard housing.

Starting in the mid-1970s, the developing countries – often with international support – began to focus on the need for the development of stronger shelter institutions. PERUMNAS in Indonesia was started from scratch during this period; the National Housing Authority of Thailand was built through the merger of several decapitalized shelter institutions. India developed Housing and Urban Development Corporation (HUDCO) and Housing Development Finance Corporation (HDFC) to support private sector shelter initiatives.

Nonetheless, even today, it is fair to say that most developing countries do not have a sufficient shelter institutional base in the public sector and almost no shelter finance institutions in the private sector, with the exception of several countries in Latin America.

This failure to develop a viable shelter institutional base, particularly shelter finance systems, has limited the ability of developing countries to implement shelter policies relevant to the needs of low-income groups.

Most developing countries continue to carry estimates of enormous shelter shortages within their shelter policies – deficits listed in the hundreds of thousands of dwelling units or even in the millions in larger countries. The shelter institutions in the public sector call for more capital contributions from their governments so that they can build more shelter for low-income groups. The developing countries in turn ask for more donor capital assistance for shelter, particularly in the form of grants or below-market interest rates.

Even after 25 years of experience by developing country governments and international donors, considerable innovation in technology, recognition of appropriate standards, growing emphasis on affordability and cost recovery, there has been relatively little net gain in solving the shelter problems facing the world's urban poor through public action.

Analysis of the recent national housing census data from many developing countries, however, has shown that, contrary to the views of developing country governments, real shelter conditions are not deteriorating in their respective countries and, in some cases, have shown improvement. In spite of talk of enormous shelter deficits, somehow the housing stock has kept pace with population growth, net densities per room have not increased, the quality of housing stock has not deteriorated. The answer to this apparent contradiction between the official government views and the census findings has been the failure to fully appreciate the significant contribution of the informal sector to provide shelter for the low-income families through their own initiative and financing.

Clearly, it is time to examine the underlying premises of national shelter policies and seek new directions.

The context of shelter in the mid-1980s

Developing country governments and international donors concerned with shelter needs must now seek new directions for shelter policies and programs within the global development context of the mid-1980s which shape and define the range of feasible choices to the end of this century. Among the factors to be considered are:

(a) The emergence of the Third World debt which now dominates the concern of policy makers in both the developed and developing world. Future borrowing capacities in many countries are seriously constrained, and the pressure to generate foreign exchange to pay for already existing debt burdens will dominate local development planning.
(b) The very high real interest rates in the USA and world markets, which are further complicated by the high value of the dollar versus most world currencies.
(c) The high public and private sector borrowing requirements in the

USA which are consuming annually US $ 80–100 billion in world savings. This funding is no longer available to support development in other countries.

(d) The collapse of the world's commodity prices which has reduced many Third World country earning capacities, particularly in Africa. The rising tide of "protectionism" which limits the potential of Third World exports, thereby frustrating industrialization efforts and increasing the difficulties of paying for already existing international debts.

(e) All of the above have combined to retard the economic growth rates of many Third World nations, and have even created negative real growth rates in some countries, particularly in Africa.

(f) The recognition of the growing failure of the internationally sponsored "basic needs" concepts to either alleviate poverty or stimulate economic growth. Many Third World countries are dependent on international capital transfers for more than 50 percent of their available investment capital. Insofar as the international donors have insisted that this capital be invested in economically unsound "basic needs" type projects, the potential of this transfer to foster strong national economic growth has been lost, with little impact on the welfare of the poverty level populations.

(g) The frequent mismanagement of Third World economies by governments in the face of the oil price shocks of the 1970s and the misuse of massive commercial borrowings which did not contribute to sustained economic development.

(h) The increasing reluctance of developed countries to provide capital assistance to the developing countries. International aid levels in real terms are declining, particularly grant and soft loan aid. The failure of the United States to commit to the IDA replenishment is but one dramatic example of this trend.

(i) The failure of the developing countries to achieve any significant and positive response to the call for a "new international economic order" or to receive any major breakthroughs in the UNTAD or GATT negotiations.

This litany of global issues, which in aggregate provides a grim climate for the development future of the world's poorest countries, suggests that shelter sector programs and projects will necessarily rank very low on the list of international donors and developing country governments. New shelter policies will need to reflect and respond to this reality.

New guiding principles for shelter are needed

Shelter policies will need to respond to new guiding principles and renewed emphasis on some of the emerging concepts of the 1970s which have not yet been adopted fully by developing country governments.

(a) The informal sector and the efforts of low-income families to provide their own shelter must be recognized and encouraged by governments. All counterproductive and negative constraints must be removed from national shelter policies, laws, and regulations. This is in recognition that developing country governments cannot, with their own resources, make a significant contribution to low-income shelter and therefore must allow the people the maximum latitude in solving their own shelter needs without hindrance or interference by government.

(b) The private sector must be encouraged to assume an ever increasing rôle in implementing shelter solutions for all income groups. Governments must reduce or even cease their efforts to provide shelter units directly.

(c) The public sector, though abandoning its direct rôle as a builder of housing units, must seek to utilize its available resources to provide serviced land and housing finance with full cost recovery; it must facilitate the private and informal sectors through the adoption of appropriate standards, laws, and procedures which foster efficiency at minimum costs, and it must provide support for training and institutional development in the public and private sector.

(d) The concept of shelter projects (whether public or private) must give way to the concept of sustainable shelter delivery systems which can operate at the national scale required.

The implementation of these guiding principles means a major shift in national shelter policies away from a concern about shelter "outputs" (numbers of dwelling units to be built as targets assigned to respective housing institutions) to a new focus on shelter "inputs" (land, finance, construction industry, building materials, and institutional development).

New directions in shelter policies

A shelter policy that is not concerned directly with dwelling unit production targets (outputs) but is concerned with the creation of a self-sustaining shelter delivery system for all income groups will be very different from most previously adopted shelter policies.

It will need to recognize that shelter policy is always evolving in any country and is never fixed or complete. It must be responsive to the political dimension present in every country. If must reflect the unique characteristics of the country, its culture, physical environment and climate, level of economic development, and natural resources. Therefore, there is no one model shelter policy that will be appropriate for all countries and for all time. The following kinds of subjects should be developed within a shelter policy based on inputs rather than outputs.

An understanding of the existing situation

The shelter policy will, as in the past, need to be based on a sound understanding of the existing situation and previous shelter sector experience. A shelter needs assessment should be undertaken which will identify the level of demand and the magnitude of the task in hand. The Office of Housing and Urban Development of USAID has developed a relatively simple and straightforward computer-based methodology for conducting shelter needs assessments of this kind.

There should be a historical review of previous public and private sector response to the shelter problems of the country that attempts to identify the shortfalls and bottlenecks which have constrained production.

There should be a clear understanding of the present institutional capacity of the public and private sector in shelter. The historical trends of investment in the shelter sector from both public, private, and informal sources should be analyzed and projections should be made of resources likely to be available in the future.

The essential case for the rôle of shelter within overall national development priorities must be constructed realistically. One common problem is for those who support housing interests to make unrealistic claims on scarce resources, leading to bad policy formulation. Only through an understanding of the country's macroresource allocation situation can appropriate goals be set for the shelter sector.

In most countries, a causality needs to be constructed which argues that economic development is the essential national goal; that urbanization will be essential to support the industrial and agricultural growth which will create the economic development; and that shelter and urban infrastructure are an essential part of the urbanization process. Based on this type of investigation, it should be possible for governments to reach major conclusions as to what needs to be done to support the shelter sector within the constraints of local conditions.

Setting shelter policy objectives

The specific objective statements in a given shelter policy need to reflect local situations. These objectives should be stated in a form which is verifiable by performance criteria. Based on shelter policy objectives that reflect the need for an inputs-oriented policy, it will be possible to discuss each of the various categories of shelter inputs which the policy seeks to influence. The following lists the kinds of specific issues which such a policy needs to address.

Land for residential settlement[1]

The land issue is usually ignored in most shelter policies and, in fact, land policy is rarely addressed in any systematic way. Yet the failure to establish a sound land policy is probably the single most important constraint in solving shelter problems. The availability of an adequate land supply for shelter at affordable prices is a critical prerequisite to achieving adequate shelter for all people, particularly lowest-income people who are the most severely disadvantaged in bidding for available land supply.

Land, by its very nature, is directly responsive to the policy signals sent by government to the land market. The price of land is to a significant extent influenced by government decisions on land tenure, taxation, cadastral information, and government investment decisions on trunk infrastructure (roads, water, etc.). Therefore, governments that are serious about solving shelter problems must address the underlying land policy issues as well.

The public sector responsibility which should be defined in a national shelter policy would include consideration of the following:

(a) Ensuring that the laws, regulations, tax policies, and tenure arrangements do not reward land speculators, and ensuring that both positive and negative incentives are established to encourage the urbanization of vacant or underutilized land which is immediately required to meet current shelter demand.

(b) Establishing appropriate procedures that are efficient, convenient, and affordable to private developers, households, and low-income groups in order to encourage the maximum legalized development of shelter.

(c) Developing land-use standards that lead to cost-efficient development related to the target group needs and ability to pay. Minimum plot sizes, road rights-of-way, open space requirements, etc. can substantially affect the total cost of shelter. Governments should calculate the minimum cost of meeting their land-use standards related to current land prices in a city and compare the results to the ability to pay of the population, based on income. In one Latin American city where this was done, it was found that 70 percent of the urban population could not afford to meet the minimum standard. In such cases, it should be obvious that standards must be reduced to reflect household income in order to allow legal settlement and obtain secure land tenure.

(d) A clear decision is required as to the extent to which government should be an active and major participant in the land market. If available land holdings are held in large tracts by a limited number of private owners, it is likely that the government must have adequate laws for the "quick taking" of private land for development and resale for shelter to all income groups. Many countries do not have adequate powers of "eminent domain," or the powers available are so constrained by legal procedures as to be unusable. In such cases, the laws and procedures must be changed if a systematic response to shelter needs is to be achieved, particularly for low-income groups.

(e) The public sector is usually the owner of large tracts of vacant or underutilized land. These land holdings are frequently divided amongst a large group of public sector institutions (such as the military, various ministries, parastatal groups, and public enterprises). Governments should establish a high-level public land policy body which would be given broad powers over the taking of surplus land from public institutions for development and resale to private entities and households in order to provide efficient urbanization patterns, reduce the pressure on land prices, and ensure an adequate supply of land to low-income groups.

(f) Conversely, many governments have been known to sell (or even give away) large tracts of public land to private entities well in advance of any possible development demand for the land. This land is then held for years until the development climate is ripe, at which time it is sold at full market prices, resulting in windfall profits for the private owners and an enormous loss of potential revenue to the public sector. This abuse of the public interest should be guarded against through the establishment of rigorous procedures of economic analysis prior to the sale of public land resources.

The new directions required in housing policy should include the elimination of the public sector rôle in shelter construction *per se* and the shifting of this responsibility to the private sector and informal sector. The many national housing corporations, authorities, etc. already well established in the public sector throughout the developing countries – which now build public shelter units – need not be abolished. Instead, consideration should be given to shifting their mandate to land development activities (without shelter construction) in order to provide the essential leverage and control that the public sector needs to assist the land market to respond to the needs of low-income groups. This effort would greatly reduce the needed public investment per unit developed and could, when well managed, result in substantial public sector income. A theoretical analysis for Mogadishu, Somalia, demonstrated that with as little as US $ 15 million in working capital a self-financing system of developing publicly owned lands could result in the creation of over 20,000 plots a year with minimal infrastructure available at affordable prices to low-income groups.

Infrastructure provision[2]

In most developing countries there is housing standing complete but vacant because of the inability of the private or public sector developer to obtain water supply, sewerage, power, or road access. This lack of coordination between house-building activities and infrastructure provision means that the stream of benefits from shelter are delayed, sometimes for many years, and the investment construction is frozen. The opportunity costs to the frozen investment add significantly to the total aggregate shelter costs of the nation.

One reason for this is that the responsibility for infrastructure provision usually rests with many diverse agencies with overlapping jurisdictions, procedures, and resources. And this is further complicated because the pricing policies of many public sector infrastructure agencies are such that insufficient cost recovery is available to provide for the operation and maintenance of existing networks (leading to breakdowns in services to existing beneficiaries) and funding is insufficient to extend the networks to new service areas.

As a result, most urban areas in the developing countries face huge deficits in infrastructure provision and, insofar as these areas are rapidly growing, there is little or no hope of providing adequate services to the new population.

The provision of minimum essential infrastructure to residential settlement areas is, next to land, the most important obstacle to meeting the shelter demand for all income groups.

An essential element in national shelter policy must be to focus on the need to meet infrastructure requirements at the scale of residential demand. Investment in essential infrastructure must of necessity be largely a public sector responsibility. It clearly should have a higher priority on public resources than investment in the shelter units themselves, which the private and informal sector can provide. The national shelter policy should therefore consider such things as:

(a)	The coordination of infrastructure provision to residential areas through the establishment of integrated sectoral plans. Here the critical policy issue is the decision concerning the priority of servicing already settled residential areas which are deficient in essential infrastructure, as opposed to investing in the provision of infrastructure to newly developing areas or proposed development areas. In the short run, it may prove impossible to do both simultaneously; therefore a choice is needed. The failure to provide infrastructure to guide new settlement area development could add substantially to the future costs of provision many years after these areas have developed. In some situations, the advance provision of infrastructure may be necessary in order to redirect settlement patterns from undesirable directions. For example, in Cairo, Egypt, it is important to provide for residential settlement in the desert lands to the east and west of the city, rather than to continue the existing trends of north and south development on vital agricultural land. However, this cannot happen unless infrastructure investment is made in advance of settlement, but huge service deficits also exist in the already built-up areas. Where should the priority of investment focus in such a complex situation?

(b)	A review of the existing institutional arrangements of the infrastructure delivery entities is required to ensure efficiency in residential provision. Overlapping responsibilities, unclear responsibilities, or gaps in the institutional structure need to be addressed. Once the appropriate institutional structures have been identified and responsibilities assigned, a specific program of institutional development and training should be considered.

(c)	The residential pricing policies for infrastructure must be reviewed in order to eliminate unnecessary subsidies to those households which do not require them. In most cases, new policies for increasing cost recovery will be needed. It will prove to be politically impossible to make single, massive increases in prices for infrastructure services; therefore consideration should be given to a long-term strategy of steady, small price increases based on an understandable set of criteria (such as adjustments with a price index, or minimum wage index, etc.). An important requirement is that a public education program accompany the revision in pricing policy that will inform the public of the reasons for the changes and the equity issues of fairness to all the citizens in providing increased access to infrastructure.

(d)	A commitment to improved operations and maintenance of existing services should also be a part of the new policy directions. The record of the developing countries on maintenance is not encouraging.

The failure of adequate maintenance provision adds enormously to the public capital investment costs in several ways. The initial capital investment is frequently larger than it has to be because of the fear that adequate maintenance will not be provided. The existing capital stock has a shortened useful life because of maintenance failures; therefore it requires either major rehabilitation or replacement much sooner than would otherwise be required.

(e) All viable alternatives which could lead to the privatization of some aspects of infrastructure provision and maintenance should be carefully considered. Housing developers should be required to provide more of the infrastructure in their projects, particularly for upper-income groups. The use of community groups and cooperatives should be considered for certain aspects of maintenance. For example, in Helwan, Egypt, community groups rather than the government operate the septic tank cleaning equipment. Solid waste collection is an infrastructure service that lends itself readily to privatization.

The commitment of human resources, management, and capital to improving the citywide delivery of infrastructure for residential settlement is a much more efficient use of resources than to attempt to undertake a series of shelter projects in which the ultimate provision of infrastructure so often remains uncertain. At the same time, settlement upgrading projects which focus infrastructure investment on a comprehensive basis, even at minimum standards, in a relatively small geographic area should not be seen as a substitute for citywide programs of infrastructure improvement.

Shelter finance availability

The availability of shelter finance to all income groups – but particularly the poor – is an essential part of a systematic response to shelter demand at a scale sufficient to impact national needs. Many developing countries have established one or two public sector shelter finance institutions but, for the most part, these organizations provide only a limited number of mortgage loans (frequently at subsidized interest rates) and rarely to the urban poor. Private sector shelter finance institutions exist in Latin America and a few other developing countries. In almost all cases, the private sector has limited its lending to only upper-income housing. More sophisticated housing finance arrangements, such as secondary mortgage markets, mortgage insurance, and title insurance, are rarely found in the developing countries.

Developing countries need to focus priority attention on the establishment of a viable nationwide shelter finance system. This will require the establishment of shelter finance policies and a longer-term strategic development plan. The key policy areas which need to be considered include:

(a) The establishment of a financial environment that allows shelter finance institutions to compete for private savings on an equal or even priority basis with other financial instruments. It has been shown that often households, even low-income households, will be willing to deposit savings in shelter finance institutions when there is likely to be an opportunity to obtain a shelter mortgage loan. Often these savings are not available to other institutions and are kept in the form of cash or gold by the family. Therefore, savings mobilization for shelter does not necessarily mean reducing deposits in other financial institutions or instruments on a one-for-one basis.

(b) The encouragement of the establishment of private sector shelter finance institutions such as savings and loan banks, credit unions, cooperatives, etc. It is unlikely that public sector shelter finance institutions can fully meet the needs for finance at scale. Insofar as the private sector can be mobilized to meet these needs, it reduces the demand for public sector equity finance of shelter.

(c) The establishment of relatively unsubsidized interest rates for shelter finance loans within public sector institutions. The history of public sector shelter finance institutions within the developing countries is filled with case histories of decapitalization and bankruptcy because of the failure to have adequate interest rate structures and to enforce cost recovery of the loans. The short-term political gain of uneconomic shelter finance mortgage loan terms must give way to the overriding need to have self-sustaining viable finance institutions.

(d) The commitment to providing access for low-income borrowers to shelter credit is essential. Most public and private sector shelter finance institutions are incorrectly convinced that the risks of lending to low-income groups are too high. Yet, ample evidence is available to demonstrate that low-income groups are good risks and will repay loans (if enforcement procedures are utilized). This is so because low-income borrowers often pay much higher real rates of interest when they use the informal credit market and therefore stand to make substantial savings if given access to formal credit markets.

(e) It has been documented in Egypt and elsewhere that when given access to home improvement loans, low-income borrowers frequently build new dwelling units for rent on their existing structure. This provides both a source of income, frequently in excess of the monthly loan payments in rents, as well as adding to the overall national housing stock at relatively low cost. Home improvement loans should be a part of an overall shelter finance system.

(f) As part of the long-term strategy for shelter finance, planning should be started and should, at the appropriate time, be implemented for the development of the capital markets for shelter finance and the establishment of a secondary market for mortgages. This, of course, requires the development of a significant institutional base of shelter finance organizations and instruments, but it should be an ultimate goal in the development of the overall shelter finance system.

Establishing the building materials industry[3]

Most shelter policies neglect the building materials industry. Since it is an industry, it is often not thought of as part of the shelter sector at all. Yet the constraints within the building materials industry often have serious negative effects on housing production. Bottlenecks in supply delay shelter program implementation and increase costs. Price escalation, because of supply imperfections, raise the cost of shelter to all income groups. Inappropriate building standards, which fail to acknowledge alternative lower-cost building materials (often locally produced) or force the inefficient use of scarce building materials, also contribute to shortages, high prices, and constraints on production.

Attention to the building materials industry is therefore a critical component in the new directions for shelter policy. Among the policy areas of concern are consideration of the following:

(a) At the macrolevel, analysis is required to determine the potential scale and mix of the building materials industry. A long-range strategic plan is needed which will determine the comparative advantage of seeking local production of various building materials versus imports. Obviously, where possible, local production is desirable over imported building materials; but it has not been unusual to find developing countries with a heavy investment in cement or steel plants (which are inherently uneconomical), for example, raising artificial trade barriers to imports to protect the local industries with the end result of increasing shortages and end-user costs.

(b) Appropriate standards for the use of building materials need to be established to encourage the efficient use of materials and the substitution of the least-cost materials, where appropriate, for more expensive materials.

(c) The use of what are often called "temporary" materials or "semi-permanent" materials should be allowed in low-cost shelter in order to stimulate supply of the housing stock. It has been shown repeatedly that houses initially built with temporary materials are upgraded by the low-income households over time as their resources permit.

(d) The most effective way to control prices and stimulate the supply of building materials is to foster a strong private sector in the building materials industry with the minimum of public sector regulation. There are many examples of situations in which the government has established monopolies or control boards for various building materials only to find increased inefficiencies in the distribution system, higher prices, and the encouragement of the black market.

(e) The building materials industry needs to develop a variety of scales of production, depending on the particular material involved. Many types of building materials, particularly those used in low-income shelter, can be produced by small-scale enterprises. When given the proper environment and encouragement by government, the small-scale building materials industry can provide significant entry points for new entrepreneurs and make a contribution to the job creation needed in most developing countries.

(f) The building materials industry often provides materials on credit to low-income households. This function supplements shelter finance credit mechanisms and, in some cases, represents one of the few means by which low-income households can obtain credit.

(g) Governments can contribute to lowering costs of materials by providing appropriate guidelines for standardization. If standardization of materials is encouraged, efficiencies in the use of materials can be obtained, since specifications can be drawn with confidence. However, in seeking standardization, it is important that quality-control standards are not set artificially high because this increases costs rather than lowering them.

(h) Governments can also consider the establishment of building materials credit facilities for the benefit of lower-income groups. The successful Banco Materiales in Peru is one example in which low-income borrowers are able to obtain a loan in the form of building materials and can pay back in cash over time. Such lending can be kept on a small scale and can be tied directly to the production of housing stock in a way that cash mortgage loans can not.

Stimulating the construction industry[4]

The establishment of a strong construction industry is essential to the achievement of national development objectives and the creation of a sustainable shelter delivery system. In many developing countries, the construction industry is inefficient, poorly managed, and monopolistic (either with public sector or private sector monopolies). The tendering process is slow and uncertain, and the potential for corruption is high. Frequently there are shortages of skilled labor. All of these things cause the cost of construction to increase. It is not unusual to find construction costs increasing at rates much more rapid than inflation in a particular country.

When the public sector attempts to be the developer of shelter projects directly, all of these problems are encountered. The cost of public sector construction is frequently considerably higher than similar construction within the private sector. This is one of the contributing reasons for transferring the shelter construction function to the private sector.

The public sector can contribute to the enhancement of the private construction sector in a variety of ways:

(a) Public sector construction contracts can be broken into their smallest viable size in order to encourage smaller construction firms to participate in the tendering process.

(b) Governments can assist private sector construction firms to obtain essential foreign exchange to import construction equipment selectively. As part of this approach, construction equipment leasing firms can be encouraged to make heavy equipment available to contractors on a job-specific basis, thereby making more efficient use of the equipment and reducing the aggregate foreign exchange costs.

(c) Governments can sponsor training programs for the construction firms in key subjects such as project management, cost control, tendering, quantity surveying, etc.

(d) Governments can sponsor training programs for skilled trades.

(e) Governments can assist in the provision of construction finance through either public or private sector finance institutions.

(f) Government can ensure that the construction industry utilizes labor-intensive technologies in order to achieve the maximum employment potential of the sector.

Developing country experience with industrialized building systems has been poor. Industrialized systems, imported from abroad, have not produced the savings in cost and time claimed by their sellers. They require scarce foreign exchange and reduce the unskilled labor component, but not the skilled labor component, which is the part of the work force in which scarcity is likely to occur.

The construction industry represents a major source of employment for unskilled low-income workers. Small-scale contractors are essential to support the commitment to informal housing which will make up the vast majority of the developing countries' shelter stock. Therefore the sustained development of the contruction sector as a matter of shelter policy formulation can make a major impact on solving housing needs.

Summary

Table 14.1 summarizes the respective public and private sector rôles within the framework of the new directions for shelter policy proposed in this chapter.

The special concern for sheltering the lowest-income groups

The focus of this analysis has been on the shift of shelter policies from a concern with shelter outputs to a concern with shelter inputs. In making such a shift, there needs to be a concern that the needs of the lowest-income groups are not forgotten. There can be little doubt that the needs of low-income groups will not be served unless the public sector provides the correct environment and incentives to the private sector to respond.

It is clear from the historical experience, however, that, even with the adoption of the newer concepts of sites-and-services projects and settlement upgrading programs, the needs of low-income people have not been adequately addressed in most developing countries.

It has now become clear that the massive resources required to carry out these projects at a scale that will alleviate needs will not be forthcoming either domestically or from the international donor community (at least in the form of grants or low-interest loans). The capital that can be mobilized will have a much greater impact on low-income shelter needs if it is used primarily to lever the mobilization of private domestic savings and to meet the essential needs for infrastructure which the informal sector cannot provide.

Furthermore, experience has shown that these public sector low-income shelter projects involve significant investment of professional and management resources which are also in short supply in the developing countries. It can be effectively argued that these scarce human resources would be better devoted to the kind of input strategy described here, rather than being focused on a limited number of low-income shelter projects.

Governments can demonstrate their concern for shelter for low-income groups by creating the environment whereby low-income people can shelter themselves. This involves ensuring the sustained supply of urbanized land with minimal infrastructure available to low-income groups at affordable prices, access to credit, and the stimulation of the building materials industries that cater to the needs of the low-income groups and the small-scale contractors required in building informal sector shelter at the scale needed.

Table 14.1 Summary of public and private rôles in a new directions housing policy.

Activity input	Public sector	Private sector
housing construction	• cease direct house construction activities	• provide all housing units through developers and individual households
land	• ensure laws do not reward speculators • adopt simplified procedures for obtaining secure land tenure • reduce land-use standards for cost-efficient development • establish land development agencies with efficient eminent domain power • utilize public land holdings efficiently	• ensure adequate access to urban land supply for low-income groups
infrastructure	• ensure coordination of provision • seek full cost recovery • work on citywide scale • improve operations and maintenance	• provide infrastructure in middle- and upper-income developments as a private cost • prioritize infrastructure services (such as septic-tank cleaning and solid-waste disposal)
shelter finance	• establish sound financial environment • use market interest rates • provide access to low-income groups	• establish private institutions, credit unions, and cooperatives • provide access to low-income groups • mobilize domestic savings
building materials	• set appropriate standards which allow use of temporary materials • stimulate standardization • avoid industrialized building systems • decontrol industry	• privatize building materials industry • provide supplier credit to low-income groups
construction industry	• stimulate small-scale private sector contractors through breaking up public sector contracts to smallest viable size • assist in meeting foreign exchange requirements • sponsor training programs	• privatize construction industry • use labor-intensive techniques

The rôle of international donors in supporting new directions in shelter policy

The international donor community has never assigned a high priority to shelter in the developing countries as compared to many other sectors. Nonetheless, the donor community has made substantial contributions to the ongoing policy dialogue and has invested in the introduction of the newer concepts of sites and services projects and settlement upgrading. A variety of international workshops and training experiences for developing country professionals has been a useful contribution toward building an international consensus on shelter policy issues.

It is clear that this international donor rôle is not expanding in shelter, and there exists some evidence that the contributions of the World Bank and the USAID Office of Housing and Urban Development are potentially declining.

It is unlikely that the developing countries can expect to obtain additional international support above present levels. However, the adoption of the new directions for shelter policies described in this chapter offers the potential to utilize available international resources, both capital and technical assistance, more efficiently to impact the needs of sheltering the urban poor.

International donor projects and programs developed in cooperation with developing country governments can provide support for the new directions through support for land development agencies, shelter finance institutions, and lending for the development of the building materials industries. Technical assistance can be provided for support of the institutional development requirements of the new directions approach, including the development of training programs.

Concluding thoughts

The quest for finding shelter solutions for the world's poor has been a long struggle to develop implementable proposals responsive to the scale of the needs. Progress has been made over the years in reducing standards, improving cost recovery, and reducing subsidies. New concepts such as sites-and-services projects and settlement upgrading have contributed to understanding the capacity and the potential of the informal sector to play a rôle in improving shelter conditions for the urban poor. But still the problem remains unsolved at the scale of world needs. The vast majority of the poor receive little or no benefit from the capital resources invested in shelter projects. The time has come to explore new directions for shelter policies in the developing countries.

By recognizing the limits of public sector resources in meeting the needs of the urban poor and providing new support and incentives to the private sector to respond to the needs of all target groups, perhaps the experience of the past can be converted into new initiatives which will meet the needs of the urban poor for shelter. This is what the new directions in shelter policy seek to address.

15

Institutional learning in shelter and settlement policies

DONALD A. SCHÖN

Introduction

MOST OF THE contributors to this volume have asked, "What *have* we learned?" They have explored the experience of shelter and settlement policies in the recent past, examined their intended and unintended consequences, considered the interactions of governmental and private institutions, and appraised the capacity of various research disciplines to explain the phenomena of shelter and settlement. They have also described the shifting policy context, asking, in Bertrand Renaud's words, "What time is it?"

Their several views have been assembled in an overview chapter advocating a new vision of shelter and settlement policy in which the idea of learning plays a central rôle.[1] They recognize the inherent complexity of the shelter–settlement processes, their limited understanding of them, and that the future of these processes is uncertain. At the same time, they see the need for new forms of action appropriate to conditions of high uncertainty. Their more modest and demanding vision calls for a range of strategic governmental interventions aimed at creating a policy environment favorable to the spontaneous, incremental shelter-creating activities of private households and microenterprises in the construction field, while reserving for central government certain functions of infrastructure development, regulation, and funding. All of this calls for an institutional capacity for learning-by-doing: learning from the experience of error and surprise, learning to build institutional capacity where little or none existed before, and learning to play new enabling rôles in a varied and continually changing policy context. Not least important, the new vision calls for a much more permeable membrane between research and practice; both central and local institutions will need to become more adept at observing and describing how incremental building processes and shelter systems actually work; how they are affected by governmental interventions; how policy moves can be treated as probes toward more effective interaction between central and local governments, public and private institutions, formal and informal systems. And researchers more distant from the locus of governmental action will need to learn to produce kinds of research more directly useful to practicing researchers in Third World governments.

Kinds and levels of learning

Perhaps all thinking about learning starts with a view of the learning agent as an individual. Individuals learn, through reflection on experience, to detect and correct errors. A familiar cycle of individual learning begins with the discovery of an error (a mismatch between what you expect and what you get from an action) and goes on to invention, production, and monitoring of an alternative action. But we are also used to speaking about collective learning, asking, for example, what a municipality has learned from a decade's experience of rent control or what a Third World nation has learned about attempts to control rural-to-urban migration. At these higher levels of aggregation, "learning" refers to the processes by which individuals in different institutions or rôles interact to produce collective perceptions, attributions, understandings, intentions, and actions. Such processes require something like the conditions of constitutional government: explicit or tacit rules that establish conditions for membership in the collectivity, decision-making, and delegation of institutional authority to individuals, who then function as learning agents.

The capacity of an institution to perform such tasks and meet such conditions depends on the institution's "learning system" – in part, the structure of rôles and rules that govern organizational inquiry and, in part, the network of interpersonal and intergroup relations "draped over" that structure. In any collectivity, individuals have different views of past experience, present situations, and future possibilities, reflecting their different positions, interests, and powers. The process of getting from these to collective perceptions, understandings, and actions is political in the colloquial sense of a win or lose struggle, games of power, negotiations. But it is also a cognitive process in which observation, data collection, reasoning, and experimentation play crucial rôles. Policy inquiry may be used to rationalize politically motivated decisions; but, even in the most overtly political bureaucracy, not any rationalization will do. There are rules of the game for policy inquiry, just as there are rules of the political game, and they constrain one another. Indeed, the inhabitants of an organizational world are sometimes able to reflect on games of political contention and convert them to more productive policy inquiry.

At the very boundaries of the terrain of institutional learning are those processes in which actions must be seen as the unintended consequences of the interactions of several learning agents, each of whom has a different perception of the meaning of events, what is to be learned from them, and what strategy of action should be pursued in the future.

Such processes occur within, as well as among, institutions. An institutional learning system consists of the totality of conditions that shape the interactions of learning agents in such a way as to enhance, or inhibit and distort, performance of the collective learning tasks of discovery, invention, production, and monitoring.

An effective learning system is not sufficient for the achievement of satisfactory shelter and settlement processes. Much depends on *what* is learned and on the purposes and values that inform it. But I shall argue that the creation of effective institutional learning systems is *necessary* to improved shelter and settlement policy and, especially, to the implementation of the new vision of policy advocated in this volume. Whether what is *necessary* is also *doable*, especially in the context of Third World countries, is a further question that must be asked; this chapter advocates an affirmative answer.

Some of the kinds of institutional learning with which we shall be concerned are:

(a) *Instrumental learning*. Here, the problem of learning is taken to be the design and choice of means to be used in order to reach settled objectives. Learning is conceived as a cumulative improvement in the performance of a complex task through ongoing detection and correction of errors in performance, in such a way as to yield what is often called a "learning curve." It is associated with learning what the task really entails, what the problems to be solved are really like, what works or does not work, what tools, skills, and models are useful, as in the cumulative refinement of sites-and-services projects over the past decade. Instrumental learning tends to be taken as a prototype; we readily understand what it means. But there are other types of institutional learning at least as important to the improvement of shelter and settlement policy.

(b) *Learning to implement policy.* In order to obtain political and institutional commitment to new policies, politicians and agency officials must grasp the operational implications of policy – what would have to be done and given up in order to implement it. Because the real significance of a policy becomes clear only in the process of attempting to carry it out, sources of resistancce to the policy, often circumvented or diluted by the vague language employed to achieve consensus in the deliberative process, re-emerge in the process of implementation. Policy means re-engaging the divergent views held by different stakeholders with different positions, interests, and powers, resolving conflicts left unresolved by the process of policy formation.

(c) *Evolving new ideas in good currency.* By "ideas in good currency," I mean ideas which become, at a particular time and in a particular political context, powerful for action. It is characteristic of ideas in good currency that there are few of them in operation at any given time, new ones tend to drive out old ones, and there are lags in the processes by which they come into being and disappear. A crucial process is the one by which, in an institution or an entire society, ideas in good currency shift to take account of a changing context, often working up hill against the resistances of individuals and organizations working to maintain the constancy of ideas to which they have attached vital interests and on which they depend for their sense of protection from uncertainty and anxiety.

(d) *Conversational learning.* Sometimes, as institutions monitor the effects of their policies, they detect outcomes so surprising that the resulting processes are best described as situational "back-talk." A case in point is Edwin Popko's study of squatter settlement upgrading and sites-and-services programs in Colombia[2]. The municipal planners involved in these projects, along with their central ministry and international aid agency counterparts, had expected that residents would be the poorest of the poor, would build their own houses to use as residences, and would depend on technical assistance in construction. Popko found that more than one-third of the residents used the structures for rental purposes, charged rental fees that were economic by prevailing standards, and were not the poorest of the poor but what might be called the "entrepreneurial poor." They tended not to build their own houses but to employ the services of small-scale contractors. The municipal planners read these results as failure and concluded that they would do best to return to fully built housing. But the same outcomes might have been read, as well or better, as signs of a misunderstanding of the market and of program objectives; sites and services might have been more appropriately understood as a means of enhancing the entrepreneurial aspirations of a group of poor people who saw the ownership and construction of shelter as key elements of their own strategies of economic survival. For planners and policy makers to listen to such back-talk would be to reframe ideas in good currency in the local context of policy implementation.

Evolution of ideas in good currency in shelter and settlement policy

Over the past 25 years, there have been periodic shifts in ideas in good currency about shelter and settlement policy in Third World countries, with significant effects on policy and practice in Third World governments, international aid agencies, and academic communities.

In the early 1960s, the emphasis was on new, fully built low-cost housing systems. At the same time, shantytowns were becoming increasingly visible in Third World cities, growing along with urban populations and rural-to-urban migration. These squatter settlements tended to be seen as a form of blight or as criminal misappropriation of land.

By the late 1960s, there was widespread disillusionment with fully built public housing. It tended to be expensive, well out of reach of the poor, and ended up mostly in the hands of middle-class citizens or, if owned by low-income families, used as an economic good to be sold at market prices. At the same time, very much as a result of the influence of John Turner's work in Peru, squatter settlements were beginning to be seen in a new way[3]. The term "self-help" began to be widely used, and squatter settlements were recognized by many observers as settings for the creation of household capital through sweat equity. Most of all, they came to be seen as vehicles for social learning through which large numbers of rural migrants were adapting to the strange demands and possibilities of urban life. A walk from the rural edge of such a settlement to the edge nearest the fully built city revealed a gradual transition from shacks made of bamboo, tar paper, and polyethylene to two-storey brick dwellings with concrete floors, indoor plumbing, and pirated access to water and electricity. Conceived in these ways, squatter settlements became the focus of a mini social movement dedicated to the reappreciation of these spontaneous, incremental building processes. But the movement was not yet forcefully connected to government shelter policies.

Out of Turner's work in Peru, as picked up and replicated by others, the idea of sites-and-services projects emerged. These embodied a novel division of labor among government agencies, community associations, and individual households. Government made land available, graded, serviced, and divided into household plots, and provided funds for construction loans. Community associations screened applicants for residency and distributed loans. Around mechanical cores provided by government, households then built their own dwellings. By the early 1970s, sites-and-services projects had become an idea in good currency in their own right. They became a bulwark of the World Bank's lending for housing in the developing world and, increasingly, a refined and proceduralized bank "product," specified and measured in every aspect of their operation.

By the early 1980s, as sites-and-services projects were in place in developing countries around the world, they had begun to provoke a much more mixed reaction. They were found not to serve the poorest of the poor but the lower middle class, or the entrepreneurial poor. Although their advantages and efficiencies were recognized, they were no longer seen as an appropriate response to large-scale shelter requirements. They sometimes carried a stigma, "teaching the natives," in the words of one development hand, "to defecate in rows." Most Third World governments did not adopt sites-and-services projects as components of their own shelter policies. Attention began to shift to a wider view of the services essential to residential settlement and to the full range of municipal capacities necessary to the provision of shelter. "Institution building" and "building municipal capacity" became new ideas in good currency.

This most recent shift of ideas in good currency is very much reflected in the new vision of policy for shelter and settlement advocated in this volume. There is a recognition of the limited rôle Third World governments should play in the actual provision of shelter. They are urged, instead, to focus on the provision of infrastructure and on the management of strategic interventions aimed at facilitating the shelter-related activities of private agents. Governments are seen as creating a policy environment conducive to spontaneous, incremental building through the manipulation of policy instruments affecting access to land, standards, construction, and finance.

Shelter is understood in terms of the full range of technological and human services essential to viable settlements, and no longer focused on the poor alone but on all segments of the population.

There is a recognition of the central importance of the municipal level of government and of the need to build municipal capacity to design, implement, and monitor local policies and programs. Interaction of central and local governments is seen as requiring a new division of labor and new modes of operation. And there is a new understanding of the limits of theory and policy knowledge. As one member of our group put it, "We understand something about the manipulation of incentives, but we cannot predict the effects of policies with precision; the situation is different in every case."

Implications for institutional learning

From this vision of policy, certain fundamental issues follow, fundamental difficulties more like paradoxes and dilemmas than technical problems. They can be grouped in terms of the interactions of central and local governments, public and private sectors, formal and informal systems.

Central and local governments

What will it mean to achieve real decentralization of policy at municipal levels when at the same time central government takes on new enabling rôles? Interactions of central and local governments can be placed within the framework of *public* learning systems, of which I shall single out two main varieties.

In a *center–periphery* system, policies are conceived and tested at a governmental center, thereafter to be diffused throughout a periphery of localities. Inquiry into new policy is the primary responsibility of the center; implementation consists in imposing a uniform, established central policy on a peripheral set of local agencies, via sanctions that consist mainly of carrots and sticks. Once they are established, policies are considered to be stable compartmentalized units which have their parallels in compartmentalized central agencies.

Within a center–periphery system, public learning proceeds through the lens of established policy categories. Agencies ask, for example, whether policy guidelines have been followed; and whether, if they have, intended outcomes have been achieved at minimal or acceptable cost.

The center–periphery model takes on the more elaborate form of a proliferation of centers when it is recognized that a given peripheral locality may also function as a center in its own region. Diffusion and implementation of central policies must accommodate to this more complex, hierarchical form.

Center–periphery systems decline and fail when the center loses control, networks disintegrate, or secondary centers and localities gain independence. These things may happen because of the limits of infrastructure connecting center to periphery, constraints on resources at the center, failure of will or competence, or because uniform and stable central policies no longer fit a world of increasing regional diversity, complexity, and change.

In an *inductive* learning system, policy implementation consists in setting in motion and guiding, around central policy themes, a network of related processes of local public learning. Within this process, the formation of policy cannot be neatly separated from its implementation, and central policy can only be constructed retrospectively from observation of local processes.

Hence, the fostering of inductive learning cannot take the form of pre-defining a policy and causing it to fan out from a center. Central policy may provide first instances or policy themes which are take-off points for chains of transformation in localities. It may help agencies to learn from one another's experience through the establishment of networks that connect local policy agents to one another.

A center–periphery system makes sense when the rate of change in the policy situation is relatively slow, when there is little regional variation, and when policy knowledge is adequate for the formation of policies suitable for diffusion over an entire nation for long periods of time. An inductive learning system makes sense when regions are seen as significantly different from one another, so that formation and imple-mentation of policy proceeds best on a local basis. A mix of center–periphery and inductive systems makes sense when both sets of conditions are present; some elements of policy are then diffused from a government center, whereas others are left to local development.

The requirement for the management of strategic policy intervention, in our vision of shelter and settlement policy, poses new demands for any public learning system. For the management of strategic policy interventions demands that new policies be treated as intervention experiments. They are undertaken, of necessity, from a base of incomplete knowledge, with a resulting inability to make reliable predictions of outcome. They must be designed to test policy hypotheses and they require learning on-line. Such policies cannot be regarded as stable over any long period of time, either for the nation as a whole or for any given locality. Further, they are unlikely to fit within the boundaries of any one agency or formal policy category. They must be crafted in their content, scale, target, and timing.

The learning system implied by our policy vision is a mix of center–periphery and inductive systems, modified to take account of the demands of strategic policy intervention.

To see what this means for central government, let us consider Richardson's[4] chapter on spatial policy and Renaud's[5] on shelter finance. Both set criteria for the crafting of strategic policy interventions. Richardson begins by admitting the limited capacity of existing theory to guide broad spatial policy, but asserts that we have qualitative knowledge of the kinds of policies likely to succeed in making small adjustments in patterns of settlement. These would call for a managed interdependence of urban and rural interventions, deployment of a mix of policies aimed at slowing down the growth of primate cities, and selective support of the "middle tier of cities and towns" as a means of revitalizing their surrounding regions. His recommendations demand continuity of attention over the long pull, a high degree of flexibility and, above all, sensitive timing – all of which depend on the elimination of obstacles "primarily institutional and political."

Renaud poses the policy problem as one of balancing conflicting requirements: the need to make home-ownership affordable to a larger number of households throughout the income spectrum and the equally important need to safeguard financial institutions against the risks of default. Renaud sees the possible utility of directed credit – in the form of tax-based housing funds, retirement systems, forced deposit schemes – but argues that it can be contributive or dissipative depending on how it is managed.

Lisa Peattie's[6] chapter on shelter systems, and William Doebele's on access to land, illustrate the meaning of strategic policy intervention at the municipal level. Peattie thinks in terms of shelter systems made up of private developers and builders, publicly sponsored shelter programs, and the incremental building activities of individual households. All are affected by policies governing the provision of roads, water, sewage, schools, clinics, and by the regulation of land tenure, standards for housing, access to materials, land, and finance. Believing in the artificiality of accounting systems that separate shelter from economically productive activity, she advocates the selective use of these policy instruments to support people in the creation of rental space, home-based production, the creation of small construction and building materials firms, the buying and selling of houses, the upgrading of shantytowns.

Doebele underlines the central rôle of access to small parcels of urban land in the incremental building processes critical to the provision of low-income shelter over the past 15 years. But he also points out a more recent tightening up of the porous urban land pattern, with a resulting rise in land prices that has created a class of "urban landless." He recommends deploying a range of mainly local policy interventions. These include investment in land-use planning, land-service systems, improved transportation to provide access to land further from the urban center, more efficient cost-recovery mechanisms to capture shares of increasing land values, measures to regularize land tenure, regularized cadastral systems, more flexible provision of construction loans, "leveraged" public deals with private developers, better systems of standards for plot sizes and building codes, and regulations that permit cooperative landownership.

In both cases, the recommended policy interventions call for local institutions capable of managing policy interventions in a strategic and concerted way. But such institutions are rare commodities at the municipal level in most Third World countries. Central governments would have to nurture them and foster their learning from one another.

Interactions of public and private sector

For many of the authors represented in this volume, recognition of the massive impact of private firms on the provision of shelter over the past 15 years is reinforced by awareness of the constraints imposed on governments by the current climate of fiscal austerity. The result is a strong disposition to see private enterprise as the principal actor in the drama of shelter and settlement, with government in a twofold, enabling rôle, providing the infrastructure within which shelter activities will unfold and creating the policy environment favorable to private action. The latter is seen as including the impacts of implicit as well as explicit policies, the choice of activities to be regulated or left unregulated, the correction of biases in procurement or taxation systems. In addition, some authors propose government competition aimed at stimulating improvement in private performance, new divisions of labor in the shelter system between public and private agencies, and direct public–private partnerships.

In his chapter on the construction industry, for example, Frederick Moavenzadeh[7] argues for the importance in the shelter system of the operation of small-scale construction and building materials firms, whose already significant contributions could be enhanced by improving their access to capital, raw materials, tools, energy, and skilled labor. He advocates the development of a local construction and building materials industry, heavily dependent on microenterprises, not only because of such an industry's potential for provision of (especially low-income) shelter but also because of its potential rôle as a source of employment for large numbers of relatively unskilled workers. He proposes, to this end, minimum construction standards, provision of seed capital, focused technical information and training, and reduction of policies and practices like wage floors, transportation subsidies, and preferential procurement policies, all of which are biased toward large producers.

Three points should be kept in mind in relation to these recommendations. First, there is, again, insufficient theoretical basis for confidence that the recommended policies will have the desired effect; they must be considered as intervention experiments to be monitored for their actual impacts on small-scale construction enterprise. Second, there is debate about the wisdom of "special windows" for credit and support to small enterprise; pursuit of such a policy must be accompanied by an attempt to monitor its effects on the health and efficiency of the larger construction industry, of which microenterprise is a part. And finally, any attempt to encourage microenterprise to the detriment of large firms will undoubtedly encounter the coalitions of interest and power that have enabled large firms to become and remain large; pursuit of the policy will depend for its effectiveness on the intelligent management of incentives and structures, economic and political.

The interactions of formal and informal incremental systems

Formal governmental interventions in support of incremental shelter systems can appear self-contradictory:

(a) How can government, committed to legality, facilitate unregistered shelter activities that escape the categories and procedures of the legal system?

(b) How can government lend its support to such a system without neutralizing its freedom of action, its spontaneity, and its capacity to improvize, the features that make it seem worth supporting in the first place?

(c) How does it make sense to say, as some of our contributors do, that incremental shelter systems are disappearing, when at the same time they recommend that government should support them?

Paradoxes such as these suggest that formal policy support of incremental systems is inherently doomed to fail. But it is possible, by moving to a more specific level of analysis, to convert paradox to experiment. We can ask, as Doebele has suggested: What parts of the incremental shelter system are disappearing as a result of government policies that might be changed? What components of the informal shelter system are most worthy of support? And what forms of support are least likely to neutralize their inherent advantages? Questions like these call for a detailed understanding of the workings of incremental building processes, a detailed mapping of the kinds of groups and households that engage in them, and an analysis of enabling strategies.

More specifically, five different approaches to government interaction with the incremental shelter system have been proposed in this volume:

(1) Free incremental building processes from inhibiting regulations by changing the regulations or by looking the other way.

(2) Create or find intermediary organizations able and willing to deal both with government and with incremental organizations.
(3) Foster the evolution of informal systems toward regularized, formal status.
(4) Gradually supplant, through outreach, the functions now filled by incremental organizations.
(5) Take clues from the observation of incremental building systems to learn what government should also be doing.

The area of credit is a good one in which to illustrate these approaches. Judith Tendler has observed, for example, that in Latin America it is not uncommon for financial institutions to lend to informal groups through the use of registered intermediaries who have established patterns of lending to, and loan-recovery from, the incremental building sector. She has also suggested that public finance institutions might take their cue from informal credit associations, providing short-term credit – for example, for the construction of rental units.

Boleat,[8] in his chapter on housing finance, suggests a number of different approaches to the problem. He begins by observing that the great bulk of incremental building is financed through direct, personal loans, with little financial mediation. The informal credit system has its advantages – personal familiarity reduces barriers to lending and also makes it easier to collect – but the system is too small and segmented to function efficiently. The effort to make such systems more efficient in themselves is, he asserts, a contradiction in terms. But he proposes a number of alternative ideas. Banks might pick up such techniques as those employed by the owners of pirate subdivisions in Columbia, financing through installment credit and delayed payment. They might reach out into the incremental building system by setting up mobile branches, permitting mutual accounts for villages or communities, or affiliating with informal credit associations. Governments might make it possible for public institutions to engage in joint financing operations with private groups. Individual bank officers can induce their institutions to move downmarket by establishing the viability of loans for kinds of shelter previously considered beyond the pale; indeed, according to Doebele,[9] some studies show that low-income households have better records of loan repayment than do higher-income residents.

It is possible, then, for the paradoxes of formal support of incremental building processes to be reframed as subjects of intervention experiment. The question is always: Which strategies are likely to be appropriate and effective in particular urban contexts at particular times?

Implications for institutional
learning systems

Bertrand Renaud has observed that "we cannot hide our mistakes any more; we have to learn what works and what does not."[5] But it is Third World governments that will have to learn. They will have to do so at both central and local levels, on a continuing basis, under conditions of incomplete understanding, regional variation, and high uncertainty. And their capacity to do so will depend on learning systems for discovering, inventing, producing, and monitoring strategic policy interventions.

Information and reporting systems

Agencies will need improved capacities to observe shelter and settlement phenomena and pick up the signals that reveal how policy interventions are working out. They will need two kinds of systems, which may be dubbed "cool and clean" and "hot and dirty." In the first category are the solid, continually updated accounting systems that contain mainly quantitative data about such things as land ownership, subsidies, rates of return on investment, and rates of cost recovery. In the second are the mainly qualitative, narrative descriptions of the workings of the shelter system and the unfolding of policy interventions. The former depend on formal reporting requirements, analytic tools, and systematic formats conscientiously applied; the latter, on insightful observations, interviewing – especially of street-level informants, whose everyday knowledge can be as useful to government agencies as "talking to customers" can be to business firms – and careful story-telling, more like good journalism than scholarly research. Both kinds of information systems depend on institutional commitments that ensure continuity of attention over long periods of time.

The reporting systems through which information is recorded and distributed must be suited to the differences between the two kinds of information. Formal reporting systems must be precise, uniformly designed, reliable, and continually updated. Informal reports must be unsanitized, containing the vivid, personal accounts usually relegated, in most agencies, to corridor conversation. They should be organized in the form of case studies usable by planners and administrators for purposes of action. In both cases, information must be allowed to flow freely within and across agencies, both vertically across layers of management and horizontally from one department to another.

Reflection on policy experience

Those who use information for purposes of analysis and design must be able to cut across the boundaries of familiar policy and accounting categories. As Lisa Peattie[6] has pointed out, the category, "housing," can be very misleading when it is taken to exclude the activities of productive work and employment; especially in low-income households, dwellings are settings for productive activity that may yield a substantial portion of family income. Similarly, analysts and designers need to be able to think across, and outside of, existing bureaucratic categories. They must think in local, context-sensitive terms, without being overly influenced by the categories of First World models or the loan packages of international aid agencies. They must be able to listen to situational backtalk, as in Popko's analysis of Colombian sites-and-services programs, and perceive its implications for the reframing of problems and objectives.[2] This requires attention to and inquiry about the experience of program difficulties and failures and the policy dilemmas often revealed by efforts at implementation.

Response to signals

The management of strategic policy interventions requires the design of new intervention experiments responsive to shifts in situation over time or from one region to another, and it requires the continual monitoring and on-line modification of interventions. This requires, in turn, that agency learning systems allow sufficient freedom of action and organizational slack to permit staff members, within broad guidelines, to invent and improvize. Rigid budgeting categories, and program structures that prevent the fluid transfer of resources and activities across categories, militate against such responsiveness. Moreover, agency staff members must be able and willing to conceive and try out new interventions, take risks, and exhibit an entrepreneurial spirit. In all of these respects, the demands for institutional learning conflict with traditional systems for institutional control – a conflict that must be carefully managed in an effective learning system.

Is it possible for a real-world organization to meet such rigorous criteria for institutional learning? One way of answering the question is by reference to the unusually effective learning systems of some real-world organizations: contemporary, First World business firms in Japan and the United States; the extraordinary Works Progress Administration which, in the 1930s, under Harry Hopkins, combined the provision of work relief with community development in ways that joined a high degree of decentralization, flexibility, and improvization to rigorously consistent principles of policy and operational control; and, in certain Latin American countries, in India, and in the People's Republic of China, examples of high-performing, learning organizations in such fields as public health, nutrition and literacy. But by examining some of the chief obstacles to the improvement of institutional learning capacity and seeing how they might be overcome, it is also possible to address the question, Is it doable?

Dynamic conservatism

Government agencies, like other organizations, are powerfully biased toward the maintenance of stability, on which they depend for the protection of individual and institutional interests, their sense of identity and order, and the avoidance of uncertainty. The term "dynamic conservatism" refers to the active, self-reinforcing processes by which organizations seek to achieve and maintain stability. Dynamic conservatism is by no means an unvarnished evil, since it is essential in some degree to the maintenance of a manageable organizational world; but it can undermine the kinds of learning necessary to the management of strategic policy interventions. Indeed, the failure to take it into account and engage it is responsible for the failure of plausible and attractive policies – such as the shelter and settlement policies advocated at the Habitat conference held in 1976 in Vancouver – to result in administrative action. Hence, it is critically important to consider the varieties of dynamic conservatism that may undermine the institutional learning systems required by the vision of shelter and settlement policy advocated in this volume.

It is useful to distinguish two kinds of dynamic conservatism. The first is rooted in coalitions of professional insiders with powerful outside stakeholders; the second, in self-reinforcing patterns of perceptions, interests, and attitudes linked to the bureaucratic structure itself.

Ralph Gakenheimer and Carlos Brando have described an example of the first kind in their account of the "unintended conspiracies" that lead to excessively high standards for infrastructure.[9] In their account, engineers, agency professionals, and elected officials are influenced by perceptions and incentives that make them far more attentive to the risks of systems breakdown than to the costs of restricted areas of service. Mistaken beliefs in "modernity," expectations of financial reward, professional alliances, links between engineers and wealthy individuals, and the disposition of elected officials to regard standards as a "technical problem" all play their parts in the self-reinforcing pattern. Gakenheimer and Brando propose a kind of remedy that has a far more general relevance to dynamically conservative systems of this sort: a restructuring of institutional arrangements aimed at shifting the direction of incentives. They recommend strengthening public agency control over whole programs of operation and maintenance, combining responsibility for design and operations, restructuring budgets and payment procedures to reward increase in area served. And they would change attitudes by emphasizing the rewards of extended service (for example, the reduction of communicable disease) and the desirability of trade-offs between the benefits of service reliability and breadth of service.

Alongside such unintended conspiracy, Gakenheimer and Brando also recognize intended conspiracies – for example, the coalitions of inside professionals with powerful, large-scale suppliers who wish to maintain existing procurement procedures or with wealthy landowners who wish to keep land registration records incomplete. In these kinds of instances, they properly describe institutional learning as requiring not only the restructuring of institutionalized incentives but the assertion of moral courage.

The second type of dynamic conservatism, linked to the internal structure of the agency itself, is a "limited learning system." I shall illustrate it with a simplified sketch of an agency that is prototypical of many of those charged with shelter and settlement policy.

Such an agency is large in scale and diversified in its scope of operations. It contains a broad division between those at its center, charged with analyzing, designing, and funding policies and programs, and those at its periphery, lower down in the organization and in more direct contact with the local settings in which programs are enacted. Center and field tend to be geographically distant from one another and distant, as well, in their understandings, languages, and styles of action. Their members may be said to live in different worlds. Critical to the performance of policy interventions are those who play intermediary rôles, moving back and forth between the rôles of center and field, and the learning system of the agency can be seen with particular clarity as it comes to bear on them.

The world of the center tends to place a high value on order, bureaucratic rationality and professional knowledge. It contains a set of espoused policies and principles governing conceptions of mission, strategies, and underlying models of the world of action. These are linked to a system of rules that translate principles into practice: reporting systems that determine what projects shall be funded and implemented; control systems that use measures of performance to manage productivity, quality, and consistency; systems of reward and punishment, including salary levels, promotions, and staff assignments; staffing policies that govern recruiting, training, deployment of staff, and career paths; procedures that shape the structure of practice, including the rhythm of visits to the field.

The world of the field tends to be messy, chaotic, and unstable. It is full of the play of local interests and powers, and it demands flexibility, innovation, improvization, and, sometimes, freewheeling entrepreneurship.

Those who play intermediary rôles must translate the center's plans and policies into field projects that call for agreements with local groups. They must assess local conditions and needs, build local interests and perceptions into project designs. Their projects must gain approval in both of the worlds to which they belong. Hence, they are continually involved in brokerage and mediation.

The agency's learning system consists in principles, procedures, and structures as staff members learn to perceive and understand them. For example, staff members, placing priority on project approval, learn to package and sanitize reports so as to increase the likelihood of approval. They learn to optimize to the measures (rather than the spirit) of performance criteria, for example, by concentrating on projects likely to be approved with minimal difficulty. Policies designed to keep staff at arm's length from the field, or reward by promotion, or move staff to areas of crisis or opportunity, tend to create staff discontinuities. When difficulties arise in the field, staff managers may attempt to "smooth" the material so as to make it appear consistent with agency policies. Staff members may find themselves caught between the flexibility and improvization demanded in the field and the center's demands for conventionality and consistency. In order to secure project approval, they may negotiate agreements they know are unlikely to be honored; and their local counterparts, wise to this game, may gladly cooperate. Under pressures of time, staff may not probe very deeply into local problems, and local counterparts, anxious to receive funding, may not volunteer to tell them. When priority is given to project approval, and field time and resources are limited, supervision and follow-up are likely to suffer.

When field staff adapt to experience in these ways, and when such patterns of behavior are widely adopted, they become matters of common knowledge. But, because they violate espoused policy, they are never publicly discussed. They become "open secrets," subject to camouflage and cover-up when there is a threat of exposure.

Within such a learning system, projects tend to be conventional, low risk, and assimilated to existing agency products; innovations, when they occur, may be hidden from official view. Authority tends to cluster at the top of the agency and relevant information – especially about the real problems of the field – at the bottom. There is little monitoring or follow-up of project activities. Failures are unlikely to receive timely detection because the signs of incipient failure tend to be sanitized away. There is little reflection on negative information that could lead to questioning of received policy; much negative information is smoothed away or interpreted in terms of the violation of standing procedures.

When top managers become aware of problems in performance, their attempts to fix things often make them worse. A perceived breach of quality standards may lead to the imposition of additional reporting requirements, perceived by staff as "one more piece of paper." Or a perceived lack of risk-taking may lead to exhortations, without awareness that staff interpret the entire context of incentives and controls as inimical to innovation. The limited learning system tends to keep itself immune to attempts at reform.

The agency's learning system might be improved if managers gained a greater awareness of it and became more attentive to the ways in which their own choices contributed to it. Such an inquiry, which Gregory Bateson has called "deutero-learning," might take the form of an organizational experiment in which inquiry into the learning system is coupled with an effort to improve substantive policy practice (organizational studies tend to be seen, by themselves, as "more paper").[10] Top management would be asked to participate in the experiment, along with middle managers and field staff; they might commit to the venture out of frustration with earlier attempts to improve performance. They would be asked not to disown their present understandings of the system but to entertain the possibility that they do not perceive what lower-level staff perceive. They would use the experiment to test their understandings. Lower-level staff would be asked, as one individual put it, to "question how we have interpreted what our managers wish us to think they want us to do."

In the substantive policy field chosen for experiment, new kinds of inquiry would be grafted onto normal procedures. Staff members would be encouraged to hold more probing conversations with local officials, include more nonsanitized information in their reports, reveal more of their personal perceptions and opinions than they are used to do. Upper-level managers would demand and respond to monitoring of implementation and would suspend the punishments usually meted out to those who break informal rules of the project approval game. Upper-level managers would have an opportunity to test their understanding of the ways in which their efforts at control and improvement have been interpreted; lower-level managers would be able to test their assumptions about possible choices and risks worth running.

Implications for research

The new vision of shelter and settlement policy proposed in this volume calls for Third World governments, central and local, to adopt enabling, facilitative rôles that focus on the management of strategic policy interventions in contexts that are poorly understood, regionally diverse, and shifting over time. Central governments are asked to manage difficult and sometimes paradoxical interactions with local governments, private firms and informal systems. These proposals depend for their viability on governmental learning systems capable of managing "hot" and "cool" information, generating and distributing nonsanitized reports that describe policy experience, reflecting broadly and flexibly on that experience, designing and conducting intervention experiments keyed to a growing understanding of shelter systems, and monitoring and modifying interventions on-line. These requirements for institutional learning are likely to founder as a result of two kinds of dynamic conservatism endemic in government agencies – the unintended conspiracies of internal professionals and external stakeholders and the self-reinforcing systems that build up around bureaucratic structures. In both cases, remedies to limited learning systems call for inquiry into the systems themselves, leading to rearrangements of the institutional structures that shape incentives and to new perceptions and understandings necessary to more effective organizational learning.

All of this has definite implications for usable research. The kinds of research supportive of the management of strategic policy interventions will be grounded in qualitative accounts of the operations of actual shelter systems. They will be closely tied to the monitoring, analysis, and design of intervention experiments. And they will need also to focus on the behavior of institutional learning systems themselves. Such research will need to be closely tied to practice. It is best undertaken by practitioners who also function as researchers, or by researchers who work in close association with practitioners. More distant researchers – in universities or research institutes – will need to learn new rôles and functions in support of practice research, developing methods, frameworks, and exemplars useful to those directly engaged in learning-by-doing.

Appendices

Appendices

Statistical Appendix A:
Trends in the growth and spatial distribution of population

PARVIZ S. TOWFIGHI

World population growth

PROBLEMS OF HUMAN settlements are related to the overall growth of
population and its distribution and movement over space. In 1950 the
population of the world was at 2.5 billion; its estimated level in the year
2000 is 6.2 billion. Although the rate of population growth has been
declining since the mid-1970s, its absolute number is still growing at an
alarming rate.

Africa will reach its highest rate of growth of 3 percent per annum
during the second half of the 1980s, declining to 2.7 percent by the year
2000. However, this will still be the highest growth rate in the world.
Africa, with 13.4 percent of the total world population, will be the third
most populated region by the year 2000.

Latin America reached its peak of growth rate in the decade of the
1960s (2.8 percent per annum), but, with a slightly lower rate of growth of
2.4 percent per annum by the year 2000, it will still rank the second
highest in the world.

South Asia and East Asia are expected to reduce their growth rates
from peak points of 2.5 and 1.9 percent per annum, respectively, in the
1960s to 1.9 and 1.0 percent per annum by the year 2000. But due to their
large population base, they will be adding 800 million to the world's
population from 1985 to the year 2000. This increase accounts for 57
percent of the additional total population in the world within that 15-

year period. In the year 2000 the two regions combined will have 3.6 billion population or 58.3 percent of the world's total.

The population of Oceania, North America, the USSR, and Europe will grow at moderate rates of 1.2, 0.6, 0.6, and 0.4 percent per annum respectively (see Table A.1).

However, the year 2000 is not the year when population growth will have stabilized, except in a few of the developed countries. According to the World Bank's projections, the population of India, for example, will not stabilize until it reaches 1.7 billion. Bangladesh, presently the most densely populated country in the world (except for Hong Kong), will stabilize at around 450 million people; and the population of Nigeria will stabilize when it has reached 650 million. Ethiopia will grow from around 40 to 230 million, Zaire from 32 million to 170 million, and Kenya from 20 to 150 million.

As a group, sub-Saharan Africa and South Asia, the world's poorest regions, would, at the time of population stabilization, account for 50 percent of the world's population, compared with 30 percent today.[1]

Urban–rural composition

Urban population

The world's urban population in 1950 was about 727 million. Only 29 percent of the world's population was urbanized. In Africa, about 15 percent lived in cities. Out of the 1.1 billion population of South Asia 16 percent lived in urban areas. A similar situation prevailed in East Asia where 17 percent of its 1.1 billion population lived in places defined as urban. The most urbanized regions of the world were North America (63.8 percent), Oceania (61.2 percent), and Europe (55 percent).

In the year 2000 the balance for the first time in history will be tilted in favour of urbanized areas with 51 percent of the world's total population living in cities.

Africa's urban population will amount to 42 percent of the total. East Asia will reach the 45 percent mark; and South Asia, though still predominantly rural, will have 37 percent of its population in urban centers.

The urbanization process of North America, Europe, Oceania, and the USSR will be reaching its peak, but that in Latin America will continue into the 21st century.

The overall urban growth rate in the world reached its peak in the 1950s at 3.4 percent per annum. This is estimated to decline to 2.7 percent per annum by the year 2000 (see Table A.2).

Table A.1 World population trend, 1950–2000: total population of the world and major regions (in thousands).

	1950 pop.	%	1960 pop.	%	1970 pop.	%	1975 pop.	%	1980 pop.	%	1985 pop.	%	1990 pop.	%	1995 pop.	%	2000 pop.	%
world total	2,513,071	100	3,026,535	100	3,676,762	100	4,033,308	100	4,415,013	100	4,830,203	100	5,275,745	100	5,733,758	100	6,199,361	100
annual growth rate (%)				1.9		2.0		1.9		1.8		1.8		1.8		1.7		1.6
Africa	219,093	8.7	274,597	9.1	353,826	9.6	405,845	10.1	469,359	10.6	544,545	11.3	630,378	11.9	725,626	12.7	828,050	13.4
annual growth rate (%)				2.3		2.6		2.8		3.0		3.0		3.0		2.9		2.7
Latin America	163,655	6.5	215,427	7.1	282,730	7.7	322,592	8.0	368,476	8.3	420,596	8.7	478,433	9.1	541,058	9.4	608,122	9.8
annual growth rate (%)				2.8		2.8		2.7		2.7		2.7		2.6		2.5		2.4
North America	166,073	6.6	198,662	6.6	226,389	6.2	236,379	5.9	246,350	5.6	258,494	5.4	270,469	5.1	280,878	4.9	289,540	4.7
annual growth rate (%)				1.8		1.3		0.9		0.8		1.0		0.9		0.8		0.6
East Asia	673,244	26.8	815,516	26.9	980,834	26.7	1,063,449	26.4	1,135,893	25.7	1,203,719	24.9	1,274,600	24.2	1,340,627	23.4	1,406,063	22.7
annual growth rate (%)				1.9		1.9		1.6		1.3		1.2		1.2		1.0		1.0
South Asia	706,318	28.1	867,062	28.6	1,110,325	30.2	1,255,320	31.1	1,421,958	32.2	1,606,407	33.3	1,802,847	34.2	2,005,197	35.0	2,205,880	35.6
annual growth rate (%)				2.1		2.5		2.5		2.5		2.5		2.3		2.2		1.9
Europe	391,968	15.6	425,158	14.0	459,461	12.5	474,171	11.8	483,538	11.0	492,405	10.2	501,178	9.5	510,443	8.9	520,232	8.4
annual growth rate (%)				0.8		0.8		0.6		0.4		0.4		0.4		0.4		0.4
Oceania	12,649	0.5	15,784	0.5	19,323	0.5	21,158	0.5	22,774	0.5	24,477	0.5	26,201	0.5	27,950	0.5	29,652	0.5
annual growth rate (%)				2.2		2.0		1.8		1.5		1.5		1.4		1.3		1.2
USSR	180,075	7.2	214,334	7.1	243,873	6.6	254,393	6.3	266,666	6.0	279,558	5.8	291,637	5.5	301,981	5.3	311,817	5.0
annual growth rate (%)				1.8		1.3		0.8		0.9		0.9		0.8		0.7		0.6

Source: Population Division, Department of International Economic and Social Affairs of the United Nations 1980. *Urban, rural and city population, 1950–2000, as assessed in 1978.* Working paper ESA/P/WP.66 (June).

Table A.2 World urban population trend, 1950–2000: the world and major regions (in thousands).

	1950 pop.	%	1960 pop.	%	1970 pop.	%	1975 pop.	%	1980 pop.	%	1985 pop.	%	1990 pop.	%	1995 pop.	%	2000 pop.	%
world total	726,673	100	1,019,847	100	1,368,169	100	1,573,913	100	1,809,439	100	2,084,844	100	2,403,092	100	2,761,798	100	3,161,815	100
percentage of total pop. (%)	28.9		33.7		37.2		39.0		41.0		43.2		45.6		48.2		51.0	
annual growth rate (%)			3.4		3.0		2.8		2.8		2.9		2.9		2.8		2.7	
Africa	32,434	4.5	50,416	4.9	80,644	5.9	103,832	6.6	134,951	7.5	174,829	8.4	229,384	9.5	282,512	10.2	349,874	11.1
percentage of total pop. (%)	14.8		18.4		22.8		25.6		28.8		32.1		35.5		38.9		42.3	
annual growth rate (%)	4.5		4.5		4.8		5.2		5.4		5.3		5.6		4.3		4.4	
Latin America	67,465	9.3	106,520	10.4	162,075	11.8	197,250	12.5	238,283	13.2	285,274	13.7	337,789	14.1	395,010	14.3	456,484	14.4
percentage of total pop. (%)	41.2		49.5		57.3		61.2		64.7		67.8		70.6		73.0		75.1	
annual growth rate (%)			4.7		4.3		4.0		3.9		3.7		3.4		3.2		2.9	
North America	106,018	14.6	133,280	13.1	159,493	11.7	170,167	10.8	181,433	10.0	194,871	9.3	208,714	8.7	221,766	8.0	233,710	7.4
percentage of total pop. (%)	63.8		67.1		70.5		72.0		73.7		75.4		77.2		79.0		80.7	
annual growth rate (%)			2.3		1.8		1.3		1.3		1.4		1.4		1.2		1.1	
East Asia	112,638	15.5	199,855	19.6	276,808	20.2	322,530	20.5	371,199	20.5	425,010	20.4	487,368	20.3	556,616	20.2	634,084	20.1
percentage of total pop. (%)	16.7		24.5		28.2		30.3		32.7		35.3		38.2		41.5		45.1	
annual growth rate (%)			5.9		3.3		3.1		2.9		2.7		2.8		2.7		2.6	
South Asia	112,507	15.5	158,717	15.6	234,924	17.2	286,228	18.2	352,827	19.5	437,409	21.0	542,181	22.6	668,955	24.2	818,067	25.9
pecentage of total pop. (%)	15.9		18.3		21.2		22.8		24.8		27.2		30.1		33.4		37.1	
annual growth rate (%)			3.5		4.0		4.0		4.3		4.4		4.4		4.3		4.1	
Europe	217,205	29.9	256,023	25.1	302,276	22.1	323,465	20.6	340,785	18.8	357,588	17.2	374,217	15.6	391,036	14.2	407,910	12.9
percentage of total pop. (%)	55.4		60.2		65.8		68.2		70.5		72.6		74.7		76.6		78.4	
annual growth rate (%)			1.7		1.7		1.4		1.0		1.0		0.9		0.9		0.8	
Oceania	7,741	1.1	10,451	1.0	13,680	1.0	15,519	1.0	17,245	1.0	19,098	0.9	20,971	0.9	22,807	0.8	24,505	0.8
percentage of total pop. (%)	61.2		66.2		70.8		73.4		75.7		78.0		80.0		81.6		82.6	
annual growth rate (%)			3.0		2.7		2.6		2.1		2.1		1.9		1.7		1.4	
USSR	70,765	9.7	104,589	10.3	138,270	10.1	154,923	9.8	172,715	9.5	190,765	9.2	207,866	8.6	223,096	8.1	237,172	7.5
percentage of total pop. (%)	39.3		48.8		56.7		60.9		64.8		68.2		71.3		73.9		76.1	
annual growth rate (%)			4.0		2.8		2.3		2.2		2.0		1.7		1.4		1.2	

Source: Population Division, Department of International Economic and Social Affairs of the United Nations 1980. *Urban, rural and city population, 1950–2000, as assessed in 1978.* Working paper ESA/P/WP.66 (June).

This represents a 21 percent rate of decline over the 50-year period which, compared with the 16 percent rate of decline of overall population growth, indicates that urban growth will come to an end before the stabilization of the world population.

Rural population

The rural population, according to the UN population studies, will grow in absolute terms from 1.8 billion in 1950 to slightly over 3 billion in the year 2000, a 70 percent increase over a 50-year period compared to 335 percent for the urban growth.

The rate of decline of the rural growth rate over the 50-year period is 67 percent, almost three times that of the urban growth rate. This means a continuing rate of decline for rural growth. It is estimated that by the year 2000 the absolute number of rural population will start to decline. This process started in North America and Oceania in the early 1970s, in the USSR in the 1960s, and in Europe in the 1950s.

In East Asia the process of decline will start in the 1990s, but Africa, Latin America, and South Asia will not experience this process of rural population decline until the 21st century (see Table A.3).

Small and medium-size towns

There are no reliable and universally acceptable definitions for small and medium-size settlements. One suggestion is to consider urban centers of between 5,000 and 20,000 population as small. Settlements above that range, up to a limit that is vaguely defined as "not yet being able to make an important contribution to national production, trade, or service provision," are classified as intermediate urban centers.[2]

If we explicitly define the upper limit of medium-size towns at 100 thousand, the regional distribution of the two categories in the developing regions of the world in the year 2000 will be as follows:

(a) In Latin America 128.5 million, or 21.1 percent of the total population, will be living in cities of less than 100,000 population, and 54 percent will be living in cities of over 100,000.

(b) In Asia 490 million, or 13.6 percent, will be living in cities of less than 100,000 as against 962.1 million, or 26.7 percent, living in cities of above that limit.

(c) In Africa 121.9 million, or 14.7 percent, will live in cities of below 100,000 population, and 228 million, or 27.5 percent, will live in cities of above 100,000.[3]

Table A.3 World rural population trend, 1950–2000: the world and major regions (in thousands).

	1950 pop.	%	1960 pop.	%	1970 pop.	%	1975 pop.	%	1980 pop.	%	1985 pop.	%	1990 pop.	%	1995 pop.	%	2000 pop.	%
world total	1,786,398	100	2,006,688	100	2,308,593	100	2,459,395	100	2,605,574	100	2,745,359	100	2,872,530	100	2,971,960	100	3,037,546	100
percentage of total pop. (%)	71.1		66.3		62.8		61.0		59.0		56.8		54.4		51.8		49.0	
annual growth rate (%)			1.2		1.4		1.3		1.2		1.1		0.9		0.7		0.4	
Africa	186,659	10.4	224,181	11.2	273,182	11.8	302,013	12.3	334,407	12.8	369,715	13.5	406,394	14.1	443,113	14.9	478,177	15.7
percentage of total pop. (%)	85.2		81.6		77.2		74.4		71.2		67.9		64.5		61.1		57.7	
annual growth rate (%)			1.8		2.0		2.0		2.1		2.0		1.9		1.7		1.5	
Latin America	96,189	5.4	108,906	5.4	120,656	5.2	125,342	5.1	130,193	5.0	135,326	4.9	140,644	4.9	146,048	4.9	151,637	5.0
percentage of total pop. (%)	58.8		50.5		42.7		38.8		35.3		32.2		29.4		27.0		24.9	
annual growth rate (%)			1.2		1.0		0.8		0.8		0.8		0.8		0.8		0.8	
North America	60,055	3.4	65,382	3.3	66,896	2.9	66,212	2.7	64,916	2.5	63,623	2.3	61,755	2.1	59,111	2.0	55,835	1.8
percentage of total pop. (%)	36.2		32.9		29.5		28.0		26.3		24.6		22.8		21.0		19.3	
annual growth rate (%)			0.9		0.2		-0.2		-0.4		-0.4		-0.6		-0.9		-1.1	
East Asia	560,605	31.4	615,662	30.7	704,026	30.5	740,919	30.1	764,694	29.3	778,709	28.4	787,233	27.4	784,010	26.4	771,979	25.4
percentage of total pop. (%)	83.3		75.5		71.8		69.7		67.3		64.7		61.8		58.5		54.9	
annual growth rate (%)			0.9		1.4		1.0		0.6		0.4		0.2		-0.1		-0.3	
South Asia	593,909	33.2	708,345	35.3	875,403	37.9	969,093	39.4	1,069,131	41.0	1,168,997	42.6	1,260,667	43.9	1,336,242	45.0	1,387,814	45.7
percentage of total pop. (%)	84.1		81.7		78.8		77.2		75.2		72.8		69.9		66.6		62.9	
annual growth rate (%)			1.8		2.1		2.1		2.0		1.8		1.5		1.2		0.8	
Europe	174,763	9.8	169,135	8.4	157,185	6.8	150,707	6.1	142,751	5.5	134,815	4.9	126,959	4.4	119,403	4.0	112,307	3.7
percentage of total pop. (%)	44.6		39.8		34.2		31.8		29.5		27.4		25.3		23.4		21.6	
annual growth rate (%)			-0.3		-0.7		-0.8		-1.1		-1.1		-1.2		-1.2		-1.2	
Oceania	4,908	0.3	5,333	0.3	5,643	0.2	5,639	0.2	5,529	0.2	5,379	0.2	5,230	0.2	5,141	0.2	5,147	0.2
percentage of total pop. (%)	38.8		33.8		29.2		26.6		24.3		22.0		20.0		18.4		17.4	
annual growth rate (%)			0.8		0.6		-0.0		-0.4		-0.5		-0.6		-0.3		0.0	
USSR	109,310	6.1	109,745	5.5	105,603	4.6	99,470	4.0	93,951	3.6	88,794	3.2	83,772	2.9	78,882	2.7	74,644	2.5
percentage of total pop. (%)	60.7		51.2		43.3		39.1		35.2		31.8		29.7		26.1		23.9	
annual growth rate (%)			0.0		-0.4		-1.2		-1.1		-1.1		-1.2		-1.2		-1.1	

Source: Population Division, Department of International Economic and Social Affairs of the United Nations 1980. Urban, rural and city population, 1950–2000, as assessed in 1978. Working paper ESA/P/WP.66 (June).

If the size definitions are changed to consider any city up to 100,000 as small, between 100 thousand and 500 thousand as intermediate, and over 500 thousand as large, a different and probably more useful classification in terms of policy implications will emerge. For instance:

(a) In Latin America by the year 2000, the middle-range cities with a total of 67.2 million will constitute 11.1 percent of the population.
(b) In Asia population of such cities will be 244 million, or 6.8 percent of the total.
(c) In Africa there will be 43.3 million, or 5.2 percent, living in cities of between 100 thousand and 500 thousand population.

When the percentages for these three continents, namely 11.1 for Latin America, 6.8 for Asia, and 5.2 for Africa, are compared to the percentages for cities of over 500,000 population, which are 42.9, 19.1, and 22.3 percent respectively, the limited number of the medium-size cities in the developing world is immediately evident.

Most policies centered around the concepts of deconcentration and decentralization often propose action to support the developmental rôles of small and intermediate centers.

The estimates and projections of the population of cities of over 100 thousand to the year 2000 are of considerable interest. When the cities of eight major regions of the world are divided into three groups, 100 thousand to 500 thousand, 500 thousand to 1 million, and more than 1 million, the emerging pattern is closely related in each region either to the level of development or to the type of economic system prevailing, or both.

For example, in Europe, probably the most developed region in the world both economically and spatially, for every 10 cities of between 100 thousand and 500 thousand population there will be 3 cities of 500 thousand to 1 million and 2 cities of over 1 million in the year 2000. Almost the same ratios can be found for the USSR.

In South Asia, for every 10 cities in the lowest category there will be around 7 cities of medium range and 7 cities of over 1 million by the year 2000. The same is true for Africa: for every 10 cities of between 100 thousand and 500 thousand population there will be around 8 cities of medium range and 11 cities of over 1 million.

In Africa, in a 50-year period between 1950 and 2000 the number of towns of between 500 thousand to 1 million will increase from 4 to 41, and the number of cities of between 100 thousand and 500 thousand will increase from 42 to 54.

In South Asia, the number of cities of 500 thousand to 1 million increases from 10 in 1950 to 91 in the year 2000, and the number of cities of 100 thousand to 500 thousand declines from 126 in 1950 to 123 in the year 2000.

The overall conclusion is that the cities of the two higher orders in Africa, East Asia (primarily China), and South Asia will grow at the expense of cities of between 100 thousand to 500 thousand population (see Tables A.12 and A.13).

The growth of large agglomerations

In 1950 there were 76 cities of over 1 million population, of which 38 were in Europe and North America. In 1980, 35 percent of the urban population in both developed and developing countries lived in cities with more than 1 million. The number of such cities is estimated to increase to 440 in the year 2000, containing 43.4 percent of the world's urban population.

The highest concentration of cities of over 1 million in the year 2000 will be in South Asia with 98 cities (22 percent), followed by East Asia with 83 cities (19 percent) and Africa with 63 cities (14 percent).

Africa's share of population of cities of over 1 million in total urban population increases from 13.9 percent (4.5 million) in 1950 to 46.3 percent (162 million) in the year 2000. All five major subregions of Africa will have higher percentages than the world average (see Table A.4).

Latin America, by 1950, had 25.6 percent (17.3 million) of its urban population concentrated in cities of over 1 million. This percentage will increase to 56.4 percent (257 million) in the year 2000. By the year 2000, the highest concentration of urban population in cities of over 1 million will be in tropical South America, where 163.7 million people (62.9 percent of total urban population) will be living in 14 cities (see Table A.5).

North America will increase its share of population of cities of over 1 million from 38.2 percent (40 million in 14 cities) in 1950 to 65.4 percent (153 million in 50 cities). The average size of these cities has remained the same (3 million) over the 50-year period (see Table A.6).

East Asia's share of population living in cities of over 1 million increases from 28.5 percent (32 million) in 1950 to 42.5 percent (270 million) in the year 2000. Out of this 270 million, about 190 million (70 percent) will be living in China (see Table A.7).

South Asia's share of population of cities of over 1 million to total urban population of the region increases from 16.7 percent (18.7 million) in 1950 to 41.2 percent (336.8 million) in the year 2000 (see Table A.8).

Europe has had the slowest rate of growth of cities of over 1 million. It will increase its share from 25.3 percent (55 million) in 1950 to 29.3 percent (120 million) in the year 2000. Two subregions northern and eastern Europe, are estimated to show a decline in the rate of growth of "million" cities (see Table A.9).

Table A.4 Share of population of cities of over 1 million in total urban population of Africa and its subregions, 1950–2000 (in thousands and percentage).

	1950 pop.	%	1960 pop.	%	1970 pop.	%	1975 pop.	%	1980 pop.	%	1985 pop.	%	1990 pop.	%	1995 pop.	%	2000 pop.	%
Africa total urban population	32,434		50,416		80,644		103,832		134,951		174,829		223,984		282,512		349,874	
population of cities of over 1 m	4,509	13.9	7,582	15.0	14,358	17.8	22,039	21.2	38,361	28.4	61,489	35.2	85,672	38.2	115,875	41.0	161,821	46.3
Eastern Africa total urban population	3,375		5,781		10,681		15,151		21,531		30,190		41,303		55,049		71,458	
population of cities of over 1 m	0	0.0	0	0.0	0	0.0	1,195	7.9	4,123	19.1	10,588	35.1	14,945	36.2	21,688	39.4	35,512	49.7
Middle Africa total urban population	4,167		6,267		10,415		13,866		18,293		23,729		30,084		37,140		44,446	
population of cities of over 1 m	0	0.0	0	0.0	1,367	13.1	2,179	15.7	4,252	23.2	7,159	30.2	10,602	35.2	14,463	38.9	19,038	42.8
Northern Africa total urban population	12,715		19,522		30,413		38,011		48,043		60,277		74,674		90,832		108,273	
population of cities of over 1 m	3,503	27.6	6,334	32.4	8,929	29.4	11,551	30.4	15,879	33.1	21,488	35.6	25,810	34.6	31,611	34.8	41,008	37.9
Southern Africa total urban population	5,941		8,245		11,062		12,890		15,337		18,413		22,081		26,329		31,160	
population of cities of over 1 m	1,006	16.9	1,248	15.1	2,641	23.9	4,012	31.1	5,645	36.8	6,444	35.0	9,567	43.3	11,117	42.2	15,025	48.2
Western Africa total urban population	6,236		10,610		18,073		23,914		31,748		42,220		55,842		73,163		94,536	
population of cities of over 1 m	0	0.0	0	0.0	1,421	7.9	3,102	13.0	8,462	26.7	15,810	37.4	24,748	44.3	36,996	50.6	51,238	54.2

Note

$$\text{Percentage} = \frac{\text{population of cities of over 1 million}}{\text{total urban population}} \times 100.$$

Table A.5 Share of population of cities of over 1 million in total urban population of Latin America and its subregions, 1950–2000 (in thousands and percentage).

	1950 pop.	%	1960 pop.	%	1970 pop.	%	1975 pop.	%	1980 pop.	%	1985 pop.	%	1990 pop.	%	1995 pop.	%	2000 pop.	%
Latin America																		
total urban population	67,465		106,520		162,075		197,250		238,283		285,274		337,789		395,010		456,484	
population of cities of over 1 m	17,286	25.6	30,962	29.1	54,944	33.9	77,096	39.1	100,114	42.0	127,671	44.8	160,503	47.5	195,269	49.4	257,439	56.4
Caribbean																		
total urban population	5,669		7,782		11,247		13,410		15,674		18,172		20,901		23,831		26,886	
population of cities of over 1 m	1,220	21.5	1,450	18.6	1,754	15.6	4,278	31.9	5,065	32.3	6,960	38.3	8,130	38.9	10,422	43.7	12,708	47.3
Central America																		
total urban population	14,238		22,774		36,187		45,203		56,340		69,841		85,734		103,892		124,405	
population of cities of over 1 m	2,967	20.8	5,122	22.5	10,566	29.2	15,677	34.7	20,941	37.2	27,154	38.9	37,537	43.8	49,337	47.5	59,187	47.6
Temperate South America																		
total urban population	16,476		22,342		27,978		30,792		33,763		36,750		39,660		42,418		45,003	
population of cities of over 1 m	6,599	40.1	10,008	44.8	12,610	45.1	14,000	45.5	16,331	48.4	18,744	51.0	20,087	50.6	21,162	49.9	21,788	48.4
Typical South America																		
total urban population	31,083		53,622		86,663		107,845		132,506		160,511		191,494		224,868		260,191	
population of cities of over 1 m	6,500	20.9	14,382	26.8	30,064	34.7	43,141	40.0	57,777	43.6	74,813	46.6	94,749	49.5	114,348	50.9	163,756	62.9

Source: Population Division, Department of International Economic and Social Affairs of the United Nations 1980. *Urban, rural and city population, 1950–2000, as assessed in 1978.* Working paper ESA/P/WP.66 (June).

Note

$$\text{Percentage} = \frac{\text{population of cities of over 1 million}}{\text{total urban population}} \times 100.$$

Table A.6 Share of population of cities of over 1 million in total urban population of North America and its subregions, 1950–2000 (in thousands and percentage).

| | 1950 | | 1960 | | 1970 | | 1975 | | 1980 | | 1985 | | 1990 | | 1995 | | 2000 | |
	pop.	%	pop.	%	pop.	%	pop.	%	pop.	%	pop.	%	pop.	%	pop.	%	pop.	%
North America																		
total urban population	106,018		133,280		159,493		170,167		181,433		194,817		208,714		221,766		233,710	
population of cities of over 1 m	40,536	38.2	60,670	45.5	86,816	54.4	99,889	58.7	110,964	61.2	123,942	63.6	136,261	65.3	146,168	65.9	152,836	65.4

Source: Population Division, Department of International Economic and Social Affairs of the United Nations 1980. *Urban, rural and city population, 1950–2000, as assessed in 1978.* Working paper ESA/P/WP.66 (June).

Note

$$\text{Percentage} = \frac{\text{population of cities of over 1 million}}{\text{total urban population}} \times 100.$$

Table A.7 Share of population of cities of over 1 million in total urban population of East Asia and its subregions, 1950–2000 (in thousands and percentage).

	1950 pop.	%	1960 pop.	%	1970 pop.	%	1975 pop.	%	1980 pop.	%	1985 pop.	%	1990 pop.	%	1995 pop.	%	2000 pop.	%
East Asia																		
total urban population	112,638		199,855		276,808		322,530		371,199		425,010		487,368		556,616		634,084	
population of cities of over 1 m	32,099	28.5	64,638	32.3	96,142	34.7	115,146	35.7	138,854	37.4	165,800	39.0	197,183	40.5	235,856	42.4	269,733	42.5
China																		
total urban population	61,219		126,837		178,368		208,522		243,165		284,202		334,447		392,269		459,268	
population of cities of over 1 m	16,634	27.2	37,975	29.9	57,224	32.1	66,969	32.1	84,020	34.6	102,841	36.2	126,174	37.7	158,673	40.5	188,933	41.1
Japan																		
total urban population	41,977		58,712		74,386		83,727		91,045		96,790		101,812		106,442		110,670	
population of cities of over 1 m	11,565	27.6	20,408	34.8	27,198	36.6	32,596	38.9	36,050	39.6	39,778	41.1	42,046	41.3	43,628	41.0	43,809	39.6
Other East Asia																		
total urban population	9,442		14,306		24,054		30,280		36,989		44,017		51,109		57,905		64,146	
population of cities of over 1 m	3,900	41.3	6,255	43.7	11,720	48.7	15,581	51.5	18,784	50.8	23,181	52.7	28,963	56.7	33,555	57.9	36,991	57.7

Source: Population Division, Department of International Economic and Social Affairs of the United Nations 1980. Urban, rural and city population, 1950–2000, as assessed in 1978. Working paper ESA/P/WP.66 (June).

Note

$$\text{Percentage} = \frac{\text{population of cities of over 1 million}}{\text{total urban population}} \times 100.$$

Table A.8 Share of population of cities of over 1 million in total urban population of South Asia and its subregions, 1950–2000 (in thousands and percentage).

	1950 pop.	%	1960 pop.	%	1970 pop.	%	1975 pop.	%	1980 pop.	%	1985 pop.	%	1990 pop.	%	1995 pop.	%	2000 pop.	%
South Asia																		
total urban population	112,407		158,717		234,924		286,228		352,827		437,409		542,181		668,955		818,067	
population of cities of over 1 m	18,754	16.7	33,807	21.3	59,381	25.3	80,186	28.0	124,511	35.3	143,797	32.9	198,508	36.6	250,241	37.4	336,810	41.2
Eastern Asia																		
total urban population	26,172		38,576		57,144		69,392		85,163		105,584		130,890		161,445		197,336	
population of cities of over 1 m	6,035	23.1	10,001	25.9	18,993	33.2	23,062	33.2	30,777	36.1	40,012	37.9	51,233	39.1	63,493	39.3	80,846	41.0
Middle South Asia																		
total urban population	75,860		101,426		145,549		175,178		214,294		266,313		331,584		412,505		509,916	
population of cities of over 1 m	12,719	16.8	22,782	22.5	36,772	25.3	47,062	26.9	63,259	29.5	86,717	32.6	124,011	37.4	157,924	38.3	207,995	40.8
Western South Asia																		
total urban population	10,374		18,715		32,231		41,658		52,770		65,513		79,706		95,005		110,816	
population of cities of over 1 m	0	0.0	2,477	13.2	6,392	19.8	13,162	31.6	18,129	34.4	26,215	40.0	33,104	41.5	40,457	42.6	47,969	43.3

Source: Population Division, Department of International Economic and Social Affairs of the United Nations 1980. *Urban, rural and city population, 1950–2000, as assessed in 1978.* Working paper ESA/P/WP.66 (June).

Note

$$\text{Percentage} = \frac{\text{population of cities of over 1 million}}{\text{total urban population}} \times 100.$$

Table A.9 Share of population of cities of over 1 million in total urban population of Europe and its subregions, 1950–2000 (in thousands and percentage).

	1950 pop.	%	1960 pop.	%	1970 pop.	%	1975 pop.	%	1980 pop.	%	1985 pop.	%	1990 pop.	%	1995 pop.	%	2000 pop.	%
Europe																		
total urban population	217,205		256,023		302,276		323,465		340,785		357,588		374,217		391,036		407,920	
population of cities of over 1 m	54,931	25.3	70,136	27.4	81,792	27.1	90,967	28.1	98,039	28.8	103,105	28.8	110,860	29.6	116,270	29.7	119,587	29.3
Eastern Europe																		
total urban population	36,709		46,325		55,013		59,671		65,158		70,618		75,816		80,811		85,780	
population of cities of over 1 m	7,671	20.9	9,269	20.0	10,202	18.5	10,718	18.0	12,367	19.0	14,137	20.0	16,004	21.1	16,850	20.9	17,645	20.6
Northern Europe																		
total urban population	53,867		58,192		65,274		67,934		69,616		71,063		72,558		74,180		75,737	
population of cities of over 1 m	23,232	43.1	23,906	41.1	23,437	35.9	24,672	36.3	24,234	34.8	23,801	33.5	26,542	36.6	26,444	35.6	26,410	34.9
Southern Europe																		
total urban population	48,362		58,422		71,810		79,665		86,840		93,887		100,761		107,417		113,764	
population of cities of over 1 m	12,760	26.4	18,570	31.8	25,366	35.3	29,831	37.4	34,947	40.2	38,956	41.5	41,666	41.4	44,933	41.8	47,260	41.5
Western Europe																		
total urban population	78,267		93,084		110,180		116,194		119,171		122,019		125,082		128,628		132,639	
population of cities of over 1 m	18,121	23.2	27,103	29.1	32,124	29.2	35,080	30.2	35,720	30.0	35,209	28.9	35,581	28.4	36,820	28.6	36,900	27.8

Source: Population Division, Department of International Economic and Social Affairs of the United Nations 1980. *Urban, rural and city population, 1950–2000, as assessed in 1978.* Working paper ESA/P/WP.66 (June).

Note

$$\text{Percentage} = \frac{\text{population of cities of over 1 million}}{\text{total urban population}} \times 100.$$

Oceania will increase its share of population of cities of over 1 million from 40.5 percent in 1950 to 49 percent by the year 2000 (see Table A.10).

The USSR shows a steady increase in the percentage share, starting from a low level of 10.5 percent (7.5 million) in 1950 and reaching 26 percent (61.4 million) by the year 2000 (see Table A.11). The average size of cities of over 1 million in the USSR is less than 1.9 million. This is well below the average size of such cities in the United States (3 million), China (2.8 million), and India (3 million).

Summary and conclusions

The trend analysis of population, urban–rural composition, and the growth of different size settlements over a 50-year period, 1950–2000, shows the following tendencies.

(a) Population growth remains one of the most important factors shaping the future of human settlements. In spite of the steady decline of the rate of growth, it will be a major concern of the developing world, especially in East Asia and South Asia and Africa.

(b) Although the urban population is stabilized in most developed countries, its growth in developing countries will continue well into the 21st century. The most formidable challenge for the developing countries in the next 2–3 decades will be how to cope with the growth of their urban settlements, especially the large urban agglomerations. Considering that over 80 percent of the growth of population of cities of over 1 million between 1985 and the year 2000 occurs in the developing countries, and the fact that the contribution of these cities to the national income of their respective countries ranges from 30 to 70 percent, the task of providing shelter and infrastructure will be crucial to the national socioeconomic development of most developing countries.

(c) The rate of growth of rural population since 1970 has steadily been decreasing. But the absolute growth will still produce significant claims for housing for the developing countries, especially those with large-size populations and scarce resources.

Table A.10 Share of population of cities of over 1 million in total urban population of Oceania and its subregions, 1950–2000 (in thousands and percentage).

	1950		1960		1970		1975		1980		1985		1990		1995		2000	
	pop.	%	pop.	%	pop.	%	pop.	%	pop.	%	pop.	%	pop.	%	pop.	%	pop.	%
Oceania																		
total urban population	7,741		10,451		13,680		15,519		17,245		19,098		20,971		22,807		24,505	
population of cities of over 1 m	3,136	40.5	4,021	38.5	5,021	36.7	5,540	35.7	5,930	34.4	7,357	38.5	10,975	52.3	11,592	50.8	11,998	49.0
Australia and New Zealand																		
total urban population	7,565		10,118		12,928		14,444		15,636		16,814		17,943		19,038		20,090	
population of cities of over 1 m	3,136	41.5	4,021	39.7	5,021	38.8	5,540	38.4	5,930	37.9	7,357	43.8	10,975	61.2	11,592	60.9	11,998	59.7
Melanesia																		
total urban population	29		85		304		583		1,008		1,561		2,173		2,778		3,296	
population of cities of over 1 m	0	0.0	0	0.0	0	0.0	0	0.0	0	0.0	0	0.0	0	0.0	0	0.0	0	0.0
Micronesia and Polynesia																		
total urban population	146		246		396		492		601		723		856		989		1,119	
population of cities of over 1 m	0	0.0	0	0.0	0	0.0	0	0.0	0	0.0	0	0.0	0	0.0	0	0.0	0	0.0

Source: Population Division, Department of International Economic and Social Affairs of the United Nations 1980. *Urban, rural and city population, 1950–2000, as assessed in 1978.* Working paper ESA/P/WP.66 (June).

Note

$$\text{Percentage} = \frac{\text{population of cities of over 1 million}}{\text{total urban population}} \times 100.$$

Table A.11 Share of population of cities of over 1 million in total urban population of the USSR, 1950–2000 (in thousands and percentage).

	1950 pop.	%	1960 pop.	%	1970 pop.	%	1975 pop.	%	1980 pop.	%	1985 pop.	%	1990 pop.	%	1995 pop.	%	2000 pop.	%
USSR																		
total urban population	70,765		104,589		138,270		154,923		172,715		190,765		207,866		223,096		237,172	
population of cities of over 1 m	7,464	10.5	12,954	12.4	21,200	15.3	23,729	15.3	37,313	21.6	44,618	23.4	52,448	25.2	56,846	25.5	61,360	25.9

Source: Population Division, Department of International Economic and Social Affairs of the United Nations 1980. *Urban, rural and city population, 1950–2000, as assessed in 1978.* Working paper ESA/P/WP.66 (June).

Note

$$\text{Percentage} = \frac{\text{population of cities of over 1 million}}{\text{total urban population}} \times 100.$$

Table A.12 Size distribution of cities of over 100,000 population, 1950–2000: the world and its subregions

AFRICA	Group	1950	1960	1970	1975	1980	1990	2000
eastern Africa	100–199	2	8	7	5	5	5	2
	200–299	1	2	5	3	1	2	3
	300–399	0	1	4	4	4	1	3
	400–499	0	0	1	1	3	0	0
	500–749	0	0	1	5	1	5	1
	750–999	0	0	1	1	4	2	1
	1,000+	0	0	0	1	3	8	14
middle Africa	100–199	4	6	9	7	4	3	2
	200–299	1	3	4	6	4	2	2
	300–399	0	0	1	3	5	2	1
	400–499	0	0	2	0	2	3	1
	500–749	0	1	0	2	1	4	5
	750–999	0	0	0	0	1	2	4
	1,000+	0	0	1	1	2	3	5
northern Africa	100–199	15	16	16	11	5	0	0
	200–299	3	9	9	12	15	5	1
	300–399	0	2	7	5	6	10	4
	400–499	2	0	0	3	2	8	7
	500–749	1	1	1	2	3	6	10
	750–999	0	1	2	1	2	2	5
	1,000+	2	3	4	5	6	8	12
southern Africa	100–199	3	5	4	5	5	3	0
	200–299	2	1	1	1	2	3	3
	300–399	0	1	1	1	0	2	2
	400–499	1	1	2	1	1	0	2
	500–749	2	2	1	2	3	1	1
	750–999	1	1	2	1	0	1	0
	1,000+	0	1	2	3	4	6	8
western Africa	100–199	4	14	14	14	14	15	5
	200–299	2	3	9	10	11	2	11
	300–399	1	2	6	4	4	7	3
	400–499	1	0	1	5	2	7	2
	500–749	0	2	2	6	9	4	5
	750–999	0	0	1	1	3	4	9
	1,000+	0	0	1	2	4	14	20
LATIN AMERICA								
Caribbean	100–199	4	3	7	6	5	3	1
	200–299	1	2	2	1	2	4	4
	300–399	1	0	0	2	1	1	2
	400–499	1	2	1	0	0	1	1
	500–749	0	1	1	2	3	0	1
	750–999	0	0	2	0	0	2	0
	1000+	1	1	1	3	3	4	6
Middle America	100–199	12	13	19	11	6	2	1
	200–299	1	6	7	11	11	4	1
	300–399	1	2	4	7	3	8	2
	400–499	2	0	4	1	9	4	4
	500–749	0	2	2	6	6	10	9
	750–999	0	1	0	1	1	3	9
	1,000+	1	1	3	3	4	10	15

	Group	1950	1960	1970	1975	1980	1990	2000
temperate South America	100–199	5	9	11	8	8	2	2
	200–299	3	3	3	6	6	8	6
	300–399	1	3	2	3	1	5	3
	400–499	1	0	2	0	2	1	4
	500–749	1	2	0	2	2	2	2
	750–999	1	0	2	2	1	1	2
	1,000+	2	3	3	3	4	5	5
tropical South America	100–199	12	31	55	38	30	7	1
	200–299	9	4	14	24	22	28	8
	300–399	2	4	7	10	13	12	24
	400–499	3	5	0	4	5	9	11
	500–749	3	3	7	4	6	13	15
	750–999	0	2	4	5	6	7	9
	1,000+	3	6	10	13	16	23	31

NORTHERN AMERICA

Northern America	100–199	66	77	64	54	47	35	24
	200–299	22	28	39	36	33	32	31
	300–399	10	18	17	21	22	25	26
	400–499	9	13	12	15	14	14	14
	500–749	11	15	19	20	26	29	31
	750–999	4	6	11	12	11	7	15
	1,000+	14	21	29	33	38	49	50

EAST ASIA

East Asia	100–199	73	65	50	37	30	25	22
	200–299	21	34	44	43	30	20	17
	300–399	4	16	18	25	28	17	18
	400–499	3	4	16	13	21	23	6
	500–749	13	13	17	22	24	26	28
	750–999	6	9	10	11	13	20	21
	1,000+	10	21	27	32	37	52	72
other East Asia	100–199	8	9	15	10	5	1	0
	200–299	2	2	4	5	8	5	3
	300–399	1	2	2	6	4	6	4
	400–499	0	0	3	0	3	2	4
	500–749	1	2	1	3	3	6	4
	750–999	0	0	1	1	2	1	5
	1,000+	3	3	4	5	5	9	10

SOUTH ASIA

eastern South Asia	100–199	16	22	33	28	14	6	1
	200–299	6	6	8	11	19	10	6
	300–399	6	5	5	4	7	12	6
	400–499	0	5	5	6	3	10	8
	500–749	2	0	5	4	7	10	15
	750–999	2	3	0	3	3	3	8
	1,000+	4	5	8	8	11	15	22
middle South Asia	100–199	56	73	97	96	82	13	3
	200–299	22	24	32	38	35	71	8
	300–399	7	14	16	17	25	21	56
	400–499	3	8	13	14	12	21	22
	500–749	2	4	16	22	22	26	37
	750–999	3	1	2	6	12	14	18
	1,000+	7	10	13	14	20	42	64

Table A.12 – *continued*

	Group	1950	1960	1970	1975	1980	1990	2000
western South Asia	100–199	6	8	14	12	8	3	2
	200–299	3	6	4	8	8	5	2
	300–399	1	0	3	2	6	7	3
	400–499	0	1	1	2	1	3	6
	500–749	1	2	3	3	3	7	6
	750–999	0	0	1	2	2	1	7
	1,000+	0	1	2	3	5	8	9

EUROPE

	Group	1950	1960	1970	1975	1980	1990	2000
eastern Europe	100–199	22	34	38	34	27	14	9
	200–299	6	8	17	17	18	23	21
	300–399	4	2	2	6	10	11	16
	400–499	1	3	1	2	3	7	4
	500–749	3	4	6	5	6	7	10
	750–999	0	1	2	3	2	2	4
	1000+	6	6	6	6	7	9	9
northern Europe	100–199	29	27	29	26	25	20	16
	200–299	11	13	14	17	18	21	21
	300–399	8	6	7	6	7	8	12
	400–499	5	4	4	5	3	4	5
	500–749	7	9	11	12	12	10	8
	750–999	1	2	2	2	4	5	6
	1,000+	8	8	9	9	9	11	12
southern Europe	100–199	37	44	40	33	27	22	17
	200–299	13	16	24	26	24	17	13
	300–399	10	7	17	20	17	11	15
	400–499	1	4	2	5	14	18	8
	500–749	3	8	6	6	8	15	25
	750–999	4	2	5	4	1	7	8
	1,000+	6	9	12	14	17	18	22
western Europe	100–199	52	65	65	63	57	55	49
	200–299	21	20	28	31	37	33	34
	300–399	6	14	16	17	13	19	21
	400–499	2	4	8	8	11	8	7
	500–749	10	6	5	5	7	13	14
	750–999	5	7	6	6	6	6	7
	1,000+	5	9	12	13	13	13	15

OCEANIA

	Group	1950	1960	1970	1975	1980	1990	2000
Australia and New Zealand	100–199	4	4	7	5	5	5	4
	200–299	1	2	2	4	2	1	1
	300–399	2	0	0	0	2	2	2
	400–499	1	2	0	0	0	0	1
	500–749	0	2	2	1	0	1	0
	750–999	0	0	2	3	3	0	1
	1,000+	2	2	2	2	3	6	6
Melanesia	100–199	0	0	0	1	0	1	1
	200–299	0	0	0	0	1	0	0
	300–399	0	0	0	0	0	0	0
	400–499	0	0	0	0	0	0	0
	500–749	0	0	0	0	0	1	0
	750–999	0	0	0	0	0	0	1
	1,000+	0	0	0	0	0	0	0

	Group	1950	1960	1970	1975	1980	1990	2000
Micronesia	100–199	0	0	0	0	0	0	0
	200–299	0	0	0	0	0	0	0
	300–399	0	0	0	0	0	0	0
	400–499	0	0	0	0	0	0	0
	500–749	0	0	0	0	0	0	0
	750–999	0	0	0	0	0	0	0
	1,000+	0	0	0	0	0	0	0
Polynesia	100–199	0	0	0	1	2	2	1
	200–299	0	0	0	0	0	0	2
	300–399	0	0	0	0	0	0	0
	400–499	0	0	0	0	0	0	0
	500–749	0	0	0	0	0	0	0
	750–999	0	0	0	0	0	0	0
	1,000+	0	0	0	0	0	0	0
USSR	100–199	55	89	112	94	77	57	41
	200–299	20	27	39	48	45	44	46
	300–399	5	15	24	24	31	27	29
	400–499	9	8	11	16	18	25	24
	500–749	11	15	10	10	20	34	36
	750–999	0	5	14	17	7	6	15
	1,000+	2	5	10	12	23	30	33

Table A.13   Size distribution of cities of over 100,000 population, 1950 and 2000: eight major regions of the world.

		Number of cities in each size category		
Region	Year	100,000–499,999	500,000–999,999	1 million and over
Africa	1950	42	4	2
	2000	54	41	59
Latin America	1950	59	5	7
	2000	75	47	57
Northern America	1950	107	15	14
	2000	95	46	50
East Asia	1950	112	20	13
	2000	74	58	82
South Asia	1950	126	10	11
	2000	123	91	95
Europe	1950	228	33	25
	2000	268	82	58
Oceania	1950	8	0	2
	2000	11	3	6
USSR	1950	89	11	2
	2000	140	51	33

Source: Population Division Department of International Economic and Social Affairs of the United Nations 1980. *Urban, rural and city population, 1950–2000, as assessed in 1978.* Working Paper ESA/P/WP.66 (June).

Appendix B:
A note on US experience on security of tenure and shelter

JACK CARLSON

Introduction

POLICY MAKERS of governments and world organizations recognize that economic and social progress comes when people are adequately rewarded, not only for work but for saving and investing.[1] Experience in the United States and some developing countries indicates that when people can achieve greater "security of tenure," such as home-ownership, instead of month-to-month tenure, this becomes an engine for greater savings and investment, as well as work. Growing documentation indicates that security of tenure, in itself, will lead to improvement in living standards, improvement in the quality of life, and more rapid economic growth for the community and country.

The United Nations has wisely recognized links between greater security of tenure and economic and social progress. A meeting of ten housing experts from all regions of the world recommended to the UN Commission on Human Settlements in 1982 that the UN should support greater security of tenure. By the end of 1983, it was adopted by the Commission on Human Settlements, the Economic and Social Council and the UN General Assembly. The UN recognizes and encourages greater security of tenure, such as long-term leases, cooperative ownership, and individual ownership. Home-ownership, a most secure form of house tenure, is recognized as benefiting society and people in many different ways:[2]

(a) Home-ownership provides greater incentives for savings and investment that, in turn, lead to higher family consumption, more jobs, and greater resources for government services.

(b) Home-ownership creates incentives for maintaining and improving dwellings, neighborhoods, and settlements.

(c) Home-ownership provides greater financial security for all members of the household, including older people, by reducing their dependency on impersonal retirement programs.

(d) Home-ownership provides incentives for family stability and fulfillment – between husband and wife, parents and children.

(e) Home-ownership is associated with lower crime rates.[3]

(f) Home-ownership enhances democracy through creating incentives for greater community involvement and social attachment – as in voting, volunteer services, and charitable contributions.

Security of tenure is important to development. In the United States, shelter accounts for one-third of the average family's consumption, whereas food is one-fifth and clothing less than one-tenth.[4] Although the poor may initially spend more of their income on food, as they experience rising incomes from better employment and redistribution of income programs, they are likely to spend a growing proportion of their income on shelter.

Repeated surveys in the United States confirm that security of tenure is a dominant preference. Between 1975 and 1981, US households were asked to rate the values that comprise the "good life". Sharing the top of the list were "a home of your own," a "happy marriage," and "children" (81 percent). A "car" was rated lower (70 percent), and, somewhat surprisingly, a job with "above-average wages" was even lower (50 percent). A color television set was at the bottom of the list (40 percent).[5]

In a more recent survey three out of four people said "It is important to me to own my own home [instead of renting]."[6]

Effects of security of tenure on economic and social progress

Public officials often champion "security of tenure" because it encourages households to be part of a community and ties them into the system of government, especially to the administration in power. Most officials, however, have not fully recognized that security of tenure is a powerful engine for economic growth and development. Now there is enough evidence to show that greater security of tenure in the form of home-ownership enhances both economic and social progress in the United States. It also has a significant impact on the behavior of lower-income and less-skilled households.[7]

Savings and investment

Most households view home-ownership as a worthwhile investment.[8] The principal reasons for the purchase of a home are a desire to own property for investment purposes (40 percent) and a more general desire to settle down in one place and be part of a community (35 percent).[9] Even in the deep recession in the early 1980s, the vast majority of US households held a favorable opinion on the investment value of home-ownership. Nine out of ten people said that owning a home was a good or excellent investment. This was true for all ages and income levels (see Table B.1).

During the early to middle 1970s, home-ownership consistently out-performed other traditional investments, generally by a factor of two to

Table B.1 Attitudes in the United States on the investment value of home-ownership (percentage distribution).

	Excellent	Good	Fair	Poor
All households	53	37	7	3
By income				
low income	47	40	9	4
middle income	63	30	5	2
high income	66	26	5	3
By age				
under 25	51	40	8	2
25–45	57	32	8	3
46–65	55	34	7	3
over 65	55	41	3	1

Source: National Association of Realtors 1981. *Attitudes of Americans concerning real estate.* October 1981 – p. 9. Washington DC.

Note: Low income is less than 75 percent of median family income (MFI); middle income is between 75 and 125 percent of MFI; high income is greater than 125 percent of MFI.

Table B.2 Comparison of return on investment from home-ownership with other investments (percent).

	1970	1976	1980
home-ownership	17.5	13.9	16.2
savings deposits	5.1	6.3	8.7
US Treasury bills (1 year)	6.5	5.5	10.9
municipal bonds (1 year prime)	4.4	3.1	6.3
certificates of deposit	7.6	5.3	13.1
corporate bonds	8.5	9.0	12.8
corporate stocks (earnings price ratio)	6.5	8.9	12.7

Source: Baker, K. 1984. *Investing in Homeownership.* Cambridge, Mass.: Joint Center for Housing Studies of MIT and Harvard University, June 1984.

one (see Table B.2). By 1980, as inflation drove up mortgage interest rates and reduced home values while increasing the return on alternative investments, the return from home-ownership was still 24 percent greater than the nearest alternative.

Long-term growth and productivity depend on savings that can be invested in longer-term needs like education and training, research and development, equipment, and structures for homes, workplaces, and shopping areas. Some policy-makers in the United States and other countries have mistakenly believed that encouring business investment alone, instead of both housing and business investment will strengthen the economy. Current and past experience in the United States shows that investment in home-ownership induces greater savings for invest-ment in shelter, settlements, and industry for an even stronger economy.

Analysis of recent surveys indicates that home-ownership induces greater savings levels. Low, middle and high-income home-owners have accumulated significantly more housing and nonhousing assets than nonhomeowners. Middle-income homeowners, for example, save and invest 56 percent more than middle-income nonhomeowners, after excluding savings used for investing in their own home. Other research has also found that homeowners consistently show higher savings and investment.[10]

Planning to own a home requires greater savings, for a downpayment of typically 5 to 25 percent of the home value in the United States. Households that plan for home-ownership tend to work more, consume

Table B.3 Savings and investment by income and house tenure status (1983 US dollars).

	Nonhomeowner	Homeowner			
		Including home		Excluding home	
			Percentage greater than non-		Percentage greater than non-
	US dollars	US dollars	homeowners	US dollars	homeowners
all households	12,000	111,000	925	44,000	367
low income	4,000	59,000	1.475	15,000	375
middle income	18,000	90,000	500	28,000	156
high income	89,000	211,000	237	102,000	115

Source: Author's calculations. Based on data from the University of Michigan, Institute of Social Research 1984. *Survey of consumer finances.* East Lansing, Mich.

Notes
(a) Assets include checking accounts, savings accounts, money-market accounts, certificates of deposit, retirement accounts (e.g. IRA and Keogh), savings bonds, stocks, corporate bonds, nontaxable holdings (municipal bonds and shares in certain mutual funds), trusts, other property assets, and equity in principal residence.
(b) Low income is less than 75 percent of median family income (MFI); middle income is between 75 and 125 percent of MFI; high income is greater than 125 percent of MFI.

Appendix B

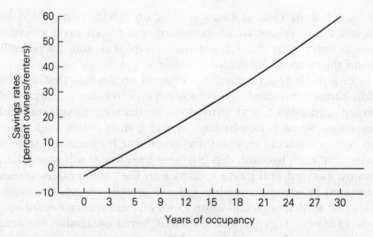

Figure B.1 Percentage difference in nonhousing savings and investment levels: continual owners in comparison with continual renters.
Source: Author's calculations based on regression analysis in Krumm, R. 1985. *Homeownership and household savings behavior: a study of panel data patterns.* Committee on Public Policy Studies, University of Chicago, unpublished.

less, save more, and invest more. The savings prior to home-ownership stimulate investment elsewhere. When the home is purchased, the prior savings are used. As income grows and house payments and operating costs require a smaller proportion of household income, homeowners continue the discipline of saving a larger proportion of income compared to nonhomeowners. Greater savings stimulated by investment in a

Table B.4 Greater savings and investment for nonhousing purposes due to home-ownership alone, by income class (1978) US dollars.

	Average nonhousing savings levels (US dollars)		
	Homeowners	Nonhomeowners	Percentage difference
low income	3,566	1,717	107.7
middle income	8,384	6,536	28.3
high income	13,203	11,354	16.3

Source: Author's calculations. Estimates are based on regression analysis in Krumm, R. 1985. *Homeownership and household savings behavior: a study of panel data patterns.* Committee on Public Policy Studies, University of Chicago – Table 14.

Notes
(a) Calculated for households with average demographic characteristics who were either continual homeowners or continual nonhomeowners from 1976 to 1979.
(b) Low income is less than 75 percent of median family income (MFI); middle income is between 75 and 125 percent of MFI; high income is greater than 125 percent of MFI.

family's home provide protection against loss of their home through illness, unemployment, and other unforeseen circumstances.

The longer the experience with home-ownership, the greater the savings. Initially homeowners save 15 to 20 percent more than nonhomeowners with the same characteristics (see Fig. B.1). But the savings rates of longer-term homeowners are significantly higher – 50–60 percent – than that of nonhomeowners. Low-income homeowners also save at significantly higher rates than middle and high-income homeowners – more than twice as much (see Table B.4). The savings generated by the discipline of home-ownership not only fully fund owner-occupied housing but may also account for 20–25 percent of total nonhousing savings in the United States – additional savings that are available for investment in infrastructure and industry.[11]

Voting participation

Political systems tend to be more stable and more responsive when citizens freely and willingly participate in decision-making. Systematic analysis of voting behavior in the United States shows that homeowners are more likely to register to vote and participate in other ways in national and local elections.

American national election studies of 1976 and 1980 show that 77 percent of the homeowners voted in these elections compared to 59 percent of nonhomeowners.[12] Similar result were reported in a 1980 US government survey when 71 percent of homeowners said they had voted in the last election compared to 42 percent of nonhomeowners.[13] A nongovernment survey also found that homeowners were more likely to vote in the presidential elections of 1980 and 1984 at all levels of education, race, and income (see Table B.5).

Most recently, a 1984 study of home-ownership and voting participation concluded that "at the national level, owners were more apt than renters to have voted in the presidential elections as well as in the primaries".[14] This was true for various occupations and levels of skill of the working members of the household. It was found that less skilled homeowners voted more often than less skilled nonhomeowners.

Greater security of tenure is shown to have a powerful influence on voting participation. Education, marital status, length of occupancy, age, and income may also affect voting behavior. In a study accounting for other influences, a typical homeowner was on average 21 percent more likely to be registered to vote and 11 percent more likely to have voted (see Table B.6). The impact may be especially significant for low-income households and for younger households (see Fig. B.2); it is even greater on the more significant decision to register to vote (see Fig. B.3).

Table B.5 United States voting percentages by tenure status, education, age, race, and household income, 1980 and 1984.

	1980 Owners (%)	Non-owners (%)	Owners greater than Non-owners (%)	1984 Owners (%)	Non-owners (%)	Owners greater than Non-owners (%)
Percentage of all persons saying they voted in the presidential election	75.5	54.1	39.6	80.7	50.9	58.5
less than high school	69.1	36.7	88.3	67.6	31.2	116.7
graduated high school	71.1	50.2	41.6	75.2	49.3	52.5
some college	86.7	70.8	22.5	91.5	69.0	32.6
under 35 years	62.3	43.2	44.2	71.1	48.6	46.3
35–55 years	79.0	73.9	6.9	85.1	57.8	47.2
over 55 years	85.9	64.9	32.4	84.9	48.3	75.8
white	76.3	59.5	28.2	80.0	49.4	61.9
nonwhite	67.0	33.5	100.0	86.9	56.7	53.3
low income	70.7	51.3	37.8	71.2	44.9	58.6
middle income	79.3	61.7	28.5	86.4	67.1	28.8
high income	83.3	63.7	31.6	90.7	61.1	48.4

Source: Author's calculations. Results are based on survey data from *ABC News/Washington Post Poll No. 3*. Study No. 8807, March 25–9, 1981; and *The Gallup Survey*, USAIPO84–1245G, November 9–11, 1984.

Notes
(a) Low income is less than 75 percent of median family income (MFI); middle income is between 75 and 125 percent of MFI; high income is greater than 125 percent of MFI.
(b) The ABC News/Washington Post question on voting participation: "In talking to people about elections, we often find out that a lot of people aren't able to vote because they were not registered, or they were sick, or they just didn't have time. How about you – do you remember for sure whether you voted in the November, 1980, presidential election when Ronald Reagan ran against Jimmy Carter?"
(c) The Gallup Survey question on voting participation: "In the election on November 6, did things come up that kept you from voting, or did you happen to vote?"

Other benefits of security of tenure

In the United States and some other countries, home-ownership is regarded as a central component of the "good life," tangible evidence of the success of prevailing settlement policies and the social order. A 1984 study found evidence of this:

...homeowners are relatively more apt to espouse traditional social values, join voluntary organizations, and to be enmeshed in local, neighborhood-based social networks. Furthermore, their traditionalism,

Table B.6 Greater likelihood of registering to vote and voting due to home-ownership alone, by income class.

	Homeowners	Nonhomeowners	Percentage difference
Likelihood of registering to vote	0.839	0.693	21.1
low income	0.729	0.538	35.4
middle income	0.827	0.675	22.5
high income	0.916	0.826	10.9
Likelihood of voting	0.782	0.706	10.8
low income	0.606	0.508	19.2
middle income	0.770	0.692	11.2
high income	0.907	0.868	4.5

Source: Author's calculations. Results are based on survey data from *ABC News/Washington Post Poll No. 3*. Study No. 8807, March 25–9, 1981.

Notes
(a) Likelihood or probability calculated for households with average demographic characteristics. Home-ownership coefficients were significant at the 95 percent level. Explanatory variables include age, marital status, sex, race, number of children, school years completed, employment status, household income, residence site location (rural or urban), political party affiliation, political ideology, and house tenure status.
(b) Low income is less than 75 percent of median family income (MFI); middle income is between 75 and 125 percent of MFI; high income is greater than 125 percent of MFI.

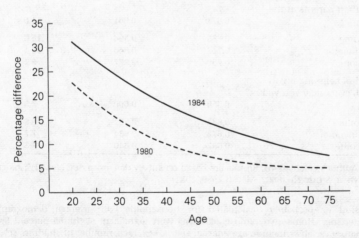

Figure B.2 Probability of voting in the 1980 and 1984 presidential elections (homeowners greater than nonhomeowners).
Source: Author's calculations based on survey data in *ASBC News/Washington Post Poll No. 3*. Study No. 8807, March 25–9, 1981: and *The Gallup Survey*. USAIPO84–1245G, November 9–11, 1984.

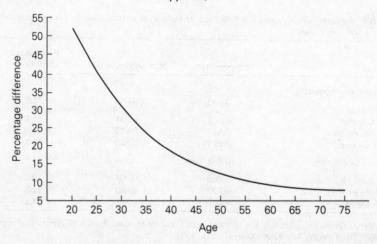

Figure B.3 Probability of registering to vote for the 1980 presidential elections (homeowners greater than nonhomeowners).
Source: Author's calculations based on survey data in *ABC/Washington Post Poll No. 3.* Study No. 8807, March 25–9, 1981.

Table B.7 Greater likelihood of financial success and positive work attitudes due to homeownership alone, by income class.

	Homeowners	Nonhomeowners	Percentage difference
Likelihood of being financially better off than parents at the same age	0.671	0.601	11.6
low income	0.635	0.564	12.6
middle income	0.712	0.646	10.1
high income	0.739	0.677	9.2
Likelihood of believing if you work hard, eventually you will get ahead	0.650	0.600	8.3
low income	0.632	0.582	8.6
middle income	0.672	0.624	7.7
high income	0.687	0.640	7.3

Source: Author's calculations. Results are based on survey data from *ABC News/Washington Post Poll No. 3.* Study No. 8807, March 25–9, 1981.

Notes
(a) Likelihood or probability calculated for households with average demographic characteristics. Home-ownership coefficients were significant at the 95 percent level. Explanatory variables include age, marital status, sex, race, number of children, school years completed, employment status, household income, residence site location (rural or urban), political party affiliation, political ideology, and house tenure status.
(b) Low income is less than 75 percent of median family income (MFI); middle income is between 75 and 125 percent of MFI; high income is greater than 125 percent of MFI.
(c) Question about financial status: "Think about your parents when they were your age. Would you say you are better off financially than they were or not?"
(d) Question on work attitudes: "Do you agree or disagree that it is true in this country that if you work hard, eventually you will get ahead?"

propensity to join, and localism are over and above that of renters of similar socioeconomic position, age, family composition, community type, and length of residence.[15]

Since an active community life may actually increase the home's value, support for prevailing settlements and the social order is in the self-interest of homeowners. Less crime, better community-based education, support of family values, all have an affect on homes, settlement, and nationhood.

Security of tenure may also have a significant effect on attitudes toward work and well-being. Homeowners are 12 percent more likely than nonhomeowners with the same average demographic characteristics to feel financially better off than their parents did at the same age. Eight percent are more likely to believe in the rewards of hard work (see Table B.7). The effect is even greater for low-income households.

Table B.8 United States volunteer work and charitable contributions by tenure status, education, age, race, and household income.

	Homeowners	Non-homeowners	Difference percentage points	Homeowners greater than non-homeowners
Percentage of all persons saying they had done volunteer work and/or had made charitable contributions in the last 12 months	91.5	78.5	13.0	16.6
less than high school	88.5	67.9	20.6	30.3
graduated high school	89.7	81.1	8.6	10.6
some college	95.7	86.5	9.2	10.6
under 35 years	86.5	74.4	12.1	16.3
35–55 years	92.6	85.9	6.7	7.8
over 55 years	94.0	82.5	11.5	13.9
white	92.0	79.3	12.7	16.0
nonwhite	87.1	75.4	11.7	15.5
low income	88.4	75.4	13.0	17.2
middle income	93.7	90.4	3.3	3.7
high income	95.1	94.1	1.0	1.1

Source: Author's calculations. Results are based on survey data from *The Gallup Survey*, USAIPO84-1245G, November 9–11, 1984.

Notes
(a) Low income is less than 75 percent of median family income (MFI); middle income is between 75 and 125 percent of MFI; high income is greater than 125 percent of MFI.
(b) Based on the following question: "On this card read off the letters of the things you have done in the past 12 months: (a) donated money to a charitable cause; (b) given money to a religious organization; (c) given a donation to be used for a relief program such as famine relief; (d) donated time to helping poor, disadvantaged, or needy people; (e) written a letter to a political official or signed a political petition; (f) donated time to religious work; (g) sent contributions to one of the television ministries; and (h) none of these."

Another study found that security of tenure affects the level of volunteer work and charitable contributions. In 1982, 92 percent of homeowners said they had engaged in volunteer work or had made charitable contributions in the last 12 months, compared to 79 percent of nonehomeowners (see Table B.8). Education, age, race, and income did not change the results.

The rôle of security of tenure in the development of the United States

Through most of United States history, officials of central and local governments have recognized the economic, social, and political benefits of security of tenure, particularly home-ownership. Today nearly two-thirds of all US citizens own the homes they live in. To encourage this, central and local policies have provided the following:

(a) tax incentives
(b) assistance in establishing privately owned institutions that channel funds into shelter and give households access to mortgage credit;
(c) insurance and credit programs to attract capital for shelter by reducing the risk to lenders and investors through unsubsidized pooling of mortgage credit;
(d) building and construction assistance and interest rate reductions to poor and moderate-income households;
(e) assistance in revitalizing neighborhoods, settlements and upgrading infrastructure – water, sewers, roads, utilities, and other needs.

Security of tenure when the United States was a developing country, before 1890

Human settlements and development in the United States benefited when people had landownership and home-ownership opportunities in addition to political, religious, and other economic opportunities. The best evidence shows that colonies encouraging security of tenure also found greater economic growth and social progress. In fact, the fastest growing colonies between 1701 and 1749 were the two newly opened land areas of Pennsylvania and North Carolina (see Table B.9). Between 1749 and 1775, rapid growth shifted south to free land in the back country of Virginia and North and South Carolina and to the newly opened territory of Georgia. New Hampshire became the fastest growing northern colony, but New York's restrictive landholding system held it to below-average growth rates. Growth and development in Massachusetts,

Table B.9 American colonial population in 1701, 1749, and 1775 (thousands)

	1701	1749	1775	Percentage increase, 1701–49	Percentage increase, 1749–75
New England					
Connecticut	30	100	262	233	162
Massachusetts	70	220	352	214	60
New Hampshire	10	30	102	200	240
Rhode Island	10	35	58	250	66
Middle Atlantic					
Delaware	–	–	37	–	–
New Jersey	15	60	138	300	130
New York	30	100	238	233	138
Pennsylvania	20	250	341	1,150	36
South					
Georgia	–	6	27	–	350
Maryland	25	85	174	240	105
North Carolina	5	45	181	800	302
South Carolina	7	30	93	329	210
Virginia	40	85	300	112	253
total	262	1,046	2,803	299	168

Source: Nicholson, A. O. P. 1854. *Statistical view of the United States: a compendium of the Seventh Census.* United States Bureau of Census. Washington, DC: US Government Printing Office – Table XI.

Note
All population figures are based on "conjectural estimates, more or less accurate," from colonial records.

Rhode Island, and Pennsylvania slowed down because of the decrease in uncommitted and accessible land.

Colonial policies encouraging security of tenure were suspended shortly after the Revolution, thus hindering growth and development in the interior of the United States. Because of the new central government's need for money, officials sold land to the highest bidder instead of dispensing it to prospective settlers on easy "first come" or "free" terms. This meant that households could no longer afford frontier land. The size of the tracts were too large and prices too high.

But in 1862 the National Homestead Act reformed security of tenure policies. Under this Act, households could obtain a tract of 160 acres for a small fee if they improved it and resided on it for five years. Along with the railroads and improved farm machinery, the Homestead Act hastened settlement and economic development in the western areas of the United States.

When the first income tax laws were enacted in 1862, primarily to help finance the Civil War, there was explicit encouragement of home-ownership. The law allowed deductions from personal income for payments of state and local property taxes and other taxes, and interest on mortgages on farms and homes and personal indebtedness. Required for ten years, it set important precedents in the United States by encouraging home-ownership through the tax system.

Security of tenure as the United States became a developed country, between 1890 and 1930

From 1890 to 1930, the US population doubled, increasing from 63 million to 123 million people; two-thirds was from natural increase and one-third from immigration. Cities grew faster than rural areas because of industrialization. Although only 36 percent of the population lived in cities and large towns in 1890, 56 percent resided in urban areas by 1930.

Security of tenure was ignored during this period. People were not offered adequate opportunity and incentive for providing their own housing either by government or industry. World War I channeled savings and investment to defense needs and away from shelter. As one observer of housing conditions in 1931 wrote:

> ... one-third of American families were living in good homes, one-third in fair homes, more or less lacking in conveniences, but not wholesome, while the last third occupied the oldest and worst castoff houses which no one else wanted. The housing of this last third was definitely sub-normal by any decent standard, and was having a deleterious influence on health, morals, and family life.[16]

This was an era of month-to-month renters. Financial systems were well established for industry and rental housing but not for owner-occupied housing. Leaders in government and industry shared the naive view that savings and investment must be done by industry, rather than recognizing that incentives for home-ownership lead not only to better housing but also to greater savings for industry. This is particularly true for the lower-income and less skilled households who suffer most from poor housing.

There were attempts to address the loss of incentive for home-ownership. There were investigations in the 1890s into urban housing problems, and in 1908 a central government commission recommended a major rehabilitation program that was never carried through. These attempts were modestly helpful three years later when, in 1913, the central government once again introduced personal income taxes in a similar form to the first tax laws of 1862–72, including incentives for home-ownership, deductions of mortgage interest and property taxes. These provisions continue today.

Security of tenure during the Great Depression in the 1930s

In a four-year period from 1929 to 1933, industrial production plunged 50 percent, real gross national product fell 30 percent, consumption spending slid 20 percent, investment fell from US $ 16 billion to less than US $ 1 billion, and one-fourth of the work force lost their jobs. Prices registered equally dramatic declines, falling 31 percent at wholesale and 25 percent on the consumer price index. Wages suffered even sharper cuts. By every known measure, the decline in the US economy was severe.

There was no one cause for the Great Depression; rather, it was a combination of many events and the failure of the central government to respond quickly, positively, and effectively. Both monetary and non-monetary factors played important rôles:

(a) *Banking and housing finance.* The first wave of bank failures in 1930 played a crucial rôle in converting a serious recession into a deep depression.

(b) *Homebuilding.* Residential construction started declining in 1927 after five of the most expansive years in US history. Although population growth in the 1930s picked up during the Depression, housing was depressed by a slowdown following 1921 and 1924 legislation limiting immigration, combined with the overbuilding of the mid-1920s.

(c) *A consumption boom.* Fueled by the strong stock market of 1928–9, a consumption boom disguised the steepness of the housing depression and spurred manufacturers of autos and other durable goods to build up excess capacity as well as burdensome inventories.

(d) *Agriculture.* Farmers' troubles had been worsening since the loss of European markets after World War I and the advent of competition from new grain exporters. In 1910, an average farmer's income had been about 40 percent of an urban worker's; by 1930, it was less than 30 percent and was still being hit hard by a vast drought and by collapsing prices. Farm defaults touched off the first wave of bank failures in 1930.

(e) *Maldistribution of income.* Despite huge gains in productivity, wages actually fell for part or all of the 1920s in mining, transportation, and manufacturing. The result was a shift to profits that pitched much of the income gains to high-income groups. From 1919 to 1929, the share of disposable income received by persons in the top 1 percent of the income distribution rose to 18.9 percent from 12.2 percent, whereas the share of the top 5 percent climbed to 33.5 percent from 24.3 percent. In the meantime, almost 60 percent of the 30 million families in the United States earned less than the income needed in 1929 to buy the basic necessities.

(f) *Overinvestment.* Capacity had been expanding at rates that could no longer be maintained, especially in 1928–9, as money from the shift to profits sought productive uses. The surplus funds flowed into stock market speculation.

(g) *International finance.* Between 1927 and 1933, the New York Federal Reserve Bank and the Federal Reserve Board in Washington, DC, struggled for dominance, until the Washington Board was finally made supreme by the Banking Acts of 1933 and 1935. During the struggle, both domestic and foreign policies became passive.

(h) *Trade barriers.* After the slowdown started, the imposition of trade barriers to protect domestic manufacturers impeded the flow of goods and capital around the world.

A loss of more than 2 million housing construction, sales and financing jobs was part of a ripple effect that left 25 percent of the labor force unemployed – 13 million persons out of 52 million in a nation of 122 million – up from 3.2 percent in 1929. This rapid increase in unemployment became the major political issue of the 1930s. Because the construction, sale, furnishing, maintenance, and operation of homes could have a strong impact on employment, one of the strategies of the central government was to return to policies encouraging greater security of tenure. Public officials believed that this would mean greater savings and investment, more jobs, and higher incomes. Home-ownership policies centered around key principles:

(a) Adequate housing should be a concern and priority of both the central and local governments.
(b) The goal is greater security of tenure, in the form of home-ownership.
(c) The central government should encourage credit markets to reduce the risk of any one investor or financial institution investing in homeowner mortgages through pooling of mortgage credit and establishing insurance against default of the loans.

In 1932, the government created the Federal Home Loan Bank (FHLB) system to serve as a central credit facility for mortgage lenders. It operates today with no significant subsidy from the government.[17] It provides lenders with a nationwide pool of mortgage credit and facilitates the flow of people's savings into housing so that homeowners can borrow at lower rates and for longer periods of time.[18] Another purpose is to enable lenders to help each other through liquidity crises so they will never have to depend on the government. In 1932 it was believed that with this system lenders would have enough confidence to invest in mortgages at lower interest rates over longer periods of time. This would then encourage home-ownership and increased employment from the rise in construction activity.

Although the FHLB system could help pool and allocate mortgage credit among mortgage lenders, it could not solve the problems of unemployed homeowners who were having difficulties with their loans. In 1933 almost 49 percent of home mortgage debt was already in default, with continued high monthly foreclosures. To combat this problem, the government created two agencies to provide for the exchange of privately financed bonds for home mortgages in default with government guarantees of interest and principal.[19] The bonds were financed by private investors at lower interest rates because of government guarantees. This represented an infusion of cash from private investors to distressed mortgage lenders, with the government as middleman and risk-taker for repayment of defaulted mortgages. These agencies offered cash loans for payments and property reconditioning. In this way, the government could provide unsubsidized liquidity to lenders by swapping privately financed bonds for defaulted home mortgages.

Although these programs were successful in offsetting the effects of foreclosure on mortgage lenders, their effect on the total volume of mortgage lending was limited. They applied only to mortgages in default.

A far-reaching attempt of the central government to encourage home-ownership was the National Housing Act of 1934, which was designed to channel idle savings into housing construction. The Act created the Federal Housing Administration (FHA) with a long-range goal to reform mortgage lending practices, to broaden housing opportunities, and to raise housing standards. Its main objective was to provide mortgage insurance against borrower default.[20] The FHA-insured mortgages, made by private lenders, involved charging a modest insurance premium to borrowers to cover cost and risk. The insurance premiums were held in an actuarially sound mutual mortgage insurance fund sufficient to cover all FHA losses from loan defaults. In this way the central government established an insurance system that helped to decrease the risk of mortgage lending. Since all the costs of this system were borne by the borrowers and lenders, it was a market-perfecting device that was not subsidized by the central government.[21]

The FHA was a great success because it helped decrease the risk of mortgage lending by private lenders. As a result, mortgage markets gradually became national in scope, and lending institutions could now rely on FHA appraisals and FHA insurance.

The Act also authorized a privately owned national mortgage association which would alleviate the liquidity problems of private mortgage lenders brought on by the Depression and unamortized home mortgages of three-year to five-year maturity. The association was also expected to counteract high interest rates, particularly in developing areas of the nation, by shifting mortgage funds from capital-rich to capital-poor areas. But private capital proved too difficult to attract, so no privately owned national mortgage association was established. It led, however, to the creation of the Federal National Mortgage Association (FNMA) in 1938, a semiprivate entity with a mandate to encourage confidence in FHA loans by buying FHA-insured mortgages. The central government had always intended FNMA to be privately owned, to be a "dealer" in mortgages, not an investor in competition with private mortgage investors. But FNMA remained a mixed-ownership corporation until 1968 when it finally became a fully privately owned corporation.

The commitment of the central government to security of tenure helped turn the economy around. Between 1933 and 1940, investment in private nonfarm residential structures rose 78 percent (after adjusting for inflation); housing starts were up 650 percent from 93,000 to 603,000; real gross national product increased 55 percent; the unemployment rate was cut in half; and the percentage of households owning their own homes began to rise.

Security of tenure after World War II

In 1944, the central government set forth basic principles to guide housing policy after World War II. Housing was vital to the health, safety, and welfare of the nation; inadequate housing should be gradually replaced; existing housing should be preserved when feasible; and the central government should do what the private sector cannot do.

These principles shaped the Housing Act of 1949. The Act delcared:

> ... the general welfare and security of the Nation and the health and living standards of its people require housing production and related community development sufficient to remedy the serious housing shortage [caused by the War], the elimination of substandard and other inadequate housing through the clearance of slums and blighted areas, and the realization as soon as feasible the *goal of a decent home and a suitable living environment for every American family*, this contributing to the development and redevelopment of communities and to the advancement of the growth, wealth, and security of the Nation.[22]

The Act authorized the central government to assist local governments in developing planned, integrated neighborhoods by upgrading or removing substandard housing. It was also meant to encourage community development by improving rural dwellings and facilities.

The central government had already enacted legislation in 1944 that guaranteed loans for the homes of returning veterans. The unique feature of this program was that it allowed mortgage lenders to make loans up to 100 percent of purchase price, with government-backed insurance against losses up to 60 percent of the amount of the loan, which in time would lead to fees paid by borrowers to cover most of the risk of default or late mortgage payments.

Security of tenure from 1950 to 1970

The major housing legislation for the 1950s was the Housing Act of 1954. It placed greater reliance on private action than on the central government, emphasizing broader programs for the conservation and rehabilitation of salvageable urban buildings. It provided greater assistance through subsidized mortgage insurance for low-income families displaced by clearance of slums and inadequate housing. The FNMA was given greater independence to obtain funds for purchasing home mortgages from private investors. The government obtained new authority flexibility to adjust the terms of government-insured and guaranteed mortgages.

In the 1960s, new emphasis was placed on providing housing for the disadvantaged, the poor, the elderly, and minorities by embarking on subsidized construction and loan programs. The purpose of the 1961 Housing Act was

... to assist in the provision of housing for moderate and low income families, to promote orderly urban development, to extend and amend laws relating to housing, urban renewal, and community facilities for other purposes.[23]

In 1964, the central government declared a "war on poverty" that had significant implications for home-ownership. The government declared:

While there are many facets to the attack on poverty, housing has a major role to play. It has long been recognized that poverty and bad housing are closely related. Each can be both cause and effect.[24]

The Housing Act of 1965 elevated the Housing and Home Finance Agency and FHA to the cabinet-level Department of Housing and Urban Development. Its centerpiece was a subsidized program providing rent supplements for low-income households.

In 1968, the central government took steps to make the 1938 FNMA a more privately owned corporation. The FNMA was partitioned into two separate entities: a new market-oriented FNMA and the government-oriented Government National Mortgage Association (GNMA).[25] The new FNMA became a government-sponsored but unsubsidized and fully private corporation. The GNMA took over the management, liquidation and special assistance functions previously carried out by the old FNMA. The special assistance function that the GNMA performs involves purchase of below-market rate mortgages. Typically these mortgages are then sold to the FNMA or other completely private investors at a market price.[26] The difference or subsidy is budgeted by the central government each year.

Security of tenure since 1970

Achieving home-ownership grew increasingly difficult after 1979. Shelter costs in the United States increased faster than median income and faster than costs for other goods and services. It has been estimated that the total cost of owning a home relative to median income increased from about 12 percent in 1968 to more than 25 percent in 1984 (see Fig. B.4). Recent purchasers, however, have experienced sharper housing cost increases, from 6 percent in 1968 to 36 percent in 1984. Even though home-ownership costs have declined during 1985 and 1986, they are still high by 1970s standards. That home-ownership costs appear to have stabilized at high levels is a serious concern for all US citizens.

In response to rising housing costs, the central government has allowed state and local governments to provide home mortgages through issuance of mortgage revenue bonds with interest earnings that are exempt from the central government's income taxes. This tax exemption reduces mortgage interest rates by 1 to 2 percentage points below nonexempt or market interest rates. From 1982 to 1985, more than 0.5 million low- and moderate-income households achieved security of tenure through this program. It can be targeted to certain depressed

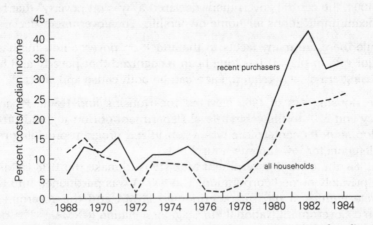

Figure B.4 Costs of owning the median-priced home as a percentage of median family income: 1968–84.

Source: Baker, K. & J. Brown 1985. *Homeownership and housing affordability in the United States: The 1985 report.* Cambridge, Mass.: Joint Center for Housing Studies of MIT and Harvard University.

areas and permits the central government to encourage housing through local officials without creating special programs.

Another major innovation since 1970 is expansion of the "secondary" mortgage market.[27] It offers more investors the conveniences and availability of investing in home mortgages. It integrates primary mortgage markets with capital markets to stimulate the flow of savings into housing. In this way it supplies a larger source of funds for home-ownership at market interest rates.

A large portion of all mortgage loans made today find their way into the secondary market. It has had a significant impact on security of tenure, especially with the introduction and growth of mortgage-backed securities. These securities represent shares in pools of home mortgages. In 1970, almost US $ 0.5 billion of these securities were issued, representing 1.3 percent of the 1–4 family residential mortgages. By 1984, mortgage-backed securities (MBS) from the major secondary market participants totaled about US $ 56 billion, accounting for 28 percent of the 1–4 family residential mortgages. Since 1970, total issuances of MBS is about US $ 360 billion or 20 percent of the US $ 1.8 trillion in family mortgages.[28] This growth has improved links between primary mortgage market lenders and other financial institutions involved in the capital markets. It has lowered mortgage interest rates by one-half to one percentage point.[29]

Another new and significant step in the secondary mortgage market has been the emergence of collateralized mortgage obligations (CMOs) and Real Estate Mortgage Investment Conduit (REMIC). By efficiently partitioning mortgage cash flows into "fast-pay, slow-pay" pools, CMOs and REMICs address investor concerns about maturity and unpredictable prepayment. These features have opened the secondary market to new sources of financing from investors who heretofore preferred more traditional capital market instruments because of greater certainty on payment. A special study prepared for the central government housing authority found that in 1983 and 1984 CMOs lowered mortgage interest rates by half of a percentage point.[30]

Conclusions

The people of the United States are better housed today than in previous generations. Home-ownership has played a major rôle. The US government, however, neglected security of tenure at times in its history and consequently the economy grew more slowly. There is a risk that this is occurring again. Since 1980, the US home-ownership rate for all households has declined by 1.1 percentage points, the first decrease

Table B.10   Home-ownership rates in the United States, 1973 to 1984.

Year	Total	Young[a]	Low income[b]
1973	64.5	43.1	51.4
1974	64.6	n.a.	48.7
1975	64.6	n.a.	47.9
1976	64.7	43.4	46.6
1977	64.8	n.a.	46.9
1978	65.0	n.a.	46.7
1979	65.2	44.7	46.3
1980	65.6	n.a.	48.8
1981	65.4	43.6	47.5
1982	64.8	n.a.	n.a.
1983	64.7	42.4	45.5
1984	64.5	n.a.	n.a.
Changes			
1973–80	+1.1	+1.6[c]	−2.6
1980–4	−1.1	−2.3[d]	−3.3[d]

Source: Baker, K. & H. Brown 1985. *Homeownership and housing affordability in the United States: the 1985 Report.* Cambridge, Mass.: Joint Center for Housing Studies of MIT and Harvard University, July 1985. Figures from the Bureau of the Census, *Annual housing survey*, various issues; *Current population survey*, Series P–20, various issues; and *Current housing reports*, Series H–111, various issues.

Notes
[a]Households under age 35.
[b]Household income under 50 percent of US median.
[c]Change through 1979.
[d]Change through 1983.

since the Depression (see Table B.10). This sharp decline has wiped out the entire gain in home-ownership since 1973. The decline in home-ownership has been twice as large for younger households and three times as great for low-income households. There are approximately 3 million fewer homeowners today than expected based on trends of the 1950s, 1960s and 1970s.

The major reason for declining home-ownership is a housing affordability problem caused in part by huge central government budget deficits. Deficits cause long-term interest rates to be higher than they would be otherwise. They increase government borrowing needs which increases the total demand for loanable funds (current crowding out), increases fears of future inflation (future crowding out), and causes a more restrictive monetary policy than otherwise. It has been estimated that central government deficits may have accounted for as much as one-quarter to one-half of the mortgage interest rate in 1984 (see Table B.11).

Should the decline in the US home-ownership rate continue, there may be serious economic and social consequences. Already personal

Table B.11   Cause of high US mortgage interest rates in 1984.

	Percentage points		Percent of total
Fiscal policy	8.3		57
central government deficit (current crowding out)	1.2	8	
inflation fears (future crowding out	7.1	49	
Monetary policy	6.2		43
Money growth			
Average 1970–9	4.3	30	
current tight monetary policy required because of central government deficits	1.9	13	
Actual mortgage interest rate	14.5		100

Source: Author's calculations. Estimates are based on an extension and update of several empirical studies, including Feldstein, M. & D. Eckstein 1970. The fundamental determinants of the interest rate. *The Review of Economics and Statistics* November, 363–75.

savings have fallen to their lowest levels since the end of World War II. Net personal savings as a percentage of net national product has averaged less than 7 percent during the last five years, compared to an 8–9 percent average for previous decades (see Fig. B.5). Although many factors have contributed to this, certainly one important reason is the decline in the home-ownership rate.

In 1981, the central government established the President's Commission on Housing to study housing and home-ownership problems, establish goals, and chart a new path for the rest of this century. The Commission's final report called on the central government to:[31]

(a) achieve fiscal responsibility and monetary stability in the economy, to lower interest rates, and allow more funds for housing;
(b) encourage free and deregulated housing markets;
(c) rely on the private sector;
(d) encourage state and local governments to play key policy rôles with less central government intervention;
(e) recognize a continuing rôle of government to address the housing needs of the poor;
(f) direct progress toward people rather than toward structures;
(g) assure maximum freedom of housing choice.

The central government, however, has not encouraged home-ownership in the 1980s as much as it did in the past. It has:

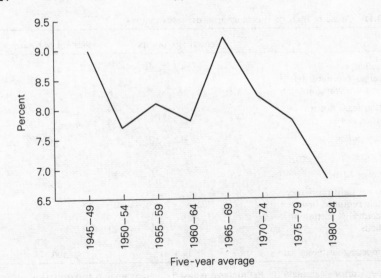

Figure B.5   Net personal savings as a percentage of net national product: 1945–84.
Source: Author's calculations based on data in United States Bureau of the Census (various dates). *Survey of current business*. Washington DC: United States Bureau of the Census.

(a) decreased taxation on renting and thus reduced the value of incentives for home-ownership;
(b) decreased the value of incentives for personal savings and investment;
(c) increased the size of the central government deficit which now takes as much as one-half of all savings from people and business for government use and thus leaves less for home-ownership and industry;
(d) proposed increasing taxes on home-ownership by no longer allowing property taxes to be deductible or allowing lower interest tax-exempt mortgages to be offered by state and local government, providing other tax changes that would artificially make short-term renting from a landlord more attractive than home-ownership or other forms of security of tenure.

Today, security of tenure is at a crossroads in the United States. There has been a clear commitment on the part of central and local governments in the past. The question is how great will that commitment be in the future. If it is less, what will be the resulting lower level of savings, investment, and economic growth?

Notes

Notes to Preface

1 Within a month, chapter assignments were commissioned with first drafts due in March 1985. A seminar for the authors and the UN/IYSH staff was scheduled to be held in April 1985 to explore the main findings and areas of agreement and disagreement. Two and a half months were then allowed for the chapters to be revised and for an overview chapter to be prepared. The function of the latter was to provide a reasonably broad-gauged analysis and an integrated set of policy recommendations. It was hoped that a semifinal draft of the entire study would be completed by late June 1985 and that the conclusions and policy recommendations in the overview chapter would be evaluated in July or August 1985 by a high-level panel of policy-making officials from Third World countries. The final manuscript – if there were no hitches – was scheduled for completion by the middle of October or November of that year.

The schedule was tight, but not inflexible. This was fortunate because the odds were against the schedule being maintained. In retrospect, however, the deviations turned out to be marginal. Almost all of the first drafts of the chapters were completed in time for the seminar to be held in April as planned. But there was some delay in the preparation of the overview chapter, which brought together the basic analyses and policy recommendations. Completed in September 1985, the subsequent review and discussions of that document by the participants and the UN/IYSH staff extended to November 1985.

Notes to Chapter 1

1 Burns, L. S. & B. Ferguson. *Criteria for future shelter and settlement policies in developing countries*. This volume, Ch. 12.
2 Peattie, L. *Shelter, development and the poor*. This volume, Ch. 11.
3 Klaassen, L. H., J. G. D. Hoogland & M. J. F. van Pelt. *Economic impact and implications of shelter investments*. This volume, Ch. 2.
4 Van Huyck, A. *New directions for national shelter policies*. This volume, Ch. 14.
5 Hall, P. *Metropolitan settlement strategies*. This volume, Ch. 10.
6 Richardson, H. *Spatial strategies, the settlement pattern, and shelter and services policies*. This volume, Ch. 9.

7   Mayo, S. K. *Household preferences and expenditures.* This volume, Ch. 3.
8   Moavenzadeh, F. *The construction industry.* This volume, Ch. 4.
9   Renaud, B. *Financing shelter.* This volume, Ch. 8.
10 Towfighi, P. *Trends in the growth and spatial distribution of population.* This volume, Statistical Appendix A.
11 Hardoy, J. E. *The legal and the illegal city.* This volume, Ch. 13.
12 Gakenheimer, R. & C. H. J. Brando. *Infrastructure standards.* This volume, Ch. 6.
13 Doebele, W. A. *Land Policy.* This volume, Ch. 5.
14 Boleat, M. *Housing finance institutions.* This volume, Ch. 7.
15 Schön, D. A. *Institutional learning in shelter and settlement policies.* This volume, Ch. 15.

Notes to Chapter 2

1   Jørgensen, N. O. 1975. *Housing finance for low income groups, with special reference to developing countries.* Rotterdam: Bouwcentrum – p. 17.
2   See, for instance, Burns, L. S., R. G. Healy, D. M. McAllister & B. K. Tjioe, 1970 *Housing: symbol and shelter,* International Housing Productivity Study, University of California, Los Angeles – p. 1; Klaassen, L. H. & W. Eizenga 1977. Some considerations on the productive capacity of consumption expenditure. In *The economics of public services.* Proceedings of the Conference held by the International Economic Association, M. S. Feldstein & R. Tuman (eds), 435–46. London and Basingstoke: The International Economic Association – p. 440.
3   Grimes, O. F., Jr. 1976. *Housing for low income urban families.* World Bank Research Publication. Baltimore and London: Johns Hopkins University Press – pp. 116, 117.
4   World Bank 1975. *Housing.* Sector Policy Paper, World Bank, Washington, DC, – p. 4.
5   Bamberger, M. 1982. The role of self-help housing in low cost shelter programmes for the Third World. *Built Environment* 8 (2), 95–107 – p. 104.
6   Krishnamurti, J. 1981 Indirect employment effects of investment. In *Technology and employment in industry* (2nd ed.), A. S. Bhalla (ed.), 65–87. Geneva: International Labor Organization – p. 83.
7   See, for instance, Bromley, R. (ed.) 1979. *The urban informal sector: critical perspectives on employment and housing policies.* Oxford: Pergamon Press; Sethuraman, S. V. 1981. *The urban informal sector in developing countries.* Geneva: International Labor Organization.
8   Sethuraman, op. cit.[7] p. 17.
9   Ibid.[8] p. 34; Linn, J. F. 1983. *Cities in the developing world.* World Bank Research Publication. Washington: Oxford University Press – p. 42.
10 Hardoy, J. E. & D. Satterthwaite, 1981. *Shelter: need and response.* Chichester: John Wiley – p. 246.
11 Sethuraman, op. cit.[7] pp. 20, 46; Peattie, L. R. 1982. Some second thoughts on sites-and-services, *Habitat International* 6 (1/2), 131–9 – p. 134; Grimes op. cit.[3] p. 53; Deneke, A. H. & M. Silva 1982. Mutual help and progressive development housing: for what purpose? In *Self-help housing, a critique,* P. M. Ward (ed.), 233–78. London: Mansell – p. 244.

12 Strassmann, W. P. 1978. *Housing and building technology in developing countries.* Michigan: Michigan State University – Ch. 1.
13 Roest, W. 1973. *Bouw en economische groei.* Deventer: Kluwer – p. 35.
14 Urquidi, V. L. & A. G. Rocha 1973. Housing construction and employment in Mexico. In *Studies on employment in the Mexican housing industry*, G. Araud, G. Boon, V. Urquidi & W. P. Strassman (eds.), 11–44. Paris: OECD Development Centre – p. 26.
15 See, for instance, ibid.;[14] Burch, D. 1979. Socio-economic variables in the construction industry. In *Housing in Third World countries*, H. S. Murison & J. P. Lea (eds.), 131–6. London: Macmillan.
16 Urquidi & Rocha, op. cit.[14] p. 34.
17 Strassman, W. P. 1975. Industrialized system building for developing countries: a discouraging prognosis. *International Chemical Cooperation Centre* 4 (13), 99–114.
18 Hardoy & Satterthwaite, op. cit.[10] p. 258.
19 See, for instance, UNIDO 1985. *The building materials industry in developing countries: an analytical appraisal.* Sectoral Studies Series No. 16, Vol. 1. Vienna: United Nations Industrial Development Organization (UNIDO) – Ch. 3; Moavenzadeh, F. & F. Hagopian 1983. *Construction and building materials industries in developing countries.* Vienna: UNIDO – Ch. 3.
20 Wegelin, E. A. 1978. *Urban low income housing and development.* Leiden and Boston: Martinus Nijhoff – pp. 74–75; Habitat Conference Secretariat 1978. *Aspects of human settlement and planning.* New York: Pergamon Press – p. 86.
21 Krishnamurty, op. cit.[6] p. 66.
22 This table is a condensed version of the diagram in Stewart, F. 1977. *Technology and underdevelopment.* London: Macmillan – pp. 270–1.
23 Urquidi & Rocha, op. cit.[14] p. 32.
24 World Bank 1980. *Shelter.* Poverty and Basic Needs Series. Washington DC: World Bank – p. 2; Hardoy & Satterthwaite, op. cit.[10] pp. 249–250.
25 Umrath, H. Housing: unlimited needs versus limited resources. *International Technical Cooperation Centre* 4 (1) (13) – p. 5.
26 Klaassen, L. H. & L. S. Burns 1963. The position of housing in national economic and social planning. In *Capital formation for housing in Latin America*, W. D. Harris & J. Gillies (eds.), 108–19. Washington DC: Pan-American Union.
27 Klaassen and Eizenga, op. cit.[2] p. 436.
28 Burns, L. S. 1966. Cost-benefit analysis of improved housing, a case study. In *Cost-benefit analysis of social projects.* United Nations Research Institute for Social Development. Report No. 7, UNRISD, Geneva.
29 For details see Burns *et al.*, op. cit.[2] Ch. 2; Burns L. S. & L. Grebler 1977. *The housing of nations.* London and Basingstoke: Macmillan – Ch. 7.
30 Burns & Grebler, op. cit.[29] p. 162.
31 Wegelin, op. cit.[20] Appendix B (for a review).
32 Wegelin, op. cit.[20]
33 Jørgensen, op. cit.[1] Ch. 5.
34 Burns & Grebler, op. cit.[29] Ch. 7; Wegelin, op. cit.[20] Appendix B.
35 World Bank, op. cit.[4] Housing p. 3.
36 Wegelin, op. cit.[20] p. 273.
37 Burns & Grebler, op. cit.[29] p. 111; Wegelin, op. cit.[20] p. 261.
38 Jørgensen, op. cit.[1] p. 197.
39 Ibid.[38] p. 44.

40 Burns *et al.*, op. cit.[2] p. 148.
41 Wegelin, op. cit.[20] Ch. 6.
42 Burns *et al.*, op. cit.[2] p. 148.
43 Roest, op. cit.[13] p. 125; Chung-Tong Wu 1979. National and regional development strategies: implications for housing policies. In *Housing in Third World countries*, H. S. Murison & J. P. Lea (eds.), 36–42. London: Macmillan – p. 38.
44 Wegelin, op. cit.[20] p. 75; Grimes, op. cit.[3] p. 32.
45 Wegelin, op. cit.[20] pp. 74–5.
46 Burns *et al.*, op. cit.[2] p. 127.
47 Wegelin, op. cit.[20] p. 82.
48 Grimes, op. cit.[3] p. 38.
49 Wegelin, op. cit.[20] p. 84.
50 Jørgensen, op. cit.[1] p. 46.
51 Burns *et al.*, op. cit.[2] p. 128.
52 Jørgensen, op. cit.[1] p. 42; Wegelin, op. cit.[20] p. 87.
53 Burns *et al.*, op. cit.[2] p. 202.
54 Wegelin, op. cit.[20] p. 86; Burns *et al.*, op. cit.[2] p. 126.
55 Burns & Grebler, op. cit.[29] p. 203.
56 Wegelin, op. cit.[20] p. 85; Burns *et al.*, op. cit.[2] p. 134.
57 Burns *et al.*, op. cit.[2] p. 136.
58 Shah, K. 1984. People's participation in housing action: meaning, scope and strategy. In *Low income housing in the developing world*, G. K. Payne (ed.), 199–208. Chichester: Wiley.
59 Ward, P. M. (ed.) 1982. *Self-help housing, a critique*. London: Mansell.
60 Murison, H. S. & J. P. Lea (ed.) 1979. *Housing in Third World countries*. London: Macmillan.
61 Peattie, op. cit., see note 11.

Notes to Chapter 3

1 Grimes, O. F. Jr. 1976. *Housing for low-income urban families: economics and policy in the developing world*. Washington, D.C.: World Bank.
2 Mayo, S. K. *et al.* 1982. *Informal housing in Egypt*. Cambridge, Mass.: Abt Associates.
3 Mayo, S. K. & D. J. Gross 1985. *Sites and services – and subsidies: the economics of low-cost housing in developing countries*, 37. Washington, D.C.: Water Supply and Urban Development Department, World Bank (mimeographed).
4 Burns, L. S. & L. Grebler 1977. *The housing of nations: analysis and policy in a comparative framework*, 47. London: Macmillan.
5 Follain, J., G.–C Lim & B. Renaud 1980. The demand for housing in developing countries: the case of Korea. *Journal of Urban Economics* 7 (3, May), 315–36.
6 Ingram, G. 1984. *Housing demand in the developing metropolis: estimates from Cali and Bogota, Colombia*. World Bank Staff Working Paper 663, World Bank, Washington DC.
7 Jimenez, E. & D. Keare 1984. Housing consumption and permanent income in developing countries: estimated from panel data in El Salvador. *Journal of Urban Economics* 15, 172–94.

8 Malpezzi, S., S. Mayo &. D. J. Gross 1985. *Housing demand in developing countries.* World Bank Staff Working Paper, World Bank, Washington DC.

9 Malpezzi *et al.*, op. cit.[8] pp. 58ff.

10 Clearly other factors also influence this fraction; some of these are analyzed in Malpezzi *et al.*, op. cit.[8]

11 For an extended discussion of how these are derived see Mayo &. Gross, op. cit.[3]

12 The horizontal axis is in 1981 US dollars. For reference, estimated monthly households incomes in most African countries and countries on the Indian subcontinent were below US $ 100; some of the countries with incomes between US $ 100 and US $ 200 were Botswana, Cameroon, Egypt, El Salvador, Indonesia, the Philippines, and Thailand; countries between US $ 200 and US $ 400 included a number of Latin and Central American countries, Nigeria and Zambia; and countries above US $ 400 included Caribbean, Latin American, and East Asian countries such as Jamaica, Bahamas, Brazil, Mexico, Panama, and Korea.

13 The basis for each figure is the estimated demand functions for renters rather than for owners. The main reasons for this are (1) that often it is homeless or renter households that represent the designated sites-and-services project target group; (2) owners' current consumption relative to current income reflects an average greater longevity and hence more chance to have upgraded housing relative to renters; and (3) in some markets, owners' current housing consumption reflects both windfall price appreciation and possibly overconsumption due to high transactions costs of moving.

14 At the peak, housing investment to GNP is about 8 percent; at very low GNP levels, the ratio is between 2 and 3 percent.

15 Annez, P. &. W. Wheaton 1984. Economic development and the housing sector: a cross-national model. *Economic Development and Cultural Change* 32 (4, July) 749–66.

16 This assumes that population growth rates are relatively constant over the relevant range; if they decline rapidly with development, then the tendency toward the inverted U type of relationship indicated by Burns &. Grebler will be enhanced. This is discussed at greater length in Mayo, S. K. &. S. Malpezzi 1985. *Cross-country models of housing demand.* Washington, DC.: Water Supply and Urban Development Department, World Bank (mimeographed).

17 Murray, M. 1983. Subsidized and unsubsidized housing starts. *Review of Economics and Statistics* LXV (November), 590–7.

18 Malpezzi, S., M. Bamberger &. S. Mayo 1982. *Planning an urban housing survey: key issues for researchers and program managers in developing countries.* Water Supply and Urban Development Discussion Paper No. 44, November, World Bank: Washington, DC.

19 Malpezzi, S. 1984. *Analyzing an urban housing survey: economic models and statistical techniques.* Urban Development Department Discussion Paper No. 52, World Bank, Washington, DC.

20 Keare, D. &. E. Jimenez 1983. *Progressive development and affordability in the design of urban shelter projects.* World Bank Staff Working Paper No. 560, World Bank, Washington, DC.

21 Follain, J. &. E. Jimenez 1985. Estimating the demand for housing characteristics: a survey and critique. *Regional Science and Urban Economics* 15, 77–107.

22 Jimenez, E. 1984. Tenure security and urban squatting. *Review of Economics and Statistics* 66 (4, November), 556–7.

23 Friedman, J., E. Jimenez & S. Mayo 1985. *The demand for secure tenure in developing countries.* Washington, D.C.: Water Supply and Urban Development Department, World Bank (mimeographed).

24 Gross, D. J. 1984. *Designing a suitable housing project: integration of a demand module into a supply side planning model.* Washington DC.: Water Supply and Urban Development Department, World Bank.

Notes to Chapter 4

1 United Nations Industrial Development Organization (UNIDO) 1985. *The building materials industry in developing countries: an analytical appraisal.* Sectoral Studies Series, Vol. 1, No. 16, UNIDO/IS.512. Vienna: UNIDO – pp. 3–6.

2 CMT, Incorporated 1982. *Role and Contribution of the Construction Industry to the Socio-Economic Growth of Developing Countries.* Paper prepared for United Nations Center for Human Settlements, Cambridge, Mass., n.p. 1980, revised 1982.

3 Moser, C. & J. Marsie-Hazen 1984. *A survey of empirical studies in the industrial and manufacturing activities in the informal sector in the developing countries.* UNIDO/IS.470. Vienna: UNIDO.

4 Riedel, J. & S. Schultz 1977. *Summary of the rôle of the construction industry in the developing countries' economic growth process.* Paper prepared for the Federal Ministry for Economic Co-operation, Munich, n.p.

5 Moavenzadeh, F. & F. Hagopian 1983. *The construction and building materials industries in developing countries.* TAP Report 83–19, Technology Adaptation Program, MIT, Cambridge, Mass. – p. 164.

6 United Nations Center for Human Settlements (UNCHS) 1984. *Small-scale building materials production in the context of the informal economy.* Nairobi: UNCHS – p. 4.

7 Riedel, J. & S. Schultz 1978. *Bauwirtschaft und Baustoffindustrie in Entwicklungslandern.* Munich: Weltform.

8 University College Environmental Research Group 1972. *Construction and development: a framework for research and action.* Paper prepared for the International Board of Reconstruction and Development, London, n.p.

9 Moavenzadeh & Hagopian, op. cit.[5] pp. 63–5.

10 Brown, D. 1984. Construction/investment spending: an engine of economic growth. *Constructor* October, 95–101 – pp. 99–101.

11 Wheeler, D. 1982. *Major relationships between construction and national economic development.* Paper prepared for the Center for Construction Research and Education, MIT, Cambridge, Mass. n.p. – p. 12.

12 Riedel & Schultz, op. cit.[4] p. 13.

13 United States Department of Labor, Bureau of Labor Statistics 1984. *Employment Projections for 1995.* March – p. 24.

14 Pitcock, D. 1984. Construction's economic role. *Constructor* April – p. 7.

15 Araud, C., G. Boon, V. Urquidi, & W. P. Strassman 1973. *Studies on employment in the Mexican housing industry,* OECD Employment Series, No. 10, OECD, Paris.

16 Strassmann, W. P. 1975. *Employment generation through residential construction in Rio de Janeiro,* East Lansing, Mich.: Michigan State University.

17 America's Infrastructure. *Constructor* (May 1983) – p. 35.

18 UNCHS, op. cit.[6] p. 14.

19 Ibid.[18] p. 15.

20 Moavenzadeh & Hagopian, op. cit.[5] p. 164.

21 Ibid.[20] p. 104.

22 Ibid.[20] p. 88.

23 Turin, D. A. 1969. *The construction industry: its economic significance and its role in development*. London: University College Environmental Research Group.

24 Pettitt, R. 1983. Computer aids to housing maintenance management. In *Systems of maintenance planning*. Rotterdam: International Council for Building Research Studies and Documentation – p. 1.

25 Rubinstein, N. 1984. Residential alterations and repairs. *Construction Review* September–October, 4–17 – p. 5.

26 Moavenzadeh & Hagopian, op. cit.[5] pp. 97–8.

27 World Bank, Transportation Department 1978. *Study of labor and capital substitution in civil engineering construction*. Washington, DC: World Bank.

28 Wheeler, D. 1982. *The economics of the building materials industry in developing countries*. Paper prepared for the Center for Construction Research and Education, MIT, Cambridge, Mass. n.p. – p. 72.

29 Strassmann, op. cit.[16] pp. 14, 22.

30 Kassimatis, P. 1976. *The construction industry in Greece*. Athens: Center for Planning and Economic Research.

31 Intermediate Technology Development Group 1978. *Appropriate technology for the production of cement and building materials*. Paper prepared for UNIDO, Working Group No. 5, New Delhi, n.p. – p. 16.

32 World Bank 1978. *World development report 1978*. Washington, DC: World Bank – p. 19.

33 UNCHS, op. cit.[6] p. 12.

34 UNIDO, op. cit.[1] pp. 151–2.

35 Anatomy of a Third World city. *The Urban Edge* September–October 1984 – p. 2.

36 Gold, B. 1983. *Changing determinants of optimal scale in production, and exploring resulting opportunities in developing countries*. Paper prepared for UNIDO, June, n.p. – pp. 19–21.

37 Keare, D. & S. Parris 1982. *Evaluation of shelter programs for the urban poor: principal findings*. World Bank Staff Working Paper No. 547, World Bank, Washington DC.

38 Ibid.[37] p. 37.

39 Ibid.[37] pp. 96–9.

40 Ibid.[37] pp. 104–6.

41 Telephone interview with Pamela Hussey, Office of Housing and Urban Programs, Bureau for Private Enterprise, Agency for International Development, March 27, 1985.

42 Keare & Parris, op. cit.[37] pp. 86–7.

43 New Directions in Bank Urban Projects. *The Urban Edge*, March 1985, 1–5.

44 Bamberger, M., E. Gonzalez-Polio & U. Sae-Hau 1982. *Evaluation of sites and services programs: the evidence from El Salvador*. World Bank Staff Working Paper No. 549, World Bank, Washington, DC – pp. 232–5.

45 Pettersson, V. 1985. Affordable housing for Thailand's urban poor. *Horizons* Winter, 21.

46 UNIDO, op. cit.[1] pp. 107–14.

47 Ibid.[46] pp. 178–9.
48 Miller, R. 1984. Steel minimills. *Scientific American* May – p. 37.
49 United States Department of Commerce 1972. *1972 Census of Manufacturing*. Washington, DC: US Department of Commerce.
50 Moser & Marsie-Hazen, op. cit[3] p. 130.
51 UNCHS, op. cit.[6] p. 15.
52 Moser & Marie-Hazen, op. cit.[3] p. 201.

Notes to Chapter 5

1 Although shelter in rural areas is a serious problem, a scarcity of land is seldom its basic cause. For this reason, this chapter will deal primarily with urban land.

2 Hardoy, J. E. & D. Satterthwaite, 1981. *Shelter: need and response: housing, land and settlement policies in seventeen Third World nations*. Chichester: Wiley – p. 236.

3 *Background paper on land use policies in the ECE region*, Paper prepared by the Economic Commission for Europe for the Expert Group Meeting on Drafting the Theme Paper on land for the Sixth Session of the Commission on Human Settlements, Nairobi, November 1–5, 1982 – p. 2.

4 According to the UN Population Division, urban populations in less developed countries had the following annual rates of increase: 1955, 4.88 percent; 1960, 5.01 percent; 1965, 4.09 percent; 1970, 4.07 percent. Projected increases were: 1975, 4.38 percent; 1980, 4.29 percent; 1985, 4.15 percent; 1990, 3.95 percent; 1995, 3.76 percent; 2000, 3.53 percent. There are, of course, major variations among countries and individual cities. Renaud, B. 1979. *National urbanization policies in developing countries*. World Bank Staff Working Paper No. 347, World Bank, Washington, DC. – p. 10.

5 In this chapter it will be necessary to make many generalizations. Conditions have, of course, differed greatly in different countries. These diversities cannot be discussed in the space available.

6 Doebele, W. A. 1977. The private market and low income urbanization: the "Pirate" subdivisions of Bogotá. *American Journal of Comparative Law* 25 (3, Summer), 531–64.

7 For a description of this process in São Paulo, Brazil, see Batley, R. 1982. Urban renewal and expulsion in São Paulo. In *Urbanization in contemporary Latin America: critical approaches to the analysis of urban issues*, A. Gilbert, J. E. Hardoy & R. Ramirez (eds.), 131–237. Chichester: Wiley.

8 For a detailed study of the dynamics of this process, see Durand-Lasserve, A. 1983. The land conversion process in Bangkok and the predominance of the private sector over the public sector. In *Land for housing the poor*, S. Angel, R. W. Archer, S. Tanphiphat & E. Wegelin, (eds.), 284–309. Singapore: Select Books.

9 United Nations Center for Human Settlements (UNCHS), 1984. *Land for human settlements: review and analysis of the present situation, recommendations for national and international action*. Nairobi, Kenya: UNCHS – HS/Op/83–15/E pp. 27 and 29.

10 "In Bangkok, the incidence of changing the land use from low-income housing to other uses is *higher* on government property than on private

property. Eighty-five percent of the families who rent land from the government face eviction or have been evicted compared with only twenty-two percent of the families on private property." (National Housing Authority of Thailand, Bouwcentrum International Education, Rotterdam; the Asian Institute of Technology, Bangkok. "Conclusions and Recommendations of the Seminar: Land for Housing the Poor: Towards Positive Action in Asian Cities," January 19, 1982, p. 2. Cited by Oberlander, H. P. 1982. *Land and human settlement policy: a review and analysis of selected recent policy developments*. Occasional Papers, No. L–1, p. 41. The Center for Human Settlements, University of British Columbia, Vancouver.

11 For an interesting account of how this happened in one city, see Payne, G. K. 1982. Self-help housing: a critique of the Gecekondus of Ankara. In *Self-help housing: a critique*, P. M. Ward (ed.), 117–39, London: Mansell – especially pp. 136–8.

12 For a comprehensive analytical treatment of the situation in Latin America, see Geisse, G. 1984. Conflicting land strategies in large Latin American cities. *Land Use Policy* 1 (4, October), 309–29. Detailed documentation of Geisse's thesis may be found in Trivelli, P. 1983. *Access to land by the urban poor: an overview of the Latin American experience*. Occasional Paper No. L–7, Center for Human Settlements, University of British Columbia, Vancouver. See also Trivelli, P. 1986. Access to land by the urban poor. *Land use policy*, 3 (2) 101–21, especially 101–9. For a discussion of the situation in some 22 countries, see Baross, P. 1983. The articulation of land supply for popular settlements in Third World cities. In *Land for housing the poor*, S. Angel, R. Archer, S. Tanphiphat & E. Wegelin (eds.), 180–210. Singapore: Select Books. "Articulation" is used by Baross to describe the systems by which prospective home builders get access to land in urban areas.

13 "The real land-price increase, keeping the consumer-price index constant, has been 29.4% per year in Japanese cities 26.2 percent in Tokyo), 20.2 percent in Seoul, 16.0 percent in Caracas, 4.9 percent in cities in the Federal Republic of Germany and 2.8 percent on public lands in Lagos." (UNCHS, op. cit.[9] p. 26.)

14 See, for example, Merrill, R. 1971. *Toward a structural housing policy: an analysis of Chile's low-income housing program*. Unpublished PhD thesis, Cornell University, Ithaca, New York; and Van der Linden, J. 1977. *The bastis of Karachi: types and dynamics*. Amsterdam: Free University. One of the best discussions of this subject is in Angel, S. 1983, Land tenure for the urban poor. In *Land for housing the poor*, S. Angel, R. Archer, S. Tanphiphat & E. Wegelin (eds.), 110–142. Singapore: Select Books. Among other things, Angel points out that legal land tenure is not always a sufficient condition for increased housing investment, particularly for persons at the lowest income levels (see pp. 117–21). Seth Opuni Asiama argues that his studies in Madina, Ghana, indicate that if the poor are given secure tenure at a very low price, further financial resources are not necessary, particularly if there is an absence of town planning and building regulations. Asiama, S. O. 1984. The land factor in housing for low income urban settlers: the example of Madina, Ghana. *Third World Planning Review*. 6 (2, May), 171–84.

In general, careful studies of the relation between varying degrees of tenure and amount of capital invested in housing are quite rare. The weight of the existing evidence is that absolute formal tenure is not so important as a "sense of security," that is, a psychological feeling that as a practical matter one's occupancy will not be disturbed by the government or another claimant. The conditions that create this sense of security may vary greatly from country to country. Thousands of families in Bogotá, Colombia, for example, have invested everything possible on the basis of a contract which is a "promise of purchase and sale." For further discussion, see Doebele, op. cit.[6].

Measuring land boundaries and recording them in an official registry is often an expensive and time-consuming process. Depending on local circumstances, it may or may not be desirable to force registration of land on low-income families. It is, however, nearly always advantageous to increase the *sense* of security of occupancy. For a good discussion of this subject, see Zetter, R. 1984. Land issues in low-income housing. In *Low-income housing in the developing world*, G. K. Payne (ed.), 228–30. Chichester: Wiley.

For land or houses to be used as collateral for credit from a formal institution, some sort of official or legally recognized tenure is normally necessary. For a comprehensive discussion of the different types of land tenure, and their implications for urban development, see Doebele, W. A. 1983. Concepts of urban land tenure. In *Urban land policy: issues and opportunities*, H. B. Dunkerley (ed.), 63–107. New York: Oxford University Press.

15　For one of the few careful studies of rental markets, see Edwards M. 1983. Cities of tenants: renting among the urban poor in Latin America. In *Urbanization in contemporary Latin America: critical approaches to the analysis of urban issues*, A. Gilbert, J. E. Hardoy, & R. Rameriz (eds.) 129–58. Chichester: Wiley. For another case study, see Strassmann, W. P. 1982. *The transformation of urban housing: the experience of upgrading in Cartagena*. Baltimore, Ind.: Johns Hopkins University Press – pp. 127–31. More generally, see Rental housing: a rediscovered priority. *The Urban Edge* 8 (2, February), 1–5. Washington DC: World Bank (1984).

16　UNCHS, op. cit.,[9] p. 25.

17　Other aspects of this theme are discussed by Klaassen L., J. G. D. Voogland and M. J. F. van Pelt. *Economic impact and implications of shelter investments*. This volume, Ch. 2; Moavenzadeh, F. *The construction industry*. This volume Ch. 4.

18　Almost all countries have had sporadic confrontations (occasionally violent) about land rights for the urban homeless. Some of these confrontations, such as those occurring in the Tondo area in the Philippines, have received international publicity.

19　For further discussion, see Peattie, L. *Shelter, development, and the poor*. This volume, Ch. 11; Hardoy, J. and D. Satterthwaite, *The legal and the illegal city*. This volume, Ch. 13. *Metropolitan Settlement Strategies*.

20　For detailed discussions of this issue, see Hall, P. This volume, Ch. 10; Richardson, H. *Spatial strategies, the settlement pattern, and shelter and services policies*. This volume, Ch. 9.

21　See Mohan, R. & R. Villamizar, 1982. The evolution of land values in the context of rapid urban growth: a case study of Bogotá and Cali, Colombia. In *World congress on land policy, 1980*, M. Cullen & S. Woolery (eds.) 217–52. Lexington, Mass.: D. C. Heath – especially pp. 248–49. In spite of their obvious importance, there have been very few careful studies of urban land markets in developing countries. See Ingram, G. K., 1982. Land in perspective: its role in the structure of cities. In *World Congress on Land Policy*, 1980, M. Cullen &

S. Woolery (eds.), 103–18. Lexington, Mass.: D. C. Heath. For a comprehensive collection of data on Latin American land markets, and their impact on areas most needed by the poor, see Trivelli, P. 1983. *Access to land by the urban poor: an overview of the Latin American experience.* Occasional Papers, No. L–7, Center for Human Settlements, University of British Columbia, Vancouver. For a well documented study of over four centuries of land ownership, political institutions and land markets in a smaller Venezuelan city, see Flores-Rangel, M. G. 1981. *Land ownership patterns as determinat of availability and accessability of urban land for residential use: case study: city of Merida, Venezuela* (2 volumes). Master's thesis, MIT Department of Urban Studies and Planning, January; also van der Berg, L. M. 1984. *Anticipating urban growth in Africa: land use and land values in the urban fringe of Lusaka, Zambia.* Lusaka: Zambia Geographical Association. (Available from the Zambia Geographical Association, PO Box 50287, Ridgeway, Lusaka, Zambia.)

22 See Walters, A. A. 1983. The value of land. In *Urban land policy: issues and opportunities* H. B. Dunkerley (ed.) 40–62. New York: Oxford University Press.

23 For a description of how improved transportation (a metro line in Valencia, Venezuela) may increase land speculation and social inequities, see Gilbert, A. 1984. Planning, invasions and land speculation: the role of the state in Venezuela. *Third World Planning Review* 6 (3, August) 225–38. See also Batley, R. Urban renewal and expulsion in São Paulo. In *Urbanization in contemporary Latin America: critical approaches to the analysis of urban issues*, A. Gilbert, J. E. Hardoy & R. Rameriz (eds.), 231–62. Chichester, Wiley, dealing with the extension of the São Paulo Metro system.

24 For further discussion of this theme, see Echenique, M. 1982. Transportation investment and urban land values: emerging empirical evidence. In *World Congress on Land Policy, 1980*, M. Cullen & S. Woolery (eds.), 255–73. Lexington, Mass.: D. C. Heath. Great care, however, must be used in carrying out this approach. Francisco Sabatini and Guillermo Geisse have shown that urban land markets are highly compartmentalized. Their analysis of Santiago, Chile, shows that merely increasing the supply of land, without consideration of locational characteristics, may not exert downward pressure on prices. See Sabatini, F. 1983. *Land prices and national economic trends: the case of Santiago, Chile, 1980–1981.* Prepared for the Second World Congress on Land Policy, Lincoln Institute of Land Policy, Cambridge, Mass., June. See also Geisse, G. 1982. *Access of the poor to land in the large cities of Latin America.* Paper prepared by the CEPAL/CELADE Joint Programme on Human Settlements at the request of the United Nations Center for Human Settlements. October. Revised version published as Geisse, op. cit., pp. 309–39.

It must also be noted that when transportation improvements are made simultaneously with a weakening of traditional informal systems of land tenure, there can be quite negative effects on low-income families, according to the study of Johan Silas in Surabaya. See Silas, J. 1983. Spatial structure, housing delivery, land tenure, and the urban poor in Surabaya, Indonesia. In *Land for housing the poor*, S. Angel, R. W. Archer, S. Tanphiphat & E. Wegelin (eds.) 211–33. Singapore: Select Books.

25 For a description of one method, see note 49. For an excellent brief general discussion see Dunkerley, H. (ed.), 1983. *Urban land policy: issues and opportunities.* New York: Oxford University Press – pp. 22–9 and Ch. 4 and 5.

26 For a comprehensive review and commentary on almost all available

mechanisms, see International Federation of Housing and Planning (IFHP) 1981. *Urban land policy*. Pre-Congress Report of IFHP Working Party, International Congress, Liège, Belgium, 26–30 September, 1981. The Hague, The Netherlands: IFHP.

27 Mabogunje, A. L., J. E. Hardoy & R. P. Misra 1978. *Shelter provision in developing countries: the influence of standards and criteria.* Chichester: Wiley – p. 29; Edited by C. Ian Jackson for the Scientific Committee on the Problems of the Environment (SCOPE): 11, 1978. Trivelli, P. 1982. *Accessability to urban land by low-income groups: an overview of the Latin American case.* Occasional Paper No. 16, Center for Human Settlements, University of British Columbia, Vancouver – p. 6. Both cited in UNCHS, op. cit.[9] p. 27. The figures on Manila and Cairo are from Hardoy, J. & D. Satterthwaite, 1981. *Shelter: need and response: housing, land and settlement patterns in seventeen third world nations.* Chichester: Wiley – pp. 87 and 34.

28 For an excellent five-page discussion of this argument, see Dunkerley, H. B. (ed.) 1983. Introduction and overview. In *Urban land policy: issues and opportunities*, pp. 6–11. New York: Oxford University Press. See also Walters, op. cit.[22]

29 An exceptionally insightful article on this point is Geisse, op. cit.[12] See also Trivelli, op. cit.[12]

30 UNCHS, op. cit.[9] p. 27.

31 In general, it is much better to improve existing systems of taxation than to substitute new ones. For a good survey of the experience in this field, see Prest, A. R. Land taxation and urban finances in less-developed countries. In *World Congress on Land Policy, 1980*, M. Cullen & S. Woolery (eds.), 369–406. Lexington, Mass: D. C. Heath.

32 de Hancock, T. M. 1980. Basic principles of land use and price controls in Japan. *International Review* I (4), 46–57. Washington, DC, US Department of Housing and Urban Development; see also Hanayama, Y. *Land market and land policy in a metropolitan area: a case study of Tokyo* (manuscript). Cambridge, Mass.: Lincoln Institute of Land Policy, forthcoming – pp. 33–4.

33 On October 2, 1976, the Republic of Korea's Minister of Construction announced plans to construct a new industrial town of 200,000 persons 35 km from Seoul and simultaneously "froze" the price of 27.7 km^2 on the site. However, speculation immediately occurred in the surrounding area, and ten weeks later the Ministry increased the frozen area to 280.19, apparently aborting the speculative activity and thereby reducing the cost and difficulty of carrying out the new town project. A similar system was contemplated for establishing a new administrative capital for the country, but it was not carried out because the new capital proposal itself was postponed. Doebele W. A. & Chan Hwang, M. 1978. *Land policies in the Republic of Korea, with special reference to decentralized development.* Unpublished report to the World Bank, April – pp. 64–6.

34 World Bank 1983. *Learning by doing: World Bank lending for urban development, 1972–82.* Washington, D.C.: World Bank – p. 44. For other case studies, and a general discussion, see UN Economic and Social Commission for Asia and the Pacific 1984. *Improvement of slums and squatter settlements: infrastructure and services.* ST/ESCAP/302 ESCAP, Bangkok. See also Strassman, W. P. 1984. *The transformation of urban housing: the experience of upgrading in Cartagena.* Baltimore, Md.: Johns Hopkins University Press.

35 Angel et al., op. cit.[58(2)], p. 541. Conclusions and recommendations.

36 As has been noted earlier, the sense of security from the threat of being displaced, rather than formal title, appears to be fundamental to the release of economic energy in the form of construction. It has been argued that formalization of title can be regressive in that it opens the poor to new forms of taxation and, more seriously, to the possibility of being "bought out" by higher-income families. In this case, the occupant low-income family may receive a substantial amount of the capital in hand to re-enter the market, but in the longer run, an area that once served the poor will be permanently converted into middle-class housing, to the disadvantage of other poor arriving in the city. Imperfect title, in other words, is excellent insurance against "gentrification."

The study of Johan Silas of the peripheral land market of Surabaya showed that improved transportation plus the "formalization" of land tenures (previously recognized by mutual consent) was a combination whose effect was quite negative for the poor. See Silas, op. cit.,[24] pp. 211–33, especially pp. 227–31.

Others argue that the total supply situation of a city is improved when lots have cadastral and tenure information fully clarified, permitting the most efficient operation of the market, which will, in the end, produce the optimum allocation of land resources and increase the supply of land. Studies of this point are, however, not conclusive. See Angel, S. 1983. Land tenure for the urban poor. In Angel *et al.*, op. cit.[8], pp. 110–42. Also Ward, P. M. 1983. Land for housing the poor: how can planners contribute? Also in Angel *et al.*, op. cit.[8], pp. 34–53, especially at p. 40.

One solution that has been offered is to make the granting of title a progressive process, or to make the final form a license which would have most of the practical advantages of full tenure but be more difficult to transfer. See a good discussion of this problem by Zetter, R. op. cit.,[14] pp. 228–30.

Jimenez has developed an economic model that attempts to explain the capitalization effects of tenure. Perceived risk of eviction is capitalized into the price of dwellings. Thus, as risk of eviction declines, prices increase. This benefits those who first receive tenure (move from an insecure to a more secure position) but may impose price barriers to turnover to succeeding low-income occupants. The theory also may explain why squatting may be found in areas where land prices are high: the poor are able to tolerate a much higher risk of eviction than the well-to-do. On the theory, see Jimenez, E. 1982. The value of squatter dwellings in developing countries. *Economic Development and Cultural Change*. 30, pp. 739–52. On its application to data from Davao, Philippines, see Jimenez, E. 1983. *Tenure security among urban squatter households in developing countries*. Draft Paper for World Bank, February 2 – pp. 21–3.

For a very useful discussion of "filtering-up" in general, see Johnson, T. E. Jr. 1985. *A study of upwards filtering of housing stock as a consequence of informal settlement upgrading in developing countries*. Paper prepared for course work at the Harvard Graduate School of Design, May 1985.

37 For comprehensive discussion of this method, see Angel, S. & Chirathamkijkul, T. 1983. "Slum reconstruction: land sharing as an alternative to eviction in Bangkok. In *Land for housing the poor*, S. Angel, R. W. Archer, S. Tanphiphat & E. Wegelin (eds.), 430–60. Singapore: Select Books.

38 San Francisco and Boston now have such so-called "linkage" requirements, and interest is being shown in other US cities. To date these have not

produced substantial numbers of housing units but have established the basic principle of linked responsibility between permission to build in the most profitable areas of the city and housing needs.

39　Such requirements have been the law for federally supported urban renewal projects in the United States since 1970.

40　Interview by author with Stuart Whitehead, Senior Financial Analyst, the World Bank, January 25, 1983.

41　"In African officially uncontrolled settlements, the insecurity of shelter due to the lack of protection of tenants, seems to be more widespread than insecurity of tenure as such, and the mechanisms of tenancy and renting speculation need to be well understood." (Barrass, F. 1982. *Relationships between squatters and land in urban sub-Saharan Africa: some comments about the situation from a lawyer's perspective.* Occasional Papers No. L–3 Center for Human Settlements, University of British Columbia – p. 42.)

42　See Dunkerley, H. B. (ed.). Introduction and overview. In *Urban land policy: issues and opportunities* op. cit., p. 38. On the implicit subsidies and equity effects of long-term leaseholds in Stockholm, see Ratzka, A. D. 1981. Land banking in Stockholm: an evaluation of municipal residential leasehold as a public finance and housing subsidy instrument. *American Planning Association Journal* July, 279–88.

43　For an interesting description of the negative effects of poor land acquisition and compensation procedures on essential projects, see Famoriyo, S. 1984. Land acquisition and irrigation in Nigeria. *Land Use Policy* 1 (1, January) 55–63. Numerous international and bilateral aid agencies are now in the process of mobilizing technical assistance and training programs to deal with this problem. However, as mentioned in note 36 above, great care must be taken that efforts to improve land measurement and registry systems are regressive in their impact on the poor. For a careful and insightful study of the politics and complexities of legal tenure in low-income areas, see Perdomo, R. P., P. Nikken, E. Fassano & M. Vilera 1982. The law and home ownership in the *Barrios* of Caracas. In *Urbanization of Latin America: critical approaches to the analysis of urban issues*, A. Gilbert, J. E. Hardoy & R. Rameriz (eds.) 205–29. Chichester: Wiley.

44　"In Nigeria, the railway company, which is a federal undertaking, owns land for one mile (1.6 km) in either side of the railway. The corporation does not regard itself as bound by town planning laws, which are a state responsibility. So prime land in the centre of many towns is therefore not subject to any form of effective land use control." (International Institute for Environment and Development 1983. *Earthscan*. Press Briefing Document No. 35, April, International Institute for Environment and Development, London – p. 24.) This is, of course, only one example of the large tracts in almost every country owned by public, semipublic or charitable and nonprofit organizations. (It is worth noting that the Kenya railway corporation has vigorously enforced its rights by evicting squatters and destroying their dwellings in Mombasa. Stren, R. 1978. *Housing the poor in urban Africa: policy, politics and bureaucracy in Mombasa.* Berkeley, Calif.: Institute for International Studies.) (Cited in Barrass, F. 1982. *Relationships between squatters and land in sub-Saharan Africa.* Occasional Papers No. L–3, Center for Human Settlements, University of British Columbia – p. 35.)

45　A good example of this type of study is Moser, C. O. N. 1982. A home of one's own: squatter housing strategies in Guayaquil, Ecuador. In *Urbanization of Latin America: critical approaches to the analysis of urban issues.* A. Gilbert,

J. E. Hardoy & R. Rameriz (eds.), 159–90. Chichester: Wiley; see also, Benjamin, S. J. 1985. *Understanding urban housing transformations: a case-study of Bhogal, India.* Thesis for the degree of Master of Science in Architectural Studies, MIT, June. Also Strassman, op. cit.[34]; Batley, R. 1982. Urban renewal and expulsion in São Paulo. In *Urbanization of Latin America: critical approaches to the analysis of urban issues*, A. Gilbert, J. E. Hardoy & R. Rameriz (eds.) 231–62, Chichester, Wiley; and Perdomo, R. P. *et. al.* 1982. In *Urbanization of Latin America: critical approaches to the analysis of urban issues*, A. Gilbert, J. E. Hardoy, R. Rameriz (eds.) 205–29. Chichester: Wiley. The classic reference is Peattie, L. R. 1970. *The view from the Barrio.* Ann Arbor: University of Michigan Press. Also Perlman, J. E. 1976. *The myth of marginality: urban poverty and politics in Rio de Janeiro.* Berkeley: University of California Press. The importance of participant-observers in improving understanding of shelter problems, and their growing use, was recently noted in "Evaluators seek 'View from the Barrio'," and in "Participant–observer method: how it works," in *The Urban Edge*, Washington, DC: World Bank, Vol. 8, No. 4, April, 1984, pp. 1–4.

Such studies might have the secondary and not insignificant effect of increasing the understanding of public agencies of cultural factors that make site planning and housing designs often unpopular with their occupants. See, for example, Muller, M. S. 1984. Traditional cultural identity in new dwellings of urban Africa. *Ekistics* 51 (307, July–August), 359–65.

For an eloquent plea to restructure the research agenda for developing countries, see Qadeer, M. A. 1985. Understanding Third World cities: perceptions and prescriptions: a review essay. In *Third World affairs 1985.* London: Third World Foundation for Economic and Social Studies, pp. 337–53 – especially pp. 352–3.

46 For an in-depth study of the illegal subdivision of Bogotá (which accounts for nearly 50 percent of all housing built in recent years), see Hamer, A. Bogotá's unregulated subdivisions. Paper for *The city study of Bogotá.* Washington: World Bank (unpublished), summarized in *The Urban Edge* 8, (8, September–October 1984), pp. 4–7. Also Doebele, W. A. 1977. The private market and low income urbanization: the "pirate" subdivisions of Bogotá. *American Journal of Comparative Law* 25 (3), 531–64.

47 Interview with Donna Haldane, Senior Urban Operations Officer, the World Bank. The credit arrangements themselves involve interesting public–private institutional interactions.

48 For more than a decade the Massachusetts Housing Finance Agency has had a successful program that has required the inclusion of specified percentages of low- and moderate-income families into conventional housing developments as a condition of granting mortgage funds at favorable interest rates to developers in the State. The so-called "linkage" legislation in American cities, op. cit.[38], is another example. Possible methods of public–private cooperation and joint development are, of course, almost unlimited.

49 For further information, see Doebele, W. A. (ed.) 1982. *Land readjustment: a different approach to financing urbanization.* Lexington, Mass.: D. C. Heath, Lexington Books. Also Minerbi, L., P. Nakamura, K. Nitz & J. Yanai, 1986. *Land readjustment: the Japanese system: a reconnaissance and a digest.* Boston, Mass.: Oelgeschlager, Gunn & Hain/Lincoln Institute of Land Policy (forthcoming).

50 A system has been proposed for Mexico that would make sites-and-service projects completely self-financing, based on supplying double-sized plots in

the original allocation. See Ward, P. 1981. Financing land acquisition for self-build housing schemes. *Third World Planning Review* 3, (1), 7–20.

51 See further discussion in note 36 above. For a general discussion of the standards issue, see Mabogunje, A. L., J. E. Hardoy & R. P. Misra 1978. *Shelter provisions in developing countries.* Chichester (UK): Wiley.

52 For a general discussion of the issues involved, see United Nations Center for Human Settlements (UNCHS) 1984. *Community participation in the execution of low-income housing projects.* HS/Op/83–16/E, UNCHS, Nairobi.

53 For the experience in Indonesia on this point, see Silas, J. 1984. The Kampung improvement programme of Indonesia: a comparative case study of Jakarta and Surabaya. In *low-income housing in the developing world*, G. K. Payne (ed.), 69–87. Chichester: Wiley – p. 80. On the importance of government goodwill in maintaining the effectiveness of community participation, see Skinner, R. Self-help, community organization and politics: Villa El Salvador, Lima. In *Self-help housing: a critique*, P. M. Ward (ed.), 209–29. London: Mansell. For an excellent general summary of the strengths and limitations of community participation, with many case studies, see United Nations Center for Human Settlements (UNCHS) 1984. *Promoting organized self-help through co-operative modes of participation.* HS/37/84/E, UNCHS, Nairobi.

54 It is also one of the best ways to give secure tenure to the poor while avoiding the possibility of "filtering up" to higher-income groups. See discussion in note 36 above.

55 Shann Turnbull. Cooperative land banks for low-income housing. In Angel *et al.*, op. cit., pp. 512–26.

56 Land Commission of New South Wales 1984. *Multiple occupancy development: feasibility study* (draft, June). Land Commission of New South Wales, Box 13, Sydney, Australia.

57 For a discussion of two land-sharing projects in Bangkok, see United Nations Center for Human Settlements (UNCHS) 1984. *Upgrading of inner-city slums.* HS/CONF/84–1 E, UNCHS, Nairobi – pp. 24–6. For a general discussion of the importance of cooperative ownership in the context of comprehensive recommendations for dealing with inner-city slums, see ibid. pp. 33–4, and Recommendations 2 and 3 (p. 40), in the same volume.

58 The problems of furnishing land for shelter for the homeless are complex ones. This chapter has been able only to touch on a few of the important aspects. In recent years we have seen the issuance of a number of excellent longer treatments of this subject. In particular, the reader is referred to four especially relevant publications.

(1) United Nations Center for Human Settlements (UNCHS) 1983. *Land for Human Settlements.* HS/Op/83–15/E. Nairobi, Kenya: UNCHS. (Available from UNCHS, PO Box 30030, Nairobi, Kenya.)

(2) Angel, S., R. W. Archer, S. Tanphiphat & E. A. Wegelin 1983. *Land for Housing the Poor.* Singapore: Select Books – especially Ch. 10, pp. 528–56, which contains 43 recommendations for action in this field. (Available from Select Books, 03–15 Tanglin Shopping Centre, 19 Tanglin Road, Singapore 1024.)

(3) Dunkerley, B. & C. M. E. Whitehead (eds.) 1983. *Urban Land Policy: Issues and Opportunities.* New York: Oxford University Press. (Distributed through the Publications Department, World Bank, 1818 "H" Street, N. W. Washington DC 20433, USA.)

(4)   International Federation of Housing and Planning (IFHP) 1981. *Urban Land Policy*. Pre-congress Report of Working Party, IFHP, The Hague, The Netherlands. (Available from IFHP, 63 Wassenaarsweg, 2596 CG, The Hague, The Netherlands.)

59   See Peattie, L. 1979. Housing policy in developing countries: two puzzles. *World Development* 7, 1017–22.

Notes to Chapter 6

1   For example, in Chapter 9 in this volume, Richardson uses "standards" to mean the quality of service rendered in the areas served and the portions of cities covered by services. These are implied in his statement "Shelter and service standards decline with movement down the urban hierarchy and from the core region to the periphery." In Chapter 8 in this volume Renaud uses "standard" to mean a level of service specifically selected for a project to match its clientele's ability to pay.

2   Moore, C. H. 1980. *Images of development: Egyptian engineers in search of industry*. Boston, Mass. MIT Press – p. 42 *et passim*.

3   Tendler, J. 1979a. *New directions: rural roads*. AID Program Evaluation Discussion Paper No. 2, March, Washington DC: US AID – p. 30.

4   Thomas, J. W. 1974. Development institutions, projects and aid: a case study of the water development programme in East Pakistan.

5   Tendler, op. cit.[3] p. 33.

6   Tendler, J. 1975. *Inside foreign aid*. Baltimore, Md.: The Johns Hopkins University Press – p. vi.

7   The assumption is that foreign exchange is very scarce, but matching local currency can always be found through committed efforts. Also, local currency management is much harder to monitor for the lender (Tendler, op. cit.[5] p. 74.)

8   Angel, S. 1985. Upgrading slum infrastructure: divergent objectives in search of a consensus *Third World Planning Review* 5 (1, February), 5–21 – p. 10.

9   One dramatic example of standards changing with political change is from São Paulo, Brazil, which embarked in 1975 on the world's largest sewerage (network and treatment) program. When the project was conceived in 1976 the state governor was Paulo Egydio Martins, a member of the old landed aristocracy that subsequently moved into banking and industry. The local authority was directed by people with roughly the same background or who at least shared the governor's views of the development process. There was strong contractor influence within the agency, which hired the study. In summary, the elite had a technocratic, modern, capitalistic view of the development process, arguing for capital intensive, high technology, "modern" solutions. As a result the project prescribed a huge, centralized, latest technology sewage treatment plant, to be the world's largest, at a scale untested elsewhere. Cheaper, simpler solutions were put aside by the numerous local and foreign consultants brought in to advise on the final choice. When Franco Montoro, the first governor directly elected by the people in 18 years, took office in 1983 a reappraisal of the adopted treatment solution was ordered, in spite of the fact that the first module of the conventional treatment plant was already under construction. The new governor represented the university establishment in São Paulo, having been

elected by a coalition of opposition and leftist forces on the basis of a populist program rich in social emphasis, and which held a more distributive, less concentrating view of the development process. Franco Montoro, who may be labeled a social democrat, had in Fernando Henrique Cardoso, the widely known development economist, one of the main architects of his proposed program of government. As a result of the tendencies of the new government, the new local authority management favored decentralization and participation, though still somewhat influenced by contracting interests. Furthermore, it faced strict budgetary limitations because of the curtailment of federal funding. The review of the treatment solution indicated that lower cost treatment ponds should be adopted instead of a conventional treatment plant, in spite of the fact that strong doubts persisted and still persist as to whether treatment ponds would be adequate at a very large scale of concentrated treatment demand. This case demonstrates that the preferences of decision makers tend to shape the types of standards and proposals that are presented and get accepted.

10   Angel, op. cit.[8] p. 18.
11   Cook, C. C., H. L. Beenhakker & R. Hartwig 1984. *Institutional aspects in rural roads projects.* Washington, DC: Transportation Department, World Bank, June 15.
12   Tendler, op. cit.[3] p. 40.
13   Tendler, J. 1979b. *Rural Electrification: Linkages and Justifications.* Washington, DC: Office of Evaluation, Bureau for Program and Policy Coordination, Agency for International Development, April 1979.
14   An example similar to that of Tendler is the program in the State of São Paulo mentioned in note 9. When Governor Montoro took office there was an urgent need for action but also an extreme shortage of funds. Aside from ideological reasons to decentralize and "make it simple," there was the very pragmatic need to lower costs. The result was the application to almost one hundred municipalities of lowered standards that the authority had already been using experimentally for three years, but which previous administrations hesitated to support. The main simplifications of the program are:

(a) Many conventional manholes are eliminated, replaced by buried junction boxes, standard joints, and rodding eyes at upstream sewer ends.
(b) Conventional manholes are used on both ends of sewers only where they receive connections from hospitals, gas stations, jails, hotels, schools, and similar institutions.
(c) Reduction of minimum diameters to 100 mm (4 in), from the conventional 150 mm (6 in).
(d) House connections are changed to allow rodding tools to be introduced through them to reach sewers.

Such simplifications have already allowed savings of at least 30 percent of total costs where tried. Studies were made and preliminary trials are under way to apply these modifications to sewer networks in the city of São Paulo itself.

15   Tendler, op. cit.[6] p. 61. *Pakistan Economic and Social Review* No. 1, Spring, 77–103 – pp. 53–6.
16   Caiden, N. & A. Wildavsky 1974. *Planning and budgeting in poor countries.* New York: Wiley – pp. 20, 47 *et passim.*
17   Continuing the case from notes 9 and 14, this revision of social contract is

what happened with the new government in São Paulo. Not only were standards lowered, with popular approval, but also municipalities were asked to provide materials. In poorer municipalities there were cases where volunteer labor was enlisted for trenching.

18 Thomas, op. cit.[4] p. 54.

Notes to Chapter 7

1 Boleat, M. J. 1985. *National housing finance systems: a comparative study*. London: Croom Helm/International Union of Building Societies and Savings Associations (IUBSSA).
2 Carlson, E. 1984. Perspectives and prospects for global housing action. *Ekistics* Vol. 51 pp. 288–302 July–August.
3 Annez, P. & W. C. Wheaton 1984. Economic development and the housing sector. *Economic Development and Cultural Change* Vol. 32, No. 4 pp. 749–71 July.
4 Renaud, B. 1984. *Housing and financial institutions in developing countries*. Chicago: International Union of Building societies and Savings Associations.
5 Strassmann, W. P. 1983. *The transformation of urban housing*. Baltimore, Md.: Johns Hopkins University Press.
6 Blaesser, E. W. 1981. *Clandestine development in Colombia*. AID Occasional Paper. Washington DC.
7 Pirate Subdivisions: low income housing in Bogotá. *The Urban Edge* 8 pp. 1–7 (8, September–October) 1984.
8 Ganjarerndee, S. 1982. *Pattern of household financial saving in Thailand*. Bangkok: Bank of Thailand.
9 United Nations 1981. *Savings for development*. Report of an International Symposium, Kingston, Jamaica, 1980. New York: United Nations.
10 UN. *Habitat News*, p. 18.
11 Christian. J. W. 1980. *Housing finance for developing countries*. Chicago: International Union of Building Societies and Savings Associations.
12 Shah, P. P. 1984. *Operational problems and potential for low income lending*. Paper presented to Asia Housing Finance Seminar, March.
13 Anatomy of a Third World City, *Urban Edge*, 8 (8), September–October 1984.

Notes to Chapter 8

1 See Renaud, B. 1984. *Housing and financial institutions in developing countries*. Chicago, Ill.: International Union of Building Societies and Savings Associations. (Also available in French, Spanish, and English from the World Bank as Staff Working Paper No. 648, 1984.)
2 This second ratio is affected by the completeness of financial reporting. It also reflects mortgage maturities, loan-to-value ratios, and the tax treatment of housing. For more details, see Boleat, M. 1985. *National housing finance systems*. London: Croom Helm.
3 See Landeau, J. F., S. Margetis, B. Renaud & J. L. Berger 1984. *Institutional housing finance in Tunisia*. Unpublished World Bank Report, World Bank, Washington DC.

4 For instance, in a very recent case in Ivory Coast, a commercial bank financing a moderate-income housing project of 500 units was appalled to find that for the lower-price units the cost of registering titles was equal to the down payment that families had accumulated over two years through a contractual savings scheme, amounting to 10 percent of the value of the unit.

5 In a Caribbean country where permits must be obtained from several administrations using different building standards and applying them inconsistently internally, it has been estimated that the cost of delays and redesigns imposed even during the construction phase might be raising the building cost of a legal unit by as much as 50 percent.

6 This is of course a mistaken impression because the real estate tax base of residential buildings is seriously eroded by rent controls. One of the better known cases is Bombay where, after many years of hesitation, the government recently came to the conclusion that rent controls had mostly negative effects and decided to take some corrective actions. In particular, because of rent control the courts had ruled that the property tax base should be determined by the rental value of buildings, which was frozen by rent controls at the date of construction. The net effect was that the property tax raised less funds in this large city than the old and ineffective octroi tax on goods entering the city limits. Without a resource base, how could a government maintain public infrastructure or expand it?

7 The recent example of Korea is very interesting. Since 1981 Korea has been restructuring its economic management strategy to take into account the new international economic environment and improve its foreign debt position. An important part of the new strategy is to have better managed public sector enterprises by giving managers greater autonomy in their decision making, together with more sharply defined external performance and internal management objectives. Since 1984, the 25 government-invested corporations are subject to the Basic Law on Management of Government-invested Business Organizations. Among these 25 organizations are the three key shelter agencies: the Korea Land Development Corporation, the Korea National Housing Corporation, and the Korea Housing Bank. Their managers are evaluated every year on the basis of publicly known criteria and they can receive bonuses or be penalized on the basis of their performances, which are reviewed by managerial committees composed of public and private experts. Ratings are reported in the press.

8 Argentina, Brazil, Chile, Indonesia, Uruguay, Israel.

9 The prior saving period which would be required for an outright cash transaction is not too difficult to evaluate as a function of the housing cost (say, 3.5 times annual income); the family savings rate (say 15 percent); and the real interest rate on financial savings (say 3 percent). For the figures quoted it is 18 years. Such long waiting periods explain the progressive investment approach followed by most households in TWCs where no long-term financing is available in the informal sector. As one should expect, given the actual market fluctuations of all these variables, the availability of financing has a positive impact on the quality of the dwelling that households own. See Struyk, R. & M. A. Turner 1985. *Housing finance and housing quality in the Philippines and Korea.* Unpublished World Bank Research Paper, January, World Bank, Washington, DC.

10 See Boleat, M. *Housing finance institutions.* This volume, Ch. 7; Boleat, M. 1985. *National finance systems: a comparative study.* London: Croom Helm.

11 For details on indexation not discussed in this chapter see, for instance, Sandilands, R. J. 1980. *Monetary correction and housing finance in Columbia, Brazil, and Chile.* Farnborough: Gower.

12 An interesting contrast can be made between the major contribution made by the provident fund of Singapore to solving the housing problem with the management of Infonavit in Mexico. Both funds draw their resources from mandatory contributions based on employment. In Singapore employers and employees contribute. In Mexico Infonavit resources come from a 5 percent tax on salaries paid by employers. Currently Infonavit still makes long-term mortgage loans at 4 percent fixed rates when inflation in the country has only declined from 100 percent to about 40 percent in the last four years.

13 For more details refer to: Burns, L. S. & L. Grebler 1976. Resource allocation to housing investment: a comparative international study. *Economic development and cultural change* 25 (1, October), 95–121; Renaud, B. 1980. Resource allocation to housing investment: comments and further results. *Economic Development and Cultural Change* 28 (2, January), 389–99; Annez, P. & W. C. Wheaton 1984. Economic Development and the Housing sector: A Cross-National Model. *Economic Development and Cultural Change*, 32 (4, July), 749–66; Buckley, R. M. & R. G. Madhusudan 1984. The macroeconomics of housing's role in the economy: an international analysis. Paper presented to the American Real Estate and Urban Economics Association, December.

Notes to Chapter 9

1 See Richardson, H. W. 1981. Defining urban population distribution goals in development planning. In *Population distribution policies in development planning*, 7–18, New York: United Nations; Richardson, H. W. 1985. *The goals of national urban policy.* Paper prepared for the Conference on Population Growth, Urbanization and Urban Policies in the Asia-Pacific Region, East–West Center, Honolulu, April 1985.

2 See Stark, O. 1980. On slowing metropolitan city growth. *Population and Development Review* 6, 95–102; Simmons, A. 1979. Slowing metropolitan city growth in Asia: policies, programs and results. *Population and Development Review* 5, 87–104.

3 See Rondinelli, D. 1983. *Secondary cities in developing countries.* Beverly Hills, Calif.: Sage; Mathur, O. P. (ed.) 1982. *Small cities and national development.* Nagoya: United Nations Centre for Regional Development.

4 Studies of the effects of implicit spatial policies include Ruane, F. 1982. *Sectoral policies and the spatial concentration of industrial activities: a factor – market adjustment approach.* Discussion Paper 12. Washington, DC: World Bank, Water Supply and Urban Development Department; Tyler, W. 1983. *The Brazilian sectoral incentives system and the regional incidence of non-spatial incentive policies.* Discussion Paper 31. Washington, DC: World Bank, Water Supply and Urban Development Department; Hamer, A. M. 1984. *Indonesian urbanization and selected sectoral policies.* Washington, DC: World Bank, mimeograph; Robinson, W. C. 1985. *Effects of implicit policies and institutional factors on urbanization.* Paper prepared for the Conference on Population Growth, Urbanization and Urban Policies in the Asia-Pacific Region, East–West Center, Honolulu, April 1985.

5 Richardson, H. W. 1977. *City size and national spatial strategies in developing countries.* Staff Working Paper 252. World Bank, Washington, DC; Richardson, H. W. 1980. Polarization reversal in developing countries. *Papers, Regional Science Association* 45, 65–78.

6 The arguments that follow draw upon earlier papers by the author: Richardson, H. W. 1981. National urban development strategies in developing countries. *Urban Studies* 18, 267–83; Richardson, H. W. 1983. Population distribution policies. *United Nations Population Bulletin* No. 15, 35–49. However, these are in turn syntheses of conclusions derived from the researches and evaluations of many other scholars and agencies.

7 See Lipton, M. 1977. *Why people stay poor: urban bias in world development.* Cambridge, Mass.: Harvard University Press; Friedmann, J. 1981. Urban bias in regional development policy. 143–59. In *Humanizing development: essays on people, space and development in honour of Masahiko Honjo*, R. P. Misra (ed.), Singapore: Maruzen Asia; Stöhr, W. B. & D. R. F. Taylor (eds.) 1981. *Development from above or below? The dialectics of regional planning in developing countries.* New York: Wiley.

8 For the most explicit statement of this position see Lipton, M. 1982. Migration from rural areas of poor countries: the impact on rural productivity and income distribution. In *Migration and the labor market in developing countries*, R. H. Sabot (ed.). Boulder: Westview Press.

9 Stark, op. cit., see note 2.

10 Mera, K. 1973. On the urban agglomeration and economic efficiency. *Economic Development and Cultural Change* 21, 309–24; Mera, K. & H. Shishido 1980. *The pattern and pace of urbanization and socio-economic development: a cross-sectional analysis of development since 1960.* DP 70, Institute of Socio-Economic Planning, University of Tsukuba, Tsukuba, Japan.

11 Qutub, S. A. & H. W. Richardson 1986. The costs of urbanization in Pakistan. *Environment and Planning A*, 18, 1089–113.

12 Vining, D. R. 1984. Population redistribution towards LDC core areas, 1950–1980. *International Regional Science Review* 9.

13 The increasing importance of circular migration and commuting for off-farm jobs supports this view.

14 See Gedik, A. 1982. *Rural to urban versus urban to urban migration in population growth of urban places in developing countries: case study of Turkey, 1970.* Columbus, Ohio: Department of City and Regional Planning, Ohio State University. "Regional Containment," whereby rural outmigrants are induced to remain in the urban centers of their home region and/or to maintain circular migratory links with the rural hinterland, is a more feasible approach than "rural rentention."

15 Linn, J. F. 1983. *Cities in the developing world: policies for their equitable, and efficient growth.* New York: Oxford University Press; Linn, J. F. 1985. *Success and failure in urban management: some lessons from the East Asian experience.* Paper prepared for the Conference on Population Growth, Urbanization and Urban Policies in the Asia–Pacific Region, East–West Center, Honolulu, April 1985.

16 See Richardson, H. W. 1985. *The goals of national urban policy.* Paper prepared for the Conference on Population Growth, Urbanization and Urban Policies in the Asia–Pacific Region, East–West Center, Honolulu, April 1985 – pp. 8–14; Richardson, H. W. Aggregate efficiency and interregional equity. In *Spatial inequalities and regional development*, H. Folmer & J. Oosterhaven (eds.), 161–83, The Hague: Martinus Nijhoff.

17 Defining the informal sector satisfactorily is impossible. See the issue of *Regional Development Dialogue* 5 (2) (1984) on the informal sector for an up-to-date discussion. Operationally, it may have to be defined residually as total employment *minus* formal sector employment, which is more easily measured. This method involves the assumption of zero unemployment in developing countries to permit the equation of the aggregate labor force with total employment. An alternative practical definition is to add the self-employed and unpaid family workers to wage employees in firms below a size threshold (often five workers) and then to deduct estimates for the professional self-employed and small-scale professional firms. These practical approaches may be unacceptable conceptually. A rougher but tolerable definition might be to equate the "informal" sector with the "unregulated" sector. However, some observers argue that the informal sector does not mean very much as an aggregate and that the appropriate mode of analysis is to divide it into subsectors such as street vendors, small-scale manufacturing and repair services, paratransit workers, informal construction, etc. The discussion here avoids a precise definition, on the ground that there is widespread agreement on how to recognize the informal sector even if defining its boundaries is somewhat fuzzy.

18 See Bairoch, P. 1976. *Emploi et taille des villes*. WEP 2–19, WP 15, International Labour Office, Geneva. El-Shakhs, S. 1984. On city-size and the contribution of the informal sector: some hypotheses and research questions. *Regional Development Dialogue* 5 (2), 77–81; Kundu, A. & P. N. Mathur 1984. Informal sector in cities of different sizes: an explanation within the core theoretic framework. *Regional Development Dialogue* 5 (2), 82–5; Hilhorst, J. G. M. 1984. City-size and the informal sector. *Regional Development Dialogue* 5 (2), 86–95; Kull, H. A note on the size of the informal sector employment in small- and medium-sized cities of Ivory Coast. *Regional Development Dialogue* 5 (2), 96–102.

19 For more details see Richardson, H. W. 1982. Policies for strengthening small cities in developing countries. In *Small cities and national development*, O. P. Mathur (ed.), 341–3. Nagoya: United Nations Center for Regional Development.

20 See Bharin, T. S. 1981. Review and evaluation of attempts to direct migrants to frontier areas through land colonization schemes. In *Population distribution policies in development planning*, 131–43. Population Studies No. 75, United Nations, Department of International Economic and Social Affairs (DIESA), New York; Martine, G. 1982. Colonization in Rondonia: continuities and perspectives. In *State policies and migration: studies in Latin America and the Caribbean*, P. Peek & G. Standing (eds.), 147–72. London: Croom Helm.

21 Consider a few illustrations. Industrial growth in rural areas may suffer from labor absenteeism at harvest and other peak times in the short run, but in the long run the rural labor force usually adjusts to industrial work habits. Industrial decentralization efforts to promote STICs may be weak in the short run, but in the longer run a critical mass may build up and industrial growth may take off. On the other hand, the short-term attraction of low wages and elastic labor supplies in STICs to entrepreneurs may disappear in the long run. Migrants to large metropolitan areas may experience short-term adjustment problems but usually adapt very well in the long run.

22 The discussion here examines only the costs of alternative settlement patterns, not the benefits. These benefits, both private and social, may be very important; the problem is that many of them are difficult to measure. No one has been able to establish, for example, that the net benefits of a highly

concentrated pattern are greater, or smaller, than those of a dispersed settlement pattern.

23 Planning and Development Corporation (PADCO) 1982. *National urban policy study – Egypt* (2 Vols.). Washington, DC: PADCO.

24 The study is summarized in Qutub & Richardson, op. cit., see note 11.

25 For more details see Garn, H. A. 1984. *The national urban policy study for Egypt: an approach to national urban settlement and investment strategies.* Washington, DC: World Bank, mimeograph.

26 Richardson, H. W. 1984. *Urban development in Bangladesh.* Washington, DC: World Bank, mimeograph. Richardson, H. W. 1985. *Obervations on the national urban development strategy project for Indonesia.* Djakarta: National Urban Development Strategy Project, mimeograph.

27 PADCO–Dacrea 1984. *Urban services inventory.* Jakarta: National Urban Development Strategy Project.

28 Richardson, H. W. 1985. The costs of urbanization: a four-country comparison. *Economic Development and Cultural Change*, forthcoming.

29 Mini-NUPS exercises have been carried out for Senegal and Ivory Coast (as well as for Nepal). These were not available to me. However, it is understood that these exercises used plausible numbers rather than hard data and were undertaken primarily to illustrate the programmability of the method rather than to generate a precise estimate of shelter and services costs. In any event, they replicated most of the assumptions of the Egyptian study on which reservations are expressed below. An earlier study on Kenya which proposed a selective urban development strategy stressing Kisumu, Eldoret, Nakuru, and Kitale suggested that "crude estimates based on housing, water supply, and sewerage costs alone suggest that the total cost of implementing the strategy is lower than accommodating spontaneous urban growth, because infrastructure costs per capita are somewhat higher in Nairobi and Mombasa than in the other towns." Richardson, H. W. 1980. An urban development strategy for Kenya. *Journal of Developing Areas* 15, (114).

30 Of course, the fact that these are annual average numbers means that they are not the numbers which will be actually absorbed. The number absorbed will start below the annual average level and subsequently rise above it.

31 My involvement in NUPS was limited to a short-term consultancy in the summer of 1981, the scope of which was restricted to preparing a framework for a "preferred strategy" urban population allocation. I had no control of the assumptions underpinning the spatial variation in shelter and services costs.

32 Interestingly, in the country where affordability is least severe (Indonesia) there are currently no serious attempts at cost recovery.

33 PADCO–Dacrea 1984. *Analysis of urban services standards, technologies and costs.* Jakarta: National Urban Development Strategy Project.

34 These data are assembled in Richardson (1985), op. cit., see note 1. p. 30.

35 See Qutub & Richardson, op. cit.[11] pp. 28–30.

36 Fertility reduction policies are an even more cost-effective approach than rural employment policies. The cost per birth averted in Bangladesh, for instance, ranges from US $ 12 to US $ 24, depending upon the type of program. This is only 2.5–3.0 percent of the shelter and services cost per capita, or 1.4–2.8 percent of total urban absorption costs per capita.

37 Comment of P. Gauru, IYSH Advisory Group Meeting, New York City, April 26, 1985.

38 This was a major argument in Richardson, H. W. 1973. *The economics of urban size.* Farnsworth, Hampshire: Saxon House.

39 See Richardson, H. W. 1981. *The future metropolitan region in developing countries.* Paper presented at the Primer Congreso International de Planeación de Grandes Ciudades, Mexico City, June 1981.
40 See Laquian, A. A. 1981. Review and evaluation of urban accommodationist policies in population redistribution. In *Population distribution policies in development planning,* 101–12. Population Studies No. 75, New York: Department of International Economic and Social Affairs (DIESA).
41 In the NHSPS project, it was estimated that the top 25 percent of households would absorb 64 percent of shelter and services resources.
42 Recovering costs is consistent with improving equity because the rich gain most from subsidies as recipients of services whereas the poor, who currently lack services, would be willing to pay for them. Willingness to pay reflects two factors: the benefits of services far exceed their costs; market substitutes (e.g., water from carriers, kerosene rather than electric power) are more expensive.

Notes to Chapter 10

1 Towfighi, P. S. *Trends in the growth and spatial distribution of population.* This volume, Statistical Appendix A – p. 381.
2 Ramachandran, A. *Foreword,* this volume.
3 Towfighi, op. cit.,[1] p. 381.
4 Hall, P. & D. Hay 1980. *Growth centres in the European urban system.* London: Heinemann Educational Books; Hall, P. 1980. New trends in European urbanization. *The Annals of the American Academy of Political and Social Science.* 451. 45–51; van den Berg, L. R. Drewett, L. H. Klaassen, A. Rossi & C. H. T. Vijverberg 1982. *Urban Europe.* Vol. 1: *A study of growth and decline.* Oxford: Pergamon; Kawashima, T. & P. Korcelli (eds.) 1982. *Human settlement systems: spatial patterns and trends.* Laxenburg: International Institute for Applied Systems Analysis; Hall. P. 1983. Decentralization without end: a re-evaluation. In *The Expanding City: Essays in Honour of Professor Jean Gottmann,* Patten, J. (ed.), 125–55 London: Academic Press; Hall, P. 1983b. Changing urban hierarchies in the development process: an international comparison. *Habitat International* 7, 129–35.
5 Richardson, H. W. 1977. *City size and national spatial strategies in developing countries.* WP 252, World Bank, Washington, DC; Richardson, H. W. 1980. Polarization reversal in developing countries. *Papers, Regional Science Association* 45, 67–85.
6 Hall & Hay, op. cit., see note 4; Hall, P. (1980), loc. cit.;[4] Cheshire, P., D. Hay & G. Carbonaro 1985. *Urban decline in Europe,* forthcoming.
7 Vining, D. R. & A. Strauss 1977. A demonstration that the current deconcentration of population in the United States is a clean break with the past. *Environment and planning, A,* 9 751–8: Vining, D. R. & T. Kontuly 1977. Increasing returns to city size in the face of an impending decline in the size of large cities: Which is the bogus fact? *Environment and Planning, A,* 9 59–62: Vining, D. R. 1982. Recent dispersal from the world's industrial core regions. In *Urbanization processes: experiences of eastern and western countries,* T. Kawashima (ed.), 171–92. Oxford: Pergamon.

8 Hall, P. (1983b) op. cit., see note 4.

9 Ibid.[8] p. 133.

10 Richardson, H. W. 1979. Metropolitan decentralization strategies in developing countries. In *Metropolitan planning: issues and policies*, Y. –E. Rho, & M. –C. Hwang (eds.). 87–101 Seoul, Korea: Korea Research Institute for Human Settlements.

11 Williamson, J. 1965. Regional inequality and the process of national development: a description of the patterns. *Economic Development and Cultural Change* 13(4) 3–45.

12 Myrdal, G. 1957. *Economic theory and underdeveloped regions.* London: Methuen; Hirschman, A. O. 1958. *The strategy of economic development.* New Haven, Conn.: Yale University Press.

13 Richardson (1980), op. cit., see note 5.

14 For American evidence see Hoch, I. 1973. Income and city size. In *Cities, regions and public policy*, G. Cameron & L. Wingo (ed.), 125–54. Edinburgh: Oliver & Boyd.

15 Richardson, H. W. 1981. National urban development strategies in developing countries. *Urban Studies* 18 267–84.

16 Hall, P. 1984. Metropolis 1890–1940: challenges and responses. In *Metropolis 1890–1940*, A. Sutcliffe (ed.). 19–66, London: Mansell.

17 Howard, E. 1946 (1898). *Garden cities of to-morrow*, London: Faber and Faber.

18 Schaefer, D. 1984. The Tennessee transplant. *Town and Country Planning* 53. 316–18.

19 Hall, P., R. Thomas, H. Gracey & R. Drewett, 1973. *The Containment of Urban England*, Vol. 2. London: Allen & Unwin – p. 358.

20 Hall, op. cit.[16] pp. 33–4.

21 Hall, P. 1982. *Urban and regional planning*, 2nd ed. London: Penguin – p. 229.

22 Hall, P. 1984. *The world cities*, 3rd ed. London: Weidenfeld & Nicolson – pp. 72–86.

23 Hall, P. 1967. Planning for urban growth: metropolitan area plans and their implications for South-East England. *Regional Studies* 1. 101–34.

24 Weaver, C. 1984. *Regional development and the local community: planning, politics and social context.* Chichester: Wiley – pp. 82–90.

25 Blacksell, M. 1981. West Germany. In *Regional development in western Europe*, 2nd edn. H. Clout (ed.) 211–39. Chichester: Wiley – p. 234–5.

26 Clout, H. 1984. *A rural policy for the EEC?* London: Methuen – p. 54.

27 Rodwin, L. 1965 Ciudad Guayana: a new city. *Scientific American* 213(3), 123–6; Cunningham, S. M. 1980. Brazilian cities old and new: growth and planning experience. In *Shaping an urban world*, G. E. Cherry (ed.) 181–202. London: Mansell – 198–9.

28 United Nations Center for Human Settlements (UNCHS) 1984a. *Land for human settlements.* Nairobi: UNCHS – p. 9.

29 Ibid.[28] p. 16; United Nations Center for Human Settlements (UNCHS) 1984. *Human settlements policies and institutions: issues, options, trends and guidelines.* Nairobi: UNCHS – p. 115.

30 UNCHS (1984b), op. cit.[29] p. 124.

31 UNCHS (1984a), op. cit.[28] p. 16.

32 UNCHS (1984a), op. cit.[28] p. 5.

33 UNCHS (1984b), op. cit.[29] p. 127.

34 UNCHS (1984a), op. cit.[28] pp. 26–7.

35 UNCHS (1984a), op. cit.[28] p. 29.

36 UNCHS (1984a), op. cit.[28] pp. 34–5.
37 UNCHS (1984b), op. cit.[29] p. 99.
38 UNCHS (1984a), op. cit.[28] p. 25.
39 United Nations Center for Human Settlements (UNCHS) (1984) *Transportation strategies for human settlements in developing countries.* Nairobi: UNCHS – p. 26.
40 Ibid.[39] p. 27.
41 Ibid.[39] p. 16.
42 Ibid.[39] pp. 46–7; Walters, A. A. 1979. *Costs and scale of bus services.* World Bank Working Paper 325, World Bank, Washington, DC: Roth, G. & G. G. Wynne, 1982. *Free enterprise urban transportation* (Learning from Abroad, 5). New Brunswick and London: Transaction Books.
43 Dunkerley, H. B. (ed.) 1983. *Urban land policies: issues and opportunities.* New York: Oxford University Press.

Notes to Chapter 11

1 Linn, J. F. 1983. *Cities in the developing world: policies for their equitable and efficient growth.* World Bank Research Publication. Oxford; Oxford University Press – pp. 138–42.
2 Juppenlatz, M. 1970. *Cities in transformation: the urban squatter problem in the developing world.* St. Lucia, Queensland; Queensland University Press; Murison, H. S. & J. P. Lea, 1979. *Housing in Third World countries: perspectives on politics and practice.* New York: St. Martin's Press.
3 Petersen, W. 1970. A general typology of migration. In *Readings in the sociology of migration.* C. J. Jansen (ed.), 49–68. Oxford: Pergamon.
4 Gugler, J. 1969. On the theory of rural–urban migration: the case of sub-Saharan Africa. In *Migration*, J. A. Jackson (ed.) Cambridge: Cambridge University Press.
5 For some evidence to the contrary see Lewis, O. Urbanization without breakdown. *Scientific Monthly* 75(1), 31–41; J. E. Perlman, 1976. *The myth of marginality: urban poverty and politics in Rio de Janeiro.* Berkeley, Calif.: University of California Press – p. 133; Nelson, J. 1969. *Migrants, urban poverty and instability in developing nations.* Occasional Papers in International Affairs, No. 22, Harvard University Center for International Affairs, Cambridge, Mass.: Reichman, R. L. 1985. *Conciencia and development in the association of Tricicleros San Jose Obrero: a grassroots labor organization in the Dominican Republic.* Ph.D. thesis, Harvard University, Cambridge, Mass.
6 Harris, J. R. & M. P. Todaro 1970. Migration, unemployment and development: a two-sector analysis. *American Economic Review* LX 126–42; R. Webb 1975. Ingreso y empleo en el sector tradicional urbano del Peru. In *America Latina: distribucion espacial de la poblacion.* R. Cardona (ed.), 257–87. Corp Centro Regional de Poblacion Bogotá; Cole, W. E. & R. D. Sanders 1972. A modified dualism model for Latin American economies. *Journal of Developing Areas* 6(2), 185–98.
7 Udall, A. 1973. *Migration and employment in Bogotá, Colombia.* Yale Ph.D. dissertation, Yale University, New Haven, Conn. Aklilu, B. & J. R. Harris 1980. Migration, employment and earnings. In G. Papanek (ed.), *The Indonesian*

Economy, 121–54. New York: Praeger. Harris, J. R. & A. Speare, Jr., Rural–urban earnings differentials and migration in Indonesia, *Economic Development and Cultural Change* (forthcoming). Collier, P. & R. H. Sabot 1982. Measuring the difference between rural and urban incomes: some conceptual issues. In *Migration and the Labor Market in Developing Countries*, R. Sabot (ed.). Boulder, Colorado: Westview Press. Livingston, I. 1981. *Rural development, employment and incomes in Kenya*, Addis Ababa: ILO/JASPA. ILO/JASPA 1983. *Basic needs in danger: a basic needs oriented development strategy for Tanzania.* Addis Ababa: ILO/JASPA, chapters 7 and 19.

8   Peattie, L. R. 1975. Tertiarization, marginality and urban poverty in Latin America. *Latin American Urban Research*, W. A. Cornelius & F. M. Trueblood (eds.), Vol. 5, 109–23. Beverly Hills, Calif.: New York: Sage Publications.

9   Jacobs, J. 1984. *Cities and the wealth of nations.* New York: Random House; Alonso, W. 1971. The economics of urban size. *Papers of the Regional Science Association* **26**, 67–83. Note also support of the large-city position by the World Bank in new directions in bank urban projects. *Urban Edge* **9** (3, March). It may be noted that since this literature and the facts it adduces is organized in terms of economic *activities*, not persons, it does not directly confront the literature of unproductive occupations, and unproductive people, and leads us to imagine that if we could only clear the people away from the activities – no doubt sweeping the streets clean in the process – everything would be well.

10 World Bank 1980. *Shelter*, Washington, DC: World Bank.

11 Angel, S., S. Benjamin & K. H. DeGoede 1977. The low-income housing system in Bangkok. *Ekistics* **44** (261), 79–84.

12 Bassuk, E. L. 1984. The homelessness problem. *Scientific American* **251** (1, July) 40–5.

13 Frieden, B. & A. Solomon 1977. *The nation's housing: 1975–1985.* Cambridge, Mass.: Joint Center for Urban Studies – ch. 4.

14 Annez, P. & W. C. Wheaton 1984. Economic development and the housing sector: a cross-national model. *Economic Development and Cultural Change* **32** (4, July) 749–66.

15 Hamberg, J. 1980. Urban development and housing policies in Cuba. Unpublished manuscript, June 1980.

16 United Nations Center for Human Settlements (UNCHS) 1984. *The construction industry in developing countries.* Nairobi, Moavanzadeh, F. *The construction industry.* This volume, Ch. 6.

17 van der Linden, J. 1977. *The Bastis of Karachi: types and dynamics.* Amsterdam: Free University; Soni, P. 1981. Self-help planning, construction and management in sites and services project in Nairobi, Kenya. *Ekistics* **48** No. 286 53–64, January–February, 61–2; Mourad, M. A. 1983. *The need for a new approach analysis of informal settlement and public housing policy in Egypt.* Thesis, MIT, Cambridge, Mass.; UNCHS (Habitat) 1984. *Small-scale building materials production in the context of the informal economy.* Nairobi: UNCHS.

18 van der Linden, op. cit., see note 17; Popko, E. 1980. *Squatter settlements and housing policy: experiences with sites-and-services in Colombia.* Agency for International Development, Office of Housing, and Department of Urban Studies and Planning, MIT, Cambridge, Mass.

19 Doebele, W. A. 1977. The private market and low-income urbanization: the private subdividers of Bogotá. *American Journal of Comparative Law* **25** 531–64 (3, Summer).

20 Collier, D. 1976. *Squatters and oligarchs: authoritarian rule and policy change in Peru.* Baltimore, Md.: Johns Hopkins University Press; Cornelius, W. 1975. *Politics and the migrant poor in Mexico City.* Stanford, Calif.: Stanford University Press; Legorreta, J. 1983. *El proceso de urbanizacion en ciudades petroleras.* Mexico D.F.: Centro de Ecodesarrollo.

21 Karst, K. L., M. L. Schwartz & A. S. Schwartz 1973. *The evolution of law in the Barrios of Caracas.* UCLA Press.

22 Peattie, L. R. 1982. Settlement upgrading: planning and squatter settlements in Bogotá, Colombia. *Journal of Planning Education and Research* 2 27–36 (1, Summer).

23 Stretton, A. W. 1981. The building industry and urbanization in Third World countries: a Philippine case study. *Economic Development and Cultural Change* 29 321–39 (2, January).

24 Goethert, R. *Unplanmässaige Sidelingsmuster in Kairo: Die Leistungsfahigkeit Inoffizieller Stadtrandentwicklung.* Band 17, Shriftenreihe, Politik und Planung, Deutscher Gemeindeverlag, Verlad W. Kohlhammer. (Translated by the author.)

25 Mayo, S. K., J. L. Katz 1981. *Informal housing in Egypt.* Cambridge, Mass.: Abt Associates; Robert R. Nathan Associates 1982. *Housing and community upgrading for low-income Egyptians,* Final Evaluation Report, Project No. 263–0066, February 1982. Robert R. Nathan Associates, Washington, D.C. Sethuraman, S. V. 1985. *Urbanization, informal sector, and employment: basic needs and the informal sector: the case of low income housing in developing countries.* Working Paper, World Employment Programme Research, Geneva International Labour Office, January 1985. In Cairo, buildings of six and eight storeys are typically constructed within the building pattern of owner management with paid workers; I do not know of data on how the costs of this private system compare to government building.

26 Strassman, P. 1978. *Housing and building technology in developing countries.* East Lansing.

27 Afshar, F. 1983. *Building technologies and materials production: their effect on construction costs, complexity and incomes and employment in the rural areas.* Sahiwal District, Punjab Pakistan, Massachusetts Institute of Technology, October 29.

28 S. V. Sethuraman, op. cit. see note 25.

29 Soni, op. cit., see note 17.

30 Soni, op. cit., see note 17

31 Edwards, M. 1982. Cities of tenants: renting among the urban poor in Latin America. In *Urbanization in Contemporary Latin America.* A. Gilbert, J. E. Hardoy & R. Ramirez (eds.), 129–58. Chichester, N.Y.: Wiley; Edwards, M. 1982. The political economy of low income housing: new evidence from urban Colombia. *Bulletin of Latin American Research,* Gilbert, A. 1983. The tenants of self-help housing: choice and constraint in the housing markets of less developed countries. In *Development and Change,* Vol. 14, 449–77, Sage, London, Beverly Hills and New Delhi; Barrada, A.-M., W. C. Wheaton & P. Annez 1978. Public policy and the economics of housing. In Joint Research Team on the Housing and Construction Industry, Cairo University and MIT, *The housing and construction industry in Egypt.* Interim Report Working Papers, Mimeographed. Department of Urban Studies, MIT.

32 Krohn, R. G., 1977. *The other economy: the internal logic of local rental housing.* Montreal: Peter Martin Associates, Ltd. – p. 5.

33 Leeds, A. 1974. Housing settlement types, arrangements for living, prolet-

arianization and the social structure of the city. In *Latin American Urban Research*, 67–99. W. A. Cornelius & F. M. Trueblood, Beverly Hills: Sage; Gilbert, A. G. & P. M. Ward 1982. Residential movement among the poor: the constraints on housing choice in Latin American cities. *Transactions of the Institute of British Geographers* N.S. 7, 129–49; Sudra, T. 1976. Housing as a support system: a case study of Mexico City. *Architectural Design* 46 (4), 222–6. Edwards, M. 1983. Residential mobility in a changing housing market: the case of Bucaramanga, Colombia. *Urban Studies* 20 131–45; Salmen, L. F. 1970. Housing alternatives for the Carioca working class: Comparison between Favelas and Casas de Comodos. *America Latina* 13 (4) 51–70; Brown, J. C. 1972. *Patterns of intra-urban settlement in Mexico City: an examination of the Turner theory*. Latin American Studies Program, Cornell University, August 1972; A. H. Deneke *et al.* 1976. *La vivienda popular urbana en El Salvador*. Fundacion de Viviendu Minima, San Salvador.

34   Rod Burgess, personal communication, 1973.

35   Mourad, op. cit., see note 17.

36   Fass, S. M. 1977. *Families in Port au Prince: a study on the economics of survival*. US Agency for International Development, Washington, DC.

37   Peattie, L. R. 1981. What is to be done with the informal sector? A case study of shoe manufacturing in Colombia. In *Towards a political economy of urbanization*, I. Safa (ed.), 208–32, New Delhi: Oxford University Press.

38   Peattie, L. R. 1983. *Small enterprises in the development process*. Working Paper, Centre for Urban Studies and Urban Planning, University of Hong Kong, February.

39   Szelenyi, I. 1983. *Urban inequalities under state socialism*. Oxford: Oxford University Press – pp. 28–33.

40   Becker, G. & R. T. Michael 1976. On the new theory of consumer behavior. In *The economic approach to human behavior*, 131–49. Chicago, Ill.: University of Chicago Press.

41   See Stretton, H. 1978. *Urban planning in rich and poor countries*. Oxford: Oxford University Press – pp. 56–8.

42   For a recent review of the literature on LDCs see *Regional Development Dialogue* 5 (2, Autumn) 1984; and Portes, A. & L. Benton 1984. Industrial development and labor absorption: a reinterpretation. *Population and Development Review* 10 (4), 589–611. On small enterprises in the developed countries, see Sabel, C. F. 1982. *Work and politics: the division of labor in industry*. Cambridge: Cambridge University Press.

43   Patricia McCarney, 1986 personal communication.

44   Peattie, L. R. 1983. Realistic planning and qualitative research. *Habitat International* 7 (5/6), 227–34.

Notes to Chapter 12

1   Hall, P. *Urban growth and shelter strategies: can we learn from experience?* This volume, Ch. 10. See also Richardson, H. *Spatial strategies, the settlement pattern, and shelter and services policies*. This volume, Ch. 9.

2   Hirschman, A. 1967. *Development projects observed*, 35. Washington, DC.: The Brookings Institution.

3 Burns, L. S. & L. Grebler 1977. *The housing of nations: analysis and policy in a comparative framework*, 12. London: Macmillan.

4 Burns, L. S. & L. Grebler 1976. Resource allocation to housing investment: a comparative international study. *Economic Development and Cultural Change* 25 (October), 95–121. See also: Renaud, B. 1980. Resource allocation to housing investment: comments and further results. *Economic Development and Cultural Change* 25 (January), 389–400; Annez, P. & W. Wheaton 1984. Economic development and the housing sector: a cross-national model. *Economic Development and Cultural Change* 32 (4, July), 749–66.

5 M. Millikan 1955. The economist's view of the rôle of housing. In *Housing and economic development*, B. Kelly (ed.), 21–8. Cambridge, Mass.: MIT Press.

6 Rodwin, L. & associates 1969. *Planning urban growth and regional development: the experience of the Guayana Program of Venezuela*. Cambridge, Mass.: MIT Press.

7 Burns, L. S. & B. K. Tjioe 1968. Housing and human resource development. *Journal of the American Institute of Planners* 34 (6, November), 396–401.

8 Linn, J. F. 1983. *Cities in the developing world: policies for their equitable and efficient growth*, 18. New York: Oxford University Press for the World Bank.

9 Klaassen, L. H., J. G. D. Hoogland & van Pelt, M. J. F. *Economic impact and implications of shelter investments*. This volume, Ch. 2.

10 Wambem, D. (n.d.) *A case for housing subsidy*. International Housing Productivity Study, University of California, Los Angeles, word-processed.

11 Klaassen, L. H. & L. S. Burns 1963. The position of housing in national economic and social policy. In *Capital formation for housing in Latin America*, W. D. Harris & J. Gillies (eds.), 108–19. Washington: Pan American Union.

12 Burns & Grebler, op. cit.[3] Ch. 5.

13 Burns & Grebler, op. cit.[3] Ch. 7.

14 Burns & Grebler, op. cit.[3] p. 141.

15 Burns, L.S. 1983. Self-help housing: an evaluation of outcomes. *Urban Studies* 20 (August), 299–309.

16 Strassmann, W. 1978. *Housing and building technology in developing countries*. East Lansing: Michigan State University.

17 Rondinelli, D. A. 1983. *Development projects as policy experiments: an adaptive approach to development administration*. London: Methuen. See also Morss, E. et. al. 1975. *Strategies for small farmer development*. Washington, DC.: Development Alternatives Incorporated.

18 Gilbert, A. 1983. The tenants of self-help housing: choice and constraint in the housing markets of less developed countries. *Development and Change* 24, 449–77 – see p. 469.

19 Shoup, D. C. 1983. Intervention through property taxation and public ownership. In *Urban land policy: issues and opportunities*, H. B. Dunkerley (ed.), 132–52. New York: Oxford University Press for the World Bank.

20 Whitehead, C. M. E. 1983. The rationale for government intervention. In *Urban land policy: issues and opportunities*, H. B. Dunkerley (ed.), 108–33. New York: Oxford University Press for the World Bank – see pp. 127–8.

21 Hardoy, J. E. & D. Satterthwaite 1981. *Shelter need and response: housing, land and settlement policies in seventeen Third World nations*, 253–4. Chichester: Wiley.

22 Deneke, A. H. & M. Silva 1982. Mutual help and progressive development

housing: for what purpose? Notes on the Salvadorean experience. In *Self-help housing: a critique*, P. M. Ward (ed.), 233–50. London: Mansell.

23 Sanyal, B. 1985. *An evaluation of Lusaka's cost recapture program. Urban Studies*, forthcoming. See also Martin, R. 1982. The formulation of a self-help project in Lusaka. In *Self-help housing: a critique*, 251–74. London: Mansell.

24 Linn, op. cit.[8] pp. 172–3.

25 Mabogunje, A. L., J. E. Hardoy & R. P. Misra 1978. *Shelter provision in developing countries*. Chichester: Wiley.

26 Payne, G. K. 1977. *Urban housing in the Third World*, 202. London: Leonard Hill.

27 Hardoy & Satterthwaite, op. cit.[21] p. 256.

28 Dwyer, D. J. 1975. *People and housing in Third World cities: perspectives on the problem of spontaneous settlements*. London: Longman.

29 Valladares, L. do Prado 1980. *Passa-se uma casa: analise do programa de remocao de favelas do Rio de Janeiro* (House for sale: analysis of the Favela Removal Program of Rio de Janeiro). Rio de Janeiro: Zahar Press.

30 Chimelli, F. 1981. Os loteamentos de periferia (Subdivisions on the periphery). In *Habitacao em questao* (Housing in question), L. do Prado Valladares (ed.), 46–69. Rio de Janeiro: Zahar Press.

31 Doebele, W. A. 1983. Concepts of urban land tenure. In *Urban land policy: issues and opportunities*, H. B. Dunkerley (ed.), 63–107. New York: Oxford University Press for the World Bank.

32 Geisse, G. G. & F. Sabatini 1982. Urban popular housing and habitat policies: the case of Santiago, Chile. *Regional Development Dialogue* 3(2), 80–98.

33 March, L. 1967. Homes beyond the fringe. *RIBA Journal* August, 334–7; March, L. 1972a. *The spatial organization of hyperurban societies*. Report of Proceedings, Town and Country Planning Summer School, Nottingham. London: The Royal Town Planning Institute; March, L. 1972b. An examination of layouts. *Built Environments* September, 374–8.

34 Turner, J. F. C. & R. Fichter (eds.) 1972. *Freedom to build*. New York: Collier Macmillan.

35 Burns, L., S., M. Hollis & D. C. Shoup 1978. *Alternative approaches to self-help housing: a comparative evaluation*. Report prepared for the World Bank, September. Washington, DC: World Bank.

36 Ward, P. M. 1982. *The practice and potential of self-help housing: a critique*, 175–208. London: Mansell.

37 Solava, M., W. L. Flinn & S. Kronus 1974. Renovation of a squatter settlement in Columbia. *Land Economics* 50 (May), 152–62.

38 Burns, L. S. & D. C. Shoup 1981. Effects of resident control and ownership in self help housing. *Land Economics* 57 (February), 107–13.

39 Araud, C. 1973. Direct and indirect employment effects of eight representative types of housing in Mexico. In *Studies on employment in the Mexican housing industry*, C. Araud et al. (eds.) 45–113. Paris: Organization for Economic Cooperation and Development.

40 Moavenzadeh, F. *The construction industry and the supply of low-cost shelter*. This volume, Ch. 4.

41 Burns & Grebler, op. cit.[3] p. 203.

42 Hardoy & Satterthwaite, op. cit.[21] p. 258.

43 Dwyer, op. cit.[28] p. 153.

44 Turner, J. F. C. 1968. The squatter settlement. Architecture that works. *Architectural Design* 38, 355–60.

45 Stokes, C. J. 1962. A theory of slums. *Land Economics* 38, 187–97.

46 Mangin, W. P. 1967. Latin American squatter settlements: a problem and a solution. *Latin American Research Review* 2(3), 65–98 – see p. 71.
47 Linn, op. cit.[8] pp. 176–7.
48 Linn, op. cit.[8] pp. 172–3.
49 Linn, op. cit.[8] p. 170.
50 Burns & Grebler, op. cit.[3]
51 Linn, op. cit.[8]
52 Hardoy & Satterthwaite, op. cit.[21] pp. 254–5.
53 Rodwin, L. 1967. Measuring housing needs in developing countries. In *Taming megalopolis*, vol. 2: *How to manage an urbanized world*, H. W. Eldredge (ed.), 1011–17. Garden City, NY: Doubleday Anchor – see p. 1011.

Notes to Chapter 13

1 Trading ports founded by the British East India Trading Company in the 17th century provided the initial stimulus for the development of Calcutta, Bombay, and Madras as cities. Although several ancient cities had at some time flourished within or close to what is today Delhi, it was the movement by the British colonial government of India's capital to New Delhi which began its rapid growth. Bangalore owes much of its early development as an important city to the fact that it became the unofficial capital of the State of Mysore, much preferred by the colonial rulers to the official capital, Mysore.

2 Cuenya, B., H. Almada, D. Armus, J. Castells, M. Di Loreto & S. Penalva 1984. *Habitat and health conditions of the popular sectors: a pilot study of participative investigation in the San Martin settlement.* Buenos Aires: Centro de Estudios Urbanos y Regionales (published in Spanish and English).

3 For discussion of the different housing sub-markets through which lower-income groups find accommodation in Third World cities, see Hardoy, J. E. & D. Satterthwaite. Shelter, infrastructure and services in Third World cities. *Habitat International* 10 (4), forthcoming.

4 Hardoy, J. E. & D. Satterthwaite 1981. *Shelter: need and response; housing, land and settlement policies in seventeen Third World nations.* Chichester: Wiley.

5 Republic of Kenya 1979. *Development Plan 1979–83*, Part 1, p. 50. Nairobi: Government Printers.

6 Linn, J. 1979. *Policies for efficient and equitable growth of cities in developing countries.* World Bank Staff Working Paper No. 342, World Bank, Washington, DC.

7 Amis, P. 1984. Squatters or tenants: the commercialization of unauthorized housing in Nairobi. *World Development* 12, 87–96.

8 Theunynck, S. & M. Dia 1981. The young (and the less young) in the infra-urban areas in Mauritania. *African Environment* 14/15/16, 206–33.

9 Harth, Dereke, A. & M. Silva 1982. Mutual help and progressive development housing: for what purpose? Notes on the Salvadorean experience. In *Self help housing: a critique*, P. Ward (ed.), 233–50. London: Mansell.

10 Keyes, W. J. 1980. Metro Manila, Philippines. In *Policies towards urban slums*, M. Sarin (ed.), 44–59. Economic and Social Commission for Asia and the Pacific (ESCAP), United Nations.

11 Moser, C. O. N. 1982. A home of one's own; squatter housing strategies in

Guayaquil, Equador. In *Urbanization in contemporary Latin America*, A. Gilbert, J. E. Hardoy & R. Ramirez (eds.), 159–90. Chichester: Wiley.

12 Harpham, T., P. Vaughan & S. Rifkin 1985. *Health and the urban poor: a review and selected annotated bibliography*. London: Evaluation and Planning Centre for Health Care, London School of Hygiene and Tropical Medicine.

13 Hardoy, J. E. & D. Satterthwaite 1986. *Small and intermediate urban centres: their role in regional and national development in the Third World*. London: Hodder & Stoughton and New York: Westview.

14 The Centre for Urban and Regional Studies (CEUR), Buenos Aires (Argentina), The Faculty of Environmental Design, Lagos University (Nigeria), the Department of Architecture, University of Khartoum (Sudan), and the International Institute for Development Research, Allahabad (India).

15 These include papers presented as a seminar on shelter policies in Third World nations organized by IIED in collaboration with Groupe de Recherche et D'Echanges Technologiques, the magazine *Trialog* and the universities of Lund and Venice.

16 See Moser, C. O. N. 1985. *Housing policy and women: towards a gender aware approach*. DPU gender and planning working paper 7, University College, London, for an analysis of how projects and programs assume "western" type nuclear families which are at odds with local realities and miss women's special needs.

17 Perez Perdomo, R. & P. Nikken 1982. The law and home ownership in the barrios of Caracas. In *Urbanization in contemporary Latin America*, J. E. Hardoy & R. Ramirez (eds.), 213–14. Chichester: Wiley.

18 McAuslan, P. 1985. *Urban land and shelter for the poor*. London and Washington, DC: Earthscan.

19 Cochrane, G. 1983. *Policies for strengthening local government in developing countries*. World Bank Staff Working Paper No. 582, World Bank, Washington, DC.

20 Rondinelli, D. A., J. R. Nellis & G. S. Cheema 1984. *Decentralization in developing countries – a review of recent experiences*, 3–4. World Bank Staff Working Paper No. 581, World Bank, Washington, DC.

21 Hardoy, J. E. & D. Satterthwaite. Government policies and small and intermediate urban centers, Chapter 8 in Hardoy & Satterthwaite, op. cit.[13]

22 Harris, N. 1983. Spatial planning and economic development. *Habitat International* 7 (5/6), 67–77.

Notes to Chapter 14

1 For an expansion on these points see Doebele, W. A. 1986. *Land policy and shelter*.

2 For additional points, see Gakenheimer, R. & C. H. J. Brando 1985. *Infrastructure building: breaking the standards stalemate*.

3 See also Renaud, B. 1985. *Financing shelter*. Boleat, M. 1985. *Housing finance institutions*. This volume, Ch. 7.

4 See also Moavenzadeh, F. 1985. *The construction industry and the supply of low-cost shelter*. This volume, Ch. 4.

Notes to Chapter 15

1 Rodwin, L. & B. Sanyal. *Shelter, settlement, and development: an overview.* This volume, Ch. 1.
2 Popko, E. 1983. PhD. thesis, unpublished, Massachusetts Institute of Technology.
3 Turner, J. F. C. 1976. *Housing by people: towards autonomy in building environments.* New York: Pantheon.
4 Richardson, H. W. *Spatial strategies, the settlement pattern, and shelter and services policies.* This volume, Ch. 9.
5 Renaud, B. *Financing shelter.* This volume, Ch. 8.
6 Peattie, L. *Shelter, development, and the poor.* This volume, Ch. 11.
7 Moavenzadeh, F. *The construction industry.* This volume, Ch. 4.
8 Boleat, M. *Housing finance institutions.* This volume, Ch. 7.
9 Doebele, W. A. *Land policy.* This volume, Ch. 5.
10 Gakenheimer, R. & C. H. J. Brando. *Infrastructure standards.* This volume, Ch. 6.
11 Bateson, G. 1972. *Steps to an ecology of mind.* New York: Ballantine.

Notes to Appendix A

1 UNCHS 1985. *Global Report.* Unpublished manuscript, April.
2 UNCHS, United Nations Commission on Human Settlements 1985. *Planning and management of human settlements, with emphasis on small and intermediate towns and local growth points.* Document HS/C/8/3, February, 1, 1985.
3 Hardoy, J. E. & D. Satterthwaite 1981. *Shelter: need and response; housing, land and settlement policies in seventeen Third World Nations.* New York: Wiley.

Notes to Appendix B

1 Economic progress can be measured by income per capita, per household, and per family. Social progress can be defined as adequate food, clothing, and shelter, with equal opportunity to share the fruits of economic growth regardless of age, race, sex, ethnic origin, or religion. It also means greater participation in the collective decision-making of community and government.

2 Community based research in the United States indicates that households with the most secure form of tenure, home-ownership, are likely to:

(i)   save more of their income every year and accumulate more wealth compared to nonhomeowners with similar characteristics;[a-f]

(ii)   be knowledgeable about community affairs;[g]

(iii) participate in national elections and in primary or preliminary elections;[h-i]

(iv) participate in local political affairs;[j-m]

(v)   be involved in volunteer work and charitable organizations;[n-o]

(vi) have higher social status and upward mobility;[p-r]

(vii) maintain their dwelling units.[s]

[a] Projector, D. S. & G. S. Weiss 1966. *Survey of financial characteristics of consumers.* Washington, DC: Board of Governors of the Federal Reserve System.

[b] University of Michigan, Institute of Social Research 1977. *Survey of consumer credit.* East Lansing, Mich.: University of Michigan, Institute of Social Research.

[c] University of Michigan, Institute of Social Research 1984. *Survey of consumer finances,* East Lansing, Mich.: University of Michigan, Institute of Social Research.

[d] Juster, F. T. 1981. Current and prospective financial status of the elderly population. In *Saving for retirement,* P. Cagan (ed.), 24–66, Washington, DC: American Council of Life Insurance and Columbia University Graduate School of Business.

[e] Krumm, R. & A. Kelly 1984. *Effects of homeownership on household savings.* Committee on Public Policy Studies, University of Chicago, unpublished, December 1984.

[f] Krumm, R. 1985. *Homeownership and household savings behavior: a study of panel data patterns.* Committee on Public Policy Studies, University of Chicago, unpublished, January 1985.

[g] Sykes, G. 1951. The differential distribution of community knowledge. *Social Forces* 29, 376–82.

[h] Ashenfelter, O. & S. Kelly, Jr. 1975. Determinants of participation in presidential elections. *Journal of Law and Economics* 18, 695–733.

[i] Kingston, P. W., J. L. P. Thompson & D. M. Eichar 1984. The politics of home-ownership. *American Politics Quarterly* 12 (April) 131–51.

[j] Alford, R. & H. Scoble 1968. Sources of local political involvement. *American Political Science Review* 62, 1192–205.

[k] Piele, P. K. & J. S. Hall 1973. *Budgets, bonds and ballots: voting behavior in school financial elections.* Lexington, Mass.: Lexington Books.

[l] Steinberger, P. 1981. Political participation and community: a cultural interpersonal approach. *Rural Sociology* 46, 7–12.

[m] Tolley, G., R. Krumm & A. Kelly 1984. *Voting participation and vote choice: an empirical examination of Massachusett's Proposition 2–1/2.* Unpublished. Committee on Public Policy Studies, University of Chicago, Chicago, Ill.

[n] Homenuck, H. P. M. 1977. A study of high rise: effects, preferences and perceptions. In *Environmental choice, human behavior and residential satisfaction,* W. Michelson (ed.). New York: Oxford University Press.

[n] Homenuck, H. P. M. 1973. *A study of high rise: effects, preferences and perceptions.* Toronto: Institute of Environmental Research, Inc.

[o] Blum, T. & P. W. Kingston 1984. Homeownership and social attachment. *Sociological Perspectives* 27 (April), 159–81.

[p] Coleman, R. P. 1973. The influence of consumer preferences on housing markets. In *America's Housing Needs: 1970 to 1980,* D. Birch et. al. (eds.), 5–71 Cambridge, Mass.: Joint Center for Urban Studies of MIT and Harvard University.

[q] Perin, C. 1977. *Everything in its place: social order and land use in America.* Princeton, NJ: Princeton University Press.

[r] Morris, E. W. & M. Winter 1978. *Housing, family, and society.* New York: Wiley.

[s] Galster, G. C. 1983. Empirical evidence on cross-tenure differences in home maintenance conditions. *Land Economics* 59 (February) 107–13.

3 See United States Department of Justice, Bureau of Justice Statistics, Washington DC, 1981. *Criminal victimization in the United States.* Figures in this report show that crime rates against homeowners are 31 percent less than crime rates against nonhomeowners.

4 Housing-related outlays in the United States were 35 percent of consumption in 1982, whereas food was 19 percent, transportation 12 percent, and clothing and shoes 9 percent. See *U.S. Long-Term Review* Winter 1983–4, Table 1.3, p. 1.43. Loungton, Mass.: Data Resources Inc.

5 Myers, D. 1983. *The impact of rising homeownership costs on family change.* Address at the annual meeting of the Population Association of America, April 15, 1983.

6 W. Apgar 1983. *Housing futures consumer survey.* Cambridge, Mass.: Joint Center for Housing Studies of MIT and Harvard University, October 1983.

7 Fragmented information in many other countries appears to confirm the same thing. Research has started which will better measure the results in some developing countries.

8 Home-ownership, however, is quite different from other investment and consumption decisions. Households must consider the long-term investment aspects of home-ownership as well as the suitability of the site to satisfy ongoing housing needs.

9 Federal National Mortgage Association 1982. *Buying a home in the 80s: a poll of American attitudes.* Washington, DC: Federal National Mortgage Association, March–April 1982 – Table 11, p. 17.

10 Security of tenure is shown to be a powerful inducement of greater savings. Education, marital status, length of occupancy, and age may also affect the level of savings. See University of Michigan, Institute of Social Research, op. cit., see note 2*b*; and Juster, op. cit., see note 2*d*.

11 Krumm, R. 1985. *Homeownership and household savings behavior: a study of panel data patterns.* Committee on Public Policy Studies, University of Chicago, unpublished, January 1985.

12 Kingston, op. cit.[2i] table 1, p. 141.

13 United States Bureau of the Census 1981. *Voting and registration in the election of November 1980.* Current Population Reports, Series p. 20, no. 359.

14 Kingston, op. cit.[2i] p. 143.

15 Blum & Kingston, op. cit.[20] p. 173.

16 E. Wood 1931. *Recent trends in American housing.* New York: Macmillan (as quoted in G. Fish (ed.) 1979. *The story of housing.* New York: Macmillan – p. 175.

17 To cover administrative costs and earn a return on equity, it relies exclusively on income from those who borrow from the credit pool.

18 The system allocates funds from mortgage lenders who have surplus lending funds to lenders in rapidly developing areas. In this way, it helps to equalize the availability of mortgage funds across the country.

19 The two agencies were the Home Owners Loan Corporation and the Farm Credit Administration.

20 By providing government loan guarantees for a longer period of time, the FHA lowered interest rates and made home-ownership affordable to millions of low- and moderate-income households. It enabled home buyers to obtain a high percentage of the appraised value of a house in a single mortgage with monthly payments stretched out over several years (initially 15 years but later changed to 30 years). The standardization of mortgage loans to the fixed-rate, level payment, fully amortized loan reduced the need for frequent refinancing of short-term debt, a factor that provided greater security to lenders and homeowners. This meant that mortgage loans guaranteed by the government could directly influence mortgage markets in the supply of mortgage credit and indirectly influence housing construction and economic development.

21 However, the government provided staffing to set standards for the loans that would be insured and to manage the fund.

22 Fish, G. (ed.) 1979. *The story of housing.* New York: Macmillan.

23 *United States Statutes at Large* 1961. 87th Congress, 1st Session, Vol. 75 –
    p. 149.

24 Housing and Home Finance Agency 1984. *18th annual report*. Washington,
    DC: Housing and Home Finance Agency – p. 2.

25 The GNMA is a government chartered and funded corporation within the
    cabinet-level Department of Housing and Urban Development.

26 The major purpose of this function is to maintain high levels of housing
    activity during periods of rising mortgage rates. Because the private market
    requires a market rate of return, the mortgages are sold at a price below
    market. The loss of GNMA is the extent of the central government's subsidy.
    However, GNMA also performs other important functions that involve
    virtually no government subsidy. For example, GNMA insures securities
    collateralized by pools of FHA-insured mortgages or mortgages generated by
    the Veterans Administration. The securities are issued by private lenders
    who originate the mortgages.

27 In the United States, the "primary" mortgage market includes those who
    want mortgage financing (home buyers) approaching those who have money
    to lend (mortgage originators). The making of a mortgage is a "primary"
    market transaction. A "secondary" market transaction occurs when the
    mortgage originator sells the mortgage from a primary transaction to another
    investor. Generally they have three sales alternatives: they may resell their
    loans to other private investors; they may sell through the markets for
    mortgage-backed securities; or they may resell to financing institutions that
    issue debt and hold mortgages in their portfolios.

28 Author's calculations based on data in Federal National Mortgage Association
    1984. *Fannie Mae housing fact book*. and Federal Home Loan Mortgage
    Corporation, Washington, DC: Federal National Mortgage Association 1985.
    Secondary mortgage markets 2 (1, Spring), 39.

29 See Hendershott, P. & K. Villani 1977. *Regulation and reform of the housing
    finance system*. American Enterprise Institute for Public Policy Research,
    Washington, DC – pp. 25–45.

30 See Corazzini, A., S. Brooks & P. Quick 1985. *CMOs and secondary mortgage
    markets*. United States Department of Housing and Urban Development,
    Washington, DC – p. 3.

31 United States President's Commission on Housing 1982. *The Report of the
    President's Commission on Housing*. Washington, DC: US Government
    Printing Office.

Acknowledgements

In the course of this enterprise I accumulated many debts.

I owe special thanks to Dr. Arcot Ramachandran and John Cox for this challenging opportunity to take a fresh look at existing policies, programs, and ways of thinking about shelter and settlements in Third World countries.

I am also very indebted to my associates, who cooperated magnificently in meeting tough deadlines for the preparation of the chapters and in suggesting effective ways of refining the ideas and handling the policy recommendations of the overview chapter.

William Doebele, Fred Moavenzadeh, Lisa Peattie, Don Schön, and Bishwapriya Sanyal served as an informal advisory group. They provided wise suggestions on every phase of the study.

I benefited from the thoughtful comments of Vaidyanathan Kandaswamy and Parviz Towfighi from the very beginning of this effort. The overview chapter also took account of the content analysis Parviz Towfighi made of the chapters contributed by the participants.

Chris Burke provided helpful résumés, suggestions, and critiques at different stages of the study.

I have also taken account of the views – expressed in the seminar held in New York and in memoranda commenting on early versions of the study – of Pietro Garau, Mark Hildebrand, Mathias Hundsalz, Bruce Hyland, Louis Menezes, all members of the UNCHS Nairobi-based professional staff.

Bhagwat Singh, Lila Patel, Laura Licchi, and Martha Martinelli, members of the UNCHS staff in New York City, solved with graciousness and efficiency the many problems of coordination, typing, and the provision of other services for the seminar held in April 1985.

Finally, I am grateful to Gerry Levinson for her exceptional patience and assistance in handling the innumerable, painstaking chores associated with this study.

Lloyd Rodwin

Notes on contributors

Mark J. Boleat is Secretary-General, the Building Societies Association, London, England and also Secretary-General of the International Union of Building Societies and Savings Associations. His books include *The building society industry* (2nd edn 1986); *National housing finance systems: A comparative study* (1984); *Housing in Britain* (1986); and *The mortgage market* (1987 with Adrian Coles).

Carlos Henrique Jorge Brando, a sanitary engineer who has worked with the water supply authorities of São Paulo, Brazil, teaches at the Agricultural College at Santo Espiritu do Pinhal, São Paulo. He is coauthor of *Institutional location and land development: medium sized cities in Egypt*, and has also engaged in the supply of agro-industrial equipment in the countries of the developing world. In addition, he is completing a doctoral dissertation in urban planning at MIT on a subject related to his contribution in this volume.

Leland S. Burns is Professor of Planning in the Graduate School of Architecture and Urban Planning, University of California (Los Angeles). His books include *Housing symbol and shelter* (1970 with R. G. Healy, D. A. McAllister & B. Khing Tjoe); *The housing of nations* (1977 with Leo Grebler); and *The future of housing markets* (1986, also with Leo Grebler).

Jack Carlson, a former professor of economics, business administration and public administration at several universities, was a member of the US delegation to the meetings of the UN Commission on Human Settlements in 1983 and 1985, and former chairman of the Senior Economic Advisors to UN's Economic Commission for Europe. From 1979 to 1986, he was Chief Executive Officer of the National Association of Realtors.

William A. Doebele is Frank Backus Williams Professor of Urban Planning and Design, Harvard University. He is the editor and major contributor to *Land readjustment: a different approach to financing urbanization* (1982); "The provision of land for the urban poor: concepts, instruments and prospects" in Shlomo Angel *et al.* (eds.), *Land for housing the poor* (1983); "Concepts of urban land tenure," in H. Dunkerley (ed.), *Urban Land Policy: issues and opportunities*.

Bruce Ferguson is a doctoral student in the Graduate School of Architecture and Urban Planning, University of California (Los Angeles). He has been a mortgage bank manager and housing consultant to cities and nonprofit groups.

Ralph Gakenheimer is Professor of Urban Studies and Planning and Civil Engineering at MIT. His publications include *Transportation planning as a response to controversy* (1976) and (as editor) *The automobile and the environment* (forthcoming).

Peter Hall is Professor, Departments of City and Regional Planning and of Geography, University of California, Berkeley and member of the Faculty of Urban and Regional Studies, University of Reading. He is the author or coauthor of more than 20 books including *The containment of urban England*, with R. Drewett, H. Gracey & R. Thomas (1973); *The world cities* (1984); and *Great planning disasters* (1981).

Jorge Enrique Hardoy is Director of the International Institute for Environment and Development's Human Settlements Programme and a Fellow of the Centro de Estudios Urbanos y Regionales in Buenos Aires. His previous books include, *PreColombian cities, urban reform in revolutionary Cuba*, and *Shelter provision in developing countries* (with A. L. Mabogunje & R. P. Misra).

Jan G. D. Hoogland is Head of the Division for Regional and Sectoral Studies, the Netherlands Economic Institute. His publications include *Habitat and policy in developing countries: definitions and features* (in Dutch, with M. J. F. van Pelt & L. B. M. Mennes), *Report for the Dutch Ministry of Housing and Physical Planning* (1985) and *Habitat and Policy in the Focus Countries of Dutch Development Cooperation* (1985, in Dutch, with M. J. F. van Pelt and L. B. M. Mennes).

Leonardus Hendrik Klaassen, currently an Advisor to the Netherlands Economic Institute, is former President, Director & Chief of Research of the NEI and Emeritus Professor at the Netherland School of Economics, Erasmus University, Rotterdam. He is the author or coauthor of more than 30 books including *Dynamics of urban development* (1971 coeditor and coauthor); *Integration of socio-economic & physical planning* (1974, with J. H. P. Paelinck); *Spatial cycles* (1985, coeditor & coauthor).

Stephen Mayo, an economist in the Water Supply and Urban Development Department at the World Bank, is Project Director of a research project on "Housing Demand and Finance in developing countries". Among his recent publications are *Housing Demand in Developing Countries, Informal housing in Egypt*, and *Sites and services – and subsidies: the economics of low-cost housing in developing countries*.

Fred Moavenzadeh is William E. Lonhard Professor of Engineering and Director of the Technology and Development Program and the Center for Construction Research & Education at the Massachusetts Institute of Technology. His publications include "Choice of appropriate technologies in the housing sector for conditions prevailing in developing countries," in *Housing planning, financing, construction*, Ed. O. Ural, Vol. 1, H33–61 (1979, Pergamon Press); "Strategy, policy options and issues for the promotion of indigenous construction industries in developing countries," UN Center for Housing Settlements, Nairobi, Kenya (Nov.

1980); and *Construction and building materials industries in developing countries* (1983 with Frances Hagopian).

Lisa Redfield Peattie, social anthropologist, is Professor Emeritus in the Department of Urban Studies & Planning at MIT. Her publications include *The view from the Barrio* (1968); *Thinking about development* (1981); and *Planning: re-thinking the Guayana Project* (in press).

Dr. Arcot Ramachandran is Under-Secretary General and Executive Director of the United Nations Center for Human Settlements (Habitat). Prior to that he has been the Secretary, Department of Science and Technology and Director-General of Scientific and Industrial Research, Government of India. A member of the editorial board of several technical journals, he has published 150 papers on heat transfer, energy, and solar energy, and delivered invited lectures on a variety of topics related to science, technology, environment and human settlements.

Bertrand Renaud is the Housing Finance Advisor, Operations Policy Staff, at the World Bank. He is responsible for coordination and direct support for policy and operations work in the six regions of the Bank. His recent publications include *Housing and financial institutions in developing countries* (1984) and co-authorship of country reviews of housing finance systems by the World Bank.

Harry W. Richardson, Distinguished Professor of Economics, Regional Planning & Public Policy, State University of New York (at Albany), and Professor of Economics & Urban & Regional Planning, University of Southern California, is the author of 18 books including *Regional economics* (1978); and *Regional growth theory* (1973).

Lloyd Rodwin is Ford International Professor at MIT, and Director of the Special Program for Urban and Regional Studies of the Third World Countries (SPURS). His books include *Planning urban growth and regional development* (editor, 1969), the experience of Guayana Program of Venezuela; *Nations and cities* (1970), a comparison of strategies for urban growth; *Cities and city planning* (1981).

Bishwapriya Sanyal is Ford International Assistant Professor in the Department of Urban Studies & Planning at MIT. His publications include *Lusaka housing project: a critical overview of low-cost housing in Zambia* (1980 with Mary Turok), Working Paper No. 92, International Labor Office, "Who gets what, where & how: a critical analysis of the housing subsidies in Zambia," *Development and Change* (1981); and co-authorship of *Evaluation of the first urban development project in Lusaka, Zambia* (1980 by the World Bank).

David Satterthwaite is a Research Associate at the International Institute for Environment & Development. His books include *Shelter, need and response: housing, land and settlement policies in seventeen Third World nations* (1981 with Jorge Hardoy) and *Small and intermediate urban centres* (1986, edited with Jorge Hardoy).

Dr. D. A. Schön, as an industrial consultant, a former government administrator, and a former president of OSTI (a non-profit social research and consulting organization) has worked as a researcher and practitioner on the problem of organizational learning and professional effectiveness. He was invited by the BBC in 1970 to deliver that year's Reith Lectures. His books include: *Invention and evolution of ideas* (1963, formerly, *The displacement of concepts*); *Technology and change* (1967); *Beyond the stable state* (1971); *Theory in practice: increasing professional effectiveness* (1974, with Chris Argyris); *The reflective practitioner* (1983); and *Educating the reflective practitioner* (1987). He is currently Ford Professor in the Department of Urban Studies and Planning at MIT.

Parviz Towfighi is a staff member of UNCHS in Nairobi. Before joining the Centre in 1983 he had been Managing Director of several construction companies; Director of Architecture and Planning with Adibi-Harris Associates; and High Advisor to the Minister of Housing and Urban Development in Iran.

Alfred P. Van Huyck, President of PADCO, Inc., has been a Senior Lecturer at the Department of Urban Studies & Planning at MIT during 1986 and 1987. His publications include *Preparing a national housing policy* (1977); *Guidelines for establishing and administering land development agencies in the developing countries* (1973) and *Urban planning in the developing countries* (1968, coeditor with J. D. Herbert).

Michiel J. F. van Pelt is Regional Economist in the Division for Regional and Sectoral Studies of the Netherlands Economic Institute. His publications include *Habitat and policy in developing countries: definitions and features* (in Dutch, with J. G. D. Hoogland and L. B. M. Mennes); *Report for the Dutch Ministry of Housing and Physical Planning* (NEI, Rotterdam, 1985); *Habitat and policy in the focus countries of Dutch development cooperation* (in Dutch, with J. G. D. Hoogland and L. B. M. Mennes; NEI, Rotterdam, 1986).

List of tables

List of figures

Index